Kölner Zeitschrift für Soziologie und Sozialpsychologie
Sonderheft 54/2014

Sonderhefte
Begründet durch René König (†), Deutschland

Jürgen Friedrichs · Alexandra Nonnenmacher (Hrsg.)

Soziale Kontexte und Soziale Mechanismen

Kölner Zeitschrift für Soziologie und Sozialpsychologie

Begründet als „Kölner Zeitschrift für Soziologie" durch *Leopold von Wiese* (1948–1954)
Fortgeführt als „Kölner Zeitschrift für Soziologie und Sozialpsychologie" durch René König (1955–1985)
Herausgeber: Prof. Dr. *Karsten Hank,* Universität zu Köln, Prof. Dr. *Thomas Schwinn,* Universität Heidelberg und Prof. Dr. *Heike Solga,* WZB Berlin
Beirat: Prof. Dr. *Eva Barlösius,* Universität Hannover; Prof. Dr. *Jens Beckert,* Max-Planck-Institut für Gesellschaftsforschung, Köln; Prof. Dr. *Hans Peter Blossfeld,* Universität Bamberg; Prof. Dr. *Bernhard Ebbinghaus,* Universität Mannheim; Prof. Dr. *Christian Fleck,* Universität Graz; Prof. Dr. *Bettina Heintz,* Universität Luzern; Prof. Dr. *Gisela Trommsdorff,* Universität Konstanz
Redaktion: PD Dr. *Volker Dreier,* Institut für Soziologie und Sozialpsychologie der Universität zu Köln
Zuschriften werden erbeten an: Redaktion der Kölner Zeitschrift für Soziologie und Sozialpsychologie, Institut für Soziologie und Sozialpsychologie, Lindenburger Allee 15, 50931 Köln. Telefon: (02 21) 4 70-2518; Fax: (02 21) 4 70-2974; E-Mail: kzfss@uni-koeln.de; Internet: http://www.uni-koeln.de/kzfss/
Die KZfSS wird u. a. in den folgenden Informationsdiensten erfasst: *Social Science Citation Index* und *Current Contents* des Institute for Scientific Information; *sociological abstracts; psychological abstracts; Bulletin signalétique; prd,* Publizistikwissenschaftlicher Referatedienst; *SRM,* social research methodology abstracts; *SOLIS,* Sozialwissenschaftliches Literaturinformationssystem; Literaturdatenbank *PSYNDEX; Juris*-Literaturdatenbank; *KrimLit* u. a. m.
Springer VS | Springer Fachmedien Wiesbaden GmbH
Abraham-Lincoln-Straße 46 | 65189 Wiesbaden
Amtsgericht Wiesbaden, HRB 9754, USt-IdNr. DE811148419
www.springer-vs.de

Verlagsleitung: Armin Gross, Peter Hendriks
Editorial Director Social Sciences & Humanities: Dr. Andreas Beierwaltes
Gesamtleitung Anzeigen und Märkte: Armin Gross
Gesamtleitung Marketing: Rolf-Günther Hobbeling

Kundenservice: Springer Customer Service Center GmbH; Springer VS-Service; Haberstr. 7, 69126 Heidelberg; Telefon: +49 (0)6221/345-4303; Telefax: +49 (0)6221/345-4229; Montag bis Freitag 8.00 Uhr bis 18.00 Uhr; E-Mail: springervs-service@springer.com
Marketing: Ronald Schmidt-Serrière M.A., Telefon (06 11) 78 78-280; Telefax (06 11) 78 78-440; E-Mail: Ronald.Schmidt-Serriere@springer.com
Anzeigenleitung: Yvonne Guderjahn, Telefon (06 11) 78 78-155; Telefax (06 11) 78 78-296; E-Mail: Yvonne.Guderjahn@best-ad-media.de
Anzeigendisposition: Monika Dannenberger, Telefon (06 11) 78 78-148; Telefax (06 11) 78 78-443; E-Mail: Monika.Dannenberger@best-ad-media.de
Anzeigenpreise: Es gelten die Mediadaten vom 1.11.2011.

Bezugsmöglichkeiten 2014: Auskünfte zum Bezug der Zeitschrift erteilt der Kundenservice Zeitschriften:
E-Mail: subscriptions@springer.com

Jährlich können Sonderhefte erscheinen, die nach Umfang berechnet und den Abonnenten des laufenden Jahrgangs mit einem Nachlass von 25% des jeweiligen Ladenpreises geliefert werden. Bei Nichtgefallen können die Sonderhefte innerhalb einer Frist von 3 Wochen zurückgegeben werden.

Jedes Abonnement Print und Online beinhaltet eine Freischaltung für das KZfSS-Archiv. Der Zugang gilt ausschließlich für den einzelnen Empfänger des Abonnements.

© Springer VS | Springer Fachmedien Wiesbaden
Springer VS ist eine Marke von Springer DE. Springer DE ist Teil der Fachverlagsgruppe Springer Science+Business Media.

Die Zeitschrift und alle in ihr enthaltenen einzelnen Beiträge und Abbildungen sind urheberrechtlich geschützt. Jede Verwertung außerhalb der engen Grenzen des Urheberrechtsgesetzes ist ohne Zustimmung des Verlags unzulässig und strafbar. Das gilt insbesondere für Vervielfältigungen, Übersetzungen, Mikroverfilmungen und die Einspeicherung und Verarbeitung in elektronischen Systemen.

Satz: Crest Premedia Solutions, Pune, India
Gedruckt auf säurefreiem und chlorfrei gebleichtem Papier.
ISSN 0023-2653   Kölner Zeitschrift für Soziologie und Sozialpsychologie (Internet)   ISSN 1861-891X

Kölner Zeitschrift für Soziologie und Sozialpsychologie

Sonderheft 54/2014

Inhaltsübersicht

Einleitung

Jürgen Friedrichs · Alexandra Nonnenmacher
Die Analyse sozialer Kontexte.. 1

I Theorie und Methodologie

Raymond Boudon
What is context?.. 17

Andreas Diekmann
Die Anderen als sozialer Kontext. Zur Bedeutung strategischer Interaktion............... 47

Lina Hedman
Compositional or contextual effects? Neighbourhoods and teenage parenthood
in Stockholm, Sweden 67

Frank Kalter · Clemens Kroneberg
Between Mechanism Talk and Mechanism Cult: New Emphases in Explanatory Sociology
and Empirical Research 91

George Galster
Nonlinear and Threshold Aspects of Neighborhood Effects 117

Jochen Mayerl · Henning Best
Theoretische und statistische Modellierung von Cross-Pressures in Kontextanalysen 135

Karl-Dieter Opp
Das Aggregationsproblem bei Mikro-Makro-Erklärungen 155

II Methodische Probleme

Georg Hosoya · Tobias Koch · Michael Eid
Längsschnittdaten und Mehrebenenanalyse 189

Manuela Pötschke
Aktuelle Probleme der Modellierung von Mehrebenen-Daten 219

III Anwendung/Bereiche

Frank van Tubergen · Tessel Mentjox
Minority Language Proficiency of Adolescent Immigrant Children in England, Germany,
the Netherlands, and Sweden 241

Eldad Davidov · Bart Meuleman · Shalom H. Schwartz · Peter Schmidt
Individual values, cultural embeddedness and anti-immigration sentiments:
Explaining differences in the effect of values on attitudes towards immigration
across Europe 263

Jürgen Friedrichs
Kontexteffekte von Wohngebieten 287

Katja Scharenberg
Schule und Schulklasse als soziale Kontexte der Entwicklung im Jugendalter 317

Rafael Wittek · Fernando Nieto Morales · Peter Mühlau
Evil Tidings: Are Reorganizations more Successful if Employees are Informed Early? 349

Alexandra Nonnenmacher · Tim Spier
Der Einfluss der Gruppengröße auf die Aktivität von Parteimitgliedern 369

Alessandro Lomi
Social Networks and Social Settings: Developing a Coevolutionary View 395

Oliver Arránz Becker · Daniel Lois · Anja Steinbach
Kontexteffekte in Familien – Angleichung von Paaren und intergenerationale
Transmission am Beispiel Religiosität 417

Die Analyse sozialer Kontexte

Jürgen Friedrichs · Alexandra Nonnenmacher

© Springer Fachmedien Wiesbaden 2014

Zusammenfassung Individuelles Verhalten ist immer eingebettet in soziale Zusammenhänge, z. B. Netzwerke, Betriebe, Wohngebiete oder ein Land. Solche Kontexte sind eine zentrale Bedingung, um individuelles Verhalten zu erklären. In dem Beitrag werden einige grundlegende Probleme der Kontextanalyse aufgeführt. Wir erörtern, was sich unter einem Kontext verstehen lässt, und geben Beispiele für Kontexte und Ihre Wirkungen. Wir erörtern, auf welche Weise Kontexte wirken, d. h. die sozialen Mechanismen. Anhand eines Mehrebenen-Modells untersuchen wir die Probleme der theoretischen Beziehungen zwischen den Ebenen und die dabei auftretenden Schwierigkeiten angemessener statistischer Modellierung. So ist weitgehend unklar, wie die Mechanismen lauten, die einen Effekt von der Aggregatebene „Land" auf die Ebene „Individuum" unterstellen.

Des Weiteren gehen wir auf „cross pressures" zwischen Kontexten ein, dabei verweisen wir auf die sehr ähnlichen Überlegungen von Simmel und Lazarsfeld. Schließlich behandeln wir zwei andere Probleme von Kontextanalysen: nicht-lineare Effekte und Selektionseffekte (unobserved variables). Wir fassen unsere Überlegungen in einer Skizze einer Theorie der Kontexte zusammen und schlagen vor, wie künftige Studien angelegt werden sollten, um Forschungslücken zu schließen.

Schlüsselwörter Sozialer Kontext · Kontexteffekte · Cross pressures · Nicht-lineare Beziehungen · Selektionseffekte · Soziale Mechanismen · Mehrebenen-Modelle

---

J. Friedrichs (✉)
Institut für Soziologie und Sozialpsychologie, Universität Köln,
Greinstr. 2, 50939 Köln, Deutschland
E-Mail: friedrichs@wiso.uni-koeln.de

A. Nonnenmacher
Dep. Erziehungswissenschaft-Psychologie, Universität Siegen,
Adolf-Reichwein Str. 2, 57068 Siegen, Deutschland
E-Mail: alexandra.nonnenmacher@uni-siegen.de

Analyzing Social Contexts

Abstract Individual behaviour is always embedded in social contexts such as networks, companies, neighbourhoods. They constitute a central condition to explain individual behaviour. We discuss major problems of context analysis. We first define context to then explore how contexts affect behaviour—the social mechanisms. We specify a multilevel model to demonstrate theoretical problems linking levels and the associated problems of adequate statistical modelling. An example is the explanation of individual behaviour by country level data.

We then discuss cross pressures between contexts; here, we show how similar theoretical approaches of Simmel and Lazarsfeld are. Finally, we turn to two other problems of context analyses: non-linear effects and selection bias. We resume our arguments by suggesting a preliminary theory of contexts and strategies for future research.

Keywords Social context · Context effects · Cross pressures · Non-linear relationships · Selection bias · Social mechanisms · Multilevel models

1 Einleitung

Drei türkische und arabische Schüler eines Gymnasiums in Berlin-Neukölln klagten 2013 vor dem Verwaltungsgericht Berlin, dass sie aufgrund eines Anteils von 63 % ausländischen Klassenkameraden, die also keine Muttersprachler waren, in der 7. Klasse in bis zu neun Fächern nur die Note 5 erhalten und das Probejahr nicht bestanden hätten. Die Klage wurde im September 2013 vom Verwaltungsgericht abgewiesen.

Die Schüler haben also, ohne es zu wissen, einen Kontexteffekt als alleinige Ursache ihrer schlechten Noten geltend gemacht. Im Prinzip war dies eine sinnvolle Hypothese, auch wenn sie vor dem Verwaltungsgericht nicht Bestand hatte. Dieses machte vielmehr die schlechten Leistungen der Schüler für ihre Noten verantwortlich. Dennoch zwang die Klage die Schule dazu, quasi wissenschaftlich zu prüfen, ob ein Kontexteffekt vorliegt: Der Direktor der Schule führte aus, in einer Parallelklasse mit einem gleich hohen Anteil ausländischer Schüler sei nur ein Schüler am Probejahr gescheitert, in einer anderen Klasse mit einem Migrantenanteil von nur 13 % dagegen fünf Schüler. Mithin könne es sich nicht um einen Einfluss (anders formuliert: Kontexteffekt) der Schulklasse handeln (SZ vom 28./29.09.2013, S. 7).

Schon immer war bekannt, dass Schulklassen das Verhalten der Schüler beeinflussen, ebenso, dass städtische Wohngebiete einen Einfluss auf das Handeln der Bewohner haben, wie frühe Studien zur Armut in London (Booth 1902–1903) oder der Chicagoer Schule (Shaw und McKay 1942) belegt haben. Fraglos gibt es bei vielen Autoren implizite Verbindungen zur Makro- und Mikroebene, denn im Grunde lautet die fundamentale Annahme der Soziologie, menschliches Verhalten sei (sehr) weitgehend durch die Umwelt geprägt; sie bestimme die Handlungsmöglichkeiten und -restriktionen der Individuen. Dennoch haben sich Makrosoziologie (Marx,

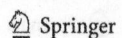

Durkheim, Luhmann) und Mikrosoziologie (Simmel, Schütz, Homans) weitgehend getrennt nebeneinander entwickelt.

Ansätze, diese Trennung zu überwinden, finden sich in den Arbeiten zu relationalen Merkmalen (Campbell und Alexander 1965; Coleman 1959). Dem Individuum werden nicht nur einzelne (absolute) Merkmale zugeschrieben, sondern auch relationale, die sich auf den Kontext beziehen. Wir messen nicht nur das Einkommen eines Haushalts, sondern auch dessen Einkommensposition im Wohngebiet: Er befindet sich im dritten Quintil. Die theoretischen Fortschritte sind in den Beiträgen zu dem Band „Quantitative Ecological Analysis in the Social Sciences" (Dogan und Rokkan 1969) zu erkennen, wobei man den Terminus „Ecological" auch durch „Kontext" ersetzen könnte. Wie sehr die Analysen dem der Makro-Mikro-Analyse entsprechen, lässt sich folgendem Zitat aus dem Aufsatz „Social Context and Individual Behavior" von Scheuch (1969, S. 143) entnehmen:

> We do note the beginning of a realization that in many of our observations on the level of individual actors we do not really take seriously the fact that there is something like social structure. Hence there has been the tendency to proceed immediately from observations on the level of individuals to statements about the character of higher-order units, and hence the inclination to equate observations of individual attributes with the state of the polity. This tendency is, however, due not merely to a particular blindness of empirical researchers but also to the gap in theorizing. Good substantive theory would need to specify the intervening processes and structures, and if this were done more explicitly, it would also be easier to develop appropriate measures.

Scheuch schlägt auch vor, den Kontext als „Umwelt" anzusehen, die „Konstellation von objektiven Merkmalen", die für eine im Kontext befindliche Gruppe kennzeichnend sind, als „subjektive Umwelt" der Gruppe.

Die erste formale Synthese von Makro- und Mikrosoziologie stammt von McClelland (1961, S. 47), der die Protestantismus-These von Weber in einem Mehrebenen-Modell expliziert. Das gleiche Modell findet sich bei Coleman (1987, 1990, S. 6 ff.); seine Arbeiten haben einen wesentlichen Beitrag zum Denken in Mikro-Makro-Modellen geleistet. In der Folge wurden zahlreiche Aufsätze darüber publiziert, wie sich Mikro- und Makroebene verbinden lassen, dokumentiert u. a. in den Sammelbänden „The Micro-Macro Link" (Alexander et al. 1987) oder „Macro-Micro Linkages in Sociology" (Huber 1991). Parallel dazu wurden statistische Verfahren der Regressionsanalyse weiterentwickelt und auf die Mehrebenenanalyse angewendet (Boyd und Iversen 1979; Bryk und Raudenbush 1992; Hox 2010; Snijders and Bosker 2012). Seitdem ist die Literatur zu hierarchischen linearen Modellen enorm angewachsen und in die gängigen Statistik-Pakete wie SPSS und Stata aufgenommen worden.

Diese Entwicklungen – auf der konzeptionellen Ebene die Modelle und der statistischen Ebene die Programme – haben sich in relativ wenigen Jahren vollzogen. Es mag übertrieben sein, aber sie stellen vermutlich den wichtigsten Beitrag zum Fortschritt der Sozialwissenschaften seit 100 Jahren dar. Wir sprechen nicht mehr von Umwelteinflüssen allgemein, sondern spezifizieren und modellieren sie. Damit werden die Theorien empirisch gehaltvoller, präziser und testbarer. Dieser Fortschritt hat auch eine Reihe von (alten) Problemen mit sich gebracht.

2 Teilprobleme

Die Analyse sozialer Kontexte lässt sich in mehrere Teilprobleme zerlegen. Wir führen sie nachfolgend auf und diskutieren die damit verbundenen Lösungen.

2.1 Was ist ein sozialer Kontext?

Die Frage, was alles ein Kontext sein kann, wird in der Literatur unterschiedlich beantwortet. Wir verstehen hierunter eine sozial-räumliche, zeitlich begrenzte Struktur – ein „soziales Gehäuse" –, die für den Handelnden mit Erwartungen, Opportunitäten und Restriktionen verbunden ist und so sein Verhalten beeinflusst. Beispiele für Kontexte sind Paare und Familien (vgl. Arránz Becker sowie Lois und Steinbach in diesem Band), Vereine, Cliquen, Netzwerke (vgl. den Beitrag von Lomi und Stadtfeld), Unternehmen (vgl. den Beitrag von Wittek sowie Morales und Mühlau), Wohngebiete (vgl. den Beitrag von Friedrichs), Schulen und Schulklassen (vgl. den Beitrag von Scharenberg), Parteien (vgl. den Beitrag von Nonnenmacher und Spier), aber auch Regionen und Länder. Eine spezifische Art, strategische soziale Kontexte, wird von Diekmann (in diesem Band) behandelt. Angesichts dieses breiten Spektrums ist es entsprechend schwierig, Opportunitäten und Restriktionen genauer zu fassen. Die in einem Kontext anzutreffenden Personen und deren Ressourcen, normative Einstellungen und dazugehörige Sanktionen stellen sicherlich Opportunitäten und/oder Restriktionen dar, die in jedem Kontext relevant sind. Darüber hinaus sind aber auch bauliche Gegebenheiten (Wohngebiet), Hierarchien (Unternehmen, Partei) oder ökonomische Faktoren wie das Bruttosozialprodukt eines Landes denkbar, um nur einige Beispiele zu nennen.

Wir können auch fragen, ob selbst das, was man als „Zeitgeist" bezeichnet, nicht ebenfalls einen Kontext darstellt. Gemeint ist damit eine kollektive Vorstellung von richtigem Handeln. Ein Beispiel ist die in England im 18. Jahrhundert vorherrschende Meinung, ein Bergbauarbeiter solle mehr verdienen als ein Soldat, das Boudon in seinem Beitrag (in diesem Band) behandelt. Ein anderes Beispiel ist die Diskussion über Päderastie in den 1960er-Jahren: Wer sich den „progressiven" Ansichten nicht anschloss, galt als konservativ, wenn nicht gar reaktionär. Die Aufarbeitung dieser Ansichten in den Jahren seit 2010 ist insbesondere unter den Grünen geführt worden. Sie zeigt rückblickend, dass es einen solchen Zeitgeist gab, und dass man sich auf ihn berufen hat, um sein Verhalten oder auch nur seine Ansichten zu entschuldigen.

In einer Gesellschaft werden sich Kontexte hinsichtlich der jeweiligen Erwartungen, Opportunitäten und Restriktionen Merkmale unterscheiden. Was aber, wenn das nicht so ist? Nehmen wir an, die Kontexte von der Schule bis zum Sportverein seien sehr ähnlich strukturiert. Eben das ist in autoritären Gesellschaftssystemen der Fall. Was im Nationalsozialismus „Gleichschaltung" hieß, war, im Sinne unserer Diskussion hier, nichts anderes, als Kontexte autoritär und normativ zu vereinheitlichen sowie ferner starke Kontrollen für angemessenes Verhalten einzuführen. Ein Element dieser Kontrolle war, entscheidende Posten in Vereinen mit Parteigenossen zu besetzen; ein anderes Element, mit Spitzeln zu arbeiten (Jahrzehnte später hießen sie dann „informelle Mitarbeiter").

2.2 Auf wen wirkt der Kontext?

Im einfachsten Fall gehen wir von der Annahme aus, ein Kontext beeinflusse alle Personen in gleichem Maße. Viele der bisher veröffentlichten Kontextanalysen gehen zumindest implizit von dieser Annahme aus, wenn beispielsweise überprüft wird, ob sich das Wohngebiet auf gewalttätiges Verhalten aller in ihm lebenden Teenager (Haynie et al. 2006) oder auf das Arbeitslosigkeitsrisiko aller Bewohner (Dujardin et al. 2008) auswirkt, oder ob die Schulklasse einen Einfluss auf die Leistungen oder den Bildungsübergang aller Schüler hat (Kristen 2002; Trautwein und Baeriswyl 2007). Wahrscheinlicher ist allerdings, dass differenzielle Effekte auf Subgruppen angenommen werden müssen, z. B. in Abhängigkeit von der (täglichen) Zeit, die im Kontext verbracht wird („exposure", vgl. Tubergen und Mentjox in diesem Band), von der Dauer seit Eintritt in den Kontext (vgl. Tolnay und Crowder 1999) oder der Stärke des Effektes – der „Dosierung", wie Galster (in diesem Band) schreibt. Die Wirkung hängt aber auch von der Position innerhalb des Kontextes ab (vgl. Haynie 2001: Wenn Jugendliche in einem dichten Netzwerk eine zentrale Position einnehmen, dann sind sie delinquentem Verhalten im Netzwerk stärker ausgesetzt und übernehmen es mit größerer Wahrscheinlichkeit als Jugendliche in einer peripheren Position in lockeren Netzwerken) oder von individuellen Merkmalen, die einen „Schutz" gegen Kontexteinflüsse bieten können oder eine erhöhte Empfänglichkeit für solche Effekte. Beispiele für Studien, die solche Differenzierungen berücksichtigen, sind Crowder und South (2003), Dittmann und Göbel (2010) sowie Small (2008). In diesem Band gehen Scharenberg am Beispiel der differenziellen Einflüsse der Schulklasse auf die Schulleistungen von Mädchen und Jungen sowie Nonnenmacher und Spier am Beispiel von Gruppengrößeneffekten auf das Aktivitätsniveau von Parteimitgliedern auf differenzielle Kontexteffekte ein. Eine weitere Möglichkeit besteht darin, dass der Einfluss individueller Merkmale auf Einstellungen und/oder Verhalten von Merkmalen des Kontextes abhängig ist (vgl. Davidov et al. in diesem Band am Beispiel des Einflusses individueller Werte auf die Einstellungen zu Migranten). Um empirisch fundierte Annahmen über solche Subgruppeneffekte formulieren zu können, wird es allerdings notwendig sein, zu klären, wie sich ein Kontext überhaupt auf seine Mitglieder auswirkt.

2.2.1 Wie wirkt der Kontext?

Dies ist die Frage nach den Kontexteffekten oder sozialen Mechanismen. Wie oder wodurch wirkt eine Bedingung eines Kontextes auf eine Person, die sich in dem Kontext befindet? Diese Wirkung sollte durch mindestens eine Hypothese erklärt werden, wahrscheinlich ist es jedoch eine Kette von miteinander verbundenen Hypothesen, also ein Theorie.

Der Kontexteffekt wird in den Modellen mit einem Pfeil eingezeichnet. Es ist jedoch nur ein Symbol, das für einen sozialen Mechanismus steht, der noch zu bestimmen ist. Auch wenn an dieser Stelle aufgrund empirischer Analysen ein Regressionskoeffizient steht, ist damit noch immer nicht klar, wie der Effekt von der Aggregatebene auf die Individuen zustande kommt. Wir sprechen von Kontexthypothesen (u. a. Coleman 1987, 1990) oder in der Analytischen Soziologie von sozialen

Mechanismen (Hedström 2005; Hedström und Swedberg 1998). Dabei sind die Auffassungen darüber, was ein Mechanismus ist, uneinheitlich (Opp 2004, 2005, 2013; Mayntz 2005; vgl. Kalter und Kroneberg in diesem Band).

Vielleicht ist es hilfreich, den der Physik entlehnten Begriff des Mechanismus auch an einem entsprechenden Beispiel zu behandeln, um zu prüfen, ob diese Analogie sinnvoll ist. Als Beispiel diene das nachfolgende Uhrwerk in Abb 1.

Hier greifen Räder ineinander, angetrieben durch eine aufgezogene Feder. Die Energie wird über eine komplizierte Kette von Verbindungsteilen in die Anzeige von Stunden, Sekunden und Wochentagen umgesetzt. Worin besteht nun die Analogie? Offenbar darin, dass wir erstens eine Kette von Annahmen benötigen, die von einem ursprünglichen Impuls oder einer Bedingung zu einem am Ende stehenden Ereignis oder Folge führen und wir zweitens das Zusammenspiel mehrerer Bauteile (Einflussfaktoren) berücksichtigen müssen.

In der technischen Definition ist Mechanismus ein automatischer Ablauf von derart miteinander verbunden Teilen, dass die Bewegung eines Elements die aller anderen auslöst. Mechanismen vermitteln zwischen Zuständen (hier: angezeigte Zeiten). Entsprechend können wir u. a. Korruption, Distinktion oder soziale Schließung (Parkin 1983) als soziale Mechanismen bezeichnen. Ein Beispiel für ein zwar noch nicht umfassend empirisch geprüftes, aber komplexes, dynamisches Erklärungsmodell, das soziale Mechanismen beinhaltet, ist das „systemische Modell" der Kriminalität, das wechselseitig Beziehungen zwischen der Sozialstruktur eines Wohngebiets, der sozialen Organisation seiner Bewohner (genauer: ihrer Bereitschaft und Fähigkeit, Normabweichungen zu sanktionieren), Kriminalität, daraus entstehende Kriminalitätsfurcht und Abwanderung aus dem Gebiet formuliert (vgl. Oberwittler 2013).

Lässt sich diese Wirkungskette auf das Mehrebenen-Modell übertragen? Im Prinzip ja, denn es wäre dann eine Kette miteinander widerspruchsfrei verbundener Hypothesen, mit denen die beiden Ebenen verbunden werden – oder anders formuliert: mit denen der Effekt erklärt wird. Dies dürfte umso schwieriger sein, je weiter

Abb. 1: Uhrwerk. (Quelle: Glashütte: A. Lange und Söhne)

Abb. 2: Mehrebenenmodell zur Erklärung der Lebenszufriedenheit

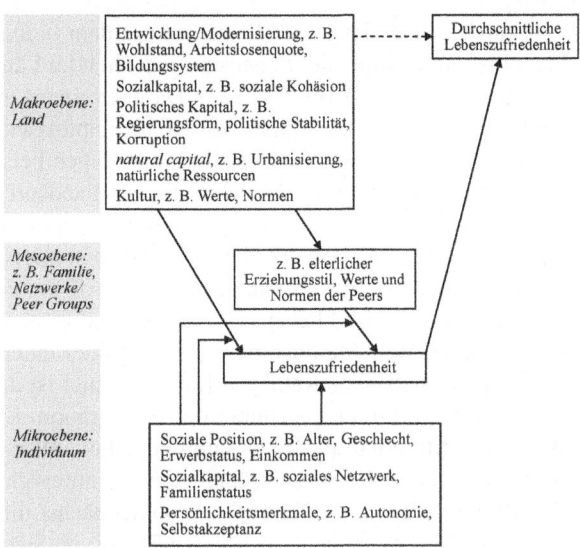

die Erklärungsebenen auseinander liegen, z. B. Gesellschaft – Individuen, wie es bei Studien zur Lebenszufriedenheit oder bei Vorurteilen (Semyonov et al. 2006) geschieht. In Bezug auf den erstgenannten Forschungsgegenstand haben Nonnenmacher und Friedrichs (2013) festgestellt, dass Ländereinflüsse auf die individuelle Lebenszufriedenheit (z. B. in Abhängigkeit vom Wohlstand des Landes, vgl. Abb. 2 unten) in der Regel nicht (ausreichend) theoretisch begründet werden.

Es stellt sich außerdem die Frage, ob, abhängig vom Forschungsgegenstand, spezifische Mechanismen wirken oder ob es möglich ist, grundlegende Prinzipien auszumachen, d. h. allgemeine Theorien der Kontexteffekte zu formulieren. Ist der Mechanismus des Effekts der peer group auf das abweichende Verhalten eines Jugendlichen der gleiche wie derjenige der Armutsquote im Wohngebiet auf den Besuch einer weiterführenden Schule? Hierzu ist auf die umfangreiche Diskussion solcher Mechanismen in der Analytischen Soziologie (u. a. Hedström 2005; Hedström und Swedberg 1998) und den Forschungen zu Effekten der Nachbarschaft (u. a. Galster 2008 sowie in diesem Band) einzugehen.

2.2.2 Welche Kontext-Ebenen?

Im vorangegangen Abschnitt wurde schon angedeutet, dass es umso schwieriger wird, den Mechanismus zu spezifizieren, je weiter die beiden Aggregatebenen auseinanderliegen; anders formuliert: je größer der Kontext ist. Deutlich wird dies vor allem in ländervergleichenden Kontextanalysen. Es kann plausibel sein, einen direkten Einfluss des Landes auf das Individuum anzunehmen, z. B. einen Effekt landesweit geltender Normen oder Gesetze auf individuelle Einstellungen oder Verhaltensweisen (vgl. Elliott und Hayward 2009; Soons und Kalmijn 2009). In vielen Fällen wird es aber vermutlich falsch sein, von nur einer Kontextebene auszugehen, sondern es ist notwendig, eine Reihe von Hypothesen, einen Mechanismus, zu spezifizieren, der die Ebene des Landes über eine Reihe von Mesoebenen, z. B. Regionen, Städte, Stadtviertel und Familien, mit dem Individuum verbindet. Abbildung 2 zeigt dies am Beispiel der Lebenszufriedenheit im Ländervergleich (vgl. Nonnenmacher und Friedrichs 2013, S. 1227). Darüber hinaus muss bedacht werden, dass das Vorhandensein oder die Stärke von Kontexteinflüssen mit individuellen Merkmalen variieren können. Bjørnskov et al. (2008) zeigen beispielsweise, dass die Höhe der *government consumption* (Anteil am Bruttoinlandsprodukt, der für öffentliche Güter verwendet wird) die Lebenszufriedenheit von Personen mit niedrigem oder mittleren Einkommen schmälert, nicht aber von Personen mit hohem Einkommen.

Ferner stellt sich das Problem, ob es sinnvoll ist, von der Landesebene direkt auf Individualebene zu schließen. Durch die Homogenisierung von Kontextmerkmalen können Kontexteffekte unentdeckt bleiben oder unterschätzt werden, wenn eine zu hohe Aggregatebene gewählt wird. Ein Beispiel ist die Studie von Semyonov et al. (2006) über Vorurteile gegenüber der Immigration. Eine erklärende Variable ist der Anteil der Minorität an der Gesamtpopulation. Wenn wir, im Gegensatz zu ihrem Vorgehen, weitere Ebenen einführen, dann könnte sich folgendes ergeben: Der Anteil der Migranten beträgt im Land 9,4 %, in der nächst-niedrigen Ebene „Bundesländer" 4,5 bis 14,5 %, in der dann niedrigeren Ebene von Städten (in Bundesländern) 3,5 bis 28,0 %, in der dann vorletzten Ebene der Stadtteile (in Städten in Bundesländern) 2,9 bis 68 % (fiktive Werte). Die Berücksichtigung dieser Ebenen könnte zeigen, dass der Einfluss des Kontextes deutlich unterschätzt wird – der relevante Kontext wäre nicht das Land, sondern das Bundesland, die Stadt oder der Stadtteil.

Noch komplexer müssen Erklärungsmodelle sein, wenn Kontexte nicht wie in Abb. 2 hierarchisch angeordnet, sondern verschachtelt sind, z. B. Wohngebiete und Schulen. Schulen werden in der Regel von Schülern besucht, die in unterschiedlichen Gebieten wohnen und dort ihre Freizeit verbringen, und Schüler aus einem Wohngebiet besuchen unterschiedliche Schulen. Auf jeden Schüler wirken also unterschiedliche Kontexte ein, deren Mitglieder wiederum durch andere Kontexte beeinflusst werden, was die Analyse von entsprechenden Effekten erheblich kompliziert. So ist z. B. bis heute unklar, wie hoch die Effekte von Nachbarschaft, Schule, Familie und peer groups auf die Schulleistungen von Jugendlichen sind. Entsprechende Studien liegen vermutlich deshalb nicht vor, weil sie mit einem sehr komplexen Design und einer großen Fallzahl zu arbeiten hätten.

Das Beispiel in Abb. 2 zeigt, wie komplex die Hypothesen sein müssen, die von der Ebene „Land" über die Mesoebene „elterlicher Erziehungsstil" und „Lebenszufriedenheit" dann auf die Mikroebene individuellen Verhaltens führt. Ohne Mesoebene hätte eine Kontexthypothese gelautet: Je höher der Wohlstand in einem Land, desto höher ist die individuelle Lebenszufriedenheit. Dieser eine direkte Effekt wird nun durch mehrere indirekte Effekte ergänzt, z. B. je höher die elterliche Toleranz, desto höher ist die Lebenszufriedenheit von Jugendlichen.

2.2.3 Cross-pressures von Kontexten?

Kontexte prägen unser Verhalten. Wir können uns einen Tagesablauf vorstellen, in dem sich eine Person nacheinander in unterschiedlichen Kontexten aufhält, z. B.: Familie – Straßenverkehr – Büro – Besprechung – Einladung bei Freunden – Familie. Diese Kontexte erfordern unterschiedliche Verhaltensmuster. Wenngleich die Kontexte wechseln, bleibt doch die Person dieselbe. Sie kann sich nicht nur je kontextspezifisch verhalten, sondern – sofern die oben formulierte Annahme zutrifft, der Kontext habe sozialisierende Wirkungen – hat sie auch die Verhaltensmuster und Normen anderer Kontexte in ihrem Verhaltensrepertoire. Daher kann es zu cross pressures zwischen den Kontexten, also zu normativen Konflikten kommen die die Person zu lösen hat (vgl. hierzu Mayerl und Best in diesem Band). Wie werden solche Konflikte gelöst? Dazu weisen wir auf eine erstaunlich Parallele hin. Georg Simmel hat in seinem Text „Die Kreuzung sozialer Kreise" (1908, S. 468) geschrieben: „Dass durch die Mehrheit der sozialen Zugehörigkeiten Konflikte äußerer und innerer Art entstehen, die das Individuum mit seelischen Dualismus, ja Zerreißung bedrohen, ist kein Beweis gegen ihre festlegende, die personale Einheit verstärkende Wirkung". Wir können das auf soziale Kontexte anwenden: Ein Akteur bewegt sich in unterschiedlichen sozialen Kontexten. Seine Individualität besteht darin, ein Schnittpunkt dieser Kreise zu sein. Simmel übersieht nicht die Konflikte, es überwiegt aber für ihn der Beitrag zur Individualität. Eine andere Sicht haben Lazarsfeld et al. (1944, S. 60 ff.), die den Begriff „cross pressures" einführten: Hier ist das Ergebnis unter anderem, dass Individuen, die solchen cross pressures unterliegen, die Entscheidung, welche Partei sie wählen wollen, vor sich hin schieben. Im Vorwort zur zweiten Auflage (1948): „In our complex society, individuals do not belong to one group only. They have a variety of major social affiliations: their social class, their ethnic group, their religious group, the informal assciations in which they partcipate. These various affiliations will make conflicting claims on some individuals" (Lazarsfeld et al. 1968, S. xxxiii).

Analog nehmen wir an, jeder Akteur handle in unterschiedlichen Kontexten, aber in einer je individuellen Ausprägung. Daraus folgt erstens, dass nicht ein, sondern mehrere Kontexte sein Verhalten geprägt haben. Zweitens: Mithin kann kein Kontext, in dem wir sein Verhalten untersuchen, einen großen Einfluss auf ihn haben; die Effekte sind gering (und können es dieser These zufolge ja auch nur sein), was erklärt, warum wir empirisch so niedrige Kontexteffekte im Vergleich zu hohen Individualeffekten feststellen. Wir folgern weiter, dass drittens der Effekt eines Kontextes K höher ist, wenn der Akteur in ihm interviewt wird, entsprechend geringer, wenn wir ihn in einem anderen Kontext Z nach den Einflüssen von K fragen. Das große Hindernis ist aber viertens, dass sich die Akteure der Effekte eines Kontexts sehr wahrscheinlich nicht bewusst sind. Die Frage, ob die Schulklasse, die Familie oder die Abteilung des Unternehmens einen Einfluss auf das Verhalten und die Einstellungen haben, können Personen sicherlich noch bejahen. Aber die viel wichtigere Frage, welche Kontexteffekte wie stark sind, dürfte sehr schwierig zu beantworten sein.

2.2.4 Ist die Wirkung linear? Und: Welches ist das geeignete Maß?

In den bisher durchgeführten Analysen wird in der Regel von linearen Kontexteffekten ausgegangen, wenngleich diese Annahme auch meist implizit ist und nicht begründet wird. Die Wirkung eines Kontextmerkmals kann allerdings auch nichtlinear sein. Es gibt eine Reihe von Hinweisen darauf, dass die Konzentration von Armut im Wohngebiet erst nach Überschreiten eines Schwellenwerts individuelles Verhalten beeinflusst und nach Überschreiten eines zweiten Schwellenwerts keine

weitere Verhaltensänderung bewirkt (Galster et al. 2000; Quercia und Galster 2000; Galster in diesem Band). Eine solche Annahme liegt auch denjenigen Erklärungen zu Grunde, die die Übernahme von Einstellungen und Verhaltensweisen der Umgebung mit einer spezifischen Form der sozialen Ansteckung (*social contagion*) begründen, den *epidemic models* (Crane 1991). Eine weitere Möglichkeit besteht darin, dass Kontexte bis zum einem Punkt positive, nach dessen Überschreiten aber negative Effekte haben (oder umgekehrt). South und Crowder (1999) haben beispielsweise gezeigt, dass die Wahrscheinlichkeit einer unehelichen Geburt mit der Benachteiligung des Wohngebiets zunächst steigt, dann aber wieder sinkt. Solche nicht-linearen Effekte können, genau wie in „herkömmlichen" Regressionsanalysen, nur entdeckt werden, wenn die Linearitätsannahme aufgegeben wird und nicht-linearen Effekten angemessene Modellierungen vorgenommen werden. Die Zerlegung des Zusammenhangs durch Spline-Regressionen ist ein methodisch anspruchsvolles Beispiel; häufig ist es aber schon ausreichend, quadratische und, wenn nötig, kubische Terme in ein Regressionsmodell einzuführen oder kontinuierliche Variablen zu Kategorien zusammenzufassen.

An die Kritik an der unreflektierten Verwendung kontinuierlicher Variablen zur Überprüfung linearer Zusammenhänge schließt sich eine weitere an: die in der Regel nicht theoretisch begründete Annahme, die der Verwendung von Mittelwerten und prozentualen Anteilen für die Messung von Kontexteigenschaften zu Grunde liegt, z. B. der Anteil an Migranten im Wohngebiet oder das Durchschnittseinkommen im sozialen Netzwerk. Es sind analytische Merkmale, sie beruhen auf mathematischen Operationen von Individualdaten (Lazarsfeld und Menzel 1961). Die hinter der Verwendung solcher Merkmale stehende Hypothese lautet genau genommen, dass allein die relative Größe einer Gruppe (Anteil Migranten im Wohngebiet) oder grundlegende Niveauunterschiede (Durchschnittseinkommen im sozialen Netzwerk) für individuelle Einstellungen oder Verhaltensweisen relevant sind. Demgegenüber ist allerdings denkbar, dass z. B. nicht (nur) das Durchschnittseinkommen im Netzwerk, sondern (auch) das Maß an Einkommenshomogenität (oder Heterogenität) von Bedeutung ist. Weitere Beispiele für solche strukturellen Merkmale des Kontextes sind hierarchische Strukturen, wie sie Wittek et al. in ihrem Beitrag in diesem Band thematisieren.

2.2.5 Wie lange wirkt ein Kontext?

Wirkt der Kontext(effekt) nur so lange, wie sich eine Person in dem Kontext aufhält? Oder gibt es Fälle, in denen der Kontext auch noch wirkt, wenn die Person sich nicht (mehr) in dem Kontext befindet? Eine Reihe von Erklärungsansätzen der Netzwerkanalyse (Theorie der differenziellen Verstärkung, Akers 1985 sowie Burgess und Akers 1966) und der Stadtsoziologie (soziale Ansteckung, kollektive Sozialisation) schreibt dem Kontext sozialisierende Wirkungen zu. Sehr wahrscheinlich trifft dies zu, deshalb kann er auch langfristige Nachwirkungen haben. So könnte ein Jugendlicher, der abweichende Verhaltensmuster im Wohngebiet in einer Gruppe erlernt hat, sich auch außerhalb des Gebietes und außerhalb der Gruppe abweichend verhalten. Nachweise für solche langfristigen Effekte liegen für den Zusammenhang zwischen

Aufwachsen in einem benachteiligten Gebiet und dem späteren Armutsrisiko im Erwachsenenalter vor (Vartanian 1999; Vartanian und Buck 2005).

2.3 Zur Weiterentwicklung von Kontextanalysen

2.3.1 Theorie

Die aus unserer Sicht wichtigste Aufgabe besteht darin, Kontexteffekte theoretisch zu erschließen; die oben zitierten Sätze von Scheuch gelten noch immer. Das bedeutet erstens, für ein Phänomen auf der Mikroebene zu überlegen, welche Kontextebenen (wie) zu seiner Erklärung beitragen können. In diesem Sinne plädieren wir für eine Erweiterung von Mikrotheorien durch die Einbindung von Kontexten. Zweitens ist es notwendig, schon empirisch nachgewiesene Zusammenhänge zwischen Makro- und Mikromerkmalen daraufhin zu überprüfen, welcher Mechanismus solche (Partial-)Korrelationen erklärt. Je nach Forschungsgegenstand kann für einen Teil der Schritte einer solchen Kausalkette auf die Theorien und Befunde bestehender Forschungsgebiete zurückgegriffen werden, nämlich bei denjenigen Forschungsgebieten, die Kontextanalysen betreiben, ohne sie so zu nennen: Studien zum Einfluss von sozialen Netzwerken (vgl. Lomi und Stadtfeld in diesem Band), von Familien (vgl. Arránz Becker et al. in diesem Band), der Schule und Schulklasse (vgl. Scharenberg in diesem Band) und anderen Sozialisationsinstanzen.[1] Drittens müssen erste Schritte hin zu einer allgemeinen „Theorie der Kontexteffekte" gemacht werden, die die grundlegenden Prinzipien beschreibt, nach denen sich Kontexte beliebiger Art auf ihre Mitglieder auswirken. Eine solche Theorie enthält zumindest folgende drei Hypothesen:

H1: Jede Person bewegt sich in unterschiedlichen Kontexten.
H2: Die Kontexten können sich gegenseitig positiv und negativ (cross pressures) beeinflussen. Das geschieht, wenn die Restriktionen unterschiedlich sind.
H3: Die Person steht vor der Aufgabe, die unterschiedlichen Kontexte für sich zu integrieren; sie strebt nach einer widerspruchsfreien Lösung.

Je länger eine Person einem Kontext ausgesetzt ist, desto stärker ist dessen Wirkung. Die Person nimmt die Kontexteffekte zum großen Teil nicht bewusst wahr. Ein erster Schritt könnte darin bestehen, Analysen aus unterschiedlichen Forschungsbereichen, möglicherweise aus unterschiedlichen wissenschaftlichen Disziplinen, auf gemeinsame Erklärungsansätze zu überprüfen. Soziales Lernen sowie die Rolle von Handlungsgelegenheiten und -restriktionen im Rahmen von rational-choice-theoretischen Ansätzen sind hier zwei Möglichkeiten, stellen aber sicher keine vollständige Aufzählung dar. Im Anschluss daran, oder parallel dazu, geht es darum, neue Anwendungsbereiche zu erschließen, das Modell also theoretisch fortzuentwickeln und empirisch in unterschiedlichen Bereichen zu fundieren.

---

[1] Kaum Vorbilder gibt es dagegen für die Verbindung zwischen Makro- und Mesoebene(n). Blaus (1994) Überlegungen zur Verteilung von Bevölkerungsgruppen als Gelegenheitsstruktur für soziale Kontakte ist in diesem Zusammenhang eines der wenigen Beispiele.

2.3.2 Dynamik von Kontexten

Ein weiteres Problem, das bisher kaum behandelt wird, ist die Dynamik von Kontexten (vgl. Esser 1993, S. 113 f.). Wenn wir davon ausgehen, dass soziale Kontexte, z. B. Nachbarschaften oder Netzwerke, einen Einfluss auf ihre Bewohner bzw. Mitglieder haben, wird damit implizit gesagt, diese Kontexte können sich im Laufe der Zeit verändern: Es sollte eine fortschreitende Homogenisierung zu beobachten sein. Wenn beispielsweise die normativen Erwartungen eines einflussreichen Teils der Bewohner einer Nachbarschaft die normativen Einstellungen aller anderen verändern, muss eine Angleichung stattfinden. Ein Beispiel für eine solche Entwicklung ist Schellings Modell zur Erklärung residenzieller Segregation als Folge individueller, von den Kontextbedingungen der Nachbarschaft abhängiger, Entscheidungen für einen Umzug (Schelling 1971, 1978). Eine ähnliche Homogenisierung aufgrund von Selektionseffekten wäre zu beobachten, wenn deutschstämmige Eltern ihre Kinder nicht in einer Schule mit hohem Migrantenanteil anmelden, weil sie Nachteile für ihre Kinder befürchten, und der Migrantenanteil in dieser Schule aus diesem Grund weiter steigt, was deutschstämmige Eltern noch stärker abhält usw. Die Theorie der differenziellen Verstärkung geht ebenfalls von einer Homogenisierung eines Netzwerks aus, in diesem Fall durch soziales Lernen.

Entgegen dieser Beispiele sprechen die von Galster (in diesem Band) festgestellten oberen Schwellenwerte allerdings dafür, dass es in Kontexten eine Art von „Sättigung" geben kann, d. h. eine Grenze, über die hinaus die stärkere Ausprägung eines Merkmals keinen zusätzlichen Effekt auf das Individuum hat. Zudem ist es möglich, dass ein Teil der Mitglieder eines Kontextes „immun" ist, d. h. aufgrund von individuellen Merkmalen Kontexteffekten nicht unterliegt, und somit einer umfassenden Homogenisierung entgegensteht. Crowder und South (2003) haben beispielsweise nachgewiesen, dass mit der Benachteiligung des Wohngebiets die Wahrscheinlichkeit, die Schule abzubrechen, für Jungen deutlich stärker steigt als für Mädchen, und begründen diese unterschiedlichen Effekte mit der für Jungen größeren Wahrscheinlichkeit, in eine Gruppe (eine „Gang") integriert zu werden, in der abweichende Normen gelten. Ein ähnliches Ergebnis erbrachte das nordamerikanische Experiment „Moving to Opportunity" (MTO), in dem Haushalte aus stark benachteiligten Gebieten randomisiert in Gebiete mit geringerer Benachteiligung umzogen. Im neuen Gebiet waren die Kriminalitätsraten der Mädchen niedriger als im alten (und niedriger als die der Jungen), die der Jungen hingegen höher (Kling et al. 2005). Ferner waren die schulischen Leistungen nur der Mädchen besser und höher als die der Jungen (Kling et al. 2007).

Um die Dynamik von Kontexten angemessen abzubilden, werden zukünftige Studien zwei Bedingungen erfüllen müssen: Erstens wird es notwendig sein, Längsschnittanalysen durchzuführen, wie es Hosoya et al. (in diesem Band) demonstrieren. Zweitens dürfen Studien nicht bei der Erklärung individuellen Verhaltens, also auf der Mikroebene, stehenbleiben, sondern müssen sich der Frage widmen, nach welchen Regeln individuelles Verhalten zu einem kollektiven Phänomen der Makroebene wird – das Aggregationsproblem (vgl. Opp in diesem Band).

2.3.3 Datenerhebung und -analyse

Mit Hilfe eines umfassenden theoretischen Modells ist es möglich, die Frage zu beantworten, welche Daten erhoben und welche Analyseverfahren angewendet werden müssen, um ein Mehrebenen-Modell angemessen zu testen (vgl. hierzu Pötschke in diesem Band). Ist es z. B. für ein zu erklärendes Phänomen notwendig, mehrere Kontexte, denen ein Individuum zugehört, gleichzeitig zu berücksichtigen? Und ist es notwendig, für andere Mitglieder dieser Kontexte wiederum deren Kontexte zu berücksichtigen? Dies könnte z. B. bedeuten, dass zur Erklärung der Schulleistungen eines Kindes nicht nur dessen Familie, peer group und Schulklasse, sondern auch die Familien und peer groups seiner Mitschüler berücksichtigt werden. Gleichzeitig muss berücksichtigt werden, dass sich erstens vermeintliche Kontexteffekte bei genauerer Betrachtung als Kompositionseffekte entpuppen können, dass zweitens die soziale Komposition eines Kontextes wiederum durch Selektionseffekte begründet ist, die es zu erklären gilt, und dass drittens bei der Überprüfung von Kontexthypothesen dieser *selection bias* kontrolliert werden muss (vgl. Hedman in diesem Band).

Um die für eine Person bedeutsamen Kontexte zu ermitteln, müssen wir nach deren Zeit- und Aktivitäten-Budget für einzelne Wochentage, Monate und unter Umständen zurückliegende Jahre fragen. Um dann die Effekte von Kontexten zu bestimmen, können wir sie berichten lassen, was sie erlebt haben, wie wichtig die Kontexte und Ereignisse waren. Hierzu kann es notwendig sein, in einem ersten Schritt weitgehend unstandardisierte Erhebungsverfahren anzuwenden. Wir können ferner projektive Verfahren anwenden und Situationen vorgeben oder geeignete experimentelle Designs entwickeln. Ein Beispiel für die Aussagekräftigkeit solcher Designs sind die von Keizer et al. (2008) durchgeführten Experimente, in denen sie einen Ansteckungseffekt (*contagion*) bei der Ausbreitung von Verwahrlosung (*disorder*) nachweisen konnten (vgl. auch Cialdini et al. 1990, 1991).

Zusammenfassend: Die hier (und in den Artikeln dieses Bands) aufgezeigten möglichen Lösungen für theoretische, methodologische und methodische Probleme tragen dazu bei, das Ziel soziologischer Analyse zu verfolgen, d. h. zu erklären, was „individual in society" umfasst.

Literatur

Akers, Ronald L. 1985. *Deviant behaviour. A social learning approach*. Belmont: Wadsworth.
Alexander, Jeffrey C., Bernhard Giesen, Richard Münch und Neil J. Smelser. Hrsg. 1987. *The micro-macro link*. Berkeley: University of California Press.
Bjørnskov, Christian, Axel Dreher und Justina A. V. Fischer. 2008. Cross-country determinants of life satisfaction: Exploring different determinants across groups in society. *Social Choice and Welfare* 30:119–173.
Blau, Peter M. 1994. *Structural contexts of opportunities*. Chicago: University of Chicago Press.
Booth, Charles. 1902–1903. *Life and labour of the people of London*. 17 Bände, 3rd ed. London: Macmillan.
Boyd, Lawrence H., und Gudmund R. Iversen. 1979. *Contextual analysis: Concepts and statistical techniques*. Belmont: Wadsworth.
Bryk, Anthony S., und Stephen W. Raudenbush. 1992. *Hierarchical linear models: Applications and data analysis methods*. Newburg Park: Sage.

Burgess, Robert L., und Ronald L. Akers. 1966. A differential association-reinforcement theory of criminal behaviour. *Social Problems* 14:128–147.
Campbell, Ernest Q., und C. Norman Alexander. 1965. Structural effects and interpersonal relationships. *American Journal of Sociology* 71:284–289.
Cialdini, Robert B., Raymond R. Reno und Carl A. Kallgren. 1990. A focus theory of normative conduct: Recycling the concept of norms to reduce littering in public Places. *Journal of Personality and Social Psychology* 58:1015–1026.
Cialdini, Robert B., Carl A. Kallgren und Raymond R. Reno. 1991. A focus theory of normative conduct. *Advances in Experimental Social Psychology* 24:201–234.
Coleman, James S. 1959. Relational analysis – the study of social organizations with survey methods. *Human Organization* 17:28–36.
Coleman, James S. 1987. Microfoundations and macrosocial behavior. In *The micro-macro link*, Hrsg. Jeffrey C. Alexander, Bernhard Giesen, Richard Münch und Neil J. Smelser, 153–173. Berkeley: University of California Press.
Coleman, James S. 1990. *Foundations of social theory*. Cambridge: Belknap Press.
Crane, Jonathan. 1991. The epidemic theory of ghettos and neighborhood effects on dropping out and teenage childbearing. *American Journal of Sociology* 96:1226–1259.
Crowder, Kyle D., und Scott J. South. 2003. Neighborhood distress and school dropout: The variable significance of community context. *Social Science Research* 32:659–698.
Dittmann, Jörg, und Jan Göbel. 2010. Your house, your car, your education: The socioeconomic situation of the neighborhood and its impact on life satisfaction in Germany. *Social Indicators Research* 96:497–513.
Dogan, Mattei, und Stein Rokkan. Hrsg. 1969. *Quantitative ecological analysis in the social sciences*. Cambridge: MIT Press.
Dujardin, Claire, Harris Selod und Isabelle Thomas. 2008. Residential segregation and unemployment: The case of Brussels. *Urban Studies* 45:89–113.
Elliott, Marta, und R. David Hayward. 2009. Religion and life satisfaction worldwide: The role of government regulation. *Sociology of Religion* 70:285–310.
Esser, Hartmut. 1993. *Soziologie. Allgemeine Grundlagen*. Frankfurt a. M.: Campus.
Esser, Hartmut. 1999. *Soziologie. Spezielle Grundlagen* (Bd. 1). Frankfurt a. M.: Campus.
Galster, George C. 2008. Quantifying the effects of neighbourhood on individuals: Challenges, alternative approaches, and promising directions. *Schmollers Jahrbuch* 128:7–48.
Galster, George C., Roberto Quercia und Alvaro Cortes. 2000. Identifying neighborhood thresholds: An empirical exploration. *Housing Policy Debate* 11:701–732.
Haynie, Dana L. 2001. Delinquent peers revisited: Does network structure matter? *American Journal of Sociology* 106:1013–1057.
Haynie, Dana L., Eric Silver und Brent Teasdale. 2006. Neighborhood characteristics, peer networks, and adolescent violence. *Journal of Quantitative Criminology* 22:147–169.
Hedström, Peter. 2005. *Dissecting the social. On the principles of analytical sociology*. Cambridge: Cambridge University Press.
Hedström, Peter, und Richard Swedberg. 1998. Social mechanisms. An introductory essay. In *Social mechanisms: An analytical approach to social theory*, Hrsg. Peter Hedström und Richard Swedberg, 1–31. Cambridge: Cambridge University Press.
Homans, George Caspar. 1961. *Social behavior. Its elementary forms*. New York: Harcourt, Brace & World.
Hox, Joop J. 2010. *Multilevel analysis. Techniques and applications*. London: Routledge.
Huber, Joan. Hrsg. 1991. *Macro-micro linkages in sociology*. Newbury Park: Sage
Keizer, Kees, Siegwart Lindenberg und Linda Steg. 2008. The spreading of disorder. *Science* 322:1681–1685.
Kling, Jeffrey R., Jens Ludwig und Lawrence F. Katz. 2005. Neighborhood effects on crime for female and male youth: Evidence from a randomized housing voucher experiment. *Quarterly Journal of Economics* 120:87–130.
Kling, Jeffrey R., Jeffrey B. Liebman und Lawrence F. Katz. 2007. Experimental analysis of neighborhood effects. *Econometrica* 75:83–119.
Kristen, Cornelia. 2002. Hauptschule, Realschule oder Gymnasium? Ethnische Unterschiede am ersten Bildungsübergang. *Kölner Zeitschrift für Soziologie und Sozialpsychologie* 54:534–552.

Lazarsfeld, Paul, und Herbert Menzel. 1969. On the relation between individual and collective properties. In *A sociological reader on complex organizations* (2. Aufl.), Hrsg. Amitai Etzioni, 422–440. New York: Holt, Rinehart and Winston.

Lazarsfeld, Paul, Bernard Berelson und Hazel Gaudet. 1944 (1948, 1968). *The people's choice*. New York: Columbia University Press.

Mayntz, Renate. 2005. Soziale Mechanismen in der Analyse gesellschaftlicher Makro-Phänomene. In *Was erklärt die Soziologie?* Hrsg. Uwe Schimank und Rainer Greshoff, 204–227. Berlin: LIT Verlag.

McClelland, David C. 1961. *The achieving society*. Princeton: Van Nostrand.

Nonnenmacher, Alexandra, und Jürgen Friedrichs. 2013. The missing link: Deficits of country-level studies. A review of 22 articles explaining life satisfaction. *Social Indicators Research* 110:1221–1244.

Oberwittler, Dietrich. 2013. Wohnquartiere und Kriminalität – Überblick über die Forschung zu den sozialräumlichen Dimensionen urbaner Kriminalität. In *Städtische Armutsquartiere – Kriminelle Lebenswelten?* Hrsg. Dietrich Oberwittler, Susann Rabold und Dirk Baier, 45–95. Wiesbaden: Springer VS.

Opp, Karl-Dieter. 2004. Erklärung durch Mechanismen: Probleme und Alternative. In *Angewandte Soziologie*, Hrsg. Robert Kecskes, Michael Wagner und Christof Wolf, 361–379. Wiesbaden: VS Verlag für Sozialwissenschaften.

Opp, Karl-Dieter. 2005. Explanations by mechanisms in the social sciences. Problems, advantages and alternatives. *Mind & society* 4:163–178.

Opp, Karl-Dieter. 2013. Rational choice theory, the logic of explanation, middle-range theories and Analytical sociology: A reply to Gianluca Manzo and Petri Ylikoski. *Social Science Information* 52:394–408.

Parkin, Frank. 1983. Strategien sozialer Schließung und Klassenbildung. In *Soziale Ungleichheiten*, Hrsg. Reinhard Kreckel, 121–136. Göttingen: Otto Schwartz.

Quercia, Roberto G., und Gerorge C. Galster. 2000. Threshold effects and neighborhood change. *Journal of Planning Education and Research* 20:146–162.

Schelling, Thomas C. 1971. Dynamic models of segregation. *Journal of Mathematical Sociology* 1:143–186.

Schelling, Thomas C. 1978. *Micromotives and macrobehavior*. New York: Norton.

Scheuch, Erwin K. 1969. Social contexts and individual behavior. In *Quantitative ecological analysis in the social sciences*, Hrsg. Mattei Dogan und Stein Rokkan, 133–155. Cambridge: MIT Press.

Semyonov, Moshe, Rebeca Raijman und Anastasia Gorodzeisky. 2006. The rise of anti-foreign sentiment in European societies, 1998-2000. *American Sociological Review* 71:426–449.

Shaw, Clifford R., und Henry D. McKay. 1942. *Juvenile delinquency in urban areas*. Chicago: University of Chicago Press.

Simmel, Georg. 1908. *Soziologie*. Berlin: Duncker & Humblot.

Small, Mario Luis. 2008. Racial differences in networks: Do neighborhood conditions matter? *Social Science Quarterly* 88:320–343.

Snijders, Tom A. B., und R. Joel Bosker. 2012. *Multilevel analysis. An introduction to basic and advanced multilevel modeling* (2. Aufl.). London: Sage.

Soons, Judith P., und Matthijs Kalmijn. 2009. Is marriage more than cohabitation? Well-being differences in 30 European countries. *Journal of Marriage and the Family* 71:1141–1157.

South, Scott J., und Kyle D. Crowder. 1999. Neighborhood effects on family formation: Concentrated poverty and beyond. *American Sociological Review* 64:113–132.

Tolnay, Stewart E., und Kyle D. Crowder. 1999. Regional origin and family stability in northern cities: The role of context. *American Sociological Review* 64:98–112.

Trautwein, Ulrich, und Franz Baeriswyl. 2007. Wenn leistungsstarke Klassenkameraden ein Nachteil sind. Referenzgruppeneffekte bei Übertrittsentscheidungen. *Zeitschrift für Pädagogische Psychologie* 21:119–133.

Vartanian, Thomas P. 1999. Childhood conditions and adult welfare use: Examining neighborhood and family factors. *Journal of Marriage and Family* 61:225–237.

Vartanian, Thomas P., und Page Walker Buck. 2005. Childhood and adolescent neighborhood effects on adult income: Using siblings to examine differences in OLS and fixed effect models. *Social Service Review* 79:60–94.

Jürgen Friedrichs, 1938, Prof. Dr., Studium der Soziologie, Philosophie, Psychologie und Volkswirtschaftslehre. Nach der Promotion Assistentenstelle im Institut für Soziologie der Universität Hamburg, dort 1974 Berufung auf eine Professur für Soziologie; 1983 auf einen Lehrstuhl für Soziologie. Seit 1991 Lehrstuhl für Soziologie an der Universität zu Köln, Direktor des Forschungsinstitutes für Soziologie und Mitherausgeber der „Kölner Zeitschrift für Soziologie und Sozialpsychologie" (bis 2012). Seit 2007 emeritiert, aber weiterhin im Institut für Soziologie und Sozialpsychologie in der Lehre und Forschung tätig. Aktuelle Forschungsprojekte: Kontexteffekte, städtische Armutsgebiete, Gentrification. Aktuelle Veröffentlichungen: „Städtische Armutsgebiete". In: Städtische Armutsquartiere – Kriminelle Lebenswelten? (Hrsg. D. Oberwittler, S. Rabold und D. Baier) Wiesbaden 2013; „Armut und räumliche Polarisierung". In: Urbane Ungleichheiten (Hrsg. P. A. Berger, C. Keller, A. Klärner und R. Neef). Wiesbaden 2014.

Alexandra Nonnenmacher, 1970, Prof. Dr., Studium der Soziologie, Psychologie und Philosophie. 2008 Promotion an der Universität zu Köln, 2008–2012 Akademische Rätin am Institut für Politische Wissenschaft der Leibniz Universität Hannover, 2009–2011 Vertretung der Professur für Empirische Sozialforschung im Fachbereich Gesellschaftswissenschaften der Universität Kassel. Seit 2012 Professorin für Methoden der empirischen Bildungs- und Sozialforschung an der Universität Siegen. Forschungsschwerpunkte: Kontexteffekte, insb. Methoden und Methodologie; städtische Armutsgebiete; politische Soziologie. Aktuelle Veröffentlichungen: „Zur Nachweisbarkeit von Kontexteffekten der sozialräumlichen Umgebung". In: Städtische Armutsquartiere – Kriminelle Lebenswelten? (Hrsg. D. Oberwittler, S. Rabold und D. Baier). Wiesbaden 2013; The missing link: deficits of country-level studies. A review of 22 articles explaining well-being. Social Indicators Research 110, 2013 (mit J. Friedrichs); Parteimitglieder in Deutschland (hrsg. mit T. Spier, M. Klein, U. von Alemann, H. Hoffmann, A. Laux und K. Rohrbach). Wiesbaden 2011.

What is Context?

Raymond Boudon†

© Springer Fachmedien Wiesbaden 2014

Abstract The notion of context should not be understood as descriptive but as analytical, in the sense that the package of features characterizing a context is dependent on the question the sociologist wants to solve. Also, the features evoked in a context should be empirically observable. This excludes introducing unobservable dispositional features in the context: a principle Weber, Durkheim and many of their modern followers endorse. The fathers of sociology have practiced since long contextual analysis in this sense. Examples drawn from their work illustrate the powerfulness of their explanation of numerous macroscopic puzzles. They illustrate how to solve the micro-macro link question. They suggest that the solution of this question is dependent on the nature of the macroscopic facts to be explained. The paper discusses the question indirectly through the accumulation of examples illustrating the powerfulness of contextual analysis. A major point of the article is also that social action includes always beliefs. Except in the cases where explaining the beliefs raises no question, it is a challenging point for social analysts. *Rational Choice Theory* is efficient in the cases where beliefs raise no question. If they do, Rational Choice Theory is doomed to introduce controversial notions as *frame* or *bias* that do not correspond to any observable reality. Because of its instrumental view on rationality, Rational Choice Theory is also unable to explain the goals different categories of individuals follow, while contextual analysis can, thanks to its broader conception of rationality.

Keywords Context · Contextual analysis · Rational choice theory · Rationality · Weber · Durkheim

R. Boudon† (✉)
University of Paris-Sorbonne,
Paris, France
e-mail: raymond.c.boudon@gmail.com

Was ist Kontext?

Zusammenfassung Der Begriff des Kontextes sollte nicht deskriptiv, sondern analytisch verstanden werden, und zwar in dem Sinne, dass das Bündel von Merkmalen, das einen Kontext kennzeichnet, von der Frage abhängt, die ein Soziologe untersuchen will. Auch sollten die Merkmale des Kontextes empirisch untersuchbar sein. Damit schließen wir Dispositions-Merkmale des Kontextes aus – ein Prinzip, das Weber, Durkheim und viele ihrer modernen Nachfolger betonen. Die Väter der Soziologie haben schon lange Kontextanalysen in diesem Sinne betrieben. Ich verwende Beispiele aus ihren Werken, um die Erklärungskraft für zahlreiche makroskopische Puzzles zu demonstrieren; sie zeigen, wie sich die Mikro-Makro-Beziehung lösen lässt. Die Lösung dieser Frage hängt von der Art der makroskopischen Sachverhalte ab, die erklärt werden sollen. Der Beitrag erörtert diese Frage indirekt, indem mehrere Beispiele vorgestellt werden, die die Stärke kontextueller Analysen belegen. Ein wichtiger Aspekt in dem Beitrag ist, dass soziales Handeln immer Glaubenssätze einschließt. Dies stellt eine Herausforderung für soziale Analysen dar, ausgenommen jene Fälle, in denen die Erklärung von Glaubenssätzen unproblematisch ist. Die Rational-Choice-Theorie ist wirkungsvoll in solchen Fällen, in denen Glaubensüberzeugungen keine Probleme aufwerfen. Wenn sie es jedoch tun, ist die Rational-Choice-Theorie gezwungen, kontroverse Begriffe wie „frame" oder „bias" einzuführen, die keiner beobachtbaren Realität entsprechen. Aufgrund ihres instrumentellen Verständnisses von Rationalität ist die Rational-Choice-Theorie auch unfähig, die Ziele unterschiedlicher Kategorien von Individuen zu erklären, was hingegen die Kontextanalyse vermag, da sie auf einer breiteren Konzeption von Rationalität beruht.

Schlüsselwörter Kontext · Kontextanalyse · Rational-Choice-Theorie · Rationalität · Weber · Durkheim

1 What context is not and what it is

I saw in the invitation of the *Kölner Zeitschrift für Soziologie und Sozialpsychologie* to write an article on "What is context?" an opportunity to questions that puzzled me since long as to why do educated people in the Western World still believe in a literal interpretation of the Bible, in the Da Vinci Code or that Americans have fomented the September 11th terrorist bomb attacks. I had the impression that the answers the current sociological literature gives to these questions are unconvincing.

Coming from a writer educated in the land of Voltaire and Diderot, these questions are obviously contextual. But Weber has clearly stated that, while questions can be contextual, answers should aim at being *a-contextual*. As he said in a time where China was seen as a high culture comparable to but far different from Western culture, a genuinely scientific sociological theory should be endorsed by Chinese. Can the above-mentioned puzzles be solved without falling in the no-theories of contemporary sociological literature on this topic?

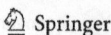

To begin with, the notion of "context" should not be taken as aiming at *describing* the social environment of a social actor[1].

As Karl Popper has claimed, physics would never have begun if its aim had been descriptive. *Explanation* is the ultimate aim of any science, *description* being an intermediary step toward this aim. But explanation implies simplification. Durkheim (1970, p. 212) has written: "abstraction is a legitimate procedure of science" (*L'abstraction est un procédé légitime de la science*). The notion of context illustrates this idea. It is an abstract one.

Contextual analysis has to satisfy a number of conditions. The first one is that the context should take the form of a set of *empirically acceptable statements*. Example: Durkheim's early Australians in his *Elementary Forms* lived in a context where they had not our modern scientific notion as to what should be done to increase the probability of gathering a good crop. Conversely, a context should exclude statements introducing unobservable data, as: these subjects were exposed to socialization effects that inclined them toward a given action.

In plain words, dispositional statements should be excluded from the content of a context, unless they refer to empirically observable data or to uncontroversial psychological laws, as: "Durkheim's Australians had no notion of our modern biology", "they wanted to survive", "they aimed consequently at generating abundant crops or a good reproduction of the cattle". All those statements are uncontroversial[2].

Another feature of the notion of context is that it should be conceived as *problem-dependent*. In other words, a context is not given once forever. It is dependent on the macroscopic facts the sociologist wants to explain. To come back to Durkheim's example, the puzzle he aimed at solving was why early Australians believed that rain rituals are efficient, while they are not. Being problem dependent, the relevant features of the context are those that will contribute to generate a convincing solution of the puzzle. Again, these features will have additionally to be empirically observable. Identifying them is not a question of technique, but of imagination.

Durkheim's example raises a typically puzzling fact. It illustrates eloquently the above-mentioned features of the notion of context: Durkheim solved the puzzle that its competitors had been unable to solve because he identified the relevant features of the context of his early Australians.

Ludwig Wittgenstein (1967) felt so uncomfortable with the puzzle that he proposed the conjuncture that early Australians did not actually believe in the efficiency of their rain rituals. Their rituals would have an expressive, not an instrumental function. They would "express a wish" *(äußern einen Wunsch)*. Wittgenstein's solution of the puzzle cannot be accepted.

---

[1] The view on *context* proposed here is close to Reynaud (2006). I have proposed in *Le Rouet de Monta*igne, Paris, Hermann, 2013, an extended version of this article.

[2] According to Popper (1976), dispositional parameters that, by difference with Durkheim's dispositional parameters (as: early Australians do not know Western biology), are unempirical, are a lasting plague to the social sciences: they are remindful of Molière's sarcasm: opium makes a sleep because of its *virtus-dormitiva*. As they spoke latin, the patients of 17th century physicians believed they mastered a science inaccessible to the common man. Classical sociologists as Durkheim or Weber as well as prominent contemporary sociologists, as Alter (2013) or Cusson (2006) on the French-speaking sociological stage, never use unempirical dispositional parameters

As Horton (1993) has shown in his studies on English-speaking black Africans, when asked, they always answer that, if they would not practice their rituals, good crop or good reproduction of the cattle would never be reached. They are aware that instrumentally efficient practices are also needed. But they are convinced that, if the rituals were not practiced, their aims would never be reached. Horton presents a second empirical argument that disqualifies definitely Wittgenstein's (1967) theory: when they convert to Christianity, the Africans who have left their village to live in cities make clear that they are happy to have converted to Christianity, since it entails a promise of a better life. But Christianity has a major flaw to their eyes: by contrast with the traditional animist African religions, it provides no means to meet the everyday problems of life, while traditional religions do, notably through rituals.

So, Wittgenstein's (1967) brilliant explanation cannot be accepted.

I will add at this point a note on my theoretical motivations in this article. I know that the development of statistical and simulation methods have in the last years made contextual analyses more sophisticated. More importantly, they have perhaps contributed to make the micro-macro question a major theoretical question. But, in spite of their importance, I will leave aside these technical questions and devote my attention to more fundamental epistemological questions.

I am speaking here from experience, having known the time when sociologists claimed that cluster analysis, Goodman's odd ratios or computer simulation would save their discipline.

My approach in this article was born from a reflection: that the question of the micro-macro link is present in the history of sociology since ever. Beside Durkheim and Weber, many contemporary sociologists owe the strength of their work to the fact that they have solved in an adequate fashion the micro-macro link question. I have for this reason chosen to multiply the examples where microscopic assumptions on behavior and context solve efficiently macroscopic questions.

Other examples deal with cases where the question of the micro macro link remains unsolved, as in the case of an important contribution of Bruno Frey (1997) or solved in a controversial fashion, as in the case of the Nobel Prize in economics Daniel Kahneman (2011).

Bronner (2009, 2013) has shown that a number of false beliefs can be explained without evoking the hidden action of *biases*. An example: when asked why an increasing number of elephants are born without tusks, most people give a Lamarckian answer: "Because tusks are useless". A few people only give the right Darwinian answer: that elephants born without tusks are less likely to be killed by hunters looking for tusks and hence are more likely to survive. It is hardly enlightening to explain that "quick thinking" (in Kahneman's parlance: everyday thinking) is exposed to biases against which "fast thinking" (scientific thinking) would be protected. People simply give the answer that appears to them as the simplest. Moreover, they probably do not even know that elephants can be born without tusks, since most familiar books present them with tusks.

The controversial notion of "bias" is not Kahneman's invention. Cognitive psychologists have used it since ever, as Shweder (1977). Thus, in a famous experiment, the following question is submitted to respondents: suppose that in a head or tail game, head is likely to fall with a probability of 0.8 and hence tail with a probability of 0.2. The respondents are supposed to guess at each of the successive tosses whether head or tail will fall. Here again, most people give the simple answer: they imitate the behavior of the coin and choose head and tail with probability respectively 0.8 and 0.2. This is wrong, since choosing head at all strikes would be a better choice. Does this experiment show though that "quick thinking" is submitted to *biases*? "Slow thinking" shows effectively that the choice of a majority of respondents is wrong[3]. But do we actually need to evoke an occult *bias* that would obscure ordinary thinking?

Priestley's theory of the phlogiston is false. But who would dare to explain that he was unconsciously guided by biases? Further question: is mankind composed of two species, slow thinking scientists and quick thinking ordinary people?

An important issue must be discussed at this point: notions as *bias, hexis, frame, framework, primitive mentality* (a notion discredited today for reasons of political correctness rather than of logics) are not only acceptable, but useful as long as they are playing a mere *descriptive* role: that they summarize factual observations. But they pollute the whole world of the social sciences as soon as they are given an *explanatory* function.

Economists, because they endorse *Rational Choice Theory*, which sees rationality as exclusively instrumental, *must* evoke notions as frame, framework, etc. since they are doomed to treat the goals, representational and normative beliefs of people as a-rational. In coherence with their definition of rationality, most of them consider goals and beliefs as mere data, to be simply registered. They run into trouble though in the cases Kahneman or Frey exemplify where the observed behavior of people contradicts the predictions of economic theory. In this case, they feel difficult not to evoke causes they recognize as hard to identify: they are sure that they exist, but express little hope that they could be identified.

Some sociologists are less prudent. They follow Lévy-Bruhl's lead, who interpreted the strange beliefs of "primitive people" with the help of the law of the three stages of human intellectual development Auguste Comte has proposed: theological, metaphysical and positive. Few sociologists accept this law today, but modern sociology has produced equivalents of this law: sociobiologists (trendy in the English-speaking world), structural sociologists (trendy in France in the 1970–1980's), memeticians (trendy today in the UK), sociologists investing their expectations in the neurosciences (trendy today in many places but already qualified as neuromania) and the list could be made longer.

Note though that neuromania is a polemical word that will be possibly discredited in a more or less remote future. Today, the neurosciences are able to display only a few contributions to the explanation of socialscientific or historical problems. But in the future they may represent more powerful tools than sociobiology or evolutionary psychology (Smail 2012).

The lesson to be drawn from this chaotic situation is that the social sciences still stand on clay feet. Popper (1976) has set the diagnosis almost forty years ago, Weber

---

[3] Since the probability of winning when using the simple answer is: 0.8 times 0.8 + 0.2 times 0.2 = 0.68, while the probability of predicting rightly a toss is 1 times 0.8 + 0 times 0.2 = 0.8, when choosing head at each toss.

explicitly, Durkheim implicitly have applied it in their empirical analyses and it can be formulated in a few words (as the principle of inertia that took centuries to be accepted!): do not try to explain behavior by a mixture of instrumentally rational factors and of a-rational factors. Still more simply: explain behavior as the effect of impersonal and personal reasons, also called "motivations". In still simpler terms: do not see rationality as merely instrumental.

2 Durkheim's example

General abstract considerations help indeed little when dealing with the question "what is context?" For this reason, already in the above pages, I tried to illustrate the definition as to what context is or is not by an example. I will now present the example drawn from Durkheim's *Elementary Forms* in its full extension (Durkheim (1979).

To me, Durkheim's explanation as to why early Australians believed in the efficiency of objectively inefficient rituals is one of his great sociological achievements. The other one, again in *The elementary forms,* is his explanation as to why the notion of Soul appears as more resilient than the notion of God. Empirical surveys as Inglehart's (1998) confirm this intuition, which I.B. Singer, the 1978 Nobel Prize of literature, expressed in a lapidary way, well after Durkheim: "Not the Soul but God does not exist" *(ce n'est pas l'Âme qui n'existe pas, mais Dieu).*

According to Durkheim's theory, to early Australians, rain rituals are instrumental, in the sense that they are supposed to generate rainfall, without which plants cannot grow. This *instrumental* side of rain dances raises no particular question. The puzzling question is why the members of traditional societies believe that rain rituals have the capacity of producing rain.

When the *primitive,* in 19th century parlance, grow some plant, they use much empirical know-how transmitted from one generation to the next. But they also need to know why plants grow, wither and die. This cannot be determined empirically. So they need to forge some biological theory. As in their context they have no access to science in the modern sense, they draw this biological theory from the religious interpretation of the world their society treats as legitimate. As to the magical rituals, they are technical procedures derived from this religious theory of the world, exactly as we derive technical applications from science. But magical techniques are unreliable. Does not this show, as Lévy-Bruhl (1960) postulates, that Durkheim's Australians follow rules of inference different from ours?

No: Durkheim's Australians not only dislike contradiction, they treat it as modern scientists do, by inventing auxiliary assumptions. We know from the Duhem-Quine thesis that, when a theory fails to explain some data, the normal reaction of any scientist is to invent auxiliary assumptions rather than to reject the theory. As he does not know *a priori* which element in the theory is wrong, it is reasonable for him to assume that an auxiliary assumption will likely reconcile the theory with the data. This is what scientists do, as the history of science shows. This is also what the magician does. In the case where his magical rituals fail, he will assume, say, that they have not been executed exactly as they should have been.

Durkheim himself raises the objection that, being ungrounded, magical techniques should fail in around 50 % of the cases. In fact, as the rain rituals are practiced in the period of the year where rain is likely to fall, a correlation between the two variables *days with/without rituals* and *days with/without rain* will be normally observed. The correlation is of course spurious. But modern Westerners ground also often their beliefs on spurious correlations.

On the whole, Durkheim's theory is much more acceptable than the alternative theories of magical rituals available on the market, as Wittgenstein's or Lévy-Bruhl's. Moreover, it explains convincingly a number of puzzling data: why magical practices were much more frequent in Europe in the 16th or 17th centuries than in the 14th, and more frequent in the modern parts of Europe. It explains on the whole many comparative data, some of which have been discovered a long time after Durkheim.

Durkheim's central thesis is that early Australians are rational in the same way as scientists are: they use the same rules of inference as modern scientists, but they do not have at their disposal the same body of knowledge: Western modern biology is unknown to them. This difference between their context and ours explain that we have trouble explaining their beliefs and behavior and incline either, as Wittgenstein, to postulate that they do not really believe in the efficiency of their rituals, or, as Lévy-Bruhland many modern anthropologists (Sanchez 2007), that they follow inference rules different from ours.

3 Two additional examples from Weber

Weber and Durkheim are often considered as offering contrasted views on sociology, Weber would be individualistic, since he claimed that individual actions are the causes of any phenomenon: that they are in his words the ideal typical "atoms" one should reach to explain any macroscopic phenomenon (Weber 1920, 1922). Durkheim would rather defend a holistic view on societies. Society would be first, individuals second.

But as soon as we look at what Durkheim does rather than at what he says he does, it is easy to show that they think the same way. Two examples from Weber will have the advantage to suggest that Durkheim and Weber share the same conception on context and on the explanation of actions and beliefs, and finally on the way to explain social phenomena.

3.1 On magical beliefs

We have the impression that people in traditional societies, as Durkheim's Australians, are both rational when they rub two pieces of wood to produce fire and irrational when they dance to produce rain (Weber 1980). The context explains this misperception: a typical modern Westerner is aware that kinetic energy can be transformed into thermic energy. For this reason, the primitive fire-maker does not surprise him, while he sees the behavior of the rainmaker as strange. As to the "primitive" himself, he has no reasons, claims Weber, to make this difference: he sees rain- and fire-making

as practices equally grounded in theories in which he believes and that ideal-typical Westerners spontaneously see as "magical".

3.2 Roman peasants against, civil servants and army officers for monotheism

Why, asked Weber (1986), were the Roman civil servants and army officers attracted by monotheistic cults imported from the Middle East, as Mithraism, while the Roman peasants felt deeply hostile to these cults and remained faithful to the traditional polytheistic Roman religion? Their hostility to Christianity was so persistent that Christians used the Latin word peasant (paganus) to describe those who were hostile to Christianity: the heathens.

Weber explains that peasants had trouble accepting monotheism because the natural phenomena that are an essential dimension of their everyday life did not seem to them compatible with the idea that the order of things would be due to a single Will: a notion that implied to their eyes a minimal degree of coherence and predictability. The natural phenomena, as e.g. the meteorological phenomena, appeared to them as too whimsical to be the effect of a single Will. This analysis explains also that an impressive body of saints appeared in the early centuries of our age in the Christian world. Thanks to the saints, Christianity was made polytheistic again, since God delegated His power to them.

The Roman civil servants and army officers lived in an entirely different context. They had the impression that Mithraism then Christianity proposed a good symbolic version of the organization of the Roman Empire they served: a single Will at the top supposed to enforce universal norms and values, a body of servants recruited with the help of formal procedures, while the host of believers were supposed to behave according to rules prescribed by the single Will.

4 Contemporary examples

I will briefly evoke some more recent examples in order to suggest that modern sociological research uses the notion of context as I have defined it.

4.1 Lazarsfeld on the invasion of Martians

A main finding of Lazarsfeld's study on the reception of Orson Welles' radio hoax announcing that Martians had invaded the Earth was that, while a correlation was observed between incredulity and level of education, categories with a low level of education, as plumbers and automobile repairers, appeared as highly incredulous (Fleck and Stehr 2011). The explanation of the "deviant cases", as Lazarsfeld called them, is that, while the level of education of plumbers and automobile repairers is low, their professional activity trains them to bear complex diagnoses: they have in common to have to reconstruct invisible processes with the help of leaky data. When a bathroom gets blocked, it may require the plumber to collect a number of indices to find out where the blockage has to be located. In other words, plumbers and automobile repairers live in a context different of the other low educated people.

4.2 An unsolved puzzle

A contemporary social scientist, Bruno Frey (1997), has shown that people accept more easily to have nuclear waste buried on the territory of their county when they are *not offered* a compensation for the risk involved than when they are. He conducted his study in Switzerland and Germany and observed the same puzzling answer in the two sites.

Bruno Frey perceived this finding as deeply uncomfortable, since it contradicts brutally the principles of economics. To economists, considerations of interest are the key of any human action. Bruno Frey evokes a vague explanation of the puzzle: that yet unexplored psychological factors would explain this deviation from the answers he would have expected on the basis of classical economic theory, or as contemporary sociologists would say, of Rational Choice Theory. Actually, we have here a contextual effect the question the respondents are asked create: if I am proposed a compensation, I perceive the offer to accept nuclear waste in my vicinity as a bad bargain. If compensation is not offered, I perceive the offer as a proposal to help the national community and may be more easily incited to accept it. The contextual effect explains the statistical data Frey was unable to explain.

This example has far going implications. It shows that as soon as a sociologist can identify a contextual effect in the sense I have defined and illustrated to begin with by an example from Durkheim, there is no need to use notions as *biases, frames, framework*, which explain nothing and recall Molière's sarcasm against those who pretended they had explained that opium makes sleepy because of its *virtus dormitiva*.

In a seminal paper, Popper (1976) claimed, rightly to me, that the social sciences would be better off if they would forget notions as *frame* or *framework*.

I do not want to go further on this issue, which I have explored elsewhere at length (Boudon 2011b, 2013). I am fully aware that it breaks with a well-implanted sociological tradition that considers as evident that its toolbox should include unempirical notions as *socialization effects, primitive mentality, bias, habitus, hexis*. For such notions are in some sense indispensable to *describe* the events of everyday life. But science begins once it is capable of substituting explanation for description.

In order to stress the importance of these ideas that, not only Popper but most philosophers of science consider now as going without saying, I will again mention Kahneman's last book on *Thinking slow and fast*. Its main thesis, resting upon a host of brilliant cognitive experiments, is that human thinking would be binary. A number of *biases* would contaminate *ordinary* thinking, but would not operate in the case of *extraordinary* scientific thinking. This is a strong thesis indeed, with a heavy metaphysical flavor: mankind made of two species!

Incidentally, one of the major findings of Durkheim in his *Elementary forms* is the opposite: religious thinking would prefigure scientific thinking. Modern historians of science confirm abundantly his thesis: the criticism Albert the Great, Buridan or William of Ockham raised against the explanation of a number of facts scholastics have inspired their scientific explanation. Thus, scholastics wondered on which forces made that an arrow went on flying after it was started by an initial *impetus*. It took centuries before the right answer emerged through the criticism of scholastics and

was finally labeled by Newton the *inertia principle:* "a body at rest needs an impetus to be put in move, a body in move needs an impetus to be put at rest".

4.3 Two further examples

Hilton Root (1994) asks why in the eighteenth century street protests against the price of bread were rare in London and frequent in Paris, although it was more favorable to consumers in Paris. The reason for the difference is that the political power was concentrated in the hands of civil servants in Paris and that Parisians knew it, while the members of the British parliament held their power from the provincial landowners who had elected them, so that the people in London knew that they had little chance to influence them. The macroscopic difference is explained by the fact that the institutions of the two countries generated two different contexts.

I have myself shown that street protests are traditionally much more frequent in France than, say, in Britain or Germany, because of the much more highly concentration of the political power at the executive level (Boudon 2011b, 2013). This explains also that everybody in France understands the expression *"le pouvoir de la rue"*, which has to my knowledge no real equivalent in English or German.

5 Are representational beliefs and actions grounded on them always contextual?

Rationality can be context-dependent or context-free. A scientific belief aims to be context-free. Individuals belonging to a context can have solid reasons to believe in some theory, while individuals belonging to other contexts can have solid reasons to reject it. Rain dances are considered as effective in some societies, not in modern societies.

On the whole, the system of reasons grounding a belief in the mind of a social actor can be *strong* or *weak* and *context-dependent* or *not*.

1. It can be context-free and strong as in the case of scientific beliefs.
2. It can be context-free and weak as in a nice example from Pareto (1968) of a syllogism the socialists of his time repeated: "Private property is not natural; what is not natural is wrong; hence private property is wrong". The syllogism is correct, but "natural" is taken as meaning "spontaneously well-accepted "in the first statement and "not artificial" in the second. This makes the syllogism wrong, but entailing nevertheless a certain power of conviction[4].
3. It can be context-dependent and strong as in the case of the belief in the effectiveness of rain dances (Durkheim).
4. It can be context-dependent and weak as when civil servants conclude from weak reasons that only state ruled agencies could serve the interests of the public: a topic Tocqueville and Weber developed at length (Table 1).

---

[4] Pareto's theory of *derivations* is a systematic exploration of the arguments that are logically wrong, although they display a certain power of conviction.

Table 1

Systems of reasons	Strong	Weak
Non contextual	Quicksilver in the barometer raises because of the weight of atmosphere	Private property is not natural
Contextual	Rain dances facilitate rainfall	The State only is motivated by the general interest

6 Principles

An important point must be raised at this point. Any system of arguments, including scientific theories, rests upon principles that by their very nature cannot be *demonstrated*, but exclusively *tested*. How? By a Bayesian procedure: when a theory resting upon some principles appears as able to explain an increasing number of facts, our confidence in the theory normally increases. But, as the Bayesian procedure takes time, theories resting on alternative principles can flourish in the meanwhile.

This explains notably the resilience of theories opposed to the neo-Darwinian theory of evolution. As the number of evolutionary data the neo-Darwinian theory convincingly explains increases slowly, it offers an opportunity to alternative theories, as today the *Intelligent Design Theory* (Boudon 2013), to be well received by those who are reluctant toward the materialist Darwinian theory of life: a macroscopic fact that is evidently puzzling. How can people in the 21th century still take literally the teachings of the Bible, in spite of the accumulation of archeological and historical data?

This can be explained by the following facts:

1. That theories rest always upon principles.
2. That principles cannot be demonstrated, but tested.
3. That the confidence in some principles increases or decreases by the application of Bayes' theorem.
4. That the application of the Bayesian procedure can take a long time.
5. That in the meanwhile, theories resting upon alternative principles can flourish on the market of ideas.

In other words, the statements 1 to 5 explain that some issues can generate two contexts, as in the case of the opposition between the Darwinians and the Anti-Darwinians. On other issues, the five statements can give birth to a greater number of contexts.

The sociological literature on the subject as to why in the 21th century people still take literally the teachings of the Bible is poor and unconvincing. In his seminal book, Hofstadter (1985) has remarked that conspiracy theories are of all time and countries, advanced and less advanced. He has shown that they are a normal ingredient of American political life. Actually, they characterize political life everywhere, in the present as in the past times. But, as a prominent scholar, Hofstadter is skeptical against the explanations produced by the social sciences and finally does not answer the question of the causes of the highly puzzling fact of the resilience of conspiracy theories in all countries, "advanced" or not and in all times.

A powerful cause of the fact that in our 21th century many people believe in strange ideas is again the slow path of the Bayesian procedure. It can be slow within the scien-

tific community itself. It took about a century before Wegener's colleagues accepted his theory of plate tectonics. He introduced it on the market of scientific ideas in 1912. The scientific community did not unanimously accept it before the 1970's.

But the Bayesian procedure can take a still much longer time to operate. To come back to an example I have already evoked, the principle of inertia was present though in a latent fashion in the critics Buridan and others raised against the answer scholastics gave to questions as to: "Why does a sailboat keeps moving once the wind has suddenly disappeared?" The right answer is again that bodies at rest need a force to be moved and bodies in move a force to be stopped. But the "principle of inertia" was not unanimously accepted before Newton, in the 17th century.

The history of science is full of stories showing that the Bayesian procedure needs time to operate. Thus, it took time before the explanation Galileo Galilei offered of the puzzle raised by the fact that bullets shouted toward the East and toward the West have the same trajectories in spite of the daily move of the Earth. Or why a stone dropped from the top of a boat in move falls at the foot of the mast and not, as scholasticism believed, behind or before the mast, depending on whether the boat moves in the direction of the rotation of the earth or in the opposite direction (Clavelin 2004).

Sociological literature on the question as to why still in the 21th century people believe in the literality of the Bible is poor because it ignores entirely that the Bayesian procedure normally used to test principles generates a sequence of contexts that affects the life of ideas.

Some current explanations are remindful of the weak theories we met earlier that imputed the beliefs in the efficiency of rain rituals to variants of Lévy-Bruhl's "primitive mentality", as when some sociologists explain that those who endorse bizarre beliefs ignore the basic principles of logical inference. Numerous empirical studies contradict pitiless this theory: people with a high level of education are not rare among those who believe in the literal truth of the Bible or in a lot of other strange ideas.

Beside the slow path of the Bayesian procedure, *dissonance effects* are at work here: As I am convinced that the Holy scripture is the voice of God, I reach consonance by taking benefit of the fact that Darwinism provides credible explanations of some facts, but is still unable to explain "big" facts, as the issue often mentioned in the anti-Darwinian literature that it does not explain the jump from one species to the next. The argument impressed political leaders in several countries, so that they imposed to teach Darwinism as a theory among others.

The explanation will likely take the form of a random mutation notably in the central parts of living organisms, possibly in the nervous cells. If so, the Darwinian theory will be completed by the discovery of a new mechanism. It will not stop the Bayesian procedure confirming the relevance of the Darwinian principles. And it will certainly not start a Bayesian procedure favorable to anti-Darwinian principles. But in the meanwhile, theories as the *Intelligent Design Theory* will be able to teach that Darwinism is unable to explain major facts, as the jump from one species to another. On such questions we retrieve the situation of the 14th century when scholasticism taught that unobservable whirlwinds where responsible for the fact that an arrow keeps on flying although the effect of the initial impetus is exhausted.

Other sociologists explain this phenomenon as a mechanical effect of socialization. As we saw, the very notion of socialization is controversial, because it induces tautological explanations, and because numerous empirical observations moreover contradict the idea of a mechanical effect of socialization. As Simmel (2003) has claimed, a liberal education can produce a liberal personality but also an authoritarian one and conversely. The strong influence of behaviorism in the United States had incited Adorno to postulate that profascist sympathies were due to authoritarian personalities. His book was severely criticized already when it came out and its basic assumption was never accepted. We understand why now: A contextual analysis following the above-mentioned rules defining a context is the only one that provides an explanation that satisfies the ordinary criteria of a genuinely scientific explanation.

May I repeat that explaining the puzzling fact that people sometimes with a good level of education believe in strange ideas was the question that originally led me to the question whether contextual analysis is able to offer a scientific answer that would dominate the current weak sociological explanations with a Levy-Bruhlian flavor or the easy tautological explanations seeing simply in these puzzling facts a "socialization effect".

I must also confess that when I began, I did not anticipate that the contextual solution to this question would take the long chain of arguments presented in this article on "What is context?"

7 Are moral beliefs always contextual?

All the examples presented in the above pages deal with representational beliefs. A complementary question is whether contextual analysis can be successfully applied to normative beliefs (as: "this type of tax is fair") and more generally to "axiological questions" (as: "Mozart is a great composer").

I deal here through the examples I present on *social beliefs* rather than on *social actions* for a simple reason: that beliefs lead any action. Even a statement as "it is a good idea to look on one's right and left before crossing over a street" rests upon beliefs: "Avoiding accidents is a good thing", "cars are dangerous for pedestrians". In such a case, the beliefs need no explanation.

My claim is that the contextual approach is useful to explain normative and axiological macroscopic empirical observations, that it can explain the phenomena of consensus which can be observed in societies on many issues and that it can explain the over time change of moral feelings and generally of collective axiological feelings (Boudon 2010).

Rational Choice Theory is well adapted to the cases where the beliefs to be explained are trivial, less so as soon as the beliefs underlying actions pose a challenge to sociological analysis. Religious beliefs are undoubtedly the category of beliefs posing the greatest challenge to sociologists. For this reason, several of my examples deal with religious beliefs[5].

---

[5] Today, "analytical sociology" is presented as an alternative to RCT (Hedström 2005). It is nothing else though than Merton's "middle range" theory. That it incorporates modern technical tools does not change

Rational Choice Theory is unprepared to deal with puzzling beliefs, as we saw when dealing with Bruno Frey's study on accepting or not nuclear waste. It simply makes them the effect of *frames*. This explains why *Rational Choice Theory* has a limited impact on sociology and political science and practically none on anthropology (Boudon 2003).

The only field in which it has been successfully mobilized is the geopolitical science, since its basic actors, its "atoms" as Max Weber would have said, are in this case governments following a simple goal—simple to describe less so to realize- i.e. meeting the challenge of other governments.

Sociology, anthropology, political science or history are neither dealing with a category of basic actors, of "atoms", given once for all, nor with goals that would be defined once forever.

The answer to the question whether contextual analysis can be successfully applied to normative and axiological reasons can be answered positively for the following reasons:

1. Theories can be built on moral, prescriptive and axiological as well as on descriptive questions. Moreover, normative, moral, prescriptive or axiological theories can be in many cases unambiguously characterized, as descriptive ones, as stronger or weaker when they are compared to one another.
2. People tend to endorse the theory they see as stronger.
3. They tend to endorse a moral, prescriptive or value statement and to experience the feeling that "X is good, bad, legitimate, fair, etc." when it appears to them, more or less vaguely depending on the circumstances, as grounded on valid reasons.
4. These reasons can be context-dependent or context-free.

The Weberian-Durkheimian sociological tradition recognizes fully the validity of the distinction postulate 4) introduces.

Scientific beliefs aim at being context-free. In the same way, the belief that a democratic regime is more likely than an authoritarian one to respect the dignity of people is commonly considered as context-free. Clearly, the citizens of democratic societies do not feel that democratic are better than dictatorial regimes simply because they have been socialized to think so and hence would have contracted the *bias, frame, hexis* or *habitus* to think so, but because they perceive their feeling as right.

In the same way, I think that Pythagoras' theorem is right, not simply because I have been socialized to think it is, but because I am able to see the reasons why it is true. As representational beliefs, normative and axiological beliefs can also be context-dependent. The belief that rain rituals are efficient is context-bound, as is the moral belief that death penalty is a legitimate form of punishment: it appears in contexts where death penalty is supposed to have a redemptory value.

---

the fact that the Mertonian paradigm underlies analytical sociology, a paradigm Weber actually already identified when he states that social phenomena should be explained by their genuine causes: the actions of the "atoms" of sociology, i.e. the individual social actors (Weber 1920). These "atoms" are of course "idealtypical" rather than concrete individuals. On the various names of "analytical sociology", see Pawson (2009).

In other words, I propose to define axiological rationality as a species of a broader category: *non-instrumental rationality* or, to qualify it positively, *cognitive rationality*. Axiological rationality is a species of cognitive rationality characterized by the fact that it deals with systems of arguments where at least one statement is axiological, as no conclusion at the imperative can be drawn from a set of statements that would be all at the indicative. As to *cognitive rationality,* the gender of which axiological rationality is a species, it can be defined as the rationality that concludes that "X is true, legitimate, adequate to reach some goal, etc." on the basis of strong mutually compatible reasons.

Thus, *cognitive rationality* is the gender that covers three species: *instrumental rationality, descriptive rationality* and *axiological rationality*.

Instrumental rationality concludes on the basis of strong mutually compatible reasons that X is an adequate means to reach goal G.

Descriptive rationality concludes on the basis of strong mutually compatible reasons for instance that the weight of atmosphere is the cause that explains that the barometer rises higher at the bottom than at the summit of a mountain. It is the form of rationality scientists use. It explains why we endorse or reject a scientific theory and also why in everyday life, we explain any event, phenomenon, or state of affairs.

Axiological rationality concludes on the basis of strong mutually compatible reasons that "X is good, legitimate, etc."

One of the causes that social sciences appear as walled up against one another, as economics against sociology and reciprocally, is that each tends to endorse exclusively a given form of rationality, *instrumental rationality* being the favorite form of economists. Inside sociology, two visions appear as chronically opposed to one another: those who swear on Rational Choice Theory and those who see human beings as conditioned by impersonal a-rational forces.

Contextual analysis in the sense defined at the beginning of this article has the positive effect of destroying these walls. It eliminates as we saw controversial notions as *frame, bias* and other notions that postulate the existence of occult causes.

It is aware that instrumental rationality can explain not only economical phenomena, but also a host of social phenomena, as Olson (1965) among others has brilliantly shown[6], and it recognizes on the other hand instrumental rationality fails to explain broad types of human behavior.

At this point, it is necessary to answer a traditional objection. As no *ought-statement* can be drawn from *is-statements,* it is often contended that normative and generally axiological theories are by their very nature basically different from representational ones. Still, as *is-statements, ought-statements* can be weaker or stronger.

To take a trivial example, under general conditions, people prefer riding a car smoothly in the city traffic because, as moving is to them a means rather than an end, they want normally the means to be as little unpleasant as possible. For this reason, they consider traffic lights as a *good* though unpleasant thing. The value statement

---

[6] In my preface to the French translation of Olson's book, I have shown that his argument can be presented, as he does, in the classical language of economic theory, but also in the more transdisciplinary language of gametheory. At any rate, *instrumental rationality* is a basic postulate of gametheory as of classical economics.

"traffic lights are a good thing" is the conclusion of a valid argument grounded on the empirical indubitable statement that traffic is more fluid with traffic lights than without.

Though elementary, this example is typical of many normative arguments. It shows that a normative argument can be as convincing as a descriptive one. This is the case when the argument involves empirical statements that can be checked and axiological statements on which all would agree, as "traffic jam is a bad thing".

The example shows also that an *ought-statement* can be derived from *is-statements,* provided the set of statements concluding to the *ought-statement* includes *at least one ought-statement.*

Weber has well seen, however, the point of utmost importance that, by difference with the example of the evaluation of traffic lights, axiological statements cannot always be considered as the conclusion of *instrumental* arguments.

By creating his notion of *axiological rationality,* he wanted to insist on the point that people may have in some circumstances subjectively strong and objectively valid *non instrumental* reasons to believe that "X is good or bad, legitimate or illegitimate, fair or unfair, etc.". He introduced by so doing a powerful idea, crucial with regard to our understanding of axiological feelings and of moral and normative feelings in particular. It provides an indispensable tool to explain the social processes whereby moral evaluations are constructed.

Once properly elaborated, the notion is also indispensable to explain the over-time change of moral feelings: Why do we consider for instance as illegitimate types of punishment that were considered earlier as normal and legitimate? Why is death penalty abolished in a growing number of countries, but not in others?

8 Axiological rationality

I would finally define *axiological rationality* formally in the following way. Let us assume that a set of statements leads to a given normative or axiological conclusion, and that the set of statements is made of acceptable and mutually compatible empirical and axiological statements. Then, if no alternative set of acceptable and mutually compatible statements leading to a different or opposite normative or axiological conclusion is available to an actor, it will be *axiologically rational* for him to assume that the given normative or axiological conclusion is right.[7]

To summarize, I would define a feeling or a statement as *axiologically rational* if people would consider it as derived from acceptable and mutually compatible arguments which can be, but are not necessarily, of the *instrumental* type, and if no set of arguments is available to them that would be as strong and would lead to a different conclusion. I propose in other words to define axiological rationality as a form of rationality characterized by the fact that it deals with arguments where at least one statement is axiological, since, again, an *ought-statement* cannot be derived from statements that would *all* be *is-statements.*

---

[7] M. Sukale (1995, 2002), a major Weber scholar, qualifies Weber's notion of axiological rationality as a dead end as a notion that would be *äußerst irreführend.*

9 An illustration of axiological rationality

While Weber was probably the first author who proposed to conceptualize the notion of *axiological rationality,* he is not the first one who has used it practically, as an example drawn from Adam Smith (1976) among other possible examples can illustrate.

This example shows that *axiological rationality* is a much more concrete and hence useful notion than Kant's general maxims of *practical reason.* This shows that sociology can solve questions ill solved by philosophy and that scientific progress can jump over the disciplines.

In his *Wealth of Nations,* Smith (1976) wonders why his fellowmen have strong collective feelings on the fairness of salaries. Thus, a strong collective feeling among 18th century Englishmen is that miners should be paid more than soldiers. What are the causes of this consensus? Adam Smith's answer consists in showing that this feeling is grounded on subjectively strong and objectively valid reasons, which can be reconstructed by the following set of statements.

A salary is the reward of a contribution. Equal rewards should correspond to equal contributions. Several components enter in the value of a contribution, as the investment required in order to generate the type of competence needed to produce the contribution and the risks involved in the realization of the contribution.

Now, the investment is comparable in the case of the miner and of the soldier. It takes about as much time and effort to train a soldier as a miner. The two jobs are characterized by similar risks. The two include above all a high risk of being wounded or killed.

Nonetheless, there are important differences between the two. The soldier serves a function that is central in any society. He contributes preserving the very existence of the nation. The miner fulfills by contrast an economic activity among others.

This difference has the consequence that the death of the two men has a different social meaning. The miner's death will be commonly identified as an *accident;* the death of the soldier on the battlefield as a *sacrifice.*

Because of this difference in the social meaning of their activities, the soldier is entitled to symbolic rewards, in terms of moral prestige, symbolic distinctions, glory notably when he has won a battle, or funeral honors in the case of death on the battlefield. For symmetric reasons, the miner is not entitled to the same symbolic rewards.

As the contributions of the two categories in terms notably of risk and investment are the same, the salaries of the miners should be higher; otherwise, an unjustifiable disequilibrium between the contributions and the rewards of the two categories would appear.

This system of reasons is responsible for the strong feeling of most people, states Adam Smith, that miners should be paid more than soldiers: they live in two different contexts.

Two remarks can be introduced at this point. The set of reasons appears as entirely convincing, *given the 18th century context.* In a context where technical progress would make possible that miners exploit the mine from the floor, instructing robots with the help of computers, the validity of the system of reasons would clearly collapse: the miners would no more run a deadly risk, but they would have to have a high level of competence and hence a long training. Second remark: the reasons grounding moral feelings are generally *metaconscious* in the mind of people: they are there, but in many cases become really conscious only from the moment when an individual asks himself or is asked why he thinks so.

These two points are of utmost importance: they explain that we can have negative feelings on the normative and axiological beliefs we observe in contexts we do not belong to. They explain also the over-time changes in our moral sensitiveness, since generations live in different contexts.

10 Lessons from Smith's example

Smith's example teaches several lessons. Systems of reasons on the salaries of miners and soldiers different from Smith's could be devised. One could argue, for instance, that soldiers are separated from their families and thus deserve more financial compensation. The argument may have been present in some minds. Would have it been sufficient by itself to create the widely shared consensus that impressed Adam Smith? Given that an empirical confirmation is in the case of this example practically impossible, it can only be stated that the reasons proposed by Smith are all straightforward, easily acceptable by anybody and compatible with one another, so that the consensus crystallized plausibly because this ideal-typical system of reasons appears as particularly convincing.

The philosopher and sociologist Max Scheler (1966) disagreed deeply with Adam Smith, since he developed himself an intuitionist theory of values. But he has the merit to have seen in full clarity that Smith's theory was of utmost importance for the explanation of normative and axiological collective values and he identified it correctly as *judicatory (urteilsartig)*. He saw well the core of Smith's theory of moral sentiments: that he proposes to analyze them as the consequence of systems of arguments that the members of a group perceive more or less implicitly as valid. It can also be noted that, while contemporary sociologists seldom consider Adam Smith as a founding father of their discipline, Talcott Parsons et al. (1961) fully recognized his importance for sociology.

Though Smith's *Wealth of Nations* is a main source of the so-called instrumental Rational Choice Theory, it contains at the same time in many passages as the one I am referring to here a powerful criticism of the limits of instrumental rationality and a proposal to overcome these limits by deriving normative and axiological feelings from processes guided by axiological rationality.

The approach Smith used can easily be illustrated by examples taken from modern writers. A contemporary theorist of ethics, Walzer (1983), proposes several analyses of our moral sentiments following the same line as Smith's analysis. To take an example close to Smith's: Why do we spontaneously consider conscription as a legitimate recruitment method in the case of soldiers but not of miners, he asks? The answer is again that the function of the former is vital to the country, while the latter is an economic activity among others. If conscription could be applied to mining, it could be applied to any kind of activities, so that it would lead to a political regime incompatible with the principles of democracy. Totalitarian regimes imposed to their citizens mining and other economic activities.

I would add in the same vein that we accept easily that soldiers are used as garbage collectors to meet situations of emergency, as when a lasting strike of garbage collectors threatens public health. But it would be considered illegitimate to use soldiers to fulfill such tasks in normal situations. Strong reasons likely to be widely shared are responsible here too for a collective moral feeling (Boudon 2011b).

In these examples, as in Smith's example, collective moral feelings are grounded on subjectively strong and objectively valid reasons. These reasons can be qualified as *trans-subjective*, since most people would likely consider them as strong. Using Smith's vocabulary, the "impartial spectator" would accept them. Thus, people who are not directly concerned in their interests because they are neither miners nor soldiers themselves and have no miners or soldiers among their parents and friends are in the position of the *impartial spectator*. They would consider as evident that miners should be paid more than soldiers.

So, Smith's analysis proposes implicitly a general theory of normative and axiological feelings. It suggests that they are grounded on reasons and that these reasons are not necessarily instrumental.

The feeling that "miners should be paid more than soldiers" is *collective* and strong because it is grounded on strong reasons in *individual* minds. The collective *feeling* in question is not a feeling in the psychological idiosyncratic sense of the word. It illustrates rather a type of feeling a social actor cannot experience without having at the same time the impression that the *Generalized other,* to use Mead's notion, would *feel* like him. Though *affective,* this feeling is associated with a system of reasons present in individual minds, though in a half-articulated intuitive fashion.

In his well-informed book on the state of the present social sciences on the question of the relation between emotion and rationality Livet (2002) has convincingly shown that emotions are a revelator of the values that guide social actions.

The philosophers of the 17th century, as Descartes, Pascal or Spinoza, wrote fascinating pages on the conflict between reason and passion. The existence of such conflicts at the individual level is not only obvious: they are omnipresent in the life of any individual. But sociology is not psychology. As Weber (1980) taught us, sociology is concerned with *social action*. Now, dealing with social action, one should be careful not to oppose affectivity and rationality.

The present fad for affectivity in sociology is possibly due to the fact that the diffusion of Rational Choice Theory appears to many sociologists as providing a chilly version of the *homo sociologicus.*

11 Moral evolution: an obsolete idea?

The evolution of norms, values and institutions is a classical issue of the social sciences from Durkheim (1967 [1893]) to Parsons (1961), Hayek (1974) or Eisenstadt (2002). They have shown that contextual analysis has the capacity of making moral evolution intelligible. None of them introduces the idea that there would be *laws* of historical development. As Pareto has written, when an idea is discredited, this situation tends to generate the view that the opposite idea is true. This figure is clearly illustrated by the case of evolutionism. From the moment when the evolutionary theories of the 19th century appeared as discredited, the idea that the notions of evolution and progress are obsolete tended to acquire the status of an evident truth. The so-called postmodern thinkers tend to adhere to the oxymoron of an absolute version of relativism, which sees the notion of progress as a mere illusion.

This radical thesis is so unacceptable that it has produced a reaction. Finally, the idea that there would be laws of history is a more or less permanent thesis developed by philosophy and the social sciences from Comte, Hegel, then Spencer, then the neo-hegelian Kojève[8] (1947) after the second World War, and close to us Fukuyama (1992), who saw in the fall of the Berlin Wall the end of history.

To *postmodern* philosophers and social scientists, the notion of progress would have been irreversibly discredited, as the notions of *truth, objectivity.* Postmodern sociology would have shown that such notions cover up mere illusions. This view is self-contradictory though, since postmodern sociologists claim to have discovered a *law:* that progress is an illusion and that this illusion would be irreversibly condemned.

Contemporary social scientists tend to treat the particular evolutions they observe and analyze as contingent. Thus, a number of writings *describe* the changes in sexual norms from *modernity* to *postmodernity,* but few attempt to *explain* why these changes give the strong feeling of being irreversible and why they probably are.

By contrast, Weber (1986) saw well that the *disenchantment* of the world was irreversible and tried to explain why. While he *explains* evolutionary phenomena, most contemporary sociologists content themselves by *describing* phenomena of *social change*, for the notion of evolution is commonly considered today as obsolete. Now, irreversibility is the feature that makes *evolution* distinct from *change*.

Again, contextual analysis in the sense defined at the beginning of this article does better than many contemporary analysts of social change. Durkheim and Weber and their followers provide through their contextual analysis of long-term social change an alternative both to postmodern relativism and to evolutionist theories.

While Durkheim recognizes fully, as Weber does, the parameterization by the social context of the reasons individuals endorse, both also stress that systems of reasons can be context-free, even on normative and moral questions. Nobody doubts that Lavoisier's theory of the composition of the air is better than Priestley's even though one can understand why Priestley was confident in his theory. In the same fashion, nobody doubts that Montesquieu's theory arguing that the distinction of powers is a *good* institution, since it makes political power both more efficient and more acceptable and dominates Bodin's or Beccaria's theory according to which political power cannot be efficient without being concentrated.

The negative feelings of the citizens of democratic countries against authoritarian or totalitarian regimes, the protest that can be observed when they feel that the distinction of powers is violated in their country and the manifestation of citizens' need

---

[8] Kojève was immensely popular in France among the young social scientists of that time, among them Raymond Aron.

for democracy in authoritarian regimes derive from the fact that they have in mind in a more or less conscious fashion the system of reasons elaborated by Montesquieu.

Other illustrations of the distinction context-free/context-bound can easily be mentioned: the value of the respect due to the dead is context-free since it is a consequence of the principle of the dignity of all human beings, while the symbolic norms expressing this value are context-bound. Politeness is context-free, but is expressed in context-bound ways. Montaigne wrote that some tribes honored their dead by eating them in order to give them the most noble sepulture and that they would be deeply shocked to learn that other tribes left their dead to the worms.

Durkheim (1970, p. 146) has answered the question as to why moral feelings can be context-free: "Individualism and freethinking were born neither with the French Revolution, nor with the Reformation, nor with the Greek and Roman antiquity, nor with the fall of the Oriental Empires; they belong to all times" *(L'individualisme, la libre-pensée ne datent ni de la révolution, ni de la réforme, ni de l'antiquité gréco-romaine, ni de la chute des empires orientaux; ils sont de tous les temps).* Durkheim means here by *individualism:* the sense individuals have for their dignity and basic needs; by *freethinking*, he means: their capacity to evaluate critically notably institutions. In other words, the dignity of human beings is a basic context-free value. This value can of course be deeply hurt in situations of war, when some categories of men are qualified as *enemies*, or in societies introducing the category of *second-class* citizens. But, even then, the value remains alive in most people's minds, excepting those who draw an advantage from the dual situation.

Context-bound moral beliefs can, as representational beliefs, be compared and evaluated. I can understand that in some contexts people believe in the efficiency of rain-rituals. But I do not need to believe it myself. I can understand that female genital mutilation is practiced is some societies because it is the consequence of a traditional system of beliefs. I need not seeing this practice as acceptable and I have reasons to think that the reasons prevailing on this issue in modern societies are stronger. I can understand that in an emergent society many people prefer an authoritarian to a democratic political organization. But I feel I have strong reasons to prefer democracy. I can *understand* that in some societies thieves run the risk of having their hand cut. But even radical relativists, if I may use this oxymoron, would find this practice inacceptable.

I feel in other words I am entitled do *judge* the practices in use in other contexts. Over-time moral change would be entirely unintelligible if the systems of reasons prevailing in various contexts could not be compared to one another.

12 The teachings of the World Value survey

Because of the broad geographical scope of Inglehart's (1998) data, since 43 countries were involved in the survey, and of their temporal depth, since the sample included three generations, they provide an ideal material for a contextual analysis of values.

By comparing the answers of the younger and older respondents, I readily checked that the younger tend to have a *rationalized* conception of moral values (Boudon 2011a). They tend to consider that the respect of other people is the ultimate ground of moral rules, that any rule that does not give the impression to be rationally grounded should be considered with skepticism, that authority is legitimate but acceptable exclusively when it is rational, that charismatic and traditional authority should be regarded with skepticism, that any rule grounded on tradition but giving the impression of not being rationally grounded is invalid.

On the whole, modern morality tends to be restricted to a single leading principle: that may be forbidden exclusively the forms of behavior that entail a negative impact on others. Conversely, the prohibition of any form of behavior entailing no detrimental effect on other people tends to be held as a *taboo:* as a rule owing its convincing power merely to tradition. Holding opinions considered by some people as shocking cannot be forbidden, since this would be contradictory with the notion of the freedom of opinion, which is itself a corollary of the principle of the respect of the dignity of all.

In the same fashion, the younger tend to have a more rational view of religious beliefs than the older: they tend to reject the elements of religious doctrines that cannot easily receive a symbolic interpretation. When they believe in God, they believe less frequently than the older in a personal God. They believe less frequently in a life after death. They tend on the whole to develop an *immanent* view of religion. Among the religious categories, Soul is much more resilient than God: an issue we already met.

As regards political values, they would like to see the political personal as more respectful of the wishes of citizens, new rights defined to the effect of protecting minorities and respecting the right of all to live their identity freely. To them, opinion democracy should correct the defaults of the representational party democracy. The younger believe less often than the older, other things equal, that political problems would have easy solutions. For this reason, they reject more often extremist political programs.

Another general finding from my reanalysis of Inglehart's study is that the effect of age reflects to a great extent the effect of education as a consequence of the overall increase of education over time: education seems in other words to be a major vector of the rationalization process going on in societies. On the whole, Inglehart's data show that the older and the younger groups live in different contexts. It suggests also that the values held by the younger express a long-time change presently in process.

13 Contextuality and relativism

Often a wrong conclusion is drawn from the idea that beliefs, actions, norms, etc. are in most cases contextual: a relativistic conclusion. It is wrong. Again I will document this point with examples.

As we saw, Durkheim maintains that self-interest is a constituent of any human being in any time and social context, and also, that depending on the parameters characterizing each society, human beings may be able to feel, express more or less clearly and satisfy more or less adequately this self-interest.

Durkheim develops these ideas in his *Division of Social Labor.* While many comments on this work insist on Durkheim's thesis that "individualism develops continuously through the course of history", most comments disregard the first part of the sentence, which states that "individualism begins nowhere". It is true that in Durkheim's mind the increasing complexity in the division of labor, because it has favored an increasing diversification of social roles and qualifications, has contributed reinforcing individualism, more precisely that it has given birth to institutions making easier the expression of individualistic values. It is true that Protestantism bears an indirect testimony in favor of the development of individualism in Renaissance time: as it stresses the freedom and responsibility of the believer in the interpretation of the Holy Scripture, Protestantism expresses, on a theological register, the fact that the development of the division of labor has increased the sense of their singularity in the mind of individuals. These statements are effectively present in Durkheim's *Division of Social Labor*. But they constitute only one part of his theory.

Again, Durkheim makes as clear as possible that, to him, if individualism grows continuously through history, it should also be recognized that "it begins nowhere". This formula indicates that individuals have always represented the reference point from which the relevance and legitimacy of norms and of institutions can be appreciated, and that in all societies, archaic as well as modern, individuals perceive institutions as more or less legitimate and acceptable. As to the criteria according to which they are judged as more or less acceptable or legitimate, they are the same in all societies: people appreciate or reject them depending on whether or not they have the feeling that they respect their dignity and vital interests.

As "individualism", in the sense Durkheim uses this word, means that people have a sense of the equal dignity of all, it assumes that a particular individual will tend to consider an institution as good or bad depending on whether he has the impression that any other individual would also have a tendency to judge it so. We can check immediately that it is difficult to state or even to believe that an institution is good or bad if one does not have the impression the other people would also tend to judge so. As conflicts of opinion in science, conflicts of opinion on moral, legal or political issues also oppose adversaries who hold different views. But they all believe that their reasons are grounded. An individual cannot consider some statement as true or some institution as good if he has not the feeling other people would also find the statement true or the institution good.

Briefly, the half sentence "individualism begins nowhere" indicates that, once an institution is proposed or imposed to a collectivity, any member of the collectivity will tend to consider it as acceptable or not, good or bad, legitimate or illegitimate, depending on whether he has the impression that it tends to be good for each of them and notably for him. That actual institutions in all societies tend to be evaluated, judged good or bad, legitimate or not, on the basis of this ideal principle does not mean of course that individuals are entitled or permitted to express this evaluation nor that they are in all cases explicitly conscious of it, nor that there are no conflicts of opinion.

Habermas (1981) has suggested that fair communication can *facilitate* the production in people's minds of the reasons justifying a normative conclusion. But communication cannot by itself make the reasons valid. On this point, Durkheim (1979, p. 624) was more clear-sighted: "in a first stage we believe in a notion because it is collective, then it becomes collective because it is true; we check its credentials before we endorse it" characterizes individual processes, not the collective evaluation of aims and goals: collecting postage stamps is collectively less positively evaluated than discovering a scientific novelty or writing an innovating novel.

Individuals are more respected in some societies than in others. The conception people have of their rights or of their dignity varies from one society to another. But there are no societies where people would not have the feeling of their dignity and of their vital interests and of the dignity and vital interests of other people. It seems advisable, as Durkheim proposes to do, to take all these facts into account: the fact that individualism begins nowhere as well as the fact that it is more developed in some societies than in others and in some conjunctures than in others.

14 Durkheim's intuition empirically confirmed

Many studies provide an empirical confirmation of Durkheim's statement according to which in all societies, traditional as well as modern, individuals have a sense of their dignity and vital interests. Popkin's (1979) *Rational Peasant* seems to me particularly illuminating in this respect.

Against a received idea defended by many anthropologists, he has convincingly shown that, in village societies of South-East Asia or Africa, the rule of unanimity is a widely accepted constitutional rule because it is perceived as the rule most likely to generate a respect for the dignity and vital interests of all.

Against this interpretation, most anthropologists have contended that the diffusion of the unanimity rule would reflect the fact that individuals in archaic societies have no sense of their singularity and would see themselves as mere parts of the collectivity.

To Popkin (1979), the unanimity rule was devised and accepted because any other decision rule would have entailed serious threats on the economically weakest members of the society.

Village societies of Africa and South-East Asia, he explains, are societies of small dimension, based on a subsistence economic system, with few exchanges with the outside environment. In such societies, the weakest members would be heavily threatened if collective decisions were taken, say, on the basis of the majority rule. Consequently, such a constitutional rule would not be considered as legitimate. Popkin's interpretation, by difference with the current interpretation of most anthropologists, recognizes the obvious fact that the unanimity rule maximizes the power of each individual, as shown by the very words, since the *unanimity rule* has another name: the *veto right*.

Moreover, Popkin's interpretation accounts for the fact that in village societies with the unanimity rule as a basic constitutional rule decisions take generally a long time and occur in a climate of confrontation and institutionalized conflict, as the word *palaver* indicates. On the whole, Popkin's study shows convincingly that the sense of all for their individuality and singularity is characteristic as well of societies where solidarity is "mechanical" to use Durkheim's vocabulary, as of societies with "organic" solidarity. Individualism meets more favorable conditions in the latter, i.e. modern societies; but it characterizes the former as well. The famous movie *12 angry men* (Lumet 1957), a sociological masterpiece, illustrates the context created by the unanimity rule. The twelve members of an American penal jury have to decide whether they decide to condemn a murderer to death penalty. After a while, eleven members have doubts and vote acquittal until the last member, who has voted for condemnation since the beginning, is finally convinced that doubts prevail.

As Durkheim, Simmel (2003) considers as evident the fact that the individualistic virus is present already at the dawn of history. It explains the abolition, in antique Germany, of the *Wergeld*, a judiciary practice that indexed the sanction on the social rank of the victim. Once it was abolished, any human life had in principle the same value. Once the abolition of the *Wergeld* was introduced, it became irreversible because it represents a step forward in the establishment of individualism. To Simmel as to Durkheim, individualism begins nowhere, but it leads the selection of ideas and institutions and explains that some ideas and institutions are irreversibly adopted.

Unfortunately, a lasting ethnocentric tendency leads on the contrary to the view that individualism is a cultural distinctive feature of modern Western society. As Durkheim and as Adam Smith before Durkheim, the economist of Indian origin AmartyaSen has stated though that the first value for any individual, Indian or European, is to be able to consider himself with respect.

On the whole, the analyses of Durkheim, Simmel, Popkin and others illustrate the powerfulness of contextual analysis in the sense I proposed at the beginning of this paper.

15 Explaining personal goals

Contextual analysis can also explain the aims and goals social actors follow. A major weakness of Rational Choice Theory is that it is unable to cope with this question. Except in one particular case: the case of addiction in the broad sense, since addiction can as well cover the case of the piano player whose practice generates a growing interest for playing the piano, or the case of the drug addict, to whom a new shoot protects him against the negative effects of the previous for the next one (Becker 1996).

I will evoke an example of my own where contextual analysis can explain the aims and goals of social actors, in this case of secondary school students. This example is developed in Boudon (1973). It rests upon the assumption that students tend to define the educational and social levels they aim to reach taking as a reference point the type of status people they are mainly in relation with have reached. They tend then to evaluate the likelihood for them to reach the educational level giving them a serious chance to reach it or to go beyond it.

This contextual model led me to a rough but on the whole right reproduction of a host of statistical data. The mechanism it hypothesizes explains more of the overall inequality of educational and social opportunities than the more popular explanation that attributes this inequality to the "cultural capital" families are able to transmit to their youngsters. If one would be able to neutralize this mechanism, it would reduce the weight of the inequality of opportunities much more significantly than if "cultural capital" would be reduced.

But contextuality is a property, not only of the objects of research, but of research itself. After others, Müller-Benedict (2007), then Müller (2009) and Relikowski et al. (2009) have confirmed the validity of the model, but they had to adapt it to the new contexts they were dealing with. In the 1970's, when I elaborated my model, immigration was marginal in Europe. This is clearly not the case in the 2000's. Relikowski et al. (2009) show for instance that the decision processes of immigrants and natives regarding the expected school and social status are not the same: another brilliant case of contextual analysis.

It should be recognized that sociology is unable to explain a host of individual choices on aims and goals. Some people have the impression they have a vocation for humanitarian causes, others for risky adventures, others for crime, others for the revolution and others for looking for scientific truth. But this "value polytheism" (Weber) is often ill perceived.

The *judicatory* theory of axiological feelings Smith's example notably illustrates has the important property that it overcomes the rigid binary distinction between affectivity and rationality: I have the strong *feeling* that some state of affairs is fair or unfair, legitimate or not, because I have strong *reasons* to believe so. The theory suggests also that the moral states of mind of the *self* depend on the way he perceives the states of mind of the *other people*: I cannot experience a reason as valid without having the feeling that the other man would share my view.

This approach to normative and axiological feelings offers moreover an analytical answer to Durkheim's question as to why any human being perceives his moral feelings as *constraining*.

Smith' example can once more help making this notion of *moral constraint* analytical, while it is often seen as a mere metaphor. It is easily checked that the individual statements used in Smith's argument have in common to be *subjectively strong,* and in Durkheim's sense *constraining,* because they are *objectively valid.* Some of these statements are empirical. For instance: "it takes as long to train a soldier as a miner", "both occupations are exposed to deadly risks". These statements are indubitable.

Uncontroversial too is the statement that reinforcing the security of a nation is a central social function, while mining is a particular economic function.

Some of the statements derive from the most familiar sociological theory: thus, exchange theory states rightly that people expect the reward they get to reflect the contribution they provide.

Some statements express familiar sociological observations: that death is not perceived as having the same meaning when it is the effect of selfsacrifice rather than of an accident or that symbolic rewards can be used to reward soldiers but not miners. These statements can also be easily accepted.

On the whole, all the individual statements used in Smith's argument are acceptable. For this reason, most people perceived its conclusion as strong.

16 Conclusion

I will just mention to conclude a practical consequence of the notion of contextual analysis I proposed in these pages. Scientific achievements are never exclusively the effect of the application of good techniques, in the social and human sciences as well as in the natural sciences.

Every scientific puzzle is unique, so that it requires scientific imagination to solve it. A practical consequence of this is that the best way to teach the complexity of the micro-macro link problem is to expose sociology students to examples where the problem has been successfully solved. They will learn then that the question as to "What is context?" has actually no general answer, but answers specifically adapted to the challenging macroscopic puzzles the sociologist wants do disentangle.

The main point of this article is that contextual analysis is the royal way of sociology at one condition, though: that the postulated dispositional features of the context are always empirical. This is the secrecy common to all the great sociological achievements, from Durkheim and Weber to contemporary sociologists.

A host of sociological publications deal with metaphors as: the *cement of society*, the *social link*, etc. without identifying satisfactorily the social mechanisms behind them. I hope this article will help clarifying this question.

Also, I hope this article will be read as a reaction against the prevailing pessimistic views on the future of societies.

References

Alter, Norbert. 2013. *La force de la différence. Itinéraires de patrons atypiques*. Paris: Presses Universitaires de France.
Becker, Gary. 1996. *Accounting for tastes*. Cambridge: Harvard University Press.
Boudon, Raymond. 1973. *L'inégalité des chances*. Paris: Armand Colin.
Boudon, Raymond. 2003. Beyond rational choice theory. *Annual Review of Sociology* 29:1–21.
Boudon, Raymond. 2010. *La sociologie comme science*. Paris: La Découverte.
Boudon, Raymond. 2011a. Modernization, rationalization and globalization. *Protosociology* 27:21–36.
Boudon, Raymond. 2011b. *Croire et savoir: penser le politique, le moral et le religieux*. Paris: Presses Universitaires de France.
Boudon, Raymond. 2013. *Le rouet de Montaigne: convictions et croyances*. Paris: Hermann.
Bronner, Gérald. 2009. *La pensée extreme*. Paris: Denoël.
Bronner, Gérald. 2013. *La démocratie des crédules*. Paris: Presses Universitaires de France.
Clavelin, Maurice. 2004. *Galiléecopernicien*. Paris: A. Michel.
Cusson, Maurice. 2006. La délinquance, une vie choisie. *Revue internationale de criminologie et de police technique et scientifique* LIX:131–148.
Durkheim, Émile. 1967. *De la division du travail social. 1893*. Paris: Presses Universitaires de France.
Durkheim, Émile. 1970. *Les études de science sociale. 1886*. Paris: Presses Universitaires de France.
Durkheim, Émile. 1979. *Les formes élémentaires de la vie religieuse. 1912*. Paris: Presses Universitaires de France.
Eisenstadt, Shmuel N. 2002. The construction of collective identities and the continual construction of primordiality. In *Making sense of collectivity. Ethnicity, nationalism and globalization*, ed. Sinisa Malešević and Mark Haugaard, 33–87. London: Pluto Press.
Fleck, Christian, and Nico Stehr, eds. 2011. *Paul F. Lazarsfeld: An empirical theory of social action, collected writings*. Oxford: Bardwell.
Frey, Bruno S. 1997. *Not just for the money: an economic theory of personal motivation*. Cheltenham: Edward Elgar.
Fukuyama, Francis. 1992. *The end of history and the last man*. New York: Free Press.
Habermas, Jürgen. 1981. *Theorie des kommunikativen Handelns*. Frankfurt a. M.: Suhrkamp.
Hayek, Friedrich A. 1974. *The pretence of knowledge, lecture*. Stockholm: Nobel Prize.org.
Hedström, Peter. 2005. *Dissecting the social: On the principles of analytical sociology*. Cambridge: Cambridge University Press.

Hofstadter, Richard. 1985. *The paranoid style in American politics, and other essays. 1965.* New York: Knopf.
Horton, Robin. 1993. *Patterns of thought in Africa and the West.* Cambridge: Cambridge University Press.
Inglehart, Ronald, Miguel Basanez, and Alejandro Moreno. 1998. *Human values and beliefs: A cross-cultural sourcebook: Political, religious, sexual, and economic norms in 43 societies: Findings from the 1990–1993 world values survey.* Ann Arbor: The University of Michigan Press.
Kahneman, Daniel. 2011. *Thinking fast and slow.* New York: Farrar, Straus and Giraux.
Kojève, Alexandre. 1947. *Introduction à la lecture de Hegel.* Leçonssur la *Phénoménologie de l'esprit* professées de 1933 à 1939 à l'École des Hautes Études. Paris: Gallimard.
Lévy-Bruhl, Lucien. 1960. *La mentalité primitive. 1922.* Paris: Presses Universitaires de France.
Livet, Pierre. 2002. *Emotions etrationalité morale.* Paris: Presses Universitaires de France.
Lumet, Sidney. 1957. *Twelve angry men (movie).* Berlin: International cinemafestival.
Müller, Walter. 2009. Benefits and costs of vocational education and training. In *Raymond Boudon, A life in sociology, vol. 3,* eds. Mohamed Cherkaoui and Peter Hamilton, 123–148. Paris: Bardwell.
Müller-Benedict, Volker. 2007. Wodurch kann die Soziale Ungleichheit des Schulerfolgs am stärksten verringert werden. *Kölner Zeitschrift für Soziologie und Sozialpsychologie* 59:615–639.
Olson, Mancur. 1965. *Logic of collective action.* Harvard University Press.
Pareto, Vilfredo. 1968. *Traité de sociologie. 1917–1919.* Genève: Droz.
Parsons, Talcott, Edward A. Shils, Kaspar D. Naegele, and Jesse R. Pitts, eds. 1961. *Theories of society. Foundations of modern sociological theory.* Glencoe, Ill.: The Free Press.
Pawson, Ray. 2009. On the shoulders of Merton: Boudon as the modern guardian of middle-range theory, In *Raymond Boudon, A life in sociology, vol. 3,* eds. Mohamed Cherkaoui and Peter Hamilton, 317–334. Paris: Bardwell.
Popkin, Samuel L. 1979. *The rational peasant. The political economy of rural society in Vietnam.* Berkeley: University of California Press.
Popper, Karl R. 1976. The myth of the framework. In *The abdication of philosophy: Philosophy and the public good,* ed. Eugine Freeman, 23–48. La Salle, Ill.: Open Court.
Raynaud, Dominique. 2006. Le context est-il un concept pertinent de l'explication sociologique? *L'Année sociologique* 56:309–330.
Relikowski, Ilona, Thorsten Schneider, and Hans-Peter Blossfeld. 2009. Primary and secondary effects of social origin in migrant and native families at the transition to the tracked German system. In *Raymond Boudon, A life in sociology, vol. 3,* eds. Mohamed Cherkaoui and Peter Hamilton, 149–170. Paris: Bardwell.
Root, Hilton L. 1994. *The fountain of privilege: Political foundations of economic markets in old regime France and England.* Berkeley: University of California Press.
Sanchez, Pascal. 2007. *La rationalité des croyances magiques.* Paris: Droz.
Scheler, Max. 1966. *Der Formalismus in der Ethik und die Materiale Wertethik. 1916.* 2 vols. Bern: Francke.
Shweder, Robert A. 1977. Likeliness and likelihood in everyday thought: Magical thinking in judgments about personality. *Current Anthropology* 18:637–659.
Simmel, Georg. 2003. *Philosophie des Geldes. 1900.* Frankfurt a. M.: Suhrkamp.
Smail, Daniel. 2012. Neuroscience and the dialectics of history. *Análise Social* 47:894–909.
Smith, Adam. 1976. *An inquiry into the nature and causes of the wealth of nations. 1793.* 7th ed. London: Strahan and Cadell.
Sukale, Michael. 1995. *Max Weber, Schriften zur Soziologie.* Stuttgart: Reclam.
Sukale, Michael. 2002. *Max Weber, Leidenschaft und Disziplin.* Tübingen: Mohr.
Walzer, Michael. 1983. *Spheres of justice: A defense of pluralism and equality.* New York: Basic Books.
Weber, Max. 1920. Letter to Robert Liefmann of march 9th, quoted by Wolfgang Mommsen. 1965. *International Social Science Journal* 17:23–45.
Weber, Max. 1922. *Gesammelte Aufsätze zur Wissenschaftslehre.* Tübingen: Mohr.
Weber, Max. 1980. *Wirtschaft und Gesellschaft, Grundriss der verstehenden Soziologie. 1922.* Studienausgabe. Tübingen: Mohr.
Weber, Max. 1986. *Gesammelte Aufsätze zur Religionssoziologie. 1920.* München: Mohr.
Wittgenstein, Ludwig. 1967. Bemerkungen über Frazer's The Golden Bough. *Synthese* 17:233–253.

Raymond Boudon†, 1934–2013. Professor, University of Paris-Sorbonne. Member: Académie des Sciences morales et politiques, Academia Europaea, British Academy, American Academy of Arts and Sciences, International Academy of Human Sciences of St Petersburg, Central European Academy of Arts and Sciences. Has been fellow at the Center for advanced study in the behavioural sciences, and invited professor notably at Harvard, Oxford, and the Universities of Geneva, Chicago, and Stockholm; founder of the European Academy of Sociology. Has published notably: Education, opportunity and social inequality (1974), The logic of social action (1981), Theories of social change (1986), The Analysis of ideology (1989), The Art of self-persuasion (1994), The Origin of Values (2000), Toqueville for Today (2006), Sociology as Science (2012); M. Cherkaoui and P. Hamilton (eds.) (2009) Raymond Boudon: A Life in Sociology. Essays in Honour of Raymond Bopudon. 4. vols.

Die Anderen als sozialer Kontext. Zur Bedeutung strategischer Interaktion

Andreas Diekmann

© Springer Fachmedien Wiesbaden 2014

Zusammenfassung Strategisches Handeln bedeutet, dass die Ergebnisse einer Handlung von „Ego" von den Handlungen der „Alteri" abhängig sind. Solche Situationen sind zahlreich im Alltagsleben, in Wirtschaft und Politik. Pioniere wie Erving Goffman oder Raymond Boudon haben die Bedeutung strategischen Handelns für die soziologische Analyse frühzeitig erkannt. Die Handlungsmöglichkeiten anderer Personen bilden den strategischen Kontext einer Person. Zwischen Kontext und Handlung besteht eine Wechselwirkung, deren Dynamik mit spieltheoretischen Modellen analysiert werden kann. Anhand der drei Beispiele Verantwortungsdiffusion, Wettbewerb und relative Deprivation, sozialer Tausch und Vertrauensproblem wird strategisches Handeln erläutert und aufgezeigt, dass strategischer Kontext die Ressourcen und die Wahrnehmung von Chancen beeinflusst, die in Analysen strategischen Handelns eben nicht als exogen angenommen werden können. Analysen des strategischen Kontexts bewegen sich sowohl auf der Mikro- als auch auf der Makroebene. Allerdings sind die strikten Rationalitätsanforderungen der Modelle nicht immer erfüllt. Oft sind evolutionäre Erklärungen angemessener, die auf weniger restriktiven Annahmen adaptiven Verhaltens basieren.

Schlüsselwörter Strategisches Handeln · Strategische Kontexte · Verantwortungsdiffusion · Relative Deprivation

---

A. Diekmann (✉)
CLU D 3, Eidgenössische Technische Hochschule Zürich,
Clausiusstraße 50, 8092 Zürich, Schweiz
E-Mail: diekmann@soz.gess.ethz.ch

Actor's Social Context. The Importance of Strategic Interaction

Abstract An action is defined as "strategic" when the consequences of ego's action depend on the action of alter. Situations of strategic interaction are numerous in daily life, business, and politics. Pioneers like Erving Goffman or Raymond Boudon recognized the importance of strategic interaction in sociological analysis long ago. Other peoples' opportunities of actions form ego's strategic context. The dynamics of the impact of the strategic context on ego's action can be modeled and analyzed by means of game theory. We will discuss three examples of strategic interaction models: "Diffusion of responsibility", Boudon's "logic of relative frustration", and the problem of social exchange and trust. We demonstrate the effects of the strategic context on the opportunities and beliefs of actors. In contrast to non-strategic rational choice theory, beliefs and opportunities are not assumed as exogenous. The analysis of the strategic context contributes to a better understanding of the micro-level effects and the macro-level implications. However, the strict rationality requirements of game models are often violated. In these situations, evolutionary models based on principles of learning and adaptions are more adequate than models based on assumptions of strict rationality.

Keywords Strategic contexts · Strategic interaction · Diffusion of responsibility · Relative deprivation

1 Einleitung: Kontext und soziales Handeln

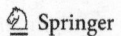

Ein Patient sucht seinen Arzt nach einem positiven Testergebnis einer Vorbeugeuntersuchung auf. Der Arzt rät zu einer speziellen Therapie. Es besteht das Risiko, dass der Arzt zwar nach bestem Wissen und Gewissen handelt, jedoch nicht auf dem neuesten Stand seiner Wissenschaft ist und eine wenig erfolgreiche Therapie verschreibt. Ein weiteres Risiko besteht darin, dass der Arzt zwar bestens informiert ist, aber nicht die optimale Therapie verschreibt, weil er selbst von einer bestimmten Behandlungsmethode profitiert. Der Patient hat also, anders als ein Flugpassagier, der der Kompetenz des Piloten vertraut, ein doppeltes Vertrauensproblem (siehe Gigerenzer 2013). Ähnlich geht es dem Kunden einer Autoreparaturwerkstatt, dem Kunden eines Anlageberaters einer Bank oder dem Klienten eines Rechtsanwalts. Max Weber definiert die Soziologie als Wissenschaft vom sozialen Handeln (Weber 1922). Er gibt ein Beispiel für eine Handlung an, die nicht unter die Kategorie „soziales Handeln" fällt: „Wenn auf der Straße eine Menge Menschen beim Beginn eines Regens gleichzeitig den Regenschirm aufspannen, so ist (normalerweise) das Handeln des einen nicht an dem des andern orientiert, sondern das Handeln aller gleichartig an dem Bedürfnis nach Schutz gegen die Nässe." Dagegen wäre es „soziales Handeln", wenn eine Person den Regenschirm aufspannt, weil dies die anderen tun und er nicht als Sonderling erscheinen möchte. Soziales Handeln erfordert nach Webers Definition, dass dem Handeln ein „subjektiver Sinn" zugeschrieben werden kann und das Handeln dem „gemeinten Sinn nach auf das Verhalten anderer bezogen wird und daran in seinem Ablauf orientiert ist" (Weber 1922). Das Verhalten gegenüber dem Arzt, dem Angestellten der Autowerkstätte, dem Anlageberater oder dem Rechtsanwalt ist in diesem Sinne soziales Handeln. Allerdings haben nicht beide Vertrauensprobleme strategischen Charakter. Das Vertrauen in die Expertise des Arztes ist eine nicht-strategische, sogenannte parametrische Entscheidung (Braun und Gautschi 2011). Dagegen ist das Vertrauen des Patienten, dass die Therapieempfehlung des Arztes im Falle eines Interessenkonflikts zugunsten des Patienten ausfallen wird, strategischer Natur. Ein misstrauischer Patient kann das erste Vertrauensproblem lösen, indem er einen als kompetent empfohlenen Arzt aufsucht. Das zweite Vertrauensproblem kann er lösen, indem er einen weiteren kompetenten Arzt aufsucht, der nicht als Therapeut tätig werden und nur eine Zweitdiagnose erstellen soll, sodass kein Interessenkonflikt besteht. Das zweite Vertrauensproblem ist strategisch, weil die Ergebnisse der Entscheidungen von Patient und Arzt, von Ego und Alter, jeweils wechselseitig von der Entscheidung des anderen Akteurs abhängig sind.

Allgemein verstehen wir unter dem „sozialen Kontext" eines Akteurs die menschengemachte Umwelt (Infrastruktur, Institutionen, soziale Normen und kulturelle Überzeugungen) und die sozialen Netzwerke und Aktivitäten, die die sozialen Handlungen eines Akteurs beeinflussen können.

Soziales Handeln im Sinne Webers kann strategisch oder parametrisch sein. Anders formuliert ist strategisches Handeln eine Teilmenge sozialen Handelns. Der andere oder die anderen strategisch handelnden Akteure bilden den sozialen Kontext, in den die Handlung eines Akteurs eingebettet ist.

Mit diesem „strategischen sozialen Kontext" und seiner Bedeutung für Erklärungen in der Soziologie werden wir uns im Folgenden hauptsächlich befassen. Hintergrund ist, dass viele soziologische Probleme strategischen Charakter haben, dieser aber in soziologischen Analysen häufig ausgeblendet wird. Ein Beispiel ist das instruktive Buch von Peter Hedström über „Die Anatomie des Sozialen" (Hedström 2007). Der strategische Kontext wurde in der analytischen Soziologie allerdings vernachlässigt (Diekmann 2010).

Im Folgenden werden in Abschn. 2 zunächst die Zusammenhänge zwischen Kontext, Handlung und Effekten auf der Makroebene erläutert. Der Abschn. 3 befasst sich anhand der Hypothese der Diffusion von Verantwortung, des Wettbewerbsmodells von Raymond Boudon und des Vertrauensspiels mit der Erklärung sozialen Handelns im strategischen Kontext. Es wird gezeigt, dass strategischer sozialer Kontext die Anwendung spieltheoretischer Methoden erfordert. Wenn Handlungen strategisch sind, können die unabhängigen Variablen der Handlungstheorie nicht mehr als exogen betrachtet werden. Zudem lösen spieltheoretische Methoden das Aggregationsproblem. Ferner richtet sich das Interesse auch auf die Entwicklung von Institutionen als Reaktion auf Probleme strategischen Handelns. Institutionen können Probleme strategischen Handelns entschärfen. Sie können aber auch neue strategische Probleme erst hervorrufen. In Abschn. 4 diskutieren wir abschließend das Problem rationalen Handelns im Kontext strategisch handelnder Akteure.

2 Kontext, Handlung, Aggregation und Makroeffekt

Um Kontexteffekte genauer erklären zu können, muss zunächst der Zusammenhang mit der Theorie sozialer Handlungen dargestellt werden. Sozialer Kontext beeinflusst die handlungsrelevanten Merkmale der Akteure. Einem einfachen heuristischen Schema zufolge, nehmen Handlungs- oder Entscheidungstheorien auf drei Kategorien unabhängiger Variablen Bezug. 1. Der Wert der Handlungsfolgen, 2. die wahrgenommene Wahrscheinlichkeit des Auftretens einzelner Handlungskonsequenzen und 3. die Handlungsressourcen. In der Formulierung von Hedström (2007) sind dies 1. „desires", 2. „beliefs", 3. „opportunities" (DBO), bei Gintis (2007) „beliefs, preferences, constraints" (BPC). Präferenzen entsprechen hier den „desires" und „constraints" (Restriktionen) entsprechen den Opportunitäten oder Ressourcen. Opportunitäten oder Ressourcen sind z. B. Zeit, Einkommen, technologische Möglichkeiten usw. Wer einen Lottoschein am Kiosk abgibt, hat den Wunsch (die Präferenz), einen möglichst hohen Gewinn zu erzielen, den „belief", dass eine bestimmte Wahrscheinlichkeit besteht, dass der Wunsch erfüllt wird (nicht notwendigerweise die objektive Wahrscheinlichkeit der Ziehung) und er hat einen entsprechenden Teil seines Einkommens zurückgelegt, um die Wette zu bezahlen. Die drei Elemente DBO (oder BPC) bilden noch keine vollständige Theorie. Dazu wären weiter a) Verfahren zur Messung von D, B und O für alle Handlungsalternativen und Handlungsfolgen erforderlich sowie b) eine Entscheidungsregel, die für jede Kombination von D, B und O angibt, welche Handlung ausgeführt wird oder mit welcher Wahrscheinlichkeit die Handlung ausgeführt wird. Abhängig u. a. von der Erfüllung mehr oder weniger restriktiver Annahmen gibt es mehrere Entscheidungs- oder Handlungstheorien (z. B. Braun und Gautschi 2011; Eisenführ et al. 2010). Die vielzitierte Wert-Erwartungstheorie oder SEU-Theorie ist nur eine Variante von mehreren. Streng genommen ist sie auf Entscheidungsprobleme nur anwendbar, wenn auch die Annahmen (Axiome) der Theorie erfüllt sind.

Entsprechend der zugrunde gelegten Theorie beeinflusst der soziale Kontext via DBO die Handlungsergebnisse, die die Akteure mit ihren Entscheidungen hervorbringen. Die aggregierten Handlungsergebnisse entsprechen dem Effekt auf der Makroebene. Coleman (1990) hat diese Zusammenhänge in einem didaktisch vereinfachten Schema dargestellt, das allerdings die Dynamik der Prozesse ausblendet (siehe auch Esser 1999).

Betrachten wir ein Beispiel. Emile Durkheim (1983) berichtet über die Analyse statistischen Materials zur Häufigkeit von Selbstmord in unterschiedlichen sozialen Gruppierungen. So zeigt sich, dass Katholiken eine geringere Selbstmordrate aufweisen als Protestanten. Bei diesem Befund bleibt Durkheim aber nicht stehen. Er versucht, die statistische Regelmäßigkeit durch einen allgemeineren Zusammenhang zu erklären, bei dem sozialer Kontext eine Rolle spielt. Der Schlüsselbegriff ist soziale Integration. Je integrierter eine soziale Gruppe ist (messbar etwa durch die Dichte von Netzwerkbeziehungen, wechselseitige Kontakte, Häufigkeit von Kirchenbesuchen usw.), desto geringer ist die Wahrscheinlichkeit eines Selbstmords. Wenn katholische Gemeinschaften in stärkerem Maße als protestantische Gemeinschaften sozial integriert sind, lässt sich so die statistische Regelmäßigkeit erklären. Der Grad der Integration ist ein Kontextmerkmal, das die Ressourcen und Handlungsziele der

Akteure beeinflusst. So wird es in sozial integrierten Gruppen seltener isolierte und vereinsamte Personen geben, was wiederum die Neigung zum „egoistischen" Selbstmord verringert.

Bei der Analyse von Kontextmerkmalen auf das Verhalten begegnet man dem interessanten Fall, dass das gleiche Merkmal als Individual- und als Kontextmerkmal unterschiedliche Effekte auf das Verhalten ausüben kann. So könnte man vermuten, dass sich katholische Wähler in katholischen Wahlbezirken anders verhalten als in mehrheitlich protestantischer Umgebung. Der Kontext, so die Annahme, moderiert die Wahrscheinlichkeit der Wahl einer sozialdemokratischen oder konservativen Partei. Ähnlich könnte soziale Integration sowohl als Kontextmerkmal (eine Person lebt in einer mehr oder minder sozial integrierten Gruppe) und als Individualmerkmal (eine Person ist in einem bestimmten Ausmaß sozial integriert) einen Effekt auf die Wahrscheinlichkeit eines Selbstmords ausüben. Während Durkheim, in der Sprache der Statistik, den „Haupteffekt" des Kontexts in den Mittelpunkt rückt, könnten zusätzlich das Individualmerkmal und der Interaktionseffekt (von Kontext und Individualmerkmal) eine Rolle spielen. Obwohl auch in diesem Fall das Aggregationsverfahren (im Unterschied zum strategischen Kontext) einfach ist und nur durch Summierung oder Bildung von Mittelwerten erfolgt, kann sich dennoch die Form des Zusammenhangs durch Aggregation qualitativ verändern.

Bezeichnen wir mit Y_{ij} die Selbstmordneigung einer Person i in der sozialen Gruppe j, mit X_{ij} das Ausmaß sozialer Integration der Person i in der Gruppe j (Individualmerkmal) und mit $X_{mj} = (1/n_j)\Sigma X_{ij}$ den Mittelwert sozialer Integration in der sozialen Gruppe j (Kontextmerkmal). Bei den sozialen Gruppen kann es sich um Nachbarschaften, Wahlbezirke oder Gemeinden handeln. Dann können wir (vereinfacht) die Hypothese in eine lineare Gleichung mit einem zusätzlichen Interaktionseffekt übersetzen und die Parameter z. B. per Regressionsverfahren schätzen: $Y_{ij} = d + aX_{ij} + b X_{mj} + cX_{ij}X_{mj}$. Der Interaktionseffekt berücksichtigt den moderierenden Einfluss des Kontexts auf den Effekt des Individualmerkmals. Zur Ermittlung des Effekts auf der Makroebene kann im vorliegenden Fall durch Mittelwertbildung über die Individuen i in Gruppe j auf einfache Weise aggregiert werden. Dann erhält man die Gleichung $Y_{mj} = d + (a+b)X_{mj} + cX^2_{mj}$. Bemerkenswert ist, dass aus einer linearen Einflussbeziehung auf Individualebene (mit „gemischtem" Interaktionseffekt) durch Aggregation eine quadratische Gleichung auf der Kontext- oder Gruppenebene resultiert.

Bei Durkheims Analyse des Selbstmords geht es im Sinne Max Webers um „soziales Handeln". Die Handlungen sind aber nicht strategisch. Die Aggregation ist einfach, da sich die Selbstmordrate in einer sozialen Gruppe als Anzahl der Selbstmorde pro Jahr, dividiert durch den Umfang der Bevölkerung, ergibt.

Anders verhält es sich, wenn Handlungen strategisch miteinander verknüpft sind. Das Aggregationsproblem ist dann nicht mehr trivial und kann wesentlich komplexere Gestalt annehmen. In alltäglichen Interaktionen, in der Politik und im Wirtschaftsleben sind die Handlungen der einzelnen Akteure oft wechselseitig voneinander abhängig. Die Ressourcen (Opportunitäten im DBO-Schema) sind dann ebenso wie die wahrgenommenen Wahrscheinlichkeiten der Handlungskonsequenzen (die „beliefs") nicht mehr exogen gegeben, sondern endogen abhängig von den Handlungen anderer.

3 Die Handlungen anderer als strategischer Kontext

3.1 Aggregationsproblem und Makroeffekt: Das Beispiel der „Diffusion von Verantwortung"

Strategisches Handeln heißt, dass die Ergebnisse einer Handlung von den Handlungen anderer Akteure abhängig sind. Betrachten wir die von Darley und Latané (1968) im Experiment untersuchte Situation, dass eine Person eine Hilfeleistung benötigt. Mehrere andere Personen wissen, dass die Person Hilfe benötigt. Sie wissen auch, dass eine einzelne Person genügt, um die Hilfe zu leisten und dass andere Personen die Situation in gleicher Weise wahrnehmen. Jede Person ist auch keineswegs völlig gleichgültig und durchaus interessiert, dass Hilfe geleistet wird. Jedoch zieht es jeder Beobachter vor, dass möglichst jemand anders die Hilfeleistung erbringt. Bekanntlich kommt es nach Darley und Latané (1968) dann zu einem Prozess der „Diffusion von Verantwortung". Je mehr Beobachter anwesend sind, desto geringer ist die Wahrscheinlichkeit, dass eine einzelne Person eingreift. Situationen der Diffusion von Verantwortung finden wir nicht nur bei Notfällen, sondern auch in vielen weniger ernsten alltäglichen Situationen ebenso wie im Wirtschaftsleben. Wenn ein Seminar von mehreren Lehrkräften durchgeführt wird, sind die einzelnen Beteiligten oftmals schlechter vorbereitet als bei alleiniger Verantwortung. Firmen warten darauf, dass andere eine Innovation entwickeln, die sie dann später kostengünstig kopieren können (Eger et al. 1992). Als allgemeines Modell für eine solche Situation ist das „Volunteer's Dilemma" (Freiwilligendilemma) vorgeschlagen worden (Diekmann 1985).

Die Situation hat eine sehr einfache Struktur. Alle Akteure sind daran interessiert, dass das Kollektivgut (Hilfeleistung, guter Unterricht, Innovation) hergestellt wird. Den Wert des Kollektivguts bezeichnen wir mit U, die Kosten der Herstellung mit K, wobei gilt: $U > K > 0$. Ein kooperativer Akteur erzielt in jedem Fall $U - K$. Ein nichtkooperativer Akteur erhält U, aber nur wenn mindestens ein anderer Akteur kooperiert, andernfalls gehen alle leer aus. Es gibt in dieser Situation eine symmetrische, rationale „Lösung", die mit den Mitteln klassischer Spieltheorie abgeleitet werden kann. Im sogenannten Nash-Gleichgewicht hat kein Akteur einen Anreiz, *einseitig* von seiner Handlungsstrategie abzuweichen, sofern die anderen Akteure die Gleichgewichtsstrategie beibehalten.

Ist p die Wahrscheinlichkeit der Kooperation und N die Anzahl der Akteure erhält man die Gleichgewichtsstrategie p* (Diekmann 1985):

$$p^* = 1 - \sqrt[N-1]{K/U}$$

Die individuelle Kooperationsneigung verringert sich, wie erwartet, mit den Kosten und wächst mit dem Wert des Kollektivguts. Genauer gesagt, und nicht ganz selbstverständlich, sinkt die Wahrscheinlichkeit mit dem *Quotienten* aus den Kosten der kooperativen Handlung und dem Wert des Kollektivguts. Weiterhin sinkt die Kooperationsneigung mit der Anzahl der Akteure N. Der in Experimenten beobachtbare Effekt der Diffusion von Verantwortung lässt sich aus dem einfachen Modell ableiten. Das vorliegende Modell einer interdependenten Handlungsstruktur kann in verschiedene Richtungen erweitert werden. Beispiele sind das asymmetrische Freiwilligendilemma (Diekmann 1993), das Freiwilligendilemma mit Kostenteilung (Weesie und Franzen 1998) und weitere Varianten. Diesen Varianten wollen wir hier nicht nachgehen, sondern uns weiter mit der Struktur der Erklärung befassen.

Die Handlungsstruktur ist gegeben durch den Typ des Spiels und die Größen N, K und U. Sie definieren den Kontext der strategischen Situation. U kann, bezogen auf das Hilfeleistungsbeispiel, interkulturell variieren. In einer egoistischen Gesellschaft wird der Wert des Kollektivguts geringer ausfallen als in einer solidarischen Gesellschaft.

Das Nash-Gleichgewicht ist ein zentrales Element zur Lösung des Aggregationsproblems bei interdependenten Handlungen. Prognostiziert man, dass die Akteure die Gleichgewichtsstrategie anwenden, errechnet sich in der symmetrischen Situation für jede Person die gleiche, individuelle Kooperationswahrscheinlichkeit. Um den Makroeffekt abzuleiten, müssen aber noch die individuellen Wahrscheinlichkeiten aggregiert werden. „Makro" bedeutet hier nur, dass der Effekt auf kollektiver oder Gruppenebene aus den individuellen Handlungen aggregiert wird. Im vorliegenden Fall ist der Makroeffekt der Handlungsstruktur die Wahrscheinlichkeit P, dass das Kollektivgut hergestellt wird. Die Anzahl der kooperativen Akteure folgt einer Binomialverteilung. Wenn wir nur wissen wollen, ob das Kollektivgut hergestellt wird, genügt es, die Wahrscheinlichkeit dafür zu berechnen, dass mindestens ein Akteur kooperiert. Dies ist eins minus der Wahrscheinlichkeit, dass niemand kooperiert oder $P = 1 - (1 - p^*)^N = 1 - (K/U)^{(N/(N-1))}$ gemäß der oben angegebenen Gleichgewichtslösung.

Durch die Diffusion von Verantwortung nimmt die Wahrscheinlichkeit einer individuellen, kooperativen Handlung mit der Zahl der Akteure ab. Gleichzeitig sorgt aber die wachsende Zahl dafür, dass die Wahrscheinlichkeit, dass mindestens eine Person kooperiert, zunimmt. Ob letzterer Trend ersteren kompensiert, hängt vom Verlauf der Funktion ab. Aus dem Modell folgt, dass auch die Wahrscheinlichkeit P der Herstellung des Kollektivguts mit der Gruppengröße N sinkt. Empirisch wurde in Experimenten zwar festgestellt, dass sich auf der individuellen Ebene die Wahrscheinlichkeit kooperativen Handelns vermindert (Diffusion von Verantwortung), das Ausmaß der Kooperation aber über der vom Modell prognostizierten Kooperationsrate liegt (z. B. Franzen 1995). Auf der Makroebene ergibt sich dann nicht, dass die Wahrscheinlichkeit der Herstellung des Kollektivguts ebenfalls mit der Gruppengröße sinkt. Goeree und Holt (2005) sowie Tutic (2014) haben auf Basis des Freiwilligendilemmas alternative Entscheidungstheorien herangezogen, um diese Diskrepanz zu erklären[1].

Zur genaueren Analyse strategischer Interaktion benötigen wir die Modelle und Lösungsbegriffe der Spieltheorie. Dies gilt besonders, wenn wir, wie in der analytischen Soziologie, an der Aufdeckung des erklärenden Mechanismus (Hedström 2007) interessiert sind. Mithilfe der Spieltheorie kann es gelingen, den sozialen

---

[1] Goeree und Holt (2005) berechnen das Gleichgewicht unter der Voraussetzung, dass die Akteure Entscheidungen mit einer gewissen Fehlerrate treffen. Für das resultierende (Quantal-Response-) Gleichgewicht können sie nachweisen, dass die Wahrscheinlichkeit, dass mindestens eine Person kooperiert, mit der Anzahl der Akteure zunimmt. Tutic (2014) erklärt den gleichen Effekt mit einem Modell begrenzter Rationalität von Rubinstein. Diese Theorien oder Modelle sind innovative Erweiterungen; ihre Validität müsste aber durch weitere empirische Tests geprüft werden.

Kontext, die Handlungsstruktur, genauer zu definieren. Weiterhin folgen aus den Modellen Hypothesen über individuelle Handlungsstrategien. Gleichzeitig verhilft das Nash-Gleichgewicht zur Aggregation der individuellen Handlungen und zur Ableitung des Makroeffekts. Die drei Schritte: Kontext – individuelle Handlung – aggregierter Makroeffekt können auf diese Weise präzise formuliert, die Ergebnisse an Daten geprüft werden.

3.2 Sozialer Kontext und Opportunitäten: Das Wettbewerbsmodell von Boudon

In der Untersuchung von Stouffer et al. (1965) wird die Zufriedenheit mit Beförderungen in zwei Armeeeinheiten berichtet. Paradoxerweise ist die Unzufriedenheit bei den häufiger beförderten Piloten höher als bei den Militärpolizisten, die im Vergleich seltener befördert wurden. Die Studie von Stouffer hat die Entwicklung und Diskussion über relative Deprivation und Bezugsgruppen stimuliert. Schon wesentlich früher hat Tocqueville (1969) auf ein ähnliches Paradox aufmerksam gemacht (Boudon 1979). Im „Alten Staat und die Revolution" entwickelt er die Hypothese, dass Unzufriedenheit und Proteste eher in prosperierenden Perioden kulminieren. Boudon (1979) hat Tocquevilles These aufgegriffen und versucht, den soziologisch interessanten Zusammenhang unter der Prämisse rationalen Verhaltens mit einem spieltheoretischen Modell zu erklären.

Die Grundzüge des Modells seien kurz skizziert (vgl. auch Berger und Diekmann 2014; Raub 1984). In einer sozialen Gruppe des Umfangs N stehen $0 \leq k \leq N$ Positionen für Beförderungen zur Verfügung. Wer befördert werden will, muss investieren. Die Kosten dafür betragen C, der Gewinn aus der Beförderung ist B. Erfolgreiche Kandidaten erzielen $\alpha = B - C$, Verlierer erhalten $\gamma = \beta - C$ und Akteure, die nicht in eine Bewerbung investieren, erhalten eine Auszahlung in Höhe von β (Abb. 1). Es gilt $\alpha > \beta > \gamma$. Die Anzahl von Investoren bezeichnen wir mit n.

Investieren heißt hier, generell Aufwand zu haben und Risiken einzugehen, um seine soziale Lage zu verbessern. Das Beispiel der Beförderung in einer Organisationseinheit von Stouffer et al. (1965) ist nur eine von vielen möglichen Anwendungen. Wer investiert, kann zum Zuge kommen oder auch nicht. Ob eine Person erfolgreich ist, hängt natürlich vom Verhalten der potenziellen Mitbewerber ab. Auf jeden Fall bleiben in einer Wettbewerbssituation n – k frustrierte Kandidaten auf der Strecke.

Abb. 1 Investieren im Wettbewerbsmodell (nach Berger und Diekmann 2014; siehe auch Hedström 2007)

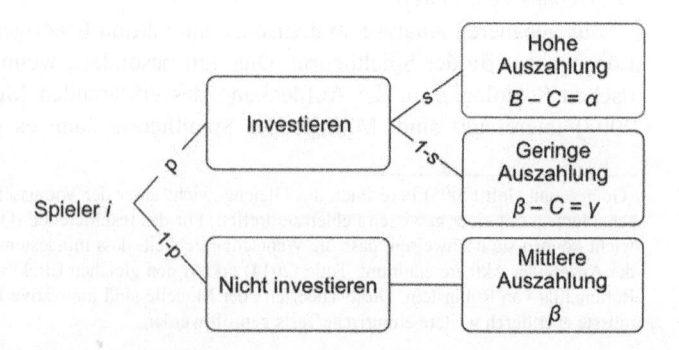

Investoren können folgende Auszahlung erwarten (Berger und Diekmann 2014):

$$E(k,n) = \begin{cases} \dfrac{k}{n}\alpha + \dfrac{n-k}{n} y & \text{für } k < n \\ \alpha & \text{für } k \geq n. \end{cases}$$

Ein rationaler Akteur wird investieren, sofern E(k, n) größer ist als β. Ist dies der Fall, unabhängig von der Zahl der Bewerber n, ist investieren eine dominierende Strategie. Etwas komplizierter ist die Situation, wenn „investieren" keine dominierende Strategie ist. In diesem Fall ist „investieren" bis zu einem Schwellenwert n* vorteilhafter als „nicht-investieren". Ist die Zahl der Konkurrenten allerdings größer als der Schwellenwert, wäre es besser, auf eine Bewerbung zu verzichten. Nur wissen die Akteure natürlich nicht, wie viele Mitbewerber jeweils investieren werden. Es gibt dann mehrere Gleichgewichte in „reinen" Strategien, die ohne Koordination nicht erreichbar sind, sowie ein Gleichgewicht in „gemischten" Strategien (Berger und Diekmann 2014; Raub 1984).

Die Handlungsstruktur ist durch die Regeln des Modells und die Parameter α, β, γ, N und k gegeben. Diese Elemente definieren den sozialen Kontext, in dessen Rahmen der Wettbewerb erfolgt. Die fünf Parameter sind exogen. Die Opportunitäten folgen dagegen endogen aus der Entscheidungsdynamik. Die Zahl der Konkurrenten, die die Chancen eines Kandidaten wesentlich beeinflusst, ergibt sich nämlich erst, wenn wir eine Hypothese über das Entscheidungsverhalten der Akteure annehmen. Wird nun, wie bei Boudon, die Rationalitäts-Annahme unterstellt, können verschiedene Hypothesen über den Effekt wachsender Chancen auf den Grad der Zufriedenheit oder Frustration abgeleitet werden. Unter bestimmten Bedingungen zeigt sich, dass die Zahl der Verlierer mit wachsenden Chancen (k) steigt und dann wieder sinkt. Gibt es wenige Chancen, werden nur wenige Akteure investieren. Entsprechend gibt es nur wenige Verlierer. Gibt es sehr viele Chancen, werden viele investieren. Es gibt dann viele Gewinner und ebenfalls wenige Verlierer. Problematisch ist die Situation zwischen den Extremen. Es gibt Gewinner, aber auch viele Verlierer. Der Verlauf der Zufriedenheit in Abhängigkeit von den Chancen ist u-förmig. Die Theorie oder das Modell gibt darüber Auskunft, unter welchen Bedingungen der abfallende Verlauf der Zufriedenheit, der „Tocqueville-Effekt", zu erwarten ist. Die aus der Theorie ableitbaren Hypothesen können sodann empirisch überprüft werden (dazu Berger und Diekmann 2014).

Der soziale Kontext definiert die Handlungsstruktur, die wiederum die Wechselwirkung zwischen Handlungsdynamik und Opportunitäten auslöst. Weil der soziale Kontext strategisches Verhalten der Akteure bewirkt, sind einfache parametrische Modelle zur Analyse der Handlungsstruktur ungeeignet. Die Opportunitäten (O im DBO-Schema) werden endogen geschaffen. Mithilfe spieltheoretischer Lösungsansätze kann die Handlungsdynamik dagegen angemessen untersucht werden. Die Nash-Gleichgewichtsstrategie ermöglicht zudem die Aggregation der Handlungsresultate. Unter bestimmten, angebbaren Bedingungen, folgt die Makrohypothese über den u-förmigen Verlauf der Zufriedenheit.

3.3 Sozialer Kontext und „Beliefs": Signale des Vertrauens

Sozialer und ökonomischer Tausch ist in der Regel mit einer doppelten Unsicherheit verbunden. Der Tausch ist zum einen zeitverzögert, d. h. einer der Tauschpartner tritt in Vorleistung. Zum andern ist nicht immer sofort ersichtlich, ob die getauschten Leistungen den Erwartungen entsprechen. Bei einem Tauschgeschäft z. B. kann es passieren, dass die gelieferte Ware von minderer Qualität ist. Es tritt ein Vertrauensproblem auf, das mit einem einfachen strategischen Modell, dem Vertrauensspiel, beschrieben werden kann.

Im Vertrauensspiel (Dasgupta 1988) interagieren zwei Akteure, der Treugeber und der Treuhänder. Der Treugeber hat die Entscheidung zwischen Kooperation (C) oder „nicht kooperieren" (Defektion D). Wählt er D, kommt kein Geschäft zustande. Keiner gewinnt und keiner verliert, die Auszahlung an Treugeber und Treuhänder ist jeweils null oder allgemein P. Kooperiert er dagegen, legt er sein Schicksal in die Hände des Treuhänders. Der Treuhänder wiederum kann kooperieren (z. B. die vorausbezahlte Ware liefern) oder defektieren, d. h. den Treugeber ausbeuten. Mit den üblichen Symbolen des Vertrauensspiels erhalten beide Akteure nach Kooperation den Gewinn R. Defektiert hingegen der Treuhänder, erhält er den Ausbeutungsgewinn T, der Treugeber macht einen Verlust S. Es gilt die Rangfolge der Auszahlungen $T>R>P>S$.

Beim einmaligen Vertrauensspiel wird ein rationaler Treuhänder, sobald er am Zuge ist, defektieren. Der Treugeber antizipiert dies und wird kein Vertrauen geben. Das Nash-Gleichgewicht in dieser Situation ist wechselseitige Defektion (mit Ergebnis P, P). Ein Geschäft kommt nicht zustande und beide verlieren im Vergleich zum Ergebnis wechselseitiger Kooperation, bei der sie jeweils R (Ergebnis R, R) erhalten hätten.

Tauschgeschäfte in kleinen Gemeinschaften sind nicht einmalig und nicht anonym. Oft werden wiederholte Tauschakte vorgenommen. Unter dieser Bedingung wird sich Kooperation entwickeln, wenn die zukünftig zu erwartenden Erträge aus der Tauschbeziehung hoch genug sind. Weiterhin kann es der Fall sein, dass der Treuhänder ethischen Normen folgt oder eine Reputation als ehrlicher Kaufmann hat, die er nicht aufs Spiel setzen möchte. Das Problem besteht dann aber darin, dass bei einmaligen Transaktionen oder am Anfang einer Serie von Transaktionen der Treugeber nicht weiß, ob sein Geschäftspartner vertrauenswürdig ist oder nicht.

Diese Überlegungen können mit einer Erweiterung des Vertrauensspiels präzisiert werden (Voss 1998). Wir gehen davon aus, dass es ehrliche und unehrliche Treuhänder gibt. Die ehrlichen Treuhänder sind an künftigen Geschäften interessiert mit Auszahlung $R^*>T$, für die unehrlichen gilt wie vorher $T>R$. Die Akteure sind in diesem Fall aufgrund ihrer Interessenlage „ehrlich" oder „unehrlich". Treugeber wissen, dass es einen Anteil von α ehrlichen und $(1-\alpha)$ betrügerischen Geschäftspartnern gibt. Wenn sie keine weiteren Informationen haben, werden sie immer kooperieren, sofern α größer ist als der Schwellenwert α^*, bei dem sie durch Kooperation mindestens so viel erzielen wie bei Verzicht auf Geschäftsbeziehungen, also mindestens P. Treugeber kooperieren immer, wenn $\alpha \geq \alpha^* = (P-S)/(R-S)$ und nehmen die Verluste durch betrügerische Partner in Kauf.

Wenn aber der Anteil betrügerischer Akteure zu groß wird ($\alpha < \alpha^*$), lohnt sich Kooperation nicht mehr. In diesem Fall würden keine Geschäfte zustande kommen. Der Markt kollabiert und sämtliche Akteure, einschließlich die betrügerischen Händler, haben das Nachsehen. In solchen Situationen ist es sehr wahrscheinlich, dass Signale entstehen, mit denen Treuhänder dem Treugeber kommunizieren, dass sie ehrlich sind (dazu genauer Przepiorka und Diekmann 2013). Die betrügerischen Treugeber sind natürlich auch daran interessiert, ehrlich zu erscheinen. Ein Signal nutzt deshalb nur, wenn es glaubwürdig ist. Anhand des Signals muss mit hoher Wahrscheinlichkeit erkennbar sein, zu welchem „Typ" ein Akteur gehört. Glaubwürdige Signale sind mit Kosten verbundene, beobachtbare Aktivitäten oder die beobachtbaren Ergebnisse von Aktivitäten. Genauer geht es um die Kostendifferenz bei der Produktion eines Signals. Diese Differenz muss so hoch sein, dass ehrliche Akteure trotz Signalkosten von der Kooperation profitieren ($R^* - s_A > P$), während betrügerische Akteure nicht gewinnen, wenn sie das Signal hervorrufen ($T - s_B < P$). s_A und s_B bezeichnen dabei die Signalkosten der ehrlichen bzw. betrügerischen Akteure. (Die Kosten der ehrlichen, aber nicht die Kosten der unehrlichen Akteure können null sein.) Unter diesen Voraussetzungen ist ein sogenanntes separierendes Signalgleichgewicht zu erwarten. Tätowierungen waren (früher) Signale, die darüber informierten, dass eine Person im Gefängnis war und bei illegalen Geschäften mit hoher Wahrscheinlichkeit vertrauenswürdig ist (Bammann und Stöver 2006; Gambetta 2009). Polizeispitzel waren dagegen mit hoher Wahrscheinlichkeit nicht tätowiert, sofern sie ein bürgerliches Leben hatten und die (sozialen) Kosten einer Tätowierung nicht auf sich nehmen konnten. Bei der Brautwerbung existiert in den meisten Kulturen das Problem, dass es ein Kandidat mit einer dauerhaften Beziehung nicht ernst meint. Kostspielige Verlobungsgeschenke sind ein Signal, das die ehrlichen von den unehrlichen Bewerbern unterscheidet. In den USA muss ein Verlobungsring heute etwa drei Monatsgehälter kosten, berichten Uhl und Voland (2002).

Ehrliche Gebrauchtwarenhändler geben eine Garantie. Wenn sie ehrlich sind (und keine Fehler passieren), sind die Kosten null. Für unehrliche Gebrauchtwarenhändler wären dagegen die Kosten prohibitiv hoch. Das Garantieversprechen ist ein Signal, das dem Kunden erlaubt, zwischen ehrlichen und betrügerischen Händlern zu unterscheiden.

Für unsere Diskussion ist von Bedeutung, dass in Signalspielen (z. B. Diekmann 2013) die subjektiven Wahrscheinlichkeiten, dass ein Akteur zu einem bestimmten Typ gehört, erst durch die Handlungen der Akteure bestimmt werden.

Der soziale Kontext besteht aus der Spielstruktur (dem Entscheidungsbaum), den Präferenzrangfolgen der Typen von Akteuren (dem D in DBO) und den Signalkosten. Diese Elemente sind exogen gegeben. Die „beliefs" (das B in DBO) folgen dagegen endogen aus der Handlungsdynamik. Der soziale Kontext beeinflusst die „beliefs" und diese wiederum die Handlungen. Im Vertrauensspiel ist dies die Entscheidung für Kooperation. Als Makroresultat ergeben sich Märkte, auf denen kooperative Tauschhandlungen vollzogen werden.

3.4 Institutionen

Signale in Vertrauensbeziehungen werden dann auftreten, wenn gesetzliche oder andere institutionelle Regelungen nicht möglich oder schwer durchsetzbar sind (z. B. auf illegalen Märkten), die meisten Transaktionen einmalig sind oder selten wiederholt werden und auch keine verlässlichen Informationen über die Reputation der Akteure vorliegen. Abhängig vom jeweiligen Kontext (einmalig versus wiederholt, Verfügbarkeit verlässlicher Informationen über Reputation, funktionierendes Rechtssystem) können jeweils unterschiedliche Kooperationslösungen in Vertrauensbeziehungen entstehen. Über die Rolle sozialer Einbettung und den empirischen Test von Hypothesen zur dyadischen, institutionellen und Netzwerkeinbettung bei Vertrauensproblemen informieren Raub und Buskens (2006). DiMaggio und Louch (1998) zeigen, dass soziale Netzwerke insbesondere bei Märkten mit Vertrauensproblemen wie dem Gebrauchtwagenmarkt einen Einfluss auf die Auswahl des Händlers ausüben.

Eine Studie von Siamwalla (1978) über die Marktstruktur agrarischer Produkte in Thailand gibt Aufschluss, dass die Lösung von Vertrauensproblemen bei Transaktionen wesentlich von den Eigenschaften der gehandelten Produkte abhängen. Reis z. B. wird von den Bauern an verschiedene Zwischenhändler verkauft. Die Bindung an einen einzelnen Aufkäufer ist hier gering. Die Qualität der Ware ist vor dem Kauf gut erkennbar, sodass kein spezifisches Vertrauensproblem bezüglich der Qualität besteht. Ganz anders verhält es sich bei Gummi. Beim Kauf des Rohprodukts kann der Händler die Qualität nicht einschätzen, während der Gummifarmer selbst sehr viel besser weiß, ob das Produkt hoch- oder geringwertig ist. Die Qualität des Rohstoffs hängt nämlich von der Sorgfalt des Farmers ab, mit der unreine Stellen beseitigt wurden sowie von der Qualität der verwendeten Säure (Siamwalla 1978). Erst sehr viel später, nach der weiteren Verarbeitung, stellt sich die Qualität des Rohprodukts heraus. Aufgrund der asymmetrischen Information besteht ein Vertrauensproblem. Im Unterschied zum Reismarkt, entstand deshalb beim Gummi eine andere Marktstruktur. Die Loyalität zwischen Verkäufer und Käufern ist hoch; ein Gummifarmer hat nur wenige Aufkäufer, die diesen Farmer kennen und der Qualität der Ware vertrauen. Hinzu kommt die „Kettenstruktur" des Handels. Ein Aufkäufer im Dorf verkauft an einen Händler im Distrikt und dieser wieder an einen Großhändler (Siamwalla 1978).

Die Eigenschaften der Ware, Gummi versus Reis, rufen in unterschiedlichem Maße Vertrauensprobleme hervor. Diese Probleme werden durch verschiedene Marktstrukturen oder Institutionen gelöst. Reismärkte sind oft Auktionsmärkte, während auf Märkten für das Rohprodukt Gummi langfristige Bindungen zwischen den Handelspartnern und Reputation charakteristisch sind (Kollock 1994). In einer experimentellen Studie hat Kollock (1994) die Märkte für Reis und Gummi simuliert. Versuchspersonen konnten unter den verschiedenen Marktbedingungen handeln, wobei sich im Ergebnis ähnliche Marktstrukturen entwickelten, wie sie für den Reis- und Gummihandel berichtet wurden. Der Kontext der Akteure, und hier insbesondere Unsicherheit der Information, beeinflusst die Handlungen der Transaktionspartner und führt auf der Makroebene zu spezifischen Marktstrukturen und Institutionen.

Im digitalen Handel entstehen Vertrauensprobleme durch die Anonymität der Marktteilnehmer, die oft über große Entfernungen und Landesgrenzen hinweg Waren per Mausklick ersteigern. Die meisten Transaktionen sind einmalig; nur ein relativ geringer Anteil von Geschäftsabschlüssen auf den bekannten Plattformen wie eBay wird wiederholt unter den gleichen Handelspartnern getätigt. Gemäß dem Standard-Vertrauensspiel sollten diese Tauschakte im Nash-Gleichgewicht gar nicht stattfinden; die anonymen Märkte kollabierten. Aber es handelt sich eben nicht um ein einfaches, einmaliges Vertrauensspiel. Mit der Einführung der Möglichkeit, den Verkäufer bewerten zu können, wurde das Vertrauensproblem wesentlich entschärft. Statt des „Schattens der Zukunft" im wiederholten Spiel wurde mit der Einführung von Reputation quasi ein „Schatten der Vergangenheit" geschaffen. Verkäufer sind im Eigeninteresse bemüht, eine Reputation aufzubauen; Käufer wiederum honorieren die Reputation. Allerdings ist es nicht ganz selbstverständlich, dass das Bewertungssystem funktioniert, denn eigennützige Akteure würden sich die Mühe der Bewertung einfach ersparen. Der homo oeconomicus gibt kein Feedback, das Bewertungssystem würde zusammenbrechen und damit auch der Auktionsmarkt. Ein kleiner Schuss Altruismus und Reziprozität, der über den Eigennutz des homo oeconomicus hinausgeht, ist das Schmieröl anonymer, elektronischer Märkte. Das Reputationssystem ist ein einfacher, aber äußerst wirksamer institutioneller Mechanismus, der diese Milliarden schweren Märkte erst ermöglicht (Diekmann et al. 2014). Allerdings hat das wechselseitige Bewertungssystem von eBay das Ausmaß positiver Bewertungen inflationiert. Eine neue institutionelle Regelung, die ein Problem entschärft, schafft oft ein neues, das im vorliegenden Fall aber mit einer Änderung des Systems behoben werden konnte[2].

Es gibt unterschiedliche institutionelle Regelungen zur Lösung von Vertrauensproblemen auf Märkten, wobei wir hier unter Institutionen dauerhafte, berechenbare Anreizmechanismen verstehen (z. B. Homann und Suchanek 2005). Neben rechtlichen Regelungen sind dies private Ordnungsmechanismen, die auf den Prinzipien von a) Loyalität (wiederholte Transaktionen unter den gleichen Partnern), b) Reputation (Bewertungen vergangener Transaktionen durch andere Handelspartner oder Bewertungen durch spezialisierte Agenturen) und c) Pfand (Hinterlegung einer Kaution) beruhen.

Die kostenlose Verfügbarkeit der Transaktionsgeschichte eines Verkäufers binnen Sekunden an jedem Ort der Welt, die Implementierung eines Reputationssystems auf Online-Plattformen, wurde erst durch die Entwicklung der Internet-Technologie ermöglicht. Andere, „alte" Institutionen wie „Pfänder" (dazu Raub und Buskens 2006) lösen Vertrauensprobleme unter der Bedingung geringer Transaktionskosten. Das Pfand muss nicht den Verlust des Treugebers von R – S bei opportunistischem Verhalten des Treuhänders ausgleichen. Es kann oft viel geringer sein, denn es muss dem Treuhänder nur den Anreiz nehmen zu betrügen (T – R). Deshalb genügt in der Regel ein Pfand von einem Euro, um Supermarktkunden zu veranlassen, ihren Einkaufswagen zurückzubringen. Ein Pfand ist die übliche Absicherung gegen Vertrauensprobleme auf dem Wohnungsmarkt. Würde es keine Kautionen geben, würden auf Vermietermärkten vermutlich in (noch) stärkerem Maße Vorurteile und Diskriminierung Platz greifen (Diekmann 2013).

Der strategische Kontext der handelnden Akteure schafft ein Vertrauensproblem. Institutionelle Regelungen können das Problem entschärfen. Welche Art von Rege-

---

[2] Auch nach Reform des Systems wechselseitiger Bewertung von Käufer und Verkäufer ist die Bewertungsrate bei eBay auf erstaunlich hohem Niveau geblieben. Siehe dazu Bolton et al. (2013).

lung entsteht, hängt von verschiedenen Bedingungen wie Informationsasymmetrien, Transaktionskosten und technologischem Fortschritt ab. Der Kontext strategisch handelnder Akteure ist dabei der Ausgangspunkt von Erklärungen der Entwicklung von Institutionen.

4 Rationales Handeln, „Beauty Contest" und begrenzte Rationalität

Kaum ein Begriff in den Sozialwissenschaften ist so stark mit Missverständnissen behaftet wie die Begriffe „Rationalität" oder „rationales Handeln". Wir verstehen hier unter Rationalität nicht mehr (und nicht weniger) als *konsistente* Entscheidungen. Konsistenz ist das Definitionsmerkmal. Es bedeutet, dass Entscheidungen in Übereinstimmung mit den Axiomen einer Rationalitäts-Theorie getroffen werden. Diese Definition wird auch von der Erwartungsnutzentheorie Neumann-Morgensterns und der Theorie des subjektiven Erwartungsnutzens (SEU) von Savage vorausgesetzt (siehe einführend Eisenführ et al. 2010). Entsprechend dieser Definition gibt es mehr oder minder restriktive Anforderungen an den Begriff „rationalen Handelns", da es unterschiedliche Entscheidungstheorien mit unterschiedlichen Axiomen-Systemen gibt.[3] Allerdings werden die meisten Entscheidungstheorien wohl die Gültigkeit eines Axioms voraussetzen, nämlich Transitivität von Präferenzen: Wenn A der Alternative B vorgezogen wird und B der Alternative C, dann sollte auch A der Vorzug gegenüber C gegeben werden.

Unsere Definition steht nicht im Gegensatz zur Definition des „frühen" Boudon, dessen Wettbewerbsmodell weiter oben behandelt wurde. Die Definition steht allerdings im Gegensatz zu Boudons (2013) Konzept von Rationalität (oder „kognitiver Rationalität"), das er in späteren Schriften ausgearbeitet hat (dazu auch Boudon in diesem Band). Es steht auch nicht im Einklang mit Konzepten, die spezifische Motive als Komponenten der Definition von Rationalität einfordern.

Rationalität erfordert nicht Eigennutz und schon gar nicht materiellen Eigennutz. Der homo oeconomicus handelt per Definitionem rational, aber rationales Handeln ist nicht gleichbedeutend mit dem Handeln des fiktiven homo oeconomicus.

Rationalität und Altruismus müssen keine Gegensätze sein. Menschen können altruistisch rational handeln im Sinne des Konsistenzkriteriums. Andreoni und Miller (2002) haben gezeigt, dass Akteure mit altruistischen Präferenzen rational in dem Sinne handeln können, dass sie die Axiome der Entscheidungstheorie erfüllen. Wenn Menschen nicht dem Bild des homo oeconomicus entsprechen und zudem noch altruistische Ziele verfolgen, folgt nicht zwangsläufig, dass sie irrational handeln. Im Sinne des Konsistenzkriteriums können ihre Entscheidungen strikt rational sein.

„Rationalität" wird „motivfrei" definiert, ohne bestimmte Präferenzen / Ziele / desires auszuschließen. Die axiomatische Nutzentheorie von Neumann-Morgenstern oder Savage (Braun und Gautschi 2011; Eisenführ und Weber 2010) hat schon immer die „weite" Version der Rational-Choice-Theorie (Opp 1999; Finkel 2008) eingeschlossen. Allerdings muss es Hinweise auf die empirische Gültigkeit der Annahmen

---

[3] Für die deskriptive Anwendung einer Entscheidungstheorie ist es ohnehin unerheblich, ob man ein Verhalten als „rational" bezeichnet oder nicht.

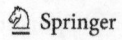

geben, die zumindest näherungsweise erfüllt sein sollten. Dieser Aspekt gerät bei Anwendungen, insbesondere in der Soziologie, allzu oft ins Hintertreffen.

Im strategischen Kontext kommt eine weitere Rationalitäts-Anforderung hinzu, die empirisch nicht immer erfüllt ist: „common knowledge". Damit ist gemeint, dass alle Akteure bestimmte (aber nicht notwendigerweise die gleichen) Informationen über die Spielstruktur und die Auszahlungen haben und alle wissen, dass alle dieses Wissen haben usw.

Betrachten wir eine Situation, in der genau diese Annahme kritisch ist. Das „Beauty-Contest-Spiel" erhielt den Namen von einem Zitat von Keynes, in dem er den Kauf von Aktien mit einem Schönheitswettbewerb vergleicht (Selten und Nagel 1998). Auf Aktienmärkten geht es nicht darum, sich für die der eigenen Meinung nach beste Aktie zu entscheiden, sondern für diejenige, von der man glaubt, dass die anderen sie für die beste Entscheidung halten. Mehr noch, nämlich von der man glaubt, dass alle glauben, dass die anderen sie als besten Kauf bewerten usw. Die Regeln des Beauty-Contest-Spiels sind einfach. Es gibt N Teilnehmer, die eine Zahl zwischen null und 100 wählen sollen. Einen Preis erhält, wer 2/3 des (arithmetischen) Mittelwerts aller genannten Zahlen am nächsten kommt. Bei mehreren Gewinnern wird der Preis geteilt.

Würde man nicht-strategisch überlegen, könnte man sagen: „Alle Zahlen sind gleichverteilt, der Mittelwert sollte daher bei 50 liegen. Ich wähle 33 1/3, denn das sind 2/3 von 50." Strategisches Denken auf der ersten Stufe geht einen Schritt weiter. „Wenn alle diese Überlegung anstellen, wird der Mittelwert 33 1/3 sein. Ich wähle deshalb 22 2/9." Auf der nächsten Stufe strategischen Denkens sind es ungefähr 15 usw., bis man sich schließlich in fortwährenden Iterationen der Null annähert.

Die Wahl von „Null" ist auch die einzige strikte Nash-Gleichgewichtsstrategie. Das Ergebnis im Gleichgewicht ist zudem Pareto-optimal, d. h. es gibt keine andere Kombination von Strategien, bei der Akteure mehr erzielen können, ohne dass andere Nachteile erleiden. Bei einem bindenden Vertrag würden, anders als im Gefangenendilemma, alle Akteure das Nash-Gleichgewicht vereinbaren. Nach üblichen Kriterien der klassischen Spieltheorie wäre die Nash-Gleichgewichtsstrategie rational. Wenn entsprechend der verhaltensorientierten Spieltheorie „Ungleichheitsaversion" als Motiv hinzukommt (Fehr und Schmidt 1999), würde sich daran nichts ändern. Im Gegenteil, es wäre ein weiterer Grund für die Wahl der Rationalitäts-Strategie, da diese auch noch zu maximaler Gleichheit führt.

In Experimenten wählen allerdings nur relativ wenige Akteure die Gleichgewichts-Strategie. Die Wahlen häufen sich typischerweise bei rund 33 oder 22. Wenn man nun die Entscheidungssituation erneut vorgibt und über den Mittelwert informiert, wird man Werte bei 15 oder 10 erhalten und mit weiteren Runden sich dem Gleichgewicht annähern (Selten und Nagel 1998). Diesen Prozess beobachtet man auch dann, wenn genauere Informationen über die Verteilung der Vorrunde gegeben werden (Diekmann 2009). Man könnte nun annehmen, dass die Akteure die Gleichgewichtsstrategie nicht wählen, weil sie diese nicht kennen. In einem Vorlesungs-Experiment wurde daher der Hälfte der Teilnehmer die Nash-Gleichgewichtsstrategie mitgeteilt, dagegen nicht den Teilnehmern in der Kontrollgruppe. Zwar lagen nun die gewählten Zahlen in der informierten Gruppe unter den Durchschnittswerten der Kontrollgruppe, aber keineswegs wurde überwiegend die „Rationalitäts-Strategie" gewählt. Warum handeln die Akteure „irrational" gemessen am Kriterium des „common knowledge"? Die Antwort lautet vermutlich: Selbst wenn man weiß, dass es rational wäre, null zu wählen, so ist doch damit zu rechnen, dass ein Teil der Mitspieler dies nicht tun wird (Selten und Nagel 1998). Dann aber ist es sinnvoller nicht die Gleichgewichtsstrategie zu wählen. Also wird man selbst auch nicht diese Strategie wählen. Die vermutete Irrationalität der Anderen hat zur Folge, dass ein Akteur sich nicht für die Gleichgewichts-Strategie entscheiden wird und somit selbst irrational handelt. Diese Entscheidung ist klug, denn in keinem der publizierten Beauty-Contest-Experimente hat jemals ein Akteur mit der Wahl der Gleichgewichtsstrategie in der ersten Runde einen Gewinn erzielt. Das Common-Knowledge-Kriterium wechselseitiger Rationalität und des Wissens darüber ist im strategischen Kontext keineswegs immer erfüllt.

Das Beauty-Contest-Spiel wurde zur Erklärung von spekulativen „Blasen" auf Aktien- oder Immobilienmärkten herangezogen. Selbst wenn man weiß, dass es sich um eine Blase handelt und man das Platzen der Blase erwartet (aber der Zeitpunkt ungewiss ist), kann es sich lohnen zu investieren. Denn die Preise können bis zum Eintreten der Katastrophe noch weiter steigen. Ähnlich wählen Akteure im Beauty-Contest-Spiel zumindest zeitweilig die „irrationale" Strategie, obwohl ihnen die Gleichgewichts-Strategie bekannt ist. Plastisch formulierte der Chef der Citygroup, Charles Prince, diese Überlegung in der „Financial Times" im Juli 2007, kurz vor Ausbruch der Krise: „When the music stops, in terms of liquidity, things will be complicated. But as long as the music is playing, you've got to get up and dance. We're still dancing" (nach Akerlof and Shiller 2010, S. XII). Im folgenden Jahr platzte die Blase!

Die stufenweise Annäherung an die Gleichgewichts-Strategie mit wachsender Rundenzahl des „Beauty Contest" demonstriert, dass Gleichgewichtspunkte im Zuge eines evolutionären Prozesses durch Lernen und adaptives Verhalten erreicht werden können. Lernen, adaptives und myopisches Verhalten beobachtet man oft in experimentellen Studien. Theorien begrenzter Rationalität („bounded rationality"), die explizit von Prinzipen adaptiven Verhaltens ausgehen, sind in diesen Fällen strikten Rationalitäts-Theorien (als deskriptive, prognostische Theorie) überlegen.

5 Ausblick

Pioniere in der Soziologie wie Goffman (1969) oder Boudon (1979) haben erkannt, dass in vielen Fällen strategisches Handeln der Schlüssel zur Erklärung gesellschaftlicher Prozesse ist. Soziale Handlungen im Sinne Max Webers haben strategischen Charakter, wenn sie nicht nur an den Handlungen anderer ausgerichtet, sondern die Ergebnisse von den Handlungen anderer *abhängig* sind. Dies unterscheidet bloße Imitation von einer Massenpanik, einem Börsenkrach oder dem Wachstum einer Protestbewegung. Heute stehen zunehmend verfeinerte Modelle der klassischen und der verhaltensorientierten Spieltheorie zur Verfügung, mit deren Hilfe es erst möglich ist, den strategischen Kontext, die Struktur strategischer Interaktionen, präzise zu beschreiben und daraus prüfbare Folgerungen abzuleiten. Die Grundlagenprobleme soziologischer Forschung haben strategischen Charakter: Die Entstehung sozialer Ordnung, die Probleme von Kooperation, Konflikt und dem Zerfall von Ordnung, die Befolgung sozialer Normen und das Problem der Sanktionierung, die Entstehung von Institutionen, sozialer Tausch und Vertrauensproblem, die Entwicklung von Protestbewegungen, soziale Dilemmas und kollektive Güter. Sowohl in der Ausbildung als auch in der Forschung der Soziologie sollten die modernen Methoden der Analyse strategischer Interaktionen größere Verbreitung finden.

Die aus Modellen strategischen Handelns ableitbaren Hypothesen können experimentell, in Feldexperimenten, Survey-Studien oder mit anderen Methoden untersucht werden. Die experimentelle Methode hat den Vorteil, dass durch Randomisierung Kausalbeziehungen genauer nachweisbar sind. Das Laborexperiment in der Verhaltensforschung ist aber nur ein erster Filter, denn die untersuchten Hypothesen sollten sich danach auch in Feldexperimenten oder anderen Studien bewähren, um als valide gelten zu können.

Die klassische Spieltheorie erfordert starke Rationalitäts-Annahmen. In Situationen, in denen diese Modelle hinreichend valide Prognosen erlauben, besteht kein Grund, alternative Entscheidungsprinzipien heranzuziehen. Zudem liefert die Theorie einen Referenzpunkt. Weicht das beobachtete Verhalten davon ab, stellt sich die Herausforderung, die „Anomalie" zu erklären. Auf diese Weise wurden oft neue Hypothesen und Erklärungen hervorgebracht. Wenn die strikten Rationalitäts-Modelle versagen, wie beim Beauty Contest demonstriert, kann auf Modelle „begrenzter" Rationalität zurückgegriffen werden. Wäre hingegen die Rational-Choice-Theorie eine mechanisch anwendbare allgemeine Theorie, könnte man die Theoriekonstruktion einem Computer überlassen. Rational-Choice-Theorie, analytische Soziologie, Spieltheorie und psychologische Entscheidungsforschung sind stattdessen als eine „Tool Box" aufzufassen. Sie liefern heuristische Prinzipien und Instrumente, um in einem konkreten Anwendungsbereich eine „Theorie mittlerer Reichweite" (Merton 1949) zu konstruieren.

Die skizzierten Anwendungen folgen der Makro-Mikro-Makro-Logik, wobei diese aber oft wesentlich komplizierter ist, als im vereinfachten „Coleman-Boot" dargestellt. Strategischer sozialer Kontext beeinflusst die unabhängigen Variablen der Entscheidungstheorie. Die Präferenzen (D), die Wahrnehmung von Chancen (B) und die Ressourcen (O) hängen vom Kontext, aber auch vom strategischen Verhalten der anderen Akteure ab. Spieltheoretische Modelle präzisieren diese Zusammenhänge, sofern die Handlungen strategisch miteinander verknüpft sind, und ermöglichen die Ableitung empirisch prüfbarer Hypothesen. Mit dem Nash-Gleichgewicht (oder dessen Verfeinerungen) liefern sie gleichzeitig eine Aggregationsregel, d. h. eine Aussage über den Effekt auf der Makroebene. Denn die Wahl einer Gleichgewichtsstrategie ist eine individuelle Entscheidung und berührt die Mikroebenene, während das aus den Handlungen aller Akteure resultierende Gleichgewicht die Makroebene betrifft. Der Begriff „Makro" kann sich auf eine kleine Gruppe von mindestens zwei Akteuren, eine große Zahl von Teilnehmern an einem Markt wie eBay oder z. B. bei Allmendemodellen zum Klimawandel auf die Weltgesellschaft beziehen.

Diese Zusammenhänge gelten auch für Modelle aus der verhaltensorientierten („behavioral") Spieltheorie, die die Annahmen der klassischen Theorie durch psychologische Motive wie z. B. „Ungleichheitsaversion" (Fehr und Schmidt 1999) ergänzen. Wie sich beim „Beauty Contest" zeigte, sind es oft nicht rationale, vorausschauende Entscheidungen, die direkt zu einer Gleichgewichtssituation führen. Vielmehr wird das Gleichgewicht (eventuell) erst im Zuge eines evolutionären Prozesses erreicht. Gürerk et al. (2006) konnten in einem bemerkenswerten Experiment zeigen, wie sich Sanktionsinstitutionen in einer Kollektivgutsituation evolutionär herausgebildet haben, obwohl die Versuchspersonen anfänglich die sanktionsfreien Institutionen bevorzugt hatten. Durch eine „Abstimmung mit den Füßen" fand die erfolgreiche, kooperationsfördernde Institution zunehmend mehr Anhänger und setzte sich schließlich gegen die sanktionsfreie Regelung durch. Evolutionäre Spieltheorie (Young 2001) untersucht die Dynamik der Prozesse und kommt mit wesentlich schwächeren Rationalitätsannahmen aus als die klassische Rational-Choice- und Spieltheorie.

Danksagung Ich bedanke mich bei Jürgen Friedrichs und den anonymen Gutachtern für Hinweise und Anregungen.

Literatur

Akerlof, George A., und Robert J. Shiller. 2010. *Animal spirits*. 9. Aufl. Princeton: Princeton University Press.
Andreoni, James, und John Miller. 2002. Giving according to GARP: An experimental test of the consistency of preferences for altruism. *Econometrica* 70:737–753.
Bammann, Kai, und Heino Stöver. Hrsg. 2006. *Tätowierungen im Strafvollzug. Hafterfahrungen, die unter die Haut gehen*. Oldenburg: BIS-Verlag.
Berger, Joël, und Andreas Diekmann. 2014. *The logic of relative frustration. Boudon's competition model and experimental evidence*. Working paper ETH Zurich.
Bolton, Gary E., Ben Greiner und Axel Ockenfels. 2013. Engineering trust: Reciprocity in the production of reputation information. *Management Science* 59:265–285.
Boudon, Raymond. 1979. *Widersprüche sozialen Handelns*. Neuwied: Luchterhand.
Boudon, Raymond. 2013. *Beiträge zur allgemeinen Theorie der Rationalität*. Tübingen: Mohr-Siebeck.
Braun, Norman, und Thomas Gautschi. 2011. *Rational Choice Theorie*. München: Juventa.
Coleman, James. 1990. *Foundations of social theory*. Cambridge, MA: Harvard University Press.
Darley, John M., und Bibb Latané. 1968. Bystander intervention in emergencies. Diffusion of responsibility. *Journal of Personality and Social Psychology* 8:377–383.
Dasgupta, Partha. 1988. Trust as a commodity. In *Trust. Making and breaking cooperative relations*, Hrsg. Diego Gambetta, 49–72. Oxford: Blackwell.
Diekmann, Andreas. 1985. Volunteer's dilemma. *Journal of Conflict Resolution* 29:605–610.
Diekmann, Andreas. 1993. Cooperation in an asymmetric volunteer's dilemma game. Theory and experimental evidence. *International Journal of Game Theory* 22:75–85.
Diekmann, Andreas. 2009. Rational choice, evolution and the „Beauty Contest". In *Raymond Boudon - A Life in Sociology*, Hrsg. Mohamed Cherkaoui und Peter Hamilton, 1–12. Oxford: Bardwell Press.
Diekmann, Andreas. 2010. Analytische Soziologie und Rational Choice. In *Die analytische Soziologie in der Diskussion*, Hrsg. Thomas Kron und Thomas Grund, 193–204. Wiesbaden: VS Verlag für Sozialwissenschaften.
Diekmann, Andreas. 2013. *Spieltheorie, Einführung, Beispiele, Experimente*. 3. Aufl. Reinbek: Rowohlt.
Diekmann, Andreas, Ben Jann, Wojtek Przepiorka und Stefan Wehrli. 2014. Reputation formation and the evolution of cooperation in anonymous online markets. *The American Sociological Review* 79:65–85.
DiMaggio, Paul, und Hugh Louch. 1998. Socially embedded consumer transactions: For what kinds of purchases do people most often use networks? *American Sociological Review* 63:619–637.
Durkheim, Emile. 1983. *Der Selbstmord*. 1897. Frankfurt a. M.: Suhrkamp.
Eger, Thomas, Manfred Kraft und Peter Weise. 1992. On the equilibrium proportion of innovation and imitation. A game-theoretic approach. *Economics Letters* 38:93–97.
Eisenführ, Franz, Martin Weber und Tomas Langer. 2010. *Rationales Entscheiden*. 5. Aufl. Berlin: Springer.
Esser, Hartmut. 1999. *Soziologie. Spezielle Grundlagen. Bd. 1 Situationslogik und Handeln*. Frankfurt a. M.: Campus.
Fehr, Ernst, und Klaus M. Schmidt. 1999. A theory of fairness, competition, and cooperation. *The Quarterly Journal of Economics* 114:817–868.

Finkel, Steven E. 2008. In defense of the „wide" rational choice model of collective political action. In *Rational Choice. Theoretische Analysen und empirische Resultate. Festschrift für Karl-Dieter Opp*, Hrsg. Andreas Diekmann, Klaus Eichner, Peter Schmidt und Thomas Voss, 23–36. Wiesbaden: VS Verlag für Sozialwissenschaften.
Franzen, Axel. 1995. Group size and one-shot collective action. *Rationality and Society* 7:183–200.
Gambetta, Diego. 2009. *Codes of the underworld: How criminals communicate*. Princeton: Princeton University Press.
Gigerenzer, Gerd. 2013. *Risiko. Wie man die richtigen Entscheidungen trifft*. München: Bertelsmann.
Gintis, Herbert. 2007. A framework for the unification of the behavioral sciences. *Behavioral and Brain Sciences* 30:1–61.
Goeree, Jacob A., und Charles A. Holt. 2005. An explanation of anomalous behavior in models of political participation. *American Political Science Review* 99:201–213.
Goffman, Erving. 1969. *Strategic interaction*. Philadelphia: University of Pennsylvania Press.
Gürerk, Özgür, Bernd Irlenbusch und Bettina Rockenbach. 2006. The competitive advantage of sanctioning institutions. *Science* 312:108–111.
Hedström, Peter. 2007. *Dissecting the social. On the principles of analytical sociology*. Cambridge: Cambridge University Press.
Homann, Karl, und Andreas Suchanek. 2005. *Ökonomik. Eine Einführung*. 2. Aufl. Tübingen: Mohr-Siebeck.
Kollock, Peter. 1994. The emergence of exchange structures: An experimental study of uncertainty, commitment, and trust. *American Journal of Sociology* 100:313–345.
Merton, Robert K. 1949. *Social theory and social structure*. New York: The Free Press.
Opp, Karl-Dieter. 1999. Contending conceptions of the theory of rational action. *Journal of Theoretical Politics* 11:171–202.
Przepiorka, Wojtek, und Andreas Diekmann. 2013. Temporal embeddedness and signals of trustworthiness: Experimental tests of a game theoretic model in the United Kingdom, Russia, and Switzerland. *European Sociological Review* 29:1010–1023.
Raub, Werner. 1984. *Rationale Akteure, institutionelle Regelungen und Interdependenzen. Untersuchungen zu einer erklärenden Soziologie auf strukturell-individualistischer Grundlage*. Frankfurt a. M.: Peter Lang.
Raub, Werner, und Vincent Buskens. 2006. Spieltheoretische Modellierungen und empirische Anwendungen in der Soziologie. In *Methoden der Sozialforschung. Sonderheft 44 der Kölner Zeitschrift für Soziologie und Sozialpsychologie*, Hrsg. Andreas Diekmann, 560–598. Wiesbaden: VS Verlag für Sozialwissenschaften.
Selten, Reinhard, und Rosemarie Nagel. 1998. Das Zahlenwahlspiel. Hintergründe und Ergebnisse. *Spektrum der Wissenschaft* 2:16–22.
Siamwalla, Ammar. 1978. Farmers and middlemen. Aspects of agricultural marketing in Thailand. *Economic Bulletin for Asia and the Pacific* 29:38–50.
Stouffer, Samuel A., Edward A. Suchman, Leland C. De Vinney, Shirley A. Star und Robin M. Williams Jr. 1965. *The American soldier*. 1949. Manhattan: Military Affairs, Aerospace Historian Publishing.
Tocqueville, Alexis de. 1969. *Der alte Staat und die Revolution*. 1856. Reinbek: Rowohlt.
Tutić, Andreas. 2014. Procedural rational volunteer. *Journal of Mathematical Sociology* 38:219–232.
Uhl, Matthias, und Eckart Voland. 2002. *Angeber haben mehr vom Leben*. Heidelberg: Spektrum.
Voss, Thomas. 1998. Vertrauen in modernen Gesellschaften. In *Der Transformationsprozess*, Hrsg. Regina Metze, Kurt Mühler und Karl-Dieter Opp, 91–129. Leipzig: Universitätsverlag.
Weber, Max. 1922. *Wirtschaft und Gesellschaft*. Tübingen: Mohr.
Weesie, Jeroen, und Axel Franzen. 1998. Cost sharing in a volunteer's dilemma. *Journal of Conflict Resolution* 42:600–618.
Young, Peyton. 2001. *Individual strategy and social structure. An evolutionary theory of institutions*. Princeton: Princeton University Press.

Andreas Diekmann, 1951, Dr. rer. pol., Professor für Soziologie an der ETH Zürich. Forschungsgebiete: Theorien sozialer Kooperation, Methoden und Modelle in der Sozialforschung, Bevölkerungs- und Umweltsoziologie, experimentelle Spieltheorie. Neuere Veröffentlichungen: Reputation formation and the evolution of cooperation in anonymous online markets. American Sociological Review 79, 2014 (mit B. Jann, W. Przepiorka und S. Wehrli); Subjective discount rates in the general population and their predictive power for energy saving behavior. Energy Policy 65, 2014 (mit H. Bruderer-Enzler und R. Meyer); The intergenerational transmission of divorce: A fifteen-country study with the fertility and family survey. Comparative Sociology 12, 2013 (mit K. Schmidheiny); Individual heterogeneity and costly punishment: A volunteer's dilemma. Proceedings of the Royal Society Biological Sciences 280, 2013 (mit W. Przepiorka); Temporal embeddedness and signals of trustworthiness: Experimental tests of a game theoretic model in the United Kingdom, Russia, and Switzerland. European Sociological Review 29, 2013 (mit W. Przepiorka); Making use of ‹Benford's law› for the randomized response technique. Sociological Methods and Research 41, 2012.

Kölner Zeitschrift für Soziologie und Sozialpsychologie

Compositional or Contextual Effects? Neighbourhoods and Teenage Parenthood in Stockholm, Sweden

Lina Hedman

© Springer Fachmedien Wiesbaden 2014

Abstract Selection bias constitutes a major problem in neighbourhood effect research but perhaps especially so for studies of effects on teenage birth rates. Results from both the U.S. and Europe are highly inconsistent: where some find substantial effects and others no effects. This inconsistency in combination with the clear correlations between neighbourhood environment and teenage birth rates where teenage mothers and mothers-to-be are overrepresented in low SES neighbourhoods makes it unclear if and to what extent neighbourhoods exerts a causal influence on teenage birth rates or whether correlations are mere reflections of differences in choices on the housing markets. This study adds to the (mainly American and British) body of literature on neighbourhood effects on teenage birth but focuses on a context—Stockholm, Sweden—where teenage birth rates are substantially lower. It offers a discussion on the potential impacts of selection bias on estimates of neighbourhood effects on teenage birth rates and empirically tests the existence of such neighbourhood effects. To account for selection bias I use a random effects model with a Mundlak correction (a hybrid model), a model that corrects for selection similarly to a fixed-effects model but also allows the inclusion of fixed parameters. The hybrid model produces coefficients that are substantially smaller compared to an OLS model that does not control for selection; selection thus biases results upwards. The neighbourhood effects estimated by the hybrid model are so small that they can be ignored.

Keywords Neighbourhoods · Teenage parenthood · Context effects

L. Hedman (✉)
Institute for Housing and Urban research, Uppsala University,
Box 514, 751 20 Uppsala, Sweden
e-mail: lina.hedman@ibf.uu.se

Nachbarschaften und Teenager-Mütter in Stockholm, Schweden

Zusammenfassung Der *selection bias* stellt ein wesentliches Problem in den Forschungen zu Nachbarschaftseffekten dar und wahrscheinlich insbesondere in Studien über Geburtenraten von Teenagern. Die Ergebnisse aus den USA und Europa sind sehr widersprüchlich; einige Studien finden substanzielle Effekte, während andere keine finden. Diese Inkonsistenz, zusammen mit der nachgewiesenen Beziehung zwischen Nachbarschaft und den Geburtenraten von Teenagern, in denen die Teenager-Mütter und werdenden Mütter in Nachbarschaften mit einem niedrigen sozialen Status überrepräsentiert sind, führt zu der Unklarheit, ob und in welchem Ausmaß eine kausale Beziehung zwischen Nachbarschaft und den Geburtenraten von Teenagern bestehen – oder aber ob diese Korrelation nur unterschiedliche Wohnstandortwahlen auf dem Wohnungsmarkt darstellen. Diese Studie trägt zu den vorliegenden, vorwiegend amerikanischen und britischen Studien bei. Sie konzentriert sich auf einen Kontext, Stockholm, Schweden, wo die Geburtenraten von Teenagern erheblich niedriger sind. In dem Artikel werden die möglichen Effekte des *selection bias* auf Schätzungen der Nachbarschaftseffekte auf die Geburtenraten untersucht und ferner empirisch getestet, ob derartige Nachbarschaftseffekte bestehen. Um den *selection bias* zu untersuchen, verwende ich ein Random-Effects-Modell mit einer Mundlak Correction, ein hybrides Modell, das die Auswahl ähnlich wie ein Fixed-Effects-Modell korrigiert, aber zugleich gestattet, feste Parameter einzubeziehen. Das hybride Modell führt auf Koeffizienten, die erheblich kleiner sind im Vergleich zu einem OLS-Modell, welches nicht den *selection bias* korrigiert; die Auswahl verzerrt die Ergebnisse daher nach oben. Die mit den hybriden Modellen geschätzten Nachbarschaftseffekte sind so gering, dass sie nicht bedeutsam sind.

Schlüsselwörter Nachbarschaft · Teenager-Mütter · Kontexteffekte

1 Introduction

Teenage parenthood is considered an important social problem in many Western countries. Previous studies have found that teenage childbearing is associated with a range of negative outcomes both preceding and following the birth of the child such as early school drop-out, low income and reliance on state benefits, lone parenthood, poor health and low life satisfaction (Lupton and Kneale 2010; Hertfelt Wahn and Nissen 2008). In addition, children of teenage mothers are less likely to obtain a high level of education and a high income as adults, and they are also more likely to become parents at an early age themselves (Francesconi 2008).

Several policy initiatives have been launched to reduce teenage birth rates and improve the situation for teenage mothers and their children. Some of these policies, like the British New Labour Policy on Teenage Parenthood, have been built partly on the assumption that high teenage birth rates is a neighbourhood related problem (Lupton and Kneale 2010). Geographical variations in teenage birth rates, where high birth rates generally are associated with neighbourhoods with low socio-economic status, may lead policy makers to think that neighbourhoods have a causal effect on teenage birth rates. However, variation in birth rates between neighbourhoods does not necessarily imply that neighbourhood-related factors have a causal effect on the propensity among girls to give birth at a young age. They may be mere reflections of variations in population patterns across neighbourhoods where girls who in general are more likely to give birth as teenagers are overrepresented in some neighbourhoods. One explanation for such spatial variations is selective mobility patterns where these girls for one reason or another move to neighbourhoods with high birth rates where girls unlikely to become teenage mothers move to other types of neighbourhoods. Selective mobility patterns are known to bias estimates of neighbourhood effects, if they are due to unoberserved factors that also are correlated with the outcome of interest (i.e. the likelihood of giving birth). To obtain results free of selection bias is by many scholars seen as one of the most important methodological challenges or neighbourhood effect research. Selection bias may be one explanation for the inconsistency in findings on whether causal neighbourhood effects on teenage childbearing exist or not. A summary of the acadmic knowledge up to this date yield that while some studies have found significant neighbourhood effects on teenage sexual behaviour, pregnancies or birth rates (South and Crowder 2010; Browning 2004; Harding 2003; Sucoff and Upchurch 1998; Brooks-Gunn et al. 1993), others find only small or no effects (Galster et al. 2007; Ginther et al. 2000; South and Crowder 1999; Thornberry et al. 1997). However, much of the early literature, just like much of the literature on the psychological causes behind the teenage childbearing (Coyle and D'Onofrio 2012), rely on correlational and cross-sectional research designs not able to accurately test causality. The "neighbourhood effects" found by these studies may thus be reflections of the (unobserved causes of) selective residential patterns of teenagers at risk of becoming parents.

In this paper, I explore the selection bias problem in relation to neighbourhood effects on teenage birth rates. I provide a theoretical discussion of the problem which aims to define the concept of selection bias, discuss how it may affect results, and what the solutions to this problem may be. This theoretical discussion is complemented by empirical analysis with: (1) a descriptive overview on the selectiveness of teenage mothers (who they are and where they live) and (2) an analysis of neighbourhood effects on the likelihood of becoming a mother during the teenage years. Neighbourhood effects are estimated with two different models; a standard OLS model not controlling for selection, and a random effects model with a Mundlak correction which controls for selection on all time-invariant variables. Results from these two models are then compared in order to give a glimpse of how selection bias may affect empirical results. The empirical analysis of neighbourhood effects on teenage childbearing makes this paper a contribution to the (inconsistent) literature on whether and to what extent neighbourhood factors affect the likelihood that a young girl will become a mother. The paper also contributes to this literature by its context of study. Most studies on teenage sexual behaviour, pregnancies and parenthood come from the U.S. and the U.K. where the birth rates are high. In this study, I use data from Sweden, a country with substantially lower teenage birth rates. The geographical pattern with teenage parents overrepresented in deprived neighbourhoods is however the same. It is thus relevant to test the neighbourhood effect hypothesis on teenage birth rates also in the Swedish context.

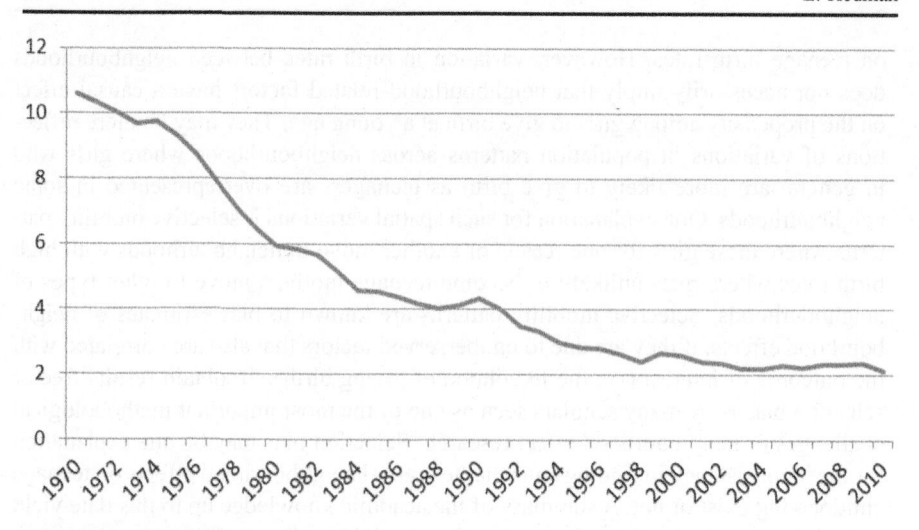

Fig. 1 Teenage (16–20) births as proportion of the total number of births, Sweden 1970–2010. (Source: Statistics Sweden)

2 Selectiveness of Swedish teenage mothers

Teenage birth rates (ages 15–19) have decreased substantially in Sweden since the early 1970s, from a birth rate of about 40 per 1000[1] (Danielsson et al. 2001) to 6 per 1000 in 2009. Comparative figures for the U.S. and the U.K. are 39 and 27 per 1000 respectively (Millennium Development Goals Indicator). Put differently, in 1970, over ten per cent of all new-born children were born to mothers aged 20 or below. Ten years later, that figure had dropped to half, and another 20 years later, it had halved again (Fig. 1). The low Swedish teenage birth rate is, according to Danielsson et al. (2001), due to a combination of compulsory education in sexual relations in school, wide spread youth health centers offering counseling and contraceptive services, and abortions free on request until week 18.

Teenage childbearing is, in Sweden, associated with a range of negative connotations from other teenagers, parents, health providers and society at large. Pregnancies are practically always unplanned and it is unusual among pregnant teenage girls to continue pregnancies and actually give birth (Danielsson et al. 2001). Teenagers who not only become pregnant but also choose to give birth can thus be expected to be a rather selective group that differs from other teenage girls in some regards.

In their review of the (mainly American) developmental psychological teenage childbearing literature, Coyne and D'Onofrio (2012; see also Coley and Chase-Lansdale 1998) categorise the identified risk factors for teenage pregnancy and fertility into three groups: socio-demographic risk factors, family-level risk factors and individual-level correlates. Risk factors belonging to the first group especially stress the positive correlations of socio-economic status (SES) and teenage fertility: teenage girls from families with low SES, whose mothers have a low level of education, and who come from single-parent families are more like to give births at a young age.

---

[1] A teenage birth rate of 40 per 1000 means that out of 1,000 teenage girls, 40 give birth.

Similar patterns have been found in Sweden (Danielsson et al. 2001). Previous U.S. based research also stresses racial differences where birth rates are especially high among African-American girls (Browning et al. 2004). Among family-level risk factors, maternal teenage childbearing is suggested to influence teenage birth rate among offspring (for Swedish evidence, see Hertfelt Wahn and Nissen 2008). This risk may be due to a similar socio-economic family characteristics of both mother and daughter at the time of giving birth (Mersky and Reynolds 2007; Barber 2001) but there are also evidence that daughters to teenage mothers are more exposed to risks associated with teenage pregnancy other than low SES, such as lower levels of parental monitoring and deviant peer norms (Meade et al. 2008). Family environment can also prevent teenage births if being positive and supportive. The third category of Coyne and D'Onofrio is individual-level correlates. It includes psychological factors, such as conduct problems, childhood mistreatment and normative developmental psychological problems, school and related risk factors, such as academic competence, educational expectations, and school-related behavioural problems, and sibling effects, i.e. whether siblings have given birth as teenagers.

Table 1 depicts some descriptive statistics of teenage (age 16–20) mothers in Stockholm, compared to teenage girls who do not give birth. The table confirms that girls from low SES and split families are overrepresented among teenage mothers. The teenage mothers were less likely to live with both parents at age 16, less likely to have parents with a university degree, less likely to have both their parents employed, and their families have lower disposable incomes. There is also clear evidence of an intergenerational transmission of teenage childbearing: girls that become teenage mothers were considerably more likely to have mothers who in turn gave birth as teenagers (until age 20). The top part of Table 1 shows some characteristics of the girls themselves, measured at age 18. These reveal that teenage mothers were less likely than other girl to have completed grade 9, compulsory school, which most children do at age 15–16. All these characteristics of teenage mothers and their families are in line with finding from previous literature. However, unlike in the U.S. where teenage motherhood is more common among African-American and Latin girls, girls with foreign background are underrepresented among teenage mothers.

Although most risk factors identified by Coyne and D'Onofrio (2012) refer to the individual or family level, they also point at the importance of context. Teenage

Table 1 Descriptive characteristics of Stockholm girls, categorised according to whether or not giving birth in ages 16–20

Values in % unless otherwise stated	Give birth	Do not give birth
Own characteristics		
Foreign background	22.8	31.3
Has completed compulsory school (9 years) at age 18	84.5	93.6
Parents' characteristic (at age 16 unless otherwise stated)		
Mother gave birth as teenager (0–20)	33.2	12.9
Parents are married/cohabitans	33.8	57.4
One or both parents have post high school education	25.0	50.3
Both parents are employed	47.4	67.5
Parents' disposable income (*mean, 10,000 SEK*)	25.6	38.6

Fig. 2 Share teenage girls (age 16–20) that become parents per neighbourhood, Stockholm 2006

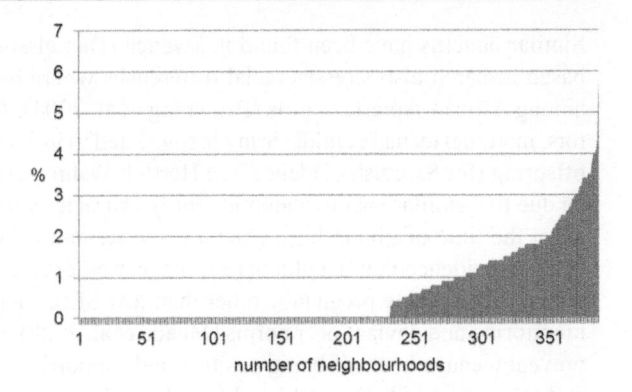

birth rates tend to vary geographically across neighbourhoods and be highest in poor areas. This is not surprising given that teenage childbearing is more common among girls from low-SES families and income is one of the most important determinants for neighbourhood allocation. Income is in turn associated with several other parental characteristics that increase the likelihood that the teenage daughter will give birth; unemployment and a low level of education generally mean lower income, as is being a single parent. In addition, teenage motherhood is, as we have seen, associated with a poor income development why daughters to teenage mothers are more likely to grow up in low-SES families. However, these other factors (employment status, education level, household composition) also have a small direct effect on neighbourhood sorting (Hedman et al. 2011).

In Stockholm, given the generally low birth rate, geographic variation means that teenage mothers are concentrated to a few neighbourhoods while most neighbourhoods do not have any teenage mothers at all among their population. Among the 388 Stockholm neighbourhoods with a least 50 inhabitants in ages 16–20 during year 2006, the number of teenage girls that became parents varied from 0 to 14 but the variation is extremely uneven. 232 neighbourhoods had no teenage mothers. Only 14 neighbourhoods had five or more. Expressed in terms of share teenagers in the neighbourhood that became parents during 2006, the number varied from 0 to 5.9 % (Fig. 2).

Descriptive characteristics of the Stockholm neighbourhoods are shown in Table 2, with neighbourhoods classified according to the share of teenage girls in neighbourhoods that gave birth during the same year. Again, it is clear that the vast majority of neighbourhoods, almost 60 %, have no teenage mothers, and in only a small fraction of neighbourhoods is the share of mothers among teenage girls 3 % or higher. The rest of the information in Table 2 provides support to the conclusion that teenage parenthood is more common in neighbourhoods with a low socio-economic status. In neighbourhoods with a high share teenage mothers, a lower share of inhabitants have a high level of education or are employed. They also have lower disposable family incomes on average. In addition, they have a higher share of immigrant residents and a higher share of inhabitants living in public rentals, two features typical for distressed neighbourhoods in Sweden.

Table 2 Descriptive statistics of neighbourhoods categorized according to new teenage mothers, Stockholm 2006

	Percentage of girls in neighbourhood that give birth		
	0	0.1–2.99	3.0–5.9
Percentage of all neighbourhoods	59.8	35.3	4.9
Percentage foreign born	13.2	22.2	31.4
Percentage with post high school education[a]	46.0	38.7	29.4
Percentage employed[a]	81.8	75.7	68.6
Disp. family income[a] (*mean, 10,000 SEK*)	48.7	34.5	27.6
Percentage living in public rentals	7.6	27.5	47.9

[a] Level of education, employment and disposable income are measured for working age population only (ages 20–64)

3 Compositional or contextual effects?

The statistical descriptions of teenage mothers and their neighbourhoods suggest that teenage childbearing is overrepresented among girls from families with low SES who live in low SES neighbourhoods. This would suggest that the girls who are most at risk of becoming teenage mothers happen to live in certain neighbourhoods, and that the spatial correlation between neighbourhood and likelihood of giving birth is (mostly?) due to variations in population composition. To the extent that correlations between neighbourhood characteristic and outcome, in this case the risk of becoming a teenage mother, are products of population composition ("compositional effects"), they will change if residential patterns change. A girl who change place of residence will not, *ceteris paribus*, experience a change in the likelihood that she will give birth during her teenage years.

However, it is also possible that the neighbourhood context exerts a causal influence of the likelihood that a teenage girl will give birth. If this is the case, a move would mean a change in the likelihood of becoming a teenage mother. For example, it has been suggested that living in a poor neighbourhood is associated with less social control, poor adult role models and a higher likelihood of having peers that encourage risky sexual behavior, while also meaning worse access to (good) educational and employment opportunities (South and Crowder 2010). If such neighbourhood-related factors affect the likelihood of giving birth, a move to a different neighbourhood would mean a change in the chance/risk of becoming a teenage mother.

Lupton and Kneale (2010) identify three overlapping explanatory frameworks for teenage motherhood that all could be expected to vary spatially (but not necessarily on the neighbourhood level): economic theory and opportunity costs, differential values, and social networks. Economic theory suggests that opportunity costs of teenage childbearing are higher among women with high qualifications (or girls with chances or expectations of obtaining such), why women with low educational credentials are more likely to become mothers early in life (Joshi 1998). Since social status tends to be transmitted across generations, the same could be applied to girls from families with low SES (see D'Addio 2007 for an overview of research). Variations in access to and quality of institutions could also explain differences in qualifications and expectations. Individuals residing in poverty neighbourhoods are generally assumed to have worse access to good quality schools and other institutions that affect their labour market prospects. Another theoretical framework explains geographical variations in birth rates with differences in norms or values related to sexual behaviour, the use of contraceptives, abortions or (teenage) childbearing. It has been argued that such norms differ across social classes where early motherhood is viewed more positively among lower classes. Other scholars study the diffusion of such norms or values across (local) social networks. They could be formed by adults, through collective socialization processes, or by peers. Crane (1991) suggests that peer pressure ("contagion") may spread epidemically in neighbourhoods when a certain threshold has been reached (i.e. when the number of teenage mothers has exceeded a critical point), and use this theory to explain the high prevalence of teenage mothers in U.S. ghettos. Using qualitative work, Arai (2007) finds that British teenage mothers do not report on having been affected by social norms, but concludes from her data that such norms may be present in some communities. South and Baumer (2000) argue in their U.S. based study that over one-third of the correlation between neighbourhood SES and teenage birth rates can be explained by differences in attitudes and behaviour of peers.

3.1 What is selection bias?

To determine whether variations in birth rates are due to causal neighbourhood effects or simply mere correlations, it is important to understand (or statistically control for) how households are allocated into neighbourhoods. The spatial allocation of different types of households is not a random process. Household choose their neighbourhoods, although the degree of choice may differ among households, given their available resources and other types of restrictions. Selection bias arises when there are unobserved factors that are statistically correlated with the allocation of people into categories or groups and these unobserved characteristics also are statistically correlated with the error term, i.e. when there are unobserved factors that affect both the choice of neighbourhood and the outcome of interest. Consider an example where a teenage girl lives in neighbourhood where teenage pregnancies are common. If the girl herself gives birth at a young age, we find a positive correlation between (the likelihood of) her giving birth and the neighbourhood teenage birth rate. This might lead us to conclude that there is a *causal* neighbourhood effect (the dashed line of Fig. 3). However, what we don't observe is that the girl (and her parents) has a religious faith which makes her unwilling to use contraceptives and thus increases the likelihood that she will get pregnant, *ceteris paribus*. This religious belief is also the reason why the teenager and her parents live in their neighbourhood; it is located near their church. Hence, the true causal relationships in this example are that religion affects residential location *and* the likelihood of giving birth (the solid lines in Fig. 3).[2] The *sorting* of girls with this certain religious faith into neighbourhoods near

---

[2] It should however be noted that scholars have found that religious faith has a negative effect on teenage childbearing (Haveman et al. 1997).

Fig. 3 Unobserved causal patterns

Neighbourhood - - - - -> Give birth   Observed

Religion   Unobserved

the church is the reason for the high local birth rates. The previous conclusion about a neighbourhood effect is consequently wrong.

A graphical illustration of the sorting and consequent selection bias problem is found in Figs. 4a–d. Figure 4a portrays four girls, two with a high likelihood of giving birth (A and B) and two with a low likelihood of giving birth (C and D) who live four different neighbourhoods, two with low share of teenage parents (A and C) and two with a low share of teenage parents (B and D). There is no correlation between the likelihood of giving birth and the share teenage parents in the neighbourhood and we would correctly not find any neighbourhood effect. In Fig. 4b, we imagine a neighbourhood effect but no residential sorting. The neighbourhood effect in this example will make the girls living in neighbourhoods with a high share teenage parents more likely to give birth while the girls who live in neighbourhoods with a low share teenage parents would become less likely to give birth ($A \rightarrow A_1 \ldots D \rightarrow D_1$). We would observe a correlation between neighbourhood characteristics and outcome in the data and correctly assume a neighbourhoods effect. However, in Fig. 4c, we assume that the girls sort into neighbourhood according to their likelihood of giving birth (or, more likely, according to some correlated feature). Hence, the girls with a high likelihood of giving birth (A and B) move to neighbourhoods with a higher share teenage parents (positions A_2, B_2), and vice versa. We again find a correlation between neighbourhood characteristic and outcome in the data as in Fig. 4b, but now the conclusion about causal neighbourhood effects would be erroneous; the pattern is solely the result of selective mobility patterns. (The same conclusion would apply if only part of the population has this type of sorting behavior). Finally, in Fig. 4d, we assume a combination of neighbourhood effects and sorting. The girls would in this example "move" as a combination of Fig. 4b and c (to positions $A_3 \ldots D_3$); the girl who lives in a high-teenage parent neighbourhood and has a high likelihood if giving birth (B) would in this example find her likelihood of giving birth even further increased by a neighbourhood effect *and* sort into a neighbourhood where the share teenage parents is even higher, which in turn is correlated with an even stronger neighbourhood effect. Girl C, who has a low likelihood of giving birth and start in a low-birth rate neighbourhood, will be affected in the opposite way while the other two girls (A and D) "move" towards the centre. Exactly where in the scatterplot these girls will end up is impossible to predict: it depends on the relative strength and timing of sorting effects and neighbourhood effects. Regardless of which, the combination of residential sorting and neighbouhood effect would most likely make us find a correlation between residential environment and outcome and we would correctly deduce a neighbourhood effect. However, due to sorting, we are unlikely to obtain correct measures of the strenght of the effect. In this example, the neighbourhood effect would be *overestimated* which can be seen by comparing the slopes of Figs. 4b and d.

The neighbourhood effect literature generally agrees that selection bias constitute a serious problem—it is by many considered as one of the most important method-

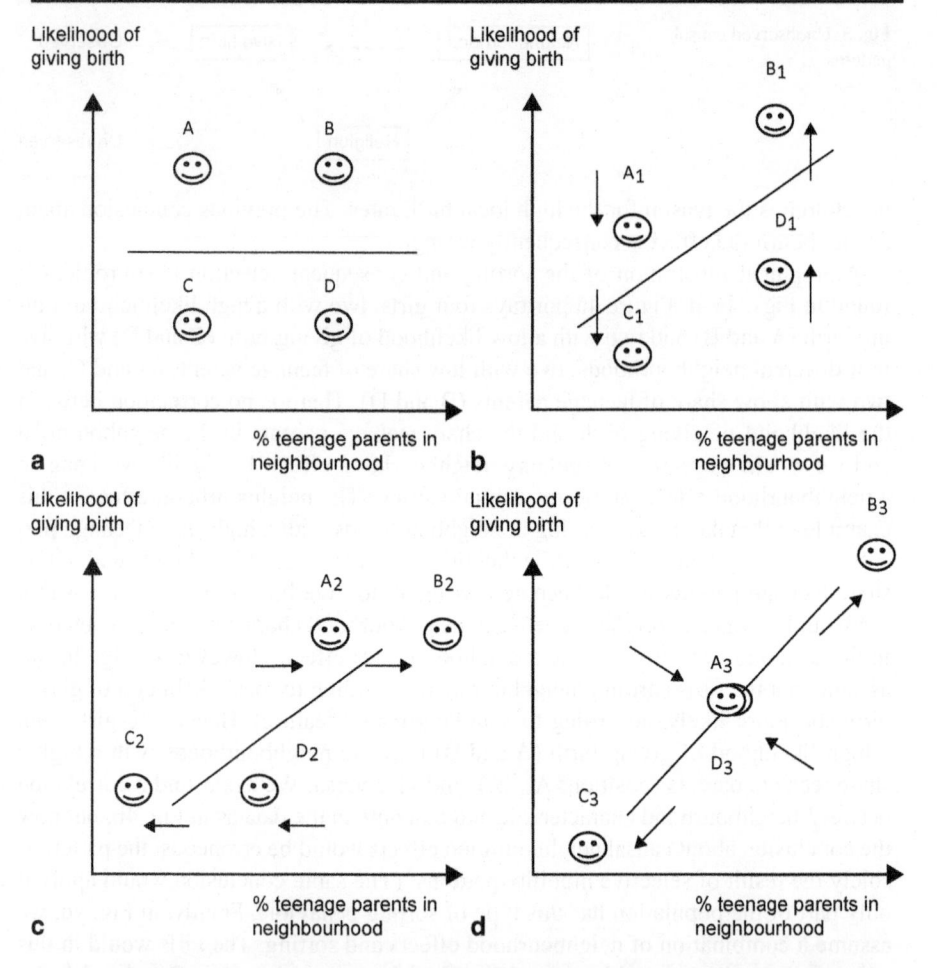

Fig. 4 a–d Illustration of selection bias and neighbourhood effects. (Fig.4a constitutes the baseline against which the other figures should be compared. The *arrows* in Figs. 4b–d signals how the individuals have moved from this baseline position). **a** No sorting, no neighbourhood effect. **b** No sorting but neighbourhood effect. **c** Sorting, no neighbourhood effect. **d** Sorting and neighbourhood effect. (The illustration builds on Hedman and Galster (2013))

ological challenges (e.g. see van Ham and Manley 2012; Galster 2008; Duncan et al. 1997; Jencks and Mayer 1990). The problem is serious enough to lead some scholars to question the existence of neighbourhood effects altogether and assume that all results are the product of selection bias, as per Fig. 4c. For example, both Oreopoulos (2003) and van Ham and Manley (2010) find correlations between neighbourhood characteristics and outcome (income, employment and welfare participation in Oreopoulos study, labour market outcomes in van Ham and Manley's study) for home owners but not for renters. Both argue that while housing allocation for renters is more or less random, home owners choose their neighbourhoods; hence results for owners are likely to be subject to bias while results for renters are no (or at least to a less extent). However, a majority of the more recent studies do find statistical evidence of neighbourhood effects also when controlling for selection bias. Selection is generally thought to bias results upwards (see Tienda 1991; Jencks and Mayer 1990 for theoretical arguments; Galser and Hedman 2013 for empirical evidence) as per Fig. 4d. It has however also been suggested that selection could bias results downwards, if, e.g., those being most negatively affected by a neighbourhood characteristic also are the first ones to move out (see Brooks-Gunn et al. 1997).

So how likely is it that there are unobservable factors that influence both residential patterns and the likelihood that young girls will give birth? This is of course impossible to say since the problematic factors are precisely *unobservable* (or they would not be problematic). It is however well known that some of the characteristics that are found to affect teenage birth rates, such as socio-economic status and household composition of the girl's family, are known to be important determinants for decisions of place of residence (Clark and Dieleman 1994). It has also been shown that households generally choose neighbourhoods where the inhabitants' characteristics match their own (Hedman et al. 2011). Given that teenage mothers more often come from families with low socioeconomic status than other girls, the residential patterns of teenage mothers described above could be assumed to be the result of a process where high-SES households sort into the most affluent neighbourhoods while low-SES households—where teenage childbearing is more common—sort into the remaining neighbourhoods. That low-SES households may have a lower degree of choice on the housing market does however not mean that they do not make a choice. Even though alternatives may be generally regarded as less attractive than more affluent areas, there is still likely to be variation in attractiveness (in the view of the moving household) among the available alternatives. The relative attractiveness of neighbourhoods may depend upon a large number of factors apart from socio-economic status or household composition, that are related to the preferences of the household: location in the city, distance to school/job, distance to previous location, aesthetic values, location of families and friends, service level etc. (see Brown and Moore 1970, for a review of studies on factors that affect neighbourhood choice, or Fransson et al. 2002, for more recent Swedish results.) Although generally unobserved in data, these factors are unlikely to be causally related to the likelihood of giving birth as a teenager and do consequently not pose a threat of biased result to the current study. However, many of the factors known to affect the chances of teenage childbearing are often not observed in data used in neighbourhood effect studies. Examples of such factors are level of parental monitoring, psychological or behavioural disorder problems, childhood abuse, or academic competence. There are also likely to be additional factors that are not observed, e.g. attitudes towards having children or level of stability in potential partner relationship. It is unclear to what extent these affect residential patterns, but if they do, neighbourhood effect estimates will be subject to selection bias.

3.2 How to control for selection bias?

The potentially best way of controlling for selection bias is to use data from experiments where the allocation of households into neighbourhood is completely random. The U.S. Moving To Opportunity (MTO) program is still considered by many as the prime example of such an experiment, partly set up by academics and launched not only as a mobility program but also as a 'natural experiment' designed to overcome selection bias through a random distribution of housing vouchers aimed to assist households to leave poverty areas (for a description of the MTO program design, see Gennetian et al. 2011). The randomisation was meant to break the link between (unobservable) family characteristics and place of residence, thus overcoming the problem of neighbourhood selection. Whether the program actually achieved this is however debated. Others have used data from "natural experiments", such as the Denver public housing allocation system where individuals who move into social housing are randomly assigned a dwelling and neighbourhood. (For a description and evaluation of the Denver housing system as means to overcome selection bias, see Galster and Santiago 2013).

Most scholars do however not have access to data from similar experiments but are bound to overcome selection bias through econometric techniques. In the European literature, where experimental data is rare, selection has been addressed through difference models, random effects models, fixed effects models and instrumental variable (IV) techniques (see Galster and Hedman 2013). *Differencing* techniques try to eliminate time-invariant individual characteristics by modeling a *change* in individual outcome as a function of a change in neighbourhood characteristics. To model change, they require data from at least two points in time. If having access to panel data, most researchers choose between fixed and random effects models with guidance of a Hausman test. Although random effect model appear occasionally in the neighbourhood effect literature (see, e.g. Propper et al 2004), the *fixed effect* approach is considerably more common The main advantage of this technique is that the fixed effects model efficiently controls for all unobserved individual time-invariant characteristics (by essentially adding an individual-specific dummy to each person in the dataset) and thus removes a substantial part of potential selection bias. An undesirable consequence is however that such fixed individual characteristics, e.g. gender and ethnicity, cannot be included in the model. The *IV* technique is the only modeling strategy that addresses both selection and endogeneity[3]. The idea behind the technique is basically to replace the endogenous neighbourhood characteristic with a exogenous variable that is strongly correlated with this charactertistic but not to the individual outcome. A first-step regression aims to obtain predicted values of the neighbourhood characteristic through these exogenous variables (instruments) while a second-step regression uses these predicted values as replacements for neighbourhood characteristic in the neighbourhood effect model. All of these models have their advantages and disadvantages. However, when comparing outcomes from the same datasets using these different models, Galster and Hedman (2013) conclude that a fixed-effects panel model with instrumental variables is preferable due to its ability to control for both selection and endogeneity. However, the use of an instrumental variable model is only beneficial under the conditions of having valid and strong instruments. Such instruments are hard to find why the number of studies using this

---

[3] Endogeneity bias arises as a consequence of mutual causality. For example, the outcome in a neighbourhood effect model, e.g. the likelihood of giving birth, may also affect residential location, which in turn affects the outcome. See Hedman and Galster (2013).

technique is low (exceptions are Hedman and Galster 2013; Sari 2012; Galster et al. 2007; Gibbons 2002). The second best model, according to Galster and Hedman, is the fixed-effects model for a non-mover population, followed by the fixed-effects approach. In this study of teenage births, I will not use the instrumental variable technique for the reason mentioned above: the difficulties of finding good instruments. Due to the small number of teenagers giving birth, I will neither restrict the sample to a non-moving population. (However, as mobility rates are low among families with teenage children, a majority of the girls can be assumed not to have moved during the years before getting pregnant.) Instead, I will use a variant of the fixed-effects model to account for selection bias.

4 Method and data

The problem of the fixed effects model, its inability to include individual time-invariant characteristics, is very relevant in this study of teenage parenthood. Not only would it be of interest to include the girls' ethnicity given racial differences in birth rates found by many U.S based studies. It would also be sensible to estimate parental characteristics, which have been argued to be important predictors of a girl's likelihood of becoming pregnant, at a given point in time when the girl still lives with her parents, and before she gets pregnant for the first time.

In their study of neighbourhood effects on income, Hedman et al. (2012) uses an approach that solves the above problem. They employ a random effects model with a Mundlak (1978) correction, which basically can be regarded as a combination between the fixed and the random effects techniques. This "hybrid" model has the advantages of both fixed and random effects: it reduces selection bias similarly to the fixed effects model but also allows the inclusion of variables that do not vary over time. In the hybrid model, time-varying variables are inserted as distance from individual mean for each year in the panel. The coefficients obtained from these demeaned variables are generally very similar to those acquired by a fixed effects model. In this study, the fixed effects and hybrid coefficients for share teenage parents in neighbourhood are in fact completely identical[4]. Hence the model arguably provides unbiased estimates to the same extent as the fixed effects model of the within individual variation. Individual means of time-varying variables are also included in the model. These represent the random effects parameters and report between-individual variation. Hedman and colleagues (2012) argue that different processes that occur as a result of neighbourhood context might affect individuals in different ways; some shown by within-individual estimates and some by between-individual estimates. Hence, obtaining estimates of both within- and between individual variations is an additional argument for using the hybrid model. Fixed characteristics are inserted in the model as they are. For a more detailed (statistical) description of the hybrid model, see Hedman et al. (2012); Jones and Subramanian (2012); Mundlak (1978). In order to get an idea about to what extent selection bias is a problem and how the hybrid model reduces bias, I will first estimate a benchmark OLS regression.

---
[4] Results from the fixed effects model are available from the author upon request.

The OLS model does not control for selection and is consequently not suitable to estimate causal neighbourhood effects. Hence, it is run for comparative purposes only.

Data are derived from the GeoSweden database. GeoSweden, administered by the Institute for Housing and Urban Research, Uppsala University, is a set of register-based data sets that can be combined through individual identifiers. For this study, I use datasets covering demographic information, geographic information, socio-economic information and data on real estates. The database covers the entire Swedish population over a 21-year period, 1990–2010. For this study, the dataset is limited to girls who turn 16 between 2002 and 2006. These individuals are followed from the year they turn 16 until the year they turn 20, i.e. for five years each. In order to give birth in ages 16–20, most individuals will get pregnant in ages 15–19, i.e. as teenagers. The number of girls who give birth at ages 15 and below is very small[5]. Although giving birth at age 20 is very different, and much more common, from giving birth at age 16, both from the girl's and society's perspective, giving birth at such a young age is unusual in Sweden and generally regarded as deviant. The dataset is further restricted to individuals who live in the Stockholm metropolitan region[6] for the entire period of follow-up.

The dependent variable in the study is the dummy giving birth or not. Individuals are allowed to have more than one child during the five years of follow-up. The definition of the dependent variable means that this is a study of having children, not of sexual behaviour or becoming pregnant. Unfortunately, I do not have access to data on sexual behaviour, pregnancies or abortions. This makes it more difficult to discuss potential transmission mechanisms of neighbourhood effects since I do not know which kind of behavior the mechanisms affect. In an attempt to shed some more light into this, I run two models which estimates control variables at different points in time. In the first model, controls are estimated the year before the potential birth, at t-1, to avoid problems of reversed causality. In this study, these control variables estimate characteristics when the pregnant girl needs to decide whether to keep her child (in most cases). In the second model, controls are measured two years before the potential birth, at t-2, thus before getting pregnant. The number of observations is somewhat smaller in the second model due to increasing problems with missing data with lower age.

Neighbourhoods are defined as SAMS (Small Area Market Statistics) areas. SAMS areas are defined by the municipalities in collaboration with Statistics Sweden and are based on homogeneity in function. They are relatively common proxies for neighbourhoods in Swedish neighbourhood effect studies. Only neighbourhoods with a minimum of 50 inhabitants in ages 16–20 during the entire period of study are included in the dataset, 388 in total. The neighbourhood variable of interest in this study is the share of teenagers, both girls and boys, in ages 16–20 that become parents. The choice to include both sexes is based on the assumption that teenage girls'

---

[5] 142 Swedes became parents at age 15 or below during years 2002–2010. Of these were 75 men and 67 women (Statistics Sweden).

[6] The Stockholm metropolitan region includes the municipalities of Stockholm and Solna, along with municipalities of the Stockholm labour market region which are areas where the majority of the commuting flow is into either Stockholm or Solna.

networks are not restricted to girls[7]. It is furthermore based on the assumption that it is the number of teenage parents that is important rather than the number of children born to teenage parents. To use percentage teenage parents as the neighbourhood variable is a slightly different approach compared to several U.S. studies that instead measures exposure to poverty (e.g. Wodtke 2013; South and Crowder 2010; Galster et al. 2007; Harding 2003; Crane 1991), although the two tend to correlate as we have seen. The chosen approach supposes a set of transmission mechanisms related to teenage childbearing rather than to poverty in general.

Control variables are mainly demographic and socio-economic and relate both to the teenager and to her parents. Control variables are chosen in accordance with reported previous findings of factors affecting teenage birth rates (Coyne and D'Onofrio 2012). Due to data limitations, it is however not possible to control for psychological or behavioural characteristics. Descriptive statistics of the variables included in the study are found in appendix Table 5.

The time-varying individual controls are household composition, level of education, the current type of occupation (student/employment/other), and whether the individual has any previous children. The latter variable may be positively or negatively correlated to whether the individual will have a child depending on timing—it is unlikely that someone will give birth just after having given birth, but teenagers who already have a child may be more inclined to have a second child at a young age. Household composition is divided into four categories: live with parents, live alone, live with partner/other, or other/unknown. These are identified through a combination of family identification number, type of family and individual position in the family, and geographical coordinates, since family ID can only be the same for a maximum of two generations. Individuals are coded as living with parents if they have the same family ID as their parents or if the individual is coded as a single parent and live within the same 100*100m coordinate as the parents. Individuals are coded as living with partner/other if they do not share family ID with any of the parents, and their family type and position suggest they have a partner. It should be noted that partners can only be identified if individuals are married or have a common child. Hence, cohabitants without children are coded as singles. Level of (completed) education is categorized into completed grade 9 (which most individuals do at age 15/16), higher level of education, and other/unknown. The only fixed individual control is background country which is measured as a dummy with categories Swedish or foreign background (born abroad or born in Sweden with two foreign born parents).

In addition, I also control for a number of parental characteristics. These are: household composition, parents' level of education, parents' employment status, parents' income and whether the mother of the teenage girl gave birth as a teenager herself. To follow parents over time would mean to risk measuring parental variables when the teenage girl has left her parental home, which teenage mothers tend to do earlier than other girls. All parental variables are fixed to the first year of the follow up, when the daughter was 16. They are categorized as dummies and estimate whether parents are married/cohabitants, whether one or both parents have a univer-

---

[7] The models are however run also for a neighbourhood variable that only includes girls/mothers with similar but slightly lower coefficients.

sity degree, whether one or both parents are employed and whether the mother gave birth at age 20 or younger. Parental income is a continuous variable, measured as the disposable income of the family where the girl lived at the age of 16. If the girl did not live in her parental home and/or had a child at age 16 (i.e. had a separate family ID from his or her parents) parental income refers to the disposable income of family of the teenager's mother. Finally, I also include control variables for year of follow-up (1–5) to account for age variations in the likelihood of giving birth, and for calendar year when the follow-up starts to account for time effects.

The sampling and restrictions, including the need of data for all control variables, result in a dataset with 38,548 individuals and 192,740 observations when the independent variables are measured at t-1. 946 births are recorded during the period. When independent variables are measured at t-2, the number of observation is reduced to 188,900 over 37,780 individuals.

5 Results

I begin by estimating an OLS model. As mentioned, the OLS model does not account for selection and is consequently presented for comparative purposes only. Some adjustments are however necessary since the OLS is based on cross-sectional rather than panel data. In the OLS, I estimate independent variables at follow-up year 3, i.e. the mid-year of the panel, when the girl is 18. The dependent variable, give birth, is however an estimate of whether the girl give birth during the entire teenage period, i.e. during age 16–20, to account for substantial age variation in birth rates.

Results of the OLS model, presented in Table 3, suggest that there indeed exist a positive correlation between neighbourhood birth rate and the likelihood of giving birth. The suggested neighbourhood effect is however small: one percentage point increase in the share teenage parents in the neighbourhood is associated with a 0.5 percentage point increase in the likelihood that a teenage girl will give birth. Household composition, both independent and parental, is also positively correlated with the likelihood of giving birth: girls who have left the parental home and girls who come from split families are more likely to become teenage parents. Other personal characteristics that are positively correlated with becoming a teenage mother are own employment (rather than being in school) and to have older children. Teenage girls with foreign background are slightly less likely to give birth. Coefficients for parental characteristics show that girls from split families, where parents have a low level of education and are unemployed are more a risk of becoming teenage mothers. There is also a positive correlation with mother's age at the birth of her first child where teenage motherhood is spread across generations.

I now move on to present results from the hybrid model, that unlike the OLS model controls for at least the part of selection bias that is related to individual characteristics that do not change over time. Model I, Table 4, presents results from a hybrid model with independent variables measured at time t-1, i.e. *the year before giving birth*. The top part of Table 4 presents deviations from the individual means for time variant variables, i.e. the within-individual variation (similar to those reported in a fixed-effects model). Model I reports a positive neighbourhood effect but it is

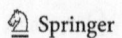

Table 3 Results from OLS regression. Dependent variable=give birth at age 16–20. Independent variables are measured at year 3 of follow-up (age 18). Dummies controlling for start year of follow-up are included in model but not shown

	Coef.	Std. Err.	Sign.
Neighbourhood variable			
Percentage teenage births in neighbourhood	0.0044	0.0009	***
Characteristics of teenager			
Single (ref=live with parents)	0.0395	0.0063	***
Live with partner (ref = live with parents)	0.1210	0.0287	***
Other/unknown household status (ref=live with parents)	0.0039	0.0031	
Compulsory school (ref = not completed compulsory school)	−0.0125	0.0045	**
High school or above (ref = not completed compulsory school)	−0.0378	0.0379	
Currently employed (ref = studying)	0.1506	0.0148	***
Other/unknown occupational status (ref = studying)	0.0174	0.0050	**
Have older children (ref = no)	0.8486	0.0140	***
Foreign background (ref = Swedish background)	−0.0032	0.0017	
Characteristics of parental household			
Parents live together (ref = other)	−0.0104	0.0014	***
One or both parents have high education (ref = other)	−0.0102	0.0016	***
One or both parents are employed (ref = other)	−0.0075	0.0015	***
Mother gave birth as teenager (until age 20) (ref = no)	0.0295	0.0019	***
Constant	0.0406	0.0048	***
R-squared	0.1113		
N	51,136		

*$p<0,05$; **$p<0,01$; ***$p<0,001$

extremely small, only 0.0013. The effect of neighbourhood context on the likelihood of becoming a teenage mother is thus basically non-existent. It is also substantially smaller than the one estimated in the OLS model. Although the two models are not directly comparable given differences in how the dependent variable is estimated and in timing of independent variables, this difference in size of neighbourhood coefficient suggests that selection bias is reduced in the hybrid model.

Results for the independent variables are in line with those reported by the OLS model. Teenagers coded as singles or who live with a partner are more likely to give birth at a young age compared to those still living with their parents, especially those with partner. The share of planned pregnancies could be expected to be higher among teenagers living with their partner one year before giving birth. This could probably also explain part of the positive correlations with being employed. As for level of education, the effect is non-existent for having completed compulsory school, and small for having completed high school. Any correlations between low education and teenage motherhood are thus likely to arise *after* birth rather than being due to a selection into giving birth. Having previous children is, unlike in the OLS model, negatively correlated with giving birth. This difference could be expected given differences in data structure. In the hybrid model, each time-varying variable are measured at t-1 rather than at age 18 and (the effect of) having previous children is strongly affected by age variations in birth rates.

The fixed variables that an ordinary fixed-effects model cannot show produce some interesting results which justify the use of the hybrid model. For example, the effect of foreign background is extremely small and negative. This result is in sharp contrast with U.S. findings where Black and Latin girls are considerably more likely than White girls to become mothers at a young age. Results for parental characteristics support previous literature and results from the OLS model; girls from split families where parents are unemployed are more likely to give birth as teenagers, as are girls whose own mothers gave birth as teenagers. The effects are however generally small and there is no effect on parents' level of education.

The bottom part of Table 4 shows the random effect parameters (representing between-individual variation). The sizes of these coefficients are generally larger than those reporting within-individual variation (the top part of the model) suggesting that there is more variation between individuals than within individuals' trajectories. This could be expected given the relatively short time period, five years. The neighbourhood effect estimate is however of roughly the same size when measuring between as within individuals.

Model II, Table 4, presents results from a hybrid model with independent variables measured at time t-2, i.e. *the year before getting pregnant*. The directions of (basically) all coefficients are the same to those of Model I, suggesting that the general conclusions are the same. There are however some differences in sizes. The neighbourhood coefficient is almost twice the size in Model II, although still being small and substantially smaller than in the OLS model. This suggests that neighbourhood effects, to the extent one can talk about such given the extremely small coefficients, affect both the likelihood of getting pregnant and the likelihood of giving birth once pregnant. The effect of own household situation and employment is weaker. A potential explanation is that most pregnancies are unplanned, as suggested by the literature, but that girls who decide to keep the child once pregnant leave their parental home and drop out of school. The effect of ethnicity and parental characteristics are roughly the same in Model I and II. This suggests that girls from low SES families are both likely to get pregnant and to give birth.

6 Conclusions

Selection bias generally constitutes a major problem in neighbourhood effect research but perhaps especially so for studies of effects on teenage birth rates where results even within the U.S. (where neighbourhood effects are reported more often and tend to be stronger than in Europe) are highly inconsistent. Many of the early studies that report significant effects fail to control for selection bias, although this does not explain all differences in results. At the same time, study after study point to selective residential patterns of teenage mothers or mothers-to-be with clear correlations between neighbourhood environment and teenage birth rates. Such patterns do not necessarily mean that selection bias is a problem but it seems probable that there are both observed and unobserved factors that make teenage girls at higher risk of child-

Table 4 Results from Random Effects model with Mundlak Correction. Dependent variable=give birth. Independent variables are measured at t-1 (Model I) or t-2 (Model II). Dummies controlling for start year of follow-up and for year of follow-up are included in model but not shown

	Model I (indep vars at t-1)			Model II (indep vars at t-2)		
	Coef.	Std. Err.	Sign.	Coef.	Std. Err.	Sign.
Time variant variables (deviation from individual mean)						
Neighbourhood variable						
Percentage teenage births in neighbourhood	0.0013	0.0003	***	0.0021	0.0003	***
Characteristics of teenager						
Single (ref = live with parents)	0.0362	0.0015	***	0.0073	0.0018	***
Live with partner (ref = live with parents)	0.1642	0.0038	***	0.0667	0.0068	***
Other/unknown household status (ref = live with parents)	0.0011	0.0017		−0.0032	0.0018	
Compulsory school (ref = not completed compulsory school)	−0.0013	0.0015		−0.0014	0,0033	
High school or above (ref = not completed compulsory school)	−0.0165	0.0017	***	−0.0004	0.0022	
Currently employed (ref = studying)	0.0236	0.0017	***	0.0132	0.0033	***
Other/unknown occupational status (ref = studying)	0.0028	0.0008	***	0.0016	0.0008	*
Have older children (ref = no)	−0.3429	0.0034	***	−0.2875	0.0048	***
Fixed variables						
Characteristics of teenager						
Foreign background (ref = Swedish background)	−0.0016	0.0004	***	−0.0013	0.0004	**
Characteristics of parental household						
Parents live together (ref = other)	−0.0007	0.0003	*	−0.0007	0.0003	*
One or both parents have high education (ref = other)	−0.0012	0.0003	***	−0.0011	0.0003	***
One or both parents are employed (ref = other)	−0.0005	0.0005		−0.0005	0.0005	
Mother gave birth as teenager (until age 20) (ref = no)	0.0027	0.0005	***	0.0024	0.0005	***
Individual means of time variant variables						
Neighbourhood variable						
Percentage teenage births in neighbourhood	0.0015	0.0003	***	0.0018	0.0004	***
Characteristics of teenager						
Single (ref = live with parents)	0.0149	0.0017	***	0.0278	0.0022	***
Live with partner (ref = live with parents)	0.2021	0.0059	***	0.2414	0.0083	***
Other/unknown household status (ref = live with parents)	0.0007	0.0008		0.0014	0.0009	
Compulsory school (ref = not completed compulsory school)	0.0032	0.,0013	*	0.0030	0.0016	
High school or above (ref = not completed compulsory school)	−0.0113	0.0019	***	−0.0115	0.0026	***
Currently employed (ref = studying)	0.0247	0.0029	***	0.0337	0.0041	***
Other/unknown occupational status (ref = studying)	0.0022	0.0013		0.0030	0.0016	
Have older children (ref = no)	0.4285	0.0039	***	0.4451	0.0051	***

Table 4 (Continued)

	Model I (indep vars at t-1)			Model II (indep vars at t-2)		
	Coef.	Std. Err.	Sign.	Coef.	Std. Err.	Sign.
Constant	−0.0068	0.0018	***	−0.0041	0.0018	*
R squared (within)	0.0672			0.0165		
R squared (between)	0.4807			0.5140		
R squared (overall)	0.1621			0.1288		
N	192,740			189,055		

$*p<0,05; **p<0,01; ***p<0,001$

bearing more prone to live in certain neighbourhoods. If such unobserved factors also are correlated with the outcome of interest selection bias will occur. Hypothetical candidates of factors that may be correlated with both place of residence and the likelihood of giving birth and furthermore often are unobserved in data are, e.g., level of parental control and family environment, and behavioural problems, academic competence and educational prospects of teenage girls.

In this study, I test the existence and scope of selection bias by running two different models, one that controls for selection bias and one that does not. The OLS model using a cross-sectional dataset does not control for selection. The OLS model in this paper produces significant neighbourhood effects, suggesting that neighbourhood processes do have a (very small) impact on the likelihood that a teenage girl will give birth. However, when running a random effects model with a Mundlak correction, a model that both controls for selection and employs a five-year panel data set, these already very small effects are further reduced to size where they are more or less irrelevant. Hence, in this study selection biases results upwards and may lead to erroneous conclusions. In this case, a (very) small "neighbourhood effect" turned so small after controlling for selection that it is basically pointless to discuss. In other contexts or if using a different dependent variable, selection bias may lead even more wrong.

The empirical analysis of this paper provides support to the literature that suggests that neighbourhood effects on teenage childbeaing are basically non-existent. At least, this seems to be the case for Sweden, a country with a low level of teenage fertility. A unit's (percentage point) increase in the share teenage parents in the neighbourhood is a relatively large change given the distribution of teenage parents across neighbourhoods and it is only associated with an extremely small increase in the likelihood that a teenage girl will become a mother. This is true regardless of whether measuring neighbourhood environment one or two years before giving birth (i.e. before giving birth or before becoming pregnant). Hence, in terms of public policy, the conclusion from this study is that if one would wish to prevent teenage motherhood, there are probably more efficient ways than to try to combat neighbourhood effects.

Like all studies, this study is not without its flaws. Three important caveats must be made. The first caveat is that although the hybrid model efficiently controls for selection of time-invariant variables, results may be affected by selection of time-variant characteristics. The model may however, according to Wodtke (2013), also underestimate effects of past environments by controlling for fixed parameters. The second caveat concerns temporal dimensions of neighbourhood effects including the point-in-time estimate of parental characteristics and the relatively short time period. Although Wodtke (2013) finds that adolescence environment is more important than child environment, it is possible that a prolonged exposure that includes potential fluctuations would provide slightly different results (see also South and Crowder 2010). However, none of these points are likely to affect the general conclusion: that neighbourhood effects are extremely small. The third caveat relates to the definition of neighbourhood and choice of context. First, these results are only relevant for the chosen neighbourhood definition: they may be different for other neighbourhood delimitations. It is also possible that effects based on similar transmission mechanisms exist in other geographical contexts, such as schools or friendship networks that are not defined by neighbourhoods. Previous studies have found that schools are more important than neighbourhoods for youth's achievements (Sykes and Musterd 2011). Whether this is the case also for teenage motherhood is a challenge for future studies.

Appendix

Table 5 Descriptive statistics of variables in hybrid model as measured at time t-1

	Mean	Std Dev	Min	Max
Give birth (dependent variable)	0.0049	0.0699	0	1
Percentage teenage births in neighbourhood	0.4714	0.7756	0	12.5
Characteristics of teenager				
Live with one or both parents	0.9277	0.2590	0	1
Single	0.0280	0.1649	0	1
Live with partner	0.0026	0.0512	0	1
Other/unknown	0.0417	0.1999	0	1
Compulsory school	0.6184	0.4858	0	1
High school or above	0.1509	0.3579	0	1
Oher/unknown	0.2307	0.4213	0	1
Studying	0.7156	0.4511	0	1
Employed	0.0105	0.1022	0	1
Other/unknown	0.2738	0.4459	0	1
Have older children	0.0042	0.0647	0	1
Foreign background	0.2446	0.4299	0	1
Characteristics of parental household				
Parents are married/cohabitans	0.5644	0.4958	0	1
One or both parents have high education	0.2250	0.4176	0	1
One or both parents are employed	0.6642	0.2496	0	1
Parents' disposable income (10,000 SEK)	37.751	37.832	0	2749.76
Mother gave birth as teenager (until age 20)	0.1426	0.3497	0	1
Time control variables				
Calendar year at start of follow-up	2003.84	1.3473	2002	2006

References

Arai, Lisa. 2007. Peer and neighbourhood influences on teenage pregnancy and fertility: Qualitative findings from research in English communities. *Health & Place* 13:87–98.
Barber, Jennifer S. 2001. The intergenerational transmission of age at first birth among married and unmarried men and women. *Social Science Research* 30:219–247.
Brooks-Gunn, Jeanne, Greg Duncan, Pamela Klebanov, and Naomi Sealand. 1993. Do neighborhoods influence child and adolescent development? *American Journal of Sociology* 99:353–395.
Brooks-Gunn, Jeanne, Greg Duncan, and Lawrence Aber (eds.). 1997. Neighbourhood poverty. Vol. 1: Context and consequences for children. New York: Russell Sage.
Brown, Lawrence A., and Eric G. Moore. 1970. The intra-urban migration process: A perspective. *Geografiska Annaler B* 52:1–13.
Browning, Christopher R., Tama Leventhal, and Jeanne Brooks-Gunn. 2004. Neighborhood context and racial differences in early sexual activity. *Demography* 41:697–720.
Clark, William A. V., and Frans M. Dieleman. 1996. *Households and housing. Choice and outcomes in the housing market*. New Brunswick: Rutgers.
Coley, Rebecca L., and Lindsay Chase-Lansdale.1998. Adolescent pregnancy and parenthood: Recent evidence and future directions. *American Psychologist* 53:152–166.
Coyne, Claire A., and Brian M. D'Onofrio. 2012. Some (but not much) progress toward understanding teenage childbearing: A review of research from the past decade. *Advances in Child Development and Behavior* 42:113–152.
Crane, Jonathan. 1991. The epidemic theory of ghettos and neighborhood effects on dropping out and teenage childbearing. *American Journal of Sociology* 96:1226–1259.
D'Addio, Anna Cristina. 2007. *Intergenerational transmission of disadvantage: Mobility or immobility across generations*. OECD Social, Employment and Migration Working Papers No. 52 OECD Publishing.
Danielsson, Maria, Christina Rogala, and Kajsa Sundström. 2001. *Teenage sexual and reproductive behavior in developed countries. Country report from Sweden*. Occasional Report No 7. New York: The Alan Guttmacher Institute.
Duncan, Greg J., James P. Connell, and Pamela K. Klebanov. 1997. Conceptual and methodological issues in estimating causal effects of neighborhoods and family conditions on individual development. In *Neighborhood Poverty: Vol. 1 Context and Consequences for Children*, eds. Jeanne Brooks-Gunn and Greg J. Duncan, 219–250. New York: Russell Sage Foundation.
Francesconi, Marco. 2008. Adult outcomes for children of teenage mothers. *Scandinavian Journal of Economics* 110:93–117.
Fransson, Urban, Gunnar Rosenqvist, and Bengt Turner. 2002. *Hushållens värderingar av egenskaper I bostäder och bostadsområden*. Research Report 2002:1. Uppsala: Uppsala University: Institute for Housing and Urban Research.
Galster, George. 2008. Quantifying the effect of neighbourhood on individuals: Challenges, alternative approaches and promising directions. *Journal of Applied Social Science Studies. Schmollers Jahrbuch* 128:7–48.
Galster, George, and Lina Hedman. 2013. Measuring neighbourhood effects non-experimentally: How much do alternative methods matter? *Housing Studies* 28:473–498.
Galster, George, and Anna Santiago. 2013. *Evaluating the potential of a natural experiment in Denver to provide unbiased evidence of neighborhood effects*. Working paper. Detroit: Wayne State University, Department of Urban studies and Planning.
Galster, George, Dave Marcotte, Marv Mandell, Hal Wolman, and Nancy Augustine. 2007. The influence of neighborhood poverty during childhood on fertility, education and earnings outcomes. *Housing Studies* 22:723–751.
Gennetian, Lisa A., Lisa Sanbonmatsu, and Jens Ludwig. 2011. An overview of moving to opportunity: A random assignment housing mobility study in five U.S. cities. In *Neighborhood and life chances. How place matters in modern America* (chapter 10), eds. Harriet B. Newburger, Eugenie L. Birch, and Susan M. Watcher. Philadelphia: University of Pennsylvania Press.
Gibbons, Steve. 2002. *Neighbourhood effects on educational achievement: Evidence from the census and national child development study*. London: London School of Economics, Center for Economics of Education.

Ginther, Donna, Robert Haveman, and Barbara Wolfe. 2000. Neighborhood attributes as determinants of children's outcomes: How robust are the relationships? *Journal of Human Resources* 35:603–642.

van Ham, Maarten, and David Manley. 2010. The effect of neighbourhood housing tenure mix on labour market outcomes: A longitudinal investigation of neighbourhood effects. *Journal of Housing and the Built Environment* 24:407–422.

van Ham, Maarten, and David Manley. 2012. Neighbourhood effects research at a crossroads. Ten challenges for future research. *Environment and Planning A* 44:2787–2793.

Harding, David J. 2003. Counterfactual models of neighborhood effects: The effect of neighbourhood poverty on dropping out and teenage pregnancy. *American Journal of Sociology* 109:676–719.

Haveman, Robert, Barbara Wolfe, Elaine Peterson, and Kathryn Wilson. 1997. *Do teens make rational childbearing choices?: Family, neighborhood, and net benefit determinants of teen nonmarital childbearing.* Discussion Paper no 1137–97. Madison, WI: University of Wisconsin-Madison, Institute for Research on Poverty.

Hedman, Lina, and George Galster. 2013. Neighbourhood income sorting and the effects of neighbourhood income mix on income. A holistic empirical exploration. *Urban Studies* 50:107–127.

Hedman, Lina, Maarten van Ham, and David Manley. 2011. Neighbourhood choice and neighbourhood reproduction. *Environment and Planning A* 43:1381–1399.

Hedman, Lina, David Manley, Maarten van Ham, and J. Östh. 2012. *Cumulative exposure to disadvantage and the intergenerational transmission of neighbourhood effects.* IZA paper no 6794. Bonn: Institute for the Study of Labour.

Hertfelt Wahn, Elisabeth, and Eva Nissen. 2008. Sociodemographic background, lifestyle and psychosocial conditions of Swedish teenage mothers and their perception of health and social support during pregnancy and childbirth. *Scandinavian Journal of Public Health* 36:415–423.

Jencks, Christopher, and Susan E. Mayer. 1990. The social consequences of growing up in a poor neighborhood. In *Inner-city poverty in the United States*, eds. L. Lynn and M. McGeary, 111–186. Washington D.C.: National Academy Press.

Jones, Kelvyn, and SV Subramanian. 2012. *Developing multilevel models for analysing contextuality, heterogeneity and change Volume 2*, 1–312. http://www.mendeley.com/profiles/kelvyn-jones/. (Accessed 26 Aug 2013).

Joshi, Heather. 1998. The opportunity costs of childbearing: More than mothers' business. *Journal of Population Economics* 11:161–183.

Lupton, Ruth, and Dylan Kneale. 2010. *Are there neighbourhood effects on teenage parenthood in the UK, and does it matter for policy? A review of theory and evidence.* London: Centre for Analysis of Social Exclusion, London School of Economics.

Meade, Christina S., Trace S. Kershaw, and Jeannette R. Ickovics. 2008. The intergenerational cycle of teenage motherhood: An ecological approach. *Health Psychology* 27:419–429.

Mersky, Joshua P., and Arthur J. Reynolds. 2007. Predictors of early childbearing: Evidence from the Chicago longitudinal study. *Children and Youth Services Review* 29:35–52.

Mundlak, Yair. 1978. On the pooling of time series and cross sectional data. *Econometrica* 46:69–85.

Oreopoulos, Philip. 2003. The long-run consequences of living in a poor neighborhood. *Quarterly Journal of Economics* 118:1533–1575.

Propper, Carol, Kelvyn Jones, Anne Bolster, Simon Burgess, Ron Johnston, and Rebecca Sarker. 2004. *Local neighbourhoods and mental health: Evidence from the UK.* ESRC Research Methods Programme Working Paper No. 6. Bristol: University of Bristol.

Sari, Florent. 2012. Analysis of neighbourhood effects and work behaviour: Evidence from Paris. *Housing Studies* 27:45–76.

South, Scott J., and Kyle D. Crowder. 1999. Neighborhood effects on family formation: Concentrated poverty and beyond. *American Sociological Review* 64:113–132.

South, Scott J., and Eric P. Baumer. 2000. Deciphering community and race effects on adolescent premarital childbearing. *Social Forces* 78:1379–1408.

South, Scott J., and Kyle D. Crowder. 2010. Neighborhood poverty and nonmarital fertility: Spatial and temporal dimensions. *Journal of Marriage and Family* 72:89–104.

Sucoff, Clea A., and Dawn M. Upchurch. 1998. Neighborhood context and the risk of childbearing among metropolitan-area black adolescents. *American Sociological Review* 63:571–585.

Sykes, Brooke, and Sako Musterd. 2011. Examining neighbourhood and school effects simultaneously what does the Dutch evidence show? *Urban Studies* 48:1307–1331.

Tienda, Marta. 1991. Poor people and poor places: Deciphering neighborhood effects on poverty outcomes. In *Macro–micro linkages in sociology*, ed. Joan Huber, 244–262. Newburgh Park: Sage Publications.

Thornberry, Terence P., Carolyn A. Smith, and Gregory J. Howard. 1997. Risk factors for teenage fatherhood. *Journal of Marriage and the Family* 59:505–522.
Wodtke, Geoffrey T. 2013. Duration and timing of exposure to neighborhood poverty and the risk of adolescent parenthood. *Demography* 50:1765–1788.

Lina Hedman, 1981, holds a PhD in human geography from Uppsala University. She is currently holding researcher positions at the Institute for Housing and Urban Research, Uppsala University, and Institute for Future Studies, Stockholm. Her main fields of research are residential segregation, patterns of residential mobility, neighbourhood choice and neighbourhood effects. Other recent publications: "Cumulative exposure to disadvantage and the intergenerational transmission of neighbourhood effects", Journal of Economic Geography, 2014, online (with D. Manley, M. van Ham and J. Östh); "Neighbourhood income sorting and the effects of neighbourhood income mix on income. A holistic empirical investigation", Urban Studies 50, 2013 (with G. Galster).

Between Mechanism Talk and Mechanism Cult: New Emphases in Explanatory Sociology and Empirical Research

Frank Kalter · Clemens Kroneberg

© Springer Fachmedien Wiesbaden 2014

Abstract The study of mechanisms has received increased attention in recent years and contributed to the formation of so-called 'analytical sociology' that has put the idea of social mechanisms at its core. We discuss the crucial characteristics of mechanism-based explanations and their relation to the longstanding tradition of explanatory sociology. Looking at the widespread and growing number of references to 'mechanisms' in the current research literature, we identify typical deviations from the ideal of a mechanism-based explanation. Many references come down to mechanism talk insofar as it is not explicated in detail how and why particular inputs tend to result in particular outputs. To this end, researchers have to give a detailed verbal account of how exactly a mechanism is thought to unfold under specified conditions, or to specify a formal generative model which can be analysed analytically or by simulation. This agenda has been at the core of methodological individualism, sociological rational choice theory, and explanatory sociology for some time, but has received a new coat of whitewash by analytical sociology. This more recent theoretical movement offers a fresh problem-centred agenda based on the well-known macro-micro-macro model and could inspire a new generation of research that places greater weight on analysing social dynamics than on developing theories of action. However, we submit that, rather than constituting a competing approach, these impulses should be located within the longstanding and multifaceted explanatory agenda in sociology. Avoiding any form of mechanism cult and

---

F. Kalter (✉)
School of Social Sciences, University of Mannheim,
68131 Mannheim, Germany
e-mail: kalter@uni-mannheim.de

C. Kroneberg
Institute of Sociology and Social Psychology, University of Cologne,
Greinstr. 2, 50939 Köln, Germany
e-mail: c.kroneberg@uni-koeln.de

choosing from the full toolbox of explanatory/analytical sociology will be crucial to answer key questions in established areas of sociological research.

Keywords Analytical sociology · Methodology of the social sciences · Macro-micro-macro scheme · Agent-based models

Zwischen Mechanismus-Gerede und Mechanismus-Kult: Neue Schwerpunkte in der Erklärendenden Soziologie und empirischen Forschung

Zusammenfassung Das Konzept der Mechanismen hat in den letzten Jahren zunehmende Aufmerksamkeit erfahren. Es bildet den Kern der sogenannten Analytischen Soziologie und hat maßgeblich zu deren Entwicklung beigetragen. Wir diskutieren die Beziehung dieses neueren Ansatzes zur Tradition der Erklärenden Soziologie und arbeiten zentrale Merkmale einer Mechanismen-basierten Erklärung heraus. In der aktuellen Forschungsliteratur wird zwar vermehrt der Mechanismus-Begriff bemüht, es lassen sich aber einige typische Abweichungen vom Ideal einer Mechanismen-basierten Erklärung identifizieren. Viele Verwendungen des Begriffs bleiben floskelhaft, weil sie nicht genau genug explizieren, warum bestimmte Anfangsbedingungen zu bestimmten Ausgängen führen. Dazu sind detaillierte und lückenlose verbale Ausführungen erforderlich oder formale Modelle, aus denen sich analytisch oder durch Simulationsmethoden die zu erklärenden Phänomene ableiten oder generieren lassen. Diese Agenda steht seit geraumer Zeit im Zentrum des Methodologischen Individualismus, der soziologischen Rational-Choice-Theorie und der Erklärenden Soziologie. Die theoretische Bewegung der Analytischen Soziologie verleiht dieser Agenda einen neuen Anstrich und gibt ihr neue Impulse: Im Rahmen des bekannten Makro-Mikro-Makro-Modells plädiert dieser Ansatz für eine neue Generation von Forschungsarbeiten, die das Gewicht und die Aufmerksamkeit von den handlungstheoretischen Grundlagen hin zur Analyse sozialer Dynamiken verlagern. Wir argumentieren, dass diese neue Schwerpunktsetzung nicht als konkurrierendes Programm zur Erklärenden Soziologie angesehen, sondern innerhalb der etablierten und vielschichtigen erklärenden Tradition der Soziologie verortet werden sollte. Anstatt eines Mechanismen-Kults um bestimmte Spezialtechniken ist substanzieller Erkenntnisfortschritt in soziologischen Anwendungsfeldern nur durch eine Ausschöpfung des vollen theoretischen Repertoires einer Erklärenden Soziologie zu erwarten.

Schlüsselwörter Analytische Soziologie · Methodologie der Sozialwissenschaften · Makro-Mikro-Makro-Schema · Agenten-basierte Modelle

1 Introduction

In recent years the notion of 'mechanisms' has become very popular, if not a buzzword, in sociology. Scanning current research articles this seems visible in almost all journals; it is well reflected also in the *Kölner Zeitschrift für Soziologie und Sozialpsychologie* (KZfSS). While in 2003 (Volume 55), 14 out of 29 (48%) articles somehow made use of the term, we find that 10 years later (Volume 65) this holds for 17 out of 23 articles (74%).

While the term appears to have been around in the discipline for quite a long time—being used, as so many important concepts in sociology, in a rather vague, inconsistent, and casual way (Mayntz 2004, p. 239; Gerring 2007, p. 178)—some highly influential books, such as 'Nuts and Bolts' by Jon Elster (1989) or 'Social Mechanisms' edited by Peter Hedström and Richard Swedberg (1998b) moved the concept explicitly to the centre of interest and tried to sharpen its meaning. The programmatic metaphor motivating the explication of the concept is that mechanisms should deliver a proper explanation of facts and regularities by revealing the 'cogs and wheels' which bring about the phenomena of interest.

Meanwhile, a distinct and visible theoretical movement, so-called 'analytical sociology', has crystallized that has put the idea of social mechanisms at its core. Important milestones of this development are the programmatic book 'Dissecting the Social', by Peter Hedström (2005), and 'The Oxford Handbook of Analytical Sociology' (Hedström and Bearman 2009a). The movement is attracting an increasing number of researchers, who now have a forum in the 'International Network of Analytical Sociology (INAS)'. It might be seen as an indicator of analytical sociology's well-established place in current sociological theory that it is also attracting an increasing number of critiques (e.g., Abbott 2007; Opp 2007; Gross 2009; Diekmann 2010; Kron and Grund 2010; Little 2012; Lizardo 2012; Santoro 2012; Opp 2013b), sometimes even on the part of those who are by no means suspected of not being in favour of the basic ideas of an explanatory approach, analytical methods, and the relevance of mechanisms.

In this article we discuss the principles and implications of this recent theoretical movement. In particular, we ask what suggestion its explicit interest in social mechanisms makes to those who feel committed to an explanatory approach and theory-guided empirical research. While some of its advocates seem to understand a mechanism-based approach and analytical sociology to be a significant turn[1] in theorizing and empirical research, other scholars tend to perceive the whole development to be nothing but old wine in new bottles.[2] We will argue that neither of these extreme views is particularly helpful, nor are recent, more scholastic, debates about which of these views might be more adequate. Rather, it seems most fruitful to perceive of the new attention given to social mechanisms as a re-emphasis on specific aspects and tasks that have been recognized before, but have been somewhat neglected, or at least have not been addressed systematically enough in prior theoretical and empirical work. In particular, the principles of analytical sociology can be read as a plea to forcefully invest in methodologies that allow sociologists to study social dynamics, even though this might mean to let go of a unifying action-theoretic agenda.

---

[1] See the notion of a 'complexity turn' in the description of 'analytical sociology' at the website of the International Network of Analytical Sociology' (INAS) at http://analyticalsociology.com/about/.

[2] Most poignantly, eminent Raymond Boudon characterized analytical sociology as not referring to something different than methodological individualism (MI) but "offering a PowerPoint-style presentation of MI" (Boudon 2013, p. 26).

To develop this argument, we will start by explicating the relation between the more recent notion of social mechanisms and previous conceptions of an explanatory approach in sociology (section II). Despite seemingly fundamental disagreement in meta-theory, especially on the status of the covering-law model, or Hempel-Oppenheim scheme, there is a great deal of overlap between these programmes that even justifies regarding them as a single approach in sociology. Their common denominator is that collective phenomena have to be explained according to the macro-micro-macro scheme and in such a precise way that it becomes possible to analytically derive the explanandum. And this is exactly how analytical sociology proposes to flesh out the idea of mechanism-based explanations in the social sciences (for other positions, see, e.g., Mayntz 2004; Cardona 2013).

Then (section III), we will briefly review to what extent the concept of social mechanisms is already driving current research. The above-mentioned trends in the journals could be seen as a (good) sign that empirical researchers are increasingly occupied with identifying and testing mechanisms, and that the days of merely relating variables and telling stories are over. However, while the use of the concept in current research indeed might partly reflect such a trend, there is also still a lot of *mechanism talk* that is only paying lip service to a truly explanatory agenda. Most importantly, even those scholars whose understanding and usage of mechanisms is in line with the refined concept seem to remain attached to types of research questions and methods that use only a part of the potential of the social mechanisms idea.

This will lead us back to a closer look at what exactly can be seen as the new impulses stemming from analytical sociology *within* the longstanding explanatory tradition in sociology (section IV). Most importantly, it focuses on the social dynamics that produce collective phenomena, rather than conceiving of them as a simple aggregation of individual behaviour, and thus corrects for a certain bias to invest foremost in the micro-foundations of sociological explanations. This emphasis on social dynamics is likely to improve our understanding of key social processes in many fields of sociology off the beaten tracks. Not least, it invites deviation from routines in empirical research, the asking of different and fresh kinds of questions, and more creativity in choosing adequate data and empirical methods.

At the same time, care should be taken that the attempt to establish analytical sociology as a new approach to theorizing and research does not mean to pre-commit to a too narrow set of techniques. As we will outline in the last section (V), such a *mechanism cult* would unnecessarily limit and divide the longstanding search for social mechanisms. This might become particularly visible when analytical sociology leaves the settings of occasionally and deliberately chosen empirical examples and makes substantive contributions to key open questions in major fields of sociology.

2 Social mechanisms, explanations, and the macro-micro-macro scheme

The concept of social mechanisms is one way to flesh out the agenda of an explanatory sociology. This agenda has been a particularly vibrant strand of European sociology for more than five decades. While it was closely intertwined with sociological rational choice theory, the approach was also articulated under an epistemological label that signifies substantive openness: 'explanatory sociology'. This label has been especially common and is meanwhile well-established in Dutch and German sociology (Verklarende sociologie, Erklärende Soziologie, see, for example, Ganzeboom and Lindenberg 1996; Hill et al. 2009; Maurer and Schmid 2010). As we will show, many of the ideas underlying analytical sociology already have been core ingredients of the tradition of explanatory sociology. It is even more remarkable then that a debate has developed between advocates of explanatory sociology and analytical sociology on the meaning and essential elements of an explanation (Opp 2013a, b; Ylikoski 2013). In particular, Hedström and Ylikoski (Hedström 2005; Hedström and Ylikoski 2010) have developed the idea of mechanism-based explanations in sharp opposition to the covering-law model, or Hempel-Oppenheim scheme, which explanatory sociology has traditionally taken as the very starting point to argue that explanations in sociology should and can be as scientific as those in other sciences (e.g., Lindenberg 1977; Wippler and Lindenberg 1987; Esser 1993). We show that this seemingly fundamental disagreement largely vanishes when taking the macro-micro-macro scheme into full and proper account. Explanatory and analytical sociology agree on the most important features of mechanism-based explanations. At the same time, however, analytical sociology offers a new emphasis in theorizing and research and this shift is already laid out in its sharp opposition to the covering-law model.

In its most simple form the covering-law model (or Hempel-Oppenheim scheme) of an explanation requires that a particular fact (B_i), the explanandum, can be logically deduced from another particular fact (A_i) via a general law (if A then B). Analytical sociology rejects this concept of explanation for two main reasons: First, empirically, such covering laws simply do not seem to exist; at least there is not a single convincing example of any truly general law in sociology by now (Hedström 2005, p. 15). This assessment is uncontroversial with respect to Durkheimian 'sociological laws' that directly relate macro-level phenomena (Lindenberg 1983). To be sure, sociology should be concerned with 'social facts', i.e., phenomena at the collective or macro level, but relations on the macro level can hardly be regarded as general laws, as they are not stable enough across time and space.

The second important objection against the covering-law model is even more fundamental. Even if sociological laws existed, a covering-law explanation would not be satisfactory because it would essentially constitute a 'black box' in need of understanding (Boudon 1998). As this argument points to the core of the mechanism idea, it is worth illustrating it with a simple example from physics: The regularity that the pressure of a gas (p) is proportional to its density (ρ) is stable enough under regular conditions to be considered a law. Density, by definition, is mass (m) per unit volume (V), so that the law can be written as $p = cm/V$, with c being a constant which needs no further elaboration here. Using this law, we could employ the covering-law scheme to 'explain' why the pressure of a gas in a given cylinder has doubled by tracing this back to the changed condition that the volume of the cylinder was reduced to half of its size by keeping the mass inside constant. The logic is sound ($p_2 = cm/V_2 = cm/(1/2 \cdot V_1) = 2 \text{ cm}/V_1 = 2p_1$) and the law can be used for valid predictions and successful interventions. Nevertheless, there is a feeling that we do not really 'understand' what is going on here, and the question of why the pressure has really doubled still feels unanswered.

As nicely described in the famous lectures of Nobel laureate Richard Feynman (Feynman et al. 1963, pp. 1–5), this black box can be opened up by recognizing that a gas consists of molecules (their weights making up the mass) that are constantly in more or less erratic movement (the velocity depending on the temperature). They therefore occasionally bounce against the walls of the cylinder and this is what leads to pressure (like bouncing tennis balls would exert pressure on a blackboard, eventually pushing it away). If we now reduce the volume of the cylinder to half of its size (keeping other things, like mass and temperature, constant) the likelihood that any molecule will bounce against a cylinder wall doubles; thus the overall pressure doubles (see Fig. 1). This insight into the cylinder immediately leads to a satisfying feeling of 'Aha, this is *why*!', a feeling that we now really *understand* the reasons behind the relation between volume and pressure. Moreover, this sense of understanding, while fallible in general (Ylikoski 2009), goes along with the ability to derive a great number of further implications: why increasing temperature leads the pressure of a gas to increase and water to evaporate, why the volume increases when water freezes, why clothes dry better in the wind, and many other regularities. All this becomes possible by identifying and understanding the 'cogs and wheels' inside the black box and this is exactly what analytical sociology regards as an ideal mechanism-based explanation.

Paying attention to the smaller elements inside is constitutive for the refined concept of mechanism. It is clearly reflected, for example, in Hedström's definition, according to which "mechanisms can be said to consist of *entities* (with their properties) and the *activities* that these entities engage in, either by themselves or in concert with other entities." (Hedström 2005, p. 24; original emphases). Analytical sociology stresses the need to open up black boxes by decomposing or 'dissecting' the social phenomena of interest into their constituent parts and processes. Hedström (2005, p. 34) makes an illuminative reference to Fodor (1994), catching up on the idea that a mechanism supposed to explain a phenomenon on a certain level L will be located at a lower level L-1 (see also Gross 2009; Demeulenaere 2011, p. 21). In our example from physics, one can consider the gas to be on level L, while the molecules and their activities are on level L-1. Referring also to example of gases and

Fig. 1 Molecule movement and pressure of a gas. (based on Feynman et al. 1963, p. 3)

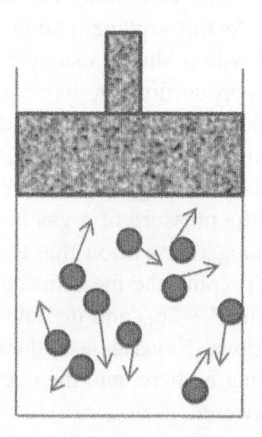

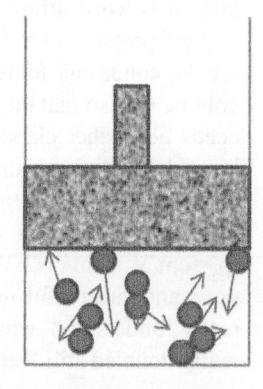

molecules, already Hempel (1965, p. 259) spoke of various 'levels of explanation' and expressed a similar view within the concept of a covering-law explanation: "It is often felt that only the discovery of a micro-theory affords real scientific understanding of any type of phenomenon, because it gives us insight into *the inner mechanism* of the phenomenon, so to speak" (Hempel 1965, p. 259; emphasis added).

Both arguments—the non-existence of general sociological laws and the need to refer to relationships on the micro level to attain a real understanding of phenomena—motivate the doctrine of methodological individualism and the famous three-step scheme which now goes under the names of 'the macro-micro-macro scheme', 'the Coleman boat', or 'the model of sociological explanation' (McClelland 1961; Coleman 1986; Wippler and Lindenberg 1987; Esser 1993; Hedström and Swedberg 1998a). In order to account for the exceptions of robust macro-level relationships and to uncover the underlying causal processes, one has to step down from the level of social phenomena to that of individual actors.[3] In other words, sociological explanations need micro-foundations.

Analytical sociology and explanatory sociology share this assessment and, consequently, the dismissal of a pure macro-sociology. In explanatory sociology, the lack of generality of macro-sociological laws and their black-box character have sometimes been called the problems of 'incompleteness' and 'meaninglessness' (see, e.g., Esser 1996; on the latter, see already Weber's concepts of 'Verstehen'/understanding and 'Sinn'/meaning). The disagreement between analytical and explanatory sociology concerns what all this implies for the covering-law model of scientific explanations. For most advocates of explanatory sociology the macro-micro-macro scheme *saves* the covering-law model and justifies its use in sociology despite the obvious problems of macro-sociological laws: The micro level is able to provide the general-laws request by the covering-law model, in form of a theory of action. Accordingly, the action theory is also referred to as the 'nomological core' of sociological explanations (Lindenberg 1981, p. 20; Esser 1999, p. 14) or, in other terms, it is seen to contain "*general* assumptions about human nature" (Wippler and Lindenberg 1987, p. 148, emphasis added). In contrast, analytical sociology avoids any reference to laws, even on the micro level of individual behaviour (Demeulenaere 2011, pp. 16–17). This difference might seem negligible at first sight as programmatic statements about analytical sociology also emphasise the role of theories of action. However, recognising it and identifying its implications is key to fully understanding the programme of analytical sociology and its implications for sociological theory and research.

Making the difference between the two approaches most poignant, explanatory sociology can be said to aim at a coherent body of knowledge unified by and reducible to law-like propositions about human behaviour (the theory of action), while analytical sociology attempts to set up a toolbox of social mechanisms based on different (not necessarily compatible or related) behavioural assumptions, each of them being more or less useful depending on the explanatory task at hand.

---

[3] While this is true in most cases, there can be instances where an adequate mechanism-based explanation might be possible by going down to entities larger than individuals. Under rare circumstances it can be justified to analyze the interaction among collective or corporative actors such as states, firms, political parties, or social movements without disaggregating these entities to the level of individual actors.

This difference in emphasis has hardly been recognised in the debate between proponents of analytical sociology and major figures of explanatory sociology and rational choice theory. The ensuing misunderstandings have partly prevented a more pragmatic discussion about different theoretical and methodological strategies. This becomes most evident in Opp's criticism that analytical sociology provides no comprehensive or fully specified theory of action (similarly, see Diekmann 2010). What seems most irritating to Opp is Hedström's proposal to use 'DBO theory' as the theory of action within analytical sociology (Hedström, 2005, p. 38–66). The acronym refers to desires (D), beliefs (B), and opportunities (O), whose interplay is assumed to determine action (see already Elster 1979). Opp criticizes that DBO theory is either not a theory at all or, if more fully specified, equivalent to a wide version of rational choice theory. Indeed, from the perspective of rational choice theory, settling for the orientating hypothesis that desires, beliefs, and opportunities shape behaviour seems a huge step backwards and ignorant of what has been achieved in the struggle for precise explanatory micro-foundations over the last decades. However, this is not the issue at stake. The real question underlying Hedström's action-theoretical proposal is not action-theoretic but rather concerns the overall theoretical strategy of explaining *collective* phenomena. The superficial character of DBO theory is indicative of analytical sociology's different emphasis that favours social dynamics (and the social networks on which they take place and which they produce) over action-theoretic details. Most recently, this point has now been made much more explicit: "Although the mechanism-based approach emphasizes the importance of action in the explanation of social phenomena, it does not subscribe to an axiomatic vision according to which a specific action theory should be used for all purposes" (Hedström and Ylikoski 2014, p. 64).

We will return to and elaborate on these different priorities and their implications in section IV when discussing new impulses stemming from analytical sociology. For the moment, we focus on the huge overlap between both approaches in order to explicate a shared understanding of mechanisms and mechanism-based explanations. Indeed, on the side of analytical sociology, the above-given definition of a mechanism likewise assumes that there are some 'regularities' in the activities of the entities. If we wouldn't accept that 'buzzing around' is what molecules of a gas 'usually do' we wouldn't accept the Feynman explanation above. Or, in Hedström and Swedberg (1998a, p. 19)'s own words: "It is important to note that the mechanisms (…) are mechanisms of some generality, and it is this generality that gives them their explanatory power." So while no reference is made to laws, analytical sociology likewise rests on the assumption of regularities in human behaviour and aims to identify mechanisms that are of 'some generality'. At the same time, on the side of explanatory sociology, most scholars would not insist that the assumptions about human behaviour must be general laws in a strict sense of the word (and this pertains even to physics, as the molecule movements would not appear under extreme conditions). This holds especially true, if we acknowledge that explanations are never final but a matter of degree and adequacy (Lindenberg 1992). In many publications, the argument in favour of methodological individualism simply refers to the fact that regularities on the micro level are *more* stable than the phenomena to be explained on the macro level (Wippler and Lindenberg 1987).

Fig. 2 The macro-micro-macro scheme

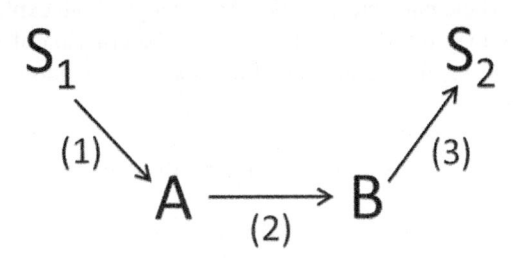

$$S_1 \searrow^{(1)} \quad\quad\quad\quad S_2 \nearrow^{(3)}$$
$$A \xrightarrow[(2)]{} B$$

So leaving aside meta-theoretical terminology, it is easily possible to identify a common ground for all those who work in the tradition of an explanatory or analytical agenda: We can improve our understanding of a (time-space dependent) fact or regularity on a given level, and thus contribute to its explanation, if we can analytically derive it from regularities of larger stability (less time-space dependency) on a lower level. And if we are interested in social facts or regularities, an explanation requires that it be derived from assumptions about relatively stable patterns of human behaviour and interaction.

Hence, the well-known macro-micro-macro scheme as depicted in Fig. 2 provides a telling representation of the idea of a mechanism-based explanation in sociology. Such an explanation must always somehow contain *all three* steps of this scheme: (1) Macro-micro links, aptly called 'bridge assumptions' by Lindenberg (1981; Wippler and Lindenberg 1987), explicating how the social conditions S_1 on the macro level influence actors A. (2) Micro-micro links, i.e., action-theoretical assumptions about what kind of conditions on the micro level will lead a typical actor A to show what kind of behaviour B. (3) Micro-macro links, also called 'transformation' rules, explicating how individual behaviour B transform into the macro phenomenon S_2 of interest.[4]

At least implicitly, the macro-micro-macro scheme meanwhile underlies a great variety of sociological approaches (Esser 1993). What sets analytical sociology and explanatory sociology apart is, amongst others, the requirement that it must be possible to *derive* the consequences S_2 from the causes S_1. This is constitutive for the concept of a mechanism-based explanation. Proponents of analytical sociology would preferably avoid the term 'derivation' because of its connotation of the idea of deduction and would rather stress that the activities of the entities are able to *generate* the outcomes of interest; to stay in the metaphor: It is not enough to lay the cogs and wheels on the table; one also has to make sure that they smoothly mesh, so that

---

[4]The same holds, by the way, for the physics example. In order to explain the explanandum, i.e. answer why the pressure has increased [to double its size] (S_2), we need the structural cause (S_1), in this case the fact that the volume has been decreased [by half], and the complete (!) causal chain. In verbal terms this would require an argument like: Holding temperature and number of molecules (mass) constant, decreasing the volume [by half] means decreasing the space for each individual molecule to move [by half] ($S_1 \to A$); as the molecules buzz around erratically ($A \to B$) this makes it [two times] likely that an individual molecule will bump into the wall of a cylinder ($S_1 \to A \to B$), as each crash of an individual molecule into the wall increases pressure on it by the same amount ($B \to S_2$); this is why decreasing the volume [by half] leads to an increase in pressure [to double its size] ($S_1 \to A \to B \to S_2$).

the whole machinery works. Accordingly, both explanatory sociology and analytical sociology place great emphasis on the criterion of precision. It therefore has to be explicated in detail how and why particular inputs tend to result in particular outputs.

3 Mechanisms and mechanism talk in current empirical research

Having sharpened our understanding of the concept of social mechanisms and its role in the general enterprise of sociological explanation, we briefly turn to its use in current sociological research articles. At first sight, the wide and growing reference to the concept seems to indicate that the view of theory as merely giving interpretations and vague ideas, and the view of empirical research as merely relating variables or giving narratives have been overcome. However, looking more closely into how the term 'mechanism' is employed, one finds considerable variation and still major deviations from the ideal-typical understanding developed above.

Given that the concept of social mechanisms is intrinsically tied to the concept of an explanation, previous work on 'incomplete explanations' may also serve as a natural starting point to classify typical deviations from the ideal of a mechanism-based explanation. Common forms of 'incomplete explanations' have been outlined by Hempel (1965, 415 ff.) and been further elaborated, for example, by Stegmüller (1969, p. 144 ff.), Opp (2014, p. 63 ff.), and Esser (1993, p. 56 ff.). Accordingly, we can distinguish at least four typical deviations from the refined concept in practical usage. The reason for identifying these types within the current literature[5] is not to point a finger, but to sensitise researchers to the fact that just using the term 'mechanism' does not solve well-known and notorious problems of incompleteness of explanations.

1. Pseudo mechanisms: Definitions and labels

One of the most problematic ways of talking about mechanisms—fortunately rare, but still existing—is to mix them up with the (macro-level) relations that are actually to be explained, examples being that the increase in inequality is explained by 'mechanisms of social closure' or that lower pay for women is explained by 'mechanisms of devaluation'. Looking more closely, what is offered as the mechanism is just another word for the phenomenon of interest; the explaining 'mechanism' is set equal to the explanandum by definition, which is called a tautology or *pseudo explanation*. The most generous interpretation of such a practice might be that using the term 'mechanism' at least expresses the implicit need to learn about the cogs and wheels underlying the phenomenon, and in the very best cases the label itself might give some associative hints about the rough direction of where to find them.

---

[5] The examples we give were inspired by scanning the latest volumes of the KZfSS as well as comparable journals like the Zeitschrift für Soziologie (ZfS) or the European Sociological Review (ESR). However, we decided against providing more detailed references to specific articles because usage often varies even within a single article and since when giving some examples we consciously exaggerate a bit to make the types very clear.

2. Ad hoc mechanisms: Descriptions, story-telling, and interpretations

Other forms of referring to mechanisms are analogous to what has been called *ad hoc explanations*. While their structure resembles that of true explanations, they miss an important criterion of adequacy, namely empirical corroboration (or even empirical accessibility). In the context of mechanism-based explanations, such ad hoc reasoning comes in different forms. Under the title 'mechanism', some authors tell a more or less comprehensive story about how particular events came about, thereby occasionally providing speculations about which micro-level processes could have generated them; but as long as there is no evidence that the processes indeed show some *generality* and do indeed *apply* under the given conditions, this misses an important aspect of the whole mechanism idea. In a sense, the case of using the label 'mechanism' to give a pure description of what actually led to a certain event can be seen as a sub-type of such ad hoc mechanisms, because it is tacitly assumed that the micro-level activities apparent in this particular case have some generality.

3. Elliptically formulated or rudimentary mechanisms: Concepts and variables

In the covering-law model an explanation is said to be elliptically formulated if it lacks some parts of the deductive argument, especially the explicit mentioning of the underlying law. In the context of mechanism-based explanations, this could mean missing (important details of) the generating regularities at the micro level. In the gas example from section II, for instance, the explanation could be said to be elliptically formulated when stating that the underlying mechanisms are 'volume (change)' and/or '(movement of) molecules'. Likewise, in sociological research articles we frequently find the term 'mechanism' used purely in reference to concepts, for example 'interest', 'power', 'social capital', 'homophily' etc., while further details on the bridge hypotheses, the action theory, and the transformation rules are missing.

While Hempel sees elliptically formulated explanations as being incomplete "in a rather harmless sense" (Hempel 1965, p. 415), Stegmüller (1969, p. 145) points out that the problem can also be more severe. It is harmless if the generating regularities are obvious and just left out for the sake of brevity; it is problematic, however, if the exact generating regularities are basically unclear—to the author, or even to anybody. The most frequent use of the term 'mechanism' in the current research literature also falls into this broad category: 'mechanisms' as intervening variables that are mistakenly seen to 'explain' the presumed causal effect of an independent variable on a dependent one.[6] Of course, mediation analysis can be suited to (partially) test mechanism-based explanations, but this presumes that the mechanisms have been clearly spelled out theoretically; in other words: Mechanisms should not be confused with potential indicators for potential concepts within potential mechanisms.

---

[6] This particular usage of the term might have been encouraged by graphical representations that place a 'mechanism' as a box in the middle of a causal diagram between input and output (Hedström and Swedberg 1998, p. 9; see also: Opp 2013, p. 332).

4. Partial mechanisms: Broader theoretical models and approaches

Another typical way of using the term 'mechanism' in the research literature is to refer to broader theoretical models or approaches. For example, authors try to explain patterns of inequality by the 'mechanism of statistical discrimination', the 'market mechanism', or the 'mechanisms of social reproduction by Bourdieu'. While many of these approaches indeed contain assumptions about micro-level regularities that are necessary and able to generate the phenomenon of interest, the problem is often that these assumptions, or additional assumptions which are also contained in the approaches, could likewise generate alternative phenomena; the mere reference to the broad approach is therefore simply not precise enough to spell out a mechanism-based explanation of the specific case. This type of incomplete explanation has been called a *partial explanation*; the statements are able to identify a set of facts in which the explanandum is contained, but they are not specific enough to single out the explanandum within this set. Again, the problem can be relatively harmless or more severe, as can be seen by comparing the first and the last examples just given: While some theoretical approaches are very precise, so that the necessary specification might be obvious and would be easy to add, other so-called theories are much too vague to allow this.

When criticizing current references to mechanisms, it has to be kept in mind that explanations, and thus the mechanisms serving within them, are never perfect and final, but a matter of degree and relative adequacy. Hence, some remnant of incompleteness is unavoidable. The first two types of references to 'mechanisms', however, have little to do with what is actually meant by this concept. The latter two types seem somewhat more 'forgivable', but, as has been mentioned, they come in many shades of grey: While most talk about mechanisms along these lines in the research literature still seems far removed from making a significant contribution to an explanation in the narrower sense, some references to concepts and theoretical models may adumbrate the generating mechanisms already sufficiently well.

Mechanism-based explanations that come close to the ideal concept can basically appear in two principle ways. Many pieces of sociological research that clearly belong to an explanatory tradition explicate the set of relevant actors, their action alternatives, and the ways in which these actors are related to each other, and continue by giving a verbal account of how their interaction produces the phenomenon of interest. Some research articles explicate mechanisms by making use of formal models that can be analysed analytically or by simulation. In terms of analytical power, such models are best suited to arrive at mechanism-based explanations because they allow an explicit analytical or computational derivation of the implications. Whatever form, verbal, formal, or a mixture of both, is chosen, the main heuristic to check whether the spelled out mechanisms might be adequate is the ability to derive as specifically as possible, and hence as informatively as possible, hypotheses for empirical tests.

Among those contributions that use formal generative models and hence often come closest to the ideal of mechanism-based explanations, it is remarkable that most articles we found in recent journal volumes focus on situational or action-formation mechanisms (within volume 55 of the KZfSS, see Berger 2013; Siegert and

Roth 2013; Weingartner 2013). For example, rational choice models of educational decision-making are used to derive hypotheses about the impact of expected costs and benefits on choosing among different educational tracks. Meanwhile much survey data is specifically collected to test such models by including direct measures of these action-theoretic concepts. Even here, however, the way this research is set up does not fully realise the potential of the programme to study social mechanisms. Most strikingly, the micro-macro transition is almost always conceptualised in a very simple fashion and merely involves aggregating educational choices by social origin and reporting the resulting association. So, although all three steps of the macro-micro-macro scheme are somehow covered, the emphasis of current research clearly lies on the first and second steps, e.g., how social origin affects the determinants of educational decisions and how individuals arrive at these decisions.

As we will show in the subsequent section, one of the most important impulses of the programme of analytical sociology is the call to go beyond this kind of analysis. This claim is also not new, as demands to pay more systematic attention to the problem of aggregation/transformation have also been made before (Lindenberg 1977; Coleman 1986). But, still, this advice has largely been ignored in practice. So, analytical sociology and the concept of social mechanisms provide a fresh and especially insistent reminder that sociological explanation is not only about bridge hypotheses and action theories.

4 Renewed emphases and accentuations

Even where the usage of the term in current empirical research comes relatively close to the refined concept of social mechanisms, the disarming charm of the prominent role models cited when outlining the programme of analytical sociology is rarely matched. Among those prototypes are Granovetter's threshold models of collective behaviour (Granovetter 1978), Coleman's explanation of the diffusion of an innovation among physicians (Coleman et al. 1957), and Schelling's famous models of segregation (Schelling 1971). What sets these famous examples apart from sociological mainstream research is that they explain social phenomena of considerable emergence and deal with dynamic social processes—which is why they also involve some formalism and math.

So, while our discussion in section II has already revealed the core idea and elements of social mechanisms, there is an important further step to be made in order to arrive at a comprehensive understanding of the concept: Most of the interesting social phenomena are dynamic in nature and can only be adequately explained when taking their process character explicitly into account. It thus has to be stressed that

Fig. 3 Social processes

the macro-micro-macro scheme is by no means restricted to static one-shot situations. Rather, specifying a mechanism-based explanation will in many cases involve reiterating the scheme several times, as depicted in Fig. 3 (Boudon 1986, p. 30; Esser 1999, pp. 17–18).

Remarkably, the importance of dynamic processes and the role model character of the above-mentioned contributions has been recognized since decades within sociological rational choice theory and explanatory sociology (Esser 2000, pp. 269–352). So it is somewhat puzzling that relatively few contributions have succeeded in following the footsteps of the famous examples and that these references still dominate recent programmatic expositions. This holds all the more as this part of sociology generally favours substantive progress over a cult of classic writers.

The major reasons for this state of affairs lie in the trade-offs that scholars who work within the macro-micro-macro-model face and the way these have been solved predominately in the past. As explicated above, in the attempt to meet the requirements of the covering-law model, explanatory sociology has put considerable emphasis on the theory of action as the nomological core of sociological explanations. This has generated considerable progress as regards the first two steps of the macro-micro-macro model. More recent theories of action make much more realistic assumptions about actors' beliefs and preferences and often incorporate additional cognitive mechanisms, such as framing or dual processes (see Kroneberg and Kalter 2012).

On the empirical side, the emphasis on developing a general theory of action has motivated prioritising primary and secondary data that allow for a close dialogue between action-theoretic arguments and empirical analysis. In particular, sociologists' interest in large-scale collective phenomena and social processes as well as the need to legitimate rational choice social research as genuinely sociological has favoured the use of representative surveys. Indeed, surveys have proven suitable to test whether choices on average respond to variations in incentives or other action-theoretic determinants of behaviour. The alliance between rational choice theory and large-scale survey data analysis (Goldthorpe 1996) has generated new insights in key areas of sociological research and considerably advanced the methodology of theory-guided survey research, elaborating both direct and indirect test strategies (see Kroneberg and Kalter 2012).

No doubt, this research tradition has generated important findings and will continue to do so. However, the use of large-scale random samples has come at a price which has already been noted some time before the recent outlines of analytical sociology, most notably by Coleman (1986, p. 1316): "The statistical tools of survey design and analysis began in the 1940s to make possible quantitatively precise statements about samples of independent individuals and the populations (again of independent individuals) they represent, as well as analysis of factors affecting individual behavior. There was no comparable development of tools for analysis of the behavior of interacting systems of individuals or for capturing the interdependencies of individual actions as they combine to produce a system-level outcome".

Coleman's major path to solving this problem is well known and still dominates economics and sociological rational choice theory: By making strong assumptions about actors' rationality and information one mathematically derives equilibria of complex social interactions in exchange models and game theory. For example, Coleman's 'linear system of action' (Coleman 1990, pp. 667–700) takes as inputs actors' interest in and control over a set of resources and allows to derive the equilibrium distribution of control (as well as the value of resources and the power of actors). This ability to derive macro-level implications from the interdependencies among actors stems from a number of strong assumptions. Among other things, actors are assumed to have preferences that follow a Cobb-Douglas utility function and to demand control over resources proportional to their interests, while taking into account their prices and their own budget (Coleman 1990, pp. 682–684). Beyond such micro-level assumptions the model also makes rather strong assumptions about social dynamics: It is based on the idea of centralised exchange among all actors under the condition of full information and the absence of externalities or transaction costs.

Likewise, solution concepts of traditional game theory rest on strong assumptions that allow derivation of macro-level outcomes from a description of the strategic interdependencies among actors. Far beyond the usual assumptions behind individual rationality, the common prediction that actors will play mutually best responses (i.e., the well-known Nash equilibrium) is based on the assumption of mutually consistent expectations, i.e., one has to assume that players *know* what the others will do (Osborne and Rubinstein 1994, p. 53). Again, it is through these assumptions that it becomes possible to formally derive the macro-level outcomes of complex interactions.

Analytical sociology tackles similar kinds of questions, but suggests a different general strategy to answer them: Schelling's and Granovetter's models provide good examples of this; these models show that it is often possible to construct mechanism-based explanations without making strong rationality assumptions (Macy and Flache 2009). The actors in Schelling's segregation models or the more general threshold models studied by Granovetter merely respond to the fraction of other individuals in their neighbourhood (or in the global population) that have a particular attribute (e.g., race) or engage in a particular action (e.g., participate in a riot). Specifically, these models do not detail action-theoretic mechanisms and do not assume that actors strategically anticipate the impact of their choices on the behaviour of other actors in order to derive emergent macro-level consequences. Rather these models place emphasis on another objective: In contrast to many traditional game theoretic and exchange or market models, they explicitly describe the process as gradually unfolding over time. It is the social dynamic of interaction that leads to the characteristics of the macro phenomenon that cannot be anticipated from the initial configuration of actors and their attributes.

Analytical sociology thus promotes a specific elaboration of the macro-micro-macro model or mechanism-based explanations: a combination of *simple* and *realistic* micro-level assumptions with a focus on a social *process* that is driven by the dynamic interactions among actors. The formal modelling technique particularly suited for this kind of theoretical analysis is agent-based modelling, which occupies a central place in the programme of analytical sociology (Hedström 2005; Hedström and Ylikoski 2010; Manzo 2014). An agent-based model (ABM) is a computational model of multiple autonomous agents that interact with each other and/or with their environments over time (Epstein 2006). In contrast to solving sets of equations mathematically as in other formal models, ABMs are programmed in a computer language and analysed inductively: By iterating the assumed agent behaviour in the context of many other agents dynamically over time, ABMs allow to investigate the macro-level consequences of this interaction. As stressed by proponents of analytical sociology, there is a natural affinity between ABMs and the concept of social mechanisms (Manzo 2007, pp. 5–6; Hedström and Ylikoski 2010, p. 63; Manzo 2010, p. 147): The objects and procedures that make up an ABM correspond to the components of mechanisms, that is "*entities* (with their properties) and the *activities* that these entities engage in, either by themselves of in concert with other entities" (Hedström 2005, p. 24; original emphases). And simulating an agent-based model means to activate "an artificial computing mechanism whose specific content is designed to mimic the detailed functioning of the real-world mechanism" (Manzo 2014, p. 31). As analytical tractability is no concern, ABMs are highly flexible and therefore particularly suited to accommodate the complexities that elude most equation-based mathematical models, such as heterogeneity of agents and spatial and network structures.

Importantly (and in contrast to the exuberant work on 'artificial societies'), analytical sociology not only favours ABMs as the theoretical modelling strategy of choice but aims to closely intertwine them with empirical research. This is done by empirically calibrating major parameters or functions of an ABM. In his analysis of youth unemployment in the Stockholm metropolitan area, Hedström (2005) uses logistic regression of register data to estimate how strongly the unemployment rate in one's district affects one's own chances to find a job. He then uses this estimate in an agent-based model of unemployment dynamics that is run on agents whose attributes mirror those of the cases in the empirical data. Bruch and Mare (2006) use vignette data on black and white respondents' neighbourhood preferences in order to estimate how these vary with the percentage of out-group members. Using empirically calibrated preference functions in their ABM allows the authors to contrast the resulting equilibria with those under the theoretical ideal-typical preferences assumed by Schelling in his classic original work. Such empirically calibrated ABMs promise to leave behind in the most uncompromising fashion the mechanism talk prevalent in many fields of sociological research. And it is by placing this research strategy at its core that analytical sociology becomes, contrary to many observers' assessment, an "original and distinctive proposal in sociology" (Manzo 2014, p. 39).

5 The principles of analytical sociology and the danger of mechanism cult

As has become clear, it is justified to regard "analytical sociology" and the tradition of "explanatory sociology" as parts of the same scientific endeavour. At the same time, analytical sociology offers a number of important suggestions on how to advance this agenda in certain respects. We now turn to a recent, particularly comprehensive statement of the principles of analytical sociology that allows us to summarize these conclusions and discuss the value and potential pitfalls of this movement. Building on previous outlines (Hedström 2005; Hedström and Bearman 2009b; Hedström and Ylikoski 2010), Manzo (2014, pp. 7–9) has characterized the principles of analytical sociology as follows:

"P1: use concepts that are as clear and precise as possible to describe both the facts to be explained and the explanatory hypotheses/facts mobilized to explain them, while avoiding all linguistic obscurity and convolutedness;

P2: mobilize the best quantitative and qualitative empirical information available and use the technical tools best suited to describing the facts to be explained;

P3: in order to explain the social outcome(s) described, first formulate a 'generative model', i.e. a model of a (set of) mechanism(s), where a mechanism is a set of entities and activities likely to trigger a sequence of events (i.e. a process) likely to bring about the outcome(s);

P4: in order to formulate the 'generative model', provide a realistic description of the relevant micro-level entities (P4a) and activities (P4b) assumed to be at work, as well as of the structural interdependencies (P4c) in which these entities are embedded and their activities unfold;

P5: in order rigorously to assess the internal consistency of the 'generative model' and to determine its high-level consequences, translate the 'generative model' into an agent-based computational model;

P6: in order to assess the generative sufficiency of the mechanisms postulated, compare the agent-based computational model's high-level consequences with the empirical description of the facts to be explained;

P7: in order to prove that the hypothesized micro- and network-level assumptions are not only generative sufficient but also empirically grounded, inject as much individual- and relational-level, quantitative, qualitative and/or experimental data as possible into the agent-based computational model and re-analyze its behavior and high-level consequences."

This set of principles has been proposed to answer questions about analytical sociology's originality and to describe the research sequence that is characteristic of the programme, but also to map "analytical sociology's internal heterogeneity" (Manzo 2014, p. 10). It allows us to clarify, again, the common denominator of explanatory and analytical sociology, as scholars in both traditions generally agree on principles P1–P4: emphasising clarity and precision, carefully establishing the explanandum, and formulating a generative model of the underlying mechanisms along the lines of structural individualism. Notably, these principles set apart this tradition from other sociological approaches, most notably variable-centred empiricism, collectivism and exercises in social philosophy. The meta-theoretical principles P1–P4 therefore implement already a specific understanding of the concept of mechanisms that rejects notions of macro-level mechanisms (in contrast to, e.g., Mayntz 2004; Cardona 2013).

By adding the principles P5–P7, Manzo moves from meta-theoretical principles to methodological ones, as they are all about agent-based models and their empirical testing and calibration. This specific understanding is effective in demonstrating that analytical sociology combines meta-theoretical and methodological elements (Manzo 2010, p. 162) and is an "original and distinctive" approach (Manzo 2014, p. 39). At the same time, these additional principles introduce a "main dividing line (…) between those who accept the entire set of principles and those who restrict analytical sociology to P1–P4" (Manzo 2014, p. 10). We therefore deem it crucial to preserve a truly foundational status as regards the meta-theoretical principles P1–P4 while relegating the additional principles to the much more pluralistic realm of methodological questions *within* analytical and explanatory sociology. This not only acknowledges that there are "analytical sociologists with different understandings of the analytical sociology research program" (Manzo 2014, p. 37), but also helps to locate analytical sociology within the longstanding tradition of explanatory sociology. In this view, analytical sociology offers a fresh problem-centred agenda that avoids old debates (Demeulenaere 2011, p. 10) and provides new priorities and methodological tools to analyse micro-macro transitions. Clearly, empirically calibrated ABMs belong to these new tools and constitute a major development in theory-guided research that enriches the toolbox of analytical sociology. However, game theory, decision theory, exchange/market models and several other models remain important tools as well, as do empirical test strategies that use lab experiments, survey data or network analysis—even if they are not used in a close dialogue with an ABM. Depending on the research setting and data situation, alternative theoretical models might even be better suited to study the relevant causal mechanisms.

To back this claim, it might suffice here to elaborate two arguments that point to limitations of empirically calibrated ABMs. The first argument relates to analytical sociology's criticism of rational choice theory for its lack of realism. As has been correctly pointed out, there is no such thing as the rational choice approach but a great variety of theories and models, and the question of their realism therefore deserves a differentiated assessment (Opp 2013b). Still, a major and reasonable argument for the superiority of ABMs over alternatives such as game theory or market models is the greater realism they would allow due to their higher flexibility. However, ABMs often replace unrealistic assumptions about choice behaviour with similarly stylised assumptions about social structures and dynamics, so that it is not straightforward to identify analytical sociologists' mission as one of increasing realism. In general, the more aspects of a phenomenon a theoretical model tries to capture, the greater is the potential to make unrealistic assumptions. As an example, consider how market models abstract from the network among exchange partners, assuming that a central auctioneer sets prices by matching demand and supply. No doubt, this is a greatly simplifying and unrealistic assumption. However, when replacing this assumption with a detailed ABM one has to specify the network structure (i.e., who exchanges with whom), the schedule of exchanges (i.e., the temporal order of exchanges), the way information about prices is transmitted among trading partners, and many more things. Whether the resulting model is more realistic overall, can be difficult to tell. And in research settings where data on these various details are missing or scarce, it might be preferable to use a simplifying assumption that gets rid of this additional complexity. In historical sociology, for example, where the scarcity of data is often particularly obvious, it can make sense to use more abstract equilibrium models and surround the conclusions with all the necessary caveats (see, e.g., Kroneberg and Wimmer 2012). And as always in such methodological affairs, which assumptions seem reasonable ultimately depends on explanatory relevance, i.e., on what a model is meant to achieve.

Secondly, even when replacing simplifying assumptions with more realistic and complex ones is worthwhile, there are alternative research agendas that sometimes allow an even closer dialogue between formalised theories and data analysis, most notably behavioural economics and experimental game theory (Camerer 2003; Fehr and Gintis 2007). Many economic experiments involve relatively sizable groups of interacting subjects so that social mechanisms and the impact of institutions can be studied systematically (see, e.g.; Gürerk et al. 2006). And their parsimonious models of choice often allow to analytically derive macro-level predictions and to fully calibrate the parameters that capture individual heterogeneity, for example in social preferences. This is obviously an advantage compared to the empirical calibration of ABMs, which often remains highly incomplete due to the paucity of data generated or collected outside the laboratory. Of course, among other problems, the issue of external validity remains, and the combination of game-theoretic models with lab experiments therefore seems most powerful if the aim is to test general propositions about social order, social norms, trust, and similar generic phenomena (Kroneberg and Kalter 2012).

In sum, the choice among research designs and modelling strategies will continue to remain a contingent and complex one and the continued pluralism of strategies to study the micro-macro transition seems most suited for theoretical and empirical progress in analytical/explanatory sociology. Elevating particular modelling or research techniques to foundational principles would yield a research agenda that is too narrow when measured against the overarching aim to develop and test generative models of social mechanisms. The movement to study social mechanisms could then easily develop into a mechanism cult that overemphasizes particular methodological tools at the expense of others.[7] The limitations of such an agenda would be especially visible when viewed from the perspective of established fields of sociological research. Empirically calibrated ABMs can make important contributions to these fields, but addressing the full spectrum of research questions and relevant dimensions (e.g., cross-country institutional or legal differences) will most likely necessitate the continued employment of more-mainstream methods and research designs.

6 Summary and outlook

While references to social mechanisms in current empirical research abound, there is a lot of mechanism talk that uses the term as a synonym for 'cause', 'explanation', 'intervening variable', or 'theoretical interpretation' but fails to explicate in detail how and why particular inputs tend to result in particular outputs. The movement of analytical sociology has put a much more specific and informative understanding of mechanisms to the core of its agenda. As we have shown, there is a great deal of overlap between analytical sociology and the longstanding explanatory tradition in

---

[7] This is certainly not the intent of Manzo's expositions of the principles of analytical sociology: "Far from simply, and naively, relying exclusively on agent-based computational modelling (for this objection, see Abbott 2007b, p. 1; Lucchini 2007, pp. 236–240, 2008, pp. 9–12; Sawyer 2007, p. 260), this strategy establishes a complex interface among multivariate statistics, computational methods, mathematics, and experiments in which each method is mobilised to accomplish specific tasks" (Manzo 2014, p. 37)

sociology. Both argue for the macro-micro-macro scheme of sociological explanations and for generative models of social mechanisms: To explain social phenomena or (time-space dependent) regularities on the macro level, one needs to analytically derive them from regularities of larger stability (less time-space dependency) on the micro level. This process entails identifying the cogs and wheels that produce the phenomenon and therefore amounts to a mechanism-based explanation.

At the same time, analytical sociology offers something new both in terms of meta-theory and, relatedly but more importantly, in terms of the practice of model building and research. In its foundations, 'explanatory sociology', well established in Dutch and German sociology, has always been an essentially action-theoretic research programme. The theory of action is seen to satisfy a crucial requirement of the Hempel-Oppenheim, or covering-law, model of scientific explanations: the usage of general laws. It followed naturally that ideally all research and theorising should be based on the same underlying theory of action. Major advocates of analytical sociology do not share this view, although they likewise allocate an important role to theories of action, and reject the covering-law model altogether. Against the backdrop of the ensuing meta-theoretical debates among proponents of both approaches, we have stressed that it is crucial to recognize both (a) the common core of these explanatory efforts that justify regarding them as a single approach to sociology and (b) the important new accentuations and tools that analytical sociology offers within this shared approach.

The common explanatory agenda consists of formulating generative models of social mechanisms along the lines of structural individualism. Analytical sociology not only provides this longstanding agenda with a new meta-theoretical suit, but it entails a certain shift in emphases at the level of actual research practices. Due to the special role attributed to a general theory of action and to the successful alliance between rational choice theory and large-scale survey data analysis (Goldthorpe 1996), most empirical work in explanatory sociology has predominately focused on situational and action-generating mechanisms. As a side effect, it has often missed out on social dynamics by focusing on simple aggregation of individual behaviour in the micro-macro link or it subscribed to at times highly unrealistic assumptions that allow a mathematical derivation of macro-level consequences.

Analytical sociology is first and foremost yet another call and attempt to shift the main focus on the micro-macro transition, by getting the priorities right and by providing new tools that allow a more realistic modelling of dynamic social processes. Being freed from the meta-theoretical demands to work with general laws, the priority is to build up a toolbox of social mechanisms while making much more pragmatic use of various behavioural assumptions. It is therefore only consequential and might help to remove misunderstandings of its mission if "programmatically, compared to the initial insistence of Hedström (2005) on the desire–belief–opportunity scheme, analytical sociology is increasingly explicit in endorsing a pluralistic stance" (Manzo 2014, p. 22).

At the same time, this clarification provides the ground for a more worthwhile debate: Rather than arguing about DBO theory, it has to be discussed whether or not it is premature to let go of the vision of common behavioural micro-foundations that united rational choice theory with its action-theoretic rivals. In contrast to Hedström's and Ylikoski's strategic disinterest in a general theory of action, there is a number of recent attempts to arrive at psychologically richer micro-foundations (Boudon 2003; Esser 2009; Lindenberg 2013; Kroneberg 2014; Wikström 2014; see our discussion in Kroneberg and Kalter 2012). These theories partly overlap and partly differ in the concepts and action-formation mechanisms assumed to drive human behaviour. But they are united by the aspiration to develop a general theory of action that is able to hold together and guide diverse explanations and models of social phenomena (Opp 2013b, p. 344 f.). It remains to be seen how much convergence will result from continued efforts to test and refine these theories and to identify ways of integrating them. This integrative action-theoretic agenda at least motivates such efforts and therefore yields somewhat different research priorities than Hedström's and Ylikoski's plea for pluralism. At the same time, this difference and potential debate does not imply different sociological approaches but should be seen as taking place within a shared explanatory and analytical agenda—united not least by a shared quest for realistic micro-foundations.

Keeping these qualifications and open questions in mind, we want to conclude by quickly pointing out a number of advantages that come with subscribing to a merely epistemological agenda, i.e., an agenda that does not commit a priori to a specific theory of action, theory of social order, and the like.

1. Often detailed data on the determinants of action are not available, making the subscription to a specific formal model of action practically irrelevant. For example, sociological analyses of learning processes often use survey data to test how far actors learn from information in their neighbourhoods, friendship networks, and so on (Matsueda et al. 2006). As these data hardly allow researchers to adjudicate among different models of learning it makes little sense to commit oneself to a particular model, such as rational Bayesian updating. Likewise, Hedström's (2005) analysis of unemployment dynamics distinguishes three different ways in which unemployment among one's peers can affect one's own chances to find a job, but data restrictions do not even allow him to operationalise these different mechanisms. Choosing among different formalised theories of action that would allow further elaboration of these mechanisms might therefore again seem a waste of time. More than that, narrating the causal story in the terminology of rational choice theory would unnecessarily detract attention from the core mechanisms of interest.

2. In many fields of sociological research, the debate about rational choice theories has resulted in a stalemate (see Kroneberg and Kalter 2012). One strategy is to develop integrative theories of action that allow one to integrate key insights from different approaches and that yield new explanations and hypotheses (see, e.g.; Kroneberg et al. 2010). Hedström and Ylikoski's (2014) disinterest in action-theoretic details can be seen as an alternative way to break the stalemate, namely through avoiding the debate altogether. By drawing rough sketches of action-generating mechanisms, the focus directly switches to social dynamics and their structural conditions and consequences.

3. Understood as a plea for other questions, analytical sociology calls for investing in other types of data that allow a study of micro-macro transitions that escape mainstream survey research. A major innovation in this regard is the increasing

collection of longitudinal data on complete networks that offers unprecedented possibilities for testing hypotheses about social mechanisms in more applied fields of sociological research. Given the close relationship between social dynamics and the network on which they take place or which they form, network analysis is a natural choice of method for analytical sociologists. As the actor-oriented statistical models for the co-evolution of networks and behaviour (Snijders 2001) are themselves agent-based simulation models, they can be used to implement the generative models supposed to produce a particular social regularity.

While our article has been led by the intention to recognise the new impulses stemming from analytical sociology, we have also pointed to the danger of a mechanism cult that would unnecessarily limit and divide the longstanding search for social mechanisms. While empirically calibrated ABMs are a major new impulse of analytical sociology and allow researchers to investigate dynamic processes both theoretically and empirically, the choice of this technique should not be ascribed the status of a foundational principle on the same level as subscription to the macro-micro-macro scheme and model building. Rather, choosing from the full toolbox of explanatory/ analytical sociology will be crucial for the most important task ahead: to answer key questions in established areas of sociological research. Analytical sociology has in some way codified and intensified a stream of theorising and research that will greatly help us to go beyond the routines of survey data analysis. But the new questions, tools, and data that will grow out of this movement will most likely have to supplement, rather than replace, established methodologies of theory-guided research on the basis of the macro-micro-macro model. Thus, treating the new development as an important impulse to advance an established and so far successful agenda, and neither as a menace nor as a cult, seems to be the most promising way to make progress in sociology.

Acknowledgements We would like to thank Gianluca Manzo for his helpful comments on an earlier draft.

References

Abbott, Andrew. 2007. Mechanisms and relations. *Sociologica* 2:1–22.
Berger, Roger. 2013. Altruistische Reziprozität. Theoretische Überlegungen und experimentelle Evidenz. *Kölner Zeitschrift für Soziologie und Sozialpsychologie* 65:31–48.
Boudon, Raymond. 1986. *Theories of social change: A critical appraisal*. Cambridge: Polity Press.
Boudon, Raymond. 1998. Limitations of rational choice theory. *American Journal of Sociology* 104:817–828.
Boudon, Raymond. 2003. Beyond rational choice theory. *Annual Review of Sociology* 29:1–21.
Boudon, Raymond. 2013. *Sociology as science: An intellectual autobiography*. Oxford: The Bardwell Press.
Bruch, Elizabeth E., and Robert D. Mare. 2006. Neighborhood choice and neighborhood change. *American Journal of Sociology* 112:667–709.
Camerer, Colin F. 2003. *Behavioral game theory*. Princeton: University Press.
Cardona, Andrés. 2013. *The programmatic bias in the discussion on social mechanisms in sociology*. SFB 882 Working Paper Series 23: Bielefeld: DFG Research Center.
Coleman, James S. 1986. Social theory, social research, and a theory of action. *American Journal of Sociology* 91:1309–1335.
Coleman, James S. 1990. *Foundations of social theory*. Cambridge: Belknap Press of Harvard University.

Coleman, James S., Elihu Katz, and Herbert Menzel. 1957. The diffusion of an innovation among physicians. *Sociometry* 20:253–270.

Demeulenaere, Pierre. 2011. Introduction. In *Analytical sociology and social mechanisms*, ed. Pierre Demeulenaere, 1–30. Cambridge: University Press.

Diekmann, Andreas. 2010. Analytische Soziologie und Rational Choice. In *Die Analytische Soziologie in der Diskussion*, ed. Thomas Grund and Thomas Kron, 193–204. Wiesbaden: VS Verlag für Sozialwissenschaften.

Elster, Jon. 1979. *Ulysses and the sirens. Studies in rationality and irrationality*. Cambridge: University Press.

Elster, Jon. 1989. *Nuts and bolts for the social sciences*. Cambridge: University Press.

Epstein, Joshua M. 2006. *Generative social science: Studies in agent-based computational modeling*. Princeton: University Press.

Esser, Hartmut. 1993. *Soziologie. Allgemeine Grundlagen*. Frankfurt a. M.: Campus.

Esser, Hartmut. 1996. What is wrong with "Variable Sociology"? *European Sociological Review* 12:159–166.

Esser, Hartmut. 1999. *Soziologie. Spezielle Grundlagen, Band 1: Situationslogik und Handeln*. Frankfurt a. M.: Campus.

Esser, Hartmut. 2000. *Soziologie. Spezielle Grundlagen, Band 4: Opportunitäten und Restriktionen*. Frankfurt a. M.: Campus.

Esser, Hartmut. 2009. Rationality and commitment: The model of frame selection and the explanation of normative action. In *Raymond Boudon: A life in sociology, vol. 2, part 2: Toward a general theory of rationality*, ed. Mohamed Cherkaoui and Peter Hamilton, 207–230. Oxford: Bardwell Press.

Fehr, Ernst, and Herbert Gintis. 2007. Human motivation and social cooperation: Experimental and analytical foundations. *Annual Review of Sociology* 33:43–64.

Feynman, Richard P., Robert B. Leighton, and Matthew L. Sands. 1963. *The Feynman lectures on physics*. Reading: Addison-Wesley Pub. Co.

Fodor, Jerry A. 1994. Jerry A. Fodor. In *A companion to the philosophy of mind*, ed. Samuel D. Guttenplan, 300–307. Oxford: Husserl.

Ganzeboom, Harry, and Siegwart Lindenberg, eds. 1996. *Verklarende sociologie. Opstellen voor Reinhard Wippler*. Amsterdam: Thesis Publishers.

Gerring, John. 2007. The mechanismic worldview: Thinking inside the box. *British Journal of Political Science* 38:161–179.

Goldthorpe, John H. 1996. The quantitative analysis of large-scale data-sets and rational action theory: For a sociological alliance. *European Sociological Review* 12:109–126.

Granovetter, Mark. 1978. Threshold models of collective behavior. *American Journal of Sociology* 83:1420–1443.

Gross, Neil. 2009. A pragmatist theory of social mechanisms. *American Sociological Review* 74:358–379.

Gürerk, Özgür, Bernd Irlenbusch, and Bettina Rockenbach. 2006. The competitive advantage of sanctioning institutions. *Science* 312:108–111.

Hedström, Peter. 2005. *Dissecting the social: On the principles of analytical sociolog*. Cambridge: University Press.

Hedström, Peter, and Peter Bearman, eds. 2009a. *The Oxford handbook of analytical sociology*. Oxford: University Press.

Hedström, Peter, and Peter Bearman. 2009b. What is analytical sociology all about? An introductory essay. In *The Oxford handbook of analytical sociology*, ed. Peter Hedström and Peter Bearman, 3–24. New York: University Press.

Hedström, Peter, and Richard Swedberg. 1998a. Social mechanism: An introductory essay. In *Social mechanisms. An analytical approach to social theory*, ed. Peter Hedström and Richard Swedberg, 1–30. Cambridge: University Press.

Hedström, Peter, and Richard Swedberg, eds. 1998b. *Social mechanisms. An analytical approach to social theory*. Cambridge: University Press.

Hedström, Peter, and Petri Ylikoski. 2010. Causal mechanisms in the social sciences. *Annual Review of Sociology* 36:49–67.

Hedström, Peter, and Petri Ylikoski. 2014. Analytical sociology and rational-choice theory. In *Analytical sociology: Actions and networks*, ed. Gianluca Manzo, 57–70. New York: Wiley.

Hempel, Carl G. 1965. *Aspects of scientific explanation and other essays in the philosophy of science*. New York: Free Press.

Hill, Paul, Frank Kalter, Johannes Kopp, Clemens Kroneberg, and Rainer Schnell, eds. 2009. *Hartmut Essers Erklärende Soziologie: Kontroversen und Perspektiven*. Frankfurt a. M.: Campus.

Kron, Thomas, and Thomas Grund, eds. 2010. *Die Analytische Soziologie in der Diskussion*. Wiesbaden: VS Verlag für Sozialwissenschaften.
Kroneberg, Clemens. 2014. Frames, scripts, and variable rationality: An integrative theory of action. In *Analytical sociology: Actions and networks*, ed. Gianluca Manzo, 97–123. New York: Wiley.
Kroneberg, Clemens, and Frank Kalter. 2012. Rational choice theory and empirical research. Methodological and theoretical contributions in Europe. *Annual Review of Sociology* 38:73–92.
Kroneberg, Clemens, and Andreas Wimmer. 2012. Struggling over the boundaries of belonging. A formal model of nation building, ethnic closure, and populism. *American Journal of Sociology* 118:176–230.
Kroneberg, Clemens, Meir Yaish, and Volker Stocké. 2010. Norms and rationality in electoral participation and in the rescue of Jews in WWII: An application of the model of frame selection. *Rationality and Society* 22:3–36.
Lindenberg, Siegwart. 1977. Individuelle Effekte, kollektive Phänomene und das Problem der Transformation. In *Probleme der Erklärung sozialen Verhaltens*, ed. Klaus Eichner und Werner Habermehl, 46–84. Meisenheim am Glan: Hain.
Lindenberg, Siegwart. 1981. Erklärung als Modellbau: Zur soziologischen Nutzung von Nutzentheorien. In *Soziologie der Gesellschaft*, ed. Werner Schulte, 20–35. Bremen: Universität.
Lindenberg, Siegwart. 1983. Zur Kritik an Durkheims Programm für die Soziologie. *Zeitschrift für Soziologie* 12:139–151.
Lindenberg, Siegwart. 1992. The method of decreasing abstraction. In *Rational choice theory. Advocacy and critique*, ed. James S. Coleman and Thomas J. Fararo, 3–20. Newbury Park: Sage.
Lindenberg, Siegwart M. 2013. Social rationality, self-regulation, and well-being: The regulatory significance of needs, goals, and the self. In *Handbook of rational choice social research*, ed. Rafael Wittek, Tom Snijders, and Victor Nee, 72–112. Stanford: University Press.
Little, Daniel. 2012. Analytical sociology and the rest of sociology. *Sociologica* 1:1–47.
Lizardo, Omar. 2012. Analytical sociology's superfluous revolution. *Sociologica* 1:1–12.
Macy, Michael, and Andreas Flache. 2009. Social dynamics from the bottom up: Agent-based models of social interaction. In *The Oxford handbook of analytical sociology*, ed. Peter Hedström and Peter Bearman, 245–268. New York: University Press.
Manzo, Gianluca. 2007. Comment on Andrew Abbott. *Sociologica* 2:1–8.
Manzo, Gianluca. 2010. Analytical sociology and its critics. *European Journal of Sociology* 51:129–170.
Manzo, Gianluca. 2014. Data, generative models, and mechanisms: More on the principles of analytical sociology. In *Analytical sociology: Actions and networks*, ed. Gianluca Manzo. New York: Wiley.
Matsueda, Ross L., Derek A. Kreager, and David Huizinga. 2006. Deterring delinquents: A rational choice model of theft and violence. *American Sociological Review* 71:95–122.
Maurer, Andrea, and Michael Schmid, eds. 2010. *Erklärende Soziologie: Grundlagen, Vertreter und Anwendungsfelder eines soziologischen Forschungsprogramms*. Wiesbaden: VS Verlag für Sozialwissenschaften.
Mayntz, Renate. 2004. Mechanisms in the analysis of social macro-phenomena. *Philosophy of the Social Sciences* 34:237–259.
McClelland, David. 1961. *The achieving society*. New York: Irvington Publ.
Opp, Karl-Dieter. 2007. Review of: P. Hedström's Dissecting the Social. *European Sociological Review* 23:115–122.
Opp, Karl-Dieter. 2013a. Rational choice theory, the logic of explanation, middle-range theories and Analytical Sociology: A reply to Gianluca Manzo and Petri Ylikoski. *Social Science Information* 52:394–408.
Opp, Karl-Dieter. 2013b. What is analytical sociology? Strengths and weaknesses of a new sociological research program. *Social Science Information* 52:329–360.
Opp, Karl-Dieter. 2014. *Methodologie der Sozialwissenschaften. Einführung in Probleme ihrer Theoriebildung und praktischen Anwendung*. Wiesbaden: Springer VS.
Osborne, Martin J., and Ariel Rubinstein. 1994. *A course in game theory*. Cambridge: MIT.
Santoro, Marco. 2012. The whole and the parts. Or: Is analytical sociology analytical enough about sociology, and itself? *Sociologica* 1:1–32.
Schelling, Thomas C. 1971. Dynamic models of segregation. *Journal of Mathematical Sociology* 1:143–186.
Siegert, Manuel, and Tobias Roth. 2013. Söhne bevorzugt? Geschlechtsspezifische Unterschiede beim Gymnasialbesuch türkischstämmiger Schülerinnen und Schülern. *Kölner Zeitschrift für Soziologie und Sozialpsychologie* 65:49–72.
Snijders, Tom A. B. 2001. The statistical evaluation of social network dynamics. *Sociological Methodology* 29:361–395.

Stegmüller, Wolfgang. 1969. *Probleme und Resultate der Wissenschaftstheorie und der Analytischen Philosophie, Band I*. Heidelberg: Springer.
Weingartner, Sebastian. 2013. Hochkulturelle Praxis und Frame-Selektion. Ein integrativer Erklärungsansatz des Kulturkonsums. *Kölner Zeitschrift für Soziologie und Sozialpsychologie* 65:3–30.
Wikström, Per-Olof H. 2014. Why crime happens: A situational action theory. In *Analytical sociology: Actions and networks*, ed. Gianluca Manzo, 74–94. New York: University Press.
Wippler, Reinhard, and Siegwart Lindenberg. 1987. Collective phenomena and rational choice. In *The Micro-Macro-Link*, ed. Jeffrey C. Alexander, Bernhard Giesen, Richard Münch, and Neil J. Smelser, 135–152. Berkeley: University of California Press.
Ylikoski, Petri. 2009. The illusion of depth of understanding in science. In *Scientific understanding: Philosophical perspectives*, ed. Henk W. De Regt, Sabina Leonelli, and Kai Eigner, 100–119. Pittsburgh: University of Pittsburgh.
Ylikoski, Petri. 2013. The (hopefully) last stand of the covering-law theory: A reply to Opp. *Social Science Information* 52:383–393.

Frank Kalter, 1964, Prof. Dr. phil., Professor of Sociology at the University of Mannheim, Director of the Mannheim Centre for European Social Research (MZES), President of the European Academy of Sociology (EAS). Main research areas: Migration and integration of ethnic minorities, formal modelling, methodology of the social sciences. Recent publications: Rational choice theory and empirical research, Annual Review of Sociology 38, 2012 (with C. Kroneberg); Intergenerational change in religious salience among immigrant families in four European countries, International Migration 51, 2013 (with K. Jacob); Migrant networks and labor market integration of immigrants from the former Soviet Union in Germany, Social Forces (advance access published March 3), 2014 (with I. Kogan).

Clemens Kroneberg, 1980, Prof., Dr. rer. soc., Professor of Sociology at the University of Cologne. Main research areas: Sociological theory, integration and migration, social boundaries, crime and deviance. Recent publications: Struggling over the boundaries of belonging. A formal model of nation building, ethnic closure, and populism. American Journal of Sociology 118, 2012 (with A. Wimmer); Rational choice theory and empirical research. Methodological and theoretical contributions in Europe. Annual Review of Sociology 38, 2012 (with F. Kalter); Die Erklärung sozialen Handelns. Grundlagen und Anwendung einer integrativen Theorie, Wiesbaden 2011; The interplay of moral norms and instrumental incentives in crime causation. Criminology 48, 2010 (with I. Heintze and G. Mehlkop).

Nonlinear and Threshold Aspects of Neighborhood Effects

George Galster

© Springer Fachmedien Wiesbaden 2014

Abstract An important frontier in context effects research is investigating nonlinear and threshold effects. There is ample theoretical foundation for suggesting that several endogenous social processes generate nonlinear relationships between measures of neighborhood social composition and a variety of outcomes for individual residents. There is also a growing international body of statistical literature testifying to the existence of nonlinear and threshold effects, though the findings are often inconsistent, especially in the European-based scholarship. Further empirical research on this topic is crucial because identifying the precise nature of nonlinear and threshold effects provides both a necessary social efficiency justification and practical programmatic guidance for policies designed to encourage more social diversity within neighborhoods.

Keywords Thresholds · Nonlinear relationships · Neighborhoods · Social mixing

Nachbarschaftseffekte: Nichtlineare Effekte und Schwellenwerte

Zusammenfassung Ein wichtiges Arbeitsgebiet in der Erforschung von Kontexteffekten ist es, nichtlineare Effekte und Schwellenwerte zu untersuchen. Es gibt umfangreiche theoretische Begründungen dafür, dass verschiedene endogene soziale Prozesse nichtlineare Beziehungen zwischen der Sozialstruktur einer Nachbarschaft

G. Galster (✉)
Department of Urban Studies and Planning, Wayne State University,
656 West Kirby Street, Detroit, MI 48202, USA
e-mail: george_galster@wayne.edu

und einer Vielzahl von Ergebnissen für die Bewohner bewirken. Zudem gibt es eine wachsende Zahl internationaler Studien, die beide Effekte belegen, obgleich die Befunde widersprüchlich sind, insbesondere der europäischen Forschung. Daher ist die weitere empirische Erforschung dieses Sachverhaltes entscheidend. Denn wenn wir in der Lage sind, die nichtlinearen Effekte und Schwellenwerte präziser zu bestimmen, erhalten wir eine notwendige soziale Rechtfertigung sowie praktische Hilfen für politische Maßnahmen, die dazu dienen, die soziale Mischung in Nachbarschaften zu erhöhen.

Schlüsselwörter Schwellenwerte · Nichtlinare Beziehungen · Nachbarschaften · Soziale Mischung

1 Introduction

Understanding how neighborhoods change in ways that manifest themselves as nonlinear or, as a special case, threshold-like relationships, has been of longstanding interest to social scientists. Past studies have explored three potentially nonlinear aspects of neighborhood change: demographic, physical, and economic (for a review, see Quercia and Galster 2000). Though accepted as conventional wisdom for a long prior period (Wolf 1963), a theoretical foundation for nonlinear change processes in a neighborhood's racial composition did not emerge until Schelling's "tipping" model (1971), which was subsequently extended by Taub et al. (1985). Numerous empirical studies have indeed found that threshold-like relationships characterize neighborhood racial transitions, though no universal tipping point exists (Card et al. 2008; Clark 1991; Crowder 2000; Giles 1975; Galster 1990; Goering 1978; Keckes and Knäble 1988; Lee and Wood 1991). Indeed, an even wider range of neighborhood socio-demographic dynamics may also be associated with nonlinear processes (Galster et al. 2000, 2007; Lim and Galster 2009). As for physical changes in neighborhoods, Taub et al. (1985), Galster (1987), and Galster et al. (2008a), have contributed theoretical models that implicitly or explicitly suggest that residential property owners' investments in their dwellings (including under-maintenance or even abandonment behaviors) will respond to changes in the neighborhood context in nonlinear or threshold-like ways. Several empirical studies have provided support (Galster 1987; Galster et al. 2004, 2006; Taub et al. 1985). The economic dimensions of neighborhood property value change in response to changing neighborhood conditions also appear strongly nonlinear, as evinced by the theoretical and empirical work of Meen (2004, 2006), Galster et al. (2006, 2007 and 2008).

Social scientists increasingly have not just been interested in how neighborhoods change, but also how neighborhoods *change people* (Sampson et al. 2002). In particular, there has been escalating interest in how the demographic and socioeconomic composition of a neighborhood may shape the attitudes and behaviors of individual residents. Here the evidence on nonlinear relationships is much less definitive, as the review below will make clear.

Yet, clarifying this nonlinear issue is of equal importance to policymakers as determining if there is any kind of substantial neighborhood effect in the first place. As I demonstrated in a series of papers (Galster 2002, 2005, 2007a, b; Galster and Zobel 1998), the particular type of nonlinear relationship between the proportion of a "disadvantaged" group in the neighborhood and the associated incidence of positive or negative externalities transpiring through intra-neighborhood social interactions hold radically different implications for the society-wide desirability and political feasibility of strategies designed to de-concentrate disadvantaged populations spatially. For example, if this relationship were linear (proportional) the spatial redistribution of the disadvantaged population would not in itself lead to any net changes in the aggregate incidence of such externalities society-wide, merely a zero-sum geographic redistribution of same. If, however, this relationship were characterized by negative social externalities ensuing only after a critical mass of disadvantaged populations were exceeded in the neighborhood, it would imply that net gains in social well-being (i.e., Pareto improvements) may be feasible by policies that kept the compositions of neighborhoods below this threshold. These points will be amplified in the last section of this chapter.

Given this important policy motivation,[1] this chapter will explore in conceptual, theoretical and empirical terms the nature and evidence related to nonlinear neighborhood effects. It first defines and explores conceptually nonlinear and threshold neighborhood effects. Second, it provides theoretical bases for why they might occur. Third, it probes several key issues related to neighborhood effects. Fourth, it reviews the international empirical evidence on nonlinear neighborhood effects. Fifth, it discusses the importance of nonlinear neighborhood effects for the formulation of social policies related to neighborhood composition. Throughout the emphasis will be on socioeconomic composition as the focal dimension of neighborhood context, as this has been of prime interest to social scientists and policy makers.

2 What are nonlinear and threshold neighborhood effects?

For the purposes of this discussion it is useful to employ a pharmacological metaphor: "dosage-response." Neighborhood effects can be thought of as a multi-element dosage of distal context that generates (through one or more causal pathways as discussed below) a response from individual residents that has physical, psychological, attitudinal and/or behavioral manifestations. A *nonlinear neighborhood effect* is one in which this dosage-response relationship is not proportional across all ranges of dosage; i.e. the relationship is not constant on the margin. A *threshold neighborhood effect* is a special case of nonlinear effects in which the marginal dosage-response relationship changes (either continuously or discontinuously) from zero to nonzero (or vice versa)[2] at a critical value (the "threshold point"). The concepts are illustrated graphically in Fig. 1, which portrays several types of relationships representing nonlinear and threshold neighborhood effects.[3]

---

[1] For more on the relationship between neighborhood effects scholarship and "social mix" strategies pursued by many governments in Europe, Australia and the U.S., see Galster (2013).

[2] The former can be termed a "lower threshold" and the latter an "upper threshold."

[3] Those shown do not exhaust the possibilities, of course.

Fig. 1 Illustrations of nonlinear and threshold neighborhood effects

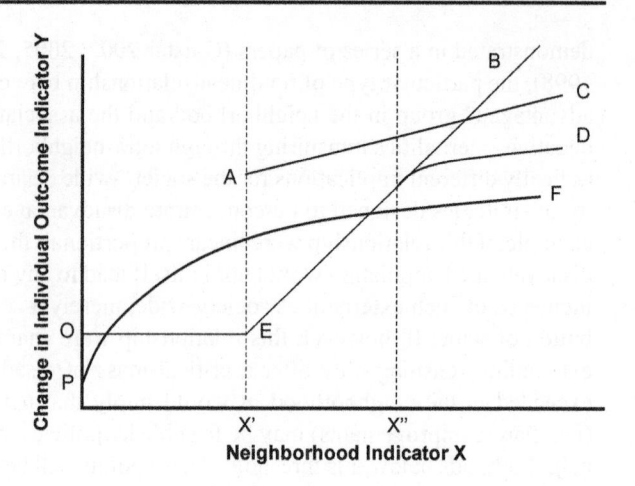

Line PF in Fig. 1 represents one nonlinear function indicating a decreasing marginal positive impact of increases in neighborhood indicator X on a particular outcome Y for a resident in the neighborhood experiencing X. Three alternative types of threshold effects are also portrayed. Line OEB represents a lower threshold at critical value X' where the marginal impact of X abruptly changes from zero to positive in a piecewise-linear fashion. Line OEAC shows a variant on this threshold with a discontinuous change in the relationship indicated by the quantum increase in impact at X' by amount A–E. Finally, line OED represents a relationship characterized by both lower and upper thresholds at "X" and X, respectively.

3 Are there theoretical bases for nonlinear neighborhood effects?

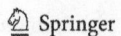

There are many potential causal mechanisms that link neighborhood context with individual outcomes; for comprehensive reviews see: Jencks and Mayer (1990), Manski (1995), Duncan et al. (1997), Gephart (1997), Dietz (2002), Sampson (2001), Sampson et al. (2002), Ioannides and Loury (2004) and Galster (2012). There are at least three, not mutually exclusive, mechanisms through which a nonlinear, or even threshold-like relationship between neighborhood characteristics and individual outcomes may be produced: socialization, collective social control, and stigmatization. The *socialization mechanism* suggests that residents can develop different attitudes, values, behaviors and expectations as a result of interactions with neighborhood peers and role models. These socialization effects transpiring through peers and role models may manifest themselves as a process of "contagion." The basic tenet of contagion models is that if decision makers live in a community where some of their respected or admired neighbors exhibit non-normative behaviors, they will be more likely to adopt these behaviors themselves. Crane (1991) proposes a formal contagion model to explain the incidence and spread of behaviors in neighborhoods with problematic social consequences, such as dropping out of school or having children as young teens. Crane states that if "the incidence of problems stays below a critical point, the frequency or prevalence of the problem tends to gravitate toward some relatively low-level equilibrium. But if the incidence surpasses a critical point, the process will spread explosively.[4] In other words, an epidemic may occur, raising the incidence to an equilibrium at a much higher level" (1991, p. 1227).

The *collective social control mechanism* suggests that pervasive community norms can shape residents' attitudes, values, and behaviors in corresponding realms because they do not wish to risk the potential social sanctions (such as ostracism) associated with violation of these norms (e.g., Simmel 1971; Weber 1978). This collective social control mechanism also implicitly suggests a threshold given its emphasis on the role that local social groups may exert on individuals. Such an effect can occur strongly only to the degree that: (1) the individual comes in social contact with the group, and (2) the group can exert more powerful threats or inducement to conform to its positions than competing groups with which the individual comes in contact. These two preconditions may involve the existence of a threshold. Given the importance of interpersonal contact in enforcing conformity, if the individuals constituting the group in question were scattered innocuously over urban space, they would be less likely to be able either to convey their normative positions effectively to others with whom they might come in contact or to exert much pressure to conform to these positions. It is only when a group reaches some critical mass of density or power over a predefined area that it is likely to become effective in shaping the attitudes, values, and behaviors of other residents. Past this threshold, as more members are recruited, the group's power to sanction non-conformists probably grows nonlinearly. This is especially likely when the position of the group becomes so dominant as to become normative in the area.

Several sociological treatises closely related to collective socialization also suggest thresholds explicitly (Granovetter 1978; Granovetter and Soong 1983; Wilson 1987). Economists also have developed several mathematical treatises involving collective socialization effects in which thresholds often emerge as solutions to complex decision problems under certain assumptions (Akerlof 1980; Brock and Durlauf 2001; Galster 1987, ch. 3).

The *stigmatization mechanism* suggests that key decision makers controlling access to private and/or public resources in the metropolitan area may allocate them differentially to individuals based on the reputations of their places of residence. For example, prospective employers may evaluate job applicants residing in certain locales based on the disrepute of the place. This neighborhood effect via stigmatization likely operates through a threshold as well. Opinions held by the larger community about the residents of a particular neighborhood are unlikely to be altered in a linear fashion by marginal changes in the population of the particular neighborhood group that is the prime basis of the stigmatization. It is only when a critical mass of this "disreputable" group has been attained that public opinion is likely to turn against this place and all its inhabitants, with concomitant restrictions on their resources and opportunities.

---

[4] More precisely, whether an epidemic occurs will be jointly determined by: (1) the length of period during which those infected can transmit the infection to others; (2) the number of non-infected people each infected person exposes; (3) the probability that an exposure will lead to infection; (4) the time it takes between exposure and becoming ill and infectious to others; and (5) whether, once healthy again, one may be infected another time.

4 What are some key attributes of threshold neighborhood effects?

Given the definitional and theoretical foundation established in the prior sections, we can now probe several questions related to threshold neighborhood effects. First, are threshold values similar in different contexts? Theory and limited empirical evidence suggests that the answer is no because of: (1) compositional differences in the individuals receiving the given neighborhood dosage: (2) doses of other neighborhood treatments being simultaneously applied that may be synergistic or protective; and (3) potential buffering actions by residents.

Careful consideration of the aforementioned mechanisms of nonlinear neighborhood effects suggest that relationships are likely heterogeneous by gender, income, age, ethnicity and perhaps other characteristics, though not necessarily in unambiguous ways (Galster et al. 2010). The key linkages rely upon the notion that intra-neighborhood social mechanisms have effects only to the extent that people: (1) spend a substantial amount of time in the neighborhood; (2) are locally oriented in their social interactions; and (3) do not marshal sufficient resources to insulate themselves from these effects. The aforementioned characteristics can potentially influence all of these three conditions. We would expect, for example, local social control in areas with more traditional, patriarchal norms may produce strict monitoring of the behaviors of women, thus potentially insulating them from neighborhood peer effects and negating their greater time spent in the neighborhood (Pinkster 2008). Such would imply a higher threshold for them. Women with child-care responsibilities, the elderly, and lower-income residents would be more likely to develop a denser network of relationships that is more focused on the neighborhood (Kleinhans 2004; Kleit 2008). Such would imply a lower threshold for them. The evidence from non-experimental and experimental studies indeed suggests that different neighborhood effect mechanisms may have varying salience across different groups (Andersson and Malmberg 2013; Bergsten 2010; Burdick-Will et al. 2010; Clampet-Lundquist et al. 2011; López-Turley 2003; Galster et al. 2010; Ludwig 2012; Musterd et al. 2012), though implied differences in measured thresholds have rarely been investigated explicitly.[5]

A second reason for deducing that threshold values will be dissimilar in different contexts is that a given neighborhood attribute is not applied as a treatment in isolation form other neighborhood attributes; neighborhood treatments are inherently "bundled." Dosages of other neighborhood treatments being administered may intensify the given dosage's expected response through synergistic interactions. Put differently, different dimensions of neighborhood treatments may not be additive but multiplicative. An analogous possibility is that there may be antidotes to the given treatment. That is, there may be dosages of other neighborhood treatments simultaneously being administered that counteract the given dosage's expected response.

The final reason for predicting heterogeneity in threshold values is potential buffering forces in the neighborhoods. People, their families, and/or their communities may respond to the given dosage in ways that counteracts its expected response. Because residents individually and collectively potentially have agency they may

---

[5]The only exceptions are Crane (1991) and Van der Klaauw and van Ours (2003), whose studies are discussed below.

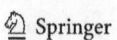

engage in compensatory behaviors that offset negative neighborhood effects, such as when parents keep their children in the home when youngsters who are bad role models are using the local playground. Such buffering actions would serve to raise threshold values.

A second question to raise concerning thresholds is whether it is the *share* of a given group that is generating the neighborhood effect, or its *absolute number* that causes the effect, once a certain threshold has been crossed. The answer likely depends on which of the three prior causal mechanisms predominates. In the case of *socialization*, it seems most plausible that it is the absolute number of neighborhood effect generators taking the form of peers and role models that defines the threshold. For any set of individuals it will be the *absolute number* of peers and role models to which they are exposed that will affect the probability that they will "catch the disease." In the case of *social control*, however, theory suggests that it is the *share* of the neighborhood's population that matters in specifying the threshold. In neighborhoods where there are multiple groups competing for normative dominance it will be the one that has the largest share that can expect to eventually have its norms collectively prevail. In the case of stigmatization, the answer probably depends on how decision makers external to the neighborhood form their stereotypes about its residents. If such stigmatization is based on generalizations based on past experiences with residents ("statistical discrimination") the answer will be that it is the *share* of the neighborhood's population that matters in specifying the threshold. If it is based on generalizations derived from vignettes or episodic media reports, the answer will more likely be that it is the *absolute number* of the neighborhood's "problem population" that matters in specifying the threshold of stigmatization. Unfortunately, the veracity of these deductions is difficult to test from extant scholarship. Virtually all studies use shares of population in various groups as measures of neighborhood context, but since the geographic neighborhood units have roughly equal populations across the sample the measure is indistinguishable for those that use absolute numbers.

The final question regarding thresholds is whether the critical value is reached by specific events. I do not believe that a general answer can be provided. Market-based forces in the housing market and household changes in preferences and economic wherewithal will shape individual decisions about whether and where to change residences and when aggregated, these individual mobility decisions will affect the aggregate characteristics of a neighborhood's population (Galster 1987). These aggregate characteristics, in turn, shape both the nature of the "treatment" being given to the residents and these residents' susceptibility to that treatment, as explained above. All these changes can happen quite gradually, and not evince any obvious triggering event. On the contrary, history is replete with examples of shocks that create highly discontinuous changes in the composition of a neighborhoods' population. This typically has come from market-oriented processes like rapid gentrification and public-generated programs like urban renewal or subsidized housing construction or demolition.

Fig. 2 Summary of U.S. studies of thresholds of neighborhood poverty rates

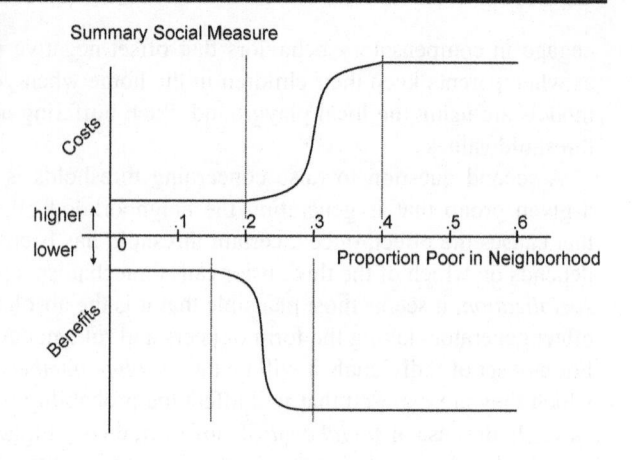

5 Empirical evidence on nonlinear and threshold neighborhood effects

Nonlinear neighborhood effects can be identified by a variety of multiple regression-like specifications that allow non-linear relationships between the measure(s) of neighborhood composition and individual outcomes to emerge (Galster et al. 2000). My review of the U.S. literature (Hannon 2002, 2005; Krivo and Peterson 1996; Vartanian 1999a, b; Weinberg et al. 2004) suggests that the independent impacts of neighborhood poverty rates in encouraging negative outcomes for individuals like crime, school leaving, and duration of poverty spells appear to be nil unless the neighborhood exceeds about 20% poverty, whereupon the externality effects grow rapidly until the neighborhood reaches approximately 40% poverty; subsequent increases in the poverty population appear to have no marginal external effect. Analogously, the independent impacts of neighborhood poverty rates in discouraging positive behaviors like working appear to be nil unless the neighborhood exceeds about 15% poverty, whereupon the effects grow rapidly until the neighborhood reaches roughly 30% poverty; subsequent increases in poverty appear to have no marginal effect (Galster 2002). This evidence suggests a dual threshold relationship, a generic summary version of which is portrayed in Fig. 2.

Though these threshold values appear quite consistent across several studies, interpretive caution must be taken before generalizing to all neighborhoods. As explained in the prior section, there are strong theoretical and empirical reasons to believe that these average threshold values do not pertain identically in all contexts.

As far as non-linear relationships between individual outcomes and neighborhood percentages of affluent residents, the work of Crane (1991), Duncan et al. (1997), Chase-Lansdale et al. (1997) and Santiago et al. (forthcoming) is relevant. Unfortunately, though they all suggest the existence of a threshold of neighborhood affluence they differ on where this occurs and for which outcomes. Crane's (1991) analysis finds strong evidence of epidemic-like effects on both secondary school leaving and teenage childbearing of the share of affluent (professional-managerial occupation) neighbors. For whites and blacks there is a threshold at 5% affluent neighbors, below which dropout rates skyrocket; for blacks not living in large cities there is another threshold at 20%, above which affluent neighbors cease having a positive impact.

These thresholds are more dramatic for black males than females. A similar threshold at low percent affluent neighbors is observed for both black and white teen women's childbearing, especially in large cities. Crane (1991, pp. 1234, 1241) interpreted these findings as consistent with intra-neighborhood social interactions, but was unable to distinguish whether the high-status neighbors created an endogenous effect (such as serving as positive role models) or a correlated effect (such as bringing resources that made local institutions and services better). Duncan et al. (1997) find a different sort of nonlinear neighborhood effect for educational attainment and the percentage of affluent neighbors. Here the threshold does not seem to occur at a small percentage of affluent, as in Crane's study.[6] The positive effect of the latter becomes dramatically stronger when the percentage exceeds the national mean for the neighborhood (for black men and women, and white women). Chase-Lansdale et al. (1997) examine how the percentage of affluent neighbors relates to a variety of intellectual and behavioral development test scores for youth. They find, controlling for family influences, that the percentage of affluent neighbors is positively associated with higher intellectual functioning scores for black children and female children only when the percentage exceeds the 25th percentile and is less than the 75th percentile; for other children the effect is linear. Santiago et al. (forthcoming) could not identify any non-linear relationships for their index of neighborhood occupational prestige in models predicting teen childbearing and school leaving. Neighborhood occupational prestige did, however, exhibit distinct threshold relationships (i.e., it only had predictive power when it exceeded sample mean values) in models predicting smoking marijuana and running away. The Duncan et al. (1997), Chase-Lansdale et al. (1997), and Santiago et al. (forthcoming) findings support the notion of collective social norms taking hold only after a substantial share of the affluent, high-prestige group is present in the neighborhood, in contrast to the implications from Crane (1991) that such forces arise when only a small threshold of the affluent has been exceeded.[7]

Most Western European evidence related to potential non-linear neighborhood effects focuses on labor market outcomes as they relate to percentages of disadvantaged neighbors. Here the findings are inconsistent in the extreme. Four studies did not observe any strong nonlinear relationships. Ostendorf et al. (2001) compared "income-mixed" neighborhoods in Amsterdam with "homogeneous" ones, to ascertain whether this aspect of neighborhood was related to an individual's chances of living in poverty. Bolster et al. (2004) compared 1-, 5- and 10-year income growth trajectories of British individuals living at the beginning of the period amid different degrees of disadvantage (measured by a composite index). Finally, McCulloch's

---

[6] Duncan et al. (1997) and Santiago et al. (forthcoming) did not explicitly test for a threshold at a below-average percentage of affluent, however.

[7] Turley (2003) analyzes behavioral and psychological test scores for youth as measured in a special supplement of the PSID. She relates these scores to the median family income of the census tract, so one cannot be certain whether the relationship is being generated by share of affluent or share of poor. She tests for non-linearities by employing a quadratic version of neighborhood income variable and finds that its coefficient is statistically significant and negative for the self-esteem outcome, implying that improving the economic environment of youth has a much greater psychological impact for those initially in disadvantaged neighborhood circumstances. Unfortunately, quadratic specifications are not precise in identifying thresholds.

(2001) multi-level analysis of British Household Panel Study data also failed to identify any strong nonlinear relationships between a ward-level index of disadvantage and such outcomes as employment status, current financial situation, financial expectations, health status, or receipt of social support. Musterd et al. (2003) related the proportion of neighboring households on social benefits to the chances of Dutch individuals' being employed consistently or not during the 1990s. Over a vast variation in neighborhoods they found no relationship. Though arguably some nonlinear relationships were evinced at the extreme values of neighborhood conditions, they involved few neighborhoods.

Other studies detected nonlinear relationships, but of highly inconsistent natures. Buck's (2001) analysis of British Household Panel Study data (but, unlike McCulloch, using unemployment rate as the neighborhood characteristic) identified substantial nonlinear relationships with the probability of not starting work and the probability of not escaping from poverty, which suggested that the worst results for individuals occurred when the share of neighborhood residents unemployed exceeded 23–24 % (i.e., the highest 5 % of all wards). Diametrically opposed results were generated by Musterd and Andersson (2006), who analyzed the national register database for the three largest metropolitan areas in Sweden to ascertain the relationship between the odds that an individual remained unemployed in both 1995 and 1999 and the percentage of unemployed residents in their neighborhood in 1995. They (like Buck) found a strong positive relationship until the neighborhood percentage unemployed exceeded 16 %; thereafter there appeared to be no further marginal impact (instead of increasing marginal impact, as per Buck). Van der Klaauw and van Ours (2003) found using data in Rotterdam administrative records that the neighborhood unemployment rate had no statistically significant negative impact on the probability of exiting welfare into work for Dutch job losers or school leavers until it surpassed 11 %, though there were no neighborhood effects for non-Dutch job losers. Finally, Hedman and Galster (2013) analyzed income of prime age workers in Stockholm as it related to the share of low-income male workers in the neighborhood.[8] Their instrumental variables panel model revealed negative impacts of this group on individual incomes only after their neighborhood share exceeded 20 %, and grew more negative once a second threshold of 50 % was exceeded.

Few studies using Western European data have investigated the potential nonlinear effects of affluent neighbors. Kauppinen (2004) used categorical variables to delineate neighborhood affluence in Helsinki and, like Duncan et al. (1997), found that only in neighborhoods with above-average educational levels does neighborhood seem to make a difference in individuals' post-secondary level of educational attainment.

Galster et al. (2008, 2011) studied the simultaneous effects of both disadvantaged and advantaged neighbors[9] on individual earnings of adults using Swedish register data from three metropolitan areas. Results related to nonlinear relationships were

---

[8] They define low-income as those earning less than the 30th percentile of the male income distribution in a given year.

[9] They define disadvantaged (advantaged) individuals as those earning less (greater) than the 30th percentile of the male income distribution in a given year.

contingent on several differences in the analyses: (1) gender of the individuals; (2) the employment status of the individual; (3) which city was studied; and (4) which statistical specification (difference model vs. fixed effect model) was employed. The strongest evidence of thresholds arose for Stockholm males, where two thresholds—one at 20% and the other at 40%—best described the strong inverse relationship between percentage of disadvantaged neighbors and subsequent earnings of individual male residents. These two studies did not reveal any clear thresholds associated with the share of advantaged neighbors and individual incomes.

In sum, this Western European evidence on nonlinear neighborhood effects arising for social composition does not paint a clear picture. It only rarely exhibits nonlinear neighborhood effects similar to those more consistently appearing in the U.S.-based research on the apparent negative consequences of concentrated poverty populations and positive consequences of affluent neighbors. This difference may be simply due to the greater variety of measures of neighborhood disadvantage and affluence and individual outcomes employed in the European evidence base. It may also be explained by trans-Atlantic differences in social welfare, transit and public finance systems. Compared to Western Europe, in the U.S. there are much starker contrasts in absolute material deprivation, compensatory national social welfare service, training and housing supports, accessibility to employment via comprehensive public transit systems, and local government fiscal capacity to fund health, safety, employment and educational services, all of which are powerfully associated with concentrations of disadvantage and affluence. These poorly measured aspects of the American neighborhood institutional and public service context may be responsible for the stronger and more consistent threshold effects observed in the U.S., not social effects emanating from these neighbors directly. Cross-cultural differences in endogenous social relationships within neighborhoods could also play important explanatory roles, of course.

It is also interesting to speculate about why (certainly in the U.S. context and possibly in the Western European context) threshold effects do not appear to be symmetric for concentrations of disadvantaged and affluent neighbors. One possible reason is that the aforementioned association with institutional and public service context is asymmetric. Another may be that the dominant endogenous social relationships generating neighborhood effects are different. For example, the impact from concentrated disadvantage may primarily arise due to changes in the dominant collective norms and peer effects, whereas that from concentrated affluence may primarily arise due to role modeling and improved collective efficacy leading to enhanced safety. There is no necessary reason why these distinctive mechanisms would transpire at the same thresholds. Clearly, these are speculations that call out for further investigations in the field.

6 Why are nonlinear neighborhood effects important?

Nonlinear neighborhood effects are important because they will determine whether a policy designed to alter the geographic distribution of social groups will prove socially efficient. By efficient I mean that a policy improves the aggregate amount of well-being summed across all members of society, with the well-being of certain individuals perhaps weighted differentially (if implicitly) according to prevailing cultural norms. This standard does not necessarily require Pareto-improvements (wherein some individuals gain and none suffer a loss of well-being), though such would be sufficient. It does, however, require adherence to the Hicks-Kaldor compensation principle. I.e., a policy is efficient if the "winners" could, in principle, compensate the "losers" sufficiently to hold them harmless and yet still be better off themselves.

The efficiency-based criterion for social policy requires considerations of the *mechanisms* of social-interactive neighborhood effects. Specifically, we must distinguish between neighborhood effects that occur because of social interactions *within* the neighborhood and those that occur because of the perceptions and actions of those *outside* of the neighborhood. First, because efficiency requires us to consider the well-being of both disadvantaged and advantaged individuals, a more comprehensive analysis of potential intra-neighborhood social externalities is required. This raises to relevance the possibility that negative social externalities imposed by disadvantaged individuals on their advantaged neighbors outweigh the positive social externalities that may flow in the opposite direction. If such were the case, it is easy to imagine a social weighting scheme (such as utilitarianism) that would register the highest values when the two groups were completely segregated residentially. Second, if *only* the extra-neighborhood process of stigmatization/resource restriction were operative, we would not need to concern ourselves with the aforementioned potential zero-sum or negative-sum aspects associated with intra-neighborhood social interactions between disadvantaged and advantaged groups. On the contrary, changing the social composition of a neighborhood by reducing the share of disadvantaged below the lower threshold so that the stigma/restriction is removed would provide a net gain for the well-being of *both* types of individuals living in the formerly stigmatized neighborhood.

What does the foregoing suggest about what sort of empirical evidence would provide *sufficient* proof that changing the social composition of a neighborhood could be justified on efficiency grounds? First, consider if intra-neighborhood social interactions were the presumed mechanism. In this case the evidence must first show that outcomes associated with greater well-being now or in the future (e.g., income, labor force participation, educational attainments) for disadvantaged individuals are either: (1) positively correlated with a higher percentage of advantaged neighbors and/or (2) negatively correlated with a higher percentage of other disadvantaged neighbors, all else equal. It also must show that advantaged individuals are neither: (1) significantly harmed by the negative social externalities generated by disadvantaged neighbors, nor (2) significantly benefited by the positive social externalities generated by other advantaged neighbors. Only if such evidence is gained about how both advantaged and disadvantaged individuals are affected by social interactions associated with neighborhood social composition can we be confident that a wide range of normative social weighting schemes would yield diverse neighborhoods as the most socially efficient outcome. Second, consider if extra-neighborhood stigmatization/resource restrictions were the presumed mechanism. In this case, the statistical evidence would not need to be stratified by group insofar as *both* advantaged and disadvantaged individuals were harmed by the stigmatization and other institutional/resource constraints associated with higher percentages of disadvantaged residents in the neighborhood. Here the evidence must show that outcomes associated with greater well-being (such as income or employment) for both groups are negatively (positively) correlated with percentages of disadvantaged (advantaged) in the neighborhood, at least past some thresholds(s).

Whether these criteria will be met depends critically on the linear or nonlinear relationships that may connect the social composition of neighborhoods and the likelihood that individual residents will reap benefits or incur costs. Suppose that each household within a social group X provides a fixed amount of positive externalities (perhaps in the form of role models) for immediate neighbors of all social groups. Such a circumstance would manifest itself as a linear relationship between the percentage of group X households in a neighborhood and the likelihood that any given resident will engage in socially beneficial behaviors. Equivalently, this situation could be represented as a linear relationship between the percentage of group X households in a neighborhood and the aggregate amount of social wellbeing there (measured by some index of behaviors and psychological satisfaction summed over all households in the neighborhood). In this case a policy that tried to alter the geographic distribution of group X households would yield no net gain in aggregate social wellbeing because the marginal benefit in neighborhood(s) that increased their percentage of X would be exactly offset in the aggregate by the marginal losses in those that decreased their percentage of X. Clearly, redistributing social groups can only create improvements in social efficiency if neighborhood composition effects on residents are nonlinear.[10]

Nonlinear neighborhood effects are a necessary but not sufficient condition, of course, for efficiency-enhancing social policies. Indeed, it is quite possible for ill-conceived policies to harm aggregate social well-being if inappropriate redistributions of social groups are undertaken, even in a regime of nonlinear neighborhood effects. I offer a simple, hypothetical numerical example as illustration in Table 1, based on the generic empirical evidence I summarized in Fig. 2. Assume a stylized city comprised of 10 neighborhoods of 100 households each. There are only two social groups, 150 households in X and 850 in Y. Finally assume that social science has established the following incidences of socially problematic behaviors by residents (expressed as an imaginary index) associated with percentages of group X households in the neighborhoods:

- $X < 20\%$: social problem index $= 5$
- $20\% \leq X < 40\%$: social problem index $= 20$
- $X \geq 40\%$: social problem index $= 30$

Here there is clearly a dual threshold neighborhood effect operative, with critical values at 20 and 40% of group X. This yields the potential for achieving a socially optimal distribution of group X (and by implication, group Y) across the ten neighborhoods. Table 1 shows several alternatives. Scenario A portrays the situation of maximum feasible concentration or segregation of the two groups; when the associated social costs associated with each of the ten neighborhoods are tallied the aggregate result is a value of 100 on our index of social costs. This serves as our baseline against which more diverse neighborhood outcomes can be compared.

---

[10] I make this argument more precisely in Galster and Zobel (1998) and Galster (2002, 2005, 2007a, b).

Table 1 Hypothetical illustration of social costs for alternative social compositions of ten neighborhoods given threshold effects

Scenario A	Social costs	Scenario B	Social costs	Scenario C	Social costs	Scenario D	Social costs
8 w/no X	8×5=40	10 w/15% X	10×5=50	7 w/no X	7×5=35	4 w/no X	4×5=20
1 w/50% X	1×30=30			3 w/50% X	3×30=90	6 w/25% X	6×20=120
1 w/100% X	1×30=30						
Total	100		50		125		140

See text for specification of groups X and Y, neighborhoods and threshold neighborhood effects

Not surprisingly, the situation with maximum neighborhood diversity (scenario B) exhibits significantly less social costs because all neighborhoods are below the lower threshold. Perhaps more surprisingly, intermediate sorts of neighborhood diversity prove substantially worse than the baseline case of maximum segregation. Scenario C shows the case were the single 100% X neighborhood is replaced by two 50% X neighborhoods. Unfortunately from the aggregate social standpoint, this necessitates pushing one more neighborhood over the 40% threshold while correspondingly failing to drop any neighborhoods below this critical value. An analogous situation is shown in Scenario D, where in no neighborhood does group X represent a majority but in six neighborhoods they exceed the 20% threshold. This scenario is also inferior to the baseline of segregation because the savings in social costs associated with dropping two neighborhoods below the 40% threshold is outweighed by pushing four neighborhoods above the 20% threshold.

The practical implication from this hypothetical illustration is that, compared to maximal segregation of two groups, maximal diversification will be a Pareto-superior outcome, but intermediate ranges of neighborhood diversification will be Pareto-inferior. Of course, this implication follows directly from the specification of at what point threshold critical values occur and how much change in social costs is associated with these values. This reinforces my claim of the practical importance of empirically investigating nonlinear neighborhood effects: one cannot assume uncritically that any policy that moves a society from segregation toward more diverse neighborhoods will enhance social efficiency.

7 Conclusion

An important frontier in neighborhood effects research is the empirical exploration of nonlinear and threshold effects. There is ample theoretical foundation for suggesting that several endogenous social processes generate nonlinear relationships between measures of neighborhood social composition and a variety of outcomes for individual residents. There is also a growing body of statistical literature testifying to the existence of nonlinear and threshold effects, though the findings are often inconsistent, especially in the European-based scholarship. Further empirical research on this topic is crucial because identifying the precise nature of nonlinear and threshold effects provides both a necessary social efficiency justification and practical programmatic guidance for policies designed to encourage more social diversity within neighborhoods.

References

Akerlof, George A. 1980. A theory of social custom, of which unemployment may be one consequence. *Quarterly Journal of Economics* 94:749–775.
Andersson, Eva, and Bo Malmberg. 2013. *Contextual effects on educational attainment in individualized neighborhoods: Differences across gender and social class*. Paper presented at ENHR Conference, Tarragona, Spain, June.
Bergsten, Zara. 2010. *Bättre Framtidsutsiker? Blandade Bostadsområden och Grannskapsffekter*. PhD dissertation. Uppsala, SWE: Department of Social and Economic Geography, Uppsala University.
Bolster, Anne, Simon Burgess, Ron Johnston, Kelvyn Jones, Carol Propper, and Rebecca Sarker. 2004. *Neighborhoods, households and income dynamics*. Bristol: University of Bristol, CMPO Working Paper Series No. 04/106.
Brock, William A., and Steven N. Durlauf. 2001. Interactions-based models. In *Handbook of econometrics*, ed. James J. Heckman and Edward Leamer, 3297–3380. Amsterdam: North-Holland.
Buck, Nick. 2001. Identifying neighborhood effects on social exclusion. *Urban Studies* 38:2251–2275.
Burdick-Will, Julia, Jens Ludwig, Stephen Raudenbush, Robert Sampson, Lisa Sanbonmatsu, and Patrick Sharkey. 2010. *Converging evidence for neighborhood effects on children's test scores: An experimental, quasi-experimental, and observational comparison*. Washington, D.C.: Brookings Institution.
Card, David, Alexandre Mas, and Jesse Rothstein. 2008. Tipping and the dynamics of segregation. *Quarterly Journal of Economics* 123:177–218.
Chase-Lansdale, P. Lindsay, Rachel A. Gordon, Jeanne Brooks-Gunn, and Pamela K. Klebanov. 1997. Neighborhood and family influences on the intellectual and behavioral competence of preschool and early school-age children. In *Neighborhood poverty: vol. 1. Context and consequences for children*, ed. Jeanne Brooks-Gunn and Greg J. Duncan, 79–118. New York: Russell Sage Foundation.
Clampet-Lundquist, Susan, Kathryn Edin, Jeffrey R. Kling, and Greg J. Duncan. 2011. Moving at-risk youth out of high-risk neighborhoods: Why girls fare better than boys. *American Journal of Sociology* 166:1154–1189.
Clark, William A. V. 1991. Residential preferences and neighborhood racial segregation: A test of the Schelling segregation model. *Demography* 28:1–19.
Crane, Jonathan. 1991. The epidemic theory of ghettos and neighborhood effects on dropping out and teenage childbearing. *American Journal of Sociology* 96:1226–1259.
Crowder, Kyle. 2000. The racial context of white mobility: An individual-level assessment of the white flight hypothesis. *Social Science Research* 29:223–257.
Dietz, Robert D. 2002. The estimation of neighborhood effects in the social sciences. *Social Science Research* 31:539–575.
Duncan, Greg J., James P. Connell, and Pamela K. Klebanov. 1997. Conceptual and methodological issues in estimating causal effects of neighborhoods and family conditions on individual development. In *Neighborhood poverty: vol. 1. Context and consequences for children*, ed. Jeanne Brooks-Gunn and Greg J. Duncan, 219–250. New York: Russell Sage Foundation.
Galster, George. 1987. *Homeowners and neighborhood reinvestment*. Durham: Duke University Press.
Galster, George. 1990. White flight from integrated neighborhoods. *Urban Studies* 27:385–399.
Galster, George. 2002. An economic efficiency analysis of deconcentrating poverty populations. *Journal of Housing Economics* 11:303–329.
Galster, George. 2005. *Neighbourhood mix, social opportunities, and the policy challenges of an increasingly diverse Amsterdam*. Amsterdam, Netherlands: University of Amsterdam, Department of Geography, Planning, and International Development Studies. http://www.fmg.uva.nl/amidst/object.cfm/objectid=7C149E7C-EC9F-4C2E-91DB7485C0839425 (Access: 3 June 2012).
Galster, George. 2007a. Neighbourhood social mix as a goal of housing policy: A theoretical analysis. *European Journal of Housing Policy* 7:19–43.
Galster, George. 2007b. Should policymakers strive for neighborhood social Mix? An analysis of the western European evidence base. *Housing Studies* 22:523–546.
Galster, George. 2012. The mechanism(s) of neighbourhood effects: Theory, evidence, and policy implications. In *Neighbourhood effects research: New perspectives*, ed. Maarten van Ham, David Manley, Nick Bailey, Ludi Simpson, and D. Maclennan, 23–56. Dordrecht: Springer VS.
Galster, George. 2013. Neighborhood social mix: Theory, evidence, and implications for policy and planning. In *Policy, planning and people: Promoting justice in urban development*, ed. Naomi Carmon and Susan S. Fainstein, 307–336. Philadelphia: University Penn Press.

Galster, George, and Anne Zobel. 1998. Will dispersed housing programmes reduce social problems in the US? *Housing Studies* 13:605–622.

Galster, George, Roberto Quercia, and Alvaro Cortes. 2000. Identifying neighborhood thresholds: An empirical exploration. *Housing Policy Debate* 11:701–732.

Galster, George, Kenneth Temkin, Chris Walker, and Noah Sawyer. 2004. Measuring the impacts of community development initiatives. *Evaluation Review* 28:1–38.

Galster, George, Peter Tatian, and John Accordino. 2006. Targeting investments for neighborhood revitalization. *Journal of the American Planning Association* 72:457–474.

Galster, George, Jackie Cutsinger, and Up Lim. 2007. Are neighborhoods self-stabilizing? Exploring endogenous dynamics. *Urban Studies* 44:1–19.

Galster, George, Jackie Cutsinger, and Ron Malega. 2008a. The costs of concentrated poverty: Neighborhood property markets and the dynamics of decline. In *Revisiting rental housing: Policies, programs, and priorities*, ed. Nicolas Retsinas and Eric Belsky, 93–113. Washington, D.C.: Brookings Institution Press.

Galster, George, Roger Andersson, Sako Musterd, and Timo Kauppinen. 2008b. Does neighborhood income mix affect earnings of adults? New evidence from Sweden. *Journal of Urban Economics* 63:858–870.

Galster, George, Roger Andersson, and Sako Musterd. 2010. Who is affected by neighbourhood income mix? Gender, age, family, employment and income differences. *Urban Studies* 47:2915–2944.

Galster, George, Roger Andersson, and Sako Musterd. 2011. *Are males' incomes influenced by the incomes of their male neighbors? Explorations into nonlinear and threshold effects*. Paper presented at European Network for Housing Research Conference, Istanbul, July.

Gephart, Martha A. 1997. Neighborhoods and communities as contexts for development. In *Neighborhood poverty: vol. I. Context and consequences for children*, ed. Jeanne Brooks-Gunn and Greg J. Duncan, 1–43. New York: Russell Sage Foundation.

Giles, Michael. 1975. White flight and percent black: The tipping point re-examined. *Social Science Quarterly* 56:85–92.

Goering, John M. 1978. Neighborhood tipping and racial transition: A review of social science evidence. *Journal of the American Institute of Planners* 44:68–78.

Granovetter, Mark. 1978. Threshold models of collective behavior. *American Journal of Sociology* 83:1420–1443.

Granovetter, Michael J., and Roland Soong. 1983. Threshold models of diffusion and collective behavior. *Journal of Mathematical Sociology* 9:165–179.

Hannon, Lance. 2002. Criminal opportunity theory and the relationship between poverty and property crime. *Sociological Spectrum* 22:363–381.

Hannon, Lance. 2005. Extremely poor neighborhoods and homicide. *Social Science Quarterly* 86:1418–1434.

Hedman, Lina, and George Galster. 2013. Neighborhood income sorting and the effects of neighborhood income mix on income: A holistic empirical exploration. *Urban Studies* 50:107–127.

Ioannides, Yannis, and Linda Loury. 2004. Job information networks, neighborhood effects, and inequality. *Journal of Economic Literature* 42:1056–1093.

Jencks, Christopher, and Susan E. Mayer. 1990. The social consequences of growing up in a poor neighborhood. In *Inner-city poverty in the United States*, ed. Laurence E. Lynn and Michael G. McGeary, 111–186. Washington, D.C.: National Academy Press.

Kauppinen, Timo. 2004. *Neighbourhood effects in a European city: The educational careers of young people in Helsinki*. Paper presented at European Network for Housing Research meetings, Cambridge, England, July.

Kecskes, Robert, and Stephan Knäble. 1988. Der Bevölkerungsaustausch in ethnisch gemischten Wohngebieten. Ein Test der Theorie von Schelling. In *Soziologische Stadtforschung*, ed. Jürgen Friedrich, 293–309. Opladen. Westdeutscher Verlag.

Kleinhans, Reinout. 2004. Social implications of housing diversification in urban renewal: A review of recent literature. *Journal of Housing and the Built Environment* 19:367–390.

Kleit, Rachel G. 2008. Neighborhood segregation, personal networks, and access to social resources. In *Segregation: The rising costs for America*, ed. James Carr and Nandinee Kutty, 237–260. New York: Routledge.

Krivo, Lauren J., and Ruth D. Peterson. 1996. Extremely disadvantaged neighborhoods and urban crime. *Social Forces* 75:619–648.

Lee, Barrett A., and Peter B. Wood. 1991. Is neighborhood racial succession place-specific? *Demography* 28:21–40.

Lim, Up, and George Galster. 2009. The dynamics of neighborhood property crime rates. *Annals of Regional Science* 43:925–945.
López-Turley, Ruth. 2003. When do neighborhoods matter? The role of race and neighborhood peers. *Social Science Research* 32:61–79.
Ludwig, Jens. 2012. Moving to opportunity: Guest editor's introduction. *Cityscape* 14:1–28.
Manski, Charles F. 1995. *Identification problems in the social sciences*. Cambridge: Harvard University Press.
McCulloch, Andrew. 2001. Ward-level deprivation and individual social and economic outcomes in the British household panel survey. *Environment and Planning A* 33:667–684.
Meen, Geoff. 2004. *Non-linear behaviour in local housing markets and the implications for sustainable mixed-income communities in England*. Unpublished paper. Reading, UK: University of Reading.
Meen, Geoff. 2006. *Modelling local deprivation and segregation in England*. Unpublished paper. Reading, UK: University of Reading.
Musterd, Sako, and Roger Andersson. 2006. Employment, social mobility and neighborhood effects. *International Journal of Urban and Regional Research* 30:120–140.
Musterd, Sako, Wim Ostendorf, and Sjoerd de Vos. 2003. Neighborhood effects and social mobility. *Housing Studies* 18:877–892.
Musterd, Sako, George Galster, and Roger Andersson. 2012. Temporal dimensions and the measurement of neighbourhood effects. *Environment and Planning A* 44:605–627.
Ostendorf, Wim, Sako Musterd, and Sjoerd de Vos. 2001. Social mix and the neighborhood effect: Policy ambition and empirical support. *Housing Studies* 16:371–380.
Pinkster, Fenne. 2008. *Living in concentrated poverty*. Unpublished PhD dissertation. Amsterdam: Department of Geography, Planning, and International Development Studies, University of Amsterdam.
Quercia, Roberto G., and George Galster. 2000. Threshold effects and neighborhood change. *Journal of Planning Education and Research* 20:146–162.
Sampson, Robert J. 2001. How do communities undergird or undermine human development? Relevant contexts and social mechanisms. In *Does it take a village? Community effects on children, adolescents and families*, ed. Alan Booth and An C. Crouter, 3–30. London: Lawrence Erlbaum Publishers.
Sampson, Robert J., Jeffrey D. Morenoff, and Thomas Gannon-Rowley. 2002. Assessing 'neighborhood effects': Social processes and new directions in research. *Annual Review of Sociology* 28:443–478.
Santiago, Anna, George Galster, Jessica Lucero, E. Lee, Karen Ishler, and Lisa Stack (forthcoming). *Opportunity neighborhoods for low-income Latino and African American youth*. Washington: U.S. Department of Housing and Urban Development.
Schelling, Thomas C. 1971. Dynamic models of segregation. *Journal of Mathematical Sociology* 1:143–186.
Simmel, Georg. 1971. *Georg Simmel on Individuality and social forms*. Chicago: University of Chicago Press.
Taub, Richard P., D. Garth Taylor, and Jan D. Dunham. 1985. *Paths of neighborhood change*. Chicago: University of Chicago Press.
Van der Klaauw, Bas, and Jan C. Van Ours. 2003. From welfare to work: Does the neighborhood matter? *Journal of Public Economics* 87:957–85.
Vartanian, Thomas P. 1999a. Adolescent neighborhood effects on labor market and economic outcomes. *Social Service Review* 73:142–167.
Vartanian, Thomas P. 1999b. Childhood conditions and adult welfare use. *Journal of Marriage and the Family* 61:225–237.
Weber, Max. 1978. *Economy and society*. 2 vols. Berkeley: University of California Press.
Weinberg, Bruce, Patricia Reagan, and Jeffrey Yankow. 2004. Do neighborhoods affect work behavior? Evidence from the NLSY79. *Journal of Labor Economics* 22:891–924.
Wilson, William J. 1987. *The truly disadvantaged*. Chicago: University of Chicago Press.
Wolf, Eleanor. 1963. The tipping-point in racially changing neighborhoods. *Journal of the American Institute of Planners* 29:217–222.

George Galster, 1948, PhD Economics (MIT) has been the Hilberry Professor of Urban Affairs at Wayne State University in Detroit since 1996. Previously he was Director of Housing Research at The Urban Institute in Washington, DC. He is the author of over 130 peer-reviewed articles, 32 book chapters, and 11 books and monographs, many of which focus on the theory and measurement of neighborhood effects. He was recently designated among the ten most-cited scholars teaching in American schools of planning. His latest book (2012) is "Driving Detroit: The Quest for Respect in the Motor City".

Theoretische und statistische Modellierung von Cross-Pressures in Kontextanalysen

Jochen Mayerl · Henning Best

© Springer Fachmedien Wiesbaden 2014

Zusammenfassung Allgemein versteht man unter Cross-Pressures das Phänomen von sozialem Druck auf individuelle Akteure, der durch Heterogenität im sozialen Umfeld und insbesondere in Form widersprüchlicher sozialer Erwartungen entsteht. Dieser Beitrag diskutiert die theoretische Einbettung von „Cross Pressures" im struktur-individualistischen Paradigma und stellt die statistische Modellierung von Cross-Pressures in Mehrebenenanalysen vor. Wir argumentieren, dass Cross-Pressures eine spezifische Klasse von Kontexteffekten (Makro-Mikro-Verbindung) und der „Definition der Situation" sind und skizzieren eine Rekonstruktion im Rahmen des Modells der Frame-Selektion. Methodisch folgt aus der handlungstheoretischen Modellierung, dass sich insbesondere Mehrebenenmodelle mit spezifizierten Cross-Level-Interaktionen zur empirisch-statistischen Analyse von Cross-Pressures eignen. Durch Verwendung von Random-Slope- und Kontext-Fixed-Effects- Modellen kann die Interaktion empirisch identifiziert werden. Abschließend demonstrieren wir die Prüfung von Hypothesen zu Cross-Pressures am Beispiel des Zusammenhangs von individuellem Postmaterialismus und individuellen Umwelteinstellungen, der durch das Kontextmerkmal „Wohlstand einer Nation" moderiert wird. Wir zeigen mit den Daten des World Value Survey, dass Postmaterialismus und Umweltbewusstsein in reicheren Gesellschaften ein integriertes Wertecluster bilden, in ärmeren Ländern jedoch getrennte Konstrukte sind.

J. Mayerl (✉)
Fachbereich Sozialwissenschaften, TU Kaiserslautern,
Erwin-Schrödinger-Str., Gebäude 57,
67663 Kaiserslautern, Deutschland
E-Mail: Jochen.Mayerl@sowi.uni-kl.de

H. Best
Institute für Politikwissenschaft und Soziologie, Universität Würzburg,
Wittelsbacherplatz 1, 97074 Würzburg, Deutschland

Schlüsselwörter Cross-Pressures · Mehrebenenanalyse · Cross-Level Interaktion · Framing · Einstellungen · Postmaterialismus

Theoretical and Statistical Modeling of Cross-Pressures in Context Analysis

Abstract Cross-pressures can be defined as individually perceived social pressure that results from heterogeneity in the social context, mainly due to conflicting social expectations of relevant social actors. In this paper we discuss the theoretical position of "cross-pressures" in the structural-individualist paradigm and present methods for modeling cross-pressures in multilevel regression models. We argue that cross pressures form a specific class of context effects, that is macro-micro links, and sketch a reconstruction as part of the problem of defining the social situation in the Model of Frame Selection. The theoretical model implies that empirical applications of the concept would ideally use multiplicative terms for the specification of cross-level interactions in multilevel models. Modeling random slopes and context fixed-effects the interaction can be identified empirically. As an example we analyze the relation between postmaterialism and environmental concern, moderated by national wealth using WVS data. Our results indicate that postmaterialism and environmental concern form an integrated value cluster in wealthy societies, but are separate constructs in poorer societies.

Keywords Cross-pressures · Multilevel analysis · Cross-level interaction · Framing · Attitudes · Postmaterialism

1 Problemstellung

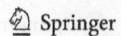

Im Kontext des strukturellen Individualismus bildet die Logik der Situation ein zentrales Element der soziologischen Analyse und Erklärung. Über sie wird die notwendige Verbindung zwischen sozialen Kontexten und Akteuren, die im Rahmen dieser Kontexte handeln, hergestellt. Relevante Kontexte, die entscheidenden Einfluss auf Akteure bei ihrer Handlungsentscheidung ausüben können, lassen sich auf unterschiedlichen Analyseebenen verorten. So zählen gesellschaftliche Makroeigenschaften, z. B. der Wohlstand eines Landes, ebenso zu situationsabhängig bedeutsamen Kontexteigenschaften wie auf der Mesoebene das soziale Nahumfeld von Akteuren, d. h. deren sozialen Netzwerke. Dass kontextuelle Faktoren die Wahrnehmungen, Bewertungen, Erwartungen und Verhaltensweisen einer Person entscheidend beeinflussen können, ist dabei sicherlich keine sozialwissenschaftliche Neuigkeit. Eine besondere Ausprägung solcher Kontexteffekte haben bereits Lazarsfeld et al. (1944) als „Cross-Pressures" beschrieben, die durch gegenläufige Einflüsse aus unterschiedlichen sozialen Gruppen auf die individuelle politische Wahlentscheidung entstehen. Gerade für moderne, stark differenzierte und pluralistische Gesellschaften ist die Zugehörigkeit von Individuen zu heterogenen sozialen Kreisen charakteristisch (vgl. z. B. Beck 1986). Da hierdurch die Wahrscheinlichkeit von heterogenen Verhaltenserwartungen und Konflikten zwischen individuellen Wertorientierungen und Werten der (Herkunfts-)Gruppe steigt, gewinnt die soziologische Analyse von Cross-Pressures besondere Bedeutung.

Etwas zugespitzt lassen sich Cross-Pressures als sozialer Druck fassen, der entweder aufgrund von widersprüchlichen normativen Forderungen an einen Akteur entsteht oder sich aus einer Inkompatibilität eigener Einstellungen und Werte mit gesellschaftlich geteilten Vorstellungen oder Constraints ergibt (z. B. Berelson et al. 1954; McClurg 2006; Mutz 2002; Nir 2005). Solche Cross-Pressures werden insbesondere durch Heterogenität im sozialen Netzwerk oder Nahumfeld eines Akteurs *unmittelbar alltagsrelevant*. Widersprechen die Einstellungen und Handlungsorientierungen eines Akteurs denjenigen ihrer wichtigsten Netzwerkpartner, dann müssen Akteure abwägen, ob sie sich zurücknehmen oder aber den direkten Konflikt mit ihrem Umfeld suchen. Entstehen Cross-Pressures durch Wirkungen gesellschaftlicher Normen oder durch den Einfluss sozialer Strukturen, beispielsweise durch das soziale Milieu, ist ihre Wirkung weniger unmittelbar. Doch auch hier können verinnerlichte Normen oder Sanktionsbefürchtungen handlungswirksam werden, selbst wenn sie eigenen Werten und Zielen widersprechen oder kontextuell widersprüchlich sind. Zusammenfassend können Cross-Pressures somit verstärkende oder vermindernde Einflüsse darauf haben, ob individuelle Präferenzen umgesetzt werden oder nicht. Wir werden im Folgenden argumentieren, dass Cross-Pressures im Rahmen eines allgemeinen Handlungsmodells auf zwei Arten handlungsrelevant werden können: entweder als zusätzlicher Kostenfaktor im deliberativen, rational abwägenden Entscheidungsmodus oder als Einflussfaktor auf die Definition der Situation oder des Handlungsrahmens. Diese beiden Typen an Wirkweisen von Cross-Pressures stehen im weiteren Verlauf dieses Textes im Vordergrund.

Im folgenden Abschnitt verorten wir Cross-Pressures zunächst theoretisch und skizzieren eine Rekonstruktion im handlungstheoretischen Kontext des Modells der Frame-Selektion (Esser 1996, 2001; Kroneberg 2005). Sodann diskutieren wir die angemessene statistisch-methodische Spezifikation von Cross-Pressures (Abschn. 3). Insbesondere wird gezeigt, wie Cross-Pressures in Mehrebenenanalysen spezifiziert und analysiert werden können. Die Mehrebenenanalyse ist ein besonders gut geeignetes statistisches Verfahren, um Beziehungen zwischen verschiedenen Aggregatsebenen zu modellieren und bietet sich daher auch zur Analyse von Cross-Pressures an. Um die empirische Analyse von Cross-Pressures zu verdeutlichen, stellen wir in Abschn. 4 eine exemplarische Anwendung zur Mehrebenenanalyse von Cross-Pressures vor und präsentieren ein Modell zur Erklärung von individueller Präferenz für Umweltschutz vor Wirtschaftswachstum. Als analyseebenen-übergreifender Cross-Pressure wird dabei der Konflikt zwischen nationalem Wohlstand einerseits und individueller Wertorientierung andererseits in Form einer Cross-Level-Interaktion modelliert. Der Beitrag schließt in Abschn. 5 mit einem Fazit.

2 Cross-Pressures: Bedeutung und Wirkweisen

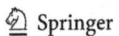

Wie eingangs erwähnt, haben Lazarsfeld und Kollegen (1944) das Konzept des Cross-Pressures eingeführt, um das Phänomen des durch Heterogenität im sozialen Umfeld entstandenen sozialen Drucks in Form widersprüchlicher Erwartungen zu beschreiben. Der Einfluss von Heterogenität im sozialen Kontext wurde und wird auch in der Netzwerkforschung aufgegriffen und erforscht (Huckfeld und Sprague 1995; McClurg 2006; Mutz 2002). Insbesondere in der politischen Soziologie wird das Konzept der Cross-Pressures intensiv verwendet, um den Einfluss konfligierender politischer Positionen auf Wahlverhalten und politische Partizipation zu untersuchen (z. B. Aars et al. 2010; Belanger und Eagles 2007; Hadler 2002; Soler 2012; Therriault et al. 2011; Wilson 2012). In theoretischen Modellen wird von „cross-pressured" Akteuren unter anderem erwartet, dass sie sich weniger politisch engagieren, eine größere Unsicherheit hinsichtlich ihrer Entscheidungen hegen, ihre Einstellungen und Verhaltensweisen weniger persistent und resistent sind, oder dass sie ein geringeres politisches Interesse aufweisen (vgl. Brader et al. 2013; Preidel und Findling 2011). Auch wenn sich diese Annahmen in empirischen Analysen z. T. uneinheitlich aufzeigen und replizieren ließen (z. B. Brader et al. 2013; Mutz 2002), so kann sicherlich konstatiert werden, dass es unzählige empirische Belege dafür gibt, dass Cross-Pressures zumindest neben anderen Bestimmungsfaktoren einen bedeutsamen Einfluss auf den Entscheidungsprozess und die Entscheidung von Akteuren ausüben können.

Allgemein betrachtet betreffen Cross-Pressures nicht nur politische, sondern alle möglichen Formen von sozialen Konflikten, die durch heterogene soziale Erwartungen entstehen können. Dabei können genauso politische wie alle anderen möglichen sozialen Bewertungen und Erwartungen in Konflikt geraten und dadurch sozialen Konflikt erzeugen. Solcher Konflikt wird auf Akteursebene als sozialer Druck wahrgenommen. So sind Cross-Pressures im familiären Umfeld beispielsweise für Akteure besonders alltagsrelevant: Wenn etwa der Erziehungsstil der Eltern mit demjenigen der Großeltern oder, allgemeiner gefasst, mit gesellschaftlichen Erziehungsnormen nicht in Einklang stehen, dann kann dies elementare Auswirkungen auf die Kinder nach sich ziehen. Zu unterscheiden sind hierbei zwei Wirkungsweisen von Cross-Pressures (Lup 2011): Einerseits können soziale Erwartungen gegensätzlich sein, sodass der soziale Kontext für einen Akteur Handlungsunsicherheit erzeugt und diesen dadurch „unter Druck setzt". Andererseits können soziale Kontexte auch dadurch Effekte von Cross-Pressures erzeugen, wenn der Erwartungsdruck des Kontexts seitens des Akteurs als einheitlich entgegen den eigenen Überzeugungen wahrgenommen wird.

Der Begriff der Cross-Pressures wurde in den letzten Jahren zunehmend erweitert. So können soziale, interpersonelle Cross-Pressures von sogenannten Issue Cross-Pressures unterschieden werden (z. B. Brader et al. 2013; Therriault et al. 2011). Während soziale Cross-Pressures den oben skizzierten Konflikt von Akteuren und Kontexten umfassen, beziehen sich Issue Cross-Pressures auf eine individuell variable Kombination an konfligierenden Präferenzen, was auch als „cross-cutting preferences" (Finseraas 2008) bezeichnet werden kann. In diesem Beitrag konzentrieren wir uns auf die Betrachtung von Cross-Pressures, die von widersprüchlichen sozialen Erwartungen der Kontextebene ausgehen. Folglich werden Issue Cross-Pressures und Cross-Pressures, die aus widersprüchlichen Erwartungen auf derselben Aggregatebene entstehen, hier nicht weiter verfolgt. Der Begriff „Cross Pressures" bezieht sich daher im Folgenden lediglich auf diese inhaltlich begrenzte Betrachtungsweise. Vor dem Hintergrund dieser Begriffsbestimmung möchten wir Cross-

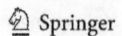

Pressures handlungstheoretisch spezifizieren. In den folgenden Absätzen ordnen wir Cross-Pressures in das struktur-individualistische Modell der soziologischen Erklärung ein und skizzieren handlungstheoretische Ansatzpunkte.

Allgemein lassen sich Cross-Pressures innerhalb des Modells der soziologischen Erklärung als ein spezifischer Typ der Makro-Mikro-Effekte verorten, der die Definition der Situation der Akteure prägt. Jede menschliche Entscheidung und Handlung findet in einem sozialen Kontext statt, der beeinflusst, wie Akteure ihre Situation deuten und welche grundlegenden, ihr weiteres Verhalten rahmenden Orientierungen sie aktivieren. Soziale Akteure sind in allen denkbaren Entscheidungssituationen immer auch externen, äußeren Bedingungen der Situation ausgesetzt. Diese beeinflussen den individuellen Entscheidungsprozess maßgeblich, begrenzen ihn und lenken ihn z. B. in sozial akzeptierte Bahnen. In der Soziologie wurde eine Fülle an theoretischen Konzepten vorgeschlagen, die versuchen, Makro-Mikro-Effekte in eine Handlungstheorie zu integrieren. Als Beispiele seien Werte, Normen, Codes, soziale Produktionsfunktionen, soziale Milieus, Habitus, Lebenswelt oder ganz schlicht Kultur genannt. Cross-Pressures können als Spezialfall sozialer Situationen begriffen werden. Mit ihnen werden spezifische Entscheidungssituationen charakterisiert, die für Akteure ein hohes *soziales Konfliktpotenzial* bergen.

Wie aber lassen sich Cross-Pressures handlungstheoretisch verorten? Mit dem Modell der Frame-Selektion (MFS, vgl. Esser 1996, 2001; Kroneberg 2005) liegt ein handlungstheoretisches Modell vor, das die Verflechtung von sozialer und subjektiver Definition der Situation bei Entscheidungsprozessen von Akteuren detailliert behandelt. Individuelles Handeln findet stets im Rahmen sozialer Kontexte statt, die die sozial institutionalisierte Situationsdefinition und damit die *soziale* Definition der Situation bestimmen. Individuelle Handlungsentscheidungen und individuelles Framing sind demnach maßgeblich durch die strukturelle Konstitution und den sozialen Sinn der Situation vorstrukturiert. Cross-Pressures entstehen aus einer solchen sozialen Definition der Situation, die entweder (aufgrund normativer Heterogenität des sozialen Umfeldes) widersprüchliche soziale Erwartungen beinhaltet oder den eigenen normativen Orientierungen des Akteurs widerspricht. Beide Wirkungsweisen beeinflussen die *subjektive* Definition der Situation der betroffenen Akteure, bei der Individuen die Situation mit einem subjektiven Sinn versehen. Individuelle Handlungsentscheidungen entstehen demnach gemäß dem MFS auf Basis mentaler, heuristischer Situationsschemata (sogenannte Frames), die die Fülle an Informationen einer Situation vorstrukturieren und komplexitätsreduzierend wirken.

Das MFS geht auf der Ebene des individuellen Entscheidungsprozesses von vier zentralen Theoriebausteinen aus (zu einer ausführlichen Diskussion vgl. Best und Kroneberg 2012; Kroneberg 2007, 2011; Mayerl 2009, 2010). Erstens wird eine Handlungsentscheidung in drei sukzessive Entscheidungsstufen unterschieden: Die Selektion eines Frames, gefolgt von der Selektion eines Handlungsskripts und der letztlichen Handlung. Dabei werden Frames als vorgefertigte Situationsdefinitionen in Form von mentalen Modellen der Situation verstanden. Framing bezeichnet dann nach Esser eine „Strategie der Vereinfachung und Zuspitzung der Situation." (Esser 1996, S. 17). Der selektierte Frame beeinflusst maßgeblich die nachfolgenden kognitiven Prozesse, reduziert deren Alternativraum und vereinfacht dadurch die Entscheidungssituation für den Akteur. Die Passung eines Frames zur aktuellen Entscheidungssituation wird als Match eines Frames bezeichnet. Entscheidende Bestandteile des Matchs sind das Ausbleiben von Störungen und insbesondere die Stärke der mentalen Verankerung, was in der Einstellungstheorie auch „attitude accessibility" bezeichnet wird (Eagly und Chaiken 1998; Fazio 1986, 1990). Zweitens wird angenommen, dass die Selektionen von Frames, Handlungsskripten und Handlungen jeweils bewusst und rational oder aber unbewusst und automatisch erfolgen können. Basierend auf Erkenntnissen aus der sozialpsychologischen Kognititionsforschung (vgl. Chaiken und Trope 1999; Fazio 1990; Petty und Cacioppo 1986) unterscheidet das MFS demnach zwei Modi der Informationsverarbeitung bei der Selektion von Frames, Skripten und Handlungen: kontrolliert-überlegte versus automatisch-spontane Informationsverarbeitung. Drittens sind die Motivation und die Möglichkeit zum überlegten Prozessieren sowie der Match eines Frames zentrale Bestimmungsfaktoren dafür, welcher Modus der Informationsverarbeitung aktiviert wird. Nur bei hoher Motivation und gegebener Möglichkeit treffen Akteure Entscheidungen im überlegt-kontrollierten Prozessmodus. Ein hoher Match reduziert dabei maßgeblich die Motivation zum elaborierten Prozessieren (vgl. Mayerl 2009, 2010). Viertens unterscheidet sich die Entscheidungslogik bei der Frame-Selektion (und entsprechend auch bei der Skript- und Handlungsselektion) zwischen den beiden Modi der Informationsverarbeitung maßgeblich. Während die Entscheidungslogik im überlegt-kontrollierten Modus derjenigen der klassischen Rational-Choice-Modelle entspricht, laufen automatisch-spontane Entscheidungen unbewusst, unaufwändig und unreflektiert ab. Automatisch-spontane Prozesse sind maßgeblich dadurch bestimmt, inwiefern Akteure bereits passende mentale Modelle der Situation in ihrem Gedächtnis verankert haben, sodass diese leicht abgerufen werden können. Kurzum: Entscheidend ist bei der automatischen Verarbeitung, ob ein Frame chronisch hoch zugänglich ist und dadurch sofort aktiviert und handlungsleitend werden kann oder nicht.

Cross-Pressures können im MFS nun auf mehrere Arten handlungsleitend werden. Die erste, sehr grundlegende Art besteht in einer Beeinflussung des Framings. Individuelle Orientierungen können nur dann unreflektiert und automatisch handlungsleitend werden, wenn die zugehörige Situationsdefinition zur tatsächlichen Situation passt, d. h. wenn das aktivierte Frame einen hohen Match aufweist. Cross-Pressures jedoch bedeuten *Irritationen der subjektiven Situationsdefinition* und können dazu führen, dass Akteure motiviert sind, reflektierte und aufwändige überlegt-kontrollierte Entscheidungen zu fällen und gegebenenfalls ein Reframing stattfindet.[1] Folglich wären bei Vorliegen von Cross-Pressures schwächere Einstellungs-Verhaltens-Zusammenhänge zu erwarten. Allgemeiner gesprochen können Cross-Pressures zu *Neutralisierungen* (z. B. Sykes und Matza 1957) von Einstellungen und Nutzenaspekten führen oder ganze Handlungsalternativen ausschließen, indem sie einen Frame aktivieren, in dem diese Aspekte nicht mehr im *choice set* enthalten sind. Des Weiteren können auch im MFS Einflüsse der Makro-Ebene in die Nutzenfunktion individueller Akteure integriert werden. Im reflektierten RC-Modus können so bei-

---

[1] Cross-Pressures sind damit beispielsweise auch Auslöser für wertrationales Handeln nach Max Weber, da sie Wertreflektionen stimulieren (vgl. Kroneberg 2007).

spielsweise Normen das abweichende Verhalten der Akteure verhindern, indem die Sanktionsdrohung zu hohe Kosten erwarten lässt.

Während die letztere Variante zu einfachen, additiven Kontexteffekten führt, werden die Kontexte in der ersten Variante als Moderatoreffekte oder Interaktionseffekte wirksam. In diesem Fall beeinflusst der Cross-Pressure das Handeln von Akteuren nicht direkt, sondern indirekt über die Wahl des Frames und die bedingte Wirkung von individuellen Entscheidungsfaktoren auf individuelle Handlungen oder Handlungsabsichten. Je nachdem, auf welcher Ebene Cross-Pressures handlungsleitend werden, ergeben sich gänzlich unterschiedliche Hypothesen, die auch eine unterschiedliche statistische Modellierung erfordern. Dies werden wir im folgenden Abschnitt genauer diskutieren.

3 Cross-Pressures in Mehrebenenanalysen

Sind soziale Cross-Pressures begrifflich als Heterogenität im sozialen Kontext leicht zu bestimmen, so ist deren Operationalisierung in empirischen Analysen hingegen weniger selbstverständlich. Sollen Cross-Pressures mehr als nur ein theoretisches Konzept sein, ist die adäquate Umsetzung in statistischen Analysen jedoch von zentraler Bedeutung. Während sich manche Forschung mit der Konstruktion eines „Cross Pressure Scores" (Brader et al. 2013) beschäftigt und in der sozialen Netzwerkforschung eine Reihe an Vorschlägen zur Operationalisierung von Heterogenität diskutiert wird (z. B. Marsden 1988, 1992; McPherson et al. 2001), erscheint es uns zunächst wichtiger, die Frage nach einem geeigneten statistischen Verfahren zu stellen. Seit einigen Jahren wird auch bei der Analyse von Cross-Pressures die Mehrebenenanalyse eingesetzt (z. B. Aars et al. 2010; Belanger und Eagles 2007; Soler 2012). Nachfolgend soll die Mehrebenenanalyse in ihren Grundzügen kurz skizziert werden, um diese anschließend mit der Analyse von Cross-Pressures zu verbinden (vgl. etwa Hox 2010; Langer 2010; Snijders und Bosker 1999).

Die Mehrebenenanalyse hat mehrere statistische Vorzüge gegenüber klassischen regressionsanalytischen Verfahren. Allem voran berücksichtigt sie die hierarchische Datenstruktur, die impliziert, dass sich Elemente eines Aggregats ähnlicher sind als Elemente aus verschiedenen Aggregaten, sodass Beobachtungen nicht mehr unabhängig voneinander sind, was eine der Grundannahmen klassischer Regressionsverfahren ist. Die Mehrebenenregression vermeidet daher Annahmeverletzungen, die bei Anwendung einer OLS-Regression entstehen würden (Autokorrelation und Korreliertheit der Residuen mit den X-Variablen) und ermöglicht die gleichzeitige Schätzung von Effekten von Variablen unterschiedlicher Aggregatebenen (Makrovariablen „Z" und Mikrovariablen „X"). Wichtig ist zudem, dass in der Mehrebenenanalyse die Gesamtvarianz einer abhängigen Individualvariablen Y in erklärbare Varianzanteile durch die Ebene zwischen Kontexten (between-Varianz) und innerhalb von Kontexten (within-Varianz) zerlegt werden kann.[2]

---

[2] Eine solche Varianzzerlegung kann in Logit-Modellen nicht vorgenommen werden. Zwar kann man auch hier die Varianz des Intercepts bestimmen, nicht aber die Residualvarianz (vgl. Gl. 5 unten).

Abb. 1 Zwei Wirkmechanismen von Kontexteigenschaften Z in der Mehrebenenanalyse **a** Individual- und Kontexteffekte **b** Zusätzliche Cross-Level-Interaktion

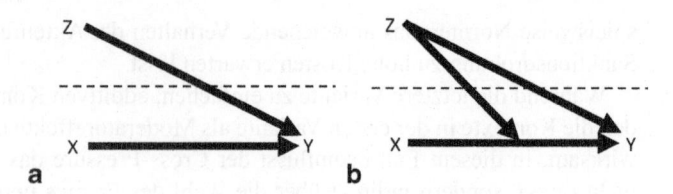

Das Herzstück der Mehrebenenanalyse besteht in der Unterscheidung von sogenannten „random" und „fixed" Koeffizienten und der Berücksichtigung verschiedener Aggregatsebenen (Levels). So kann in einem Beispiel mit Haushalten als Level 2 und Haushaltsmitgliedern als Level 1 die Konstante (auch Intercept genannt) einer Regression des Individualmerkmals Y auf den Individualprädiktor X zwischen sozialen Kontexten, hier also zwischen Haushalten, variieren. Lässt man diese Variation zu, so wird ein Mehrebenemodell mit *random Intercept* geschätzt. Wird die Konstante hingegen in allen Kontexten als gleich restringiert, ergibt sich ein fixed Intercept-Modell. Variable Regressionskonstanten bedeuten, dass sozusagen das Basisniveau bei der Schätzung von Y unterschiedlich hoch ist, je nach Haushaltskontext. Ebenso kann der Steigungskoeffizient des Effekts der Individualvariablen X auf Y von Kontext zu Kontext variieren. Lässt man auch diese Variation bei der Schätzung eines Regressionskoeffizienten zu, so handelt es sich um *random Slopes*, andernfalls um *fixed Slopes*. Die Varianz des random Intercept oder der random Slopes gibt Hinweise auf die Frage, wie stark die jeweiligen Parameter zwischen den Kontexten variieren. In diesem Sinne ergibt sich bei einem linearen Modell ohne erklärende Variablen, aber mit random Intercept, eine Zerlegung der Varianz von Y zwischen den Ebenen in die Varianz der Konstante (Kontext) und die Residualvarianz (individuell).

Zentral für eine soziologische Analyse von Cross-Pressures ist nun die Frage, *warum* sich ein X-Y-Effekt zwischen verschiedenen Kontexten unterscheidet. Die Antwort hierfür kann nur in Unterschieden in den Eigenschaften Z zwischen den Kontexten gefunden werden. Beeinflusst Z also nicht nur die Ausprägung von Y, sondern auch den Effekt von X auf Y, so ist Z eine Form von Moderatorvariable. Man spricht hier von einer sogenannten *Cross-Level-Interaktion* – die Kontexteigenschaft Z moderiert den Effekt der Individualvariablen X auf die Individualvariable Y. In Abb. 1 werden die beiden Wirkweisen von Kontexteigenschaften grafisch veranschaulicht.

Formal betrachtet kann die herkömmliche lineare Regressionsgleichung bei einem Random-Intercept-Random-Slope Modell (ohne Cross-Level-Interaktion) wie folgt erweitert werden:

$$Y_{ij} = b_{0j} + b_{1j}X_{1ij} + e_{ij} \tag{1}$$

$$b_{0j} = b_0 + b_{01}Z_{1j} + u_{0j} \tag{2}$$

$$b_{1j} = b_1 + u_{1j} \tag{3}$$

mixed model: $Y_{ij} = b_0 + b_{01}Z_{1j} + u_{0j} + (b_1 + u_{1j})X_{1ij} + e_{ij}$ \tag{4}

Gleichung (1) entspricht der herkömmlichen linearen Regressionsgleichung. Bei einem Random-Intercept Modell mit Level 2-Prädiktoren (Z) ist der Intercept der

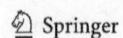

Regressionsgeraden jedoch abhängig von Z sowie einem zufälligen Störterm (Gl. 2). Da in unserem Fall auch der Slope über die Kontexte hinweg variiert, wird auch der Slope durch einen zufälligen Störterm beeinflusst (Gl. 3). Setzt man die Gl. (2) und (3) in Gl. (1) ein, so erhält man das sogenannte mixed model (Gl. 4).

Die Spezifikation von Cross-Level-Interaktionen erfolgt nun durch die simple Erweiterung von Gl. (3) hin zu Gl. (3.1) durch die Einführung der Moderatorvariablen Z:

$$Y_{ij} = b_{0j} + b_{1j}X_{1ij} + e_{ij} \quad (1)$$

$$b_{0j} = b_0 + b_{01}Z_{1j} + u_{0j} \quad (2)$$

$$b_{1j} = b_1 + b_{11}Z_{1j} + u_{1j} \quad (3.1)$$

mixed model: $Y_{ij} = b_0 + b_{01}Z_{ij} + u_{0j} + b_1 X_{1ij} + b_{11}\left(Z_{1j}X_{1ij}\right) + u_{1j}X_{1ij} + e_{ij}$ (4.1)

Im mixed model (Gl. 4.1) ist leicht zu erkennen, warum es sich bei der Cross-Level-Interaktion tatsächlich um einen Interaktionseffekt handelt, da der Term Z*X entsteht. Und das ist es ja genau, was erreicht werden soll, nämlich dass der Effekt von X auf Y durch die Kontextvariable Z verstärkt oder abgeschwächt wird.

Genau dasselbe Prinzip kann auch auf andere Formen der Regressionsanalyse angewandt werden. Für die binär-logistische Regression, die im nachfolgenden Kapitel als Anwendungsfall verwendet wird, gilt dann für ein Random-Intercept-Random-Slope Modell mit Z-Prädiktor und Cross-Level-Interaktion entsprechend:

$$\hat{P}_{ij} = \frac{\exp\left(b_{0j} + b_{1j}X_{1ij}\right)}{1 + \exp\left(b_{0j} + b_{1j}X_{1ij}\right)} \quad (5)$$

$$b_{0j} = b_0 + b_{01}Z_{1j} + u_{0j} \quad (6)$$

$$b_{1j} = b_1 + b_{11}Z_{1j} + u_{1j} \quad (7)$$

mixed model: $\hat{P}_{ij} = \dfrac{\exp\left(b_0 + b_{01}Z_{1j} + u_{0j} + b_1 X_{1ij} + b_{11}Z_{1j}X_{1ij} + u_{1j}X_{1ij}\right)}{1 + \exp\left(b_0 + b_{01}Z_{1j} + u_{0j} + b_1 X_{1ij} + b_{11}Z_{1j}X_{1ij} + u_{1j}X_{1ij}\right)}$ (8)

Wieder ist im mixed model in Gl. (8) leicht die Cross-Level-Interaktion zwischen Z und X zu erkennen. Da es sich bei dem hier aufgezeigten Effekt um einen *variablenspezifischen Interaktionseffekt* handelt, der eine interaktive Wirkung auf den Nutzen oder die latente abhängige Variable des Logit Modells nahelegt (siehe z. B. Nagler 1994; Berry et al. 2010), kann der Interaktionseffekt auch im nichtlinearen Wahrscheinlichkeitsmodell einfach mit einem Produktterm modelliert werden (siehe z. B. Best und Wolf 2010 für eine Diskussion von Interaktionseffekten in der logistischen Regression).

Entscheidend für die adäquate Implementation von Cross-Pressures in der Mehrebenenanalyse ist nun, dass konkrete Annahmen über die exakte Wirkweise des Konflikte und „sozialen Druck" ausübenden Kontexts benötigt werden. In der Mehrebenenanalyse lassen sich drei verschiedene Formen unterscheiden, die auch jeweils bereits zur Analyse von Cross-Pressures in Mehrebenenalysen in der Literatur angewendet wurden:

Erstens kann der Cross-Pressure als Level 2-Prädiktor Z operationalisiert und geschätzt werden. In diesem Fall geht man davon aus, dass konfligierende Kontexteigenschaften direkt die abhängige Individualvariable Y beeinflussen, weshalb wir dies auch als „additive Cross-Pressures" bezeichnen. So ließe sich z. B. klären, ob die Kontexteigenschaft Z oder die Individualeigenschaft X einen stärkeren Effekt auf Y ausüben. In der Sprache der Mehrebenenenalyse kann Z als direkter Prädiktor jedoch immer nur den Intercept der Regressionsgleichung beeinflussen, also sozusagen die Basis von Y. Dass dies so ist, liegt schlicht daran, dass sich die Individuen innerhalb eines Kontexts hinsichtlich Z ja nicht unterscheiden. Als Anwendungsfall haben in diesem Sinne z. B. Belanger und Eagles (2007) politische Heterogenität im Haushalt als Z-Variable eingeführt (binäre Variable Z), und Aars et al. (2010) haben u. a. die Standardabweichung des Einkommens innerhalb von Stadtregionen als Heterogenitätsmaß verwendet, um dieses als Z-Prädiktor einzusetzen. Zu beachten ist jedoch, dass es sich bei dieser Variante vor allem dann um Cross-Pressures im eigentlichen Sinne handelt, wenn die Z-Variable bereits als Konfliktmaß operationalisiert ist (z. B. politische Uneinigkeiten im Haushalt). Gegeben die oben dargestellte handlungstheoretische Modellierung, dass Cross-Pressures insbesondere über Unsicherheiten und den Match oder Wahl eines Handlungsframes wirken, halten wir additive Cross-Pressures jedoch für theoretisch weniger bedeutsam.

Der Cross-Pressure-Effekt kann und sollte daher zweitens auch als Cross-Level-Interaktion geschätzt werden. Diesen „multiplikativen Cross-Pressures" liegt die Annahme zugrunde, dass der konfligierende Kontext die Wirkweise von individuellen Bestimmungsfaktoren beeinflusst (vgl. z. B. Belanger und Eagles 2007; Soler 2012). In Abschn. 2 haben wir auf Basis des Modells der Frame-Selektion argumentiert, dass dies über Irritationen der subjektiven Situationsdefinition geschieht. Während im ersten, additiven Fall also ein Einfluss des Kontexts direkt auf die individuelle Y-Variable modelliert wird, wird im zweiten, multiplikativen Fall der Kontexteinfluss auf die Wirkweise der Individualvariablen X spezifiziert. Diese Form der Umsetzung von Cross-Pressures als Cross-Level-Interaktion kann als direkteste Form der statistischen Spezifikation von Cross-Pressures aufgrund eines Konflikts zwischen eigenen Wertorientierungen und denen des sozialen Umfelds betrachtet werden, da hier Beziehungsgeflechte zwischen zwei unterschiedlichen Aggregatebenen geschätzt werden. Die Spezifikation und theoretische Einbettung eines Mehrebenenmodells verhilft daher nicht nur dazu, ein statistisch angemessenes Verfahren einzusetzen, sondern häufig auch dazu, sich der exakten Wirkweise der Kontexteigenschaften erst bewusst zu werden und dadurch die theoretischen Annahmen zu präzisieren.

Eine dritte Art, Cross-Pressures in Mehrebenenmodellen zu implementieren, besteht darin, intrapersonell konfligierende Einstellungen und Präferenzen als X-Variable einzusetzen (z. B. Finseraas 2008; Völkl 2007). Diese Issue Cross-Pressures behandeln dann keine Konflikte zwischen Aggregatebenen, sondern rein auf Individualebene, und die Mehrebenenanalyse ist einzig dann anderen klassischen Verfahren vorzuziehen, wenn eine hierarchische Datenstruktur vorliegt und Annahmen der klassischen Regressionsanalyse verletzt sind.

4 Anwendung: Kontextabhängigkeit der Wirkung von individuellen Wertorientierungen

Wir möchten nun die Analyse von Cross-Pressures anhand einer empirischen Anwendung beispielhaft darstellen. Ein mittlerweile Jahrzehnte altes Puzzle in der sozialwissenschaftlichen Werte- und Umweltforschung ist der Umstand, dass einerseits hohe Quoten an umweltbewussten Personen sowohl in relativ reichen als auch in relativ armen Ländern vorzufinden sind, andererseits aber auch kein klarer Zusammenhang zwischen dem Umweltbewusstsein und dem Anteil an Postmaterialisten an der Bevölkerung vorzufinden ist (vgl. Abb. 2a und b; Daten des World Value Survey 2005–2009). Es scheint demnach, zumindest auf Aggregatebene, kein klares Muster erkennbar zu sein, wie Umwelteinstellungen mit nationalem Wohlstand und allgemeinem Wertewandel oder konkreter der Ausbreitung des Postmaterialismus

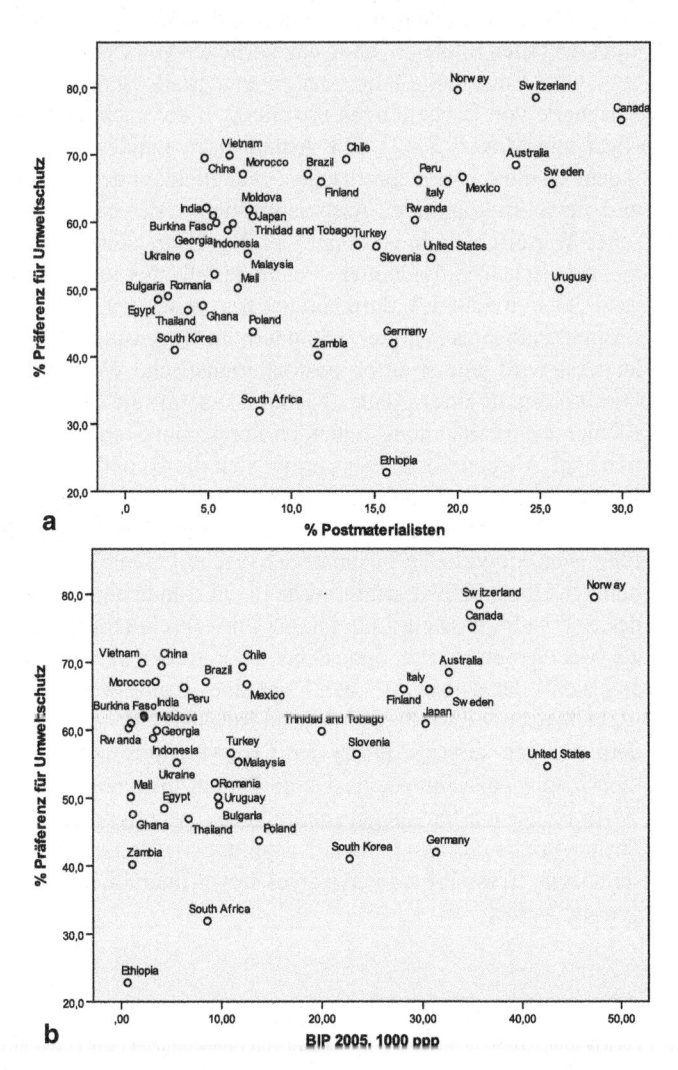

Abb. 2 Weltweite Präferenz für Umweltschutz, Postmaterialismus und nationaler Wohlstand (40 Länder; Daten: World Value Survey 2005–2009). **a** Postmaterialismus und Umweltschutz **b** Nationaler Wohlstand und Umweltschutz

zusammenhängen. In der Literatur ist eine kontrovers geführte Debatte über diese Fragen entbrannt, die jedoch nicht zu einer endgültigen Klärung führte (siehe insbes. Franzen und Meyer 2010; Franzen und Vogl 2013; Dunlap und Mertig 1995, 1997; Dunlap und York 2008; Inglehart 1995; Brechin und Kempton 1994, 1997).

Eine mögliche Lösung der Frage, ob Wohlstand oder Postmaterialismus Bedingungen für die Verbreitung von Umwelteinstellungen sein können, wurde schon früh im Rahmen der „Objective Problems – Subjective Values" (OPSV)-Hypothese vorgeschlagen (Brechin 1999; Inglehart 1995). Brechin und Inglehart argumentieren, dass es verschiedene Quellen der Umwelteinstellungen gebe: Individuelle Betroffenheit von Umweltbelastungen in ärmeren Ländern und Postmaterialismus in reicheren Ländern. Zwar wird der theoretische Mechanismus von den Autoren nicht exakt oder handlungstheoretisch begründet spezifiziert, die Hypothese kann jedoch als Grundlage genommen und handlungstheoretisch als Cross-Pressure gefasst werden. In diesem Sinne lässt sich argumentieren, dass eine postmaterialistische Wertebasis in einer neutralen Situation, ohne das Vorliegen von Cross-Pressures, kausal zu umweltbewussten Einstellung führt. Der postmaterialistische Wertekern wird dabei um eine Peripherie von Einstellungen erweitert, zu der auch das Umweltbewusstsein gehört (Best und Mayerl 2013). Die Armut eines Landes agiert nun als Cross-Pressure, indem sie die mentale chronische Zugänglichkeit der Umwelteinstellungen reduziert und sie so im kognitiven Assoziationsnetzwerk von Akteuren von postmaterialistischen Wertorientierungen trennt – es liegt dann keine ausreichende Passung (Match) mehr zwischen individuellem Postmaterialismus und der Handlungssituation während des individuellen Entscheidungsprozesses vor. Dies bedeutet zwar nicht, dass Postmaterialismus in ärmeren Ländern im Gegensatz zum Umweltbewusstsein steht, letzteres wird jedoch durch postmaterialistische Werte nicht automatisch aktiviert. Der Wohlstand eines Landes beeinflusst somit die Definition der Situation und die Elemente eines handlungsleitenden Frames im Sinne des Modells der Frame Selektion (vgl. Abschn. 2). Hieraus ergibt sich die Hypothese eines variablenspezifischen Interaktionseffektes zwischen nationalem Wohlstand und individuellen postmaterialistischen Wertorientierungen in ihrer Wirkung auf Umwelteinstellungen.[3] Demnach führt eine individuelle postmaterialistische Orientierung vor allem dann zu einem höheren Umweltbewusstsein, wenn die Person in einem ökonomischen Kontext lebt, der es erlaubt, dass ein Individuum Umweltschutz gegenüber Wirtschaftswachstum als wichtiger einschätzt, ohne dabei unter großen ökonomischen oder sozialen Druck angesichts der wirtschaftlichen Lage eines Landes zu geraten. Dies ist insbesondere in reichen, entwickelten und postindustriellen Ökonomien der Fall. In ärmeren Ländern dagegen kann die durch den Cross-Pressure ausgelöste Dissonanz und Reflexion häufig dazu führen, dass eine Person trotz postmaterialistischer Orientierung Wirtschaftswachstum gegebenenfalls als wichtiger einschätzt als Umweltschutz. Postmaterialismus und Umwelteinstellungen wären entkoppelt. Statistisch kann dieser soziale Cross-Pressure als Cross-Level-Interaktion in einem Mehrebenenmodell getestet werden.

---

[3] Wir wenden das handlungstheoretische Modell der Frame-Selektion hier also nicht direkt auf Handlungsentscheidungen, sondern auf die Erklärung von Einstellungen oder Präferenzen an.

Abb. 3 Analysemodell zur Erklärung von individueller Präferenz für Umweltschutz

Makro
- Makro-Kontrollvariablen
- Nationales Wirtschaftswachstum
- Nationaler Wohlstand

Cross-Pressure

Mikro
- Individueller Postmaterialismus
- Wahrg. Umweltbelastung
- Mikro-Kontrollvariablen

Präferenz für Umweltschutz

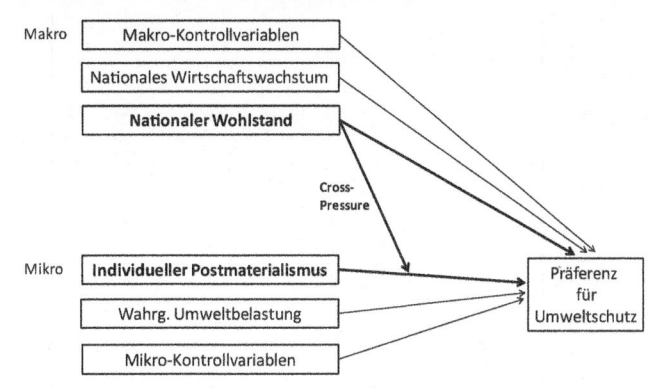

Tab. 1 Deskriptive Statistiken der Variablen im Modell

Variable	Range	Mittelwert	SD
Präferenz für Umweltschutz (AV)	{0; 1}	0,56	0,50
OECD	{0; 1}	0,35	0,48
BIP Wachstum (10 J)	[−52,28; 106,51]	0	35,79
BIP/p (1000 ppp) (BIP)	[−13,02; 33,65]	0	13,00
Wahrgenommene lokale Luftverschmutzung	[0; 3]	1,89	1,13
Postmaterialist (PM)	{0; 1}	0,12	0,32
Alter (10 J)	[1,5; 9,7]	4,15	1,64
Geschlecht (weiblich)	{0; 1}	0,51	0,50
Relatives Einkommen	[1; 10]	4,69	2,30
Höherer sek. Schulabschluss	{0; 1}	0,37	0,48

Abbildung 3 zeigt das zu schätzende Mehrebenenmodell. Als Datensatz dient der World Values Survey 2005–2009. In das empirische Modell gehen 40 Länder aus allen Kontinenten ein, zu denen aus der Datenbank *World Development Indicators* (World Bank 2011) zusätzliche Makrovariablen zugespielt wurden. Umweltbewusstsein wird operationalisiert als dichotomes Maß einer Ranking-Frage, welches gesellschaftliche Ziel höher eingeschätzt wird: ökonomisches Wachstum versus Umweltschutz. Aufgrund der binären abhängigen Variablen „Präferenz für Umweltschutz" schätzen wir eine binär-logistische Mehrebenenanalyse. Als Makrovariablen (Z) gehen das Bruttoinlandprodukt (BIP/Kopf in 1000 ppp), das BIP-Wirtschaftswachstum in den letzten 10 Jahren und die OECD-Mitgliedschaft (0/1) in das Modell ein. Als Individualvariablen (X) verwenden wir Postmaterialismus (basierend auf der klassischen 4-Item-Ranking-Skala; dichotom 0/1; der Code 1 bedeutet dabei „reiner Postmaterialist"), lokale Umweltprobleme (4-Punkte Ratingskala), und soziodemographische Kontrollvariablen (Alter, Bildungsabschluss, Geschlecht und subjektiv wahrgenommenes relatives Einkommen auf einer 10-Punkte Rating-Skala). Tabelle 1 stellt deskriptive Statistiken der Variablen zusammen.

In Tab. 2 werden insgesamt fünf Modellschätzungen vorgestellt. Das Nullmodell (M0) dient lediglich dem Test, ob die Intercepts signifikant zwischen den Kontexten, im vorliegenden Beispiel also Länder, variieren und damit ein Random-Intercept-Modell angebracht ist. Dies ist hier der Fall, wie man an der Varianz des Intercepts erkennen kann. Das Mikromodell (M1) zeigt die Ergebnisse, wenn ausschließlich

Tab. 2 Ergebnisse der Mehrebenenanalyse von Präferenz für Umweltschutz

	M0 (Null-modell) b	se	M1 (Mikro-modell) B	se	M2 (Mehrebenenmodell) b	se	M3 (Cross-Level-Interaktion) b	se	M4 (Country Fixed-Effects) b	se
Makro-Prädiktoren										
OECD					−0,116	(0,237)	−0,112	(0,237)		
BIP Wachstum (10 J)					0,005*	(0,002)	0,004*	(0,002)		
BIP/p (1000 ppp) (BIP)					0,021*	(0,009)	0,020*	(0,009)		
Mikro-Prädiktoren										
Wahrgenommene lokale Luftverschmutzung			0,083***	(0,010)	0,084***	(0,010)	0,084***	(0,010)	0,084***	(0,010)
Postmaterialist (PM)			0,353***	(0,070)	0,353***	(0,070)	0,322***	(0,057)	0,321***	(0,055)
Alter (10 J)			0,139***	(0,032)	0,138***	(0,032)	0,137***	(0,032)	0,136***	(0,032)
Alter²			−0,016***	(0,003)	−0,016***	(0,003)	−0,016***	(0,003)	−0,016***	(0,003)
Geschlecht (weiblich)			0,038	(0,020)	0,038	(0,020)	0,038	(0,020)	0,038	(0,020)
Relatives Einkommen			0,017***	(0,005)	0,017***	(0,005)	0,017***	(0,005)	0,017***	(0,005)
Höherer sek. Schulabschluss			0,267***	(0,023)	0,266***	(0,023)	0,266***	(0,023)	0,266***	(0,023)
Cross-Level-Interaktion										
Interaktion BIP × PM							0,018***	(0,004)	0,017***	(0,004)
Intercept	0,329***	(0,081)	−0,357**	(0,112)	−0,323*	(0,137)	−0,322*	(0,137)	−0,099	(0,125)
Var(PM)			0,141***	(0,045)	0,140***	(0,045)	0,073***	(0,031)	0,065***	(0,029)
Var(Intercept)	0,263***	(0,059)	0,246***	(0,055)	0,195***	(0,044)	0,195***	(0,044)		
N	45656		45656		45656		45656		4565610	
AIC/N	1305		1294		1294		1294		1292	
LL	−29800,35		−29538,19		−29533,49		−29526,48		−29437,1210	

*** $p<0,001$; ** $p<0,01$; * $p<0,05$ (Bemerkung: Länder-Dummies in M4 nicht abgedruckt)

Abb. 4 Durchschnittlicher marginaler Effekt des Postmaterialismus auf die Präferenz für Umweltschutz in Abhängigkeit vom nationalen Wohlstand (BIP)

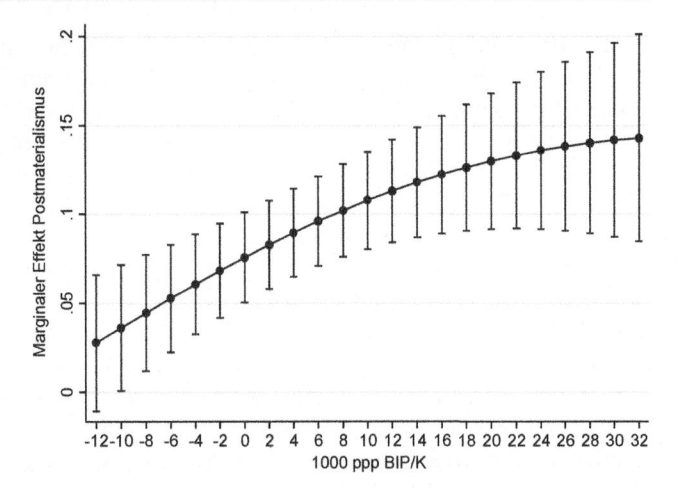

X-Prädiktoren berücksichtigt werden. In diesem Modell werden zusätzlich random Slopes für Postmaterialismus zugelassen. Inhaltlich zeigt sich, dass individueller Postmaterialismus einen positiven, statistisch signifikanten Effekt auf die Präferenz für Umweltschutz vor Wirtschaftswachstum ausübt. Postmaterialisten haben im Durchschnitt ein höheres Umweltbewusstsein als Nicht-Postmaterialisten. Ein Blick auf die Varianzen der random Slopes zeigt jedoch, dass der Effekt von Postmaterialismus signifikant zwischen den Ländern variiert. Das Mehrebenenmodell (M2) fügt diesem Modell Variablen der Makroebene hinzu, sodass sich ein Random-Intercept-Random-Slope Modell mit Level-2 Prädiktoren ergibt. In diesem Modell geht von den Makrovariablen „Nationaler Wohlstand" und in geringerem Umfang auch von „Wirtschaftswachstum" ein signifikanter positiver Effekt auf die Umweltschutzpräferenz aus. Das Umweltbewusstsein ist demnach in reicheren Ländern und in Ländern mit höherem Wachstum stärker ausgeprägt. Die Effekte der Mikrovariablen bleiben unverändert.

Diese Modelle geben jedoch noch keine Hinweise auf die zentrale Frage dieses Artikels nach dem Cross-Pressure im Sinne einer Abhängigkeit des Postmaterialismus-Effektes vom Reichtum eines Landes. Um die zugehörige Hypothese zu prüfen, fügen wir in M3 einen multiplikativen Term hinzu und modellieren eine Cross-Level-Interaktion von BIP und Postmaterialismus. Modell 3 zeigt nun, dass die Interaktion von Postmaterialismus und nationalem Wohlstand statistisch signifikant mit positivem Vorzeichen ist. Das heißt, wie theoretisch mit der OPSV-Hypothese erwartet: In sozialen Kontexten mit hohem ökonomischem Wohlstand ist es für ein Individuum deutlich leichter, postmaterialistische Wertorientierungen in Umweltschutzpräferenzen umzusetzen im Vergleich zu Kontexten mit niedrigem ökonomischem Wohlstand. Abbildung 4 stellt den Interaktionseffekt grafisch dar. Man sieht an den durchschnittlichen marginalen Effekten (vgl. Best und Wolf 2012), dass in reichen Ländern die Wahrscheinlichkeit, eine Präferenz für Umweltschutz vor Wirtschaftswachstum zu haben, bei Postmaterialisten um knapp 15 Prozentpunkte höher ist als bei Nicht-Postmaterialisten. In extrem armen Ländern hingegen gibt es keinen statistisch signifikanten Effekt mehr, und auch substanziell ist er mit unter 5 Prozentpunkten vergleichsweise wenig bedeutsam.

Ein Blick auf die Varianz des random Slope zeigt, dass die Cross-Level-Interaktion ungefähr die Hälfte der Länderunterschiede im Zusammenhang zwischen Postmaterialismus und der Präferenz für Umweltschutz ausmacht.

Im letzten Modell (M4) führen wir statt der inhaltlichen Kontextvariablen Länder-Dummies ein. Hierdurch ergibt sich ein Country-Fixed-Effect-Modell, in dem *alle* Länderunterschiede kontrolliert sind. Diese Fixed-Effects-Modellierung führt zu einem Modell, in dem die Koeffizienten nicht mehr durch unbeobachtete Heterogenität auf Länderebene verzerrt werden können. Diese Kontrolle ist umso wichtiger, da die Zahl der Einheiten auf der Makroebene recht gering ist und hier Ergebnisse durch Endogenität und Fehlspezifikationen der Modelle leicht verzerrt werden können. Im Fixed-Effects-Modell kann die Cross-Level-Interaktion hingegen unverzerrt identifiziert werden. Auch in M4 ist die Interaktion statistisch signifikant und positiv.[4]

Zusammengefasst haben wir in diesem Abschnitt die „Objective Problems, Subjective Values"-Hypothese theoretisch als ein Cross-Pressure zwischen nationalem Wohlstand als Handlungsbedingung der Kontextebene und individuellen Werthaltungen und Umwelteinstellungen aufgefasst. Dieser Cross-Pressure-Effekt wurde mit einer Mehrebenenregression mit random Slopes, einer Cross-Level-Interaktion zwischen Postmaterialismus und dem BIP und Country-Fixed-Effects modelliert. Wir konnten zeigen, dass in der Tat eine Interaktion zwischen den beiden Konstrukten existiert; selbst im restriktiven Fixed-Effects-Modell. Der Zusammenhang zwischen Umweltbewusstsein und postmaterialistischen Werten ist also in der Tat kontextabhängig: Während in reichen Ländern die beiden Konstrukte ein integriertes Wertecluster bilden, sind Umwelteinstellungen und postmaterialistische Werte in ärmeren Ländern voneinander getrennt.

5 Zusammenfassung und Fazit

Ziel dieses Beitrags ist es, das von Lazarsfeld und Kollegen (1944) in die politische Soziologie eingeführte Konzept der Cross-Pressures theoretisch genauer zu bestimmen und angemessene Spezifikationen in statistischen Modellen zu diskutieren. Auf der allgemeinsten Ebene versteht man unter Cross-Pressures das Phänomen von sozialem Druck auf individuelle Akteure, der durch Heterogenität im sozialen Umfeld und insbesondere in Form widersprüchlicher sozialer Erwartungen entsteht. Vor allem in der politischen Soziologie, aber auch in der Netzwerkanalyse wird das Konzept der Cross-Pressures intensiv verwendet, um etwa den Einfluss konfligierender politischer Positionen im sozialen Umfeld auf Wahlverhalten und politische Partizipation zu untersuchen (z. B. Huckfeld und Sprague 1995; Mutz 2002).

Zunächst verorten wir Cross-Pressures im Makro-Mikro-Makro-Modell des struktur-individualistischen Erklärungsparadigmas und argumentieren, dass Cross-Pressures eine spezifische Klasse des Makro-Mikro-Links und der „sozialen Definition der

---

[4] Zusätzlich wurde das Modell mit einigen Modifikationen erneut geschätzt. Die besagte Cross-Level-Interaktion blieb stets in Richtung und Größenordnung unverändert und statistisch signifikant: Ein Modell mit Postmaterialisten-Anteil als Z-Variable (nicht signifikant), Cross-Level-Interaktion aus Wirtschaftswachstum und Postmaterialismus (nicht signifikant), Cross-Level-Interaktion aus nationalem Wohlstand und wahrgenommener lokaler Luftverschmutzung (nicht signifikant).

Situation" sind, die die „subjektive Definition der Situation" maßgeblich prägt. Auch eine genauere handlungstheoretische Spezifikation auf Basis von Dual-Process-Modellen (Chaiken und Trope 1999) und dem Modell der Frame-Selektion (Esser 2001; Kroneberg 2007) verweist auf die Bedeutung der Situationsdefinition: Cross-Pressures aus dem sozialen Umfeld eines Akteurs erzeugen Unsicherheit und Irritationen, was zu einer schlechteren Passung des Handlungsframes führt und dadurch ein überlegtes Reflektieren und letztlich ein Reframing wahrscheinlicher macht. Wir argumentieren, dass Cross-Pressures auf zwei Arten wirksam werden können: Erstens auf additive Weise und zweitens als multiplikativ wirkende Moderatorbedingung, wobei der multiplikative Fall theoretisch stärker fundiert werden kann. Die additive Wirkung basiert auf der Annahme, dass Cross-Pressures als gesonderte Terme in die individuelle Nutzenfunktion eingehen und Akteure die drohenden Kosten ihres potenziell nonkonformen Handelns zu vermeiden suchen. Die multiplikative Wirkung kann hingegen, wie skizziert, mit Hilfe des Modells der Frame-Selektion theoretisch fundiert werden, indem Cross-Pressures zentrale Faktoren des Framings beeinflussen und somit als moderierende Bedingung beeinflussen, ob individuelle Orientierungen unbewusst und automatisch die nachfolgenden kognitiven Entscheidungsprozesse leiten oder nicht.

Methodisch folgt aus dieser handlungstheoretischen Spezifikation, dass sich insbesondere Mehrebenenmodelle mit spezifizierten Cross-Level-Interaktionen zur empirisch-statistischen Analyse von Cross-Pressures eignen. Dies gilt insofern, als dass wir in diesem Beitrag Cross-Pressures als Konflikte zwischen zwei unterschiedlichen Aggregatsebenen thematisieren. Wie gesehen eignen sich sowohl Random-Slope-Modelle als auch Fixed-Effects-Modelle für die angemessene Modellierung dieses Typs von Cross-Pressures durch Cross-Level-Interaktionen.

Schließlich haben wir am Beispiel des Zusammenhangs zwischen individuellen postmaterialistischen Wertorientierungen und umweltbezogenen Präferenzen im internationalen Vergleich eine Anwendung der Mehrebenenanalyse zum statistischen Nachweis von Cross-Pressures demonstriert. Im Zuge der „Objective Problems – SubjectiveValuse"-Hypothese nach Brechin (1999) und Inglehart (1995) wurde argumentiert, dass der nationale Wohlstand als Kontexteigenschaft eine moderierende Wirkung auf den Zusammenhang zwischen individuellen Wertorientierungen und umweltbezogenen Präferenzen ausübt. Je ärmer demnach ein Land ist, in dem sich ein Akteur aufhält, desto schwächer ist die Wirkung postmaterialistischer Orientierungen auf Umweltbewusstsein. Der nationale Wohlstand wirkt demzufolge als Cross-Pressure auf den individuellen Entscheidungsprozess, indem ein bestimmter Zusammenhang zwischen Werten und Einstellungen unterdrückt werden kann (oder im Umkehrschluss erst wirksam wird, wenn der Cross-Pressure wegfällt). Für Personen aus armen Nationen wird dabei, so die Annahme, der soziale Druck, sich unabhängig von individuellen postmaterialistischen Werten zugunsten von ökonomischen und gegen ökologische Präferenzen zu stellen, so groß, dass die postmaterialistische Orientierung nicht mehr in Umweltbewusstsein mündet. Als theoretischer Unterbau dieses Wirkungszusammenhangs wird argumentiert, dass in armen Nationen keine Passung (Match) mehr zwischen individuellen Werteorientierungen (Postmaterialismus) und der Einstellung zum Umweltschutz (Umweltschutz vs. Wirtschaftswachstum) besteht und dadurch der automatische Framing-Prozess gestört oder unterbrochen wird.

Zusammengefasst eignen sich Mehrebenenmodelle aus zweierlei Gründen besonders gut für soziologische Kontextanalysen: Sie ermöglichen die adäquate Umsetzung komplexer theoretischer Modelle und sie erlauben die direkte Spezifikation der Beziehungsgeflechte zwischen einzelnen Aggregatebenen. Damit kann die Mehrebenenanalyse insbesondere zur theorieadäquaten Umsetzung der Makro-Mikro-Verbindung im struktur-individualistischen Modell einer soziologischen Erklärung in empirisch-statistischen Analysen beitragen.

Literatur

Aars, Jacob, Dag Arne Christensen und Tor Midtbo. 2010. *Diversity, uniformity and urban political participation*. Stein Rokkan Centre for Social Studies Working Paper Series 2010 (4).
Beck, Ulrich. 1986. *Risikogesellschaft auf dem Weg in eine andere Moderne*. Frankfurt a. M.: Suhrkamp.
Belanger, Paul, und Munroe Eagles. 2007. Partisan cross-pressure and voter turnout: The influence of micro and macro environments. *Social Science Quarterly* 88:850–867.
Berelson, Bernard R., Paul F. Lazarsfeld und William N. McPhee. 1954. *Voting: A study of opinion formation in a presidential campaign*. Chicago: Chicago University Press.
Berry, William D., Jacqueline H. R. DeMerrit und Justin Esarey. 2010. Testing for interaction in binary logit and probit models: Is a product term essential? *American Journal of Political Science* 54:248–266.
Best, Henning, und Christof Wolf. 2010. Logistische Regression. In *Handbuch der sozialwissenschaftlichen Datenanalyse*, Hrsg. Christof Wolf und Henning Best, 827–854. Wiesbaden: VS Verlag für Sozialwissenschaften.
Best, Henning, und Christof Wolf. 2012. Modellvergleich und Ergebnisinterpretation in Logit- und Probit-Regressionen. *Kölner Zeitschrift für Soziologie und Sozialpsychologie* 64:377–395.
Best, Henning, und Clemens Kroneberg. 2012. Die Low-Cost-Hypothese. Theoretische Grundlagen und empirische Implikationen. *Kölner Zeitschrift für Soziologie und Sozialpsychologie* 64:535–561.
Best, Henning, und Jochen Mayerl. 2013. Values, beliefs, attitudes: An empirical study on the structure of environmental concern and recycling participation. *Social Science Quarterly* 94:691–714.
Brader, Ted, Joshua A Tucker und Andrew Therriault. 2013. Cross pressure scores: An individual-level measure of cumulative partisan pressures arising from social group memberships. *Political Behavior* (online advance access).
Brechin, Steven. 1999. Objective problems, subjective values, and global environmentalism: Evaluating the postmaterialist argument and challenging a new explanation. *Social Science Quarterly* 80:793–809.
Brechin, Steven R., und Willett Kempton. 1994. Global environmentalism: A challenge to the postmaterialism thesis? *Social Science Quarterly* 2:245–269.
Brechin, Steven R., und Willett Kempton. 1997. Beyond postmaterialist values: National versus individual explanations of global environmentalism. *Social Science Quarterly* 78:16–20.
Chaiken, Shelly, und Yaacov Trope. Hrsg. 1999. *Dual-process theories in social psychology*. New York: Guilford Press.
Dunlap, Riley E., und Angela G. Mertig. 1995. Global concern for the environment: Is affluence a prerequisite? *Journal of Social Issues* 51:121–137.
Dunlap, Riley E, und Angela G. Mertig. 1997. Global environmental concern: An anomaly for postmaterialism. *Social Science Quarterly* 78:24–29.
Dunlap, Riley E, und Richard York. 2008. The globalization of environmental concern and the limits of the postmaterialist values explanation: Evidence from four multinational surveys. *Sociological Quarterly* 49:529–563.
Eagly, Alice H., und Shelly Chaiken. 1998. Attitude structure and function. In *The Handbook of Social Psychology*, vol. I, Hrsg. Daniel T. Gilbert, Susan T. Fiske und Gardner Lindzey, 269–322. Oxford: Oxford University Press.

Esser, Hartmut. 1996. Die Definition der Situation. *Kölner Zeitschrift für Soziologie und Sozialpsychologie* 48:1–34.
Esser, Hartmut. 2001. *Soziologie. Spezielle Grundlagen, Band 6: Sinn und Kultur.* Frankfurt a. M.: Campus.
Fazio, Russell H. 1986. How do attitudes guide behavior? In *The handbook of motivation and cognition: Foundations of social behavior*, Hrsg. Richard M. Sorrentino und Edward T. Higgins, 204–243. New York: Guildford Press.
Fazio, Russell H. 1990. Multiple processes by which attitudes guide behaviour: The MODE-model as an integrative framework. In *Advances in experimental social psychology*, Hrsg. Mark P. Zanna, 75–109. San Diego: Academic Press.
Finseraas, Henning. 2008. Immigration and preferences for redistribution: An empirical analysis of European survey data. *Comparative European Politics* 6:407–431.
Franzen, Axel, und Dominikus Vogl. 2013. *Two decades of measuring environmental attitudes: A comparative analysis of 33 countries. Global Environmental Change.* Social Science Research Network (published online).
Franzen, Axel, und Reto Meyer. 2010. Environmental attitudes in cross-national perspective: A multilevel analysis of the ISSP 1993 and 2000. *European Sociological Review* 26:219–234.
Hadler, Markus. 2002. Wählen als Gruppenerfahrung? Ein Test des wahlsoziologischen Ansatzes von Paul F. Lazarsfeld. *Österreichische Zeitschrift für Soziologie* 27:53–77.
Hox, Joop J. 2010. *Multilevel analysis. Techniques and applications.* London: Routledge.
Huckfeld, Robert, und John Sprague. 1995. *Citizens, politics, and social communication: Information and influence in an election campaign.* New York: Cambridge University Press.
Inglehart, Ronald. 1995. Public support for environmental protection: Objective problems and subjective values in 43 societies. *Political Science and Politics* 28:57–71.
Kroneberg, Clemens. 2005. Die Definition der Situation und die variable Rationalität der Akteure. Ein allgemeines Modell des Handelns. *Zeitschrift für Soziologie* 34:344–363.
Kroneberg, Clemens. 2007. Wertrationalität und das Modell der Frame-Selektion. *Kölner Zeitschrift für Soziologie und Sozialpsychologie* 59:215–239.
Kroneberg, Clemens. 2011. *Die Erklärung sozialen Handelns. Grundlagen und Anwendung einer integrativen Theorie.* Wiesbaden: VS Verlag für Sozialwissenschaften.
Langer, Wolfgang. 2010. Mehrebenenanalyse mit Querschnittsdaten. In *Handbuch der sozialwissenschaftlichen Datenanalyse*, Hrsg. Christof Wolf und Henning Best, 741–774. Wiesbaden: VS Verlag für Sozialwissenschaften.
Lazarsfeld, Paul F., Bernard R. Berelson und Hazel Gaudet. 1944. *The people's choice – How the voter makes up his mind in a presidential campaign.* New York: Columbia University Press.
Lup, Oana. 2011. *The relevance of micro-social contexts for individual political engagement.* A comparative analysis. Budapest: Dissertation Central European University.
Marsden, Peter V. 1988. Homogeneity in confiding relations. *Social Networks* 10:57–76.
Marsden, Peter V. 1992. Network diversity, substructures and opportunities for contact. In *Structures of power and constraint: Papers in honor of Peter Blau*, Hrsg. Craig Calhoun, Marshall Meyer und Richard S. Scott, 397–410. New York: Cambridge University Press.
Mayerl, Jochen. 2009. *Kognitive Grundlagen sozialen Verhaltens. Framing, Einstellungen und Rationalität.* Wiesbaden: VS Verlag für Sozialwissenschaften.
Mayerl, Jochen. 2010. Die Low-Cost-Hypothese ist nicht genug. Eine Empirische Überprüfung von Varianten des Modells der Frame-Selektion zur besseren Vorhersage der Einflussstärke von Einstellungen auf Verhalten. *Zeitschrift für Soziologie* 39:38–59.
McClurg, Scott D. 2006. The electoral relevance of political talk: Examining disagreement and expertise effects in social networks on political participation. *American Journal of Political Science* 50:737–754.
McPherson, Miller, Lynn Smith-Lovin und James M Cook. 2001. Birds of a feather: Homophily in social networks. *Annual Review of Sociology* 27:415–444.
Mutz, Diana C. 2002. The consequences of cross-cutting networks for political participation. *American Journal of Political Science* 46:838–855.
Nagler, Jonathan. 1994. Scobit: An alternative estimator to logit and probit. *American Journal of Political Science* 38:230–255.
Nir, Lilach. 2005. Ambivalent social networks and their consequences for participation. *International Journal of Public Opinion Research* 17:422–442.
Petty, Richard E., und John T. Cacioppo. 1986. *Communication and persuasion: Central and peripheral routes to attitude change.* New York: Springer.

Preidel, Caroline, und Valentina Findling. 2011. Cross-Pressures und politische Partizipation in Deutschland. *Konstanzer Journal für Politik und Verwaltung* 1:38–51.
Snijders, Tom A. B., und Roel J. Bosker. 1999. *Multilevel analysis. An introduction to basic and advanced multilevel modeling*. London: Sage.
Soler, Joan Barcelo. 2012. *Contextual effects on subjective national identity and nationalist vote in Catalonia*. ICPS, Working Paper Series 311.
Sykes, Gresham M., und David Matza. 1957. Techniques of neutralization – a theory of delinquency. *American Sociological Review* 22:664–670.
Therriault, Andrew, Joshua A. Tucker und Ted Brader. 2011. Cross-pressures and political participation. http://opensiuc.lib.siu.edu/pnconfs_2011 (zugegriffen: 18.6.2014).
Völkl, Kerstin. 2007. Nichtwahl- die Alternative für parteilich Ungebundene am Wahltag? In *Der gesamtdeutsche Wähler*, Hrsg. Hans Rattinger, Oscar W. Gabriel und Jürgen W. Falter, 15–35. Baden Baden: Nomos.
Wilson, Tracy. 2012. *Cross-pressured voters: Reconciling ideologies in European parliament elections*. ELECDEM closing conference, „Advancing Electoral Research". Florence: European University Institute.
World Bank. 2011. World development indicators. http://data.worldbank.org/data-catalog/world-development-indicators (zugegriffen: 18.6.2014).

Jochen Mayerl, 1974, Jun.-Prof. Dr. rer. pol., Juniorprofessor für Methoden der empirischen Sozialforschung am Fachbereich Sozialwissenschaften der Technischen Universität Kaiserslautern. Forschungsgebiete: Surveyforschung, Strukturgleichungsmodellierung, Einstellungs-Verhaltens-Forschung, Framing. Veröffentlichungen: Strukturgleichungsmodellierung: Ein Ratgeber für die Praxis. Wiesbaden 2014 (mit D. Urban); Die Low-Cost-Hypothese ist nicht genug. Empirische Überprüfung von Varianten des Modells der Frame-Selektion zur besseren Vorhersage der Einflussstärke von Einstellungen auf Verhalten. Zeitschrift für Soziologie 39, 2010; Antwortlatenzzeiten in der survey-basierten Verhaltensforschung. Kölner Zeitschrift für Soziologie und Sozialpsychologie 59, 2007 (mit D. Urban).

Henning Best, 1975, Prof. Dr., Institut für Politikwissenschaft und Soziologie, Julius-Maximilians-Universität Würzburg. Forschungsinteressen: Handlungs- und Entscheidungstheorie, Umweltsoziologie, quantitative Methoden. Zuletzt veröffentlicht: Values, beliefs, attitudes: an empirical study on the structure of enviornmental concern and recycling participation. Social Science Quarterly 94, 2013 (mit J. Mayerl); Die Low-Cost-Hypothese: Theoretische Grundlagen und empirische Implikationen. Kölner Zeitschrift für Soziologie und Sozialpsychologie 64, 2012 (mit C. Kroneberg); Modellvergleich und Ergebnisinterpretation in Logit- und Probit-Regressionen. Kölner Zeitschrift für Soziologie und Sozialpsychologie 64, 2012 (mit C. Wolf); Handbuch der Sozialwissenschaftlichen Datenanalyse. Wiesbaden 2010 (hrsg. mit C. Wolf).

Das Aggregationsproblem bei Mikro-Makro-Erklärungen

Karl-Dieter Opp

© Springer Fachmedien Wiesbaden 2014

Zusammenfassung In diesem Aufsatz steht eine Komponente des Mikro-Makro-Erklärungsmodells (d. h. des individualistischen Forschungsprogramms) im Mittelpunkt der Überlegungen: Es geht um die Frage, ob und gegebenenfalls wie Kollektivmerkmale (oder, gleichbedeutend, Makrovariablen) durch Eigenschaften von Individuen (d. h. Mikroeigenschaften) gebildet werden können. Dies ist das Aggregationsproblem. Nach einer kurzen Beschreibung der Vorgehensweise bei Mikro-Makro-Erklärungen und ihrer möglichen Probleme wird der Stand der Forschung zum Aggregationsproblem skizziert. Sodann werden zwei Arten von Aggregationen behandelt: analytische Aggregationen (d. h. die Mikro-zu-Makro-Beziehung ist logischer Art) und empirische Aggregationen (d. h. die Mikro-zu-Makro-Beziehung ist empirischer Art). Es wird weiter diskutiert, ob es Kollektivmerkmale gibt, die nicht individualistisch rekonstruiert werden können. Da viele kollektive Sachverhalte unbeabsichtigte Ergebnisse individuellen Handelns sind, fragt es sich, ob Aggregationen oder die Struktur von Mikro-Makro-Erklärungen verschieden sind, wenn die Folgen individuellen Handelns beabsichtigt oder unbeabsichtigt sind. Diese Frage wird verneint. In einem letzten Teil wird argumentiert, dass es zwar emergente Eigenschaften gibt, dass diese jedoch nicht gegen die Möglichkeit von Mikro-Makro-Erklärungen sprechen. In diesem Zusammenhang wird gefragt, ob ontologische Analysen (d. h. Unterscheidungen verschiedener „Seinsebenen") für die Lösung theoretischer Probleme in den Sozialwissenschaften und auch für das Aggregationsproblem hilfreich sind. Diese Frage wird verneint.

K.-D. Opp (✉)
Institut für Soziologie, Universität Leipzig,
Sulkyweg 22, 22159 Hamburg, Deutschland
E-Mail: opp@sozio.uni-leipzig.de

Schlüsselwörter Mikro-Makro-Erklärungen · Aggregationsprobleme · Unbeabsichtigte Konsequenzen

The Aggregation Problem in Micro-Macro Explanations

Abstract The present paper discusses a component of the micro-macro explanatory model (i.e. the individualistic research program): the question is whether and, if so, how collective properties (or, equivalently, macro variables) can be constructed by properties of individuals (i.e. by aggregating micro variables). This is the aggregation problem. After sketching the procedure of micro-macro explanations and its possible problems the state of research in regard to the aggregation problem is described. Then two kinds of aggregation are analyzed in detail: analytical aggregations (i.e. the micro-to-macro relationship is a logical one) and empirical aggregations (i.e. the micro-to-macro relationship is empirical). It is further discussed whether there exist collective properties that cannot be reconstructed individualistically. Many collective properties emerge by the unintended consequences of individual action. It is argued that the structure of micro-macro explanations do not differ if these consequences are intended or unintended. In the final part it is claimed that there are emergent properties but that they do not invalidate methodological individualism. In this context it is argued that "ontological" arguments are not helpful for solving explanatory problems of the social sciences.

Keywords Micro-macro explanations · Aggregation · Unintended consequences

1 Einführung

Im Mittelpunkt dieses Aufsatzes steht die Beziehung zwischen kollektiven und individuellen Merkmalen. Bei der „Aggregation" individueller Merkmale geht es darum, wie kollektive Merkmale (z. B. Kohäsion oder Kriminalitätsrate) auf der Grundlage individueller Merkmale gebildet werden können. Dies wird als „Aggregationsproblem" bezeichnet. Nach Coleman (1990, S. 6) ist dieses das Hauptproblem von Mikro-Makro-Erklärungen. Im Folgenden wird zuerst gezeigt, in welcher Weise das Aggregationsproblem mit dem individualistischen Forschungsprogramm zusammenhängt und welche Probleme bei Erklärungen im Rahmen dieses Programms, d. h. bei Mikro-Makro-Erklärungen, auftreten können. Nach einer Darstellung des Standes der Forschung zum Aggregationsproblem werden zwei Arten der Aggregation behandelt: analytische und empirische Aggregationen. Weitere Fragen, die im Folgenden diskutiert werden, sind: Können alle Kollektivmerkmale durch Individualmerkmale aggregiert werden? Unterscheiden sich Aggregationen beabsichtigter und unbeabsichtigter Folgen sozialen Handelns? Schließt die Existenz „emergenter" Eigenschaften Aggregationen aus?

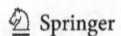

Springer

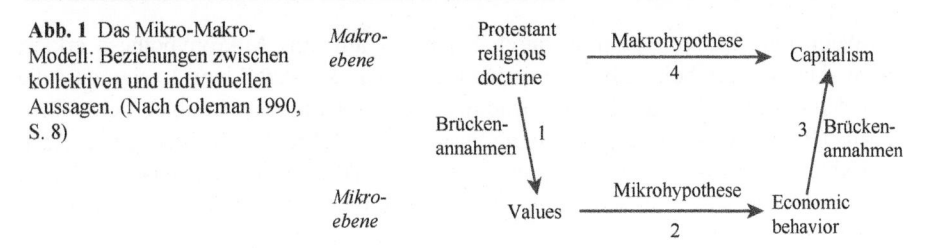

Abb. 1 Das Mikro-Makro-Modell: Beziehungen zwischen kollektiven und individuellen Aussagen. (Nach Coleman 1990, S. 8)

```
Makro-        Protestant           Makrohypothese
ebene         religious         ─────────────────▶  Capitalism
              doctrine                  4
                                                         ▲
              Brücken-    ╲  1                     3  ╱ Brücken-
              annahmen     ╲                         ╱  annahmen
                            ▼
Mikro-                             Mikrohypothese         Economic
ebene                   Values  ─────────────────▶        behavior
                                        2
```

2 Die Vorgehensweise bei Mikro-Makro-Erklärungen

Die grundlegende These des individualistischen Forschungsprogramms[1] ist, dass kollektive Sachverhalte als Ergebnis der Eigenschaften individueller Akteure erklärt werden können. Wir wollen diese Art der Erklärung und die dabei auftretenden Probleme mit dem Standardbeispiel illustrieren: Es geht um die These, dass ein wichtiger Faktor für die Entstehung des Kapitalismus die protestantische Ethik ist. Diese Hypothese Max Webers (Weber 2004) verwendet Coleman zur Illustration des individualistischen Forschungsprogramms (Coleman 1990, S. 8). Abbildung 1 fasst diese Erklärung zusammen. Die Graphik wird auch als „Coleman-Boot" oder „Coleman-Badewanne" bezeichnet.[2]

Erklärt wird eine empirische Beziehung zwischen zwei Makrovariablen: Protestantismus und Kapitalismus. Die Frage ist, warum die protestantische Ethik eine Bedingung für die Entstehung des Kapitalismus ist. Bei dieser Makrohypothese handelt es sich nach Coleman um eine kausale Beziehung, wie Pfeil 4 in Abb. 1 andeutet.

Die Erklärung der Makrohypothese lautet, kurz gesagt, dass die protestantische Ethik bei ihren Anhängern (und vielleicht auch generell bei Mitgliedern einer Gesellschaft) zur Entstehung bestimmter Werte führt (Pfeil 1). Diese Werte beeinflussen das ökonomische Handeln der Individuen (Pfeil 2). Die Beziehung 1 gilt für viele Individuen, sodass auch das ökonomische Handeln einer Vielzahl von Individuen beeinflusst wird. Dieses wiederum erzeugt eine kapitalistische Ordnung (Pfeil 3).[3]

Betrachten wir dieses Erklärungsmodell etwas genauer. Neben der Makrohypothese, die aus einer unabhängigen und einer abhängigen Variablen besteht, ist ein weiterer Bestandteil der Erklärung eine Mikrohypothese, ebenfalls bestehend aus einer unabhängigen und einer abhängigen Variablen. Das Erklärungsmodell in Abb. 1 wird Mikro-Makro-Modell (oder Makro-Mikro-Modell) genannt.

---

[1] Vgl. im deutschen Sprachbereich z. B. Bohnen (2000), Boudon (1980), Esser (1993), Opp (2009, 2011) und Vanberg (1975). Udéhn (2001, 2002) gibt einen informativen Überblick über die Geschichte und die verschiedenen Versionen des individualistischen Forschungsprogramms. Vgl. weiter die Sonderhefte 1 bis 3 (Jg. 35, 2011) des Journal of Mathematical Sociology, die auch als Buch vorliegen (Buskens et al. 2012).

[2] Die Graphik und das Beispiel findet man bereits bei McClelland (1961, S. 47). Vgl. auch Hummell und Opp (1971, S. 15) sowie Hernes (1976).

[3] Colemans Analyse wird von Cherkaoui (2005) vernichtend kritisiert. Er wirft Coleman vor, Weber völlig missverstanden zu haben. Da es im vorliegenden Aufsatz nicht um eine Diskussion der Protestantismusthese, sondern um die Struktur von Mikro-Makro-Erklärungen geht, soll auf die Kritik Cherkaouis nicht eingegangen werden.

Wenn eine Makrohypothese durch Rückgriff auf eine Mikrohypothese erklärt wird, dann werden beide Ebenen miteinander verbunden. Abbildung 1 zeigt, dass die unabhängige Variable der Makroebene mit der unabhängigen Variablen der Mikroebene (Pfeil 1) und dass die abhängige Variable der Makroebene mit der abhängigen Variable der Mikroebene in Beziehung gesetzt wird (Pfeil 3). Inhaltlich bedeutet dies, dass der Protestantismus den Kapitalismus hervorgebracht hat, *weil* die protestantische Ethik individuelle Werte verändert hat (Verbindung der unabhängigen Variablen der Makro- und Mikrohypothese) und weil diese Werte ökonomisches Handeln beeinflusst haben (Mikrohypothese). Dieses Handeln führt dann zur kapitalistischen Ordnung; dies ist die Verbindung der abhängigen Variablen der Mikro- und Makroebene (Pfeil 3). Der Rekurs auf die Mikroebene erklärt also die Makrobeziehung (Pfeil 4).

Diese Verbindungen zwischen Mikro- und Makroebene bezeichnen wir als *Brückenannahmen*. In der Literatur findet man hierfür unterschiedliche Bezeichnungen. Der Ausdruck „Brückenannahmen" erscheint zweckmäßig, da offengelassen wird, welcher Art diese Annahmen sind, d. h. ob sie analytisch oder empirisch sind. Wir werden hierauf noch zu sprechen kommen. Weiter ist der Ausdruck „Brückenannahme" intuitiv einleuchtend, da es sich tatsächlich um die Überbrückung von Mikro- und Makroebene handelt. Will man genauer zum Ausdruck bringen, welche Variablen miteinander verbunden werden, kann man von Makro-zu-Mikro-Annahmen oder Mikro-zu-Makro-Annahmen sprechen.

Mikro-Makro-Erklärungen in der konkreten sozialwissenschaftlichen Forschung sind weitaus komplizierter als das einfache Erklärungsmodell von Abb. 1. Es gibt eine Vielzahl von Variationen dieses Modells. Erstens bestehen Makrohypothesen und die angewendete Mikrotheorie normalerweise nicht nur aus einer einzigen unabhängigen Variablen. Zweitens weisen viele Erklärungen nicht nur eine Mikro- und eine Makroebene, sondern z. B. auch eine Meso-Ebene auf. Drittens wird oft nicht eine Makro*beziehung*, sondern ein einzelnes Makro*explanandum* erklärt, wie z. B. die Veränderung der Kriminalitätsrate in einem Land. Da dieser Artikel nicht Mikro-Makro-Erklärungen generell, sondern nur einen Bestandteil dieser Erklärungen, nämlich das Aggregationsproblem oder Mikro-zu-Makro-Beziehungen, zum Gegenstand hat, soll auf Variationen von Mikro-Makro-Erklärungen nicht eingegangen werden. Es geht vielmehr um die Struktur dieser Erklärungen, dass nämlich Makrohypothesen in der beschriebenen Weise durch Rückgriff auf die Mikroebene erklärt werden und dass dabei das Aggregationsproblem von Bedeutung ist. Um die Vorgehensweise und die Probleme einer Mikro-Makro-Erklärung zu analysieren, ist das vereinfachte Modell ausreichend.

3 Probleme von Mikro-Makro-Erklärungen

Die möglichen Probleme von Mikro-Makro-Erklärungen fasst Abb. 2 zusammen. Diese Probleme sollen nur kurz behandelt werden, da wir uns auf Mikro-zu-Makro-Beziehungen (also auf das Aggregationsproblem) konzentrieren (vgl. zum Folgenden im Einzelnen Opp 2009, 2011).

Abb. 2 Mögliche Probleme einer Mikro-Makro-Erklärung. (Aus: Opp 2009, S. 35)

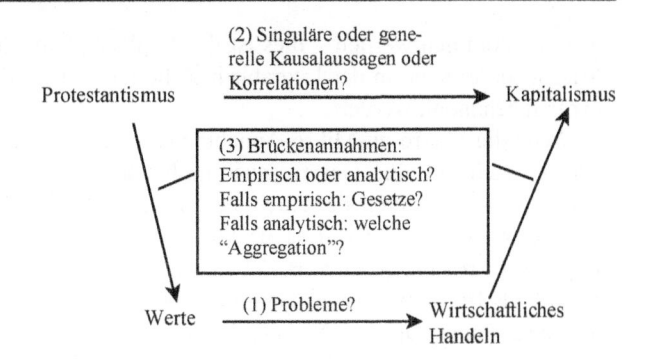

```
                          (2) Singuläre oder gene-
                          relle Kausalaussagen oder
                          Korrelationen?
        Protestantismus ─────────────────────► Kapitalismus
                  \      (3) Brückenannahmen:       ▲
                   \     Empirisch oder analytisch? │
                    \    Falls empirisch: Gesetze?  │
                     \   Falls analytisch: welche   │
                      \  "Aggregation"?             │
                       ▼                            │
                     Werte ──(1) Probleme?──► Wirtschaftliches
                                               Handeln
```

Die Makrohypothese. In den Abb. 1 und 2 ist die Makrohypothese (Pfeil 4 in Abb. 1) eine singuläre Kausalaussage, d. h. eine Kausalaussage, die sich auf ein bestimmtes Raum-Zeitgebiet bezieht. Die Makrohypothese könnte jedoch auch eine generelle Aussage, d. h. ein Gesetz, sein, z. B.: Für alle Gesellschaften gilt: Je größer die Ungleichheit ist, desto wahrscheinlicher gewinnen sozialistische Parteien Wahlen.

Besonders zweifelhaft ist, ob es sich bei der Makroaussage wirklich um eine Kausalaussage handelt. Wenn die Beziehung zwischen Protestantismus und Kapitalismus durch Rückgriff auf die Individualebene erklärt werden kann, dann bedeutet dies, dass eben keine kausale Beziehung auf der Makroebene besteht: Es wird ja behauptet, dass die Beziehung zwischen Protestantismus und Kapitalismus existiert, *weil* Protestantismus zu Werten führt usw. D. h. die Makrobeziehung wird erklärt. „Protestantismus" hat keinen direkten, sondern nur einen indirekten kausalen Effekt auf den Kapitalismus. Der Pfeil zwischen „Protestantismus" und „Kapitalismus" ist also nicht zutreffend: Hier müsste eine (gerade oder geschwungene) Linie gezeichnet werden, die eine bloße Korrelation, d. h. eine nicht-kausale Beziehung, symbolisiert.

Die Mikrohypothese. Vertreter des individualistischen Forschungsprogramms verwenden normalerweise die Theorie rationalen Handelns. Wenn diese auch umstritten ist, so wird sie doch angewendet, weil, so wird argumentiert, gegenwärtig keine der Theorie rationalen Handelns klar überlegene alternative Theorie existiert. Weniger umstritten erscheint eine weite Version der Theorie, in der insbesondere von den Wahrnehmungen der Akteure ausgegangen wird und in der angenommen wird, dass Akteure nicht im objektiven Sinne maximieren, sondern dass sie die aus ihrer Sicht beste Handlung wählen (vgl. zur Diskussion im Einzelnen Opp 1999, 2004).

Die Makro-zu-Mikro-Annahmen. In den Abb. 1 und 2 ist die Beziehung 1 eine singuläre Kausalhypothese: In einem bestimmten Raumzeitgebiet führte der Protestantismus zu bestimmten individuellen Wertorientierungen. Bei solchen singulären Kausalaussagen besteht immer das Problem, welches die Argumente dafür sind, dass nicht andere Faktoren zu dem Explanandum geführt haben. Normalerweise werden Gesetzesaussagen angewendet. So könnte im Beispiel ein Gesetz lauten: Wenn in einer Gesellschaft eine Religion mit bestimmten Wertorientierungen existiert, dann führt dies zur Internalisierung dieser Werte bei den Mitgliedern der Religionsgemeinschaft. Der Protestantismus ist eine solche Religion – dies ist die Anfangsbedingung. Diese führt dann gemäß dem Gesetz dazu, dass die entsprechenden Wertorientierungen übernommen werden – dies ist das Explanandum. Ein Problem bei Makro-zu-Mikro-Erklärungen in der Literatur besteht darin, dass die Gesetzesaussagen selten explizit behandelt werden.

Wenn die Makro-zu-Mikro-Annahme empirischer Art ist, dann könnte es sich im Prinzip auch um eine Gesetzesaussage handeln. Gibt es solche Gesetzesaussagen und, falls ja, wie lauten sie? Auch diese Frage ist in der Literatur ungeklärt.

Es wäre auch denkbar, dass die Makro-zu-Mikro-Beziehungen analytischer (d. h. logischer) Art sind. Wenn z. B. der Einfluss eines Individuums in einer Gruppe definiert ist als 1/Gruppengröße, dann folgt der Einfluss eines Individuums in der Gruppe logisch aus der Gruppengröße und der genannten Definition. So wäre in einer Gruppe von 1000 Mitgliedern der Einfluss eines einzelnen Mitglieds 1/1000; in einer Gruppe von 2 Personen ist der Einfluss einer Person 1/2. Liegt eine analytische Beziehung vor, müsste der Pfeil 1 z. B. durch eine Linie ersetzt werden, die eine analytische Beziehung symbolisiert. Die Unterscheidung zwischen analytischen und empirischen Beziehungen wird selten getroffen, sie ist aber wichtig für die Beurteilung eines Erklärungsarguments. Liegen analytische Beziehungen vor, muss die entsprechende Annahme nicht empirisch überprüft werden. Existieren analytische Beziehungen, dann fragt es sich, welcher Art genau solche Beziehungen sind. Bei empirischen Beziehungen treten andere Probleme auf. So wäre bei singulären Kausalaussagen zu fragen, welche Argumente für die Kausalbehauptung angeführt werden können.

Mikro-zu-Makro-Annahmen: Da diese Gegenstand der folgenden Überlegungen sind, sollen sie hier nicht behandelt werden.

4 Das Aggregationsproblem in der soziologischen Literatur. Zum Stand der Diskussion

Der Pionier des individualistischen Forschungsprogramms in der Soziologie ist George C. Homans mit seinem Aufsatz „Social Behavior as Exchange" (1958). Weder in diesem Aufsatz noch in den beiden Auflagen von „Social Behavior" (Homans 1974) werden Brückenannahmen im Detail analysiert. D. h. die Fragen, die in dem Kasten von Abb. 2 aufgeführt werden, bleiben offen. Diese Fragen werden auch in anderen Schriften der verhaltenstheoretischen Soziologie nicht behandelt (vgl. z. B. Burgess und Bushell 1969; Opp 1972), die, wie Homans, lerntheoretische Hypothesen anwenden.

Ende der 1950er Jahre wird das Aggregationsproblem in einem grundlegenden Aufsatz von Lazarsfeld und Menzel (1961) analysiert. Hier werden detaillierte Funktionen zwischen individuellen und kollektiven Merkmalen behandelt. Auch Coleman (1964, insbes. S. 24–92, 253–268) befasst sich mit Mikro-Makro-Funktionen, ohne allerdings die Schrift von Lazarsfeld und Menzel (1961) zu erwähnen. In dieser Tradition steht auch der Aufsatz von Hummell (1973) und fast 50 Jahre nach dem Aufsatz von Lazarsfeld und Menzel die Schrift von Jasso (2010). In diesen Schriften geht es nicht grundsätzlich um die Haltbarkeit des individualistischen Forschungsprogramms, sondern um Konstruktionsmöglichkeiten kollektiver Merkmale aus individuellen Merkmalen. Allerdings sind diese Schriften für die Beurteilung des individualistischen Forschungsprogramms von zentraler Bedeutung, da an vielen Beispielen demonstriert wird, wie genau auf der Basis individueller Eigenschaften Kollektivmerkmale konstruiert werden können.[4]

Einige Anmerkungen zur Terminologie. In der Schrift von Hummell und Opp (1971, s. a. 1968), in der u. a. das Aggregationsproblem behandelt wird, sprechen die Autoren nicht von „Aggregation", sondern von der „Definierbarkeit" von Kollektivbegriffen durch Begriffe der Individualebene (1971, z. B. S. 7). In der Terminologie des vorliegenden Aufsatzes bedeutet dies, dass analytische Mikro-zu-Makro-Beziehungen behandelt werden. Es wird darauf hingewiesen, dass oft nur Vermutungen über die Bedeutung der Kollektivbegriffe angestellt werden können, da diese häufig nicht klar definiert sind. Hummell und Opp vertreten die „Rekonstruktionsthese", d. h. dass Kollektivbegriffe durch Individualbegriffe (d. h. durch Eigenschaften von Individuen) „rekonstruiert" werden können.[5] Die Brückenannahmen werden als „Koordinationsregeln" bezeichnet (1971, S. 13). Das Mikro-Makro-Schema, wie es später Coleman zugeschrieben wird, findet sich bereits in dieser Schrift (S. 15). Weiter wird zwischen definitorischen (also analytischen) und empirischen Koordinationsregeln unterschieden (S. 17–18). Spezifische Funktionen zwischen Mikro- und Makroebene werden allerdings nicht behandelt. Es geht vielmehr darum, *ob* Kollektivbegriffe individualistisch rekonstruiert werden können, und nicht darum, *wie* dies geschehen könnte.

Lindenberg (1977, s. a. Lindenberg und Wippler 1978) hat die Problematik der Brückenannahmen aufgegriffen und in mehreren späteren Publikationen weiter diskutiert (vgl. hierzu und zu Hummell und Opp auch Raub und Voss 1981). Das Aggregationsproblem nennt Lindenberg „Transformationsproblem". Unseres Erachtens trifft die Bedeutung des Ausdrucks „Aggregation" das, was geschieht, genauer als „Transformation". Mikro-zu-Makro-Beziehungen heißen bei Lindenberg „Transformationsregeln". Streng genommen geht es beim Aggregationsproblem nicht um „Regeln" (wie auch aus den Ausführungen von Lindenberg hervorgeht), sondern um bestimmte Annahmen. Auch Lindenberg unterscheidet zwischen empirischen und analytischen Brückenannahmen. Eine detaillierte Diskussion der Funktionen, die individuelle Merkmale in Kollektivmerkmale „transformieren", finden wir auch bei Lindenberg nicht.[6]

Lindenberg glaubt, dass sein „transformatorischer Ansatz" sich von dem Ansatz von Hummell und Opp unterscheidet (s. Lindenberg 1977, S. 64 – hierzu auch Opp

---

[4] Dies wird illustriert in den Beiträgen im Sonderheft des Journal of Mathematical Sociology (2011, Hefte 1 bis 3) über „Micro-Macro Links and Microfoundations in Sociology" (als Buch s. Buskens et al. 2012). Abgesehen von zwei Beiträgen, die sich generell mit Mikro-Makro-Erklärungen befassen, zeigen die übrigen Beiträge an konkreten Beispielen, wie aus bestimmten Mikro-Annahmen Makro-Eigenschaften gebildet werden.

[5] Hummell und Opp sprechen anstatt von „Kollektivbegriffen" von „soziologischen" und anstatt von Begriffen der individuellen Ebene von „psychologischen" Begriffen. „Soziologische" Begriffe werden als Kollektivbegriffe und „psychologische" als Individualbegriffe definiert.

[6] Auf die Details der Analysen Lindenbergs soll hier nicht eingegangen werden. Es sei nur angemerkt, dass einige Punkte präzisierungsbedürftig sind. So wäre der Unterschied zwischen Anfangsbedingungen und Randbedingungen (S. 54) bei der Ableitung „kollektiver Effekte" zu klären. Entsprechend ist die relativ komplizierte Struktur der Ableitungen nicht klar. Zu einer Alternative siehe das Kapitel „Die Elementarstruktur kollektiver Erklärungen" in Opp (1979, S. 12–20).

2009, S. 28). Da ein solcher möglicher Unterschied auch für das Aggregationsproblem von Bedeutung ist, soll auf die Argumente Lindenbergs kurz eingegangen werden. Erstens behauptet Lindenberg, ein „reduktionistischer Ansatz" berücksichtige keine kognitiven Elemente. Dies ist jedoch unrichtig: Ein solcher Ansatz ist prinzipiell offen für die Art der angewendeten Mikrotheorie. Zweitens führe ein reduktionistischer Ansatz dazu, „kollektive Phänomene individualistisch zu definieren" (S. 64). Was auch immer damit gemeint ist: Richtig ist, dass bei Hummell und Opp die Bedeutung der vorliegenden Kollektivbegriffe, u. a. bei der Aggregation individueller Merkmale, ermittelt wird und dass dann geprüft wird, ob diese individualistisch rekonstruiert werden können. Dies entspricht genau der Vorgehensweise von Lindenberg. Schließlich behauptet Lindenberg, ein „reduktionistischer" Ansatz wende gegebene Individualhypothesen an, wobei Probleme dieser Hypothesen nicht ermittelt werden könnten (S. 64). Selbstverständlich können sich bei der empirischen Überprüfung von Mikro-Makro-Erklärungen im Programm von Hummell und Opp die Individualtheorien als falsch erweisen. Es ist keine Frage, dass sowohl das von Hummell und Opp als auch das von Lindenberg vertretene Programm darauf abzielen, kollektive Sachverhalte durch Anwendung von Individualtheorien zu erklären. In der Schrift von Hummell und Opp wird immer wieder betont, dass „Reduktion" dasselbe wie „Erklärung" bedeutet. In diesem Sinne ist also eine „reduktionistischer Ansatz" identisch mit einem „transformatorischen Ansatz". Lediglich die Terminologie ist unterschiedlich. D. h. der „transformatorische Ansatz" ist keineswegs eine „(hoffentlich progressive) Problemverschiebung" (Lindenberg 1977, S. 50). Für das Aggregationsproblem folgt, dass sich die Ansätze von Lindenberg und Hummell und Opp nicht unterscheiden.

Vor allem im deutschen Sprachbereich werden das individualistische Forschungsprogramm und insbesondere das Aggregationsproblem nach wie vor intensiv diskutiert (vgl. insbesondere Esser 1993; Greshoff 2012; Greve et al. 2008; Schmid 2009; vgl. auch die folgende Kontroverse: Kelle und Lüdemann 1995; Lindenberg 1996a; Kelle und Lüdemann 1996; Opp und Friedrichs 1996; Lindenberg 1996b). Diese Literatur behandelt jedoch nicht im Detail die Fragen, die im Mittelpunkt der folgenden Ausführungen stehen.

5 Makrovariablen als analytische Funktionen von Mikrovariablen

In diesem Abschnitt werden wir zwei Arten analytischer Aggregation behandeln: die Aggregation *einstelliger* Merkmale (die nur einem Individuum zukommen) und *zweistelliger* bzw. – gleichbedeutend – *relationaler* Merkmale (die mindestens zwei Individuen gleichzeitig haben können).

5.1 Die Aggregation einstelliger Mikrovariablen

Die Coleman'sche Badewanne, wie sie in Abb. 1 dargestellt ist, wird in zahlreichen Publikationen wiedergegeben. Dabei wird immer die Mikro-zu-Makro-Beziehung als empirische Beziehung angesehen: Typischerweise steht in der Graphik ein Pfeil. Dies gilt auch für den Artikel Colemans von 1987, der viele Beispiele für Mikro-

Makro-Modelle diskutiert und bei dem Mikro-zu-Makro-Beziehungen immer empirischer Art sind. Eine empirische Beziehung liegt jedoch keineswegs immer vor. Es gibt Makrovariablen, bei denen ist es offensichtlich, dass sie durch mathematische Aggregation individueller Merkmale gebildet werden. Ein einfaches Beispiel ist die Kriminalitätsrate. Diese ist gleich der Summe der Straftaten von Individuen einer Stadt oder eines Landes, dividiert durch die Bevölkerungsgröße (oder die Größe der strafmündigen Bevölkerung). Zwischen Mikro- und Makrovariablen liegt also keineswegs eine empirische Beziehung vor. *Aggregation* bedeutet, dass Merkmale von Individuen zu einem Makromerkmal zusammengefasst werden. Dies ist eine rein analytische oder mathematische Operation, d. h. die Makrovariable ist eine mathematische Funktion der Eigenschaften individueller Akteure. Akteure sind etwa Politiker, Frauen, Männer, Vorbestrafte und Parteimitglieder. Es handelt sich hier um Kategorien oder *Mengen* von Individuen. Man könnte auch von Populationen sprechen (Jasso 2010). Diese Populationen können durch *Merkmale* (d. h. Variablen) charakterisiert werden. Bei der Aggregation werden aus Merkmalen von Individuen neue Makromerkmale gebildet.

Dies illustriert unser Beispiel: Ein Merkmal von Individuen sei „kriminell sein" oder „vorbestraft sein" (d. h. eine Straftat begangen zu haben). Die Population „Bewohner einer Stadt" wird also charakterisiert durch das Merkmal „vorbestraft sein". Angenommen, es handele sich um ein dichotomes Merkmal: Man kann entweder (mindestens einmal) vorbestraft sein oder nicht. Wie könnte man aus diesen individuellen Merkmalen andere Merkmale konstruieren? Man könnte z. B. die Anzahl von Personen, die vorbestraft sind, zählen. Das neue Merkmal wäre dann die „Anzahl der Vorbestraften" der Stadt. Man könnte auch den „Prozentsatz der Vorbestraften" ermitteln, indem man die Anzahl der Vorbestraften durch die Größe der (strafmündigen) Bevölkerung dividiert. „Vorbestraft sein" könnte auch als quantitative Variable definiert werden: Vorstrafen einer Person können zwischen 0 und einer positiven Zahl variieren. Man könnte dann die durchschnittliche Anzahl der Vorstrafen aller Individuen oder auch die Standardabweichung berechnen. In jedem Falle werden also durch mathematische Operationen aus individuellen Merkmalen Kollektivmerkmale konstruiert.

Die Aggregationen sind dabei Werte neuer Makrovariablen (Jasso 2010, S. 5). Aggregiert man z. B. die Scheidungshäufigkeit von Städten, indem man pro Stadt die Häufigkeit von Scheidungen durch die Anzahl der Ehepaare, die in der Stadt wohnen, dividiert, dann lautet die neue Variable „Scheidungsrate". Die konkreten Scheidungsraten, etwa von Köln, Hamburg oder Leipzig, sind dabei Werte der Variable „Scheidungsrate".

Man kann auch Eigenschaften von Mengen von *Aggregaten* (z. B. Staaten, Städte, Familien) zu neuen Merkmalen zusammenfügen. So könnte man die Scheidungsraten von Städten bilden und hieraus etwa das Merkmal „durchschnittliche Scheidungsrate" konstruieren. Man könnte hier von *Kollektivmerkmalen zweiter Ordnung* sprechen. Hier sind die Einheiten der Analyse Kollektive, die verwendet werden, um andere Kollektivmerkmale zu bilden. Wir beschränken uns der Einfachheit halber zunächst auf Individuen.

Es sei noch einmal betont, dass die Funktionen, die bisher zur Diskussion standen, analytischer (d. h. logischer) Art sind, d. h. man kann sie nicht empirisch testen. Dies ist anders, wenn behauptet wird, dass das Ausmaß der individuellen Kriminalität eine Funktion der Opportunitätsstrukturen ist. Dies ist eine empirische Hypothese, die falsch sein kann.

Die Frage, welches genau die Funktionen sind, durch die Makrovariablen gebildet werden können, wird als das *Aggregationsproblem* bezeichnet. Zum ersten Mal wurde dieses, wie bereits erwähnt, von Lazarsfeld und Menzel (1961) ausführlich behandelt. Sie definieren „analytische Merkmale" von Kollektiven in folgender Weise: „These are properties of collectives which are obtained by performing some mathematical operation upon some property of each single member [of a group]" (S. 427). Es handelt sich hier um algebraische Operationen. Die Autoren erwähnen z. B. einfache *Summierungen* individueller Eigenschaften. Die „Größe einer Gruppe" ist einfach die Summe der Mitglieder. Die Autoren nennen weiter *Durchschnittsbildungen* (z. B. die Durchschnittsmiete in einem Stadtbezirk) und *Prozentsätze bzw. Proportionen* (Kriminalitätsrate). Die *Standardabweichung* oder Varianz individueller Merkmale ist ein weiterer Typ der Aggregation. „Soziale Ungleichheit" oder generell die „Heterogenität" einer Gruppe kann durch die Standardabweichung von individuellen Merkmalen berechnet werden.

Bei den individuellen Merkmalen handelt es sich immer um *einstellige Merkmale*. Dies sind Merkmale, die nur einem Individuum zukommen können. Beispiele sind Einkommen, Geschlecht, Vorstrafe oder Religionszugehörigkeit. „Mehrstellige" Merkmale werden mindestens zwei Individuen gleichzeitig zugeschrieben, z. B. Paaren von Individuen. „Verheiratet sein mit" oder „interagieren mit" sind Beispiele.

Die Arbeit von Jasso (2010) kann als eine Weiterentwicklung der Überlegungen von Lazarsfeld und Menzel (1961) gesehen werden. Dabei ist es merkwürdig, dass Jasso diesen Aufsatz nicht erwähnt. Jasso zeigt im Detail eine Vielzahl von möglichen Arten der Aggregation. Sie führt z. B. aus, dass bei der Existenz von zwei Mikrovariablen aus deren Beziehung eine ganze Reihe neuer Makrovariablen gebildet werden kann. So könnte eine Regressionsgleichung geschätzt werden. „The population can now be described by the parameters of the regression line – intercept and slope – magnitude of linear correlation, various sums of squares, and so on" (S. 8). Zu Einzelheiten sei auf die Ausführungen von Jasso verwiesen.

Will man eine Makroeigenschaft durch den Rückgriff auf Eigenschaften individueller Akteure erklären, sollten zwei Fragen beantwortet werden. Erstens ist zu klären, was genau die Makroeigenschaft ist, die erklärt werden soll. Oft sind die kollektiven Explananda in der Soziologie unklar formuliert. Beispiele sind die Erklärung der Entstehung von „Gesellschaften", die Frage, welche Wirkungen die hohe „Kohäsion" einer „Gruppe" hat oder wie „Institutionen" entstehen. Alle die in Anführungszeichen gesetzten Begriffe sind unklar oder haben verschiedene Bedeutungen. Solange solche Begriffe nicht erheblich präzisiert werden, kann nur schwer oder gar nicht entschieden werden, ob oder in welcher Weise sie eine Funktion individueller Eigenschaften sind.

Ist die zu erklärende Makroeigenschaft klar definiert, dann sollte der zweite Schritt darin bestehen, herauszuarbeiten, auf welche individuellen Merkmale sich die Makroeigenschaft bezieht. Hier ist also zu klären, *ob* eine individualistische Rekonstruktion möglich ist. Dies ist in vielen Fällen einfach zu entscheiden, wie etwa bei der Wahlbeteiligung. „Wahl" ist ein relativ klarer Begriff und „Beteiligung" (d. h. Stimmabgabe) ebenfalls. Die Variable „Rate der Beschäftigten" ist klar, wenn die offiziellen Daten verwendet werden. Will ein Forscher selbst diese Rate ermitteln, ist zu klären, was genau unter „Beschäftigten" zu verstehen ist. Soll man etwa nur Vollzeit-Beschäftigte ermitteln? Sollen auch Personen unter diesen Begriff fallen, die in der Schattenwirtschaft arbeiten? Im Folgenden gehen wir davon aus, dass die verwendeten Kollektivbegriffe klar sind. Wenn klar ist, *dass* eine individualistische Rekonstruktion möglich ist, ist also nächstes zu fragen, *wie* genau die Rekonstruktion erfolgen kann.

5.2 Die analytische Aggregation relationaler individueller Merkmale

Aggregationen werden oft mit zweistelligen Merkmalen von Individuen vorgenommen. Diese werden auch „Relationen" oder „relationale Merkmale"[7] genannt. So kommt das Merkmal „arbeitslos" genau einem Individuum zu, es handelt sich also um ein einstelliges Merkmal. Dies gilt nicht für „Interaktion": Person A hat nicht eine mehr oder weniger häufige Interaktion wie etwa ein bestimmtes Einkommen, vielmehr betrifft „Interaktion" zwei Individuen gleichzeitig. Die Unterschiede zwischen einstelligen und zweistelligen Merkmalen werden besonders deutlich durch eine Formalisierung oder Symbolisierung. In der formalen Logik wird ein einstelliges Merkmal durch ein Prädikat oder Merkmal und einen einzigen Argumentausdruck (der sich auf Einheiten wie z. B. Individuen bezieht) dargestellt. So heißt Aa „a ist arbeitslos" (dabei ist A das Merkmal und a der Argumentausdruck). Dies ist ein einstelliges Merkmal. Der Ausdruck „Iab" heißt Person a interagiert mit b. „Interaktion" ist also ein zweistelliges Merkmal.[8]

Die Makromerkmale, die durch die Aggregation individueller relationaler Merkmale entstehen, heißen nach Lazarsfeld und Menzel (1961) „strukturelle" Merkmale. „These are properties of collectives which are obtained by performing some operation on data about the relations of each member to some or all of the others" (S. 428). Ein Beispiel ist die „Cliquenbildung" („cliquishness") einer Schulklasse. Diese kann definiert werden als „the number of subgroups into which a class can be divided so that no choices cut across subgroups" (S. 428). D. h. bestimmte Mitglieder einer Gruppe (wie z. B. einer Schulklasse) interagieren nur miteinander und nicht mit anderen Mitgliedern. Abbildung 3 ist ein Beispiel für eine Clique – die Buchstaben bezeichnen Personen, die Linien Interaktionen. Man könnte aber auch dann von einer „Clique" sprechen, wenn bestimmte Personenmengen *relativ häufig* miteinander interagieren. So läge eine Clique vor, wenn in Abb. 3 z. B. zusätzlich C und F interagieren. Eine solche Struktur mit zwei Cliquen ist der einfachste Fall einer Cliquenstruktur. Wie kompliziert reale soziale Netzwerke sind, wird beispielhaft in der Untersuchung von Bearman et al. (2004) gezeigt, die u. a. „the structure of adolescent romantic and sexual networks in an American high school" beschreiben.

---

[7] Relationale Merkmale können auch mehr als zwei Individuen zugeschrieben werden. So könnte ein Merkmal heißen „Person a bestraft Person b in der Weise c". Wir beschränken uns im Folgenden auf zweistellige Relationen, die also nur zwei Individuen zugeschrieben werden können.

[8] Zu diesen elementaren Unterscheidungen vgl. z. B. Rautenberg (2008), Zoglauer (2008) oder die elementare Einführung in Opp (2014, S. 183–202).

Abb. 3 Beispiel für eine Cliquenstruktur

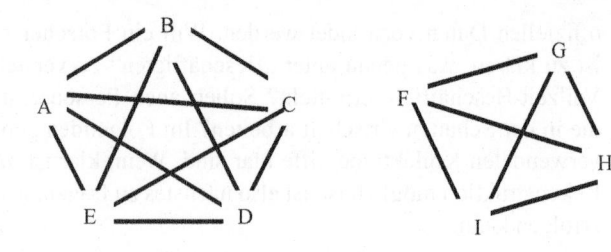

Analysieren wir Art der Aggregation bei relationalen Merkmalen etwas genauer. Zunächst ist festzuhalten, dass es sich um eine *analytische Aggregation* handelt. Dies bedeutet, dass zwischen den Individuen und deren Merkmalen einerseits und dem Gruppenmerkmal andererseits keine empirischen, sondern nur logische oder analytische Beziehungen bestehen: Wenn wir wissen, welche Individuen mit welchen anderen Individuen interagieren (oder eine sonstige Beziehung haben), dann konstruieren wir das Kollektivmerkmal durch mathematische Operationen.

Illustrieren wir dies an unserem Beispiel. Hierzu wollen wir die in Abb. 3 dargestellte Cliquenstruktur in Form einer Matrix darstellen (Tab. 1). Für jedes Paar der Gruppe wird in das betreffende Feld eine 1 eingetragen, wenn eine Beziehung zwischen den beiden Personen besteht, ansonsten enthält das betreffende Feld eine 0. Eine Person kann keine Beziehung zu sich selbst haben. In der Diagonale der Tabelle steht also immer eine 0. „Interaktion" ist symmetrisch (d. h. wenn A mit B interagiert, dann interagiert auch B mit A). Dies hat z. B. zur Folge, dass dann, wenn A (Person in der Reihe) mit B (Person in der Spalte) interagiert, auch B (Person in Reihe) mit A (Person in Spalte) interagiert. „Interaktion" ist so definiert, dass eine Person nicht mit sich selbst interagieren kann. Es lassen sich auf den ersten Blick, wie in der Graphik, zwei Gruppen identifizieren (s. die schattierten Felder).

Die Matrix-Darstellung erleichtert es zu zeigen, wie individuelle Beziehungen zu Kollektivmerkmalen aggregiert werden. Ein solches Merkmale ist die *Kohäsion* einer Gruppe (s. z. B. Jansen 2006, Kap. 5; Diekmann 2007, S. 497). Dieses Kollektivmerkmal könnte definiert werden als die Anzahl der tatsächlich bestehenden Beziehungen, bezogen auf die Anzahl der möglichen Beziehungen. Die Matrix enthält 32 mal die Zahl 1. Da eine Beziehung zwischen zwei Personen zweimal durch eine 1 dargestellt ist, bestehen tatsächlich 32/2, also 16 Beziehungen. Wenn jede Person mit jeder anderen Person interagiert (dies sind die möglichen Beziehungen),

Tab. 1 Beispiel für eine Cliquenstruktur mit zwei Cliquen

	A	B	C	D	E	F	G	H	I
A	0	1	1	1	1	0	0	0	0
B	1	0	1	1	1	0	0	0	0
C	1	1	0	1	1	0	0	0	0
D	1	1	1	0	1	0	0	0	0
E	1	1	1	1	0	0	0	0	0
F	0	0	0	0	0	0	1	1	1
G	0	0	0	0	0	1	0	1	1
H	0	0	0	0	0	1	1	0	1
I	0	0	0	0	0	1	1	1	0

dann würde es 9 x 8 = 72 Beziehungen geben. Diese müssten durch 2 dividiert werden, da eine Beziehung zwischen zwei Personen nach dieser Berechnung doppelt gezählt würde. Die Zahl der möglichen Beziehungen ist also 36.[9] Entsprechend ergibt sich die Kohäsion als 16/36 = 0,44. Dies ist der Kohäsionsindex. Eine Kohäsion von 1 liegt entsprechend vor, wenn jede Person mit jeder anderen Person interagiert. Dies ist der Fall für die Personen A bis E und F bis I. Entsprechend kann eine Clique der Größe r definiert werden als eine Teilmenge von r Personen, bei denen der Kohäsionsindex den Wert 1 hat.

Das Beispiel illustriert nicht nur, dass Gruppenmerkmale aus relationalen individuellen Merkmalen analytisch konstruiert werden. Weiter ist Folgendes von Bedeutung. Einstellige Merkmale (z. B. vorbestraft sein) werden aggregiert, indem Operationen mit den Merkmalen einzelner Individuen ausgeführt werden, wie vorher gezeigt wurde. Einheiten der Aggregation sind also *einzelne* Individuen. Dies ist anders bei zweistelligen Merkmalen. So werden bei der Konstruktion des Merkmals „Kohäsion" Beziehungen, die *Paaren* von Individuen zukommen, aggregiert. Kohäsion wird gebildet durch eine Aggregation der Werte in den Feldern der Matrix. Jede Zahl in einem Feld bezieht sich auf Paare von Individuen. Ein Paar ist das kleinstmögliche Kollektiv. Dies bedeutet, dass bei der Aggregation zweistelliger Merkmale die Einheiten, die aggregiert sind, bereits Kollektive „niedriger Ordnung" sind – man könnte von der *Aggregation von Kollektiven erster Ordnung sprechen*. Allerdings kommen solche Kollektive durch Entscheidungen individueller Akteure zustande: Jeder der Akteure entscheidet, ob er oder sie eine Beziehung eingeht oder nicht. Man kann also auch bei der Aggregation von relationalen Merkmalen sagen, dass Kollektivmerkmale das „Ergebnis" individuellen Handelns sind, wie das individualistische Forschungsprogramm behauptet.

In der beschriebenen Weise wird eine Vielzahl anderer Eigenschaften von Kollektivmerkmalen, die sich auf soziale Netzwerke beziehen, aggregiert wie z. B. die Dichte oder die Zentralität von Netzwerken.[10]

5.3 Aggregationen und institutionelle Regeln

Oft handelt es sich bei Makroeigenschaften nicht um bloße mathematische Aggregationen individueller Merkmale. Angenommen, die Makroeigenschaft sei die „Annahme eines Gesetzes in einem Parlament". Dies scheint zunächst nur zu heißen, dass mehr Mitglieder des Parlaments für als gegen das Gesetz gestimmt haben. Mit anderen Worten:

„Annahme" eines Gesetzes = df. die Anzahl der Befürworter ist größer als die Anzahl der Nicht-Befürworter eines Gesetzes.

Dies ist eine analytische Aggregation. Dabei wird implizit angenommen, dass die Abstimmungsregel die Mehrheitsregel ist. Es wäre aber denkbar, dass bei mehrheit-

---

[9] Diese Zahl ergibt sich auch, wenn man nur die Felder oberhalb der Diagonalen zählt.
[10] Vgl. z. B. McGlohon et al. (2011). Vgl. weiter die umfangreiche Literatur zur Netzwerkanalyse, z. B. Jansen (2006), Kadushin (2012), Trappmann et al. (2010) oder Vega-Redondo (2007) – jeweils mit weiteren Literaturhinweisen.

licher Befürwortung das Gesetz nicht als angenommen gilt. Dies würde etwa der Fall sein, wenn die Mehrheit der Mitglieder für das Gesetz gestimmt hat, wenn aber für dessen Annahme eine Zwei-Drittel-Mehrheit erforderlich ist. Bei der genannten Aggregationsregel müsste also hinzugefügt werden: „Bei Abstimmungen gilt die Mehrheitsregel".

Handelt es sich immer noch um eine analytische Aggregation? Diese Frage ist zu bejahen. Denn wenn man das Abstimmungsverhalten und die Abstimmungsregel kennt, dann kann die Aggregation immer noch vorgenommen werden, ohne dass zusätzliche Daten herangezogen werden müssen.

5.4 „Partielle Aggregationen": Können die Ziele kollektiver Akteure auf der Grundlage individueller Ziele aggregiert werden?

Auch Vertreter des individualistischen Forschungsprogramms sprechen von den Zielen kollektiver Akteure. So haben Unternehmen das Ziel der Gewinnmaximierung. Es gibt Staatsziele (z. B. Meinungsfreiheit zu garantieren). Soziale Bewegungen und Interessengruppen haben das Ziel, Regierungen zu bestimmten Entscheidungen zu veranlassen. Wie ermittelt man die Ziele von Kollektiven? Bei Individuen kann man die Ziele empirisch messen, z. B. im Rahmen einer Umfrage. So könnte man in einer Bevölkerungsumfrage ermitteln, wo die Befragten ihren nächsten Urlaub verbringen wollen. Offensichtlich kann man nicht ein Unternehmen, den Staat oder eine soziale Bewegung nach ihren Zielen fragen, man kann nur Personen fragen, z. B. Mitglieder eines Kollektivs. Aber wen sollte man in einem Unternehmen auswählen, um die Ziele „des" Unternehmens zu ermitteln?

Es gibt verschiedene Möglichkeiten, die Ziele von Kollektiven zu ermitteln. Eine Möglichkeit ist, das Ziel eines Kollektivs zu definieren als die Ziele aller Mitglieder des Kollektivs. Wenn z. B. das Ziel einer Fußballmannschaft darin besteht, das nächste Spiel zu gewinnen, dann ist dieses kollektive Ziel identisch mit den Zielen aller Mitglieder. Ein Problem dieser Definition ist, dass die Ziele der Mitglieder oft unterschiedlich sind. In diesem Falle kann aufgrund der genannten Definition „das" Ziel des Kollektivs nicht bestimmt werden. So könnte es bei einer Fußballmannschaft auch Spieler geben, die mit einem Unentschieden zufrieden sind. Was ist dann „das" Ziel der Fußballmannschaft?

Zweitens könnte das (oder auch ein) Ziel einer Gruppe als das Abstimmungsergebnis der Mitglieder über ein Ziel definiert werden. So mag ein Fußballverein darüber abstimmen, ob man neue Spieler einstellen soll, um in eine höhere Liga aufzusteigen. Wenn die Mehrheit der Mitglieder (bei Mehrheitsregel) dafür stimmt, dann kann man sagen, das Ziel „des" Vereins ist, in die höhere Liga aufzusteigen.

Häufig findet aber bei der Ermittlung von Zielen eines Kollektives, z. B. von Organisationszielen, keine einfache Aggregation der Ziele aller Mitglieder statt. Es gibt vielmehr „eine Minderheit leitender Personen innerhalb einer Organisation", die dieser die Ziele vorgeben (Mayntz 1963, S. 64). D. h. „high level executives" legen Ziele fest und versuchen sie zu realisieren (Simon 1997, S. 163). „Ziele" eines Kollektivs sind also oft die Aggregation der Ziele der Mitglieder einer bestimmten *Teilgruppe* eines Kollektivs, z. B. des Vorstandes. Die Aggregation ist also „partiell" in dem Sinne, dass nur die Ziele eines Teils der Mitglieder aggregiert werden.

Wenn die Ziele eines Kollektivs von einer Teilgruppe gesetzt werden, dann bedeutet dies keineswegs, dass nur diese Teilgruppe diese Ziele verfolgt, d. h. zu realisieren versucht. Normalerweise werden diese Ziele empirisch durchgesetzt, d. h. es werden Maßnahmen der Art ergriffen, dass jedes Mitglied der Gruppe die Ziele akzeptiert und dazu beiträgt, die Ziele zu erreichen. Aber selbst wenn dies bei manchen Mitgliedern nicht gelingt, wird man noch von „den" Zielen des Kollektivs sprechen, solange diese faktisch verfolgt werden. Typischerweise werden Personen, die die Ziele nicht akzeptieren, negativ sanktioniert oder als Mitglieder ausgeschlossen. So sind die im Grundgesetz verankerten Staatsziele für alle Bürger verpflichtend. Abweichungen werden sanktioniert (formell oder informell). D. h. die Formulierung der Ziele ist ein erster Schritt, der zu Entscheidungsprozessen führt, die die Durchsetzung der Ziele beabsichtigen. Da es hier nur um die Aggregation geht, wollen wir uns mit diesen Prozessen nicht weiter befassen.

Man könnte bei der Ermittlung von Zielen eines kollektiven Akteurs auch in folgender Weise vorgehen: Man zieht Dokumente heran, die die Ziele der Gruppe beschreiben. So ergeben sich die Staatsziele aus dem Grundgesetz. Gegen diese Vorgehensweise lassen sich mehrere Einwände erheben. Erstens gibt es eine Vielzahl von Kollektiven, bei denen keine derartigen Dokumente vorliegen. Hier gäbe es also keine Möglichkeit, die Ziele zu ermitteln.

Selbst wenn es Dokumente gibt, die die Ziele eines Kollektivs festlegen, fragt es sich, wessen Ziele hier beschrieben werden. Ist ein solches Dokument die Beschreibung der Ziele aller Mitglieder einer Gruppe oder nur das Ergebnis einer Abstimmung von Teilgruppen wie des Vorstandes eines Unternehmens? Selbst wenn es Dokumente gibt, weiß man also nicht, wessen Ziele beschrieben werden. Ein weiteres Problem ist, dass die in Dokumenten festgelegten Ziele vielleicht nicht die Ziele sind, die die Akteure tatsächlich verfolgen. So wird unterschieden zwischen den proklamierten (oder offiziellen) und den operativen (tatsächlichen) Zielen der Entscheider. Wenn man die Ziele eines Kollektivs als Variablen verwenden will, um dessen Verhalten zu erklären oder vorauszusagen, dann ist es sinnvoll, die operativen Ziele zu heranzuziehen. D. h. selbst wenn man Dokumente verwendet, liegt faktisch eine Aggregation von Zielen vor, die schriftlich festgelegt wurden. Die Dokumente lassen aber normalerweise offen, welcher Art die Aggregation ist.

Resümierend kann man sagen, dass bei allen beschriebenen Möglichkeiten, die Ziele eines Kollektivs zu ermitteln, analytische Aggregationen der Ziele der Mitglieder oder von Teilen der Mitglieder vorgenommen werden.

6 Empirische Aggregationen von Mikroeigenschaften

Wir haben uns bisher mit *analytischen* Mikro-zu-Makro-Beziehungen befasst. In diesem Abschnitt stehen *empirische* Aggregationen im Mittelpunkt der Analyse. Wir beginnen mit einigen Beispielen und behandeln dann Probleme dieser Art von Aggregation.

6.1 Einige Beispiele für empirische Aggregationen

1. Einzelne Autofahrer schalten am späten Nachmittag gleichzeitig ihre Scheinwerfer ein (Mikroebene). Dies hat auf der Makroebene den Effekt, dass der Prozentsatz (anderer) Autofahrer, die ihre Scheinwerfer einschalten, steigt (s. zu diesem Beispiel Schelling 1978, S. 13–14 und die Beispiele auf S. 91–110).
2. Angenommen, eine bestimmte Menge von Personen protestiert für den Bau neuer Kindertagesstätten (Mikroebene). Diese Proteste führen zur Vermehrung der Anzahl von Tagesstätten (Makrovariable).
3. Das Sparen individueller Akteure (Mikroebene) erhöht das Wirtschaftswachstum (Makrovariable).
4. Angenommen, einzelne Individuen erfahren, dass die Abweichung von einer Norm größer ist als erwartet (Mikroebene). Dies führt zur Abschwächung der Norm (Makroebene). Dies ist die Präventivwirkung des Nichtwissens (Popitz 1968; hierzu im Einzelnen Opp 2011; Rauhut 2013).
5. Zuwanderung (Mikrovariable) führt zur Verminderung der Vorurteile in der Gesellschaft (Makrovariable).
6. Das Einkommen von Individuen (Mikroebene) hat einen Effekt auf das Aspirationsniveau der Bevölkerung (Makroebene).
7. Der CO_2-Ausstoß der einzelnen Akteure (Mikroeben) hat einen positiven Effekt auf die Krebserkrankungen in der Gesellschaft (Makroebene).
8. Die Sanktionierung von Rauchern (Mikroebene) führt zur Entstehung einer Nichtraucher-Norm (Makroebene).

In allen diesen Beispielen ist der Ausgangspunkt eine Menge individueller Akteure mit bestimmten Merkmalen. Dies ist die Mikroebene. Diese Merkmale haben *kausale Effekte* auf Variablen der Makroebene. Es handelt sich hier also um Mikro-zu-Makro-Beziehungen, aber es findet keine analytische, sondern eine empirische Aggregation statt. So hat das Anschalten der Scheinwerfer einzelner Akteure die *Wirkung*, dass der Prozentsatz anderer Akteure steigt, die das Licht einschalten. Hier handelt es sich nicht um eine analytische Aggregation im vorher genannten Sinne, dass nämlich ein Makromerkmal (z. B. die Kriminalitätsrate einer Stadt) eine analytische Funktion von Mikromerkmalen (Kriminalität einzelner Akteure) ist. Vielmehr *führen* Merkmale einzelner Akteure auf der Mikroebene zu bestimmten Makromerkmalen. Die Einschaltung der Scheinwerfer einzelner Akteure hat z. B. die Wirkung, dass andere Akteure das Licht einschalten. Das Makromerkmal ist also eine *empirische Funktion* der Mikromerkmale, keine analytische Funktion. Hier wird nicht aggregiert im Sinne eines logischen oder analytischen „Zusammenfügens" von Merkmalen individueller Akteure zu einem Makromerkmal. Man kann aber sagen, dass das „Aggregat" der individuellen Akteure einen Effekt auf der Makroebene hat. So beeinflussen die einzelnen Autofahrer, die das Licht eingeschaltet haben, *insgesamt* ein Aggregat anderer Autofahrer. Man kann entsprechend von einer *empirischen Aggregation* sprechen. Umständlicher, aber klarer ist der Ausdruck „empirische Mikro-zu-Makro-Beziehungen".

Die Beispiele enthalten zwei Arten von Effekten. Erstens haben bestimmte Merkmale von Akteuren Effekte auf andere Merkmale *dieser Akteure*. In Beispiel 7 führt eine Erhöhung des Einkommens von Personen zu einer Erhöhung des Aspirationsniveaus *dieser* Personen – so wollen wir jedenfalls annehmen. Zweitens beziehen sich die Beispiele auf Einflussprozesse, d. h. Merkmale einzelner Individuen haben Wirkungen auf Makrovariablen, die sich auf *andere Individuen* beziehen. Dies gilt etwa für die Beispiele 2 (Proteste und Verhalten Dritter) und 5 (Zuwanderung und Vorurteile). Drittens gibt es Beispiele, bei denen nicht klar ist, auf welche Merkmale von Akteuren sich die Makrovariable bezieht. Dies gilt für Beispiel 3, in dem ein Einfluss individueller Merkmale auf das Wirtschaftswachstum behauptet wird. Um welche Kombination von Handlungen individueller Akteure es sich bei „Wirtschaftswachstum" handelt, ist zumindest nicht offensichtlich und bedarf der genaueren Analyse. Vielleicht kann ja Wirtschaftswachstum überhaupt nicht durch Aggregation individueller Merkmale gebildet werden.

Beispiel 7 weist eine Besonderheit auf: Hier haben bestimmte individuelle Handlungen Wirkungen, die *aufgrund von Naturgesetzen* zu erwarten sind. Dies gilt z. B. auch bei der Tragik der Allmende. Hier führt die zu starke Nutzung einer Ressource (z. B. einer Wiese) durch Individuen dazu, dass sich die Ressource nicht regeneriert. Diese Wirkung tritt aufgrund von Naturgesetzen auf.

6.2 Empirische Aggregationen mit mehrfacher analytischer Aggregation

Betrachten wir nun die Aggregationen in den Beispielen etwas genauer. Wir fragen: Wie genau wirken die individuellen Merkmale auf die Makrovariablen? Handelt es sich hier wirklich um direkte kausale Effekte oder werden implizit analytische Aggregationen vorgenommen?

Beispiel 1: Die unabhängige Mikrovariable ist eine Menge von Individuen i, die die Scheinwerfer einschalten (s. den unten links eingerahmten Text in Abb. 4, Teilgraphik A1). Das Verhalten dieser Individuen kommt unabhängig von dem Verhalten anderer Individuen zustande – so wollen wir annehmen. Das Verhalten der Individuen i hat einen Effekt auf andere Individuen j: diese schalten die Scheinwerfer ein, nachdem die Individuen i die Scheinwerfer eingeschaltet haben. Dies sei ein kausaler Effekt. In Abb. 4 werden beide Variablen eingerahmt und durch einen gestrichelten Pfeil verbunden. Dieser symbolisiert die empirische Aggregation. Liegt hier wirklich ein direkter kausaler Effekt vor? Zunächst wird im Beispiel angenommen, dass die Individuen j nicht jeweils ein einzelnes Individuum i, sondern die Gesamtheit der Individuen i (oder mindestens eine Teilmenge dieser Individuen) beobachten und daraufhin das Licht einschalten. Dies ist ein Kontexteffekt. D. h. zunächst einmal erfolgt bei dem Beispiel implizit eine *analytische Aggregation*: Das aggregierte Merkmal i, also die Makrovariable, ist der „Prozentsatz der Personen i, die das Licht einschalten" (s. „Analytische Aggregation 1" in Abb. 4).

Warum ändert das Anschalten der Scheinwerfer der Individuen i das Verhalten der Individuen j? Offensichtlich beeinflusst das Handeln des Aggregates i („% i Scheinwerfer") die Anreize bei den Individuen j, das Licht einzuschalten. So könnten Personen der Gruppe j befürchten, dass die Unfallwahrscheinlichkeit steigt, wenn ihr Auto nicht beleuchtet ist. Es wäre auch plausibel, dass das Anschalten der Scheinwerfer von i bei j die akzeptierte Norm aktiviert, dass man bei Dämmerung das Licht

Abb. 4 Zwei Beispiele für empirische Aggregationen

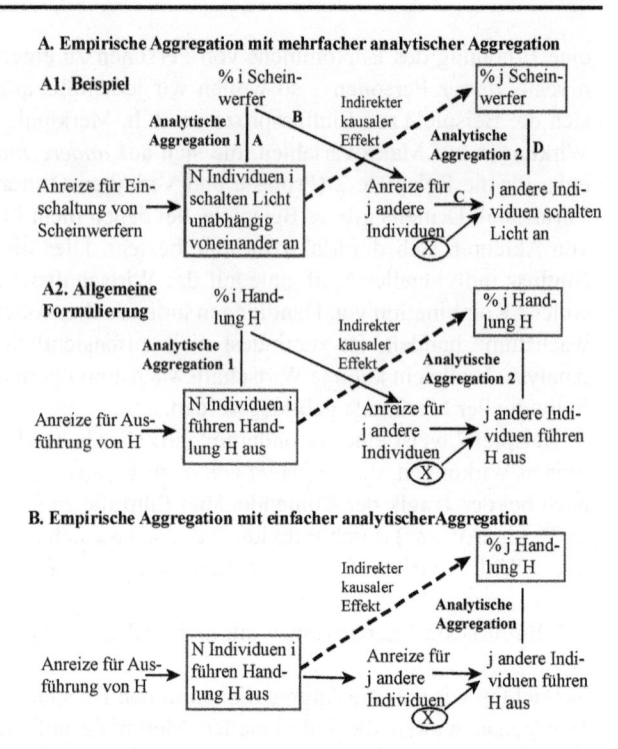

A. Empirische Aggregation mit mehrfacher analytischer Aggregation

A1. Beispiel

Anreize für Einschaltung von Scheinwerfern → N Individuen i schalten Licht unabhängig voneinander an (Analytische Aggregation 1, A) → % i Scheinwerfer (B) → Anreize für j andere Individuen (C, X) → j andere Individuen schalten Licht an (Analytische Aggregation 2, D) → % j Scheinwerfer

Indirekter kausaler Effekt

A2. Allgemeine Formulierung

Anreize für Ausführung von H → N Individuen i führen Handlung H aus (Analytische Aggregation 1) → % i Handlung H → Anreize für j andere Individuen (X) → j andere Individuen führen H aus (Analytische Aggregation 2) → % j Handlung H

Indirekter kausaler Effekt

B. Empirische Aggregation mit einfacher analytischer Aggregation

Anreize für Ausführung von H → N Individuen i führen Handlung H aus → Anreize für j andere Individuen (X) → j andere Individuen führen H aus (Analytische Aggregation) → % j Handlung H

Indirekter kausaler Effekt

anschalten muss. Diese und vielleicht andere Anreize führen dazu, dass die Individuen j ihre Scheinwerfer anschalten. Nun erfolgt die zweite analytische Aggregation von den einzelnen Individuen j zu „% j Scheinwerfer" (s. die obere Abbildung von Abb. 4).

Der kausale Prozess besteht also aus den Beziehungen A bis D (s. die Linien und Pfeile in der oberen Graphik von Abb. 4). Er beginnt also mit der analytischen Aggregation 1; die aggregierte Makrovariable hat dann einen Effekt auf die Mikroebene, und zwar auf eine unabhängige Variable einer Mikrohypothese. Diese Variable beeinflusst das Handeln einzelner Akteure (Mikroebene), das dann wiederum aggregiert wird. Der gestrichelte Pfeil ist also ein indirekter und nicht ein direkter kausaler Effekt. Weiter ist von Bedeutung, dass der beschriebene kausale Prozess zwei analytische Aggregationen enthält.

In der Abbildung wird weiter angenommen, dass nicht nur der Prozentsatz derer, die die Scheinwerfer einschalten, für das Handeln der Individuen j von Bedeutung ist. Andere Faktoren, die als „X" angedeutet sind, beeinflussen ebenfalls das Verhalten der anderen Individuen. So könnte jemand seine Batterie schonen wollen und das Unfallrisiko in Kauf nehmen, d. h. das Licht nicht oder später einschalten. Dieser Faktor würde also den Einfluss der Anreize von Seiten der Individuen i vermindern.

In welcher Beziehung steht die Abb. 4 zum Coleman-Boot? Dieses würde aus den Beziehungen B, C und D bestehen. D. h. „% i Scheinwerfer" ist die unabhängige und „% j Scheinwerfer" die abhängige Makrovariable. Die Wirkung von „Anreize für j…" auf „j andere Individuen…" ist die Mikrotheorie. Die analytische Mikro-zu-Makro-Annahme ist die Beziehung zwischen „j andere Individuen…" (Mikroebene) und

„% j Scheinwerfer" (Makroebene). Die erste analytische Aggregation würde nicht Bestandteil des Coleman-Schemas sein. Die Abbildung ist also eine Erweiterung des Coleman-Bootes.

Bei den empirischen Aussagen im Beispiel handelt es sich um singuläre Kausalaussagen. Somit gelten die vorher beschriebenen Probleme (s. Abb. 2). Woher weiß man z. B., dass das Einschalten der Scheinwerfer bestimmte Anreizeffekte hat? Oder woher weiß man, dass die in der Mikrohypothese (Beziehung C) beschriebenen Anreize tatsächlich einen kausalen Effekt haben? Diese Fragen werden nicht beantwortet.

Inwieweit illustriert unser Beispiel generell die Struktur empirischer Aggregationen? Graphik A2 in Abb. 4 beschreibt das vorangegangene Beispiel (Graphik A1) in genereller Weise. Ausgangspunkt ist eine empirische Aggregation der Art, dass auf der individuellen Ebene eine Menge einzelner Personen i eine bestimmte Handlung H ausführen, die bei einem Aggregat anderer Personen j zur Ausführung dieser Handlung führt. Dies ist der indirekte kausale Effekt. Die „Analytische Aggregation 1" betrifft die Ausgangsvariable („% i Handlung H") und entspricht der Aggregation „% i Scheinwerfer" in der oberen Graphik. Dieses aggregierte Kollektivmerkmal der ersten Aggregation führt dazu, dass ein Aggregat anderer Personen diese Handlung ausführt (% j Handlung H). Dies ist die empirische Aggregation. Sie entspricht einer Hypothese, die man häufig in der Literatur findet, dass nämlich dann, wenn bestimmte Individuen eine Handlung ausführen, dies andere Individuen dazu veranlasst, diese Handlung ebenfalls auszuführen.

Beispiel 2: Hier findet die empirische Aggregation zwischen den individuellen Protesten und der Erfüllung der Forderungen der Protestierer statt. Wiederum hat das Aggregat der Protestierer (also etwa eine Demonstration oder deren Teilnehmerzahl) zunächst eine Wirkung auf die Anreize der Dritten, die über die Annahme der Forderungen entscheiden. Es erfolgt eine kollektive Entscheidung in Form einer Abstimmung, also eine analytische Aggregation. Die Argumentation ist also identisch mit der von Beispiel 1.

Beispiel 3: Das Sparen individueller Akteure wird zunächst aggregiert, da die Sparrate eine Wirkung auf das Wirtschaftswachstum hat. Diese Sparrate müsste nun die Anreize individueller Akteure beeinflussen, die bestimmte Handlungen ausführen. Diese sind die abhängige Variable der Mikrohypothese. Hier müsste dann die Aggregation zu „Wirtschaftswachstum" erfolgen. Wir haben dieses Beispiel gewählt, weil es typisch ist für Beispiele in der Literatur, in denen das Mikro-Makro-Schema angewendet wird: Es ist nicht klar, welche Bedeutung genau das Makromerkmal hat. Entsprechend kann auch nicht gesagt werden, welcher Art die vorzunehmende Aggregation ist. Dies gilt etwa auch für das Standardbeispiel des Coleman-Bootes, bei dem die abhängige Makrovariable „Kapitalismus" ist. Es ist äußerst unklar, welche ökonomischen Handlungen von Individuen in welcher Weise die Entstehung des „Kapitalismus" beeinflussen. In Beispiel 3 kann also der letzte Schritt der Argumentation nicht vollzogen werden, weil die abhängige Makrovariable zu unklar ist.

Beispiel 4: Ausgangspunkt sind einzelne Individuen, die bestimmte Informationen über das Verhalten anderer Individuen erhalten. Das Verhalten dieser anderen Individuen führt zu einer Normabschwächung der zuerst genannten Individuen. Hier sind diejenigen, deren Abweichung bekannt wird, die Individuen i – also z. B. ein Prozentsatz dieser Individuen. So könnte die Nachricht sein, dass ein unerwartet hoher Prozentsatz der Steuerzahler Steuern hinterzieht. In Graphik A2 von Abb. 4 ist dies „% i Handlung H". Das Bekanntwerden bei den einzelnen Individuen j führt bei diesen zu Anreizen, d. h. zu Bedingungen, die die Norminternalisierung vermindern. Diese aggregiert sich analytisch zu der Abschwächung sozialer Normen auf der Makroebene.

Beispiel 5: Auch hier hat das Aggregat der Zuwanderer eine Wirkung auf die Anreize der einzelnen Mitglieder der restlichen Bevölkerung, die bei einer Teilgruppe zur Verminderung von Vorurteilen führen. Diese Teilgruppe wird aggregiert. Dieses Beispiel entspricht also ebenfalls Graphik A2 in Abb. 4.

Beispiel 6: Dieses hat das gleiche Muster: Das Einkommen einer Menge von Personen – eine Makrovariable, die aufgrund einer analytischen Aggregation konstruiert wird, hat einen Effekt auf Bedingungen (Anreize) einer Vielzahl von Individuen j, die bei diesen zu einer Änderung des Aspirationsniveaus führen, das dann analytisch aggregiert wird zu den Vorurteilen „der" Bevölkerung.

6.3 Empirische Aggregationen mit einfacher analytischer Aggregation

Bei den bisherigen Beispielen hatte immer ein Aggregat von Individuen einen Einfluss auf Anreize anderer Individuen; diese Anreize führten dann dazu, dass die anderen Individuen bestimmte Handlungen ausführten, die wiederum aggregiert wurden. Unser letztes *Beispiel 8* entspricht nicht diesem Muster. Hier gilt, dass *einzelne* Individuen i Sanktionen ausführen, die bei anderen *einzelnen* Individuen j (den Sanktionierten) die Anreize verändern, die dann bei diesen Individuen zu bestimmten Handlungen oder Merkmalen (Aufgeben des Rauchens oder Internalisierung einer Nichtraucher-Norm) führen; diese werden dann analytisch aggregiert. Graphik B in Abb. 4 zeigt diese Argumentationsstruktur.

Man könnte Graphik B in Abb. 4 noch um Kontextmerkmale (Makroebene) erweitern. Beim Nichtraucher-Beispiel könnte die Verabschiedung eines Nichtraucher-Gesetzes eine solche Makrovariable sein, die dann einen zusätzlichen Effekt auf die „Anreize…" hat. Solche Kontextmerkmale können im Übrigen auch bei den anderen Beispielen hinzugefügt werden. Dies ändert aber nichts Grundsätzliches an unserer Argumentation. Lediglich die theoretischen Argumente werden komplizierter.

Auch die in diesem Abschnitt beschriebene Art der empirischen Aggregation weicht von dem üblichen Coleman-Schema ab. Es existiert keine Makro-zu-Mikro-Beziehung. Weiter ist die Mikro-zu-Makro-Beziehung analytischer Art.

6.4 Resümee

Unsere detaillierte Analyse empirischer Aggregationen legt die Vermutung nahe, dass zwei Arten empirischer Aggregation unterschieden werden können, die in Abb. 4 dargestellt sind. Wir haben diese Arten durch Beispiele illustriert. Es ist uns nicht gelungen, Beispiele zu finden, die die Existenz weiterer Arten der empirischen Aggregation vermuten lassen.

Es ist wichtig zu beachten, dass die vorher behandelten Probleme von Mikro-Makro-Erklärungen (s. Abb. 2) bei empirischen Aggregationen nicht gelöst sind. So bestehen die empirischen Aussagen aus singulären Kausalaussagen, deren Probleme vorher behandelt wurden. Trotzdem ist es für Mikro-Makro-Erklärungen wichtig, welche möglichen Strukturen solche Erklärungen haben können. Die hier behandelten empirischen Aggregationen erweitern das übliche Mikro-Makro-Erklärungsschema. Es handelt sich um bestimmte kausale Prozesse, d. h. Mechanismen, die genauer untersucht werden sollten.

7 „Globale" Merkmale: Gibt es Kollektivmerkmale, die nicht auf der Grundlage individueller Merkmale konstruiert werden können?

Diese Frage bejahen Lazarsfeld und Menzel (1961, S. 428): „Often collectives are characterized by properties which are not based on information about the properties of individual members." Solche Merkmale nennen die Autoren „global properties". Diese These widerspricht dem individualistischen Forschungsprogramm und damit auch der These, dass kollektive Eigenschaften immer Aggregationen individueller Eigenschaften sind. Die „Rekonstruktionsthese" behauptet dagegen, dass alle Kollektivbegriffe individualistisch rekonstruiert werden können (Opp 2009, S. 35; s. bereits die ausführliche Diskussion bei Hummell und Opp 1971).

Welche These trifft zu? Bevor man diese Frage zu beantworten versucht, erscheint es sinnvoll zu analysieren, ob und ggf. wie die Rekonstruktionsthese überprüft werden kann. Es geht um eine Bedeutungsanalyse von Begriffen, die sich auf Kollektive beziehen. Ob sich diese individualistisch rekonstruieren lassen, kann nicht a priori sondern nur nach einer detaillierten Analyse der Bedeutung der entsprechenden Kollektivbegriffe entschieden werden. Ob z. B. Begriffe wie Globalisierung, Wirtschaftswachstum oder Kapitalismus als Merkmale von Individuen rekonstruiert werden können, kann nur eine detaillierte Analyse der Bedeutung dieser Begriffe ergeben.

Entsprechend müsste man aus der Literatur Makrovariablen auswählen und untersuchen, inwieweit diese durch Individualmerkmale aggregiert werden können. Dabei müsste man solche Merkmale aussuchen, bei denen es scheint, dass ihre individualistische Rekonstruktion besonders schwierig ist. In dieser Weise gingen Hummell und Opp (1971) vor. Für die von diesen Autoren ausgewählten Makrovariablen zeigte sich, dass sie ohne Ausnahme individualistisch rekonstruiert werden konnten. Uns ist keine andere Schrift bekannt, in der die genannte These in dieser Weise systematisch überprüft wurde.

Aufgrund des genannten Problems, dass viele Makrovariablen, die in der Soziologie verwendet werden, äußerst unklar sind, bleibt nichts anderes übrig, als Vermutungen (also Hypothesen) über die Bedeutung der zu analysierenden Makromerkmale zu formulieren und zu prüfen. Hummell und Opp (1971) gehen in dieser Weise vor. Dabei analysieren sie auch die Bedeutung der bei Lazarsfeld und Menzel (1961) erwähnten globalen Merkmale (Hummell und Opp 1971, S. 36–38). Wir wollen diese Analyse hier nicht wiederholen, sondern nur das erste Beispiel, das Lazarsfeld und Menzel (1961) erwähnen, herausgreifen: Amerikanische Indianerstämme können charakterisiert werden durch die „frequency with which themes of ‚achievementmotive' make their appearance in their folktales" (S. 428). Das Kollektiv sind also Indianerstämme. Diese werden durch kulturelle Artefakte charakterisiert. Entsprechend könnte man moderne Gesellschaften durch die Anzahl der Bücher in Haushalten oder durch die Anzahl der Fahrräder charakterisieren, die sie besitzen. Ein anderes Beispiel ist das Vorhandensein einer U-Bahnstation in einem Wohngebiet (s. den Beitrag von Jürgen Friedrichs in diesem Band). Kann man diese Merkmale individualistisch rekonstruieren? Die „folktales" werden von Personen verfasst. Es liegt also eine zweistellige Relation der Art „Person P verfasst Erzählung E" vor. Wenn man nun lediglich den einen „Teil" der Relation auszählt, dann ändert dies nichts daran, dass hier individuelle Merkmale aggregiert werden. Bei dem Beispiel der U-Bahnstation wird ebenfalls einem Kollektiv (dem Wohngebiet) ein Merkmal (Vorliegen einer U-Bahnstation) zugeschrieben. Auch dieses Merkmal entsteht durch bestimmte Aktivitäten von Personen. Das Ergebnis dieser Handlungen ist dann die U-Bahnstation.

Für die Rekonstruktionsthese spricht weiter die kaum mehr zu überblickende Anzahl von „agent-based"-Computersimulationen (vgl. z. B. Macy und Flache 2009; Helbing 2012). Hier werden Makroeigenschaften auf der Grundlage individueller Merkmale konstruiert. Die Anzahl der Kollektivmerkmale, die erklärt werden, ist so umfassend, dass man diese Analysen als eine Bestätigung der Rekonstruktionsthese ansehen kann.

Gegen die zuletzt angeführten Argumente für die Rekonstruktionsthese – die große Anzahl vorliegender Mikro-Makro-Erklärungen, in denen Aggregationen vorgenommen wurden, und die Vielzahl von agentenbasierten Simulationen – könnte Folgendes eingewendet werden. In den genannten Schriften wurden nur solche Kollektivmerkmale ausgewählt, die individualistisch rekonstruiert werden konnten. So könnten Vertreter des individualistischen Programms sich nur mit solchen Makro-Explananda befassen, bei denen eine individualistische Rekonstruktion leicht möglich ist. Dieser Einwand ist nicht von der Hand zu weisen. Es wäre deshalb sinnvoll, einmal zu analysieren, ob es soziologische Explananda gibt, die nicht in den genannten Analysen enthalten sind und bei denen eine individualistische Rekonstruktion schwierig oder unmöglich ist. Vielleicht sollte man dabei auf Kollektivmerkmale der „grand theories" zurückgreifen wie die soziologische Systemtheorie und prüfen, inwieweit diese in den genannten Analysen enthalten sind und individualistisch rekonstruiert werden können. Solange jedoch keine Evidenz dafür vorliegt, dass Aggregationen oder individualistische Rekonstruktionen von Kollektivmerkmalen nicht möglich sind, ist die Rekonstruktionsthese vorläufig als bestätigt anzusehen.

Viele Gegner des individualistischen Forschungsprogramms machen sich nicht die Mühe, die große Zahl vorliegender theoretischer und empirischer Beiträge zu diesem Programm im Detail daraufhin zu prüfen, wie Aggregationen vorgenommen werden oder ob es Beispiele gibt, bei denen Aggregationen nicht möglich sind. Oft werden lediglich Thesen vertreten, die eher wie Dogmen klingen und nicht wie Ergebnisse detaillierter Analysen. So heißt es lapidar bei Gorski (2013, S. 662): „... social structures are more than the simple aggregation of individual persons, whence the perennial failures of methodological individualism in the social sciences." Man erwartet vergeblich eine Erläuterung, z. B. was mit „simple aggregations" gemeint ist, und Argumente, etwa Beispiele, bei denen Aggregationen nicht möglich sind. Man möchte auch wissen, was die „perennial failures of methodological individualism" sind.

8 Unterscheiden sich die Aggregationen beabsichtigter und unbeabsichtigter Folgen sozialen Handelns?

Gehen wir von einem Beispiel aus: Ein kollektiver Akteur, z. B. eine Gemeinde, trifft eine Entscheidung, nämlich ein Jugendzentrum einzurichten. Das Ziel sei, die Kriminalität von Jugendlichen zu vermindern. Das Jugendzentrum soll dabei Freizeitmöglichkeiten anbieten, die die Jugendlichen von kriminellen Handlungen abhalten. Die Verminderung der Kriminalität der Jugendlichen ist das explizit formulierte Ziel, das durch die Errichtung des Jugendzentrums erreicht werden soll. Wird das Ziel erreicht, dann handelt es sich um eine beabsichtigte Folge sozialen Handelns. Dieses Handeln ist die Einrichtung des Jugendzentrums.

Die Modellierung dieser Situation ist in Abb. 5 zusammengefasst. Das Modell für die *beabsichtigte Konsequenzen sozialen Handelns* zeigt Teil A von Abb. 5. Die beabsichtigte Wirkung, die Verminderung der Kriminalität durch Errichtung eines Jugendzentrums, ist eine Makrobeziehung. Wir nehmen also an, dass die Kriminalitätsrate verändert werden soll. Wir zeichnen einen Pfeil auf der Makroebene, da es sich aus der Sicht der Akteure um einen kausalen Effekt handelt. In Wirklichkeit ist dies eine Korrelation, wie wir vorher gesehen haben. Beabsichtigt sei weiter, dass das Jugendzentrum die Anreize zur Kriminalität vermindert. Dies führt dann zu verminderter Kriminalität und entsprechend zu einer verminderten Kriminalitätsrate. Beabsichtigt sind also die negative Makrobeziehung und die negative Anreizwirkung des Jugendzentrums (d. h. die Verminderung der Anreize für kriminelles Handeln) – siehe die eingekreisten Minuszeichen. Wenn die Mikrotheorie zutrifft, dann wird das Ziel erreicht: die Verminderung der Kriminalitätsrate.

Wie ändert sich die Modellierung, wenn der Bau des Jugendzentrums die *unbeabsichtigte Konsequenz* hat, dass die Kriminalitätsrate nicht sinkt, sondern steigt? Das neue Jugendzentrum könnte eine Gelegenheit für Jugendliche sein, sich zu treffen und dabei kriminelle Handlungen vorzubereiten. D. h. die Errichtung des Jugendzentrums führe zu kriminalitätsfördernden Anreizen, die eine Erhöhung der Kriminalitätsrate zur Folge hatten. Teil B der Abb. 5 stellt diese Situation dar: die Anreize zur Kriminalität steigen, was zur Erhöhung der Kriminalität und damit zu einer unbeabsichtigten Erhöhung der Kriminalitätsrate führt. Die unbeabsichtigten Beziehungen zwischen den Variablen sind wieder eingekreist.

Betrachten wir die Unterschiede in der Modellierung, wenn die Folgen sozialen Handelns beabsichtigt oder unbeabsichtigt sind. Die Unterschiede in den beiden Situ-

Abb. 5 Ein Beispiel für die Aggregation bei unbeabsichtigten und beabsichtigten Folgen sozialen Handelns

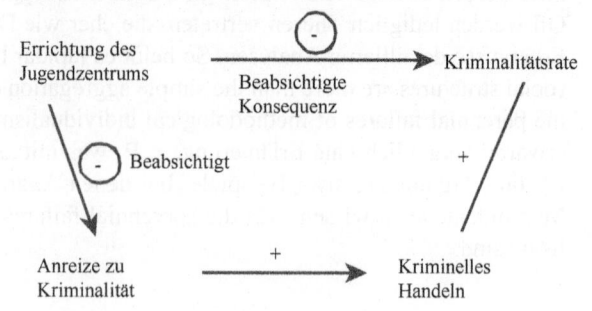

A. Beabsichtigte Folgen sozialen Handelns

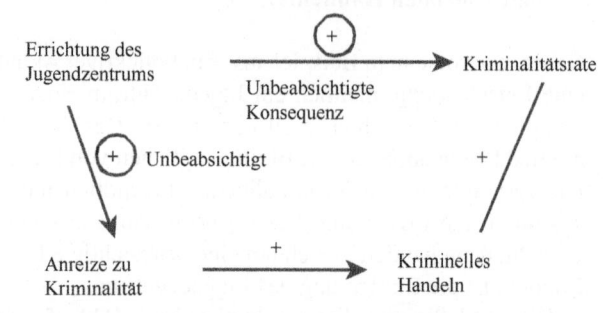

Errichtung des Jugendzentrums —(−)→ Kriminalitätsrate
Beabsichtigte Konsequenz

(−) Beabsichtigt

Anreize zu Kriminalität —(+)→ Kriminelles Handeln

(+)

B. Unbeabsichtigte Folgen sozialen Handelns

Errichtung des Jugendzentrums —(+)→ Kriminalitätsrate
Unbeabsichtigte Konsequenz

(+) Unbeabsichtigt

Anreize zu Kriminalität —(+)→ Kriminelles Handeln

(+)

ationen bestehen darin, dass bestimmte Handlungen von Akteuren zum einen Anreize verändern, die die beabsichtigten Folgen haben (oberer Teil von Abb. 5), im anderen Falle Anreize so verändern, dass unbeabsichtigte Folgen auftreten (unterer Teil von Abb. 5). In beiden Fällen unterscheidet sich die Struktur der Mikro-Makro-Erklärung nicht.

Dies zeigt Abb. 6 in genereller Weise. Es ist für die Modellierung unerheblich, ob die Veränderung der Anreize, die durch das Handeln der Akteure entsteht, beabsichtigt oder nicht beabsichtigt ist. Für die Erklärung der Wirkungen des Handelns kommt es darauf an, *in welcher Weise* welche Anreize tatsächlich verändert werden – siehe Pfeil 1 in Abb. 6. Ein anderes Beispiel mag dies illustrieren: Nehmen wir an, eine Person, die ihre Autoscheinwerfer einschaltet, beabsichtige nicht, die Reaktionen anderer Autofahrer zu beeinflussen. Die Beeinflussung könnte trotzdem auftreten, genau so, als wenn beabsichtigt ist, die anderen Autofahrer dazu zu veranlassen, die Scheinwerfer einzuschalten. Auch hier kann der Anreizeffekt von Handlungen unterschiedlich sein. Die Art der Modellierung bleibt aber gleich. Abbildung 6 zeigt, dass die Makro-zu-Mikro-Effekte unbeabsichtigt sein können. Dies hat dann insgesamt die unbeabsichtigt Konsequenzen, dass die Kriminalitätsrate steigt. Entsprechend werden die Ziele der Akteure, eine negative Beziehung auf der Makroebene (in Abb. 6 haben wir eine Linie gezeichnet), nicht erreicht.

Wir sind davon ausgegangen, dass in den Abbildungen die Akteure zutreffende Informationen über die Mikrotheorie haben. Wenn diese falsch ist, können ebenfalls unbeabsichtigte (oder auch beabsichtigte!) Folgen entstehen. Aber auch in diesem Falle ist die Art der Modellierung dieselbe.

Abb. 6 Allgemeines Modell zur Aggregation unbeabsichtigter und beabsichtigter Folgen sozialen Handelns

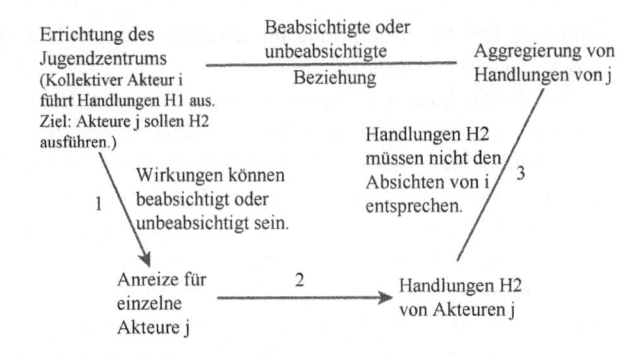

Errichtung des Jugendzentrums (Kollektiver Akteur i führt Handlungen H1 aus. Ziel: Akteure j sollen H2 ausführen.)

Beabsichtigte oder unbeabsichtigte Beziehung

Aggregierung von Handlungen von j

Handlungen H2 müssen nicht den Absichten von i entsprechen.

1 Wirkungen können beabsichtigt oder unbeabsichtigt sein.

3

Anreize für einzelne Akteure j

2

Handlungen H2 von Akteuren j

Aus diesen Überlegungen folgt nicht, dass es für sozialwissenschaftliche Analysen uninteressant ist, ob soziales Handeln beabsichtigte oder unbeabsichtigte Konsequenzen hat. Unser Beispiel in Abb. 5 illustriert dies. Die Gemeinde hätte das Jugendzentrum nicht gebaut, wenn die Erhöhung der Kriminalität zutreffend vorausgesagt worden wäre. Weiter dürfte das Bekanntwerden der unbeabsichtigten und unerwünschten Konsequenzen dazu führen, dass neue Handlungen ausgeführt werden, mit denen versucht wird, die unerwünschten Konsequenzen aus der Welt zu schaffen. Aber für die Art der Erklärung des Handelns der Akteure spielt es keine Rolle, ob Konsequenzen beabsichtigt sind oder nicht.

9 Emergenz und „Figurationen": Gibt es einen dritten Weg jenseits von Individualismus und Kollektivismus?

In diesem Abschnitt wollen wir uns zunächst mit dem Begriff der Emergenz befassen. Unser Argument lautet, dass es emergente Eigenschaften gibt, dass diese jedoch nicht implizieren, dass Aggregationen nicht vorgenommen werden können. Sodann diskutieren wir einige Argumente von Gert Albert (2013), der diese These bestreitet.

9.1 „Emergenz" und die Aggregation individueller Merkmale

Wenn auch der Begriff der Emergenz oft in unklarer und mehrdeutiger Weise verwendet wird (vgl. vor allem die detaillierte Darstellung bei Sawyer 2005), so bezieht er sich oft auf die Beziehung zwischen Individuum und Kollektiv, es geht also um Mikro-Makro-Beziehungen. „Many accounts of the micro-macro link use the philosophical notion of emergence to argue that collective phenomena are collaboratively created by individuals yet are not reducible to individual action" (Sawyer 2001, S. 552 – der Autor zitiert eine umfangreiche Literatur, die diese These belegt). Eine Illustration ist die V-Formation eines Vogelzuges (Sawyer 2002, S. 229). Ein einzelner Vogel hat nicht die Eigenschaft einer „V-Formation", diese ist Eigenschaft des Vogelzuges. Ein weiteres Beispiel ist die Arbeitsteilung. Diese, so Blau (1964, S. 3) „is an emergent property of communities that has no counterpart in a corresponding property of individuals". Blau erwähnt weiter die „Altersverteilung". Diese sei ein Gruppenmerkmal: „individuals have no age distribution, only an age" (S. 3). Die Emergenzthese wird auch oft so formuliert, dass das Ganze mehr sei als die Summe seiner Teile.[11] So besteht eine Interaktionsstruktur nicht nur aus der Menge der Individuen, wie wir vorher sahen.

Bei der Diskussion der Emergenzthese müssen drei Fragen unterschieden werden. 1) Trifft die Emergenzthese für den sozialen Bereich zu, d. h. gibt es tatsächlich emergente Eigenschaften, die Kollektiven, aber nicht Individuen zukommen? Angenommen, die Emergenzthese trifft zu. In diesem Falle entstehen zwei weitere Fragen. 2) Schließt die Emergenzthese aus, dass Kollektivmerkmale durch eine Aggregation individueller Merkmale *konstruiert* werden können? 3) Schließt die Emergenzthese aus, dass Kollektiveigenschaften individualistisch *erklärt* werden können? Auf diese Fragen soll im Folgenden kurz eingegangen werden.[12]

Zunächst muss aber eine andere Frage geklärt werden. Wenn ein Begriff in unklarer und vieldeutiger Weise verwendet wird, ist zunächst festzulegen, welche Bedeutung bei einer Analyse zugrunde gelegt werden soll. Es ist nicht auszuschließen, dass unterschiedliche Definitionen zu unterschiedlichen Antworten auf die genannten Fragen führen. Im Folgenden wird der Emergenzbegriff, wie angedeutet, in folgender Weise verwendet: Merkmale von Kollektiven heißen „emergent", wenn sie nicht Individuen zugeschrieben werden können. Begriffe wie Altersverteilung oder Globalisierung sind Beispiele. Wir gehen von diesem Begriff aus, weil er in der Literatur häufig in dieser Weise definiert wird.

Zur ersten Frage ist festzustellen, dass es ohne Zweifel Individualmerkmale gibt, die nicht Kollektiven zugeschrieben werden können. Ein Individuum hat z. B. weder ein Wirtschaftswachstum noch eine Scheidungsrate. Man kann sogar soweit gehen und behaupten, dass kaum ein Individualmerkmal (oder vielleicht sogar überhaupt kein Individualmerkmal) auch Kollektiven zugeschrieben werden kann. Selbst wenn die *Wörter* identisch sind, so unterscheidet sich doch deren *Bedeutung*. So bezieht sich der Ausdruck „Alter" auf die Dauer der Existenz eines Gegenstandes. Aber das Objekt, das ein Alter haben kann, ist zum einen ein Individuum, zum anderen ein Kollektiv. Somit unterscheidet sich die Bedeutung von „Alter", wenn es Individuen oder Kollektiven zugeschrieben wird.

Die zweite Frage – können Kollektivmerkmale auch dann individualistisch rekonstruiert werden, wenn die Emergenzthese zutrifft? – ist klar zu bejahen. Wir verweisen hier auf die vorangegangene Diskussion zur Rekonstruierbarkeit von Kollektivbegriffen durch Individualbegriffe. Wir werden im Übrigen auf diese Frage im nächsten Abschnitt zurückkommen.

Schließlich folgt aus der Geltung der Emergenzthese keineswegs, dass emergente Eigenschaften von Kollektiven nicht durch Eigenschaften von Individuen *erklärt* werden können. Wenn man davon ausgeht, dass Kollektiveigenschaften generell emergent sind, dann bestätigt die umfassende Literatur des individualistischen Forschungsprogramms, dass Emergenz kein Hinderungsgrund für individualistische Erklärungen ist.

---

[11] Zur Explikation dieser vieldeutigen These vgl. z. B. Nagel (1965) und Schlick (1965).

[12] Zu diesen Fragen gibt es eine kaum mehr zu überblickende Literatur. Eine gute Zusammenstellung von Aufsätzen und weiterführender Literatur enthält Greve und Schnabel (2011).

9.2 Emergenz und „Figurationen"

Im Folgenden sollen einige Argumente von Gert Albert (2013) diskutiert werden, der eine Alternative zum individualistischen Forschungsprogramm skizziert und damit auch die Möglichkeit der Aggregation in Zweifel zieht: Albert führt u. a. einen neuen Emergenzbegriff ein und argumentiert, dass die ontologische Struktur der sozialen Realität „Reduktion", und dies heißt auch Aggregation, ausschließt. Schließlich vertritt Albert die These, es sei sinnvoll, auf die Formulierung von Gesetzen zu verzichten, da die soziale Realität so heterogen ist, dass sie nicht unter generelle Gesetze subsumiert werden kann. Diese Argumente sollen im Folgenden diskutiert werden.[13]

Der neue Emergenzbegriff. Dieser soll das bekannte Mikro-Makro-Schema in zentraler Weise erweitern. In der neuen Definition wird „die Emergenz zu einer Emergenz der Teile, nicht des Ganzen" (S. 212). Damit ist gemeint, dass das „Ganze" die „Teile" beeinflusst. So ist Kreativität emergent: Es gibt soziale Voraussetzungen von Kreativität „wie auch die sozialen Einwirkungen auf die Routinisierung kreativer Praktiken bei der Prägung des Habitus…" (S. 200). Wenn das „Ganze" eine Wirkung auf die „Teile" hat, dann bedeutet dies, dass Makroeigenschaften einen kausalen Effekt auf individuelle Eigenschaften haben oder haben können (s. auch das „neue" Mikro-Makro-Schema auf S. 215). So beeinflussen die sozialen Bedingungen (Makroebene) die Kreativität von Individuen (Mikroebene). Es handelt sich also um Makro-zu-Mikro-Beziehungen. Bei der These, dass Kreativität den Habitus prägt, handelt es sich um eine Mikrotheorie: „Kreativität" und „Habitus" sind individuelle Eigenschaften, wobei die erste Variable einen Einfluss auf die zweite hat.

Man kann selbstverständlich Makro-zu-Mikro-Beziehungen ebenfalls als „Emergenz" bezeichnen. D. h. man kann von Emergenz auch dann sprechen, wenn Mikroeigenschaften sozusagen hervorgebracht werden durch Makroeigenschaften. Normalerweise bezieht sich der Begriff auf emergente Makroeigenschaften, die also auf Mikroeigenschaften beruhen. Hier handelt es sich also um Mikro-zu-Makro-Beziehungen. Es steht jedem frei, Begriffe neu zu definieren, da Begriffsdefinitionen bekanntlich nicht wahr oder falsch sein können. Um aber Unklarheiten zu vermeiden, wäre es in diesem Falle zweckmäßig, zwischen Emergenz von oben (dies ist der neue Emergenzbegriff) und Emergenz von unten (so wird der Emergenzbegriff normalerweise verwendet) zu unterscheiden. Diese Neudefinition des Emergenzbegriffs ist also für unsere Diskussion des Aggregationsproblems irrelevant. Hier geht es um Mikro-zu-Makro-Beziehungen, bei Albert um Makro-zu-Mikro-Brückenannahmen. Diese sind selbstverständlich im individualistischen Forschungsprogramm enthalten, wie oben bei der Darstellung des Mikro-Makro-Modells (Abb. 1) gezeigt wurde.

Nebenbei bemerkt: Das individualistische Forschungsprogramm schließt keineswegs aus, dass Makro-zu-Mikro-Beziehungen auch analytisch sein können, wie Albert anscheinend glaubt (im Schema S. 215 ist von „Definitionen" die Rede). Wie

---

[13] Die Überlegungen von Albert erwecken den Eindruck, dass der Erklärungsansatz von Elias unvereinbar mit dem individualistischen Forschungsprogramm ist. Dies ist zumindest zweifelhaft bei seinem Werk „Der Prozess der Zivilisation" (Elias 1997), bei dem offensichtlich ein individualistischer Ansatz implizit verwendet wird (vgl. im Einzelnen Opp 1983, S. 149–175).

wir gezeigt haben, ist eine solche These abwegig (s. z. B. unser Beispiel zur Definition des persönlichen politischen Einflusses).

Ontologie und Erklärung. Gert Albert vertritt die These, dass eine „ontologische Unterschiedlichkeit" der sozialen Realität auch „verschiedene methodologische Vorgehensweisen empfehlen lässt" (S. 195). Nach Elias, so Albert, gibt es eine Hierarchie von Einheiten unterschiedlicher Integrationsstufen. „Das Kennzeichen der Gebilde/Integrate auf höheren Ebenen ist nun aber, dass sie weder ontologisch noch epistomologisch reduzierbar sind" (S. 200). D. h. „ontische Autonomie" impliziert „die Unmöglichkeit der reduktiven Erklärung der Eigenschaften höherer Ebenen" (vgl. hierzu auch z. B. Sawyer 2005, S. 63).

Mit „ontischer Autonomie" dürfte gemeint sein, dass man im sozialen Bereich unterschiedliche Arten von Einheiten unterscheiden oder auch abgrenzen kann wie Individuen, Kleingruppen (z. B. Familien), Organisationen und Gesellschaften. Gebilde sozialer Art (also Kollektive) werden bei Elias als „Figurationen" bezeichnet. „Figurationen sind Menschen-in-Beziehungen" (Albert 2013, S. 196). Wenn diese Einheiten so grundlegend verschieden sind, dann folgt, dass Aggregationen nicht möglich sind, da sich die „Natur" von Einheiten der Mikro- und Makroebene grundlegend unterscheidet.

Zunächst einmal hat unsere Diskussion des Aggregationsproblems gezeigt, dass Vertreter des individualistischen Forschungsprogramms nicht bestreiten, dass es unterschiedliche Einheiten gibt – man kann, wenn man will, auch von einer „ontischen Autonomie" der Einheiten sprechen. Warum es zweckmäßig sein soll, einen solchen sicherlich eindrucksvollen Ausdruck einzuführen, ist nicht ersichtlich. Die zentrale Frage ist aber, wie man von der „ontischen Autonomie" auf die Unmöglichkeit schließen kann, Individualmerkmale zu Kollektivmerkmalen zu aggregieren (und Makroeigenschaften individualistisch zu erklären). Selbst wenn man Kollektive als real existierend ansieht, fragt es sich, warum dies eine Aggregation und eine Erklärung durch Theorien über individuelles Handeln ausschließen soll. Wieso folgt aus „ontischer Autonomie", dass man spezielle Theorien für jede „Seinsschicht" benötigt (und dass, wohl als Folge, nicht aggregiert werden kann)? Was sind die Argumente dafür, dass aus der „ontischen Autonomie" von Kollektiven die Unmöglichkeit folgt, diese individualistisch zu rekonstruieren und zu erklären? Die bloße Tatsache, dass Sachverhalte verschieden sind, impliziert noch nichts darüber, dass sie mit unterschiedlichen Theorien erklärt werden müssen oder dass keine Aggregation möglich ist. Diese Frage, warum „ontische Autonomie" „Irreduzierbarkeit" zur Folge haben soll, wird von Albert an keiner Stelle auch nur gestellt, geschweige denn überzeugend beantwortet. Noch einmal: Wieso ist es auszuschließen, dass es *Theorien* geben kann, die die Eigenschaften von sehr unterschiedlichen „Seinsebenen" oder „Figurationen" erklären können und dass eine Aggregation möglich ist?

Zur Prüfung der These der „Irreduzierbarkeit" hätte man die sozialwissenschaftliche Literatur analysieren können, in der verschiedene soziale „Seinsebenen" behandelt werden. Es hätte sich dann gezeigt, dass sehr unterschiedliche Kollektivmerkmale individualistisch rekonstruiert und erklärt werden. Man blättere nur einmal Zeitschriften wir „Rationality & Society" oder „Public Choice" durch. Nun könnten

Vertreter der These der „Irreduzibilität" argumentieren, dass diese Arbeiten schwerwiegende Mängel aufweisen. Wenn das so ist, warum wird dies nicht gezeigt?

Das folgende Beispiel mag illustrieren, wie einfach „Konfigurationen" individualistisch zu erklären sind. Eine Dyade (z. B. eine Ehepaar) ist eine Konfiguration. Lässt sich deren Entstehung individualistisch erklären? Von Bedeutung sind die Anreize zur Aufnahme von Interaktionen und zu deren Fortführung. Sind solche Anreize gegeben, dann würde dies dazu führen, dass eine Dyade (also die einfachste Art einer Gruppe) entstanden ist. Tauschbeziehungen (und auch Interaktionen) werden dadurch erklärt, dass sich Individuen besser stehen, wenn sie eine Beziehung eingehen. Das Beispiel illustriert, dass unterschiedliche „ontische Seinsebenen" – Individuen und Gruppen – kein Hindernis sind, die höhere „Seinsebene" durch eine Theorie zu erklären, die sich auf die unterste „Seinsebene" (Individuen) bezieht. Dieses Beispiel setzt eine Aggregation voraus. Wie gezeigt, wird eine „Dyade" aggregiert aus Eigenschaften von Individuen.

Es fragt sich generell, inwieweit „ontologische" Fragen für die Beurteilung der Fruchtbarkeit des individualistischen Forschungsprogramms und damit für die Möglichkeit von Aggregationen überhaupt von Bedeutung sind. Solche Fragen „zielen auf die Grundstrukturen des Sozialen und versuchen zu bestimmen, worin die Seinsweise des Sozialen überhaupt besteht. In welchem Sinne gibt es soziale Phänomene und in welchem Sinne individuelle? Sind Soziales und Individuelles distinkte Entitäten oder handelt es sich um Kategorien zur Analyse einer Wirklichkeit, in der beides immer gemeinsam auftritt, in der vielleicht Soziales ‚nichts anderes' ist als ein aggregiertes Mikro?" (Greve et al. 2008, S. 10). Zunächst einmal fragt es sich, wie solche Fragen überhaupt beantwortet werden können. Wie stellt man z. B. fest, ob „Soziales ‚nichts anderes' ist als ein aggregiertes Mikro"? Im individualistischen Forschungsprogramm geht es um Erklärung konkreter sozialer Sachverhalte und nicht um das Wesen oder die „Seinsweise" des Sozialen. Beim Aggregationsproblem ist nicht die Frage, ob „Soziales ‚nichts anderes' ist als ein aggregiertes Mikro". Die Frage ist, ob sich Begriffe, die sich auf Kollektive beziehen, rekonstruieren lassen als Merkmale von Individuen (genauer: als Begriffe, die sich auf Individuen beziehen). Zur Erklärung von Makrovariablen ist es dann von Bedeutung, wie Individualmerkmale (die abhängige Variablen einer Mikrotheorie sind) aggregiert werden können. Es ist sehr fraglich, ob Reflexionen über die „Seinsweise" des Sozialen zur Beantwortung solcher Fragen hilfreich sind.

Die folgenden Überlegungen sollen diese These weiter verdeutlichen. Es wird behauptet, dass allein Individuen real sind, aber keineswegs Kollektive. Daraus folgt dann, dass es nicht möglich ist, etwas Reales zu etwas Irrealem zu aggregieren. Die erste Frage in diesem Argument ist, was „real" bedeutet. Ist gemeint, dass man nur Individuen direkt beobachten (z. B. berühren) kann – wie etwa ein Auto oder einen Vogel, aber nicht Kollektive? Wenn dies gemeint ist, dann kann man zustimmen: Kollektive sind nicht real. Man kann aber „real" auch anders definieren: „real" ist etwas, das man identifizieren kann und über das man somit Aussagen treffen kann, die empirisch geprüft werden können. So kann man feststellen, dass die USA eine „Gesellschaft" ist, und man kann verschiedene Hypothesen über die USA formulieren und überprüfen – obwohl die USA ein Kollektiv ist und in der ersten Bedeutung von „real" gar nicht existiert. Weiter kann man fragen, ob Eigenschaften der USA etwa die Kriminalitätsrate oder die Kohäsion, individualistisch rekonstruiert werden können und ob diese Eigenschaften erklärt werden können. Ist es für die Beantwortung dieser Fragen wirklich von Bedeutung, ob die USA in irgendeinem Sinne „real" ist? Offensichtlich ist die Antwort „nein". Im individualistischen Programm geht es um theoretische und nicht um „ontologische" Fragen. Zu dem Argument, dass aus der „Realität" von Individuen und der „Nicht-Realität" von Kollektiven folge, dass Merkmale von Kollektiven nicht individualistisch erklärt und rekonstruiert werden können, möchte man wissen, wieso das eine aus dem anderen „folgt". Ist dies ein logischer Schluss? Wenn ja: wie lautet die Schlussregel? Oder bezieht sich „folgt" lediglich auf eine Plausibilitätsbeziehung? Dann möchte man Argumente hören.

Sollte man auf die Formulierung von Gesetzen verzichten? Liegen keine sozialwissenschaftlichen Gesetze vor, dann ist auch eine Mikro-Makro-Erklärung kaum sinnvoll. Damit verliert das Aggregationsproblem an Bedeutung: wenn Mikro-Makro-Erklärungen mangels Mikrogesetzen fragwürdig sind, wen interessiert dann noch das Aggregationsproblem? Es ist also sinnvoll, ein Argument zu diskutieren, das die Existenz sozialwissenschaftlicher Gesetze in Zweifel zieht. Die These von Gert Albert lautet, dass es aufgrund der „Wandelbarkeit des menschlichen Erfahrens und Verhaltens" sinnlos ist, nach allgemeinen Handlungsgesetzen Ausschau zu halten. „Diese Wandelbarkeit... impliziert die Wandelbarkeit der damit verbundenen theoretischen Gesetze und erfordert von daher eine auf diese Sachverhalte zugeschnittene Methodologie". Dies ist ein zentrales Missverständnis über die Möglichkeit, Theorien zu formulieren und anzuwenden. Die Wenn-Komponente (oder Je-Komponente) einer informativen Theorie umfasst extrem unterschiedliche Arten von empirischen Sachverhalten. Diese sind in konkreten Anwendungssituationen die Anfangsbedingungen. So beziehen sich lerntheoretische Hypothesen auf alle Arten von Belohnungen und Bestrafungen; die weite Version der Theorie rationalen Handelns umfasst ebenfalls alle möglichen Arten von Präferenzen und Restriktionen. Diese Theorien sind entsprechend in extrem unterschiedlichen Situationen anwendbar, seien es Stämme in der Steinzeit, Entwicklungsländer, Agrar- oder Industriegesellschaften. Entsprechend können diese Theorien auch sehr unterschiedliche Sachverhalte wie Handlungen in sehr unterschiedlichen Situationen erklären. Es ist also abwegig zu behaupten, die Heterogenität der sozialen Realität mache die Formulierung von Gesetzen unmöglich oder sinnlos. Ist z. B. ein Gesetz des freien Falls nicht möglich, weil die Heterogenität der Gegenstände, die fallen können, extrem groß ist? Derartige Argumente wurden in der Literatur seit langem behandelt und zurückgewiesen – vgl. hierzu bereits Nagel (1961, S. 459–466). Wenn Albert entsprechend den Gesetzesbegriff aufweichen möchte, wäre es hilfreich gewesen, wenn er die Art der Gesetze, die er im Auge hat, etwas näher charakterisiert hätte. Wie müsste man z. B. die Wert-Erwartungstheorie modifizieren? Solche konkreten Fragen werden jedoch auch nicht ansatzweise behandelt.

10 Diskussion

Wie könnte eine fruchtbare Diskussion des Aggregationsproblems weitergeführt werden? Wenn man an der Weiterentwicklung der Sozialwissenschaften interessiert ist, d. h. an der Beantwortung konkreter Erklärungsfragen und der Weiterentwicklung sozialwissenschaftlicher Theorien, dann sind die eher *philosophischen* Debatten wenig hilfreich. So fragt es sich, inwieweit z. B. die Beiträge in den Bänden von Greve und Schnabel (2011) über Emergenz und von Greve et al. (2008) über Mikro-Makro-Erklärungen für die Lösung der Erklärungsprobleme, an denen Sozialwissenschaftler arbeiten, hilfreich sind. Angenommen, Forscher sind interessiert an den Wirkungen von Mindestlöhnen auf die Höhe der Arbeitslosigkeit, an den Wirkungen der Globalisierung auf die Entwicklung der Armut oder an den Wirkungen von Bestrafungen auf das bestrafte Verhalten. Inwieweit tragen die Beiträge in den genannten Bänden (und generell die Art der philosophischen Analysen, die diese Bände repräsentieren) dazu bei, dass diese Forscher bessere Erklärungen finden – und dies bedeutet auch, methodologische Fehler in ihren Beiträgen vermeiden? Für den Autor dieses Aufsatzes ist die Lektüre derartiger Schriften ein äußerst frustrierendes Unternehmen. Es ist meist unmöglich, die Beziehungen derartiger Analysen zur Theoriebildung oder Forschung in der Soziologie herzustellen. Man hat sogar oft den Eindruck, dass die Autoren wenig von der konkreten sozialwissenschaftlichen Theoriebildung und Forschung wissen oder nicht daran interessiert sind. Dies gilt auch für das Aggregationsproblem, das nicht im Detail behandelt wird. Wie wissenschaftstheoretische Analysen aussehen können, die für Sozialwissenschaftler hilfreich sind, zeigen Schriften von Hempel (1965) oder Nagel (1961), in denen z. B. der Gehalt funktionalistischer Analysen oder die Logik der Typenbildung analysiert werden. Zu erwähnen ist auch Little (1991, 1998), dessen Analysen konkrete sozialwissenschaftliche Schriften zum Gegenstand haben. Man kann nur hoffen, dass sich in Zukunft Philosophen stärker als bisher den Praktiken der Sozialwissenschaften widmen und auch so konkrete Fragen wie das Aggregationsproblem im Detail analysieren.

Literatur

Albert, Gert. 2013. Figuration und Emergenz. Zur Ontologie und Methodologie des Ansatzes von Norbert Elias. *Kölner Zeitschrift für Soziologie und Sozialpsychologie* 65:193–222.
Bearman, Peter, James Moody und Katherine Stovel. 2004. Chains of affection: The structure of adolescent romantic and sexual networks. *American Journal of Sociology* 110:44–91.
Blau, Peter M. 1964. *Exchange and power in social life*. New York: Wiley.
Bohnen, Alfred. 2000. *Handlungsprinzipien oder Systemgesetze*. Tübingen: Mohr Siebeck.
Boudon, Raymond. 1980. *Die Logik des gesellschaftlichen Handelns. Eine Einführung in die soziologische Denk- und Arbeitsweise*. Darmstadt: Luchterhand.
Burgess, Robert L., und Don Jr. Bushell. Hrsg. 1969. *Behavioral sociology. The experimental analysis of social process*. New York: Columbia University Press.
Buskens, Vincent, Werner Raub und Marcel A. L. M. Van Assen. 2012. *Micro-macro links and microfoundatins in sociology*. London: Routledge.
Cherkaoui, Mohamed. 2005. *Invisible codes: Essays on generative mechanisms*. Oxford: Oxford University Press.
Coleman, James S. 1964. *Introduction to mathematical sociology*. Glencoe: Free Press (Ill).
Coleman, James S. 1987. Microfoundations of macrosocial behavior. In *The micro-macro link*, Hrsg. Jeffrey C. Alexander, Bernhard Giesen, Richard Münch und Neil Smelser, 153–173. Berkeley: University of California Press.
Coleman, James S. 1990. *Foundations of social theory*. Cambridge: Belknap Press of Harvard University Press.

Diekmann, Andreas. 2007. *Empirische Sozialforschung. Grundlagen, Methoden, Anwendungen.* Reinbek: Rowohlt.
Elias, Norbert. 1997. *Über den Prozeß der Zivilisation.* Bd. 1 und 2. Frankfurt a. M.: Suhrkamp.
Esser, Hartmut. 1993. *Soziologie. Allgemeine Grundlagen.* Frankfurt a. M.: Campus.
Gorski, Philip S. 2013. What is critical realism? And why should you care? *Contemporary Sociology* 42:658–670.
Greshoff, Rainer. 2012. Soziale Aggregationen als Erklärungsproblem. *Zeitschrift für theoretische Soziologie* 1:109–122.
Greve, Jens, und Annette Schnabel. Hrsg. 2011. *Emergenz. Zur Analyse und Erklärung komplexer Strukturen.* Berlin: Suhrkamp.
Greve, Jens, Annette Schnabel und Rainer Schützeichel. 2008. Das Makro-Mikro-Makro-Modell der soziologischen Erklärung – zur Einleitung. In *Das Mikro-Makro-Modell der soziologischen Erklärung. Zur Ontologie, Methodologie und Metatheorie eines Forschungsprogramms,* Hrsg. Jens Greve, Annette Schnabel und Rainer Schützeichel, 7–17. Wiesbaden: VS Verlag für Sozialwissenschaften.
Helbing, Dirk. Hrsg. 2012. *Social self-organization. Agent-based simulations and experiments to study emergent social behavior.* Berlin: Springer VS.
Hempel, Carl G. 1965. *Aspects of scientific explanation and other essays in the philosophy of science.* New York: Free Press.
Hernes, Gudmund. 1976. Structural change in social processes. *American Journal of Sociology* 82:513–547.
Homans, George C. 1958. Social behavior as exchange. *The American Journal of Sociology* 63:597–606.
Homans, George C. 1974. *Social behavior. Its elementary form* (1. Aufl. 1961). New York: Harcourt, Brace & World.
Hummell, Hans J. 1973. Methodologischer Individualismus, Struktureffekte und Systemkonsequenzen. In *Soziales Verhalten und soziale Systeme,* Hrsg. Karl-Dieter Opp und Hans J. Hummell, 61–134. Frankfurt a. M.: Athenäum.
Hummell, Hans J., und Karl-Dieter Opp. 1968. Sociology without sociology. The reduction of sociology to psychology: A program, a test, and the theoretical relevance. *Inquiry* 11:205–226.
Hummell, Hans J., und Karl-Dieter Opp. 1971. *Die Reduzierbarkeit von Soziologie auf Psychologie. Eine These, ihr Test und ihre theoretische Bedeutung.* Braunschweig: Vieweg.
Jansen, Dorothea. 2006. *Einführung in die Netzwerkanalyse. Grundlagen, Methoden, Forschungsbeispiele.* Wiesbaden: VS Verlag für Sozialwissenschaften.
Jasso, Guillermina. 2010. Linking individuals and societies. *Journal of Mathematical Sociology* 34:1–54.
Kadushin, Charles. 2012. *Understanding social networks: Theories, concepts, and findings.* Oxford: Oxford University Press.
Kelle, Udo, und Christian Lüdemann. 1995. „Grau, Teurer Freund, ist alle Theorie…" Rational Choice und das Problem der Brückenannahmen. *Kölner Zeitschrift für Soziologie und Sozialpsychologie* 47:249–267.
Kelle, Udo, und Christian Lüdemann. 1996. Theoriereiche Brückenannahmen? Eine Erwiderung auf Siegwart Lindenberg. *Kölner Zeitschrift für Soziologie und Sozialpsychologie* 48:542–545.
Lazarsfeld, Paul F., und Herbert Menzel. 1961. On the relation between individual and collective properties. In *Complex organizations. A sociological reader,* Hrsg. Amitai Etzioni, 421–440. New York: Holt, Rinehart & Winston.
Lindenberg, Siegwart. 1996a. Die Relevanz theoriereicher Brückenannahmen. *Kölner Zeitschrift für Soziologie und Sozialpsychologie* 48:126–140.
Lindenberg, Siegwart. 1996b. Theoriegesteuerte Konkretisierung der Nutzentheorie. Eine Replik auf Kelle/Lüdemann und Opp/Friedrichs. *Kölner Zeitschrift für Soziologie und Sozialpsychologie* 48:560–565.
Lindenberg, Siegwart. 1977. Individuelle Effekte, kollektive Phänomene und das Problem der Transformation. In *Probleme der Erklärung sozialen Verhaltens,* Hrsg. Klaus Eichner und Werner Habermehl, 46–84. Meisenheim am Glan: Hain.
Lindenberg, Siegwart, und Reinhard Wippler. 1978. Theorienvergleich: Elemente der Rekonstruktion. In *Theorienvergleich in den Sozialwissenschaften,* Hrsg. Karl Otto Hondrich und Joachim Matthes, 219–231. Darmstadt: Luchterhand.
Little, Daniel. 1991. *Varieties of social explanation. An introduction to the philosophy of social science.* Boulder: Westview Press.
Little, Daniel. 1998. *Microfoundations, method, and causation. On the philosophy of the social sciences.* New Brunswick: Transaction.

Macy, Michael, und Andreas Flache. 2009. Social dynamics from the bottom up: Agent-based models of social interaction. In *The Oxford handbook of analytical sociology*, Hrsg. Peter Hedström und Peter Bearman, 245–268. Oxford: Oxford University Press.
Mayntz, Renate. 1963. *Soziologie der Organisation*. Reinbek: Rowohlt.
McClelland, David C. 1961. *The achieving society*. New York: The Free Press.
McGlohon, Mary, Leman Akoglu und Christos Faloutsos. 2011. Statistical properties of social networks. In *Social network data analytics*, Hrsg. Charu C. Aggarwal, 17–42. New York: Springer.
Nagel, Ernest. 1961. *The structure of science. Problems in the logic of scientific explanation*. London: Routledge & Kegan Paul.
Nagel, Ernest. 1965. Über die Aussage „Das Ganze ist mehr als die Summe seiner Teile". In *Logik der Sozialwissenschaften*, Hrsg. Ernst Topitsch, 225–235. Köln: Kiepenheuer & Witsch.
Opp, Karl-Dieter. 1972. *Verhaltenstheoretische Soziologie. Eine neue soziologische Forschungsrichtung*. Reinbek: Rowohlt.
Opp, Karl-Dieter. 1979. *Individualistische Sozialwissenschaft. Arbeitsweise und Probleme individualistisch und kollektivistisch orientierter Sozialwissenschaften*. Stuttgart: Enke.
Opp, Karl-Dieter. 1983. *Die Entstehung sozialer Normen. Ein Integrationsversuch soziologischer, sozialpsychologischer und ökonomischer Erklärungen*. Tübingen: Mohr Siebeck.
Opp, Karl-Dieter. 1999. Contending conceptions of the theory of rational action. *Journal of Theoretical Politics* 11:171–202.
Opp, Karl-Dieter. 2004. Die Theorie rationalen Handelns im Vergleich mit alternativen Theorien. In *Paradigmen der akteurszentrierten Soziologie*, Hrsg. Manfred Gabriel, 43–68. Wiesbaden: VS Verlag für Sozialwissenschaften.
Opp, Karl-Dieter. 2009. Das individualistische Erklärungsprogramm in der Soziologie. Entwicklung, Stand und Probleme. *Zeitschrift für Soziologie* 38:26–47.
Opp, Karl-Dieter. 2011. The beneficial and unintended consequences of false beliefs about norm violation. When Is there a ‚preventive effect of ignorance'? In *Sociology and the unintended. Robert Merton Revisited*, Hrsg. Adriana Mica, Arkadiusz Peisert und Jan Winczorek, 257–283. Frankfurt a. M.: Peter Lang.
Opp, Karl-Dieter. 2014. *Methodologie der Sozialwissenschaften. Einführung in Probleme ihrer Theorienbildung und praktischen Anwendung*. Wiesbaden: Springer VS.
Opp, Karl-Dieter, und Jürgen Friedrichs. 1996. Brückenannahmen, Produktionsfunktionen und die Messung von Präferenzen. *Kölner Zeitschrift für Soziologie und Sozialpsychologie* 48:546–559.
Popitz, Heinrich. 1968. *Über die Präventivwirkung des Nichtwissens. Dunkelziffer, Norm und Strafe*. Tübingen: Mohr Siebeck.
Raub, Werner, und Thomas Voss. 1981. *Individuelles Handeln und gesellschaftliche Folgen. Das individualistische Forschungsprogramm in den Sozialwissenschaften*. Darmstadt: Luchterhand.
Rauhut, Heiko. 2013. Beliefs about lying and spreading of dishonesty: Undetected lies and their constructive and destructive social dynamics in dice experiments. *PLOS One* 8:1–8.
Rautenberg, Wolfgang. 2008. *Einführung in die mathematische Logik: Ein Lehrbuch*. Wiesbaden: Vieweg + Teubner.
Sawyer, Keith. 2001. Emergence in sociology: Contemporary philosophy of mind and some implications for sociological theory. *American Journal of Sociology* 107:551–585.
Sawyer, Keith. 2002. Durkheim's dilemma: Towrd a sociology of emergence. *Sociological Theory* 20:227–247.
Sawyer, R. Keith. 2005. *Social emergence. Societies as complex systems*. Cambridge: Cambridge University Press.
Schelling, Thomas C. 1978. *Micromotives and macrobehavior*. New York: W.W. Morton and Company.
Schlick, Moritz. 1965. Über den Begriff der Ganzheit. In *Logik der Sozialwissenschaften*, Hrsg. Ernst Topitsch, 213–223. Köln: Kiepenheuer & Witsch.
Schmid, Michael. 2009. Das Aggregationsproblem – Versuch einer methodologischen Analyse. In *Hartmut Essers Erklärende Soziologie. Kontroversen und Perspektiven*, Hrsg. Paul Hill, Frank Kalter, Johannes Kopp, Clemens Kroneberg und Rainer Schnell, 135–167. Frankfurt a. M.: Campus.
Simon, Herbert A. 1997. *Administrative behavior. A study of decision-making processes in administrative organizations. 1945*. New York: The Free Press.
Trappmann, Mark, Hans J. Hummell und Wolfgang Sodeur. 2010. *Strukturanalyse sozialer Netzwerke. Konzepte, Modelle, Methoden*. Wiesbaden: VS Verlag für Sozialwissenschaften.
Udéhn, Lars. 2001. *Methodological individualism*. London: Routledge.

Udéhn, Lars. 2002. The changing face of methodological individualism. *Annual Review of Sociology* 28:479–507.
Vanberg, Viktor. 1975. *Die zwei Soziologien. Individualismus und Kollektivismus in der Sozialtheorie.* Tübingen: J.C.B. Mohr.
Vega-Redondo, Fernando. 2007. *Complex social networks.* Cambridge: Cambridge University Press.
Weber, Max. 2004. *Die protestantische Ethik und der Geist des Kapitalismus. Vollständige Ausgabe* (hrsg. und eingeführt von Dirk Käsler). München: C.H.Beck.
Zoglauer, Thomas. 2008. *Einführung in die formale Logik für Philosophen.* Göttingen: Vandenhoeck & Ruprecht.

Karl-Dieter Opp, 1937, Professor Emeritus an der Universität Leipzig und Affiliate Professor an der University Washington (Seattle). Forschungsschwerpunkte: Soziologische Theorie (insbes. „Rational Choice"-Theorie), kollektives Handeln und politischer Protest, Normen und Institutionen und Methodologie der Sozialwissenschaften. Neuere Buchpublikationen: Methodologie der Sozialwissenschaften. Wiesbaden 2014; Theories of political protest and social movements. A multidisciplinary introduction, critique and synthesis. London 2009. Neuere Aufsätze: Modeling micro-macro relationships: Problems and solutions. In: Micro-macro links and microfoundations in sociology. London 2012; Collective identity, rationality and collective action. Rationality & Society 24, 2012; Die Produktion historischer „Tatsachen". Wie die falsche Teilnehmerzahl der Leipziger Montagsdemonstration am 9. Oktober 1989 Allgemeingut wurde. Soziologie 41, 2012; What is analytical sociology? Strengths and weaknesses of a new sociological research program. Social Science Information 52, 2013; Norms and rationality. Is moral behavior a form of rational action? Theory & Decision 74, 2013.

Längsschnittdaten und Mehrebenenanalyse

Georg Hosoya · Tobias Koch · Michael Eid

© Springer Fachmedien Wiesbaden 2014

Zusammenfassung In dem vorliegenden Beitrag werden exemplarisch anhand der Daten des australischen Household, Income and Labor Dynamics in Australia Surveys 10 (HILDA 10) einige basale Multilevelmodelle für längsschnittliche Daten vorgestellt. Hierbei handelt es sich um Übertragungen des Random-Intercept-Only-Modells, des Random-Intercept-Modells und des Random-Intercept-Random-Slope-Modells mit Level-1- und Level-2-Prädiktoren auf längsschnittliche Daten. Es wird auf die Modellierung von Kontexteffekten eingegangen. Eine Besonderheit bei längsschnittlichen Daten liegt darin, dass der Kontext der zeitvariierenden Beobachtungen auf Ebene-1 die Person (Ebene-2) darstellt. Um Effekte der soziologischen Makro-Ebene zu berücksichtigen, ist es notwendig, die Modelle um eine dritte Ebene zu erweitern. Ein Modell mit drei Ebenen wird vorgestellt und weitere Modelle zur Modellierung von Daten im Längsschnitt, wie ein Wachstumskurvenmodell und ein multivariates Multilevelmodell, werden kurz behandelt.

Schlüsselwörter Multilevelmodelle · Längsschnittliche Daten · Panel-Daten · Kontexteffekt

---

G. Hosoya (✉) · T. Koch · M. Eid
Fachbereich Erziehungswissenschaft und Psychologie, Freie Universität Berlin,
Habelschwerdter Allee 45, 4195 Berlin, Deutschland
E-Mail: georg.hosoya@fu-berlin.de

T. Koch
E-Mail: tkoch@zedat.fu-berlin.de

M. Eid
E-Mail: eid@zedat.fu-berlin.de

Longitudinal Data and Multilevel Analysis

Abstract In the present article a few basic multilevel models for longitudinal data are introduced and applied to the Household Income and Labor Dynamics in Australia Survey 10 (HILDA) for demonstrational purposes. The covered models are adaptions of the random-intercept-only model, the random-intercept models and the random- intercept random-slope model with and without level-1 and level-2 predictors to longitudinal data. The modeling of contextual effects is covered. One particularity in longitudinal data is the fact that persons (level-2) may be regarded as the context of the time-varying observations on level-1. To incorporate the macro-level of sociology, it is necessary to expand the model to a third level. A model with three levels is introduced and in addition a simple growth curve model and a multivariate multilevel model are presented.

Keywords Multilevel modeling · Longitudinal data analysis · Panel data · Contextual effects

1 Einleitung

Mehrebenenmodelle, wie gemischte Modelle oder hierarchisch lineare Modelle (siehe z. B. Bryk und Raudenbusch 1992; Snijders und Bosker 1999; Gelman und Hill 2007; Hox 2010; Pinheiro und Bates 2000; Rabe-Hesketh und Skrondal 2012; Hedeker und Gibbons 2006), sind eine elegante Möglichkeit der Datenanalyse, sofern die Unabhängigkeitsannahme der multiplen Regression verletzt ist. Dies ist typischer Weise dann der Fall, wenn Beobachtungen oder Messwerte ineinander verschachtelt sind. Bei querschnittlichen Untersuchungen, z. B. im erziehungswissenschaftlichen Kontext, sind Schüler (Level-1) in Klassen (Level-2) geschachtelt. Die Klassen wiederum sind in Schulen (Level-3) geschachtelt. Im soziologischen Kontext könnte die unterste Ebene (Level-1) das Individuum oder die Mikro-Ebene sein. Das Individuum ist in eine definierte Einheit, wie z. B. dem Wahlkreis geschachtelt (Level-2, Meso-Ebene-1), der Wahlkreis wiederum ist in einen Bezirk geschachtelt (Level-3, Meso-Ebene-2) und so fort bis zur Makro-Ebene.

Ferner ist die Anwendung der Mehrebenenanalyse bei längsschnittlichen Daten indiziert, weil in diesem Fall Messwerte oder Beobachtungen (Level-1) innerhalb von Personen (Level-2) geschachtelt sind. Bei Panel-Daten kommt als weitere besondere Eigenschaft hinzu, dass die Messwerte nicht nur in Personen geschachtelt, sondern die Personen in unterschiedlichen soziologischen Kontexten oder Regionen (Level-3) geschachtelt sind. Da die Personen zu unterschiedlichen Wellen befragt werden, kann sogar eine weitere Kreuzungsebene (Messzeitpunkt) hinzukommen.

Ein großer Vorteil der Mehrebenenanalyse besteht darin, dass es möglich ist, Effekte einer höheren Ebene auf eine niedrigere Hierarchieebene zu bewerten. Ebenso kann geprüft werden, inwiefern Zusammenhänge auf einer unteren Ebene durch Eigenschaften einer höheren Ebene moderiert werden. Ferner hat die Mehrebenenanalyse den Vorteil, dass bekannte Techniken der multiplen Regression, wie z. B. die simultane Berücksichtigung von kategorialen und kontinuierlichen Kovariaten oder Prädiktoren, problemlos möglich sind, da die Mehrebenenanalyse nichts weiteres ist, als eine Erweiterung der multiplen Regression um Effekte, die zwischen den Ebenen variieren können. Diese Effekte werden auch als Zufallseffekte oder Random-Effects bezeichnet. Insofern stellt die Mehrebenenanalyse ein interessantes methodisches Instrument dar, das es erlaubt, psychologische *und* soziologische Fragestellungen mit einem Modellierungsansatz zu prüfen. Psychologisch könnte es z. B. von Interesse sein, inwiefern die Lebenszufriedenheit eines Individuums von dem Vorliegen eines Arbeitsverhältnisses abhängt und inwiefern das Eintreten der Arbeitslosigkeit im Sinne eines kritischen Lebensereignisses sich auf die individuelle Lebenszufriedenheit auswirkt. Soziologisch kann es von Interesse sein, inwiefern Eigenschaften des soziologischen Kontexts mit der individuellen Lebenszufriedenheit zusammenhängen und ob Eigenschaften des Kontexts den Effekt der Arbeitslosigkeit auf die Lebenszufriedenheit moderieren.

Die in der Soziologie und Ökonometrie bekannten Fixed-Effects-Regressionsmodelle (FE-Modelle) (siehe z. B. Rabe-Hesketh und Skrondal 2012, S. 257 und Brüderl und Ludwig, im Druck) sind den Random-Intercept-Modellen der Mehrebenenanalyse formal sehr ähnlich. Ein Unterschied besteht darin, dass im Random-Intercept-Modell angenommen wird, dass die Intercepts normal verteilt sind, während diese Annahme bei FE-Modellen nicht getroffen wird. Die Random-Effects (RE-Modelle) oder Random-Coefficient-Regressionsmodelle der Ökonometrie sind formal den Random-Intercept-Random-Slope-Modellen der Mehrebenanalyse sehr ähnlich. Die in der Mehrebenenanalyse verwendeten Modelle wiederum sind Spezialfälle der verallgemeinerten gemischten Modelle. Im vorliegenden Artikel wird aus Konsistenzgründen durchgängig die Terminologie der Mehrebenenanalyse verwendet und es werden Hinweise gegeben, wie die entsprechenden Konzepte in der soziologischen Literatur bezeichnet werden.

2 Einfache längsschnittliche Mehrebenenmodelle

Zielsetzung des vorliegenden Beitrags besteht darin, Schritt für Schritt einige sehr basale Mehrebenenmodelle für längsschnittliche Daten vorzustellen und anhand einiger praktischer Beispiele zu erläutern. Zunächst wird das Random-Intercpet-Only-Modell vorgestellt, mit dem bewertet werden kann, ob eine Personenheterogenität hinsichtlich der längsschnittlich erhobenen abhängigen Variablen vorliegt. Dieses Modell wird um einen Prädiktor erweitert, mit dem geprüft werden kann, ob eine zeitvariierende Kovariate mit der abhängigen Variablen zusammenhängt. Das resultierende Modell wird Random-Intercept-Modell genannt. In einem nächsten Schritt wird das Random-Intercept-Modell um einen nach den Personen variierenden Effekt einer zeitvariierenden Prädiktorvariable erweitert. Das resultierende Modell ist ein Random-Intercept-Random-Slope-Modell. Zur Berücksichtigung von Effekten zeitstabiler Eigenschaften der Personen auf die abhängige Variable und der Prüfung einer möglichen Moderation von Zusammenhängen auf Level-1 durch personenbezogene Variablen auf Level-2 wird das Modell um einen zeitinvarianten, personenbezogenen Prädiktor erweitert. Das resultierende Modell ist das Random-Intercept-Random-Slope-Modell mit Level-2-Kovariaten. Um die Behandlung von Kontexteffekten im Längsschnitt zu verdeutlichen, werden zunächst Kontexteffekte im Querschnitt besprochen und das Prinzip wird direkt auf längsschnittliche Daten übertragen. Auf die Auswirkung der unterschiedlichen Möglichkeiten der Zentrierung auf die Interpretation der Koeffizienten wird eingegangen. Das längsschnittliche Kontextmodell wird um eine dritte Ebene erweitert, um Auswirkungen zeitstabiler Eigenschaften der Makro-Ebene auf Zusammenhänge auf den unteren Ebenen zu berücksichtigen. Es wird auf die Verwendung von zeitvariierenden Variablen, die auf der Makro-Ebene erhoben wurden, eingegangen und schließlich werden ein einfaches Wachstumskurvenmodell und ein einfaches multivariates Multilevelmodell vorgestellt.

2.1 Das Random-Intercept-Only-Modell bei längsschnittlichen Panel-Daten

Panel-Daten, wie diejenigen des deutschen Sozio-oekonomischen Panels (SOEP) (Schupp 2009) oder die Daten des australischen *Household, Income and Labor Dynamics in Australia Surveys* (HILDA) (Summerfield et al. 2011) haben typischerweise eine längsschnittliche Form. Individuen werden mehrfach zu unterschiedlichen Messzeitpunkten oder Wellen befragt. Aufgrund der längsschnittlichen Natur der Daten ist zu erwarten, dass die Unabhängigkeitsannahme der Residuen in der multiplen Regression verletzt ist, da Personen sich stabil über die Messzeitpunkte hinweg auf einer abhängigen Variablen unterscheiden können. Wird Personenheterogenität in der Analyse nicht berücksichtigt, kann es sein, dass der Forscher oder die Forscherin bei der Interpretation der Ergebnisse den sogenannten ökologischen Fehlschluss begeht (siehe z. B. Robinson 1950). Dies bedeutet, dass Zusammenhänge, die zwischen den Personen existieren, fälschlicher Weise auf der Ebene innerhalb der Person interpretiert werden. Darüber hinaus werden die Standardfehler verzerrt geschätzt, wodurch die Validität inferenzstatistischer Schlüsse gefährdet ist. Zur Bewertung des Ausmaßes der Personenheterogenität auf einer Variablen im Längsschnitt kommt das sogenannte Random-Intercept-Only-Modell zum Einsatz. Auf Basis dieses Modells lässt sich der Intraklassenkorrelationskoeffizient berechnen, mit dem bewertbar ist, wie viel Varianz in der abhängigen Variable auf Personenheterogenität zurückzuführen ist. Das Random-Intercept-Only-Modell wird in der Literatur auch als Random-Intercept oder Nullmodell bezeichnet. Das Modell und die damit verbundenen Verteilungsannahmen auf Populationsebene werden nun dargestellt.

Level-1-Gleichung (Messwerte):

$$y_{ti} = \beta_{0i} + \varepsilon_{ti} \tag{1.1}$$

Level-2-Gleichung (z. B. Personen):

$$\beta_{0i} = \gamma_{00} + \upsilon_{0i} \tag{1.2}$$

Gesamtgleichung:

$$y_{ti} = \gamma_{00} + \upsilon_{0i} + \varepsilon_{ti} \tag{1.3}$$

Die Level-1-Gleichung besagt, dass der Wert y_{ti} einer Person i zum Zeitpunkt t sich aus einem personenspezifischen Effekt β_{0i} und einem Level-1-Residuum ε_{ti} zusammensetzt. In der Level-2-Gleichung wird dieser Effekt in eine globalen Effekt γ_{00} und eine personenspezifische Abweichung υ_{0i} zerlegt. Diese personenspezifische Abweichung wird auch als Level-2-Residuum bezeichnet. Wird die Level-2-Geichung in die Level-1-Gleichung eingesetzt, ergibt sich die Gesamtgleichung. Diese Gleichung entspricht einem sehr einfachen Fixed-Effects-Modell der Soziologie und Ökonometrie ohne Prädiktoren und mit personenspezifischen Achsenabschnitten (siehe Brüderl und Ludwig, im Druck). Allerdings wird bei Fixed-Effects-Modellen keine Verteilungsannahme über die Intercepts getroffen. γ_{00} ist ein globaler y-Achsenabschnitt und υ_{0i} erfasst zeitkonstante Personenheterogenität. In der Mehrebenenanalyse werden Verteilungsannahmen bezüglich der Residuen auf Level-1 und Level-2 getroffen. Typischerweise wird angenommen, dass die Residuen auf Level-1 normal verteilt mit einem Erwartungswert von 0 und einer Varianz von σ_ε^2 sind:

$$\varepsilon_{ti} \sim N(0, \sigma_\varepsilon^2).$$

Es sind auch andere Residualstrukturen denkbar. So kann es gerade bei längsschnittlichen Daten sinnvoll sein, einen autoregressiven Effekt auf den Residuen zu modellieren, um verbleibende Autokorrelationen zwischen den Messzeitpunkten, die nicht durch das Modell abgefangen werden, zu berücksichtigen. Ferner ist es denkbar, dass die Residualvarianz zwischen den Individuen heterogen ist (Heteroskedasdizität), was es aus theoretischer Sicht sinnvoll macht, diese Heterogenität, sofern möglich, mit zu modellieren. Die Thematik der Modellierung von Residualstrukturen in Mehrebenenmodellen ist relativ komplex und sprengt den Rahmen einer einführenden Darstellung (siehe hierzu ausführlicher z. B. Singer und Willet 2003). Harring und Blozis (2013) und Fitzmaurice et al. (2004) widmen sich der Thematik für die Software SAS. Pinheiro und Bates (2000) behandeln das Thema für das R-Paket nlme. Ferner ist eine entsprechende Funktion nicht in jeder Analysesoftware verfügbar.

Die Residuen auf Level-2 sind normalverteilt mit einem Erwartungswert von 0 und einer Varianz von $\sigma_{\upsilon_0}^2$:

$$\upsilon_0 \sim N(0, \sigma_{\upsilon_0}^2).$$

Ferner sind die Level-1-Residualvarianz und die Level-2-Residualvarianz bei Annahme der Normalverteilung der Level-1-Residuen stochastisch unabhängig, von daher ergibt sich ein einfacher Satz der Varianzzerlegung, auf dem sich der Intraklassenkorrelationskoeffizient zur Bewertung der Personenhomogenität aufbauen lässt. Dieser Koeffizient lautet auf Populationsebene:

$$\rho = \frac{\sigma_{\upsilon_0}^2}{\sigma_{\upsilon_0}^2 + \sigma_\varepsilon^2}.$$

Der Intraklassenkorrelationskoeffizient bezeichnet den Anteil der Varianz zwischen den Level-2-Einheiten auf der abhängigen Variable an der Gesamtvarianz. Ist diese Varianz substanziell, ist auf jeden Fall eine Mehrebenenanalyse oder Fixed-Effects-

Regression angebracht. Dieses Modell eignet sich zur Prüfung substanzieller, zeitstabiler Unterschiede zwischen den Personen auf der abhängigen Variablen.

2.2 Das Random-Intercept-Modell mit Kovariaten bei längsschnittlichen Panel-Daten

Bei der Analyse von Panel-Daten ist es zusätzlich von Interesse, inwiefern Kovariaten oder Prädiktoren mit der abhängigen Variablen zusammenhängen. Im Folgenden wird anhand eines einfachen Modells mit einem Prädiktor gezeigt, wie Kovariaten, die zeitgleich mit Personenmerkmalen erhoben werden, in der Analyse berücksichtigt werden können. Diese Kovariaten werden auch Level-1-Kovariaten oder zeitvariierende Kovariaten genannt, da sie auf der untersten Ebene des Modells erhoben werden und über die Zeit und über die Personen hinweg schwanken können.

Ein einfaches Multilevel-Modell mit einer Level-1-Kovariate wird im Folgenden dargestellt (siehe z. B. Rabe-Hesketh und Skrondal 2012, Abschn. 3.3 für die allgemeine Form).

Level-1-Gleichung (Messwerte, Mikro-Modell):

$$y_{ti} = \beta_{0i} + \beta_{1i} x_{1ti} + \varepsilon_{ti} \quad (2.1)$$

Level-2-Gleichungen (Personen, Meso-Modell):

$$\beta_{0i} = \gamma_{00} + \upsilon_{0i} \quad (2.2)$$

$$\beta_{1i} = \gamma_{10} \quad (2.3)$$

Gesamtgleichung:

$$y_{ti} = (\gamma_{00} + \upsilon_{0i}) + \gamma_{10} x_{1ti} + \varepsilon_{ti} \quad (2.4)$$

In der Level-1-Gleichung wird ein zeitvariierender Prädiktor x_{1ti} in die Regression aufgenommen, dem ein entsprechender Koeffizient β_{1i} zugeordnet ist. Dieser Koeffizient kann potenziell über die Level-1-Einheiten (Personen) variieren. Allerdings wird dieser Prädiktor in den Level-2-Gleichungen auf γ_{10} „fixiert". Diese restriktive Annahme bedeutet, dass der Effekt des Prädiktors x_{1ti} auf die abhängige Variable für alle Individuen identisch ist. Aus Perspektive der soziologischen oder ökonometrischen Methodik handelt es sich hierbei um ein Fixed-Effect-Modell (FE-Modell) mit einem zeitvariierenden Prädiktor und einer Verteilungsannahme auf den variierenden Intercepts β_{0i}. Personenheterogenität wird durch das Level-2-Residuum υ_{0i} erfasst. An den Annahmen hinsichtlich der Verteilung der Level-1- und Level-2-Residuen ändert sich gegenüber dem Random-Intercept-Only-Modell nichts. Selbstverständlich kann das Modell um weitere zeitvariierende Prädiktoren auf Ebene-1 erweitert werden. Diese Prädiktoren können zeitvariierende Eigenschaften der Person sein, aber auch zeitvariierende Eigenschaften des Kontexts, in dem die Person lokalisiert ist. Das Erkenntnisinteresse der Anwendung dieses Modells liegt darin zu prüfen, ob die abhängige Variable mit zeitvariierenden Kovariaten zusammenhängt, wobei gleichzeitig die Heterogenität zwischen den Personen berücksichtigt wird.

2.3 Das Random-Intercept-Random-Slope-Modell bei längsschnittlichen Panel-Daten

Eine Annahme des Random-Intercept-Modells ist, dass der Effekt des zeitvariierenden Prädiktors x_{1ti} über alle Level-2-Einheiten hinweg konstant ist. Diese Annahme ist sehr restriktiv. Es ist psychologisch sinnvoll anzunehmen, dass der Effekt des Prädiktors zwischen den Personen variieren kann. Um Hypothesen diesbezüglich der Prüfbarkeit zuzuführen, ist es notwendig im Modell eine Variation des Effektes des Prädiktors über die Personen i zuzulassen. Modelle dieser Art werden im Kontext der Mehrebenenanalyse als Random-Intercept-Random-Slope-Modelle oder als Random-Coefficient-Modelle bezeichnet (siehe z. B. Rabe-Hesketh und Skrondal 2012, Kap. 4).

Level-1-Gleichung (Messwerte, Mikro-Modell):

$$y_{ti} = \beta_{0i} + \beta_{1i} x_{1ti} + \varepsilon_{ti} \tag{3.1}$$

Level-2-Gleichungen (Personen, Meso-Modell):

$$\beta_{0i} = \gamma_{00} + \upsilon_{0i} \tag{3.2}$$

$$\beta_{1i} = \gamma_{10} + \upsilon_{1i} \tag{3.3}$$

Gesamtgleichung:

$$y_{ti} = (\gamma_{00} + \upsilon_{0i}) + (\gamma_{10} + \upsilon_{1i}) x_{1ti} + \varepsilon_{ti} \tag{3.4}$$

In der zweiten Level-2-Gleichung wird die Restriktion auf dem Parameter β_{1i} gelöst und eine Variation nach der Ebene-2 (z. B. Personen) zugelassen. Dies geschieht durch das Hinzufügen des Level-2 Residuums υ_{1i}. Auf diese Weise ist es möglich zu bewerten, inwiefern der Effekt des Prädiktors x_{1ti} über die Personen schwankt. Dies ist im Kontext psychologischer Forschung interessant, da geprüft werden kann, ob interindividuelle Differenzen hinsichtlich der Wirkung des Prädiktors vorliegen. In einem weiteren Schritt können diese Differenzen durch personenbezogene, zeitstabile Kovariaten aufgeklärt werden.

Da nun zwei Level-2-Residuen existieren, ist es nötig, zusätzlich zu der Verteilungsannahme der Level-1-Residuen ε_{ti} eine Annahme über die Verteilung der Level-2-Residuen υ_{0i} und υ_{1i} zu treffen. Es wird angenommen, dass die Level-2-Residuen multivariat normal verteilt mit Mittelwerten von Null und einer Varianz-Kovarianz-Matrix Σ sind (siehe z. B. Eid et al. 2010). Über diese Matrix lässt sich bewerten, ob der Random-Koeffizient β_{0i} über die Level-2-Einheiten variiert, ob der Effekt des Prädiktors x_{1ti} über die Level-2-Einheiten variiert und ob ein Zusammenhang zwischen den variierenden Koeffizienten des Modells besteht.

Aus der Perspektive der ökonometrischen oder soziologischen Methodik handelt es sich um ein Random-Coefficient-Modell mit einer Verteilungsannahme auf den variierenden y-Achsenabschnitten und Steigungen. Prinzipiell ist es möglich, das Modell um weitere zeitvariierende Kovariaten zu erweitern und für diese Kovariaten nach der Person variierende Effekte aufzunehmen.

2.4 Das Random-Intercept-Random-Slope-Modell mit Level-2 Prädiktoren

Aus psychologischer Perspektive ist es interessant zu prüfen, inwiefern der Effekt des zeitvariierenden Prädiktors x_{1ti} von zeitstabilen Eigenschaften der Person, wie z. B. dem Geschlecht oder Persönlichkeitsmerkmalen, abhängt. Ferner kann von Interesse sein, inwiefern die Personenheterogenität, die durch den Koeffizienten β_{0i} erfasst wird, von den Persönlichkeitsmerkmalen abhängt. Um derartige Hypothesen zu prüfen, ist es notwendig die Level-2-Gleichungen um Level-2-Prädiktoren zu erweitern. Diese Prädiktoren heißen Level-2-Prädiktoren, da sie *zeitstabile* Eigenschaften der Level-2-Einheiten, z. B. der Personen darstellen.

Level-1-Gleichung (Messwerte, Mikro-Modell):

$$y_{ti} = \beta_{0i} + \beta_{1i}x_{1ti} + \varepsilon_{ti} \tag{4.1}$$

Level-2-Gleichungen (Personen, Meso-Modell):

$$\beta_{0i} = \gamma_{00} + \gamma_{01}z_{1i} + \upsilon_{0i} \tag{4.2}$$

$$\beta_{1i} = \gamma_{10} + \gamma_{11}z_{1i} + \upsilon_{1i} \tag{4.3}$$

Gesamtgleichung:

$$y_{ti} = (\gamma_{00} + \upsilon_{0i}) + \gamma_{01}z_{1i} + (\gamma_{10} + \upsilon_{1i})x_{1ti} + \gamma_{11}z_{1i}x_{1ti} + \varepsilon_{ti} \tag{4.4}$$

Die Modellerweiterung erfolgt durch die Aufnahme des Level-2-Prädiktors z_{1i} in die Level-2-Gleichungen. Auf diese Weise ist es möglich zu prüfen, ob die Koeffizienten β_{0i} und β_{1i} von der zeitstabilen Personeneigenschaft z_{1i} abhängen. γ_{00} ist der erwartete Wert des Koeffizienten β_{0i}, wenn der Level-2-Prädiktor z_{1i} eine Ausprägung von 0 besitzt. γ_{01} ist der Effekt des Level-2-Prädiktors z_{1i} auf den Koeffizienten β_{0i}, also der Effekt der zeitinvarianten Personenvariable z_{1i} auf die Personenheterogenität. υ_{0i} ist das Residuum der Level-2-Regressionsgleichung. γ_{10} ist der erwartete Effekt des Prädiktors x_{1ti} auf die abhängige Variable y_{ti}, wenn der Level-2-Prädiktor z_{1i} eine Ausprägung von Null besitzt. γ_{11} gibt an, inwiefern der Effekt des Level-1-Prädiktors x_{1ti} auf die anhängige Variable y_{ti} durch den Level-2-Prädiktor z_{1i} moderiert wird. υ_{1i} ist das Residuum der entsprechenden Regression. Auch bei diesem Modell wird eine multivariate Normalverteilung der Level-2-Residuen angenommen. Mittels dieses Modells ist also bewertbar, inwiefern zeitstabile Eigenschaften der Level-2-Einheiten (z. B. Personen) sich auf die abgängige Variable auswirken und ob der Zusammenhang zwischen einer Level-1-Kovariate und der abhängigen Variable durch die zeitkonstante Level-2-Variable moderiert wird.

Aus psychologischer Perspektive ist das Random-Intercept-Random-Slope-Modell im Längsschnitt äußerst attraktiv, da sich in längsschnittlichen Daten bewerten lässt, inwiefern Effekte von zeitvariierenden Prädiktoren durch Persönlichkeitseigenschaften moderiert werden und inwiefern die zeitvariierenden Ausprägungen auf der abhängigen Variablen von Eigenschaften der Person abhängen. Aus soziologischer Sicht fehlt allerdings die Makro-Ebene. Um die Makro-Ebene zu berücksichtigen, ist es notwendig eine dritte Ebene in das Modell einzufügen. Diese Ebene könnte die Nachbarschaft, der Landkreis, die Region oder das Land sein, in der eine Person lokalisiert ist. Die entsprechenden Level-3-Variablen wären in diesem Fall *zeitstabile* Eigenschaften der Level-3-Einheit.

2.5 Zentrierungstechniken

An dieser Stelle sind einige Erläuterungen zur Technik der Zentrierung von Prädiktorvariablen angebracht (siehe hierzu z. B. auch Enders und Tofighi 2007 und Kreft et al. 1995). Beim Betrachten der Gleichungen fällt auf, dass die Bedeutung einiger Koeffizienten in der Mehrebenenanalyse vom Nullpunkt der beteiligten Prädiktorvariablen abhängt. Beispielsweise ist im Random-Intercept-Random-Slope-Modell β_{0i} der erwartete Wert der Level-2-Einheit i, wenn die Ausprägung des Level-1-Prädiktors x_{1ti} Null ist. Um dem Koeffizienten β_{0i} eine sinnvoll zu interpretierende Bedeutung zu geben, kann es sinnvoll sein, die Prädiktorvariable x_{1ti} zu zentrieren. Dies ist umso wichtiger, da der Koeffizient β_{0i} auf Level-2 selbst durch den Level-2-Prädiktor z_{1i} modelliert wird. Ebenso kann es sinnvoll sein, die Prädiktoren auf Level-2 zu zentrieren, um dem Koeffizient γ_{00} eine sinnvoll interpretierbare Bedeutung zu geben. In der Mehrebenenanalyse wird zwischen zwei Arten der Zentrierung unterschieden. Zentrierung von Prädiktorvariablen am Gesamtmittelwert (*grand mean centering, centering at the grand mean, CGM-Zentrierung*) und Zentrierung am Clustermittelwert (*group mean centering, centering within cluster, CWC-Zentrierung*). Die Auswirkungen auf die Interpretation der Koeffizienten seien am Beispiel des Random-Intercept-Random-Slope-Modells kurz erläutert. Eine Zentrierung der Prädiktorvariable x_{1ti} auf Ebene-1 lässt sich wie folgt darstellen:

$$x_{1cgm} = x_{1ti} - x_{1..} \tag{5.1}$$

Die Zentrierung der Prädiktorvariable am Gesamtmittelwert $x_{1..}$ bewirkt, dass der Koeffizient β_{0i} auf Ebene-1 die erwartete Ausprägung der Level-2-Einheit i auf der abhängigen Variable darstellt, wenn der Prädiktor x_{1ti} eine global mittlere Ausprägung besitzt.

Eine Zentrierung am Clustermittelwert lässt sich wie folgt darstellen:

$$x_{1cwc} = x_{1ti} - x_{1.i} \tag{5.2}$$

Hier wird die Variable x_{1ti} am individuellen Mittelwert $x_{1.i}$ zentriert. Der Koeffizient β_{0i} ist nun die erwartete Ausprägung auf der abhängigen Variablen, wenn der Prädiktor x_{1ti} eine Level-2-spezifisch mittlere Ausprägung besitzt. Ist z. B. die abhängige Variable das Wohlbefinden einer Person und der Prädiktor die Wachheit, so ist β_{0i} das erwartete Wohlbefinden einer Person bei personenspezifisch über die Messzeitpunkte hinweg betrachteter mittlerer Wachheit. Für die Zentrierung von Prädiktorvariablen auf unterschiedlichen Ebenen können keine pauschalen Empfehlungen gegeben werden, da die Wahl einer Zentrierungsart auch von der Art der vorliegenden Variablen und dem verwendeten Modell abhängt. Allerdings sollte in der Praxis dargestellt werden, welche Zentrierungstechnik verwendet wurde. Zu diesem Thema sei die Lektüre der Arbeiten von Enders und Tofighi (2007) und Kreft et al. (1995) auch im Zusammenhang mit Kontexteffekten empfohlen.

2.6 Exkurs: Kontexteffekte bei querschnittlichen Daten

Um Kontexteffekte in der längsschnittlichen Mehrebenenanalyse und deren Besonderheiten zu verstehen, ist es zweckmäßig, sich zu verdeutlichen, wie Kontexteffekte bei *querschnittlicher* Datenlage behandelt werden. Im Rahmen der querschnittlichen Mehrebenenanalyse kann zwischen zwei unterschiedlichen Kontextvariablen unterschieden werden. Einmal sind Kontextvariablen Eigenschaften einer Level-2-Einheit, die direkt erhoben werden können. Im erziehungswissenschaftlichen Kontext könnte diese Variable beispielsweise die Anzahl der Schüler in einer Klasse (Level-2) sein. Diese Anzahl ist für jeden Schüler in einer Klasse gleich. Auch die zeitstabile Persönlichkeitseigenschaft eines Klassenlehrers ist eine Level-2-Variable, da die Ausprägung für jede Schülerin oder jeden Schüler einer Klasse identisch und technisch betrachtet eine Eigenschaft des Kontexts ist. Ferner wird unter Kontextvariable eine Prädiktorvariable verstanden, die durch Aggregation von Beobachtungen auf Individualebene (Level-1) hervorgegangen ist. Durch die Verwendung dieser Variable lässt sich z. B. bewerten, inwiefern die Leistung einer Schülerin oder eines Schülers mit der individuelle Gewissenhaftigkeit (Individualeffekt) einerseits und mit der mittleren Gewissenhaftigkeit in der Klasse (Kontexteffekt) andererseits zusammenhängt. Je nachdem, ob oder wie die Prädiktorvariable auf Ebene 1 zentriert wurde, ist es ferner möglich, den Zusammenhang zwischen Leistung und Gewissenhaftigkeit innerhalb der Klassen *(within effect)* vom Zusammenhang zwischen den Klassen *(between effect)* zu trennen (siehe hierzu besonders Kreft et al. 1995 und auch Rabe-Hesketh und Skrondal 2012, Abschn. 3.7).

Zur Verdeutlichung von querschnittlichen Kontextmodellen mit aggregierten Variablen werden im Folgenden zwei Modelle vorgestellt. Erstens ein Modell mit am Gesamtmittelwert zentrierter Prädiktorvariable auf Ebene-1 (CGM-Zentrierung) und zweitens ein Modell mit am Gruppenmittelwert zentrierter Prädiktorvariable auf Ebene-1 (CWC-Zentrierung). Die Ziele sind zunächst die Erläuterung der Sachverhalte im Querschnitt, um mit den Eigenheiten der Analyse von Kontexteffekten vertraut zu werden. In einem zweiten Schritt werden die Konzepte auf längsschnittliche Analysen übertragen. Zunächst wird das Modell mit CGM-zentrierter, aggregierter Kontextvariable dargestellt.

Level-1-Gleichung (z. B. Schüler, Mikro-Modell):

$$y_{ij} = \beta_{0j} + \beta_{1j}\left(x_{ij} - x_{..}\right) + \varepsilon_{ij} \tag{6.1}$$

Level-2-Gleichungen (z. B. Klassen, Makro-Modell):

$$\beta_{0j} = \gamma_{00} + \gamma_{01}\left(x_{.j} - x_{..}\right) + \upsilon_{0j} \qquad (6.2)$$

$$\beta_{1j} = \gamma_{10} \qquad (6.3)$$

Gesamtgleichung:

$$y_{ij} = \gamma_{00} + \gamma_{01}\left(x_{.j} - x_{..}\right) + \gamma_{10}\left(x_{ij} - x_{..}\right) + \upsilon_{0j} + \varepsilon_{ti} \qquad (6.4)$$

In der Level-1-Gleichung ist nun der Index t für die Zeit durch den Index j ersetzt, der im Querschnitt für eine Level-2-Einheit (z. B. eine Klasse) steht, in der die individuellen Messwerte der Schüler (Level-1) verschachtelt sind. Zudem wurde die Prädiktorvariable x_{ij} am Gesamtmittelwert $x_{..}$ zentriert, um dem Koeffizienten β_{0j} eine sinnvolle Bedeutung zu geben. β_{0j} ist nun die erwartete Ausprägung einer Person auf der abhängigen Variablen in einer Level-2-Einheit j, wenn eine global mittlere Merkmalsausprägung auf dem Prädiktor x_{ij} vorliegt. In der ersten Level-2-Gleichung werden diese gruppenspezifischen Koeffizienten auf Basis der am Gesamtmittelwert zentrierten und aggregierten Kontextvariablen $x_{.j}$ modelliert. In Folge der Zentrierung ist γ_{00} die erwartete Ausprägung auf der abhängigen Variable für eine Person mit *global mittlerer Ausprägung* auf dem Level-1-Prädiktor x_{ij} in einer Level-2-Einheit mit *global mittlerer Ausprägung* auf der aggregierten Variablen $x_{.j}$. γ_{01} ist der Kontexteffekt (*contextual effect*) und γ_{10} ist der Individualeffekt. Das heißt, es lässt sich mit diesem Modell bewerten, inwiefern die Ausprägung auf der abhängigen Variablen neben dem Unterschied auf Personenebene (Individualeffekt) von Unterschieden zwischen den Level-2-Einheiten (Kontexteffekt) abhängt.

Bei der Bewertung von Kontexteffekten mittels der Zentrierung am Gesamtmittelwert ist die aggregierte Prädiktorvariable $x_{.j}$ mit den unaggregierten Werten x_{ij} auf Level-1 korreliert; somit lassen sich Effekte innerhalb einer Ebene nicht von Effekten zwischen den Ebenen trennen. Soll der Effekt innerhalb der Ebene-1 (*within effect*) vom Effekt zwischen den Ebenen (*between effect*) getrennt werden, muss die Prädiktorvariable auf Level-1 am *Gruppenmittelwert* oder Clustermittelwert zentriert werden. Um γ_{00} eine sinnvoll interpretierbare Bedeutung zu geben, kann die aggregierte Variable $x_{.j}$ zusätzlich am Gesamtmittelwert $x_{..}$ zentriert werden. Die resultierende Gesamtgleichung ist:

$$y_{ij} = \gamma_{00} + \gamma_{B}\left(x_{.j} - x_{..}\right) + \gamma_{W}\left(x_{ij} - x_{.j}\right) + \upsilon_{0j} + \varepsilon_{ti} \qquad (6.5)$$

γ_{B} ist nun der reine Effekt der Prädiktorvariable auf die abhängige Variable auf Level-2 (*between effect*). γ_{W} ist der reine Effekt der Prädiktorvariable auf die abhängige Variable auf Level-1 (*within effect*). Praktisch lässt sich hiermit z. B. der Effekt der Gewissenhaftigkeit auf die Leistung zwischen Schulklassen (γ_{B}) vom Effekt innerhalb der Klassen (γ_{W}) trennen. Ferner ist der Kontexteeffekt (*contextual effect*) die Differenz des Between-Effektes und des Within-Effektes ($\gamma_{B} - \gamma_{W}$) des Modells mit Group-Mean-Zentrierung (siehe hierzu ausführlich z. B. Skrondal und Rabe-

Hesketh 2012, S. 151; Enders und Tofighi 2007 und Kreft et al. 1995). Aus soziologisch-methodischer Sicht sind die hier dargestellten Modelle zur Bewertung von Kontexteffekten Fixed-Effects-Modelle mit aggregierten und unterschiedlich zentrierten Prädiktorvariablen. Personenheterogenität wird durch das Level-2-Residuum v_{0j} erfasst.

2.7 Kontexteffekte bei längsschnittlichen Panel-Daten

Wird die Konzeption der Kontexteffekte im Querschnitt direkt auf längsschnittliche Daten übertragen, wird deutlich, dass der untere Kontext (Level-2) der längsschnittlich erhobenen Messwerte nicht etwa das Land oder die Region oder die Gemeinde darstellt, sondern die Personen (Level-2) sind der Kontext der zeitvariierenden Messwerte (Level-1). Auf Basis einer CGM-zentrierten Prädiktorvariablen auf Level-1 ergibt sich direkt folgendes Modell:

$$y_{ti} = \gamma_{00} + \gamma_{01}(x_{.i} - x_{..}) + \gamma_{10}(x_{ti} - x_{..}) + \upsilon_{0i} + \varepsilon_{ti}. \tag{7.1}$$

γ_{00} ist die erwartete Ausprägung einer Person i auf dem Kriterium y_{ti} bei einer global mittleren Ausprägung auf der Prädiktorvariablen x_{ti}. γ_{01} ist der Kontexteffekt (*contextual effect*). Anhand dieses Koeffizienten lässt sich bewerten, inwiefern Unterschiede der *mittleren, über die Messzeitpunkte aggregierten Ausprägungen der Personen auf der Prädiktorvariablen* mit Unterschieden im Kriterium einhergehen. γ_{10} gibt an, inwiefern Abweichungen der individuellen Ausprägungen der Prädiktorvariablen x_{ti} auf Level-1 vom Gesamtmittelwert x mit Unterschieden im Kriterium einhergehen. Da die individuellen Ausprägungen der Prädiktorvariablen auf Level-1 nicht am Clustermittelwert zentriert sind, ist es nicht möglich, den Effekt zwischen Personen (*between effect*) sauber vom Effekt innerhalb der Personen *(within effect)* zu trennen. Ist das Ziel der Analyse diese Trennung, so ist es nötig die Prädiktorvariablen auf Level-1 am personenspezifischen Level-2-Mittelwert $x_{.i}$ zu zentrieren. Hierdurch wird die Varianz zwischen den Personen auf der Prädiktorvariablen auf Level-1 eliminiert. Um dennoch die Varianz zwischen den Personen in der Analyse zu berücksichtigen, werden die CGM-zentrierten Mittelwerte der Personen auf der Prädiktorvariable in die Analyse mit aufgenommen. So ist eine Trennung zwischen Within-Effekt und Between-Effekt möglich.

Für das Modell mit Zentrierung der Prädiktorvariable am Level-2-Mittelwert (CWC-Zentrierung) ergibt sich bei Übertragung auf längsschnittliche Daten direkt folgendes Modell:

$$y_{ti} = \gamma_{00} + \gamma_{B}(x_{.i} - x_{..}) + \gamma_{W}(x_{ti} - x_{.i}) + \upsilon_{0i} + \varepsilon_{ti}. \tag{7.2}$$

Mittels dieses Modells ist es möglich, Effekte des Prädiktors *innerhalb* der Personen von Effekten des Prädiktors *zwischen* den Personen zu trennen. So kann es sein, dass innerhalb der Personen längsschnittlich ein positiver Zusammenhang (γ_W) zwischen der Prädiktorvariablen und dem Kriterium besteht, was allerdings nicht ausschließt, dass zwischen den Personen auf aggregierter Ebene ein negativer Zusammenhang (γ_B) zwischen Prädiktor und Kriterium besteht. Zum Beispiel könnten Wohlbefinden und Wachheit innerhalb einer Person längsschnittlich positiv assoziiert sein, was allerdings nicht bedeutet, dass Personen, die ständig wach sind, sich insgesamt wohler fühlen.

2.8 Kontexteffekte bei längsschnittlichen Panel-Daten mit drei Ebenen (Messwert, Person, Makro-Ebene)

Bei den längsschnittlichen Kontextmodellen mit zwei Ebenen ist es eine Limitierung, dass der soziologisch gemeinte Kontext oder die Meso- oder Makro-Ebene nicht auftauchen. Die Lösung besteht darin, eine weitere Modellierungsebene (Level-3) mit dem Index j einzufügen. Diese Möglichkeit ist nach Kenntnis der Autoren noch wenig exploriert. Erläuterungen finden sich bei Rabe-Hesketh und Skrondal (2012, Kap. 8) und Long (2012, Kap. 13). Fest steht, dass die resultierenden Modelle sehr schnell relativ komplex werden können. Im Folgenden wird ein Kontextmodell mit aggregierten Variablen auf Level-2 und Level-3 spezifiziert. Der Prädiktor x_{tij} auf Level-1 wird am Gesamtmittelwert zentriert. Ferner werden Kontextvariablen durch Aggregation innerhalb der Personen ($x_{.ij}$) und innerhalb der Regionen ($x_{..j}$) gebildet und am Gesamtmittelwert ($x_{...}$) zentriert.

Level-1-Gleichung (z. B. Messwert, Mikro-Modell):

$$y_{tij} = \beta_{0ij} + \beta_{1ij}(x_{tij} - x_{...}) + \varepsilon_{tij} \qquad (8.1)$$

Level-2-Gleichungen (z. B. Person, Meso-Modell):

$$\beta_{0ij} = \gamma_{00j} + \gamma_{01j}(x_{.ij} - x_{...}) + \upsilon_{0ij} \qquad (8.2)$$

$$\beta_{1ij} = \gamma_{10j} \qquad (8.3)$$

Level-3-Gleichungen (z. B. Region, Makro-Ebene):

$$\gamma_{00j} = \gamma_{000} + \gamma_{001}(x_{..j} - x_{...}) + \upsilon_{00j} \qquad (8.4)$$

$$\gamma_{01j} = \gamma_{010} \qquad (8.5)$$

$$\gamma_{10j} = \gamma_{100} \qquad (8.6)$$

Gesamtgleichung:

$$y_{tij} = [\gamma_{000} + \gamma_{001}(x_{..j} - x_{...}) + \upsilon_{00j}] + \gamma_{010}(x_{.ij} - x_{...}) + \upsilon_{0ij} + \gamma_{100}(x_{tij} - x_{...}) + \varepsilon_{tij} \qquad (8.9)$$

$$= \gamma_{000} + \gamma_{001}(x_{..j} - x_{...}) + \gamma_{010}(x_{.ij} - x_{...}) + \gamma_{100}(x_{tij} - x_{...}) + \upsilon_{00j} + \upsilon_{0ij} + \varepsilon_{tij} \qquad (8.10)$$

In der Level-1-Gleichung wird das Basismodell zur Modellierung des Messwerts y_{tij} der Person i zum Zeitpunkt t in Region j spezifiziert. β_{0ij} ist der erwartete Messwert der Person i in Region j auf dem Kriterium, wenn die zeitvariierende Prädiktorvariable x_{tij} eine insgesamt mittlere Ausprägung aufweist, da am Gesamtmittelwert $x_{...}$ zentriert wurde. In der ersten Level-2-Gleichung werden die nach den Personen variierenden Koeffizienten β_{0ij} auf Basis eines nach der Region variierenden Intercepts γ_{00j} und eines nach der Region variierenden Effektes γ_{01j} des zentrierten, über die Messzeitpunkte aggregierten, zeitstabilen Prädiktors $x_{.ij}$ einer Person i in Region j modelliert. v_{0ij} ist ein Level-2-Residuum. Die nach der Region variierenden Koeffizienten γ_{00j} werden auf Level-3 auf Basis einer festen Konstante γ_{000} und des zentrierten, über die Personen und Messzeitpunkte aggregierten Prädiktors $x_{..j}$ modelliert. $x_{..j}$ variiert somit lediglich *zwischen den Regionen*. v_{00j} ist ein Level-3 Residuum. Der nach den Personen variierende Effekt β_{1ij} des Prädiktors x_{tij} wird der Einfachheit halber über die Level-2-Gleichungen auf γ_{100} restringiert. In der Gesamtgleichung zeigt sich, dass γ_{001} den Kontexteffekt der Region auf die abhängige Variable darstellt, γ_{010} den Effekt der aggregierten Personenvariable und γ_{100} denjenigen der Abweichungen der individuellen, zeit-variierenden Prädiktorvariable auf Level-1 vom Gesamtmittelwert. Das Erkenntnisinteresse der Anwendung dieses Modells liegt darin zu prüfen, inwiefern die Ausprägungen der abhängigen Variablen von Effekten der zeitvariierenden Variablen x_{tij} auf Level-1, von Effekten der innerhalb der Personen aggregierten Variablen $x_{.ij}$ und von Effekten der innerhalb der Regionen aggregierten Variablen $x_{..j}$ abhängen.

Wird die Prädiktorvariable auf Level-1 am personenspezifischen Mittelwert zentriert, ergibt sich direkt folgende Gesamtgleichung:

$$y_{tij} = \gamma_{000} + \gamma_{001}(x_{..j} - x_{...}) + \gamma_{010}(x_{.ij} - x_{...}) + \gamma_{100}(x_{tij} - x_{.ij}) + v_{00j} + v_{0ij} + \varepsilon_{tij}$$

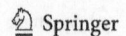

γ_{000} ist die erwartete Ausprägung auf der Prädiktorvariable einer Person mit mittleren Ausprägungen auf der innerhalb der Regionen aggregierten Variablen $x_{..j}$, der innerhalb der Personen (Level-2) aggregierten Variablen $x_{.ij}$ und einer *personenspezifisch* mittleren Ausprägung auf der Variablen x_{tij} zum Zeitpunkt t auf Level-1. γ_{001} ist der Effekt der Unterschiede der Level-3-Einheiten auf die abhängige Variable, γ_{010} ist der Effekt der Unterschiedlichkeit der Level-2-Einheiten auf die abhängige Variable und γ_{100} ist der Effekt der Variabilität der Prädiktorvariable x_{tij} *innerhalb* einer Person auf die abhängige Variable y_{tij}. v_{00j} ist das Residuum der Level-3-Regression und v_{0ij} ist das Residuum der Level-2-Regression. Es wird für die Random-Effects jeweils separat eine Normalverteilung angenommen. Die Level-2- und Level-3-Residuen sind somit voneinander unabhängig. Ferner wird angenommen, dass das Level-1-Residuum ε_{tij} normalverteilt mit einem Erwartungswert von 0 ist. Auch bei diesem Modell ist in Folge der CWC-Zentrierung des Level-1 Prädiktors x_{tij} am Personenmittelwert $x_{.ij}$ der Effekt des Prädiktors innerhalb einer Person vom Effekt zwischen den Personen trennbar. γ_{010} ist der Effekt des Prädiktors zwischen den Personen (*between effect*), der nicht bereinigt ist von Level-3 Einflüssen, und γ_{100} ist der Effekt des Prädiktors innerhalb der Personen (*within effect*). Der Kontexteffekt der innerhalb der Region aggregierten Variable $x_{..j}$ auf die abhängige Variable ist γ_{001}. Dieses Modell ist dann indiziert, wenn das Interesse darin besteht, den Effekt der Prädiktorvariable zwischen den Personen vom Effekt der Variable innerhalb der Personen zu trennen und zudem den Effekt des Kontextes auf Ebene-3 zu berücksichtigen.

2.9 Kontexteffekte bei längsschnittlichen Panel-Daten mit zeitvariierender Kontextvariable

Bisher wurden lediglich aggregierte Messwerte auf Ebene-2 und Ebene-3 als Kontextvariablen betrachtet. Allerdings ist es durchaus denkbar, dass in Panel-Daten auch Variablen vorliegen, die zeitvariierende Eigenschaften einer Region abbilden, wie z. B. die Arbeitslosigkeitsrate in einem bestimmten Jahr. Technisch betrachtet handelt es sich hierbei um eine Level-1-Variable, obwohl sie Eigenschaften der Region repräsentiert. Der wichtige Unterschied zu den obigen Kontextmodellen besteht darin, dass die zeitvariierende Eigenschaft der Region eine Variable ist, die auf einer höheren Ebene erhoben worden sein kann (z. B. die Arbeitslosigkeit in einer Region zum Messzeitpunkt t), allerdings auf Level-1 modelliert wird, da es sich um eine zeitvariierende Variable handelt. „Echte" Level-2- oder Level-3-Prädiktorvariablen variieren lediglich zwischen den entsprechenden Ebenen und zeigen keine Variabilität auf einer der unteren Ebenen. Da die auf Makro- oder Meso-Ebene erhobene Variable auf Ebene-1 variiert, wird sie auch auf Ebene-1 modelliert. Ein Modell, dass gleichzeitig den Effekt einer zeitstabilen Level-2-Eigenschaft und den Effekt einer zeitvariierenden Variable auf die Messwerte auf Level-1 abbildet wird nun dargestellt.

Level-1-Gleichung (z. B. Messwert, Mikro-Modell):

$$y_{ti} = \beta_{0i} + \beta_{1i}(x_{1ti} - x_{1..}) + \beta_{2i}x_{2ti} + \varepsilon_{ti} \quad (9.1)$$

Level-2-Gleichung (z. B. Person, Meso-Modell):

$$\beta_{0i} = \gamma_{00} + \gamma_{01}(x_{1.i} - x_{1..}) + \upsilon_{0i} \quad (9.2)$$

$$\beta_{1i} = \gamma_{10} \quad (9.3)$$

$$\beta_{2i} = \gamma_{20} \quad (9.4)$$

Gesamtgleichung:

$$y_{ti} = \gamma_{00} + \gamma_{01}(x_{1.i} - x_{1..}) + \gamma_{10}(x_{1ti} - x_{1..}) + \gamma_{20}x_{2ti} + \upsilon_{0i} + \varepsilon_{ti} \quad (9.5)$$

In der Level-1-Gleichung ist $(x_{1ti} - x_{1..})$ eine zeitvariierende Prädiktorvariable, die CGM-zentriert wurde. x_{2ti} ist eine unzentrierte, zeitvariierende Prädiktorvariable, die zeitvariierende Eigenschaften der Makro-Ebene oder Meso-Ebene abbilden kann.

In den Level-2 Gleichungen ist $(x_{1.i} - x_{1..})$ eine innerhalb der Level-2-Einheiten i über die Messzeitpunkte t hinweg aggregierte Prädiktorvariable, die CGM-zentriert wurde. Zudem werden die nach den Level-2-Einheiten variierende Koeffizienten β_{1i}

und β_{2i} auf γ_{10} und γ_{20} restringiert und somit als konstant angenommen. Somit ist in der Gesamtgleichung γ_{00} die erwartete Ausprägung auf y_{ti} bei einer mittleren Ausprägung auf der aggregierten Prädiktorvariablen $x_{1.i}$, einer Level-2 spezifisch mittleren Ausprägung der zeitvariierenden Prädiktorvariable x_{1ti} und einer Ausprägung von Null auf der auf Makroebene erhobenen, zeitvariierenden Prädiktorvariable x_{2ti}. γ_{01} ist der Effekt der aggregierten Prädiktorvariable, γ_{10} ist der Effekt der Prädiktorvariable innerhalb einer Level-2-Einheit und γ_{20} ist der Effekt der Variablen x_{2ti}. υ_{0i} ist ein Level-2-Residuum und ε_{ti} ist das Residuum auf Level-1. Mit diesem Modell ist es möglich zu bewerten, inwiefern z. B. die Lebenszufriedenheit von a.) der Variation der Prädiktorvariablen x_{1ti} über die Messzeitpunkte, b.) von der innerhalb der Level-2-Einheiten (z. B. Personen) aggregierten Prädiktorvariable und c.) von der zeitvariierenden Variable x_{2ti} abhängt.

2.10 Wachstumskurvenmodelle

Die bisher vorgestellten Modelle gehen davon aus, dass es einen zeitstabilen, personenspezifischen Effekt υ_{0i} gibt. In der Terminologie der Veränderungsmessung sind dies sogenannte Variabilitätsmodelle (Eid et al. 2008). Die zu verschiedenen Messzeitpunkten erhobenen Zustände schwanken um einen personenspezifischen, zeitstabilen Wert, den man in der Psychologie *Trait* nennt. Diese Annahme kann zu streng sein, insbesondere dann, wenn Veränderungsprozesse auf Ebene der Person stattfinden, z. B. wenn die Ausprägung eines Merkmals über die Zeit kontinuierlich wächst oder abnimmt. In solchen Fällen müssen diese Modelle erweitert werden, um solche Prozesse adäquat abzubilden. Eine solche Möglichkeit bieten Wachstumskurvenmodelle.

Bei längsschnittlichen Datenanalysen kann es angebracht sein, den Erhebungszeitpunkt oder die Welle als Prädiktor in das Modell mit aufzunehmen. Auf diese Weise ist es möglich, Hypothesen über funktionale Verläufe auf der abhängigen Variablen über die Erhebungszeitpunkte zu prüfen. Im Rahmen der Multilevelanalyse ist es zudem möglich, individuelle Trajektorien abzubilden und zu prüfen, inwiefern diese Trajektorien von Eigenschaften höherer Ebenen abhängen. Modelle dieser Art werden auch Wachstumskurvenmodelle genannt. Im Folgenden sei ein sehr einfaches lineares Wachstumskurvenmodell mit 2 Ebenen mit zeitstabiler Level-2-Kovariate dargestellt.

Level-1-Gleichung (z. B. Messwert, Mikro-Modell):

$$y_{ti} = \beta_{0i} + \beta_{1i}T_{ti} + \varepsilon_{ti} \tag{10.1}$$

Level-2-Gleichungen (z. B. Person, Meso-Modell):

$$\beta_{0i} = \gamma_{00} + \gamma_{01}z_i + \upsilon_{0i} \tag{10.2}$$

$$\beta_{1i} = \gamma_{10} + \gamma_{11}z_i + \upsilon_{1i} \tag{10.3}$$

Gesamtgleichung:

$$y_{ti} = \gamma_{00} + \gamma_{01}z_i + \upsilon_{0i} + (\gamma_{10} + \gamma_{11}z_i + \upsilon_{1i})T_{ti} + \varepsilon_{ti} \quad (10.4)$$

$$= (\gamma_{00} + \upsilon_{0i}) + \gamma_{10}z_i + (\gamma_{10} + \upsilon_{1i})T_{ti} + \gamma_{11}z_iT_{ti} + \varepsilon_{ti} \quad (10.5)$$

In diesem Modell wird pro Individuum i je eine lineare Wachstumskurve modelliert. Der kontinuierliche Level-1-Prädiktor T_{ti} enkodiert den Erhebungszeitraum oder den Messzeitpunkt. β_{0i} ist die erwartete Ausprägung der Person i auf der Kriteriumsvariable, wenn der Prädiktor T_{ti} eine Ausprägung von Null besitzt. β_{1i} ist der Steigungskoeffizient der Wachstumskurve für Person i. Die Koeffizienten β_{0i} und β_{1i} werden in den Level-2 Gleichungen auf Basis des zeitstabilen Prädiktors z_i modelliert, der z. B. eine zeitstabile Persönlichkeitseigenschaft abbilden kann. γ_{00} ist die erwartete Ausprägung des Koeffizienten β_{0i}, wenn z_i eine Ausprägung von Null besitzt. γ_{01} ist der Effekt des Prädiktors z_i auf den Koeffizienten β_{0i}. γ_{10} ist der erwartete Steigungskoeffizient β_{1i}, wenn der Prädiktor z_i eine Ausprägung von Null besitzt und γ_{11} ist die erwartete Änderung des Steigungskoeffizienten β_{1i}, wenn der Prädiktor z_i sich um eine Einheit erhöht. υ_{0i} und υ_{1i} sind Level-2-Residuen, die miteinander kovariieren können und ε_{ti} ist das Level-1-Residuum. Ein typischer Anwendungsfall dieses Modells in der psychologischen Forschung ist die Prüfung der Hypothese, ob die Gruppenzugehörigkeit z_i (z. B. Kontroll- und Experimentalgruppe) mit dem linearen Verlauf auf der abhängigen Variable (z. B. Therapieverlauf) in Zusammenhang steht. Das hier dargestellte Modell ist sehr einfach. Es können auch andere funktionale Verläufe auf Ebene-1 (z. B. quadratisch, kubisch, logarithmisch, exponentiell, etc.) angenommen werden (siehe z. B. Skrondal und Rabe-Hesketh 2012, Kap. 7 und Biesanz et al. 2004). Ferner lassen sich weitere Level-1- und-Level-2 Prädiktoren in das Modell aufnehmen und es ist denkbar, das Modell um weitere Ebenen (z. B. die Makro-Ebene als Level-3) zu erweitern. Diese Erweiterungen sind notwendig, wenn es darum geht zu prüfen, ob zeitstabile Eigenschaften des Kontexts oder der Makro-Ebene mit individuellen Veränderungsprozessen einhergehen.

2.11 Multivariate Multilevelmodelle

In den vorherigen Abschnitten wurden Wachstumskurvenmodelle besprochen. Wachstumskurvenmodelle sind vermutlich die beliebteste Klasse von Modellen der Veränderungsmessung im Rahmen der Multilevelanalyse. Allerdings haben diese Modelle einen Nachteil: Es muss eine funktionale Annahme über den Verlauf der abhängigen Variablen über die Zeit getroffen werden. Diese Annahme ist unter Umständen zu restriktiv. Auch die Annahme der Random-Intercept-Modelle oder Fixed-Effekt-Modelle, dass es einen zeitstabilen, personenspezifischen Random-Effekt gibt, ist unter Umständen zu restriktiv und unrealistisch. Eine Alternative ist die Verwendung von multivariaten Multilevelmodellen (siehe z. B. Snijders und Bosker 1999, Abschn. 2.1.3 und Hox 2010, Kap. 10). Diese Modelle machen keine funktionale Annahme über den Verlauf, sondern es wird über eine Dummy-Kodierung der Messzeitpunkte ermöglicht, die individuellen Werte der abhängigen Variable zu jedem einzelnen Messzeitpunkt zu modellieren. Im Vergleich zu Wachstumskurvenmodellen muss keine funktionale Annahme über den Verlauf über die Zeit getroffen werden und es ist auch nicht nötig anzunehmen, dass es einen *zeitstabilen*, personenspezifischen Random-Effekt gibt, wie dies bei Fixed-Effects-Modellen der Fall ist. Vielmehr werden die Personenparameter zu jedem Messzeitpunkt modelliert. Ein relativ einfaches multivariates Multilevelmodell mit zwei Ebenen für 4 Erhebungszeitpunkte ist auf Ebene-1 wie folgt definiert:

Level-1-Gleichung:

$$y_{ti} = \beta_{1i}T_{1i} + \beta_{2i}T_{2i} + \beta_{3i}T_{3i} + \beta_{4i}T_{4i} \tag{11.1}$$

Die Variablen T_{1i} bis T_{4i} repräsentieren dummy-kodierte Indikatoren für den Erhebungszeitpunkt. Abhängig von der Kodierung können auch mehrere Messzeitpunkte zu einer Phase zusammengefasst werden. Repräsentieren diese Variablen beispielsweise die Wellen 2006 bis 2009 in Panel-Daten, so erhält die Variable T_{1i} den Wert 1, wenn das Kriterium y_{ti} im Jahr 2006 erhoben wurde, anderenfalls den Wert 0. Gleiches gilt für die Variablen T_{2i} bis T_{4i} und die Jahre 2007 bis 2009. Auf diese Weise bedeuten die Koeffizienten β_{1i} bis β_{4i} die erwartete Ausprägung der Person i auf dem Kriterium zum entsprechenden Erhebungszeitpunkt. β_{1i} ist somit zum Beispiel die erwartete Lebenszufriedenheit der Person i im Jahr 2006. Die Level-1-Gleichung des multivariaten Mehrebenenmodells besitzt kein Residuum. Dies hat zur Folge, dass alle Variabilität der abhängigen Variablen in den Koeffizienten β_{1i} bis β_{4i} abgebildet wird. Die variierenden Koeffizienten β_{1i} bis β_{4i}, welche personenspezifische Ausprägungen auf der abhängigen Variablen zum jeweiligen Messzeitpunkt darstellen, können nun durch Level-2-Gleichungen und zeitstabile Prädiktoren modelliert werden.

Level-2-Gleichungen:

$$\beta_{1i} = \gamma_{00} + \gamma_{01}z_{1i} + \upsilon_{0i} \tag{11.2}$$

$$\beta_{2i} = \gamma_{10} + \gamma_{11}z_{2i} + \upsilon_{1i} \tag{11.3}$$

$$\beta_{2i} = \gamma_{20} + \gamma_{21}z_{3i} + \upsilon_{2i} \tag{11.4}$$

$$\beta_{3i} = \gamma_{30} + \gamma_{31}z_{4i} + \upsilon_{3i} \tag{11.5}$$

Die Koeffizienten γ_{00}, γ_{10}, γ_{20} und γ_{30} stellen die erwarteten Lebenszufriedenheitswerte der Personen zum jeweiligen Messzeitpunkt dar, wenn die Level-2-Prädiktorvariable einen Wert von 0 aufweist. Die Koeffizienten γ_{01}, γ_{11}, γ_{21} und γ_{31} repräsentieren die erwarteten Veränderungen auf der Kriteriumsvariable zum jeweiligen Messzeitpunkt, wenn sich der Prädiktor z_i um eine Einheit erhöht. Von den Level-2-Residuen wird angenommen, dass diese multivariat normalverteilt mit einer Kovarianzmatrix

Σ und Erwartungswerten von Null sind. Diese Kovarianzmatrix macht es möglich zu bewerten, inwiefern die Ausprägungen der Personen auf der abhängigen Variable über die Erhebungszeitpunkte bei $z_i=0$ kovariieren. Somit sind Aussagen über die Stabilität und die Autokorrelation der Kriteriumswerte möglich, ohne Autokorrelationen in der Residualstruktur abbilden zu müssen. Technisch betrachtet, handelt es sich bei dem vorgestellten Modell um eine multivariate Erweiterung der Mehrebenenanalyse oder die mehrebenenanalytische Formulierung einer MANOVA oder MANCOVA, wobei die multivariate Verteilung der Kriteriumsvariable zu den jeweiligen Messzeitpunkten modelliert wird. Das Modell lässt sich auch als lineares Strukturgleichungsmodell darstellen. Die manifesten Variablen sind die abhängigen Variablen zum jeweiligen Messzeitpunkt, welche durch latente Variablen mit einem Messfehler von Null abgebildet werden. Die Interkorrelationsmatrix und die Varianzen der latenten Variablen entsprechen der Kovarianzmatix der Level-2-Residuen. Die Modellierung der Faktorwerte durch einen Prädiktor z_i entspricht den Level-2-Regressionsgleichungen. Selbstverständlich kann diese Modell um Prädiktorvariablen auf Level-1, Level-2 und um weitere Ebenen und Messzeitpunkte erweitert werden. Allerdings werden die dabei auftretenden Modelle relativ schnell recht komplex. Angenommen, es werden 20 Messzeitpunkte modelliert, so hat die entsprechende Kovarianzmatrix der Level-2-Residuen eine Dimensionalität von 20×20. Derzeit verfügbare Software zur Mehrebenenanalyse erreicht hier recht schnell die Grenzen. Ferner bietet nicht jede Software zur Multilevelanalyse die Möglichkeit, das Level-1-Residuum auf Null zu restringieren. Es ist also immer genau abzuwägen, wann ein wenig restriktives multivariates Multilevelmodell oder ein einfacheres Multilevelmodell zur Anwendung kommt.

3 Praktische Beispiele

Die Darstellung der Modelle wurde bewusst abstrakt gehalten. Um die Modelle mit Leben zu füllen und die praktische Relevanz zu verdeutlichen, ist es zweckmäßig, Beispielanalysen durchzuführen. Als Datenbasis dienen die Wellen der Jahre 2001 bis 2010 des australischen HILDA-Surveys (Summerfield et al. 2011). Die abhängige Variable ist durchgehend die jährlich erhobene Lebenszufriedenheit. Als Prädiktorvariable wird der Arbeitslosigkeitsstatus der Panelteilnehmerinnen und -teilnehmer und deren Alter und Geschlecht verwendet. Die Arbeitslosigkeitsvariable wurde dummy-codiert (0: arbeitslos, 1: in Arbeit). Alle Personen, die im jeweiligen Jahr nicht dem Arbeitsmarkt zur Verfügung standen, wurden aus der Analyse entfernt. Ebenso wurden alle Datenpunkte entfernt, für die keine Angaben zum Alter, Geschlecht, zur Lebenszufriedenheit oder keine Regionalinformationen vorliegen. Zur Erstellung einer Regionen-Variable wurde aus den Variablen *section of state (hhsos)* und *major statistical region (hhmsr)* im HILDA-Datensatz eine neue Variable mit 45 Stufen gebildet, welche zusätzlich zwischen *major urban, other urban, bounded locality, rural balance* und *migratory* innerhalb der 13 *major statistical areas* in Australien differenziert. Zur Prüfung von Regionaleffekten ist es allerdings günstiger, auf feingliedrigere geografische Informationen zurückzugreifen. Insgesamt verbleiben so 5964 Individuen und 49 505 Datenpunkte in der Analyse.

Zur Analyse wird das R-Paket nlme (Pinheiro et al. 2013) eingesetzt, mit dem Mixed-Effects oder Mehrebenenmodelle angepasst werden können. Zudem ist es möglich, die Residualstruktur zu modellieren. In den meisten dargestellten Modellen wird ein autoregressiver Prozess der Ordnung 1 auf den Residuen angenommen. Dieser ist dann sinnvoll anzunehmen, wenn es eine gewisse Trägheit des Veränderungsprozesses gibt und die Autokorrelation umso höher ist, je geringer der zeitliche Abstand zweier Messzeitpunkte ist. Für das Kontextmodell mit drei Ebenen kommt das R-Paket lme (Bates et al. 2011) zum Einsatz. Mit diesem Paket ist es möglich, Modelle mit gekreuzten Zufallseffekten anzupassen (siehe z. B. Baayen et al. 2009 für experimentelle Designs). Allerdings können keine Residualstrukturen modelliert werden. Insgesamt scheint die Modellierung der Residualstruktur bei komplexen Zufallseffekten softwaretechnisch schwierig und noch nicht in jeder Software implementiert zu sein. Die hier dargestellten Modelle wurden testweise sowohl mit als auch ohne Modellierung einer autoregressiven Struktur auf den Residuen angepasst. Dabei zeigte sich, dass sich an den festen Effekten der Modelle, deren Standardfehlern und den t-Werten nur marginal etwas ändert. Allerdings zeigen sich geringe Unterschiede auf den geschätzten Varianzkomponenten. Auch die informationstheoretischen Indices (AIC, BIC) für die Modelle mit autoregressiven Effekten auf Ebene der Level-1-Residuen sind geringer, was anzeigt, dass es sinnvoll ist, autoregressive Effekte aufzunehmen.

3.1 Das Random-Intercept-Only-Modell im Längsschnitt

Das Erkenntnisinteresse der Anwendung des Random-Intercept-Only-Modells besteht darin zu prüfen, inwiefern eine Personenheterogenität der Lebenszufriedenheit der Personen des HILDA-Panels über die Messzeitpunkte vorliegt. Die Ergebnisse der Analyse sind in Tab. 1 dargestellt.

In der Sektion der festen Effekte zeigt sich ein $\hat{\gamma}_{00}$ von 7,854. Das bedeutet, dass die geschätzte, mittlere Ausprägung der Lebenszufriedenheit über alle Personen, Regionen und Messzeitpunkte 7,854 Punkte beträgt. Zudem zeigt sich eine geschätzte Level-2 Residualvarianz von $\hat{\sigma}^2_{v_0} = 0,925$ und eine geschätzte Level-1 Residualvarianz von $\hat{\sigma}^2_\varepsilon = 0,952$. Damit ist der geschätzte Intraklassenkorrelationskoeffizient $\widehat{ICC} = 0,52$. Insgesamt sind also 52 % der Variabilität der Daten auf Ebene-1 auf Unterschiede der Personen hinsichtlich der Lebenszufriedenheit zurückzuführen und eine Multilevelanalyse ist indiziert. Zudem zeigt sich eine geschätzte Autokorrelation der Residuen von $\hat{\rho} = 0,214$.

Tab. 1 Random-Intercept-Only-Modell

	Parameter	Schätzer	SE	df	t
Intercept	γ_{00}	7,854**	(0,014)	43514	574,38
Zufällige Effekte		Varianz			
Intercept	$\sigma^2_{v_0}$	0,925			
Residualvarianz	σ^2_ε	0,952			
Autokorrelation AR (1)		0,214			

Anzahl der Beobachtungen = 49505; Anzahl der Personen = 5946; AIC = 147101,6; BIC = 147136,9
**$p<0,01$; *$p<0,05$

Tab. 2 Random-Intercept-Modell mit Level-1-Kovariate

	Parameter	Schätzer	SE	df	t
Intercept	γ_{00}	7,870**	(0,014)	43 540	575,84
Arbeitslosigkeit	γ_{10}	−0,339**	(0,029)	43 540	−11,81
Zufällige Effekte			Varianz		
Intercept	$\sigma^2_{v_0}$		0,914		
Residualvarianz	σ^2_ε		0,950		
Autokorrelation AR(1)	0,213				

Anzahl der Beobachtungen = 49 505; Anzahl der Personen = 5946; AIC = 146 964,5; BIC = 147 008,9
**$p<0,01$; *$p<0,05$

3.2 Das Random-Intercept-Modell mit Level-1-Kovariate im Längsschnitt

Das Erkenntnisinteresse der Anwendung des Random-Intercept-Modells mit Kovariaten besteht darin zu prüfen, inwiefern die abhängige Variable des Modells mit den aufgenommenen Prädiktorvariablen oder Kovariaten zusammenhängt, wobei gleichzeitig ggf. vorliegende, zeitstabile Personenheterogenität mitmodelliert wird. Im hiesigen Beispiel wird die dummy-kodierte Arbeitslosigkeitsvariable (0: nicht arbeitslos, 1: arbeitslos) als zeitvariierender Prädiktor in das Modell aufgenommen. Die Ergebnisse sind in Tab. 2 dargestellt.

In der Sektion der festen Effekte zeigt sich ein geschätztes $\hat{\gamma}_{00}$ von 7,870. Dies ist die erwartete, mittlere Lebenszufriedenheit der Personen, die arbeiten. In Folge der Dummy-Codierung der Arbeitslosigkeitsvariablen ist der geschätzte Koeffizient $\hat{\gamma}_{10}$ der Kontrast der arbeitslosen Personen zu der Referenzgruppe der arbeitenden Personen. Dieser Kontrast beträgt −0,339 Punkte auf der Lebenszufriedenheitsskala.

3.3 Das Random-Intercept-Random-Slope-Modell im Längsschnitt

Random-Intercept-Random-Slope-Modelle werden typischerweise dann eingesetzt, wenn es darum geht zu prüfen, ob der Effekt der Prädiktorvariablen über Gruppenstrukturen variiert. Diese Variabilität lässt sich in einem zweiten Schritt durch Level-2 Variablen aufklären. Für das hiesige Beispiel wird die Restriktion des Random-Intercept-Modells gelockert, dass der Effekt der Arbeitslosigkeit über alle Personen stabil ist. In Folge dessen taucht ein weiteres Level-2-Residuum v_{1j} in der Modellgleichung auf, dessen geschätzte Varianz die Variabilität des Effektes der Arbeitslosigkeit abbildet. Ferner wird die Korrelation der Level-2 Residuen geschätzt. Die Ergebnisse sind in Tab. 3 dargestellt.

Der geschätzte Koeffizient $\hat{\gamma}_{00} = 7,870$ ist die erwartete Lebenszufriedenheit der arbeitenden Personen. Der geschätzte Kontrast der arbeitslosen Personen zur Referenzgruppe der Arbeitenden beträgt im Mittel $\hat{\gamma}_{10} = -0,316$. Die geschätzte Varianz der Intercepts, d. h. der erwarteten Lebenszufriedenheitswerte der Personen, wenn der Prädiktor der Arbeitslosigkeit eine Ausprägung von 0 aufweist, ist 0,893. Die geschätzte Varianz des Effektes der Arbeitslosigkeit beträgt $\hat{\sigma}^2_{v_1} = 0,888$. Diese Varianz ist substanziell und kann gegebenenfalls durch Prädiktorvariablen auf Ebene-2 aufgeklärt werden.

Tab. 3 Random-Intercept-Random-Slope-Modell

Parameter		Schätzer	SE	df	T
Intercept	γ_{00}	7,870**	0,014	43 540	582,15
Arbeitslosigkeit	γ_{10}	−0,316**	0,042	43 540	−7,54
Zufällige Effekte		*Varianz*	*Korrelation*		
Intercept	$\sigma^2_{v_0}$	0,893			
Arbeitslosigkeit	$\sigma^2_{v_1}$	0,888	0,064		
Residualvarianz	σ^2_ε	0,926			
Autokorrelation AR (1)		0,209			

Anzahl der Beobachtungen = 49 505; Anzahl der Personen = 5964; Devianz = 146 594,6; BIC = 146 656,2
**$p<0,01$; *$p<0,05$

3.4 Das Random-Intercept-Random-Slope-Modell mit zeitkonstantem Level-2 Prädiktor

Liegt eine Varianz des Effekts einer Prädiktorvariablen über die Level-2 Einheiten vor, so ist es zweckmäßig diese Varianz durch zeitstabile Level-2 Variablen aufzuklären. Hierzu kommt das Random-Intercept-Random-Slope-Modell mit Level-2 Prädiktor zum Einsatz. Für das vorliegende Beispiel wird geprüft, ob die Lebenszufriedenheit und der Effekt der Arbeitslosigkeit von dem Geschlecht der Personen abhängen. Die Ergebnisse der Analyse sind in Tab. 4 dokumentiert.

Die erwartete Lebenszufriedenheit von Männern, die nicht arbeitslos sind, beträgt $\hat{\gamma}_{00} = 7,839$ Punkte auf der Lebenszufriedenheitsskala. Der erwarte Effekt der Arbeitslosigkeit für Männer beträgt $\hat{\gamma}_{10} = -0,355$ Punkte auf der Lebenszufriedenheitsskala und ist statistisch signifikant. Ferner zeigt sich ein signifikanter Effekt des Geschlechts auf die Lebenszufriedenheit. Die erwartete Lebenszufriedenheit von arbeitenden Frauen liegt geschätzte $\hat{\gamma}_{10} = 0,062$ Punkte über der erwarteten Lebenszufriedenheit von arbeitenden Männern. Dieser Effekt ist statistisch signifikant. Der negative Effekt der Arbeitslosigkeit auf die Lebenszufriedenheit für Frauen fällt geschätzte $\hat{\gamma}_{11} = 0,070$ Punkte *geringer* aus als derjenige der Männer, allerdings ist dieser Kontrast statistisch nicht signifikant.

Tab. 4 Random-Intercept-Random-Slope-Modell mit zeitkonstantem Level-2 Prädiktor

Parameter		Schätzer	SE	df	t
Intercept	γ_{00}	7,839**	0,019	43 539	405,56
Arbeitslosigkeit	γ_{10}	−0,355**	0,062	43 539	−5,76
Geschlecht	γ_{01}	0,062*	0,027	5962	2,31
Arbeitslosigkeit x Geschlecht	γ_{11}	0,070	0,084	43 539	0,83
Zufällige Effekte		*Varianz*		*Korrelation*	
Intercept	$\sigma^2_{v_0}$	0,891			
Arbeitslosigkeit	$\sigma^2_{v_1}$	0,887		0,064	
Residualvarianz	σ^2_ε	0,926			
Autokorrelation AR (1)		0,209			

Anzahl der Beobachtungen = 49 505; Anzahl der Personen = 5964; Devianz = 146 592,3; BIC = 146 671,6
**$p<0,01$; *$p<0,05$

Tab. 5 Random-Intercept-Random-Slope-Modell mit zeitvariierendem Level-2 Prädiktor

	Parameter	Schätzer	SE	df	t
Intercept	γ_{00}	7,902**	0,014	43 538	554,23
Arbeitslosigkeit	γ_{10}	−0,444**	0,052	43 538	−8,51
Alter (zentriert)	γ_{01}	0,006**	0,001	43 538	6,37
Arbeitslosigkeit x Alter (zentriert)	γ_{11}	−0,013**	0,003	43 538	−4,22
Zufällige Effekte		*Varianz*	*Korrelation*		
Intercept	$\sigma^2_{v_0}$	0,879			
Arbeitslosigkeit	$\sigma^2_{v_1}$	0,871	0,063		
Residualvarianz	σ^2_ε	0,927			
Autokorrelation (AR1)		0,209			

Anzahl der Beobachtungen = 49 505; Anzahl der Personen = 5964; Devianz = 146 544,8; BIC = 146 624,0
**$p<0,01$; *$p<0,05$

3.5 Das Random-Intercept-Random-Slope-Modell mit zeitvariierendem Level-2 Prädiktor

Im vorhergehenden Beispiel handelte es sich bei der Level-2 Variable „Geschlecht" um eine zeitkonstante Variable. Im Rahmen von längsschnittlichen Erhebungen ist „Alter" eine Variable, die zwar der Person zukommt, allerdings nicht zeitstabil ist. Um diese Variable in einer Multilevel-Analyse zu modellieren, kann diese als Level-1-Variable in ein Modell aufgenommen werden. Im folgenden Beispiel wird geprüft, inwiefern der Effekt der Arbeitslosigkeit vom Alter der Person abhängt. Die Variable Alter wurde am Stichprobenmittelwert über alle Messzeitpunkte zentriert (42,54 Jahre), um den variierenden Intercepts eine sinnvolle Bedeutung zu geben. Ferner wird angenommen, dass die Intercepts und der Effekt der Arbeitslosigkeit über die Personen variieren können. Die Ergebnisse der Analyse sind in Tab. 5 dargestellt.

Die erwartete Lebenszufriedenheit von arbeitenden Personen im mittleren Alter beträgt $\hat{\gamma}_{00} = 7,902$ Punkte. Der erwartete Effekt der Arbeitslosigkeit für Personen im mittleren Alter beträgt $\hat{\gamma}_{10} - 0,444$ Punkte. Dieser Effekt ist statistisch signifikant. Ferner wird der Effekt durch das Alter moderiert. Pro Jahr Alterszuwachs verändert sich die erwartete Lebenszufriedenheit bei Arbeitslosigkeit um weitere $\hat{\gamma}_{11} = -0,013$ Punkte. Dieser Effekt ist statistisch signifikant. Zudem existiert ein signifikanter Alterseffekt. Pro Jahr steigt die Lebenszufriedenheit bei arbeitenden Personen um $\hat{\gamma}_{01} = 0,006$ Punkte. Es zeigt sich also insgesamt, dass der negative Effekt der Arbeitslosigkeit auf die Lebenszufriedenheit sich mit dem Alter verstärkt. Allerdings sind diese Effekte mit Vorsicht zu interpretieren, da das Alter mit den Messzeitpunkten konfundiert ist. Im vorliegenden Beispiel wurde eine zeitvariierende Level-2-Variable in die Analyse mit aufgenommen. Aber es ist auch durchaus denkbar, eine zeitvariierende Level-3-Variable, wie z. B. die Arbeitslosigkeitsrate als Prädiktor auf Level-1 mit aufzunehmen.

3.6 Ein Kontextmodell mit zwei Ebenen ohne Zentrierung der Level-1 Prädiktorvariable

Zur Prüfung von Effekten des Level-2-Kontexts kann die Prädiktorvariable innerhalb der Level-2-Einheiten aggregiert und als Prädiktor in das Modell mit aufgenommen

Tab. 6 Kontextmodell mit zwei Ebenen ohne Zentrierung der Level-1-Prädiktorvariablen

	Parameter	Schätzer	SE	df	t
Fixed Effects					
Intercept	γ_{00}	7,900**	0,014	43540	556,43
Arbeitslosigkeit	γ_{10}	−0,271**	0,030	43540	−9,01
Arbeitslosigkeit Person	γ_{01}	−0,730**	0,099	5962	−7,36
Random Effects		*Varianz*			
Intercept	$\sigma^2_{\upsilon_0}$	0,904			
Residualvarianz	σ^2_e	0,950			
Autokorrelation AR (1)		0,213			

Anzahl der Beobachtungen = 49505; Anzahl der Personen = 5964; Devianz = 146912,6; BIC = 146965,5
**$p<0,01$; *$p<0,05$

werden. Der geschätzte Effekt der aggregierten Variablen entspricht dem Kontexteffekt (*contextual effect*) auf Personenebene. Im vorliegenden Beispiel interessiert, inwiefern die Lebenszufriedenheit neben dem Effekt auf Ebene-1 zusätzlich von dem Effekt der Arbeitslosigkeitsrate der Personen im Beobachtungszeitraum abhängt. Zu diesem Zweck wurden die Jahre der Arbeitslosigkeit innerhalb einer Person aggregiert. Ein Wert von 1 auf dieser Variablen bedeutet, dass die Person im gesamten Untersuchungszeitraum arbeitslos war und ein Wert von 0 zeigt an, dass die Person im gesamten Untersuchungszeitraum nicht arbeitslos war. Der Wert bildet also die relativen Jahre der Arbeitslosigkeit ab. Die Person (Ebene-2) ist hier der Kontext der Messwerte auf Ebene-1. Der Indikator für die Arbeitslosigkeit auf Ebene-1 wurde nicht zentriert, da der Kontexteffekt (*contextual effect*) interessiert und nicht die Zerlegung in einen *within*- und *between*-Effekt. Zudem handelt es sich bei Arbeitslosigkeit um eine dichotome Indikatorvariable, bei der eine Zentrierung nicht sinnvoll ist. Die Ergebnisse der Analyse sind in Tab. 6 dokumentiert.

Die erwartete Lebenszufriedenheit einer Person, die im Untersuchungszeitraum nie arbeitslos war, ist $\hat{\gamma}_{00} = 7,900$. Der erwartete Effekt der Arbeitslosigkeit für eine Person, die nie arbeitslos war, beträgt $\hat{\gamma}_{10} = -0,271$ Punkte auf der Lebenszufriedenheitsskala. Dieser Effekt ist statistisch signifikant. Pro Prozentpunkt Anstieg der relativen Zeit der Arbeitslosigkeit im Untersuchungszeitraum steigt dieser Effekt um geschätzte $(\hat{\gamma}_{01} / 100) = -0,007$. Punkte. Dieser Effekt ist statistisch signifikant. Praktisch legt dies die Vermutung nahe, dass die Länge der Arbeitslosigkeit negativ mit der Lebenszufriedenheit zusammenhängt. Nehmen wir an, eine Person ist arbeitslos und war 100 % der Zeit im Untersuchungszeitraum arbeitslos, so ist die erwartete Ausprägung auf der Lebenszufriedenheitsskala $7,900 - 0,271 + (1*-0,730) = 6,899$ Punkte. Die erwartete Lebenszufriedenheit einer arbeitslosen Person, die sich in 50 % des Untersuchungszeitraums in Arbeitslosigkeit befindet, ist dementsprechend $7,900 - 0,271 + (0,5*-0,730) = 7,264$ Punkte. Das bedeutet, dass neben dem Eintritt der Arbeitslosigkeit innerhalb einer Person, die Dauer der Erfahrung der Arbeitslosigkeit sich zusätzlich negativ auf die Lebenszufriedenheit auswirkt.

3.7 Kontextmodell mit drei Ebenen und ohne Zentrierung der Level-1 Prädiktorvariable

Im Rahmen von längsschnittlichen Panel-Daten ist die Ebene-2 die Person. Um zu prüfen, ob eine aggregierte Prädiktorvariable auf Makro-Ebene (Level-3) zusätzlich einen Effekt auf die abhängige Variable ausübt, kann die über die Personen und Messzeitpunkte in den Regionen aggregierte Prädiktorvariable in das Modell mit aufgenommen werden. Hierdurch kann geprüft werden, inwiefern die relative Häufigkeit der über die Messzeitpunkte aggregierten Arbeitslosigkeit in einer Region zusätzlich zu den Effekten der zeitvariierenden Arbeitslosigkeit auf Ebene-1 und der Arbeitslosigkeitsrate der Person (Ebene-2) einen Effekt auf die abhängige Variable ausübt. Ferner wird ein über die Regionen variierendes Level-3-Residuum mit in die Regressionsgleichungen aufgenommen. Für das vorliegende Beispiel wird also geprüft, ob die aggregierte Arbeitslosigkeitsrate der Regionen über alle Messzeitpunkte sich zusätzlich negativ auf die Lebenszufriedenheit auswirkt. Die Ergebnisse der Analyse sind in Tab. 7 dargestellt.

Die erwartete Lebenszufriedenheit von Personen, die im Untersuchungszeitraum nie arbeitslos waren und in einer Region ohne Arbeitslosigkeit leben ist $\hat{\gamma}_{000} = 7,995$ Punkte. Der erwartete Effekt der Arbeitslosigkeit innerhalb einer Person beträgt $\hat{\gamma}_{100} = -0,287$ Punkte. Zusätzlich sinkt die erwartete Lebenszufriedenheit einer Person um $(\hat{\gamma}_{010} / 100) = -0,007$ Punkte pro Prozentpunkt Arbeitslosigkeit im Untersuchungszeitraum. Der erwartete Effekt der Region auf die Lebenszufriedenheit beträgt $(\hat{\gamma}_{001} / 100) = -0,010$ Punkte auf der Lebenszufriedenheitsskala pro Prozentpunkt Unterschied der relativen Häufigkeit der Arbeitslosigkeit in der Region. Dieser Effekt ist statistisch allerdings nicht signifikant, was darauf hindeutet, dass die innerhalb der Regionen über Messzeitpunkte und Personen aggregierte Arbeitslosigkeitsrate in der definierten Region nicht mit der Lebenszufriedenheit auf Ebene-1 zusammenhängt und eher die individuelle Häufigkeit des Erlebens der Arbeitslosigkeit über die Jahre ausschlaggebend für die Lebenszufriedenheit ist. Natürlich ist die Interpretation dieses Effektes an die Definition der regionalen Einheiten gebunden. Für das vorliegende Beispiel wurden künstliche Regionalvariablen gebildet, ggf. zeigt sich hier ein

Tab. 7 Kontextmodell mit drei Ebenen ohne Zentrierung der Level-1 Prädiktorvariablen

	Parameter	Schätzer	SE	t
Intercept	γ_{000}	7,995**	0,046	173,20
Arbeitslosigkeit	γ_{100}	−0,287**	0,030	−9,61
Arbeitslosigkeitsrate (Person)	γ_{010}	−0,710**	0,099	−7,19
Arbeitslosigkeitsrate (Region)	γ_{001}	−1,013	1,161	−0,87
Random Effects		*Varianz*		
Intercept (Person)	$\sigma^2_{v_0}$	0,951		
Intercept (Region)	$\sigma^2_{v_{00}}$	0,013		
Residualvarianz	σ^2_ε	0,892		

Anzahl der Beobachtungen=49 505; Anzahl der Personen=5964; Anzahl der Regionen=45; Devianz=148 125; BIC=148 212

**$p<0,01$; *$p<0,05$

Effekt, wenn auf wesentlich feingliederige Regionalinformationen zurückgegriffen wird. Ferner zeigt sich, dass die geschätzte Varianz der Lebenszufriedenheit über die Regionen relativ gering ist ($\hat{\sigma}^2_{v_{00}} = 0,013$). Die geschätzte Variabilität zwischen den Personen unter der Berücksichtigung der verwendeten Prädiktorvariablen ist weitaus höher ($\hat{\sigma}^2_{v_0} = 0,951$).

3.8 Wachstumskurvenmodell mit zeitvariierender Level-1 Kovariate

Im Folgenden wird ein sehr einfaches Wachstumskurvenmodell an die Daten angepasst. Prädiktoren auf Level-1 sind einerseits die Wellen 2001 bis 2010 des HILDA-Surveys und die zeitvariierende Arbeitslosigkeit, welche dummy-codiert vorliegt (1: arbeitslos, 0: nicht arbeitslos). Mit dem Modell soll geprüft werden, ob die lineare Veränderung der Lebenszufriedenheit über die Zeit durch die Arbeitslosigkeit moderiert wird. Die Ergebnisse der Analyse sind in Tab. 8 dargestellt.

Der Koeffizient $\hat{\gamma}_{00}$ ist die erwartete Lebenszufriedenheit arbeitender Personen im HILDA-Panel im Jahr 2001. $\hat{\gamma}_{10}$ ist der erwartete Effekt der Arbeitslosigkeit im Jahr 2001. Dieser Effekt beträgt $-0,232$ Punkte auf der Lebenszufriedenheitsskala. Pro Jahr verändert sich die Lebenszufriedenheit der arbeitenden Personen um erwartete $\hat{\gamma}_{20} = -0,009$ Punkte. Der Kontrast bei Arbeitslosigkeit zu diesem Effekt ist $\hat{\gamma}_{30} = -0,024$ Punkte. Inhaltlich bedeutet dies nach dem Modell, dass eine Beschleunigung des Abfalls der Lebenszufriedenheit eintritt, sobald Arbeitslosigkeit vorliegt. Die Annahme eines linearen Verlaufs der Lebenszufriedenheit über die Zeit ist sehr restriktiv. Im nächsten Abschnitt wird ein Phasenmodell verwendet, um zu prüfen, ob der Effekt der Arbeitslosigkeit sich über die Zeit verändert.

3.9 Multivariates Multilevelmodell mit Level-1 Kovariate

Um detaillierter zu prüfen, ob die Arbeitslosigkeit im Zusammenhang mit der Lebenszufriedenheit steht und um detailliert zu klären, wie dieser Effekt sich zwischen den Jahren unterscheidet, wird ein Phasenmodell an die Daten des HILDA-Surveys der Wellen 2005 bis 2010 angepasst. Insgesamt gehen 5574 Personen in die Analysen ein. Das Modell wurde mittels der R-Funktion lavaan (Rosseel 2012) zur Struktur-

Tab. 8 Wachstumskurvenmodell mit zeitvariierender Level-1 Kovariate

	Parameter	Schätzer	SE	t
Intercept	γ_{00}	7,908**	0,016	506,26
Arbeitslosigkeit	γ_{10}	$-0,232$**	0,060	$-3,97$
Jahr	γ_{20}	$-0,009$**	0,002	$-4,82$
Arbeitslosigkeit x Jahr	γ_{30}	$-0,024$*	0,010	$-2,28$
Random Effects		*Varianz*	*Korrelation*	
Intercept (Person)	$\sigma^2_{v_0}$	0,892		
Arbeitslosigkeit	$\sigma^2_{v_1}$	0,893	0,06	
Residualvarianz	σ^2_e	0,925		
Autokorrelation (AR1)			0,208	

Anzahl der Beobachtungen = 49 505; Anzahl der Personen = 5964; AIC = 146 565,9; BIC = 146 645,2
**$p < 0,01$; *$p < 0,05$

gleichungsmodellierung angepasst. Zeitvariierender Prädiktor auf Level-1 ist der Status der Arbeitslosigkeit. Tabelle 9 zeigt die Ergebnisse der Analyse.

Die Koeffizienten $\hat{\gamma}_{10}$ bis $\hat{\gamma}_{60}$ sind die geschätzten Lebenszufriedenheitswerte (Mittelwerte) der arbeitenden Personen in den jeweiligen Jahren. Die Koeffizienten $\hat{\gamma}_{70}$ bis $\hat{\gamma}_{12.0}$ sind die geschätzten Kontraste der arbeitslosen Personen zur Lebenszufriedenheit der arbeitenden Personen in den jeweiligen Jahren.

Tabelle 10 zeigt die geschätzten Varianzen und Kovarianzen der Zufallseffekte. Es zeigt sich eine deutliche Heterogenität der Varianzen.

Diese Heterogenität ist im Gegensatz zu FE-Modellen nicht über die Wellen konstant, sondern darf über die Jahre variieren. An den Autokorrelationen ist erkennbar, dass die erwarteten Lebenszufriedenheitswerte arbeitender Personen über die Wellen hinweg recht stabil sind. Ferner zeigt sich ein typischer autoregressiver Abfall der Korrelationen in Abhängigkeit der zeitlichen Distanz zweier Wellen. Das diese Korrelationen höher ausfallen als die Autokorrelation in Residualstrukturen bei Random-Intercept-Modellen liegt vermutlich daran, dass ein Teil der Kovarianz zwischen den Messzeitpunkten bei Random-Intercept-Modellen durch die über die Personen variierenden Intercepts abgefangen wird. Übrigens können in allen Mehrebenenmodellen spezifische Kontrasthypothesen getestet werden. Somit lässt sich beispielsweise die Hypothese prüfen, dass die Lebenszufriedenheit der arbeitenden Personen im Jahr

Tab. 9 Multivariates Multilevelmodell mit Level-1 Kovariate

	Parameter	Schätzer	SE	z
2005	γ_{10}	7,806**	0,020	
2006	γ_{20}	7,784**	0,020	381,52
2007	γ_{30}	7,807**	0,020	390,49
2008	γ_{40}	7,810**	0,019	388,73
2009	γ_{50}	7,849**	0,020	403,37
2010	γ_{60}	7,809**	0,020	401,96
Arbeitslosigkeit 2005	γ_{70}	−0,245**	0,107	392,54
Arbeitslosigkeit 2006	γ_{80}	−0,101	0,128	−2,30
Arbeitslosigkeit 2007	γ_{90}	−0,360**	0,134	−0,79
Arbeitslosigkeit 2008	$\gamma_{10.0}$	−0,348**	0,119	−2,69
Arbeitslosigkeit 2009	$\gamma_{11.0}$	−0,589**	0,119	−2,92
Arbeitslosigkeit 2010	$\gamma_{12.0}$	−0,629**	0,107	−4,93

$N=5574$; AIC$=31\,977{,}44$; BIC$=32\,184{,}72$; $\chi^2(30)=83{,}96$, $p<0{,}001$; RMSEA$=0{,}02$; CFI$=1{,}00$
**$p<0{,}01$; *$p<0{,}05$

Tab. 10 Geschätzte Varianz-Korrelations-Matrix der Zufallseffekte

	Varianz	Korrelation					
2005	1,634						
2006	1,560	0,589					
2007	1,583	0,545	0,597				
2008	1,471	0,526	0,571	0,598			
2009	1,495	0,525	0,530	0,526	0,584		
2010	1,546	0,478	0,509	0,499	0,568	0,590	

Für alle Korrelationen gilt $p<0{,}01$

2005 sich von der Lebenszufriedenheit der arbeitslosen Personen im Jahr 2010 unterscheidet. Zur Prüfung von spezifischen Kontrasthypothesen im Rahmen gemischter linearer Modelle geben Hothorn et al. (2008) für die Software R Hinweise.

4 Diskussion

In vorliegenden Beitrag wurde an einigen einfachen Beispielen gezeigt, wie Mehrebenenmodelle zur Analyse von längsschnittlichen Panel-Daten verwendet werden können, um Hypothesen hinsichtlich der Zusammenhänge zwischen einer abhängigen Variable und auf mehreren Ebenen anfallenden Prädiktoren zu prüfen. Zudem wurde darauf eingegangen, wie aggregierte Kontextvariablen auf unterschiedlichen Ebenen in der Analyse berücksichtigt werden können und welche Auswirkungen unterschiedliche Arten von Zentrierung auf die Interpretation der Prädiktoren haben. Ferner wurde kurz auf Wachstumskurvenmodelle und multivariate Multilevelmodelle eingegangen. Vergleichen wir die Modelle, die an einen Datensatz angepasst wurden anhand der informationstheoretischen Maße, so zeigt sich, dass das Wachstumskurvenmodell die Daten am sparsamsten beschreibt.

In diesem Beitrag wurde nur ein sehr kleiner Ausschnitt von möglichen Mehrebenenmodellen, die sich für längsschnittliche Analysen eignen, berichtet. Auch sind die Modelle sehr einfach gehalten, um einen Einstieg in die Materie zu erleichtern. Bei allen Modellen ist es möglich, diese um weitere Prädiktoren auf Ebene-1, Ebene-2 und Ebene-3 zu erweitern. Zudem können theoretisch weitere Ebenen eingefügt werden. Allerdings sind Modelle mit 3 und mehr Ebenen bisher wenig exploriert. Um im Längsschnitt Effekte der soziologisch gemeinten Makro-Ebene zu berücksichtigen, ist es notwendig eine dritte Ebene in die mehrebenenanalytischen Modelle einzubauen. Die dabei auftretenden Modelle werden je nach Anzahl der Prädiktoren auf den Ebenen relativ schnell sehr komplex. Auch die Auswirkungen der Zentrierung von Prädiktoren auf die Interpretation der Regressionskoeffizienten erschweren die Interpretierbarkeit. Um dennoch den Überblick zu behalten, ist es günstig, die Modelle Schritt für Schritt hypothesengeleitet aufzubauen und sich *vor* einer Analyse zu verdeutlichen, was die geschätzten Koeffizienten einer Analyse *inhaltlich* bedeuten und ob die Koeffizienten es erlauben, eine interessierende Hypothese angemessen zu prüfen. Hierbei ist eine Kenntnis des formalen Aufbaus der Modelle unvermeidlich. Zur Vertiefung der Thematik wird die angeführte Literatur, insbesondere das Buch von Rabe-Hesketh und Skrondal (2012), empfohlen, das sich durch eine relativ umfassende Darstellung und klare Notation auszeichnet.

Ein weiterer Aspekt, der in diesem Beitrag nur kurz angerissen wurde, ist die Modellierung von Residualstrukturen auf Ebene-1. Die Annahme der identischen und unabhängigen Verteilung der Residuen auf Level-1 ist unter Umständen zu restriktiv. Bei längsschnittlichen Modellen kann es angemessen sein, eine gegebenenfalls vorliegende autoregressive Struktur auf den Residuen und gruppenbedingte Heteroskedasdizität mit zu berücksichtigen. Die Modellierung dieser Strukturen ist nicht mit jeder Software möglich und bei komplexen Zufallseffekten, wie sie bei der Berücksichtigung einer dritten Ebene bei Panel-Daten auftreten, kann die Modellierung schwierig sein. Ein informeller Vergleich der hier dargestellten Modelle mit und ohne Modellierung der Residualstruktur hat gezeigt, dass sich an den festen Effekten und den Standardfehlern im Wesentlichen nichts verändert, allerdings wäre eine systematischere Untersuchung wünschenswert. Im Zweifel ist die Modellierung der Residualstruktur – sofern möglich – der bessere Weg.

Eine weitere Möglichkeit der Berücksichtigung autoregressiver Effekte besteht darin, diese in den Parametern des Modells und nicht in der Residualstruktur abzubilden. Das hier dargestellte multivariate Multilevelmodell ist ein Beispiel, welches konzeptuell der klassischen MANOVA ähnelt. Allerdings werden auch hier die Modelle in einer mehrebenenanalytischen Formulierung relativ schnell sehr komplex, da diese Analysemethode sich hauptsächlich für die Untersuchung lediglich einer abhängigen Variable eignet und multivariate Anwendungen der Mehrebenenanalyse scheinen eher selten zu sein. Eine Alternative für den multivariaten Fall könnten längsschnittliche und dynamische Multilevel-Strukturgleichungsmodelle sein.

Abschließend lässt sich sagen, dass Mehrebenenmodelle sich im univariaten Fall gut zur Modellierung von längsschnittlichen Daten eignen. Anwendungsbeispiele finden sich bei Luhmann und Eid (2009) und Luhmann et al. (2014) für dyadische Daten. Ein besonderer Vorteil der Mehrebenenanalyse liegt darin, dass sich Effekte von Eigenschaften einer höheren Ebene (z. B. der Makro-Ebene) auf verschachtelte Ebenen (z. B. das Individuum) abbilden lassen.

Allerdings sind gerade Modelle mit drei oder mehr Ebenen, wie sie z. B. bei der Analyse von Panel-Daten auftreten können, wenig exploriert. Hier bieten sich interessante methodische und inhaltliche Kooperationsmöglichkeiten zwischen Ökonometrie, Soziologie und Psychologie. Günstig wäre es zunächst, die Unterschiede in den Begrifflichkeiten und die Gemeinsamkeiten in der mathematischen Form der verwendeten Modelle in den unterschiedlichen Disziplinen zu klären. Hiernach könnten einige prototypische Modelle z. B. für Panel-Daten entwickelt werden, um den potenziellen Anwenderinnen und Anwendern eine methodische Orientierung zu bieten, mit der sich substanzwissenschaftliche Fragestellungen aus den Fachgebieten klären lassen.

Literatur

Baayen, Harald, Doug Davidson und Douglas Bates. 2009. Mixed-effects modeling with crossed random effects for subjects and items. *Journal of Memory and Cognition* 59:390–412.

Bates, Douglas, Martin Maechler und Ben Bolker. 2011. lme4: Linear mixed-effects models using S4 classes. http://CRAN.R-project.org/package=lme4. Zugegriffen: 15. Feb. 2014.

Biesanz, Jeremy C., Natalia Deeb-Sossa, Alison A. Papadakis, Kenneth A. Bollen und Patrick Curran. 2004. The role of coding time in estimating and interpreting growth curve models. *Psychological Methods* 9:30–52.

Brüderl, Josef, und Volker Ludwig. Im Druck. *Fixed-effects panel regression*. In *Regression analysis and causal inference*, Hrsg. Henning Best und Christoph Wolf. London: Sage.

Bryk, Anthony S., und Stephen W. Raudenbush. 1992. *Hierarchical linear models in social and behavioral research: Applications and data analysis methods*. Newbury Park: Sage.

Eid, Michael, Christian Geiser und Fridtjof Nussbeck. 2008. Neuere psychometrische Ansätze der Veränderungsmessung. *Zeitschrift für Psychiatrie, Psychologie und Psychotherapie* 56:181–189.

Eid, Michael, Mario Gollwitzer und Manfred Schmitt. 2010. *Statistik und Forschungsmethoden*. Weinheim: Beltz.

Enders, Craig K., und Davood Tofighi. 2007. Centering predictor variables in cross-sectional multilevel models: A new look at an old issue. *Psychological Methods* 12:121–138.
Fitzmaurice, Garrett M., Nan Laird und James Ware. 2004. *Applied longitudinal data analysis*. Hoboken: Wiley.
Gelman, Andrew, und Jennifer Hill. 2007. *Data analysis using regression and multilevel/hierarchical models*. Cambridge: Cambridge University Press.
Harring, Jeffrey R., und Shelley A. Blozis. 2013. Fitting correlated residual error structures in nonlinear mixed effects models with SAS PROC NLMIXED. *Behavioral Research Methods*. doi:10.3758/s13428-013-0397-z.
Hedeker, Don, und Robert D. Gibbons. 2006. *Longitudinal data analysis*. Hoboken: Wiley.
Hothorn, Torsten, Frank Bretz und Peter Westfall. 2008. Simultaneous inference in general parametric models. *Biometrical Journal* 50:346–363.
Hox, Joop J. 2010. *Multilevel analysis: Techniques and applications*. 2. Aufl. New York: Routledge.
Kreft, Ita G. G., Jan De Leeuw und Leona S. Aiken. 1995. The effect of different forms of centering in hierarchical linear models. *Multivariate behavioral research* 30:1–21.
Long, Jeffrey D. 2012. *Longitudinal data analysis for the behavioral sciences using R*. Los Angeles: Sage.
Luhmann, Maike, und Michael Eid. 2009. Does it really feel the same? Changes in life satisfaction following repeated life events. *Journal of Personality and Social Psychology* 92:363–381.
Luhmann, Maike, Pola Weiss, Georg Hosoya und Michael Eid. 2014. Honey I got fired! A longitudinal dyadic analysis of the effect of unemployment on life satisfaction in couples. *Journal of Personality and Social Psychology* 107:163–180.
Pinheiro, José C., und Douglas Bates. 2000. *Mixed-effects models in S and S-PLUS*. New York: Springer.
Pinheiro, José C., Douglas Bates, Saikat DebRoy, Sarkar Deepayan und R Core Team. 2013. nlme: linear and nonlinear mixed effects models. (Software Manual). http://CRAN.R-project.org/package=nlme (Zugegriffen: 15. Feb. 2014).
Rabe-Hesketh, Sophia, und Anders Skrondal. 2012. *Multilevel and longitudinal modeling using Stata – volume I: Continuous responses*. College Station: Stata Press.
Robinson, William S. 1950. Ecological correlations and the behavior of individuals. *American Sociological Review* 15:351–357.
Rosseel, Yves. 2012. lavaan: An R package for structural equation modeling. *Journal of Statistical Software* 48:1–36.
Schupp, Jürgen. 2009. 25 Jahre Sozio-oekonomisches Panel – Ein Infrastrukturprojekt der empirischen Sozial- und Wirtschaftsforschung in Deutschland. *Zeitschrift für Soziologie* 38:350–357.
Singer, Judith D., und John B. Willett. 2003. *Applied longitudinal data analysis: Modeling change and event occurence*. Oxford: Oxford University Press.
Snijders, Tom A. B., und Roel J. Bosker. 1999. *Multilevel analysis: An introduction to basic and advanced multilevel modeling*. 2. Aufl. London: Sage.
Summerfield, Michelle, Ross Dunn, Simon Freidin, Markus Hahn, Peter Ittak, Milica Kecmanovic, Ning Li, Ninette Macalalad, Nicole Watson, Roger Wilkins und Mark Wooden. 2011. *HILDA user manual – release 10*, Melbourne: Institute of Applied Economic and Social Research, University of Melbourne.

Georg Hosoya, 1972, Dr. phil., wissenschaftlicher Mitarbeiter, Freie Universität Berlin. Forschungsgebiete: Item Response Theorie. Veröffentlichungen: Ein probabilistisches Testmodell zur Erfassung intraindividueller Variabilität, Unveröffentlichte Dissertation Berlin 2013. Honey I got fired! A longitudinal dyadic analysis of the effect of unemployment on life satisfaction in couples. Journal of Personality and Social Psychology. 2014 (mit M. Luhman, P. Weiss und M. Eid).

Tobias Koch, 1983, Dr. phil., wissenschaftlicher Mitarbeiter. Forschungsgebiete: Multilevel Analysen, Strukturgleichungsmodelle, MTMM Analysen, Veränderungsmessung. Veröffentlichungen: Multilevel structural equation modelling of multitrait-multimethod-multioccasion data. Unveröffentlichte Dissertation Berlin 2013.

Michael Eid, 1963, Prof. Dr., Professor für Psychologie an der Freien Universität Berlin. Seine Hauptforschungsinteressen liegen im Bereich der Psychometrie insbesondere in der Modellierung multimethodal erhobener Daten und von Veränderungsprozessen. Darüber hinaus beschäftigt er sich mit Fragen der Wohlbefindensmessung, der Emotionsregulation und der Hautkrebsprävention.

Aktuelle Probleme der Modellierung von Mehrebenen-Daten

Manuela Pötschke

© Springer Fachmedien Wiesbaden 2014

Zusammenfassung Mehrebenenanalysen finden für zahlreiche Forschungsfragen in unterschiedlichen Wissenschaftsgebieten Anwendung. Sie erlauben die adäquate statistische Abbildung von Modellvorstellungen, die durch die Einbettung individueller Zusammenhänge in Kontexte geprägt sind. Im Beitrag geht es um einen Überblick über aktuelle Diskussionen im Zusammenhang mit der Modellierung und Interpretation von Mehrebenenanalysen. Sie beziehen sich sowohl auf Fragen der Datenerhebung (Fallzahlen und Datenstruktur) als auch auf Fragen der Schätzung (Auswahl der Schätzverfahren, Güteinterpretation, Zentrierung).

Schlüsselwörter Cross Classified-Strukturen · REML-Schätzverfahren · FML-Schätzverfahren · Zentrierung · Fallzahlen

Problems of modeling in multilevel analyses

Abstract Multilevel analyses are applied for many research problems in different research domains. They allow for adequate statistical modelling of individual characteristics embedded in contexts. The contribution reviews the present discussion of the relation between modelling and interpretation of multilevel analyses. Both the problems of data (number of cases and structure of data) and of estimation (selection of estimation procedure, validity and centering) are assessed.

Keywords Cross-classified structures · REML estimates · FML estimates · Centering · Number of cases

---

M. Pötschke (✉)
FB Gesellschaftswissenschaften, Universität Kassel,
Nora-Platiel-Str. 1, 34127 Kassel, Deutschland
E-Mail: manuela.poetschke@uni-kassel.de

1 Einleitung

Mehrebenenmodelle finden mittlerweile in zahlreichen Fachwissenschaften weite Verbreitung. Die zunehmend feiner ausgearbeitete theoretische Einbettung von Individualverhalten in Kontexte trug dazu ebenso bei, wie die Entwicklung von Schätzverfahren und Maßzahlen (vor allem auch für nicht lineare Modelle) sowie die Verbesserung der computergestützten Rechenleistungen. Dadurch waren neben den inhaltlich motivierten Anwendungen vor allem vielfältige Simulationsstudien möglich, die die statistischen Voraussetzungen für Mehrebenenmodelle und Konsequenzen ihrer Verletzung sowie die Beurteilung der geschätzten Parameter auf eine sicherere Basis stellen.

Aspekte wie eine hinreichende Datenbasis oder eine angemessene Interpretation unterschiedlicher Schätzergebnisse werden im Zusammenhang mit Mehrebenen-Designs aber nach wie vor auch kontrovers diskutiert. Hierzu zählen ein angemessener Stichprobenumfang genauso wie Konsequenzen aus der Verletzung der hierarchischen Datenstruktur oder die Entscheidung für oder gegen ein spezifisches Schätzverfahren. Auch wenn es um die Interpretation der Modellparameter geht, sind bisher noch offene Fragen geblieben. Sie beziehen sich auf Zentrierungsverfahren und die Beurteilung der Modellgüte. Diesen generellen Fragen wird im ersten Teil des vorliegenden Überblicks über Probleme bei der Modellierung von Mehrebenen-Daten nachgegangen.

Der zweite Teil wendet sich dann den Problemen spezifischer Modelle zu, die den linearen Regressionsansatz in vielfältiger Hinsicht erweitern. Zwar wird in Einführungen zur Idee der Mehrebenenanalysen und zur anschaulichen Entwicklung der entsprechenden Schätzgleichungen oft auf das lineare Modell zurückgegriffen. In der praktischen Forschung liegen aber häufig Daten mit kategorialem Skalenniveau vor oder die Modelle beziehen sich auf latente Strukturen, die sich der direkten Messung entziehen. Darüber hinaus gewinnen Daten mit Zeitverlaufsinformationen an Bedeutung. Auch für die aus diesen unterschiedlichen Forschungsinteressen resultierenden Verfahren sind mittlerweile mehrebenenanalytische Ansätze entwickelt.

2 Generelle Probleme der Modellierung von Mehrebenmodellen

In den nachfolgenden Ausführungen beziehen wir uns in der Regel auf ein lineares Zwei-Ebenen-Modell. In ihm wird ein sogenannter Fixer Part, der die Schätzung der mittleren Regressionskoeffizienten beinhaltet, vom sogenannten Random Part unterschieden, der die Variation der Schätzungen zwischen den Gruppen und die Residualvarianz auf der ersten Ebene enthält.

Für das Ausgangsmodell ergibt sich die Schätzung der Verteilung der abhängigen Variable ohne erklärende Variable durch

$$y_{ij} = \gamma_{00} + u_{0j} + e_{ij}$$

wobei: y_{ij} = beobachteter Wert der abhängigen Variable;
γ_{00} = geschätzter mittlerer Wert über alle Personen in allen Gruppen hinweg;

u_{0j} = Abweichungen der Gruppenmittelwerte in der abhängigen Variable zum Gesamtmittelwert;
e_{ij} = der Residualabweichung auf der erste Ebene.

Werden in das Modell Erklärungsvariablen einbezogen, kann entweder unterstellt werden, dass die Wirkungen in allen Kontexten gleich ausfallen (Random Intercept Model) oder, dass sie kontextabhängig variieren (Random Coefficient Model). Im ersten Fall werden die Varianzkomponenten der Effekte auf null festgesetzt.

$$y_{ij} = \gamma_{00} + \gamma_{10j}x_{1ij} + u_{0j} + u_{1j}x_{1ij} + e_{ij}$$

wobei: y_{ij} = beobachteter Wert in der abhängigen Variable,
γ_{00} = geschätzter mittleren Wert über alle Personen in allen Gruppen hinweg,
γ_{10} = mittlerer Effekt der Variable x_1,
u_{0j} = Abweichungen der Gruppenmittelwerte in der abhängigen Variable zum Gesamtmittelwert,
u_{1j} = Variation des Effektes ß1 zwischen den Gruppen,
e_{ij} = der Residualabweichung auf der erste Ebene.

Dieses Modell kann nun um weitere erklärende Variablen oder aber Interaktionseffekte erweitert werden. Besonders interessant scheinen Cross Level-Interaktionen, die die Wirkung einer Aggregatvariable auf die Ausgestaltung der Beziehung zwischen zwei Variablen der erste Ebene zum Ausdruck bringt. Anhand dieser grundlegenden Modelle sollen nun zentrale Fragen diskutiert werden, die im Rahmen der praktischen Anwendung von Mehrebenenmodellen relevant sind.

2.1 Anforderungen an die Datenbasis

2.1.1 Stichprobenumfang

Eine seit langem diskutierte Frage bezieht sich auf die notwendige Fallzahl an Daten auf den einzelnen Ebenen. Als Ausgangspunkt dieser Debatte kann die 30/30-Regel angesehen werden, die auf Kreft (1996) zurückgeht. Basierend auf Erfahrungen in der Schulforschung ist damit gemeint, dass in einem 2-Ebenenmodell für unverzerrte Schätzungen mindestens 30 Elemente der zweiten Ebene und jeweils mindestens 30 Elemente der ersten Ebene notwendig sind. Kreft (1996) unterscheidet in ihrer Beurteilung nicht zwischen den Schätzungen für die fixen Effekte und den Schätzungen der Varianzparameter.

In der Folge wurden wiederholt Simulationsstudien zur Frage der notwendigen Fallzahlen präsentiert. Hier zeigte sich, dass die Fallzahlen unterschiedliche Auswirkungen auf das Verzerrungspotenzial für fixe Effekte und Varianzkomponenten haben. Als gemeinsames Ergebnis vielfältiger Forschungen hat sich gezeigt, dass die Regressionskoeffizienten mit Blick auf die Fallzahlen in der Regel robust ausfallen. Schätzprobleme ergeben sich aber für die Varianzkomponenten (Afshartous 1995; Mok 1995; Maas und Hox 2005; Schulz 2010).

Insbesondere Hox (2010) und Maas und Hox (2005) leiteten aus ihren Ergebnissen das Fazit ab, dass eine große Anzahl an Elementen der zweiten Ebene wichtiger sei als eine große Anzahl an Elementen der ersten Ebene. In ihren Simulationen ergab sich für Konstellationen mit 30 Gruppen ein relevant verzerrter Standardfehler für die Varianz der zweiten Ebene (Maas und Hox 2005, S. 91). In den anderen simulierten Bedingungen mit 50 oder 100 Gruppen und bei Gruppengrößen von 5, 30 oder 50 Elementen sind unverzerrte Schätzungen für die Regressionskoeffizienten und ihre Standardfehler und für die Varianzparameter zu beobachten gewesen (Maas und Hox 2005, S. 90).[1] Sie schlagen als Mindestanforderung deshalb ein Verhältnis der Fallzahlen auf der zweiten zur ersten Ebene von 50/20 vor. Wenn die Varianzkomponenten von besonderem Interesse sind, sollte sich das Verhältnis sogar auf 100/10 ändern.

In zahlreichen Studien wurde der Frage nach Schätzproblemen durch ungünstige Fallzahlen detaillierter nachgegangen. So untersuchten Theall et al. (2008) die Auswirkungen von Gruppengrößen kleiner als fünf auf die Schätzgüte der Effekte und Varianzparameter in einem Mehrebenenmodell. Insbesondere die Standardfehler steigen mit kleiner Gruppengröße. Wenn sehr viele Gruppen nur über wenige Fälle verfügen, dann kann unter Umständen ein bestehender Gruppeneffekt unentdeckt bleiben (Theall et al. 2008, S. 12 f.). Analoge Ergebnisse nicht nur für metrische sondern auch für dichotome Variablen legte Clarke (2008) vor. Lediglich im Fall der Kombination geringer Fallzahlen auf der ersten Ebene und fehlender Werte waren auch die Regressionskoeffizienten überschätzt. Sie schlussfolgert, dass der Mehrebenenansatz auch dann ein robustes Analysetool darstellt, wenn nur wenige Elemente der ersten Ebene pro Gruppe enthalten sind. Die Schätzung eines Modells unter Vernachlässigung der Ebenenstruktur stellt deshalb keine zwingende Alternative dar (Clarke 2008, S. 757 f.). Raudenbush (2008, S. 207) verweist in diesem Zusammenhang auf zahlreiche inhaltliche Fragestellungen, die die Anwendung des Mehrebenansatzes erfordern und für die die Datenbasis gleichzeitig *per se* geringe Fallzahlen auf der erste Ebene aufweist. Er zeigt, dass durch die Auswahl geeigneter Schätzverfahren wie einer Laplace-Schätzung auch in diesen Fällen gute Ergebnisse erzielt werden können (Raudenbush 2008, S. 234).

Moinedding et al. (2007) gehen explizit der Frage hinreichender Fallzahlen in logistischen Regressionen nach und stellen im Ergebnis fest, dass die empfohlene Fallzahl auf erster und zweiter Ebene nicht generell die Güte der Schätzungen in diesen Modellen garantiert, sondern dass die Verteilung der Ausprägungen der abhängigen Variable in die Überlegungen einzubeziehen ist. Je seltener die untersuchten Ereignisse eintreten, desto mehr Elemente sind in den Gruppen nötig. Unabhängig davon, wirkte sich eine geringe Gruppengröße kleiner als fünf auch darauf aus, ob das Modell konvergierte. Deshalb sollten in logistischen Mehrebenenanalysen eher jeweils 50 Elemente in mindestens 50 Gruppen eingebettet sein.

Schulz (2010) geht mit seiner Simulationsstudie darüber hinaus und untersucht neben den kleinen Gruppen vor allem sehr schiefe Verteilungen der Gruppengrößen.

---

[1] Auch für die Simulationsbedingungen mit 50 Gruppen waren Verzerrungen der Standardfehler zu beobachten. Maas und Hox bewerteten sie zwar als nicht vernachlässigbar, gleichzeitig aber als akzeptabel für die praktische Forschung (Maas und Hox 2005, S. 90 f.).

Das Simulationsdesign orientiert sich an den in der Literatur berichteten Empfehlungen und unterscheidet zwischen folgenden Konstellationen von Gruppen- und Personenanzahlen: 100/100, 75/20; 50/50 und 50/20. Für jede Kombination schätzt Schulz drei Variationen. In der ersten Versuchsanordnung sind alle Gruppen gleich stark besetzt. In der zweiten variiert die Gruppenbesetzung zufällig zwischen 5 Personen und einem maximal festgelegtem Wert. In der dritten Variation sind die Gruppengrößen extrem unterschiedlich, sodass jeweils wenige Gruppen sehr viele Elemente aufweisen und sehr viele Gruppen mit jeweils nur einem Element besetzt sind (vgl. zur ausführlichen Beschreibung und Begründung Schulz 2010, S. 79). Im Ergebnis zeigt sich eine Zunahme der Streuung der Varianz auf Aggregatebene, wenn die Verteilung der Fälle schiefer wird. Die Simulationen ergeben darüber hinaus eine systematische Unterschätzung der Varianz im Aggregat bei gleichzeitiger Überschätzung der Varianz der Effekte (Schulz 2010, S. 103 f.).

Mit einem anderen Fokus argumentieren Snijders und Bosker (2012) zur Fallzahl auf den einzelnen Ebenen. Sie betonen die Abhängigkeit der Empfehlung für ein spezifisches Design von den Forschungsinteressen und der notwendigen Power mit Blick auf unterschiedliche Tests im Rahmen einer Analyse (Snijders 2005; Snijders und Bosker 2012, S. 176 ff.).[2]

Wie in anderen Analysestrategien, stellen fehlende Werte eine Herausforderung für Mehrebenanalysen dar. Sie sind sowohl mit inhaltlichen als auch mit schätztheoretischen Problemen verbunden. Deshalb galt es lange Zeit als Common Sense, dass mit Mehrebenenmodellen nur vollständige Datensätze analysiert werden können (Goldstein 1987). Mittlerweile liegen zahlreiche Beiträge vor, die sowohl die Imputation in Mehrebenen-Designs als auch die Implementierung dieser Imputations-Ansätze in Mehrebenen-Software thematisieren (auch mit weiteren Nachweisen van Buuren 2011, S. 173 f.). In Abhängigkeit der Muster fehlender Werte[3] können klassische komplexe Imputations-Verfahren danach auch für Mehrebenen-Daten herangezogen werden. Das Ziel besteht darin, eine Balance zwischen guter Schätzung und Beibehaltung vollständiger Fallzahlen zu bieten.

Einen Ausschluss von Fällen mit fehlenden Werten erleichtert zwar möglicherweise die praktische Analyse, bringt aber gleichzeitig einen Verlust an Power mit sich und die Ergebnisse sind nur unter der Annahme der Zufälligkeit des Fehlens der Werte unverzerrt. Van Buuren (2011) diskutiert deshalb darüber hinausgehende mögliche Vorgehensweisen für zwei Varianten: für fehlende Werte in der abhängigen Variable und für fehlende Werte sowohl in der abhängigen als auch in der unab-

---

[2] In ihren Beispielen beziehen sich Snijders und Bosker (1999, 2012) häufig auf Designs mit 10 Gruppen. Maas und Hox (2005, S. 90 f.) konnten allerdings zeigen, dass die Verzerrungen der Varianz-Komponenten in diesen Fällen bis zu 25 % betrugen und dass die Standardfehler zu klein ausfielen. Sie ziehen daraus den Schluss, dass zehn Gruppen in einem Mehrebenendesign zu wenig sind.

[3] Unterschieden werden klassischerweise drei Muster fehlender Werte, deren Beschreibung auf Little und Rubin (1987) zurückgeht: MCAR (Missing Completely at Random) liegt dann vor, wenn die Wahrscheinlichkeit einer Beobachtung weder von den beobachteten Werten noch von den nicht beobachteten Werten für einen Fall abhängt. Dieses Muster kann als Spezialfall von MAR (Missing at Random) verstanden werden, in dem die Wahrscheinlichkeit für fehlende Beobachtungen von den beobachteten, jedoch nicht von den unbeobachteten Daten abhängt. Für beide Fälle gibt es Strategien des Umgangs mit fehlenden Werten. Für das dritte Muster NMAR (Not Missing at Random), in dem Wahrscheinlichkeit fehlender Fälle von den unbeobachteten Werten selber abhängt, gibt es keine Strategie der Integration in Modelle.

hängigen Variablen.[4] Theoretisch bieten sich Likelihood basierte Schätzmethoden und multiple Imputationen an, um mit fehlenden Werten umzugehen.[5] Van Buuren (2011) vergleicht drei Techniken der multiplen Imputation für konkretere Empfehlungen miteinander: Die Ebenenstruktur der Daten wird bei der multiplen Imputation ignoriert (flat file), die Imputations-Routine enthält einen Gruppenfaktor und multiple Imputation unter Verwendung des Mittelwertes aus einem Gibbs Sampling. Aus seinen Simulationen ergibt sich, dass das letztere Verfahren das gewinnträchtigste ist (van Buuren 2011, S. 193). Andere Autoren empfehlen die Verwendung verschiedener Verfahren wie des EM-Algorithmus (Heck und Thomas 2009, S. 117) zur Schätzung der maximierten Likelihoods. In diesem iterativen Verfahren werden die beobachteten Werte durch die fehlenden Werte auf der Basis vorgegebener Verteilungsannahmen so lange ergänzt, bis sich die Schätzwerte nur noch marginal verändern.

2.2 Hierarchische Datenstruktur

In der Regel wird eine hierarchische Datenstruktur vorausgesetzt, wenn Mehrebenenanalysen Verwendung finden. Das bedeutet, dass die Elemente der einzelnen Ebenen dem Inklusionsprinzip folgend gerade immer genau einem Element der nächst höheren Ebene zuzuordnen sind. Das ist empirisch jedoch nicht immer der Fall. Zwei Abweichungen können hier unterschieden werden: Cross Classified-Strukturen und multiple Mitgliedschaften (Beretvas 2011). Im ersten Fall besteht nicht zwischen allen Ebenen eine hierarchische Beziehung. Werden beispielsweise Schülerleistungen in Abhängigkeit der besuchten Grund- und weiterführenden Schule untersucht, ist in der Regel nicht davon auszugehen, dass alle Schüler einer Grundschule gemeinsam in die weiterführende Schule wechseln und in dieser dann auch nur Schüler aus diesen spezifischen Grundschulen sind.[6] Ein weiteres Beispiel bezieht sich auf die Untersuchung der Abhängigkeit von Schulleistungen vom schulischen und persönlichen Kontext in Gestalt der Familiensituation oder der Nachbarschaften von Schülern.

Multiple Mitgliedschaften stellen eine zweite Abweichung vom Anspruch hierarchischer Datenstrukturen dar. Sie bestehen dann, wenn die Elemente einer unteren Ebene nicht nur einer aggregierten Gruppe, sondern mehreren zugeordnet werden kann. Ist ein Arbeitnehmer nicht nur in einer Firma angestellt, kann es zu multiplen Mitgliedschaften kommen, die eine Anpassung der Datenstruktur mit Blick auf den

---

[4] Für die denkbaren Varianten, dass fehlende Werte in den Variablen der zweiten Ebene vorliegen oder die Zuordnung eines Elements zur übergeordneten Ebene wegen des Fehlens des Schlüssels nicht gelingt, gibt es bisher keine einheitlichen Bewertungen und Lösungsvorschläge (van Buuren 2011, S. 178).

[5] Darüber hinaus beschreibt van Buuren (2011) auch das Vorgehen durch fallweisen Ausschluss, die Schätzung von fehlenden Werten nach einem Drop Out auf der Basis der letzten Beobachtung und für eine Imputation der Mittelwerte. Diese Verfahren sind mit gravierenden Problemen behaftet, was zu ihrer Ablehnung führt (van Buuren 2011, S. 182).

[6] Beretvas (2011, S. 315 f.) beschreibt auch für diesen Fall die Chance der hierarchischen Datenstruktur, wenn jede weiterführende Schule ihre Schüler eindeutig aus genau anzugebenden Grundschulen rekrutiert.

mehrebenenanalytischen Ansatz erfordern (Skrondal und Rabe-Hesketh 2004, S. 63; Beretvas 2011).

Während sich die Cross Classified-Strukturen also dadurch ergeben, dass mehrere Klassifizierungsmerkmale nebeneinander stehen, entstehen multiple Mitgliedschaften durch die Zugehörigkeit eines Elements aus der unteren Ebene zu mehreren Elementen des einen Klassifizierungsmerkmals, das die zweite Ebene bildet (Beretvas 2011, S. 321).

Für die Schätzung von Modellen mit Cross Classified-Strukturen stehen zwei einfache Strategien zur Verfügung. Einerseits kann eines der Klassifizierungsmerkmale der zweiten Ebene aus den Analysen ausgeschlossen werden. Im obigen Beispiel würde das bedeuten, dass die Zugehörigkeit zu einer Grundschule nicht modelliert wird, sondern die beiden Ebenen lediglich durch die Schüler in weiterführenden Schulen gebildet werden. Beretvas (2011, S. 324) berichtet als mögliche Konsequenz daraus von verzerrten Standardfehler- und ungenauen Varianzschätzungen. Die zweite Strategie besteht darin, die Elemente, die die Cross Classified-Struktur bilden, aus den Analysen auszuschließen. Im Schulbeispiel würden alle Schüler aus den Analysen ausgeschlossen, die eine überkreuzende Zuordnung zu Grund- und weiterführenden Schulen aufweisen. Das hat zwei nicht zu ignorierende Folgen: die Reduktion der Fallzahl führt zu sinkender Power der Erklärung und die Generalisierbarkeit der Ergebnisse wird beschnitten (Beretvas 2011, S. 325).

Elaborierte Strategien des Umgangs mit Cross Classified-Daten bestehen in der Aufnahme der Strukturen in das zu schätzende Modell.

$$y_{i(j_1,j_2)} = \gamma_{00(j_1,j_2)} + u_{0j} + u_{00j_2} + u_{00(j_1 \times j_2)} + e_{i(j_1,j_2)}$$

Die Fehlerterme beschreiben hier die individuellen Abweichungen e für die Personen i in den Cross Classified-Kontexten j_1 und j_2, die Gruppenabweichungen u jeweils vom generellen Mittelwert über die Cross Classified-Strukturen hinweg (u_{0j}) und bezogen auf ein Strukturelement der zweiten Ebene (u_{00j2}) sowie die Abweichung, die sich aus der Wechselwirkung zwischen den Cross Classified-Elementen ergibt ($u_{00(j1,j2)}$) (Beretvas 2011, S. 326).

Skrondal und Rabe-Hesketh (2004, S. 60 ff.) beschreiben für den Umgang mit Cross Classified-Strukturen den „Trick", ein virtuelles Level einzuführen, das die spezifischen Kombinationen der Elemente einer zweiten Ebene beinhaltet. Es wird die Ebene z. B. durch die Zuordnung zu der Einheit definiert, die später zu beobachten war und die davor liegenden Zugehörigkeiten zu den kreuzenden Elementen werden über Dummy-Variablen abgebildet. Die Definition der virtuellen Ebene muss nicht von inhaltlicher Relevanz sein, vielmehr orientiert sie sich an den Ausprägungen der einen Klassifikationsvariable. Skrondal und Rabe-Hesketh (2004) weisen darauf hin, dass eine Schätzung umso schwieriger wird, je mehr Kombinationen empirisch beobachtet werden und schlagen dann Markov-Ketten-Monte-Carlo-Methoden vor (Skrondal und Rabe-Hesketh 2004, S. 62).

Um multiple Mitgliedschaften für eine Person zu modellieren, werden den (möglicherweise mehreren) Elementen der zweiten Ebenen, denen die Person zuzuordnen ist, Gewichte zugewiesen, die sich für jede Person auf eins summieren (Beretvas 2011, S. 332). Diese Gewichte gehen in die Schätzung der kontextspezifischen

Abweichungen von der generellen mittleren Schätzung ein $(w_{ih}u_{0j})$. Formal kann das Nullmodell folgendermaßen dargestellt werden.

$$y_{i\{j\}} = \gamma_{00} + \sum_{h \in \{j\}} w_{ih}u_{0j} + e_{i\{j\}}$$

Auch für die Kombination aus beiden Verletzungen der hierarchischen Datenstruktur liegen Modellentwicklungen vor. Für das Nullmodell ergibt sich eine Adaption aus den beiden vorangegangen Lösungen in der Form

$$y_{i(\{j_1\},j_2)} = \gamma_{000} + \sum_{h \in \{j_1\}} w_{ih}u_{0h0} + u_{00j_2} + e_{i(\{j_1\},j_2)}$$

Diese Modelle können nun um Erklärungsvariablen auf den Ebenen wie üblich erweitert werden.[7] Allerdings sind die Schätzungen für die vorgestellten Modelle insbesondere der multiplen Mitgliedschaften nicht in vielen Softwareprogrammen möglich.

3 Entscheidung für ein Schätzverfahren

Die Ergebnisse aus Mehrebenenanalysen resultieren in der Regel aus Maximum Likelihood-Schätzungen. Es werden iterativ Anpassungen von geschätzten Populationsparametern so vorgenommen, dass die empirischen Daten möglichst gut auf der Basis der Modellparameter repliziert werden (Heck und Thomas 2009, S. 113 f.; Rabe-Hesketh und Skrondal 2012, S. 101; Hox 2010, S. 43). Ausgehend von Startwerten, die zumeist aus einer Regression mit einer Ebene stammen, werden die geschätzten Parameter schrittweise so verändert, dass sich die Modellanpassung verbessert. Als Maß für die Güte dieser Anpassung dient der Likelihood für das Modell. Besteht kein relevanter Unterschied mehr zwischen zwei nachfolgenden Modellen wird der iterative Prozess beendet und das Modell konvergiert mit den zuletzt geschätzten Parametern.[8] Die Algorithmen, die zur Maximierung des Likelihood herangezogen werden können, sind vielfältig.[9] Die Anwendung eines spezifischen Algorithmus hängt nicht nur von inhaltlichen Überlegungen ab, denn nicht jedes Verfahren ist in allen verfügbaren Softwaren implementiert.

---

[7]Beretvas (2011, S. 332 ff.) gibt verschiedene Erweiterungsmöglichkeiten an und führt in die formalen Formulierungen der Modelle ein.

[8]Probleme bei der Konvergenz der Modelle treten häufig dann auf, wenn zu viele Varianzparameter geschätzt werden sollen, die Werte nahe Null aufweisen oder wenn die Modelle falsch spezifiziert sind. Aber auch für korrekt spezifizierte Modelle können unter Umständen keine Lösungen gefunden werden, wenn die Stichprobengröße klein ausfällt (Hox 2010, S. 42). In den Fällen eines nicht konvergierenden Modells auf der Basis der ML-Schätzung kann auf die Generalized Least Square-Methode zurückgegriffen werden. Als Verallgemeinerung des OLS-Ansatzes der linearen Regression führt ihre Anwendung bei großen Fallzahlen zu analogen Ergebnissen wie die ML-Schätzung. Allerdings sind die GLS-Schätzer weniger effizient und die resultierenden Standardfehler sind ungenau (Kreft 1996).

[9]Skrondal und Rabe-Hesketh (2004, S. 159 ff.) diskutieren in einer umfassenden Übersicht neben dem EM-Verfahren weitere Maximierungs-Algorithmen, die je nach der konkreten Zielrichtung der Analyse und der Qualität der verwendeten Daten anzuwenden sind.

Im Rahmen der ML-Schätzungen wird zwischen zwei grundsätzliche Verfahren unterschieden: Full Maximum Likelihood (FML) und Restricted Maximum Likelihood (RML). Während bei ersterem alle zu schätzenden Parameter in die iterative Anpassung einbezogen werden (Regressionskoeffizienten und Varianzkomponenten) ist das zweite dadurch gekennzeichnet, dass in einem ersten Schritt nur die Varianzkomponenten in die Anpassung eingehen und die Regressionskoeffizienten in einem zweiten, separaten Schritt geschätzt werden (Kreft und de Leeuw 1998, S. 131; Hox 2010, S. 41).

Im Ergebnis zeigen sich geringere Verzerrungen der Varianzkomponenten, die auf der Basis des RML geschätzt wurden als im FML Verfahren[10] und gleichzeitig entsprechen die Schätzparameter dann den Ergebnissen einer Varianzanalyse, wenn die Gruppengrößen gleich ausfallen. Eine Reihe von Autoren verweisen darauf, dass für die inhaltliche Interpretation von Koeffizienten eher auf das RML zu setzen sei, vor allem dann wenn die Anzahl der Gruppen im Vergleich zu den geschätzten Parametern klein ausfällt (Skrondal und Rabe-Hesketh 2004, S. 185; Hox 2010, S. 41).

Allerdings sind zwei Vorteile des FML-Verfahrens gegenüber dem RML-Verfahren zu konstatieren, die in der Praxis zu seiner weit verbreiteten Anwendung führen. Zum einen ist die Schätzung einfacher und schneller zu realisieren. Zum anderen ist für den Vergleich von unterschiedlichen Erklärungsmodellen auf der Basis eines Chi-Quadrat-basierten Tests die Verwendung der FML-Methode angezeigt, da hier die fixen Modellteile in die Maximierungsfunktion mit aufgenommen wurden.

Skrondal und Rabe-Hesketh (2004, S. 185) resümieren, dass die eine Empfehlung für oder gegen eines der beiden Likelihood maximierenden Verfahrens nicht prinzipiell ausfallen kann, sondern immer von zahlreichen Bedingungen abhängt. Hier ist für die praktische Forschung relevant, dass die Unterschiede in den gefundenen Schätzern häufig trivial sind (Hox 2010, S. 43 ff.; Kreft und de Leeuw 1998).

Die Schätzung auf der Basis der Likelihood Maximierung kann in die, sich zunehmender Verbreitung erfreuende, Strategie des Bootstrapping eingebettet werden (Hox 2010, S. 264 ff.). Es werden aus dem bestehenden Sample wiederholt Stichproben gezogen,[11] die Parameter unter Verwendung des FML oder RML Verfahrens geschätzt und dann eine Lösung über alle Bootstrappiterationen hinweg erzeugt.[12] Im Ergebnis entsteht eine Verteilung der „synthetischen" (Carpenter et al. 1999) Modellparameter, durch die bessere Punkt- und Standardfehlerschätzungen generiert werden können.[13]

---

[10] Allerdings weisen Skrondal und Rabe-Hesketh (2004, S. 185) darauf hin, dass der Restricted Maximum Likelihood dann verzerrt sein kann, wenn die Gruppengrößen stark variieren.

[11] Hox (2010, S. 264) verweist auf spezifische Studien, die zeigen, dass für eine erfolgreiche Schätzung auf der Basis von Bootstrappiterationen eine Fallzahl von mindestens 150 vorliegen muss. Für kleine Fallzahlen scheint das Verfahren nicht geeignet. Die Zahl der Iterationen liegen üblicherweise zwischen 1000 (Hox 2010, S. 44) und 2000 in speziellen Verteilungen können aber auch 5000 Iterationen notwendig werden (Hox 2010, S. 264).

[12] Für einen grundlegenden Überblick vgl. van der Leeden et al. (2008, S. 401 ff.).

[13] Carpenter et al (1999) stellen parametrische und nicht parametrische Bootstrapverfahren gegenüber. Im ersten Fall werden die Parameterschätzungen auf der Basis des gesamten Modells generiert, im zweiten Fall auf der Basis der Residuen Matrizen.

Der Vorteil besteht darin, dass keine theoretischen Verteilungsannahmen getroffen werden müssen. Bei der Anwendung des Verfahrens ist aber zu beachten, dass der Ziehungsprozess im Bootstrap-Verfahren dem originalen Prozess zur Datengewinnung gleichen muss. Daraus entstehen für Mehrebenmodelle besondere Herausforderungen, da die Bootstrapsamples die gleiche hierarchische Struktur aufweisen müssen wie das originale Sample. Das ist bisher für das fallweise Bootstrapping nicht möglich, deshalb findet in Mehrebenenmodellen nur parametrisches oder nicht parametrisches Bootstrapping der Residuen Anwendung (Hox 2010, S. 268).

Ein Schätzverfahren, das sich aufgrund gestiegener Rechenkapazität von PCs und der Ausarbeitungen zu den Markov-Ketten-Monte-Carlo-Verfahren zunehmend leichter umsetzen lässt, ist die Bayesianische Schätzung (Hamaker und Klugkrist 2011). Als zentralen Unterschied zu klassischen Schätzverfahren machen Hamaker und Klugkrist (2011, S. 137) das Verständnis von Wahrscheinlichkeiten aus. Hier werden Wahrscheinlichkeiten als Grad der Unsicherheit über die Populationsparameter und nicht als Maß der Replizierbarkeit empirischer Verteilungen aufgefasst. Vielmehr werden die Populationsparameter als zufällige Größen mit einer bekannten Wahrscheinlichkeitsverteilung verstanden und auf der Basis der empirischen Beobachtungen mit ihrer Posteriori-Wahrscheinlichkeitsverteilung geschätzt (Hamaker und Klugkrist 2011; Kreft und de Leeuw 1998, S. 132). Die Festlegung der A-priori-Verteilung ist eine große Herausforderung für den Forscher. Allerdings lassen sich auch für den Fall unzureichender Kenntnis der A-priori-Verteilung mit diffusen Verteilungsannahmen Parameterschätzungen generieren. Auch erfordert dieser Ansatz keine Normalverteilung, was ihn insbesondere für Analysen mit kleinen Fallzahlen oder für sehr komplexe Modelle attraktiv werden lässt. Darüber hinaus führen Bayes'-ianische Schätzungen nicht zu unplausiblen (negativen) Varianzschätzungen oder zu Korrelationen größer eins (vgl. dazu die Ausführungen in Abschn. 4.2.2) und sie sind auch anwendbar, wenn fehlende Werte im Datensatz auftreten. Als weiteren Vorteil führen Hamaker und Klugkrist (2011, S. 139) die anschauliche Präsentation der Schätzergebnisse an, da sie sich auf Konfidenzintervalle beziehen.

4 Aspekte der Interpretation von Mehrebenmodellen

4.1 Datenzentrierungen

Nach wie vor wird bei der Anwendung von Mehrebenenanalysen die Datenzentrierung[14] thematisiert. Damit ist gemeint, dass die erhobenen Daten unter bestimmten Voraussetzungen nicht in ihrer ursprünglichen Form sondern als Abweichungen von Mittelwerten in die Analysen eingehen (sollten). Prinzipiell sind zwei Vorgehensweisen zu unterscheiden: entweder werden die Differenzen zwischen dem beobachteten Wert und dem generellen Mittelwert über alle Gruppen hinweg (Grand Mean Cen-

---

[14] Paccagnella (2006) verweist auf unterschiedliche Bezugspunkte für die Zentrierung wie den Median oder das arithmetische Mittel und darauf, dass die Orientierung am Mittelwert am häufigsten Verwendung findet. Die Ausführungen hier beziehen sich deshalb auch lediglich darauf.

tering) oder die Differenzen zwischen dem beobachteten Wert und dem jeweiligen Gruppenmittelwert (Group Mean Centering) betrachtet.

Langer (2010, S. 760) nennt drei Vorteile der Verwendung von zentrierten Daten: Aufhebung von Multikollinearität zwischen Individualdaten und Kontextmerkmalen, die aus Individualdaten hervorgingen, Reduzierung der Kovarianzen zwischen Regressionskoeffizienten und Konstanten und die Beschleunigung iterativer Prozesse (analog Enders und Tofighi 2007).

Enders und Tofighi (2007, S. 122) heben wie schon Kreft und de Leeuw (1998, S. 114) hervor, dass die Entscheidung über eine Zentrierung nicht auf der Basis empirischer Befunde getroffen, sondern nur aus inhaltlichen Gründen im Anschluss an das Forschungsinteresse begründet werden kann. Paccagnella (2006) betont differenzierter, dass sie von drei Sachverhalten abhänge: der Art der Zentrierung, der Spezifizierung von Cross Level Interaktionen und vom Analyseziel.

Die Zentrierung am generellen Mittelwert erleichtert insbesondere die Interpretation der Regressionskonstanten, weil die Zentrierung für sie eine inhaltliche Bedeutung für die Merkmalsausprägung null der unabhängigen Variablen sicherstellt. Positive Abweichungen werden dann als überdurchschnittliche und negative Abweichungen als unterdurchschnittliche Ausprägungen in der erklärenden Variable verstanden. Die Konstante stellt die Schätzung für eine Person dar, die in allen unabhängigen Variablen mittlere Werte aufweist. Ein Effekt kann vor dem Hintergrund mittlerer Ausprägungen in allen anderen zu kontrollierenden Variablen interpretiert werden. Enders und Tofighi (2007, S. 136) resümieren, dass die Zentrierung am generellen Mittelwert dann angezeigt sei, wenn die Forschungsfrage auf Effekte der zweiten Ebene unter Kontrolle der Zusammenhänge der ersten Ebene gerichtet ist und wenn Interaktionseffekte der zweiten Ebene einbezogen werden (so auch Langer 2010, S. 760).

Erfolgt die Zentrierung nicht am generellen Mittelwert sondern am Gruppenmittelwert, dann wird die Konstante als Schätzung für die abhängige Variable bei einer Person geschätzt, die in den unabhängigen Variablen jeweils mittlere Ausprägung bezogen auf ihre eigene Gruppe aufweist. Mit der Relativierung absoluter Werte an der für eine Gruppe typischen Gruppenkonstellation soll dem sogenannten „Froschteicheffekt" begegnet werden. Damit ist gemeint, dass eine spezifische Ausprägung in Abhängigkeit von der Komposition der Gruppe unterschiedliche Bedeutung haben kann. Es macht einen Unterschied, ob man ein großer Frosch in einem Teich mit anderen großen Fröschen ist oder ob man als großer Frosch in einem Teich mit vielen kleinen Fröschen lebt (Hox 2010, S. 68).

Paccagnella (2006, S. 72 f.) zeigt bezugnehmend auch auf Kreft et al. (1995), dass die Zentrierung am Gruppenmittelwert das zu schätzende Modell derart verändert, sodass von einer Äquivalenz der Modelle ohne und mit Zentrierung nicht mehr auszugehen ist.[15] Trotzdem sprechen auch statistische Gründe für die Zentrierung von Daten. Werden Gruppenmittelwerte als Erklärungsvariablen der zweiten Ebene in das Modell einbezogen, besteht üblicherweise die Gefahr hoher Multikollinearität

---

[15] Ebenso argumentieren Kreft und de Leeuw, wobei sie den Begriff der Äquivalenz präziser ausführen. Sind zwei Modelle äquivalent heißt das, dass ihre Parameter ineinander überführt werden können, nicht aber, dass sie die gleichen Parameter aufweisen (Kreft und de Leeuw 1998, S. 108 f.).

mit den zugehörigen Individualdaten. Durch die Verwendung der Differenzen zum Gruppenmittelwert anstelle der Originaldaten wird dieser Zusammenhang aufgelöst. Enders und Tofighi (2007, S. 136) empfehlen die Verwendung von Gruppenmittelwerten, wenn Zusammenhänge auf der Individualebene von zentralem Forschungsinteresse sind oder wenn Interaktionseffekte auf der ersten Ebene oder Cross Level Interaktionen in das Modell einbezogen werden.

4.2 Modellgüte

4.2.1 Erklärte Varianz

Analog zu anderen multiplen Regressionsmodellen können auch in Mehrebenendesigns Anteile erklärter Varianzen der abhängigen Variable als ein Gütemaß der Erklärungskraft der vorgelegten Modelle verstanden werden.

$$R^2 = 1 - \frac{\sigma^2_{(M_0)} - \sigma^2_{(M_1)}}{\sigma^2_{(M_0)}}$$

wobei: σ^2_{M0} = Gesamtvarianz des Nullmodells,
σ^2_{M1} = Gesamtvarianz des Erklärungsmodells.

Mit steigender Komplexität der Modelle erhöht sich dann in der Regel die Erklärungskraft oder bleibt zumindest gleich. In Mehrebenmodellen kann sich nun aber der überraschende Befund größerer Varianzen bei Modellerweiterungen zeigen, was in der Konsequenz zu negativen R^2-Werte führt (Snijders und Bosker 2012, S. 109 f.). Snijders und Bosker (2012, S. 113) oder Kreft und de Leeuw (1998) führen als Gründe dafür entweder Fehlspezifikationen des Modells im fixen Part oder Zufallsschwankungen an. Darüber hinaus beschreibt Hox (2010, S. 73) die Interpretation der Varianzkomponenten in Abhängigkeit der Skalierung der beteiligten Variablen. Wenn die Variablen zentriert in die Analysen eingehen, ist von einer stabileren Schätzung der Varianzkomponenten auszugehen, ohne dass jedoch das Phänomen negativer Erklärungskraft vollständig beseitigt wäre. Zur Erklärung des Phänomens ist auf die Annahme der Regressionsschätzung zurückzugehen, dass die Stichprobengenerierung in einem Zufallsprozess für alle Variablen erfolgt. Für Aggregatdaten sind die Verteilungen aber auf der ersten Ebene konstant, sodass die Normalverteilungsannahme hier nicht zutrifft und Korrekturfaktoren nicht die gewünschte Wirkung entfalten können (Hox 2010, S. 75).

Da die Varianzkomponenten auf die einzelnen Ebenen verteilt sind, ist es über die allgemeine Erklärungskraft hinaus instruktiver, ebenen-spezifische R^2-Maße zu verwenden. Für die erste Ebene wird dazu die Differenz aus den Varianzen der Residuen der ersten Ebene des Nullmodells und des Erklärungsmodells ins Verhältnis zur Varianz des Nullmodells gesetzt.

$$R^2_w = 1 - \frac{\sigma^2_{e_{M0}} - \sigma^2_{e_{M1}}}{\sigma^2_{e_{M0}}}$$

wobei: σ^2_{eM0} = Varianz auf der ersten Ebene des Nullmodells,
σ^2_{eM1} = Varianz auf der ersten Ebene des Erklärungsmodells.

Ein analoges Vorgehen bezogen auf die Varianzen der zweiten Ebene führen zur Interpretation der Erklärungsleistung für aggregatbezogene Sachverhalte.

$$R_b^2 = 1 - \frac{\sigma^2_{u_{M0}} - \sigma^2_{u_{M1}}}{\sigma^2_{u_{M0}}}$$

wobei: σ^2_{uM0} = Varianz auf der zweiten Ebene des Nullmodells,
σ^2_{uM1} = Varianz auf der zweiten Ebene des Erklärungsmodells.

Für die Verwendung der grundlegenden Berechnungen in Modellen mit variierenden Effekten und unterschiedlichen Gruppengrößen wurden verschiedene Korrekturmöglichkeiten entwickelt. Hox (2010, S. 77) zeigt, dass im Ergebnis die geschätzte Erklärungskraft recht ähnlich ausfällt. Snijders und Bosker (1994) ersetzen die Varianz der zweiten Ebene durch eine mittlere Gruppenvarianz oder durch das harmonische Mittel der Gruppenvarianzen. Im Ergebnis ergeben sich ähnliche Werte aber auch bei Verwendung des Medians der Gruppengröße (Hox 2010, S. 76). Snijders und Bosker (2012, S. 114) schlagen als einfacheren Weg allerdings vor, die Berechnung der Erklärungskraft auf der Basis eines Modells mit fixen Effekten zu berechnen, da diese Ergebnisse sehr nahe bei den Werten für Modelle mit Zufallseffekten lägen.

Eine Möglichkeit der Information über Anteile erklärter Varianz ohne den direkten Rückgriff auf die Varianzkomponenten der Modelle bietet Maddalas R^2 (Langer 2010, S. 756).

$$R_M^2 = 1 - e^{\frac{-(-2\log(lh)_{M_0} - (-2\log(lh)_{M_1})}{n_{ij}}}$$

wobei: $-2log(lh)_{M0}$ = Devianzwert des Nullmodells,
$-2log(lh)_{M1}$ = Devianzwert des Erklärungsmodells,
n_{ij} = Stichprobenumfang.

4.2.2 Modellanpassung

Für den Modellvergleich wird üblicherweise der Devianzwert verwendet. Berechnet als -2loglikelihood enthält er eine Information über den Abstand zwischen den modellgenerierten Parametern und den empirischen Beobachtungen. Inhaltliche Bedeutung gewinnt er im Vergleich der Modelle, wenn gezeigt werden soll, ob der Einbezug von Erklärungsvariablen zu einer entscheidenden Verbesserung der Modellanpassung an die Daten beiträgt. Die Differenz aus zwei Devianzwerten ist Chi-Quadrat-verteilt, die Freiheitsgrade ergeben sich aus der Differenz der einbezogenen Parameter.[16]

---
[16] Beim Modellvergleich ist darauf zu achten, dass Modelle auf der Basis der RML-Schätzung nur dann miteinander verglichen werden können, wenn der fixe Modellpart gleich bleibt. Wenn er sich zwischen den Modellen unterschiedet, soll die FML-Schätzung Verwendung finden, da hier alle Modellteile in die Maximierung der Likelihoodfunktion einbezogen werden.

Weitere Maße, die in aktueller Software für Mehrebenenmodelle berichtet werden, finden sich mit den Fitmaßen AIK (Akaikes Information Criterion) und dem BIC (Schwarzes Bayesian Information Criterion). Beide beziehen die Komplexität des Modells in die Berechnung mit ein.

$$BIC = d + q \ln(N) \qquad AIC = d + 2q$$

wobei: d = Devianz
q = Anzahl der geschätzten Parameter
N = Stichprobenumfang

Diese Maße sind nicht explizit für die Mehrebenenanalyse entwickelt, sondern stellen umfassendere Konzepte dar, die sich aus der Informationstheorie (AIK) oder dem Bayesianischen Ansatz (BIC) speisen (Hamaker et al. 2011, S. 232). Die Vorteile dieser Maße im Vergleich zu sehr viel häufiger diskutierten Tests, die sich auf Entscheidungen über eine Nullhypothese beziehen, bestehen darin, dass multiple Modellvergleiche simultan erfolgen können und dass eine bessere Entscheidung über das beste der gefundenen Modelle getroffen werden kann.

Für ihre Interpretation ist zu beachten, dass nicht der Wert des Information Criterion *per se* interessiert, sondern es im Modellvergleich um die Differenz zwischen zwei Werten geht. Hamaker et al. (2011, S. 233 f.) stellen zwei Transformationen vor, die eine anschauliche Interpretation der Werte in dem Sinne erlauben, dass ein Modell mit einem höheren Gewicht die beobachteten Daten generiert und deshalb als erklärungsmächtiger gilt oder dass ein Modell in einem bestimmten Verhältnis zu einem anderen eine bessere Replikation der empirischen Daten erlaubt.

In Kontextanalysen gewinnen die Fragen, welchen Einfluss der Einbezug von variierenden Effekten auf die Gütemaße hat und wie die Fallzahl zu verstehen ist, die in die Berechnung des BIC eingeht, an Bedeutung. Obwohl die Maße in der praktischen Anwendung in der Regel zu ähnlichen Ergebnissen kommen, weisen Hamaker et al. (2011) auf ihre unterschiedlichen Hintergründe und Zielmodelle hin. Diese sind bei der Beurteilung von Modellen, die in Abhängigkeit des verwendeten Maßes unterschiedlich ausfallen kann, einzubeziehen. Bei der Entscheidung für eines der Maße ist zu beachten, dass für den Modellvergleich immer das gleiche Maß genutzt wird und dass bei verschiedenen Ergebnisse bezüglich des besten Modells mehrere Modelle als Ergebnis zu berichten sind (Hamaker et al. 2011, S. 253 f.).

5 Komplexe Mehrebenenmodelle

Die Modellierung unter Einbezug von Kontexten ist nicht auf die lineare Beziehung zwischen erklärender und zu erklärender Variable beschränkt. Mittlerweile liegen für alle komplexen Analyseverfahren entsprechende Abhandlungen vor. Es überlagern sich verfahrensspezifische Aspekte mit den Besonderheiten von Mehrebenenmodellen. Im Folgenden soll ein kurzer Überblick über aktuelle Anwendungen gegeben werden.

5.1 Logistische Modelle

Mehrebenenmodelle für dichotome Variablen oder Anteile folgen der prinzipiellen Logik verallgemeinerter linearer Modelle. Die drei definierenden Komponenten bestehen in der zugrunde liegenden Parameterverteilung, der linearen Schätzgleichung des verallgemeinerten Modells und der Linkfunktion, die die Verknüpfung zwischen der abhängigen Variable und dem durch die lineare Gleichung geschätzten Ausdruck beinhaltet. Die Verbindung über die Linkfunktion ist notwendig, da das lineare Modell zu unplausiblen Schätzwerten führt und die Normalverteilungsannahme über die Variablen nicht zutreffend ist (Hox 2010, S. 124 ff.). Häufig kann eine binomiale Verteilung zugrunde gelegt und die Logitfunktion als Link verwendet werden.[17] Die große Verbreitung erklärt Hox (2010, S. 115) damit, dass die Anwendung der Exponentialfunktion auf die gefundenen Logitparameter eine direkte Interpretation der Odds Ratios erlaubt.

Im Ergebnis kann das Modell formuliert werden in der Form

$$\ln \frac{p}{1-p} = \gamma_{00} + \gamma_{10} x_1 + u_{0j}$$

Die Interpretation der Koeffizienten unterscheidet sich nicht von ihrer Interpretation in Modellen mit einer Ebene. Zu beachten ist, dass sie sich auf eine Veränderung des Logits beziehen und dass eine Aussage über die abhängige Variable selbst erst durch die Transformation

$$p = \frac{e^{(\gamma_{00} + \gamma_{10} x_1 + u_{0j})}}{1 + e^{(\gamma_{00} + \gamma_{10} x_1 + u_{0j})}}$$

möglich ist (Hox 2010, S. 123, 126).

Eine Besonderheit besteht nun darin, dass keine Varianz der ersten Ebene geschätzt wird (Gelman und Hill 2007, S. 86), da die Varianz in direkter Abhängigkeit vom Anteil selber anzugeben ist (Snijders und Bosker 2012, S. 293). Das Logit ist für die Identifizierung des Modells mit einem Mittelwert von null und einer Varianz von etwa $\pi^2/3$ standardisiert, sodass eine direkte Interpretation der Varianzkomponenten unterschiedlicher Modelle nicht sinnvoll ist. Für die Varianzzerlegung auf die einzelnen Ebenen wird deshalb ein Skalierungsfaktor (in der Regel eins) verwendet, der zur Berechnung der Intraklassenkorrelation Rho mit

$$\rho = \frac{\sigma_u^2}{\sigma_u^2 + \frac{\pi^2}{3}}$$

führt (Guo und Zhao 2000, S. 451; Hox 2010, S. 128).

---

[17] Hox gibt auf der Basis der speziellen Literatur einen Überblick über verschiedene Linkfunktionen (Hox 2010, S. 112 ff.) und konstatiert eine große Ähnlichkeit der Funktionen, so lange die Verteilung nicht extrem schief ist (weniger als 10 % der Fälle weisen eine der beiden Ausprägungen auf) (Hox 2010, S. 115).

Die standardisierte Varianz auf der ersten Ebene führt auch dazu, dass aus den Varianzkomponenten nicht direkt auf die Güte des Modells geschlossen werden kann.[18] Werden Erklärungsvariablen in das Modell aufgenommen, kann erwartet werden, dass sich die unerklärte Varianz vermindert. Die auch für dieses Modell vorgenommene Standardisierung führt aber zum gleichen Ausdruck der Varianz auf der ersten Ebene. Deshalb werden für die Einschätzung der Modellgüte häufig Maße herangezogen, die den Devianzwert einbeziehen.[19] Diese Pseudo-R^2 Maße können aber lediglich globale Güteinformationen geben und differenzieren nicht zwischen den Ebenen. Darüber hinaus sind sie auf eine gute Schätzung des Loglikelihoods des Modells angewiesen.

Snijders und Bosker (2012, S. 305 f.) präferieren einen anderen Ansatz, der auf McKelvey und Zavoina (1975, S. 111) zurückgeht und die Idee erklärter Varianzen in latenten Konstrukten aufgreift.[20] Danach wird das Logit als latentes Konstrukt verstanden, dessen Varianz sich aus der standardisierten Residualvarianz der ersten Ebene, der Residualvarianz der Konstanten im Regressionsmodell und der systematischen Varianz der einbezogenen Regressionskoeffizienten zusammensetzen lässt. Für den Anteil erklärter Varianz lässt sich dann

$$R^2_{MZ} = \frac{\sigma^2_{10}}{\sigma^2_{10} + \sigma^2_{u0} + \sigma^2_e} \text{ formulieren,}$$

wobei: σ^2_{10} = Varianz des Regressionskoeffizienten,
σ^2_{u0} = Varianz der Konstanten zwischen den Gruppen,
σ^2_e = Residualvarianz auf der ersten Ebene.

Nach der Re-Skalierung der Ergebnisse aus einem Erklärungsmodell auf das Nullmodell durch σ_0/σ_m und σ^2_0/σ^2_m können Regressionskoeffizienten und Varianzkomponenten unterschiedlicher Modelle verglichen werden (Hox 2010, S. 136).

Die Schätzung der logistischen Mehrebenenmodelle erfolgt auf der Basis von Taylorreihen als sogenannte Quasi-Likelihood-Verfahren. Es ist eine Entscheidung über die Verwendung der Taylor-Schätzung erster oder zweiter Ordnung zu treffen, wobei letztere akkurater ausfällt gleichzeitig aber auch mehr Rechenkapazität beansprucht. Eine zweite Entscheidung im Zusammenhang mit dem Schätzverfahren bezieht sich darauf, ob in die Schätzung lediglich der fixe Part des Modells einbezogene wird (MQL: Marginal Quasi Likelihood) oder auch die Varianzkomponenten (PQL: Predictive Quasi Likelihood) (Hox 2010, S. 118 ff.). Insbesondere dann, wenn die Zufallseffekte groß und die Gruppengrößen klein sind, wären PQL Schätzungen zu präferieren. Da in diesen Fällen häufig Konvergenz-Probleme auftreten, werden in der Forschungspraxis aber auch MQL Schätzungen genutzt. Bezogen auf beide

---

[18] Eine weitere Konsequenz besteht drin, dass die Regressionskoeffizienten aus unterschiedlichen Modellen nicht direkt miteinander vergleichen werden können.

[19] Hier kann auf die Diskussion der Vor- und Nachteile zu Mc Faddens R2, Cox und Snells R2 und Nagelkerkes R2 verwiesen werden, wie sie in der allgemeinen Literatur zu logistischen Modellen ohne Kontextbezug diskutiert werden (Long 1997; Backhaus 2011, S. 249 ff.).

[20] Auch Long (1997) konstatierte bereits das besondere Potenzial des Ansatzes von McKelvey und Zavoina (1975).

Verfahren ist von einer Unterschätzung der Regressionskoeffizienten auszugehen. Deshalb zieht Hox (2010, S. 123) den Schluss, dass eine bessere Schätzung auf der Basis einer numerischen Integration im Rahmen des FML vorliegt. Rabe-Hesketh und Skrondal (2012, S. 541) verweisen explizit auf die Anforderungen an Rechenkapazität, wenn diesem Vorschlag gefolgt wird und empfehlen die Spezifikation nach Laplace, die nur einen Integrationspunkt verwendet.[21]

5.2 Einbezug latenter Konstrukte

Die Entwicklung von Verfahren, die latente Konstrukte in die Modellbildung einbeziehen erfuhr in den letzten Jahren eine ähnlich rasante Entwicklung wie die Erweiterung der Mehrebenenmodelle auf nicht lineare Beziehungen. In der aktuellen Diskussion ist nun eine Integration der Vorstellung von mehreren Ebenen in die Modellierung der Beziehungen zwischen latenten Konstrukten zu beobachten. Es ist zu beachten, dass noch nicht für alle komplexen Modelle ausreichend abgesicherte Erfahrungen und Methoden zu berichten sind. Aber der Einbezug latenter Konstrukte auf der Aggregatebene, die Spezifizierung von variierenden Effekten und von Faktorenmodellen zur fehlerfreien Messung und von Pfadanalysen zur Unterscheidung von direkten, indirekten und totalen Effekten sind vor allem mit dem Pogrammpaket Mplus (Heck und Thomas 2009, S. 101) oder mit GLAMM möglich (Rabe-Hesketh et al. 2004; Rabe-Hesketh und Skrondal 2012).

Generell wird in Strukturgleichungs-Ansätzen[22] zwischen Mess- und Pfadmodellen unterschieden (Muthén und Asparouhov 2011; du Toit und du Toit 2008). Die Messmodelle implizieren Faktorenanalysen, wobei die latenten Faktoren die konkrete Ausprägung in den beobachteten manifesten Indikatoren bestimmen. Die Beobachtung kann dann durch ein Regressionsmodell dargestellt werden, dass aus einem Koeffizienten (Faktorladung) und der individuellen Residualvarianz besteht. Die Basis zur Identifizierung der zugrunde liegenden latenten Konstrukte bildet die Kovarianzmatrix der manifesten Indikatoren. Die Beziehung zwischen den latenten Konstrukten wird im Rahmen des Pfadmodelles abgebildet. Die Modelle können einen sehr hohen Komplexitätsgrad erreichen, da es möglich ist, die latenten Konstrukte gleichzeitig als abhängig und unabhängig zu modellieren und weil mehrere abhängige Konstrukte parallel geschätzt werden können.

Im Mehrebenmodell wird die Kovarianzmatrix nun in zwei Matrizen zerlegt, die Kovarianz-Matrix der individuellen Beobachtungen innerhalb der Gruppen und die Kovarianz-Matrix, die die Beziehungen der Gruppenmittelwerte zum Ausdruck bringen. Für die Schätzung der Kovarianz-Matrizen zwischen und innerhalb der Gruppen stehen verschiedene Wege zur Verfügung. Hox (2010, S. 299 ff.) resümiert, dass der

---

[21] Die konkrete Anwendung eines Schätzverfahrens hängt auch davon ab, welche Formen in welcher Software implementiert sind. Hox (2010, S. 123) berichtet unterschiedliche Ansätze in Abhängigkeit der Verwendung von MlwiN, HLM und SuperMix und schlägt die Verwendung von Bayes'ianischen Schätzungen oder Bootstrapverfahren vor, wenn keine numerische Integration möglich ist (2010, S. 139). Rabe-Hesketh und Skrondal (2012, S. 540 f.) geben Empfehlungen mit Blick auf die Optimierung mit STATA.

[22] Auch für den spezifischeren Fall latenter Klassenanalysen liegen Abhandlungen zur Integration des Mehrebenen-Modells vor (Vermunt 2003, 2011).

MUML-Ansatz (Muthén 1994) und das zweistufige Vorgehen[23] nach Goldstein (2003) am wenigstens geeignet sind, akkurate Schätzungen zu liefern. Dagegen ergeben die Schätzungen gewichteter Kovarianz-Matrizen (Asparouhov und Muthén 2007; Muthén und Asparouhov 2011) und die Full Maximum Likelihood-Methode ähnlich gute Ergebnisse. Letzteres Verfahren hat den Vorteil, dass variierende Regressionskoeffizienten modelliert werden können. Allerdings heißt das für das Messmodell, dass gruppenabhängige Messungen erfolgen.

Für die Beurteilung der Modelle kann in Strukturgleichungsmodellen generell auf zahlreiche Maße zurückgegriffen werden, die zumeist Chi-Quadrat-basiert und deshalb anfällig für Veränderungen des Stichprobenumfangs sind. Außerdem geben diese Maße ein globales Gütemaß über alle Ebenen wieder, wobei die erste Ebene durch die größeren Fallzahlen ein stärkeres Gewicht erlangt als die höheren Ebenen (Hox 2010, S. 307).[24]

Ein sehr häufig genutztes Maß stellt das RMSEA (Root Mean Square Error of Approximation) dar, das zum Ausdruck bringt, wie nahe das geschätzte Modell dem wahren Modell kommt.

$$RMSEA = \sqrt{\frac{\chi^2 - df}{Ndf}}$$

wobei: χ^2 = Chi-Quadrat Wert für das Modell,
df = Freiheitsgrade,
N = Stichprobenumfang.

Werte kleiner als 0,05 sprechen für eine gute Modellanpassung, Werte unter 0,08 sind gerade noch akzeptabel. Ergibt sich ein negativer Wert aus der Differenz von Chi-Quadrat und der Anzahl der Freiheitsgrade wird der RMSEA-Wert auf null festgesetzt (Skrondal und Rabe-Hesketh 2004, S. 271; Hox 2010, S. 309).

5.3 Panelanalysen

Immer dann, wenn individueller Wandel oder Stabilität im Fokus des Forschungsinteresses steht, muss auf wiederholte Messungen bei den gleichen Individuen zurückgegriffen werden. Der Einbezug der mehrfachen Messungen in ein Mehrebenendesign ist nicht kompliziert: die Messungen stellen die erste Ebene in der Datenhierarchie dar, die Personen bilden die zweite Ebene usw. Im Ergebnis kann die Variation der ersten Ebene als individuelle Entwicklung verstanden werden und die Variation der zweiten Ebene als Unterschiede zwischen Personen. Als Erklärungsvariable wird in einem ersten Schritt der Zeitpunkt der Messung einbezogen. Wird der erste Zeitpunkt mit null kodiert, kann in diesem Modell die Regressionskonstante inhaltlich als mitt-

---

[23] Hier wird zuerst auf der Basis des Mehrebenmodells für jede Ebene eine separate Kovarianz-Matrix erzeugt, die dann in die Schätzung eines Strukturgleichungsmodells direkt eingehen. Hox (2010, S. 296) weist darauf hin, dass es sich hierbei selber um Schätzungen handelt, die dann wiederum die Basis für Schätzungen bilden. Außerdem kann den so erhaltenen Standardfehlern und Testparametern nur dann vertraut werden, wenn vollständige Daten vorliegen, die multivariat normal verteilt sind.

[24] Hox (2010, S. 307 f.) schlägt deshalb vor, separate Fit-Indices per Hand zu berechnen.

lerer Schätzwert der abhängigen Variable über alle Personen hinweg zum Zeitpunkt der ersten Messung verstanden werden. Wie oben bereits berichtet, kann sich auch für Panelmodelle der unplausible Befund negativer Varianzerklärung ergeben (Hox 2010, S. 88), dem durch die Schätzung eines spezifischen Basismodells begegnet werden kann (Snijders und Boker 2012).

Das Potenzial von Panelanalysen im Mehrebendesign ist vielfältig. An erster Stelle ist anzumerken, dass sie tatsächliche individuelle Entwicklung adäquat abbilden und gleichzeitig zeitkonstante und zeitvariante Variablen in die Erklärung einbeziehen kann. Darüber hinaus sind die Schätzungen nicht auf gleiche Zeitabstände zwischen den einzelnen Messungen bzw. die gleiche Anzahl an Messungen bei allen Personen angewiesen und die Modellierung der Kontexte erfolgt angemessen (Hox 2010, S. 98, 106 ff.).

6 Fazit

Als generelles Fazit lässt sich festhalten, dass Mehrebenenanalysen heutzutage eine breite Anwendung finden, weil die Einbettung in Kontexte offensichtlich inhaltlich für eine Vielzahl von Fragestellungen gut zu begründen ist.

Auch wenn die Anforderungen an die Daten hoch sind, scheinen komplexe Erhebungsprojekte zunehmend an Akzeptanz zu gewinnen. Darüber hinaus verheißt die Entwicklung von Verfahren für nicht hierarchische Datenstrukturen eine weitere Verbreitung der Mehrebenenanalyse und darüber hinaus auch eine bessere Erklärung für interessante sozialwissenschaftliche, psychologische und andere Phänomene.

Für zahlreiche Schätzprobleme liegen mittlerweile Lösungen vor, sodass statistisch gut abgesicherte Interpretationen geleistet werden können. Die häufigsten Beschränkungen sind sicher nach wie vor in der spezifischen Implementierung unterschiedlicher Algorithmen in den verschiedenen Softwareprogrammen und in der zur Verfügung stehenden Rechenkapazität zu finden.

Literatur

Afshartous, David. 1995. Determination of sample size for multilevel model design. http://citeseerx.ist.psu.edu/viewdoc/summary?doi=10.1.1.49.4318 (Zugegriffen: 19. Juni 2014).
Asparouhov, Tihomir, und Bengt O. Muthén. 2007. *Computationally efficient estimation of multilevel highdimensional latent variable models*. Proceedings of the Joint Statistical Meeting, August 2007, Salt Lake City.
Backhaus, Klaus, Bernd Erichson, Wulff Plinke und Rolf Weiber. 2011. *Multivariate Analysemethoden*. Berlin: Springer.
Beretvas, Natasha. 2011. Cross-classified and multiple-membership models. In *Handbook of advanced multilevel analysis*, Hrsg. Joop J. Hox und J. Kyle Roberts, 313–334. New York: Routledge.
Carpenter, James, Harvey Goldstein und Jon Rasbash. 1999. A non-parametric bootstrap for multilevel models. *Multilevel Modelling Newsletter* 11:1.
Clarke, Philippa. 2008. When can group level clustering be ignored? Multilevel models versus single-level models with sparse data. *Journal of Epidemiology and Community Health* 62:752–758.
Du Toit, Stephen, und Mathilda Du Toit. 2008. Multilevel structural equation modeling. In *Handbook of multilevel analysis*, Hrsg. Jan De Leeuw und Erik Meijer, 435–478. New York: Springer.

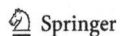

Enders, Craig, und Davood Tafighi. 2007. Centering predictor variables in cross-sectional multilevel models: A new look at an old issue. *Psychological Methods* 12:121–138.
Gelman, Andrew, und Jennifer Hill. 2007. *Data analizing using regression and multilevel/hierarchical models*. New York: Cambridge University Press.
Goldstein, Harvey. 1987. *Multilevel analysis in educational and social research*. London: Griffin.
Goldstein, Harvey. 2003. *Multilevel statistical models*. London: Edward Arnold.
Guo, Guang, und Hongxin Zhao. 2000. Mulitlevel modeling for binary data. *Annual Review of Sociology* 26:441–462.
Hamaker, Ellen L., und Irene Klugkrist. 2011. Bayesian estimation of multilevel models. In *Handbook of advanced multilevel analysis*, Hrsg. Joop J. Hox und Kyle J. Roberts, 137–162. New York: Routledge.
Hamaker, Ellen L., Pascal van Hattum, Rebecca M. Kuiper und Herbert Hoijtink. 2011. Model selection on information criteria in multilevel modeling. In *Handbook of advanced multilevel analysis*, Hrsg. Joop J. Hox und Kyle J. Roberts, 231–255. New York: Routledge.
Heck, Ronald H., und Scott L. Thomas. 2009. *An introduction to multilevel modeling techniques*. New York: Routledge.
Hox, Joop J. 2010. *Multilevel analysis. Techniques and applications*. New York: Routledge.
Kreft, Ita.1996. Are multilevel techniques necessary? An overview, including simulation studies. Los Angeles: California State University. http://www.eric.ed.gov (Zugegriffen: 18. Juni 2014).
Kreft, Ita, und Jan de Leeuw.1998. *Introducing multilevel modeling*. Thousand Oaks: Sage.
Kreft, Ita, Jan de Leuuw und Leona Aiken. 1995. The effect of different forms of centering in hierarchical linear models. *Multivariate Behavioral Research* 30:1–21.
Langer, Wolfgang. 2010. Mehrebenenanalyse mit Querschnittsdaten. In *Handbuch der sozialwissenschaftlichen Datenanalyse*, Hrsg. Christof Wolf und Henning Best, 741–774. Wiesbaden: VS Verlag für Sozialwissenschaften.
Little, Roderick J., und Donald B. Rubin. 1987. *Statistical analysis with missing data*. New York: Wiley.
Long, J. Scott. 1997. *Regression models for categorical and limited dependent variables*. Thousand Oaks: Sage.
Maas, Cora J., und Joop J. Hox. 2005. Sufficient sample size for multilevel modeling. *Methodology* 1:89–92.
McKelvey, Richard D., und William Zavoina. 1975. A statistical model fort the analysis of ordinal level dependent variables. *The Journal of Mathematical Sociology* 4:103–120.
Moineddin, Rahim, Flora I. Matheson und Richard H. Glazier. 2007. A simulation study of sample size for multilevel logistic regression models. *Medical Research Methodology* 2007:7–34.
Mok, Magdalena. 1995. Sample size requirements for 2-level designs in educational Research. *Multilevel Modelling Newsletter* 7:11–15.
Muthén, Bengt O. 1994. Multilevel covariance structure analysis. *Sociological Methods and Research* 22:376–398.
Muthén, Bengt O., und Tihomir Asparouhov. 2011. Beyond multilevel regression modeling. In *Handbook of advanced multilevel analysis*, Hrsg. Joop J. Hox und Kyle J. Roberts, 15–40. New York: Routledge.
Paccagnella, Omar. 2006. Centering or not centering in multilevel models? The role of group mean and the assessment of group effects. *Evaluation Review* 30:66–85.
Rabe-Hesketh, Sophia, und Anders Skrondal. 2012. *Multilevel and longitudinal modeling using STATA*. College Station: STATA Press.
Rabe-Hesketh, Sophia, Anders Skrondal und Andrew Pickles. 2004. GLAMM manual. U.C. Berkely, Division of Biostatistics. Working Paper Series. WP 160. http://www.gllamm.org/docum.html.
Raudenbush, Stephen W. 2008. Many small groups. In *Handbook of multilevel analysis*, Hrsg. Jan De Leeuw und Erik Meijer, 207–236. New York: Springer.
Schulz, Arne Hendrik. 2010. *Einfluss von Kontexteffekten auf den Medieneinsatz in Schulen*. Kassel: unveröffentlichte Masterarbeit.
Skrondal, Anders, und Sophia Rabe-Hesketh. 2004. *Generalized latent variables modeling. Multilevel, longitudinal, and structural equation models*. London: Chapman Hall.
Snijders, Tom A.B. 2005. Power and sample size in multilevel linear models. In *Encyclopedia of statistics in behavioral science*, 3, Hrsg. Brian S. Everitt und David C. Howell, 1570–1573. Chicster: Wiley.
Snijders, Tom A.B., und Roel J. Bosker. 1994. Modeled variance in two-level models. *Sociological Methods and Research* 22:342–363.
Snijders, Tom A.B., und Roel J. Bosker. 2012. *Multilevel analysis. An introduction to basic and advanced multilevel modeling*. 1999. Thousand Oaks: Sage.

Theall, Katherine P., Richard Scribner, Sarah Lynch, Neal Simonsen, Matthias Schonlau, Bradley Carlin und Deborah Cohen. 2008. Impact of small size on neighborhood influences in multilevel models. Munich Personal RePEc Archive, No. 11648.
Van Buuren, Stef. 2011. Multiple imputation of multilevel data. In *Handbook of advanced multilevel analysis*, Hrsg. Joop J. Hox und Kyle J. Roberts, 173–195. New York: Routledge
Van der Leeden, Rien, Erik Meijer und Frank M. T. A Busing. 2008. Resampling multilevel models. In *Handbook of multilevel analysis*, Hrsg. Jan De Leeuw und Erik Meijer, 401–433. New York: Springer.
Vermunt, Jeroen K. 2003. Multilevel latent class models. *Sociological Methodology* 33:213–239.
Vermunt, Jeroen K. 2011. Mixture models for multilevel data sets. In *Handbook of advanced multilevel analysis*, Hrsg. Joop J. Hox und Kyle J. Roberts, 59–81. New York: Routledge.

Manuela Pötschke, Dr. ist Akademische Oberrätin am Fachbereich 05 der Universität Kassel und verantwortet dort das Lehrgebiet Angewandte Statistik. Forschungsgebiete: Mehrebenenanalyse, Evaluation akademischer Lehre, E-Learning im Bereich Statistik. Veröffentlichungen: Mehrebenenanalyse. In: Methoden der empirischen Sozialforschung. Wiesbaden 2014 (Hrsg. J. Blasius und N. Baur, i. Erscheinen); Mehrebenenmodelle: angemessene Modellierung von Evaluationsdaten. In: Lehre und Studium professionell evaluieren: Wie viel Wissenschaft braucht die Evaluation? Bielefeld 2010 (Hrsg. P. Pohlenz und A. Oppermann); Nonresponse und Stichprobenqualität. Frankfurt 2004 (zus. mit U. Engel, Ch. Schnabel und J. Simonson).

Kölner Zeitschrift für Soziologie und Sozialpsychologie

Minority Language Proficiency of Adolescent Immigrant Children in England, Germany, the Netherlands, and Sweden

Frank van Tubergen · Tessel Mentjox

© Springer Fachmedien Wiesbaden 2014

Abstract We study minority language proficiency of adolescent immigrant children in England, Germany, the Netherlands and Sweden. We elaborate on theoretical mechanisms of exposure, efficiency and non-economic incentives of minority language acquisition. Using data from adolescent immigrant children in England, Germany, the Netherlands and Sweden, we find evidence for the role of exposure in that immigrant children who were born abroad were more proficient than those born in the host country. Exposure via the percentage of co-ethnics at school is positively related to minority proficiency, whereas parental proficiency in the destination language is negatively associated. Also belonging to a larger immigrant group increases exposure to the minority language and results in language retention. Efficiency in terms of cognitive abilities does not play a role. Non-economic incentives to retain the minority language, indicated by the ethnic identification of parents, is positively related to the child's minority language proficiency and this relationship is stronger when the quality of the parent-child relationship is higher.

Keywords Ethnic minorities · Immigration · Language proficiency · Mother tongue

F. van Tubergen (✉) · T. Mentjox
Department of Sociology, Utrecht University,
Padualaan 14, 3584 Utrecht, the Netherlands
e-mail: f.vantubergen@uu.nl

T. Mentjox
e-mail: T.R.Mentjox@students.uu.nl

Herkunfts-Sprachkompetenz von jugendlichen Immigranten in England, Deutschland, den Niederlanden und Schweden

Zusammenfassung Wir untersuchen die Minoritäts- (Herkunfts-) Sprachkompetenz von jugendlichen Immigranten in England, Deutschland, den Niederlanden und Schweden. Wir spezifizieren theoretische Mechanismen wie Ausgesetztsein (exposure), Wirksamkeit und nicht-ökonomische Anreize auf das Erlernen der Sprache von Minoritäten. Wir verwenden Daten von jugendlichen Immigranten in den vier Ländern. Die Ergebnisse sind, dass Kinder von Immigranten, die nicht im Gastland geboren wurden, kompetenter in der Herkunftssprache waren als solche, die im Gastland geboren wurden. Die Sprachkompetenz stieg mit dem Anteil eigenethnischer Jugendlicher in der Schule, war aber geringer, wenn die Eltern die Sprache des Gastlandes beherrschen. Weiter zeigte sich, dass die Zugehörigkeit zu einer großen Gruppe von Immigranten dazu führt, der Sprache der Minorität stärker ausgesetzt zu sein, was dann dazu führte, die Herkunftssprache beizubehalten. Hingegen sind kognitive Fähigkeiten nicht bedeutsam für das Ausmaß der Kompetenz. Nicht-ökonomische Anreize, die Sprache der Minorität beizubehalten, z. B. durch das Ausmaß der ethnischen Identifikation der Eltern, weisen einen positiven Zusammenhang mit der Herkunfts-Sprachkompetenz der Kinder auf, und diese Beziehung ist stärker, wenn die Eltern-Kind-Bindung höher ist.

Schlüsselwörter Ethnische Minoritäten · Immigration · Sprachkompetenz · Muttersprache

1 Introduction

Immigration is a worldwide phenomenon that changes the ethnic composition of nations and raises questions about the incorporation of immigrants (Castles and Miller 2003). One important aspect of integration concerns the language use and proficiency of immigrants (Alba and Nee 2003; Chiswick and Miller 2001; Tran 2010). Whereas first generation immigrants are generally fluent in the minority language or 'mother tongue', many immigrants have difficulties in learning to speak and write the host country language. A considerable number of studies investigated patterns and causes of destination language use and proficiency of adult first-generation immigrants, i.e. immigrants who were born outside the destination country (e.g. Akresh 2007; Chiswick and Miller 2001; Espenshade and Fu 1997; Van Tubergen and Wierenga 2011; Veltman 1983).

For the children of immigrants, who grow up in the host country and learn the destination language at school, maintaining the minority language is additional to learning the destination language. Studies conducted in the United States show that quite some immigrant children do not speak and write their minority language well (e.g. Arriagada 2005; Rumbaut et al. 2006), which makes it an interesting topic for research. What explains individual differences in minority language skills? This question has become even more relevant nowadays, as the population of children of immigrants in traditional immigrant countries like the United States and in Europe is rapidly growing (Stoeldraijer and Garssen 2011). Furthermore, research findings suggest that maintaining the minority language in addition to the destination language ("bilingualism") has benefits for immigrant children over the use of only the destination language (e.g. Alba et al. 2002). For example, bilingual children were found to have higher educational outcomes (Portes and Rumbaut 1996). The minority language is also important because it is part of the ethnic identity (Phinney et al. 2001).

The few studies that have been done on minority language found that over generations, immigrants lose their mother tongue in favour of the destination language (Arriagada 2005; Rumbaut et al. 2006). The size of the immigrant group was found to have a protective effect, leading to more frequent use of minority language and higher proficiency (Linton 2004; Linton and Jiménez 2009; Lutz 2006; Stevens 1992). Family cohesion, as indicated by having non-divorced parents, positively influences language maintenance (Arriagada 2005; Lutz 2006; Tannenbaum and Berkovich 2005). Mixed results were found for residential segregation (Linton 2004; Vervoort et al. 2012), parental involvement (Tannenbaum and Berkovich 2005), and gender (Lutz 2006; Portes and Schauffler 1994).

The first aim of this study is to provide a coherent theory of minority language proficiency, in which mechanisms and assumptions are clearly specified. Most studies in this field of research tend to be descriptive, and theoretical mechanisms are not spelled out, resulting in a 'variable-oriented' approach (e.g. Arriagada 2005; Lutz 2006; Tran 2010). Instead, our study is theory-driven. We come up with a coherent theory, and identify key individual-level mechanisms of the acquisition of the minority language among adolescents. These mechanisms are partly taken from the Chiswick-Miller (1995, 2001) theory of language learning, which has been developed and applied in the context of foreign-born adults who acquire the destination language (Esser 2006; Van Tubergen 2010; Van Tubergen and Wierenga 2011). We discuss expansions and restrictions of this theory, identifying which of the mechanisms can (not) be applied to *minority* language learning among *adolescents*. We extend this standard theory by proposing a new mechanism that might be particularly relevant when studying minority languages. We then come up with assumptions about the connection between social contexts and the individual-level (behavioural) mechanisms, and formulate testable hypotheses.

The current study also contributes to the state of the art by examining minority language skills of adolescent immigrant children in Europe. Previous studies were mainly conducted in the United States (e.g. Arriagada 2005; Lutz 2006; Rumbaut et al. 2006; Tran 2010), and most of these studies examined Mexicans and other Spanish-speaking immigrant groups, which together make up a substantial language minority. In contrast to this large population of Spanish speaking immigrants in the United States, the language situation in European nations is more diverse. Many European countries host a variety of immigrant groups, many of them having a different language. Possibly, this might result in a fast loss of minority languages in Europe, but to date little is known about the proficiency in minority languages among immigrant children. We are not aware of any large-scale, comparative research on minority language proficiency of adolescent immigrant children in Europe.

We make use of the "Children of Immigrants Longitudinal Survey in four European countries" (CILS4EU; Kalter et al. 2013). An advantage of this dataset is that it contains information provided by both children and parents. By using information provided by parents it is better possible to study the effects of parental characteristics than has been done in previous studies, which had to rely on information of the children. CILS4EU is a school-based survey that contains more than 6,000 immigrant children around 14–15 years of age, spread over almost 100 schools per country.

2 Theoretical background

To explain the minority language proficiency of adolescent children of immigrants we partly rely on Chiswick and Miller's influential theory of adult destination-language acquisition (Chiswick and Miller 1995, 2001). Chiswick and Miller (1995, 2001), and later on also Esser (2006) and Van Tubergen (2010) distinguish three theoretic mechanisms that are important for language learning, namely *exposure*, *efficiency* and economic *incentives*. These are individual-level behavioural mechanisms, which, in combination with bridge assumptions about macro-micro linkages, allow one to study the importance of social contexts.

In our study, we theoretically elaborate on the notions of exposure and efficiency, below. Economic incentives of language investments are relevant when studying adults, as they are participating in the labour market. Since our study involves immigrant children from around 14–15 years of age, we do not consider *economic* incentives to be relevant. In addition to the Chiswick-Miller theory, however, we do come up with a rather underdeveloped mechanism about *non-economic* incentives and motivations for language learning, which has to do with ethnic identification.

2.1 Exposure

The first mechanism identified by the Chiswick-Miller theory is *exposure*. It is defined as "the extent to which others, whether in person or through the media, use the destination language in one's presence and the extent to which the person himself or herself utilizes it" (Chiswick and Miller 1995, p. 249). In this original framing, Chiswick and Miller relate exposure to the destination language, i.e. the official language of the host society. The exposure mechanism has frequently been used in this context, and it is generally regarded as a major determinant of destination language proficiency of adult immigrants (e.g. Hwang and Xi 2008; Stevens 1992; Van Tubergen and Kalmijn 2009). Exposure to the destination language prior to migration, in the origin country, and after migration positively affect destination language skills (Chiswick and Miller 1995, 2001). Exposure to language can occur via media, but also in interaction with family members, friends, colleagues, neighbours, and so forth.

We use this mechanism to derive hypotheses about the acquisition of *minority* languages among *adolescents*. Consequently, we expect that when adolescents are more exposed to the minority language, they will be more proficient in this language. To do so, we need to relate this individual-level mechanism with auxiliary assumptions that link social contexts to the degree of individual exposure to the minority language. For immigrant adolescents, the degree of exposure to their minority language might be critically dependent on how often they hear and speak that language in the social contexts in which they participate. We study the potential role of exposure in four (exogenously determined) social contexts in which adolescents are embedded: their *immigrant group*, their *school setting*, their *family*, and the *country of birth* in which they were born.

First, immigrant groups strongly differ in size. There are numerous smaller groups, and the language experience of growing up in such a smaller group might be dramatically different than when adolescents belong to a numerically large group. Larger immigrant groups provide a language environment in which immigrant children are frequently exposed to their minority language. In larger groups, immigrant children have more opportunities to meet co-ethnics, resulting in more co-ethnic contacts and higher levels of active and passive exposure to their mother tongue (Linton 2004; Linton and Jiménez 2009; Stevens 1992). Furthermore, the size of the immigrant group may also be related to the provision of media in the minority language. A higher supply and demand of media in the minority language is more likely with larger immigrant groups (Chiswick and Miller 2001). For these reasons, we hypothesize that *the higher the percentage of co-ethnics in the country of destination, the higher the minority language proficiency of adolescent immigrant children* (Hypothesis 1).

Another, more local context, that might affect exposure is the school. Exposure to the minority language can be determined by the ethnic composition of the school that immigrant children attend. Some schools mainly consist of minority youth, often even from the same background, whereas other schools predominantly consist of majority children. It can be assumed that a higher presence of co-ethnic students increases the exposure to the minority language, subsequently affecting the maintenance and proficiency in the minority language. The more immigrants from the same ethnic group are present at school the more opportunities immigrant children have to interact in their language and are exposed to the minority language use of other immigrant children. We therefore hypothesize: *The higher the percentage co-ethnics at school, the higher the minority language proficiency of immigrant children* (Hypothesis 2).

The family is probably the most important language environment (Ishizawa 2004). Immigrant children learn the minority language predominantly from their parents (Lutz 2006). Here, we study the possible consequences when parents are proficient in the destination language –which might change the language used when communicating with their children. We assume that children's exposure to the minority language at home will be less intense when the parents are more skilled in the destination language. When parents are not well proficient in the host language, they will tend to communicate in the minority language with their children. It is therefore hypothesized that *the more proficient parents are in the destination language, the lower the minority language proficiency of their children* (Hypothesis 3).

Finally, we study the socialization context and earlier exposure to minority language. As said, the adolescents we study here are around 14–15 years of age. Some of them were born abroad, whereas others were born and raised in the destination country. This can have important consequences for the exposure to the minority language when they were younger. Immigrant children who are born abroad (i.e., so-called first generation) have been solely exposed to the minority language for a number of years before they migrated. Other adolescent immigrant children were born in the destination country (i.e., second generation) and they have been immediately exposed to both the minority and destination language. We expect to see consequences of this differential exposure for their command of the minority language. We therefore hypothesize: *First-generation immigrant children are more proficient in the minority language than second-generation immigrant children* (Hypothesis 4).

2.2 Efficiency

The theory of Chiswick and Miller (1995, 2001) also proposed an efficiency mechanism to explain individual differences in destination language proficiency of adult immigrants (cf. Esser 2006; Van Tubergen 2010; Van Tubergen and Kalmijn 2009). Efficiency is defined as "the extent of improvement in destination-language skills per unit of exposure" (Chiswick and Miller 1995, p. 394). This implies that adult immigrants who are more efficient in learning new languages will become more proficient in the host-country language. This individual-level learning mechanism has often been tested by considering the educational level of immigrants. In their work, Chiswick and Miller (2001) mainly focused on schooling as a proxy for the efficiency with which people learn new languages. Higher levels of schooling may indicate a greater ability to learn, which might carry over to the ability to learn languages.

Although this efficiency mechanism has been exclusively applied to adult immigrants who learn the host-country language, we argue that the scope of the mechanism might actually be larger and equally applied to research on minority language proficiency of adolescents. We assume that higher efficiency in language learning also entails higher efficiency in acquiring minority languages. We use the cognitive abilities of adolescents as a proxy for their efficiency in learning, and expect to see that this has a positive effect on the proficiency in the minority language. We hypothesize that *the higher the cognitive abilities, the higher the minority language proficiency of immigrant children* (Hypothesis 5).

2.3 Non-economic incentives

Chiswick and Miller's theory (1995, 2001) focuses on economic incentives as the third mechanism of acquiring the host-country language of adult immigrants (cf. Esser 2006; Van Tubergen 2010). This mechanism states that language learning is on the one hand costly, as it involves opportunity costs (i.e., forgone earnings while not working), but also direct costs in terms of course fees or books needed for language learning. On the other hand, the mechanism states that learning the new language is economically beneficial for adult immigrants, given the human capital value of language abilities, and the increasing opportunities in the labour market. Such as an explicit calculation of the economic costs and labour market benefits seems less relevant when studying adolescents, who are still far away from participating in the labour market.

This is not to say that there are no incentives for adolescents to acquire the minority language, and that all that matters is learning via (passive) exposure and individual differences in efficiency. We propose that non-economic incentives might be relevant for understanding investments in the minority language. A prime motivation for adolescents to acquire the minority language could be that such skills and knowledge promotes their ethnic group-belongingness. When adolescents learn the language of their minority group, they become part of their ethnic group, and learn about its culture, norms, values and traditions (Cheng and Kuo 2000; Ishizawa 2004). How important the motivations for adolescents are to acquire such knowledge about the ethnic and cultural tradition might in turn be dependent on how strongly the ethnic identity is emphasized by their parents. When parents strongly identify with their ethnic origin group, and put much effort in transmitting the cultural, ethnic and religious norms and values of their group, this presumably increases the non-economic incentives of adolescents to acquire the minority language of their parents. Importantly, parents differ in how strongly they identify with their ethnic group, and consequently how much they socialize their children in the ethnic traditions. It can be expected that parents who stronger identify with their ethnic group perceive the minority language as more important and take a more active stance in transmitting their culture and language to their children, which would have a positive effect on the motivations for adolescents to acquire the minority language. We hypothesize: *parental ethnic identification will have a positive effect on the minority language proficiency of immigrant children (*Hypothesis 6).

The non-economic motivations for adolescents to acquire the minority language might be conditional upon the relationship with their parents. When parents strongly identify with their ethnic origin group, and have a strong incentive to transmit the ethnic-cultural traditions to their children, its success depends on the quality of the parent-child relationship. In case there is a good relationship, socialization should work rather well and their adolescent children will acquire the minority language. When instead the children do not have a good relationship with their parents, they might not learn the minority language, even when parents strongly identify with their ethnic group and want their children to learn their ethnic language. Therefore, it is hypothesized that: *the more parental involvement, the stronger the positive effect of parental ethnic identification on the minority language proficiency of immigrant children* (Hypothesis 7).

3 Data and methods

To test our hypotheses, we use the first wave of the Children of Immigrants Longitudinal Survey (CILS4EU). Data were collected among students around 14–15 years of age in England, Germany, the Netherlands and Sweden during the academic year 2010–2011. High efforts were undertaken to standardize sampling frames, sampling, questionnaires, survey methods and data cleaning (Kalter et al. 2013). Nevertheless, country differences appear in response rates of schools and parents. Because the response rates among parents were too low in England and Sweden, we leave these countries out in the analysis of the role of parents. In some countries, we can match the CILS4EU data to contextual data on group size, whereas in other countries we cannot. We carefully pay attention to these issues in our study, as we will discuss below.

In each country, children filled in written questionnaires in their class at school. Around 5,000 children and 100 schools participated in the survey in each country. Children received a questionnaire to be filled out by one (not pre-determined) parent. Schools were sampled on their percentage of immigrants at school, stratified in four categories: (1) 0–10%; (2) 10–30%; (3) 30–60%; and (4) 60–100%. Schools with a high number of immigrant children were oversampled, and the dataset thus contains a large number of immigrant children.

Only children that meet one of the following two conditions were selected for this study: (1) child is born abroad; or (2) at least one of the parents is born abroad, and thus only first and second generation immigrants were selected. We used the migration background of children to determine immigrant group size at the national level and school level. In some countries, the migration background of third generation immigrant children could not be specified. Therefore, our sample only contained first and second generation immigrant children. Finally, we excluded children whose migration background refers to a country in which the destination language is dominant, since for these children it is very likely that the minority language is equal to the destination language. This leaves us with 5,878 children in the four countries.

3.1 Dependent variables

So far, we captured proficiency in the minority language as a general concept. However, four aspects of language proficiency are often distinguished; speaking, understanding, writing and reading. In previous research on immigrant children, the effects of the determinants have never been compared over different aspects. Some authors studied listening abilities (Cheng and Kuo 2000), speaking abilities (Lutz 2006; Portes and Hao 1998), speaking and understanding (Vervoort et al. 2012), or a combined scale of the four aspects (Arriagada 2005; Tran 2010). Possibly, some determinants differently affect language dimensions. We therefore investigate whether the proposed factors hold across different dimensions.

Minority language proficiency—Children were asked whether another language than the host language is spoken at home. When another language was indicated, they were asked about their proficiency in this language, measured by four questions: How well do you think you can (1) speak; (2) understand; (3) read; (4) write this <second> language?; The answering categories, on a 5-point scale, range from (1) 'not at all' to (5) 'excellently'. For children who did not report another language to be spoken at home, we assumed these children to not be proficient in their minority language and therefore we assigned the lowest value of (1) 'not at all' to these children.

We distinguished between two dimensions of proficiency: (1) oral dimension (speaking and understanding), and (2) written dimension (reading and writing). Speaking and understanding were found to correlate 0.88, and reading and writing 0.91. The correlations are higher within dimensions than between dimensions, with the other possible dimensions correlating below 0.72. This convinced us that the two dimensions are empirically an appropriate distinction. For both dimensions a scale has been created (Cronbach's alpha respectively 0.94 and 0.95).

3.2 Independent variables

Group size—The size of the immigrant group in the country is based on the migration background of the child. Specifically, we rely on figures on the number of first and second generation immigrants (children and adults) in the host country, per immigrant group (Central Bureau of Statistics Netherlands 2011). Group size is divided by the total number of inhabitants in the country. This variable could only be studied for the Netherlands, because reliable data on group size are not available for the other three countries.

Presence co-ethnics at school—The presence of co-ethnics at school is measured as the proportion of students at school that are from the same national origin. The relative size of the immigrant groups is based on migration background, and was acquired by aggregating our own data. Although we do not have precise figures on the entire school, at least two classes per school participated in the survey, and these classes were randomly selected.

Parental proficiency in the destination language—Parental proficiency in the destination language was measured by four questions: How well do you think you can (1) speak; (2) understand; (3) read; (4) write <host language>? The answering categories are on a 5-point scale ranging from (1) 'not at all' to (5) 'excellently'. We use the same distinction as used for the child's minority language proficiency also for their parents. In models to explain the oral proficiency of the child, the parent's oral proficiency in the destination language is included. Likewise, when explaining the written proficiency of the child, the parent's written proficiency in the destination language is included. Two separate scales are created (Cronbach's alpha oral: 0.92; written: 0.91).

Generation—We distinguished between first and second generation immigrants, with the former being those children being born outside the host country, and the latter being those children being born in the host country (and having at least one parent born outside the host country).

Cognitive abilities—The abilities of children were tested during one school hour. We used the overall test score on puzzles made by the children during class, which indicates the number of puzzles answered correctly. These puzzles capture the abilities of children to reason and think logically and analytically.

Parental ethnic identification—The parent who filled out the questionnaire was asked whether he or she feels to belong to another group than the majority population. When another group was pointed out, it was asked how strongly the parent feels to belong to this group. The four answering categories range from (1) 'very strongly' to (4) 'not at all strongly'. For parents who did not indicate to identify with another group than the majority group, we expected that they identify with the minority group even less than those who did report a minority group but identified 'not at all strongly'. For these parents, we assigned a value of (5) that indicates less ethnic identification than (4) 'not at all strongly. The variable is reverse coded.

Relationship quality—To measure the quality of the relationship between parents and children, six statements are used: (1) My parents show interest in grades and achievement in school; (2) My parents tell me that they are proud when I do well at school; (3) My parents encourage me to work hard for school; (4) Whenever I feel sad, my parents try to comfort me; (5) My parents try to understand what I think and feel; and (6) My parents show me that they love me. On all statements the answering categories range from (1) 'strongly agree' to (5) 'strongly disagree' on a five-point scale. Although the first three variables refer to involvement in school matters and the latter three statements are more general, the statements altogether load on one factor (i.e. all factors are above .56). The scale is found to be reliable, with a Cronbach's alpha of 0.82. The scale is reverse coded with a higher value representing more parental involvement.

3.3 Control variables

Gender of child—We control for gender of the respondent. Previous studies showed that girls are more proficient in the minority language than boys (Lutz 2006; Portes and Hao 1998; Portes and Schauffler 1994; Tran 2010). A value of '1' indicates that the child is a girl and '0' indicates that the child is a boy.

Gender of parent—We have information on one of the parents and this is in most cases (i.e. 71 %) the mother. To capture possible biases arising from gender differences in parents' behaviour, we control for the gender of the parent.

Intermarriage—When parents are from different countries of origin, the transmittance of the minority language is argued to be lower than when both parents are from the same origin (Alba et al. 2002; Stevens 1985). Intermarriage was taken into account in combination with generation. As mentioned, we excluded all children whose migration background is 'mixed'. For first generation immigrant children this means that the parents were born in the same country outside the host country and intermarriage could thus not be specified. For the second generation we distinguished two categories. The 'secondmono' category includes all second generation immigrant children whose parents are born in the same country outside the host country. The 'secondmixed' category indicates the second generation immigrant children who have one foreign-born and one native-born parent.

Intact families—Previous studies stated that living in an intact family is beneficial for the proficiency in the minority language (e.g. Arriagada 2005; Lutz 2006; Portes and Hao 1998). We included a dummy variable whether the child is living together with both biological parents.

Destination country—We included dummy variables for the destination countries.

Continent of origin—Children stem from different migration backgrounds and to control for differences between these backgrounds we included continent of origin. Due to the large number of different immigrant groups we could not control for them separately.

Table 1 provides the descriptive statistics of the dependent, independent and control variables.

3.4 Analytical method

We apply linear multilevel analyses to test our hypotheses. Individual observations are interdependent, because children are nested in school, their immigrant group and their host country. Standard statistical tests assume observations to be independent

Table 1 Descriptive statistics dependent, independent and control variables

Variable name	Mean/proportion	S.D.	Range
Minority language proficiency			
Oral	3.34	1.34	1–5
Written	2.54	1.34	1–5
Percentage co-ethnics country	1.34	1.01	0.0002–2.3353
Percentage co-ethnics school	12.35	14.93	0.7299–79.2453
Parental proficiency destination language (L2)			
Oral	3.48	0.91	1–5
Written	3.38	1.01	1–5
Generation			
First	0.25	0.43	0/1
Second mono	0.45	0.50	0/1
Second mixed	0.30	0.46	0/1
Cognitive abilities	17.65	4.56	0–27
Parental ethnic identification	3.19	1.68	1–5
Relationship quality	4.29	0.65	1–5
Girl	0.50	0.50	0/1
Parent is mother	0.72	0.45	0/1
Intact family	0.70	0.46	0/1
Destination country			
England	0.20	0.40	0/1
Germany	0.32	0.47	0/1
Netherlands	0.18	0.38	0/1
Sweden	0.30	0.46	0/1
Continent of origin			
Africa	0.17	0.37	0/1
Asia	0.46	0.50	0/1
Europe	0.30	0.46	0/1
North America	0.04	0.20	0/1
Oceania	0.004	0.06	0/1
South America	0.02	0.15	0/1

and by using these standard tests spurious results might occur (Snijders and Bosker 2011). For this reason, multilevel analysis is needed.

On the first level we have children. Immigrant children are then nested within the combination of immigrant groups and schools. To indicate this second level, unique combinations were created for all immigrant groups at all schools. The third level concerns the immigrant groups at the country level. Unique combinations were created for all immigrant groups in all countries. For example, Turkish children in the Netherlands have a different code than Turkish children in Germany, and Turkish children in the Netherlands have a different code than Moroccan children in the Netherlands.

We estimated four models for both oral and written language skills. In the first model we included only the respondents in the Netherlands and for this model all hypotheses could be tested. For the second model we added Germany, but because group size is unknown in Germany, we excluded group size at the national level in this model. The third model included Germany and the Netherlands but did not contain information on parental characteristics and group size at the country level. We exclude these variables in order to compare the results with the identical model 4. In this model 4, we included all four countries and included the same variables as in model 3. Note that due to high non-response on the parental survey in Sweden and England, we only estimate the effect of parental characteristics in the Netherlands and Germany (model 2).

3.5 Multiple imputation

To deal with missing data, we used multiple imputation, which is a simulation-based statistical technique, and the only way to correctly deal with missing data (see Stata manual 2011). An advantage of this method over listwise deletion is that it avoids issues of selectivity. In our data we see that those children whose parent did not fill out the questionnaire have higher minority language proficiency than those children whose parent did fill out the questionnaire. This might hint at selectivity regarding parental characteristics. It can be expected that those parents not fluent in the destination language participated less often.

Multiple imputation is conducted with the chained function in Stata. All variables for our analyses are predicted by each other. Several other variables that are theoretically assumed to be associated with the imputed variables are also incorporated. A causal relationship is not necessarily assumed. To impute continuous and ordinal variables we used predictive mean matching (PMM). For categorical variables we used logistic regression (logit). 20 imputations were used to reduce the sampling error (reference manual of StataCorp 2011).

For the different models, we used different imputation files. The first files concerned imputations for Germany and the Netherlands and was used for models on the Netherlands and Germany. The second file concerned the imputation for all four countries together. This file did not include variables based on information provided by the parents, and was used for the fourth model. In both files, the imputation was done separately for the countries, because differences in associations might exist between countries.

4 Results

4.1 Descriptive patterns

We first discuss some descriptive findings on proficiency in minority languages in England, Germany, the Netherlands and Sweden. Quite some immigrant children reported that they do not at all read (15%) and write (18%) the minority language (findings not presented here). Only about 1–2% of the immigrant children stated that they do not at all speak or understand the minority language. Second generation immigrants reported more often to not at all speak the minority language, on all four aspects.

In a study by Rumbaut et al. (2006) on the United States, the percentage of immigrants who speak the minority language very well is examined by immigrant genera-

Table 2 Mean on oral and written minority language proficiency for two largest immigrant groups per country (scale 1–5)

England			Germany			Netherlands			Sweden		
	Oral	Written		Oral	Written		Oral	Written		Oral	Written
Total	3.26	2.25	Total	3.40	2.69	Total	3.12	2.35	Total	3.46	2.68
Pakistan	3.65	2.10	Turkey	3.67	3.14	Turkey	3.67	3.21	Iraq	3.93	2.62
India	3.50	2.06	Russia	3.18	2.08	Morocco	3.51	2.21	Serbia	3.87	3.57

tion. To compare whether the trend in the United States resembles the trend in Europe we examined the percentage of immigrant children who speak the minority language very well for which we combined our categories 'very well' and 'excellently'. We find that among the first generation 66% of the children speak the minority language 'very well'. This percentage drops for the children classified as 'secondmono' to 51%. Among the secondmixed category, only 24% speak the minority language very well. Rumbaut et al. (2006) found a similar decline in speaking the minority language very well.

To provide some insight into the minority language proficiency of different immigrant groups in the four countries, Table 2 presents a description of the mean of the oral and written language scales for the total immigrant population, but also for the two largest immigrant groups. The lowest oral skills are found for Russians in Germany and the highest for Serbians in Sweden. Serbians in Sweden also have the highest written proficiency whereas the Indian immigrant group in England has the lowest. Based on this table, the only immigrant group that can be compared across destination countries are Turks in Germany in the Netherlands. The table shows that their proficiency in the oral dimension in both countries is almost equal; however Turks in the Netherlands are somewhat better in reading and writing the minority language than Turks in Germany.

4.2 Multilevel analyses

We calculated the intraclass correlation based on the variance components in the intercept-only models (Table 3) and on the variance components presented in Tables 4 and 5. It shows that there is significant clustering at the combined groups-school level,

Table 3 Variance components in intercept only models

	Model 1—Netherlands	Model 2/Model 3 -Germany and Netherlands	Model 4—England, Germany, Netherlands, Sweden
Oral dimension			
Variance immigrant groups country	0.422	0.444	0.564
Variance immigrant groups school	0.180	0.122	0.189
Variance individuals	1.238	1.199	1.209
Written dimension			
Variance immigrant groups country	0.254	0.231	0.389
Variance immigrant groups school	0.028	0.069	0.128
Variance individuals	1.350	1.300	1.316

Table 4 Linear multilevel analysis: oral dimension of minority language proficiency

Oral dimension	Model 1– Netherlands		Model 2– Germany and Netherlands		Model 3– Germany and Netherlands (incomplete)		Model 4– England, Germany, Netherlands, Sweden	
	B	S.E.	B	S.E.	B	S.E.	B	S.E.
Intercept	3.444***	0.321	3.356***	0.180	2.819***	0.148	2.909***	0.124
% co-ethnics country	0.071	0.094						
% co-ethnics school	0.005*	0.004	0.005***	0.002	0.006***	0.002	0.006***	0.002
Parental proficiency oral L2	−0.043	0.056	−0.115***	0.029				
First generation	0.178*	0.109	0.322***	0.057	0.368***	0.057	0.418***	0.041
Second generation mono	0		0		0		0	
Second generation mixed	−0.868***	0.113	−0.704***	0.058	−0.907***	0.055	−0.954***	0.040
Cognitive abilities	0.008	0.009	0.004	0.005	0.003	0.005	0.002	0.004
Parental ethnic identification	0.163***	0.031	0.147***	0.016				
Relationship quality	0.146**	0.067	0.198***	0.032	0.189***	0.032	0.167***	0.023
Parental ethnic identification * Relationship quality	0.056	0.046	0.007	0.022				
Girl	−0.165**	0.071	−0.015	0.040	0.009	0.040	0.049*	0.029
Gender parent (1 = mother)	−0.112	0.096	−0.107**	0.050				
Family structure (1 = intact family)	0.091	0.083	0.163***	0.048	0.232***	0.048	0.239***	0.034
Destination county								
England							0.215*	0.110
Germany			0.311***	0.087	0.313***	0.092	0.273**	0.107
Netherlands			0		0		0	
Sweden							0.395***	0.103
Continent of origin								
Africa	−0.166	0.189	0.020	0.119	0.041	0.125	−0.026	0.098
Asia	−0.374**	0.180	0.031	0.106	0.054	0.113	−0.020	0.092
Europe	0		0		0		0	
North America	−0.264	0.243	0.179	0.181	0.111	0.192	−0.122	0.159

Table 4 (Continued)

Oral dimension	Model 1– Netherlands		Model 2– Germany and Netherlands		Model 3– Germany and Netherlands (incomplete)		Model 4– England, Germany, Netherlands, Sweden	
	B	S.E.	B	S.E.	B	S.E.	B	S.E.
Oceania	0.038	0.420	−0.123	0.318	−0.171	0.332	0.050	0.302
South America	0.263	0.311	0.343*	0.200	0.341	0.210	0.302*	0.156
No. observations	1055		2948		2948		5878	
No. groups country	89		190		190		389	
No. groups school	558		1516		1516		3202	
Variance immigrant groups country	0.109		0.105		0.130		0.231	
Variance immigrant groups school	0.051		0.030		0.051		0.061	
Variance individuals	1.126		1.052		1.085		1.105	

Hypotheses tested one-sided; control variables tested two-sided

*$P<0,1$; **$P<0,05$; ***$P<0,01$

Table 5 Linear multilevel analysis: written dimension of minority language proficiency

Written dimension	Model 1– Netherlands		Model 2– Germany and Netherlands		Model 3– Germany and Netherlands (incomplete)		Model 4– England, Germany, Netherlands, Sweden	
	B	S.E.	B	S.E.	B	S.E.	B	S.E.
Intercept	2.583***	0.329	2.362***	0.188	2.085***	0.155	2.155***	0.126
% co-ethnics country	0.198**	0.098	0.007***	0.002	0.008***	0.002	0.008***	0.002
% co-ethnics school	0.005*	0.003						
Parental proficiency written L2	−0.008	0.055	−0.042*	0.027				
First generation	0.251**	0.112	0.458***	0.060	0.484***	0.060	0.625***	0.043
Second generation mono	0		0		0		0	
Second generation mixed	−0.413***	0.119	−0.381***	0.062	−0.511***	0.057	−0.551***	0.042
Cognitive abilities	0.005	0.009	0.004	0.005	0.004	0.005	0.003	0.004
Parental ethnic identification	0.138***	0.035	0.113***	0.017				
Relationship quality	0.150**	0.070	0.215***	0.034	0.212***	0.034	0.173***	0.025
Parental ethnic identification * relationship quality	0.066*	0.048	0.032*	0.022				
Girl	−0.098	0.072	0.072*	0.042	0.089**	0.042	0.071**	0.031
Gender parent (1 = mother)	−0.233*	0.130	−0.120*	0.065				
Family situation (1 = intact family)	−0.028	0.085	0.124**	0.051	0.178***	0.050	0.193***	0.036
Destination country								
England							0.238**	0.109
Germany			0.247***	0.095	0.251**	0.098	0.221**	0.106
Netherlands			0		0		0	
Sweden							0.434***	0.102
Continent of origin								
Africa	−0.339*	0.195	−0.244**	0.129	−0.230	0.133	−0.332***	0.097
Asia	−0.687***	0.186	−0.461***	0.116	−0.451***	0.121	−0.465***	0.091
Europe	0		0		0		0	
North America	−0.065	0.252	0.243	0.197	0.207	0.204	−0.017	0.158

Table 5 (Continued)

Written dimension	Model 1– Netherlands		Model 2– Germany and Netherlands		Model 3– Germany and Netherlands (incomplete)		Model 4– England, Germany, Netherlands, Sweden	
	B	S.E.	B	S.E.	B	S.E.	B	S.E.
Oceania	0.401	0.436	0.044	0.342	0.002	0.350	0.168	0.305
South America	0.507	0.321	0.502**	0.217	0.523**	0.222	0.397**	0.157
No. observations	1055		2948		2948		5878	
No. groups country	89		190		190		389	
No. groups school	558		1516		1516		3202	
Variance immigrant groups country	0.122		0.136		0.153		0.207	
Variance immigrant group school	0.000		0.027		0.030		0.075	
Variance individuals	1.234		1.175		1.207		1.205	

Hypotheses tested one-sided; control variables tested two-sided

*$P<0.1$; **$P<0.05$; ***$P<0.01$

and at the groups-country level, which means that both random components need to be taken into account.

The findings from the linear multilevel analyses are presented in Table 4 (oral skills) and 5 (written skills).

The first set of hypotheses was derived from the exposure mechanism. Our findings suggest that the size of the immigrant group in the host country positively affects written skills in the minority language (Table 5). We do not find a relationship between group size and oral skills (Table 4). Therefore, the support for hypothesis 1 is mixed. In line with hypothesis 2, the relative size of the co-ethnic immigrant group at school is positively related to the minority language proficiency. The higher the percentage of co-ethnics at school, the more proficient the child is in both the oral and written dimension of the minority language.

We find support for hypothesis 3, when we look at the results for both Germany and the Netherlands (Model 2). When studying only the Netherlands, results do not reach significance. But when analysed together with Germany, we clearly see that parents' proficiency in the host-country language is negatively associated with their children's written and oral minority language skills. We also observe differences across immigrant generation. As expected by hypothesis 4, we find the first generation to be less proficient in the minority language than the second generation.

Regarding the efficiency mechanism, we find no evidence for hypothesis 5. Cognitive abilities seem to have no effect on the minority language proficiency. The non-significant result is consistent across all models.

The third set of hypotheses reflected the non-economic incentives. The main effect of ethnic identification of the parents is positive and significant, indicating that the more parents identify with their ethnic group, the more proficient their children are in the minority language. We find this effect for both the oral and written dimension, and in both Model 1 (without Germany) and 2 (with Germany). This finding is in line with hypothesis 6. We also hypothesized about the interaction effect between parental ethnic identification and relationship quality. We expected the positive effect of parental ethnic identification to be stronger when parents have a better relationship with their children. We find this to be the case for the written dimension of language, but not for the oral dimension. Thus, the positive association between parental ethnic identification and written knowledge of the minority language is stronger when the parent-child relationship is stronger.

The control variables show some interesting patterns. Living with both biological parents is positively related to both oral and written language proficiency (Model 2–4). Furthermore, we find differences across our four destination countries. Children in Sweden are more proficient in the minority language than children in the Netherlands, with children in England and Germany being in between these two extremes.

5 Conclusion and discussion

We studied patterns and causes of minority language proficiency of adolescent immigrant children in Germany, Sweden, England and the Netherlands with data from CILS4EU. It is the first large-scale research on minority language skills in Europe.

Moreover, our study attempted to formulate a coherent theory of language learning, deviating from prior work which has been rather descriptive and variable-oriented. Theoretically, we formulated hypotheses from the mechanisms that emphasize the role of the degree of *exposure* to minority language (at home, at school, in other contexts), the *efficiency* with which children learn languages, and *non-economic motivations* (associated with the importance of the maintenance of ethnic traditions) and the resulting willingness to learn the mother tongue. The first two mechanisms were taken from the Chiswick-Miller theory, which has been developed and tested on foreign-born adults who acquire the destination language.

Three general conclusions can be drawn from our study.

First, virtually all immigrant children in the four European countries can speak their minority language and have at least some understanding of their mother tongue. Much more difficulties arise for adolescents when they have to read or write in their minority language. Learning to read and write typically requires more formal education and training, whereas speaking and understanding can be learnt more easily by practicing informally. For both oral and written dimensions, however, there are strong individual differences in skills.

Second, such individual differences in oral and written minority language skills partly arise because of differences in exposure to that language. Even when analysing children aged 14–15, we find that when they were born and socialized abroad, their command of the minority language is much better than when they were born in the host country. Such early exposure to the minority language apparently has an enduring effect on language maintenance. After arrival in the host country, another social context that affects the degree of exposure is their immigrant group. Some immigrant children belong to a relatively small group, which means they will be very little exposed to their minority language via daily social interactions in the neighbourhood, with friends and acquaintances, but also to a limited extent on social media. Indeed, we find that the language retention is stronger among children who grow up in numerically larger groups. On a more local level, we see that exposure works in schools as well. Schools can provide a protective social context for language maintenance, when there are many immigrant children who speak the same minority language. This provides ample opportunities to speak and hear their ethnic language on a daily basis. Also the social context at home matters. Naturally, parents are the prime source of exposure to the minority language, and it is obvious to assume a strong impact of parents. But in our study, we even showed that when parents have more knowledge of the host country language, their children have fewer oral and written command of the minority language. Presumably, when parents are more proficient in the host language, they use the minority language less often in communications with their children, resulting in fewer exposure and eventually a lack of minority proficiency among the children. All in all, these results confirm the testable hypotheses that were derived from the exposure mechanism.

Third, non-economic incentives play a role in acquiring the minority language, as learning this language is part of the ethnic-cultural tradition of the parents. When parents more strongly identify with their ethnic group, their children have more command of their parents' language, presumably due to the importance parents and their children attach to their cultural background. This parental transmission however is conditional upon the quality of the parent-child relationship. When children have a good relationship with their parents, they will more strongly internalise the norms, values and traditions of their parents. Our study indeed shows that the positive effect of the ethnic identification of the parents on minority language proficiency is stronger when the parent-child relationship is qualitatively better.

The study can be improved in various ways, raising new questions and stimulating follow-up research. First, against expectations, we do not find evidence for the efficiency mechanism. We find that cognitive abilities are not related to minority language skills. Possibly, this means that the ability to think logically and analytically does not spill over to the ability to acquire new languages. Alternatively, there is such a linkage, but adolescents with higher cognitive abilities underestimate their minority skills, or use their talents for investments in the destination language at the cost of acquiring their mother tongue. As our study relied on only one measure, no strong conclusions about the role of efficiency can be drawn yet. Second, minority language proficiency was only measured for children who indicated another language to be spoken at home. Although that number was fairly high in our study (i.e., over 85 %), little is known about the true minority language skills of the small group who report not to speak another language at home. Third, we used a self-rated proficiency in the minority language. Although so far most studies have employed measures of self-reported proficiency, it is more reliable to rely on actual tests of minority language skills. Fourth, results were not always the same for the oral and written dimension of language proficiency. In the theory used here, no differences were expected. Further research is encouraged to elaborate theoretically on differential effects on these two language dimensions. Finally, although our study included four different European countries, we did not formulate explicitly hypotheses on country differences, due to the low number of countries. Our exploratory comparative approach, however, showed that –after taking into account for various individual, family, and school characteristics– adolescent immigrant children in Sweden are more proficient in their minority language than in other countries, particularly the Netherlands. Further research is encouraged to explain such country differences.

References

Akresh, Ilana R. 2007. Contexts of English language use among immigrants to the United States. *International Migration Review* 41:930–955.

Alba, Richard, John Logan, Amy Lutz, and Brian Stults. 2002. Only English by the third generation? Loss and preservation of the mother tongue among the grandchildren of contemporary immigrants. *Demography* 39:467–484.

Alba, Richard, and Victor Nee. 2003. *Remaking the American mainstream: Assimilation and contemporary immigration.* Harvard University Press.

Arriagada, Paula A. 2005. Family context and Spanish-language use: A study of Latino children in the United States. *Social Science Quarterly* 86:599–619.

Castles, Stephen, and Mark J. Miller. 2003. *The age of migration. International population movements in the modern world. 1993.* Basingstoke: Palgrave Macmillan.

Central Bureau of Statistics Netherlands. 2011. Statline. www.statline.cbs.nl.

Cheng, Simon H., and Wen H. Kuo. 2000. Family socialization of ethnic identity among Chinese pre-adolescents. *Journal of Comparative Family Studies* 31:463–484.

Chiswick, Barry R., and Paul W. Miller. 1995. The endogeneity between language and earnings: International analyses. *Journal of Labor Economics* 13:246–288.
Chiswick, Barry R., and Paul W. Miller. 2001. A model of destination-language acquisition: application to male immigrants in Canada. *Demography* 38:391–409.
Espenshade, Thomas J., and Haishan Fu. 1997. An analysis of English-language proficiency among U.S. Immigrants. *American Sociological Review* 62:288–305.
Esser, Hartmut. 2006. *Sprache und Integration: Die sozialen Bedingungen und Folgen des Spracherwerbs von Migranten*. Frankfurt: Campus Verlag.
Hwang, Sean-Shong, and Juan Xi. 2008. Structural and individual covariates of English language proficiency. *Social Forces* 86:1079–1104.
Ishizawa, Hiromi. 2004. Minority language use among grandchildren in multigenerational households. *Sociological Perspectives* 47:465–483.
Kalter, Frank, Anthony F. Heath, Miles Hewstone, Jan O. Jonsson, Matthijs Kalmijn, Irena Kogan, and Frank van Tubergen. 2013. Children of immigrants longitudinal survey in four European countries (CILS4EU). Cologne: GESIS Data Archive. ZA5353 Data file Version 1.0.0, doi:10.4232/cils4eu.5353.1.0.0.
Linton, April. 2004. A critical mass model of bilingualism among U.S.-Born Hispanics. *Social Forces* 83:279–314.
Linton, April, and Tomás Jiménez. 2009. Contexts for bilingualism among US-born Hispanics: 1990 and 2000. *Ethnic and Racial Studies* 32:967–995.
Lutz, Amy. 2006. Spanish maintenance among English-speaking Latino youth: The role of individual and social characteristics. *Social Forces* 84:1417–1433.
Phinney, Jean S., Irma Romero, Monica Nava, and Dan Huang. 2001. The role of language, parents, and peers in ethnic identity among adolescents in immigrant families. *Journal of Youth and Adolescence* 30:135–153.
Portes, Alejandro, and Lingxin Hao. 1998. E Pluribus Unum: Bilingualism and loss of language in the second generation. *Sociology of Education* 71:269–294.
Portes, Alejandro, and Rubén G. Rumbaut. 1996. *Immigrant America: A portrait*. Berkeley: University of California Press.
Portes, Alejandro, and Richard Schauffler. 1994. Language and the second generation: Bilingualism yesterday and today. *International Migration Review* 28:640–661.
Rumbaut, Rubén G., Douglas S. Massey, and Frank D. Bean. 2006. Linguistic life expectancies: Immigrant language retention in Southern California. *Population and Development Review* 32:447–460.
Snijders, Tom A.B, and Roel J. Bosker. 2011. *Multilevel analysis: An introduction to basic and advanced multilevel modeling*. Sage.
StataCorp. 2011. Stata: Release 12. Statistical software. College Station, TX: StataCorp LP
Stevens, Gillian. 1985. Nativity, intermarriage and mother-tongue shift. *American Sociological Review* 50:74–83.
Stevens, Gillian. 1992. The social and demographic context of language use in the United States. *American Sociological Review* 57:171–185.
Stoeldraijer, Lenny, and Joop Garssen. 2011. Prognose van de bevolking naar herkomst, 2010–2060. In *Bevolkingstrends 1e kwartaal*, 24–31. Den Haag: Centraal Bureau voor de Statistiek.
Tannenbaum, Michal, and Marina Berkovich. 2005. Family relations and language maintenance: Implications for language educational policies. *Language Policy* 4:287–309.
Tran, Van C. 2010. English gain vs. Spanish loss?: Language assimilation among second-generation Latinos in young adulthood. *Social Forces* 89:257–284.
Van Tubergen, Frank. 2010. Determinants of second language proficiency among refugees in the Netherlands. *Social Forces* 89:515–534.
Van Tubergen, Frank, and Matthijs Kalmijn. 2009. A dynamic approach to the determinants of immigrants' language proficiency: The United States, 1980–2000. *International Migration Review* 43:519–543.
Van Tubergen, Frank, and Menno Wierenga. 2011. Language acquisition of male immigrants in a multilingual destination: Turks and Moroccans in Belgium. *Journal of Ethnic and Migration Studies* 37:1039–1057.
Veltman, Calvin. 1983. *Language shift in the United States*. Berlin: Mouton.
Vervoort, Miranda H.M., Jaco Dagevos, and Hek Flap. 2012. Ethnic concentration in the neighbourhood and majority and minority language: Study of first and second-generation immigrants. *Social Science Research* 41:555–569.

Frank van Tubergen, 1976, Professor at the Department of Sociology/ICS, Utrecht University, Utrecht, the Netherlands, and Distinguished Adjunct Professor at the King Abdulaziz University, Jeddah, Saudi Arabia. His research interests include social networks, religion and immigration. He recently published "Discrimination of Arabic-named applicants in the Netherlands: An internet-based field experiment examining different phases in online recruitment procedures" (with Blommaert and Coenders), Social Forces, in press.

Tessel Mentjox, received her master's degree of Sociology at Utrecht University, where she participated in the two-year English research master Sociology and Social Research.

Individual values, cultural embeddedness, and anti-immigration sentiments: Explaining differences in the effect of values on attitudes toward immigration across Europe

Eldad Davidov · Bart Meulemann · Shalom H. Schwartz · Peter Schmidt

© Springer Fachmedien Wiesbaden 2014

Abstract During the last decade, many European countries have faced sizeable immigration inflows accompanied by high prevalence of negative sentiments toward immigrants among majority members of the host societies. We propose that basic human values are one important determinant of such negative attitudes, and we seek to explain variation across countries in the strength of the effects of values. Based on Schwartz' (1992, 1994) basic human value theory, we hypothesize that universalism values are conducive to positive attitudes toward immigration, while conformity-tradition reinforce anti-immigration sentiments. We furthermore hypothesize that these value effects are moderated by two contextual variables. Both value effects are expected to be weaker in countries with a higher level of cultural embeddedness. Furthermore, negative effects of conformity-tradition values are hypothesized to be cushioned by a lower proportion of immigrants in the country. A multilevel analysis of data from 24 countries from the fourth round of the European Social Survey (2008–2009) supports these hypotheses. Moreover, we demonstrate

E. Davidov (✉)
Institute of Sociology, University of Zurich,
Andreasstraße 15, 8050 Zurich, Switzerland
e-mail: davidov@soziologie.uzh.ch

B. Meulemann
Centre for Sociological Research, University of Leuven,
Parkstraat 45, 3000 Leuven, Belgium
e-mail: bart.meuleman@soc.kuleuven.be

S. H. Schwartz
Department of Psychology, The Hebrew University of Jerusalem,
Mount Scopus, 91905 Jerusalem, Israel
e-mail: msshasch@mscc.huji.ac.il

P. Schmidt
Institut für Politikwissenschaft, Justus-Liebig-Universität Gießen,
Karl-Glöckner Str. 21 E, 35394 Giessen, Germany
e-mail: peter.schmidt@sowi.uni-giessen.de

that the measurement properties of the theoretical constructs exhibit equivalence across countries, thereby justifying statistical comparisons.

Keywords Basic human values · Attitudes toward immigration · Multilevel analysis · Cross-level interaction · European Social Survey · Measurement equivalence

Individuelle Werte, kulturelle Einbettung und immigrations-feindliche Einstellungen: Wie sich die Unterschiede in den Wirkungen von Werten auf Einstellungen zur Immigration in Europa erklären lassen

Zusammenfassung Im letzten Jahrzehnt sind viele europäische Länder von einer beträchtlichen Zuwanderung betroffen gewesen, begleitet von negativen Einstellungen der Majorität gegenüber den Immigranten. Wir schlagen vor, dass Werte eine wichtige Determinante solcher negativen Einstellungen sind, und erklären die Variation in der Stärke der Effekte von Werten in den einzelnen Ländern. Auf der Grundlage der Theorie grundlegender menschlicher Werte von Schwartz (1992, 1994) nehmen wir an, dass Universalismus Werte zu positiver Einstellung gegenüber der Zuwanderung führen werden; im Gegensatz dazu führen Konformität und Tradition zu immigrationsfeindlichen Gefühlen. Wir nehmen ferner an, dass diese Wirkungen von Werten durch zwei Kontext-Variablen moderiert werden. Beide Effekte von Werten sind niedriger in Ländern mit einem höheren Grad von kultureller Einbettung, und weiter, negative Effekte der Werte-Konformität und Tradition werden vermutlich durch einen niedrigen Anteil von Immigranten in einem Land gedämpft. Eine Mehrebenen-Analyse mit Daten von 24 Ländern der vierten Welle des European Social Survey (2008 bis 2009) stützen diese Hypothesen. Darüber hinaus zeigen wir, dass die Messeigenschaften der theoretischen Konstrukte über die Länder hinweg äquivalent sind und deshalb die statistischen Vergleiche rechtfertigen.

Schlüsselwörter Menschliche Werte · Einstellungen zur Einwanderung · Mehrebenenanalyse · Cross-level-Interaktion · European Social Survey · Äquivalenz von Messungen

1 Introduction

European countries have faced a constant increase of immigration in recent decades (Hooghe et al. 2008). Approximately 3.4 million people immigrated into countries belonging to the EU-27 in 2004, the number increased to 3.8 million in 2008, and this trend appears to be continuing.[1] Not surprisingly, substantial sociological research has been devoted to understanding the consequences and implications of this upsurge in migration. Much of this research has focused on one implication that is considered particularly worrisome, i.e., the level of anti-immigrant sentiment among members

---

[1] See http://epp.eurostat.ec.europa.eu/portal/page/portal/eurostat/home/.

of the host societies. Several studies reveal a rapid rise and/or a high level of antiforeigner sentiment: Substantial proportions of the population of host societies favor denying equal rights to immigrants and perceive them as a threat to social cohesion and order, culture, and traditions, and their economic well-being (Raijman et al. 2008; Scheepers et al. 2002; Schlüter et al. 2008). In many European countries the popularity of anti-immigrant politicians or parties has risen and public opinion has shifted to a less welcoming position (Lubbers et al. 2002).

Previous research has sought to delineate the mechanisms underlying the genesis of negative attitudes of majority members toward immigrants. It has focused on both individual and contextual determinants of such attitudes. A first line of research maintains that socioeconomic vulnerability, reflected in low education levels, weak labor market positions, and economic deprivation, accounts for the negative attitudes. Various studies have tested these propositions with international datasets like the European Social Survey and conclude that vulnerable individuals fear losing their jobs due to competition from newcomers to the labor market who are willing to accept lower wages (Gorodzeisky 2011; Kunovich 2004; Pichler 2010; Raijman et al. 2003; Semyonov and Glikman 2009; Semoyonov et al. 2006, 2008). Yet some studies also demonstrate reductions of perceived threat due to contact with immigrants (e.g., Semyonov and Glikman 2009).

A second line of research proposes that ideological dispositions are an important source of anti-immigrant attitudes and that political conservatism mobilizes negative sentiments that induce hostility to and prejudice against immigrants. Empirical studies have demonstrated repeatedly that right-wing individuals tend to reject immigration more strongly (Gorodzeisky 2011; Raijman et al. 2003; Semyonov et al. 2006, 2008).

A third set of studies explains the emergence of anti-immigrant prejudice as due to *contextual* variables that affect negative attitudes directly or that moderate the effects of individual-level variables. These studies suggest that unfavorable economic conditions on the country level accompanied by large-scale immigration are perceived as a threat to the economy and may induce hostile attitudes (Gorodzeisky 2011; Meulemann et al. 2009; Pichler 2010; Quillian 1995, 1996; Scheepers et al. 2002; Semyonov et al. 2006). Other contextual variables identified as sources of hostile attitudes are negative media coverage (Schlüter and Davidov 2011) and national immigration policies (Schlüter et al. 2013; Weldon 2006).

In recent years, a number of authors have also noted the important role that human values play in the explanation of negative attitudes toward immigrants (Davidov and Meuleman 2012; Davidov et al. 2008a; Sagiv and Schwartz 1995; Schwartz 2006a, 2007). These studies adopted Schwartz' (1992) definition of basic human values as beliefs about the importance of broad goals as guiding principles in life. They used individual differences in values to explain negative attitudes toward immigrants over and above the effects of social structural position. Values are found to exert robust effects, some of which varied across countries.

Research has yet to examine the *conditions* that affect the influence of basic human values on attitudes toward immigration, that is, the circumstances under which values contribute more or less to the explanation of anti-immigrant sentiments. Nor have researchers proposed a theory that might explain the variation in value effects across countries. This study investigates *variation* in the effects of values on attitudes toward immigration across 24 European countries from different European regions. We will argue that an aspect of cultural values—cultural embeddedness (Schwartz 2006b), that is, the extent to which individuals in the society are expected to strive toward shared goals rather than their own—serves as a moderator of the impact of values on anti-immigration attitudes. By trying to explain variation in the effect of individual values on attitudes toward immigration across countries in a systematic way, our study contributes to a better understanding of the conditions under which values are more prominent in explaining negative sentiments toward immigration.

To test these hypotheses empirically, we utilize an internationally comparable dataset that includes large samples from many European countries, the European Social Survey (ESS; Jowell et al. 2007). We derive latent variables that take measurement errors into account (Bollen 1989) for our main theoretical constructs, and we test the equivalence of our constructs across countries (Billiet 2003). Testing for construct equivalence has rarely been practiced in studies that apply multilevel analysis, although such equivalence is a necessary condition for a meaningful interpretation of multilevel analyses (Kim et al. 2012). Before turning to the empirical analyses, we present the theoretical background and propositions of the study.

2 Theoretical considerations

2.1 The value theory

Human values are 'desirable transsituational goals, varying in importance, that serve as guiding principles in the life of a person or other social entity' (Schwartz 1994, p. 21). Individuals' values are ordered in a hierarchy of importance that is quite stable across time and situations.[2] Schwartz (1992)[3] has postulated that the full range of values recognized across societies form a motivational continuum; extensive research in over 80 countries has supported this theory that distinguishes 10 values (universalism, benevolence, tradition, conformity, security, power, achievement, hedonism, stimulation, and self-direction). We will focus on the two values universalism and the unified value conformity-tradition, because they have been found to predict attitudes

---

[2] In contrast to values, attitudes are not ordered hierarchically, are less stable, and refer to positive and negative evaluations of objects rather than to the importance of goals (Rokeach 1968; Schwartz 2006a). Values, but not attitudes, serve as standards to judge people, actions, and events.

[3] We employ the Schwartz value theory rather than the Inglehart theory (e.g., Inglehart and Baker 2000) mainly for three reasons. First, Schwartz (1992, 1994) makes a better theoretical and empirical distinction between values and attitudes. Such a distinction is crucial for using values to explain attitudes and for guaranteeing discriminant validity between the concepts. Second, Schwartz makes a clear distinction between individual-level and societal-level values whereas Inglehart does not make such a distinction on the measurement level. We propose mechanisms to explain attitudes toward immigration on the individual level. Therefore, the Schwartz theory is better suited to test them empirically. Finally, the database we chose to test our propositions is the European Social Survey, which includes measures of anti-immigrant sentiments across a large set of European countries. This dataset included measurements for Schwartz' rather than Inglehart's values. See Becker et al. (2012) and Datler et al. (2012) for a discussion about differences between the two theories.

toward immigration[4] (Davidov and Meuleman 2012; Davidov et al. 2008a; Sagiv and Schwartz 1995; Schwartz 2007).

2.2 Relations of values to attitudes toward immigration

2.2.1 The individual level

What mechanism links values to attitudes toward immigration? Values whose expression, attainment, or motivation may be promoted or blocked by immigration to a country are likely to affect attitudes toward immigration (Sagiv and Schwartz 1995). This mechanism is particularly relevant for two values, namely, universalism and conformity-tradition. Universalism values express the motivation to appreciate differences among individuals as well as to understand, tolerate, and protect the welfare of all people, with an emphasis on the weak and vulnerable who are different from the self (Schwartz 2006a). Admitting immigrants who left or even fled their country of birth in search of a better life provides opportunities to realize the goal of promoting the welfare of the weak and vulnerable. Therefore, we expect a positive effect of universalism on attitudes toward immigration (hypothesis *H1*).

In contrast, we hypothesize that tradition and conformity values lead to negative attitudes toward immigration (hypothesis *H2*). This is because these values express the motivation to maintain the beliefs, customs, and practices of one's culture and family and to avoid violation of conventional expectations and norms. The arrival of newcomers threatens the attainment of these values because immigrants from different cultures are liable to introduce new and unfamiliar practices and beliefs, to question common norms and conventions or to violate them out of ignorance, and to bring about change in the existing societal order.

Previous individual-level research has demonstrated the effects of the values universalism, tradition, and conformity on attitudes toward immigration in numerous countries (e.g., Davidov et al. 2008a; Davidov and Meuleman 2012; Sagiv and Schwartz 1995; Schwartz 2007). The current study will provide a rigorous test of Hypotheses *H1* and *H2* by trying to replicate the finding across 24 countries. But at the same time, we take current knowledge a step further by addressing the following questions: How do value effects vary across countries, and how can this variation be explained?

2.2.2 Variability in value effects

The above hypotheses and the reasoning underlying them are stated as applicable across societies. We expect, however, that the strength of the effects of these basic human values varies across societies. In order for values to affect attitudes and behav-

---

[4] In many empirical studies it was not possible to distinguish between tradition and conformity (see, e.g., Davidov 2010). Therefore, we decided to unify them in this study. This does not contradict the theory due to their shared motivation and proximal location in the value space. We did not use security as a predictor because of the different meaning it may have across countries which may lead to conceptual confusion. Furthermore, in additional exploratory analyses, security only has a relatively small effect because of its close content to conformity and tradition.

ior, they must be activated in specific situations or contexts (Schwartz 2006a). Contextual variables are likely to influence the intensity with which values relevant to immigration attitudes are activated.

The first contextual variable we consider is cultural embeddedness, a cultural dimension for comparing societies (Schwartz 2006b). In so-called 'embedded cultures', people are viewed as entities embedded in the collectivity. Meaning in life comes largely through social relationships, through identifying with the group, participating in its shared way of life, and striving toward its shared goals rather than pursuing one's own goals. Embedded cultures emphasize maintaining the status quo and restraining individuals' actions that might disrupt in-group solidarity or the traditional order. In contrast, in less embedded cultures, people are viewed as autonomous entities who are encouraged to cultivate and express their own preferences, feelings, ideas, and abilities, and to find meaning in their own uniqueness.

Embeddedness assumes that a person's roles in and obligations to collectivities are more important than her unique ideas and aspirations, and in less embedded societies individuals are encouraged to express their uniqueness and independence in thought, action, and feelings (Schwartz 2006b). As such, cultural embeddedness should be distinguished from Hofstede's (2001) concept of collectivism: Whereas collectivism refers to the way in which individuals and the surrounding group are actually related, embeddedness refers in addition to the norms that dictate how they should be related.[5]

This analytical framework implies that individuals' personal values are more likely to be salient, to be activated rather than suppressed, and to influence their attitudes and behavior in societies with less embedded cultures. Lesthaeghe and Moors (2000, p. 11) also inferred that 'value orientations are ... predictive for choices... in contexts with ... high degrees of individual autonomy'. On these bases, we hypothesize that values have stronger effects on attitudes toward immigration in less embedded societies (hypothesis *H3*).

Our second contextual variable is the proportion of immigrants in a country. Group threat theory posits that people who live in conditions of intense competition for scarce goods are more likely to perceive immigrants as a threat (Stephan et al. 2005; Coenders 2001; Scheepers et al. 2002; Quillian 1995, 1996). A high proportion of immigrants in a country has been associated with negative attitudes toward immigration at the country level (Scheepers et al. 2002; Semyonov et al. 2006). We hypothesize that this is also the case across the 24 European countries we study here (hypothesis *H4*). Empirical evidence for an effect of the proportion of immigrants on attitudes toward immigration is mixed with some authors finding support while others do not. For example, Quillian (1995, 1996) or Coenders et al. 2004) found supportive evidence for the effect of immigrant group size, but Semyonov et al. (2004) or Strabac and Listhaug (2008) did not. The test of Hypothesis *H4* in the current study provides a rigorous test of this effect across numerous countries.

---

[5] *Our* choice to focus on cultural embeddedness rather than on collectivism is not only justified based on theoretical considerations, but is also supported by empirical arguments. We reproduced the analyses presented below using collectivism as a moderator for value effects (results not shown but are available upon request). Cross-level interactions for collectivism are insignificant (with Tradition-Conformity) or considerably weaker than is the case for cultural embeddedness.

Yet more central to the purpose of this study, we hypothesize that the higher the proportion of immigrants in the country, the stronger the negative effect of conformity and tradition on attitudes toward immigration will be (hypothesis *H5*). As noted above, immigration threatens the attainment of these values by introducing new and unfamiliar practices and beliefs. It increases the number of people who may question or violate common norms and conventions. The greater the proportion of immigrants from dissimilar cultural backgrounds, the greater the pressure for change in the societal institutions that people who emphasize conformity and tradition values cherish. Hence, we expect that these values will then show a stronger relationship with anti-immigration sentiment.

There is mixed evidence for an effect of immigration levels on relations of values to immigration attitudes. Davidov et al. (2008a) found that values had a weaker effect on attitudes in countries with higher immigration levels. But Davidov and Meuleman (2012) found no variation across countries that differed in immigration levels in the effects of conservation values on immigration attitudes. Immigration levels are not equivalent to the proportion of immigrants. However, the two are sufficiently related so that the mixed findings for the former are relevant to the interaction of the latter with values that we predicted (hypothesis *H5*). No studies have examined the possible cross-level interaction effect of cultural embeddedness on relations of individual values with attitudes toward immigration which are postulated in hypothesis *H3*.

3 Data and measurement

3.1 Data

The analyses utilize the data of the fourth round (2008–2009) of the European Social Survey (ESS) (Jowell et al. 2007). In each of 24 European countries, strict probability samples of the noninstitutionalized populations aged 15 years and older were selected. In all, 41,965 respondents reported their attitudes and opinions regarding various social and political issues, their basic values, and a full list of background variables. The following countries, with their abbreviation and effective sample sizes in parentheses, were included in the analyses: Belgium (BE; 1,586), Bulgaria (BG; 2,210), Cyprus (CY; 1,119), Czech Republic (CZ; 1,968), Denmark (DK; 1,505), Estonia (EE; 1,207), Finland (FI; 2,138), France (FR; 1,907), Germany (DE; 2,501), Great Britain (GB; 2,100), Greece (GR; 1,946), Hungary (HU; 1,513), Ireland (IE; 1,476), Latvia (LV; 1,643), Netherlands (NL; 1,602), Norway (NO; 1,412), Poland (PL; 1,595), Portugal (PT; 2,228), Romania (RO; 2,007), Slovakia (SK; 1,755), Slovenia (SI; 1,175), Spain (ES; 2,341), Sweden (SE; 1,611), and Switzerland (CH; 1,368).[6]

---

[6] For further documentation about the data collection procedures, see http://www.europeansocialsurvey.org/. Data can be downloaded from http://ess.nsd.uib.no/

3.2 Variables

Attitudes toward Immigration. Respondents were asked three questions: To what extent do you think [your country] should allow people (1) of the same race or ethnic group (2) of a different race or ethnic group (3) from poorer countries outside Europe, to come and live in your country? Response categories ranged from 1 (allow many to come and live here) to 4 (allow none). We recoded responses so that higher scores indicate greater willingness to allow immigrants into the country. Confirmatory factor analysis (CFA) (Bollen 1989; Jöreskog 1971) demonstrated that the three questions load positively and strongly on a single factor. These questions were averaged to form an index that we named Allow.

Values. The ESS Human Values Scale is a modification of the Portrait Values Questionnaire (Schwartz 2007). It includes brief verbal portraits of 21 different people, gender-matched to the respondent. Each portrait describes a person's goals, aspirations, or wishes that point implicitly to the importance of a single value. For example, the following item describes a person for whom universalism values are important: "She thinks it is important that every person in the world be treated equally. She believes everyone should have equal opportunities in life." For each portrait, respondents answer the question: 'How much like you is this person?' choosing one of six labeled boxes ranging from 'very much like me' (1) to 'not like me at all' (6). Respondents' own values are inferred from their self-reported similarity to people who are described in terms of particular values. We reversed the scores so that higher scores indicate greater value importance.

We used the three universalism items that tap the importance of tolerance, equality, and environmental concern, two tradition items that tap the importance of tradition, customs, religion, and modesty, and two conformity items that tap the importance of following rules, doing what one is told, and behaving properly. In CFA analyses, all items loaded strongly on their respective value factor. We therefore averaged the items to form two indices that we named Universalism (UN) and Conformity-Tradition (COTR).

Cultural embeddedness. In each country, we utilized scores based on responses of urban school teachers and university students to the Schwartz Value Survey (for details see Schwartz 2006b). School teachers' values are considered a good proxy of society's values as in their educational function in schools they are expected to convey and disseminate norms and values among young pupils and future generations. Data were gathered between 1990 and 2007. Evidence in Schwartz (2006b) reveals very little change in cultural embeddedness scores across extended periods of time even in countries that underwent major political and institutional change. We therefore combined the data from this whole period for the index. The items included were validated empirically as indicators of cultural embeddedness by means of multidimensional scaling with countries as the unit of analysis (Schwartz 2006b). The cultural embeddedness score was the average ratings in each country of the importance of 15 value items: social order, tradition, forgiving, obedience, politeness, being moderate, honoring elders, national security, cleanliness, devoutness, wisdom, self-discipline, protection of one's public image, family security, and reciprocation of favors.

Both the individual values and the country scores for embeddedness were derived from questionnaires distributed among individuals. However, embeddedness is a characteristic of national cultures on which societies differ whereas conformity and tradition values are variables on which individuals differ. The former refers to the prescriptions in a society for how people should relate, the latter to the goals that motivate individuals. The former emerges in analyses in which country means are the unit of analysis, the latter emerge in analyses in which individuals' value priorities are the unit of analysis. These two levels of analysis are conceptually and statistically independent. Moreover, the value items that fit together in theory and emerge empirically to measure conformity-tradition and cultural embeddedness, while partially overlapping, differ in a number of particulars. Of the 15 embeddedness items, seven measure individual values from conformity-tradition, but the other seven measure security, power, benevolence, and universalism values at the individual level. The latter include, for example, 'wisdom' and 'forgiving'.[7]

Proportion of immigrants in a country. We operationalized this variable as the percentage of non-EU immigrants (foreign born) in the population of each country.[8] The data for 2007 were downloaded from the website of the MIMOSA project (http://mimosa.gedap.be/).

Control variables. Gender was scored 0 for males and 1 for females. Age was measured in years. Education was measured by the highest level of education achieved (0 = no education up to 5 = tertiary education completed). Subjective income was measured by responses to the question "Which of the descriptions … comes closest to how you feel about your household's income nowadays?" on a 4-point scale (1 = living comfortably on present income, 4 = finding it very difficult on present income). Political orientation was measured by self-placement on a 0 (left) to 10 (right) scale. Finally, religiosity was measured by responses to the question "…how religious would you say you are?" on a scale ranging from 0 (not at all religious) to 10 (very religious).

3.3 Modeling strategy

We used multilevel analysis to take account of the two-level structure of the data, where individuals are nested within countries. We estimated a series of increasingly more complex models as proposed by Hox (2010). After estimating a so-called empty model, we included the sociodemographic variables as control variables. In the third

---
[7] Data on embeddedness across countries may be provided by the 4th author upon request.

[8] The two countries with the largest share of non-EU immigrants are Estonia and Latvia. These countries host a very large minority group of ethnic Russians who have lived there for an extended period of time but did not receive citizenship after the collapse of the Soviet Union. Because of this specific context in the Baltic States, the percentage of non-EU immigrants might represent a different reality and our indicator might lack comparability. To rule out the possibility that this distorts our conclusions, we replicated all analyses in this paper excluding Estonia and Latvia. Results (available upon request) are virtually identical, and do not alter the conclusions.

model, we added the universalism and conformity-tradition values at the individual level and the cultural embeddedness score and the percentage of non-EU immigrants at the country level. Finally, we included random slopes for the values and cross-level interactions to test the hypothesized variations in the effect of individual values across countries.

We estimated all models with the restricted maximum likelihood procedure implemented in SPSS 19. To deal with item nonresponse, we used multiple imputation (Rubin 1996; Schafer 1997). All variables were standardized (over the pooled dataset), so all effects can be interpreted as standardized effects (Hox 2010; Snijders and Bosker 1994). Furthermore, the two value scales were group-mean centered (Hox 2010, p. 68) before standardization, in order to avoid confusion between processes operating at the individual and country level. This procedure guarantees that the interaction effects we observe are actually cross-level interactions (as our theoretical framework predicts) rather than interactions at the country level (Hofmann and Gavin 1998).

4 Results

4.1 Testing for equivalence

As a first step, we ensured that our measurement of attitudes toward immigration and of individual values of universalism and conformity-tradition, our main constructs, were equivalent across countries (Billiet 2003). Equivalence of concepts is a necessary condition before cross-cultural studies may be meaningfully conducted. In line with previous studies (Davidov 2008; Davidov and Meuleman 2012; Davidov et al. 2008b), we employed multiple group confirmatory factor analysis (MGCFA: Bollen 1989; Brown 2006; Jöreskog 1971) to test for measurement equivalence across the 24 groups (countries) in this study. The tests supported full metric and partial scalar equivalence, thereby permitting meaningful interpretation of a multilevel analysis (Davidov 2010).[9]

4.2 Descriptive overview

Table 1 provides country averages for the scales measuring attitudes toward immigration (Allow) and value priorities (Universalism and Conformity-Tradition) as well as scores on the two contextual variables (cultural embeddedness and the proportion of non-EU immigrants).

Willingness to accept immigrants varied substantially across countries. Attitudes were most positive in Sweden, followed by Poland, Norway, Germany, and Bulgaria. Rejection of immigration was strongest in Greece followed by Latvia, Hungary, Portugal, and to a lesser extent, Cyprus and the Czech Republic. As shown in Table 1, the mean willingness score varied considerably across countries. The difference between the most (Sweden) and least (Greece) positive country was 1.46, which is consider-

---

[9] The full analyses are available from the first author.

Table 1 Country scores for attitudes toward immigration, the value scales, and the contextual variables

Country	Allow (country average)	Universalism (country average)	Conformity-Tradition (country average)	% non-EU foreigners	Cultural Embeddedness Score
BE	0.17	0.12	0.03	6.10	3.25
BG	0.30	−0.12	0.32	0.39	3.87
CH	0.28	0.37	−0.29	9.56	3.28
CY	−0.33	0.30	0.43	7.67	4.04
CZ	−0.33	−0.37	−0.10	0.93	3.59
DE	0.32	0.08	−0.27	7.72	3.06
DK	0.22	−0.02	−0.25	5.84	3.19
EE	−0.24	−0.19	−0.30	15.56	3.81
ES	−0.24	0.38	0.39	7.53	3.31
FI	0.00	0.11	−0.16	2.24	3.37
FR	0.03	0.12	−0.38	7.65	3.20
GB	−0.12	−0.07	−0.16	6.96	3.34
GR	−0.63	0.41	0.45	8.22	3.41
HU	−0.46	0.01	−0.04	0.76	3.60
IE	0.07	0.20	0.18	3.97	3.41
LV	−0.51	−0.28	−0.07	14.58	4.46
NL	0.16	−0.03	−0.15	8.34	3.19
NO	0.37	−0.28	−0.21	5.61	3.45
PL	0.50	0.05	0.30	1.14	3.86
PT	−0.45	−0.40	−0.19	5.33	3.43
RO	0.04	−0.24	0.20	0.44	3.78
SE	0.83	−0.19	−0.41	8.05	3.12
SI	0.09	0.15	0.21	9.95	3.71
SK	0.09	0.03	0.43	0.94	3.82

The allow, universalism, and conformity-tradition scales are standardized (Note that in the multilevel models, the value scales were group-mean centered before standardizing in order to guarantee that the interactions with context variables are due to actual cross-level interactions rather than macro-level processes)

able knowing that this is a standardized variable. The multilevel analysis sheds light on the sources of variation in willingness to accept immigrants both within countries and between them.

Embeddedness varied considerably across countries as well. Scores were highest in Latvia, Estonia, Cyprus, Bulgaria, and Poland and lowest in Germany, Sweden, the Netherlands, and Denmark. In the former countries we expect values to exert stronger effects whereas in the latter we expect them to operate less strongly.

4.3 Multilevel analysis

The results of the series of multilevel model analyses are reported in Tables 2 (Models 1–4) and 3 (Models 5–7).

Model 1 included only a random intercept to enable us to determine how much of the variance in the dependent variable is accounted for by individual-level variability and how much by between-country variability. Twelve percent of the variance is due

Table 2 Multilevel models explaining attitudes toward immigration (Models 1–4). (Source: ESS 2008–2009, own calculations)

	Model 1		Model 2		Model 3		Model 4	
	Par.	SE	Par.	SE	Par.	SE	Par.	SE
Fixed effects								
Intercept	0.01	0.07	0.00	0.07	0.00	0.07	0.01	0.06
Gender			0.01*	0.00	−0.01	0.00	−0.01	0.00
Age			−0.12***	0.00	−0.11***	0.00	−0.11***	0.00
Educational level			0.12***	0.00	0.10***	0.00	0.10***	0.00
Subjective income			−0.09***	0.01	−0.10***	0.01	−0.10***	0.01
Conformity-Tradition (COTR)					−0.12***	0.01	−0.12***	0.01
Universalism (UN)					0.14***	0.01	0.14***	0.01
Left-right position					−0.08***	0.01	−0.08***	0.01
Religiosity					0.05***	0.01	0.05***	0.01
Context variables								
Embeddedness							−0.09	0.06
% non-EU immigrants							−0.07	0.06
Cross-level interactions								
COTR x embeddedness								
UN x embeddedness								
COTR x % non-EU immigrants								
Variance components								
Residual variance	0.882***	0.006	0.838***	0.006	0.809***	0.006	0.809***	0.006
Random intercept	0.124**	0.037	0.103**	0.031	0.103**	0.030	0.096**	0.030
Slope COTR								
Slope UN								
Intra Class Correlation	0.12		0.11		0.11		0.11	
Explained variance								
% reduced variance residual			0.05		0.08		0.08	
% reduced variance intercept			0.17		0.17		0.23	

Ni=41,965; Nj=24

Multiple imputation is used to handle missing data. All entries are standardized effects

COTR conformity-tradition, *UN* Universalism

*$p<0,05$; **$p<0,01$; ***$p<0,001$

to country-level variability; hence, it is important to use multilevel analysis (Hox 2010).

Model 2 regressed Allow (the index of attitude toward immigration) on the sociodemographic variables gender, age, education, and subjective income. Compared to the empty model, the individual- and country-level variances dropped by 5.0% and 17%, respectively, indicating that these variables explain considerable

Table 3 Multilevel models explaining attitudes toward immigration (Models 5–7). (Source: ESS 2008–2009, own calculations)

	Model 5		Model 6a		Model 6b		Model 6c		Model 7	
	Par.	SE	Par.	SE	Par.	SE	Par.	SE	Par.	SE
Fixed effects										
Intercept	0.01	0.06	0.01	0.06	0.01	0.06	0.01	0.06	0.01	0.06
Gender	−0.01	0.00	−0.01	0.00	−0.01	0.00	−0.01	0.00	−0.01	0.00
Age	−0.11***	0.00	−0.11***	0.00	−0.11***	0.00	−0.11***	0.00	−0.11***	0.00
Educational level	0.10***	0.00	0.10***	0.00	0.10***	0.00	0.10***	0.00	0.10***	0.00
Subjective income	−0.10***	0.01	−0.10***	0.01	−0.10***	0.01	−0.10***	0.01	−0.10***	0.01
Tradition-Conformity	−0.11***	0.01	−0.11***	0.01	−0.11***	0.01	−0.11***	0.01	−0.11***	0.01
Universalism	0.14***	0.01	0.14***	0.01	0.14***	0.01	0.14***	0.01	0.14***	0.01
Left-right position	−0.08***	0.01	−0.08***	0.01	−0.08***	0.01	−0.08***	0.01	−0.08***	0.01
Religiosity	0.05***	0.01	0.05***	0.01	0.05***	0.01	0.05***	0.01	0.05***	0.01
Context variables										
Embeddedness	−0.09	0.06	−0.09	0.06	−0.09	0.06	−0.09	0.06	−0.09	0.06
% non EU immigrants	−0.07	0.06	−0.07	0.06	−0.07	0.06	−0.07	0.06	−0.07	0.06
Cross-level interactions										
COTR x embeddedness			0.03**	0.01					0.03***	0.01
UN x embeddedness.					−0.05***	0.01			−0.05***	0.01
COTR x % non-EU immigrants							−0.02*	0.01	−0.02*	0.01
Variance components										
Residual variance	0.804***	0.006	0.804***	0.006	0.804***	0.006	0.804***	0.006	0.805***	0.006
Random intercept	0.096**	0.030	0.096**	0.030	0.096**	0.030	0.096**	0.030	0.096**	0.030
Slope COTR	0.003**	0.001	0.002*	0.001	0.003**	0.001	0.003*	0.001	0.002*	0.001
Slope UN	0.003**	0.001	0.004**	0.001	0.001*	0.001	0.003**	0.001	0.001*	0.001
ICC	0.11		0.11		0.11		0.11		0.11	

Table 3 (Continued)

	Model 5		Model 6a		Model 6b		Model 6c		Model 7	
	Par.	SE	Par.	SE	Par.	SE	Par.	SE	Par.	SE
Explained variance										
% reduced variance residual	0.09		0.09		0.09		0.09		0.09	
% reduced variance intercept	0.23		0.23		0.23		0.23		0.23	
% reduced var. slope COTR			0.25		0.00		0.16		0.51	
% reduced var. slope UN			−0.05		0.65		0.01		0.67	

Ni=41,965; Nj=24

Multiple imputation is used to handle missing data. All entries are standardized effects

COTR conformity-tradition, *UN* universalism

*$p<0.05$; **$p<0.01$; ***$p<0.001$

variance on both levels of analysis. Women and those with higher education and income were more positive toward immigration whereas older people were considerably more negative. These findings are in line with what has been reported in the literature (e.g., Semyonov et al. 2006).

Model 3 added the individual values of universalism and conformity-tradition and also level of religiosity and left-right political orientation. These individual characteristics added to the explanation of variance in attitudes toward immigration over and above the effects of the sociodemographic variables, primarily at the individual level. In line with previous studies (Davidov et al. 2008a; Davidov and Meuleman 2012), attitudes toward immigration were more positive among those high in universalism values and low in conformity-tradition values. The two basic values had the strongest effects among the individual-level predictors. The inclusion of universalism and conformity-tradition is responsible for the lion's share in the drop of residual variance between Models 2 and 3 at the individual level. Furthermore, attitudes toward immigration were more positive among more religious individuals and among those with left-wing political orientations. This finding is also in line with previous studies (see, e.g., Scheepers et al. 2002).

Model 4 added the macro-level variables, cultural embeddedness levels, and percentage of non-EU residents in each country, in order to examine their effect on variation between countries in attitudes toward immigration. Based on group threat theory (Quillian 1995, 1996), we hypothesized that greater proportions of immigrants in a country would increase competitive threat and, therefore, lead to rejecting immigration. This hypothesis was not confirmed; proportion of immigrants in a country did not account for significant between-country variability in attitudes to immigration. We had no reason to expect a direct effect of cultural embeddedness on attitudes toward immigration, nor did the analysis reveal such an effect. Thus, neither contextual variable had a direct effect on attitudes toward immigration.

Model 5 investigated whether the effect of individual values on attitudes varied across countries and, if so, to what extent. In this model, we allowed the slopes of universalism and conformity-tradition values to vary across countries. The random slope variances of the two values were significant, indicating that the effects of the values do indeed vary across countries. The random slope variances provide a clear estimate of the size of the difference in the effects of the values. The standard deviation of both random slopes equaled 0.055 (namely, the square root of the random slope variances). This indicates that country-specific value effects deviate on average by 0.055 from the mean value effects over all countries. Inspection of the country-specific value effects (not shown) indicates that—in spite of the considerable cross-national variance in effect sizes—the direction of the effects of universalism and conformity-tradition values on attitudes toward immigration is the same across 24 European countries.

Subsequently, we examined whether the variation across countries in the effects of values could be explained by the contextual variables, thus testing Hypotheses *H3* (cultural embeddedness) and *H5* (percentage of immigrants in country). Because the sample size at the country level is quite limited ($N=24$), three separate models were estimated, each containing one cross-level interaction effect: universalism X cultural embeddedness (Model 6a), conformity-tradition X cultural embeddedness

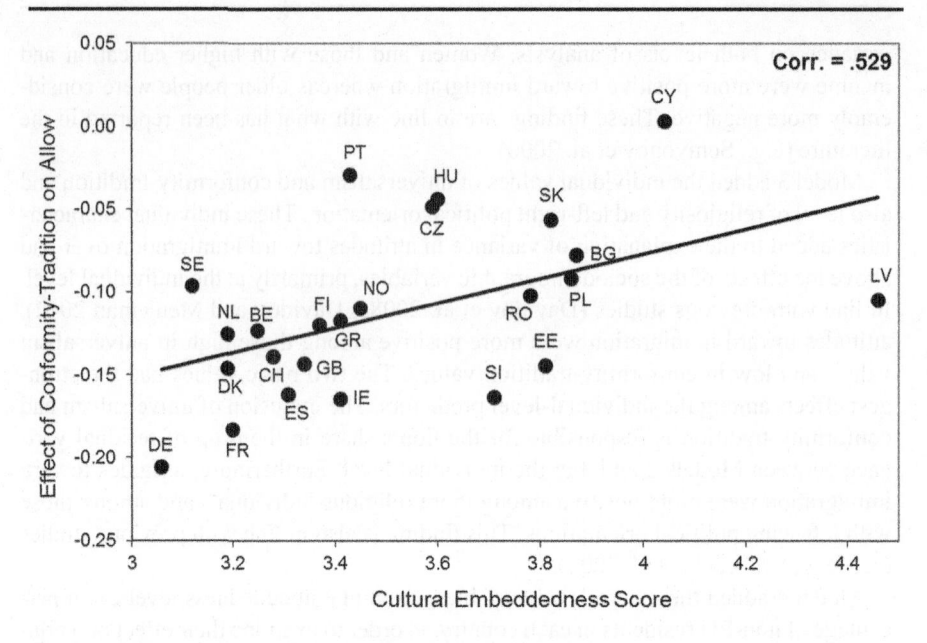

Fig. 1 Variation across countries in the effects of conformity-tradition values on attitudes toward immigration as a function of the level of cultural embeddedness in the country. (Source: ESS 2008–2009, own calculations. For country abbreviations see text)

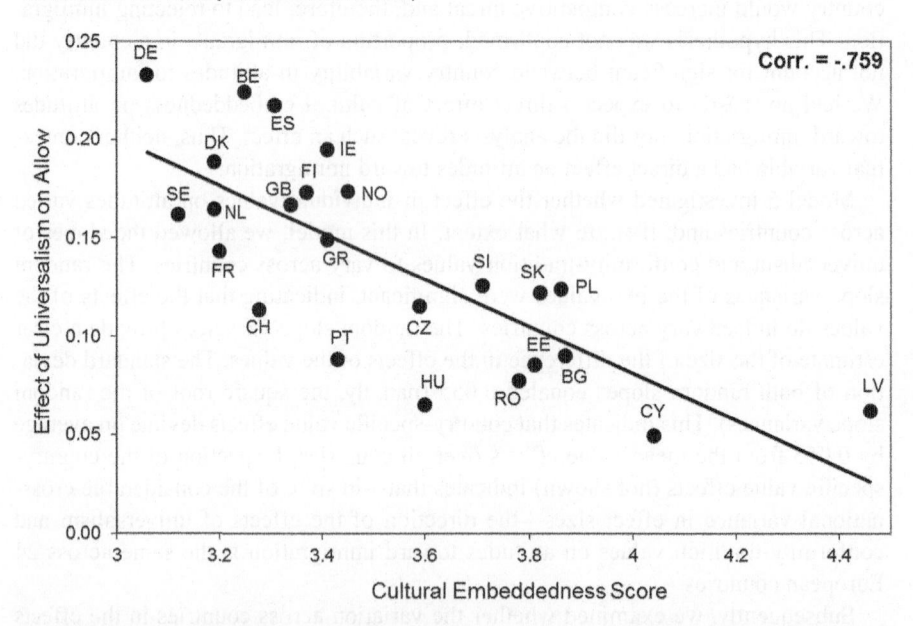

Fig. 2 Variation across countries in the effects of universalism values on attitudes toward immigration as a function of the level of cultural embeddedness in the country. (Source: ESS 2008–2009, own calculations. For country abbreviations see text)

(Model 6b), and conformity-tradition X percentage non-EU immigrants in the country (Model 6c). Additionally, Figs. 1, 2, and 3 visualize how variation in the effects

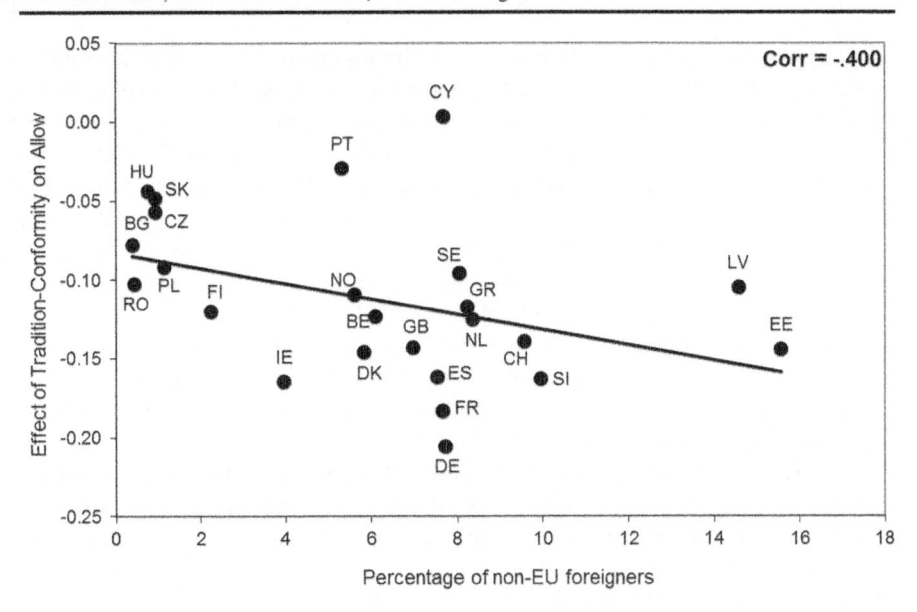

Fig. 3 Variation across countries in the effects of conformity-tradition values on attitudes toward immigration as a function of the percentage of non-EU population in the country. (Source: ESS 2008–2009, own calculations. For country abbreviations see text)

of the basic individual values is related to the contextual variables. The cross-level interaction terms estimate the size of these relationships.

Models 6a and 6b indicate that the interaction terms of cultural embeddedness were significant with both conformity-tradition values and with universalism values. Thus, the level of cultural embeddedness in a country moderated the effects of universalism and conservation on attitudes toward immigration. In less culturally embedded societies, values had stronger effects on attitudes. The negative coefficient for the interaction between cultural embeddedness and universalism values indicates that the positive main effect of universalism values on attitudes toward immigration was weaker in countries high on embeddedness and stronger in countries low on embeddedness. The positive coefficient for the interaction between cultural embeddedness and conformity-tradition values indicates that the negative main effect of these values on attitudes toward immigration was weaker in countries high on embeddedness and stronger in countries low on embeddedness. In sum, in countries high in cultural embeddedness, individual values had a weaker effect on attitudes toward immigration. Cultural embeddedness can explain 25 % of the variation in the effect of conformity-tradition and no less than 65 % of the variation in the effect of universalism. These findings fit the theoretical argument that individual values are more likely to be activated and to guide attitudes in less culturally embedded societies, that is, societies whose culture encourages pursuing one's own goals and expressing one's unique preferences.

Model 6c reveals a significant coefficient for the interaction term between the percentage of non-EU foreigners in a country and conformity-tradition values. The negative coefficient of this interaction indicates that the negative main effect of conformity-tradition values on attitudes toward immigration was stronger in countries where the proportion of the immigrant population is higher, that is, people high in conformity-tradition values reject immigration more strongly in countries with larger immigrant populations, confirming our fifth hypothesis. This fits the theoretical argument that a larger proportion of immigrants in a country increases the potential for societal change, intensifying the threat experienced by people for whom it is especially important to preserve convention, social norms, and customs. Consequently, these people reject immigration even more strongly in countries with large proportions of immigrants. Sixteen percent of the variability in the effect of conformity-tradition on attitudes toward immigration was explained by this cross-level interaction.

Model 7, finally, includes all three cross-level interactions simultaneously. The finding that the results are virtually identical to those of Models 6a–6c essentially corroborates the robustness of the results.

The full set of findings reveals that universalism and conformity-tradition values exert strong effects on attitudes toward immigrants in many different countries. Moreover, the strength of these effects varies significantly across countries. This variation depends to a substantial extent on the level of cultural embeddedness and the proportion of non-EU immigrants in each country.

5 Summary and conclusions

European countries have faced a constant increase of immigration in recent decades, accompanied by a rapid rise in and/or a high level of anti-foreigner sentiment. In many European countries the popularity of anti-immigrant politicians or parties has risen and public opinion has shifted to a less welcoming position. This study built upon previous studies that have shown the important role of basic human values as determinants of negative attitudes to immigrants. We hypothesized that more positive attitudes toward immigration would be found among individuals who give higher priority to universalism values, and contrastingly, more negative attitudes would be found among individuals who give higher priority to conformity-tradition values. The present study sought to explain variation across countries in these effects of values on attitudes. We identified two contextual variables likely to explain this variation, cultural embeddedness and proportion of immigrants in the population. We expected cultural embeddedness to play an important role in moderating these effects across countries.

We hypothesized that the effects of the two basic individual values are weaker in societies whose culture is higher on embeddedness (vs. autonomy). The rationale behind this cross-level interaction is that in more embedded societies, people are socialized and encouraged to maintain group solidarity and to find meaning in life through identifying with and pursuing the goals of the groups of which they are members. In less embedded societies they are socialized and encouraged to cultivate their own unique preferences and ideas and to pursue their own personal goals. Thus, personal values are more likely to be salient, readily activated, and hence to influence attitudes more in less embedded societies. We further hypothesized that the negative effect of conformity-tradition values on attitudes toward immigration is stronger in countries with a higher percentage of immigrants. Immigrants potentially threaten the maintenance of accepted customs, traditions, and norms, and the larger the proportion of immigrants the greater the threat to the status quo. This threat directly challenges the goals of conformity-tradition values and is, therefore, likely to activate them as sources of influence on attitudes.

To test our hypotheses, we utilized the data of 24 European countries from the fourth round of the European Social Survey (2008–2009). We analyzed the data with multilevel models because we wished to examine effects at both the individual and country level and to test cross-level interactions. Because constructs are not comparable across countries unless their measurement is equivalent, we used multigroup confirmatory factor analysis to establish the necessary metric and partial scalar equivalence of the value and attitude constructs. This permitted meaningful interpretation of the multilevel analysis.

The analyses largely supported the hypotheses. Previous findings of significant effects of universalism, conformity, and tradition values on attitudes toward immigration were replicated. Universalism values predicted more positive attitudes and conformity-tradition values predicted more negative attitudes. These effects were robust in the sense that they were significantly positive (for universalism) and negative (for conformity-tradition) in virtually all countries. Nonetheless, the strength of these value effects varied across countries. The hypothesized effects of the two country-level contextual variables on the strength of value effects were supported by the data. In countries with less embedded cultures, both values had stronger effects than in countries with more embedded cultures. Moreover, in countries with higher proportions of non-EU immigrants, the effect on attitudes of conformity-tradition values was stronger. The proportion of non-EU immigrants in a country had no direct effect on attitudes toward immigration, replicating previous studies (e.g., Semyonov et al. 2004; Strabac and Listhaug 2008).

The findings demonstrated that individuals' values play an important role in the explanation of attitudes toward immigration even after controlling their sociodemographic characteristics. Indeed, underlining the significance of values, their effects were stronger than the effects of the sociodemographic characteristics in standardized terms. Thus, when designing policies to increase public support for immigration, values within the population should be taken into account. Values are largely shaped and crystallized during adolescence and remain relatively stable thereafter, barring major traumas or therapy (Hitlin and Piliavin 2004; Inglehart 1997). This suggests that policies should be aimed at young people in order to affect the impact of values on attitudes to immigration.

The findings for cultural embeddedness demonstrate that this cultural dimension does not affect attitudes directly. However, its importance and that of the proportion of immigrants in the society may primarily be through increasing or decreasing the likelihood that the values relevant to attitudes will be activated. Indeed, individuals' personal values are more likely to be salient, to be activated rather than suppressed, and to influence their attitudes and behavior in societies with less embedded cultures. Our findings suggest that the individual level effects of values are highly robust, yet they are nonetheless moderated.

This is study is not without limitations. In particular, our conclusions regarding the cross-level interaction might be challenged by the fact that this dimension of national culture correlates substantively with other contextual variables, such as a lower GDP, a lower human development index (HDI), poorer education on average, and having a communist past. Such factors may have reduced the quality of responses to the values questionnaire in high embedded countries and as a result could account for the moderation. Unfortunately, the small sample size at the country level does not allow us to control for these factors and to rule out the possibility that the cross-level interaction is spurious.

Our findings suggest that variability across countries in attitudes toward immigration may be accounted for to a large extent by variability in individual values combined with the level of cultural embeddedness and size of the immigrant population in the country. However, to understand shifts in such attitudes over time, we may need other explanations. Values tend to display high stability over time and do not offer a convincing mechanism for studying longitudinal change in anti-immigrant sentiments. Studies suggest instead that worsening economic conditions (Semyonov et al. 2006, 2008), immigration policies (Schlüter et al. 2013) or change in media coverage (Schlüter and Davidov 2011) may offer, at least in part, explanations for such longitudinal variation in negative attitudes toward immigration.

Given the continuing increase of immigration around the world and the persistence and growth of negative attitudes toward immigration, it is critical to understand the sources of these attitudes. Promoting positive attitudes toward immigration may be beneficial both for immigrants and for their receiving societies. In the long run, immigration has generally strengthened societies economically (Borjas 1995; Dustmann et al. 2010), but opposition from members of the host society undermines social cohesion. In the present study we have (1) identified two relevant values that could be targets of socialization, (2) suggested mechanisms through which these values influence attitudes, and (3) investigated the circumstances in which these mechanisms operate more strongly. Theorizing that identifies other relevant variables and that investigates possible cross-national variation in their effects on attitudes toward immigration is needed. Equally important, it is necessary to deal with the methodological issue of equivalence of measurement when studying these new variables. By ensuring this critical prerequisite, we were able to study the effects of values on a key attitude across countries and to draw reliable conclusions.

Acknowledgments The authors would like to thank Lisa Trierweiler for the English proof of the manuscript. The work of the first author was supported by the Scientific Exchange Programme—SCIEX (Switzerland) and the URPP program, Social Networks, University of Zurich. The work of the third and fourth authors on this paper was supported by the Higher School of Economics (HSE), Moscow, Basic Research Program (International Laboratory of Socio-Cultural Research).

References

Beckers, Tilo, Pascal Siegers, and Anabel Kuntz. 2012. Congruence and performance of value concepts in social research. *Survey Research Methods* 6:13–24.
Billiet, Jaak. 2003. Cross-cultural equivalence with structural equation modeling. In *Cross-cultural survey methods*, ed. Janet Harkness, Frons Van de Vijver, and Peter Mohler, 247–264. Hoboken: Wiley.

Bollen, Kenneth A. 1989. *Structural equations with latent variables*. New York: Wiley.
Borjas, George J. 1995. The economic benefits from immigration. *Journal of Economic Perspectives* 9:3–22.
Brown, Timothy, A. 2006. *Confirmatory factor analysis for applied research*. New York: The Guilford Press.
Coenders, Marcel. 2001. Nationalistic attitudes and ethnic exclusionism in a comparative perspective: An empirical study of attitudes toward the country and ethnic immigrants in 22 countries. Nijmegen: ICS dissertation.
Coenders, Marcel, Merove Gijsberts, and Peer Scheepers. 2004. Resistance to the presence of immigrants and refugees in 22 countries. In *Nationalism and exclusion of migrants: cross-national comparisons*, ed. Merove Gijsberts, Louk Hagendoorn, and Peer Scheepers, 97–120. Aldershot: Ashgate.
Datler, Georg, Wolfgang Jagodzinski, and Peter Schmidt. 2012. Two theories on the test bench: Internal and external validity of the theories of Ronald Inglehart and Shalom Schwartz. *Social Science Research* 42:906–925. doi: http://dx.doi.org/10.1016/j.ssresearch (Accessed: 2012.12.09).
Davidov, Eldad. 2008. A cross-country and cross-time comparison of the human values measurements with the second round of the European Social Survey. *Survey Research Methods* 2:33–46.
Davidov, Eldad. 2010. Testing for comparability of human values across countries and time with the third round of the European Social Survey. *International Journal of Comparative Sociology* 51:171–191.
Davidov, Eldad, and Bart Meuleman. 2012. Explaining attitudes towards immigration policies in European countries: The role of human values. *Journal of Ethnic & Migration Studies* 38:757–775.
Davidov, Eldad, Bart Meuleman, Jaak Billiet, and Peter Schmidt. 2008a. Values and support for immigration. A cross-country comparison. *European Sociological Review* 24:583–599.
Davidov, Eldad, Peter Schmidt, and Shalom Schwartz. 2008b. Bringing values back. *Public Opinion Quarterly* 72:420–445.
Dustmann, Christian, Tommaso Frattini, and Caroline Halls. 2010. Assessing the fiscal costs and benefits of a8 migration to the UK. *Fiscal Studies* 31:1–41.
Gorodzeisky, Anastasia. 2011. Who are the Europeans that Europeans prefer? Economic conditions and exclusionary views toward European immigrants. *International Journal of Comparative Sociology* 52:100–113.
Hitlin, Steven, and Jane Allyn Piliavin. 2004. Values: Reviving a dormant concept. *Annual Review of Sociology* 30:359–393.
Hofmann, David. A., and Mark B Gavin. 1998. Centering decisions in hierarchical linear models: Implications for research in organizations. *Journal of Management* 24:623–641.
Hofstede, Geert. 2001. *Cultures consequences: Comparing values, behaviours, institutions and organizations across nations*. 2nd ed. Thousand Oaks: Sage.
Hooghe, Marc, Ann Trappers, Bart Meuleman, and Tim Reeskens. 2008. Migration to European countries: A structural explanation of patterns, 1980–2004. *International Migration Review* 42:476–504.
Hox, Joop J. 2010. *Multilevel analysis. Techniques and applications*. New York: Routledge.
Inglehart, Ronald. 1997. *Modernization and postmodernization: Cultural, economic and political change in 43 societies*. Princeton: Princeton University Press.
Inglehart, Ronald, and Wayne E. Baker. 2000. Modernization, cultural change, and the persistence of traditional values. *American Sociological Review* 65:19–51.
Jöreskog, Karl G. 1971. Simultaneous factor analysis in several populations. *Psychometrika* 36:408–426.
Jowell, Roger, Caroline Roberts, Rory Fitzgerald, and Eva Gillian. 2007. *Measuring attitudes cross-nationally: Lessons from the European Social Survey*. Los Angeles: Sage.
Kim, Eun Sook, Oi-man Kwok, and Myeongsun Yoon. 2012. Testing factorial invariance in multilevel data: A Monte-Carlo study. *Structural Equation Modeling* 19:250–267.
Kunovich, Robert M. 2004. Social structural position and prejudice: An exploration of cross-national differences in regression slopes. *Social Science Research* 33:20–44.
Lesthaeghe, Ron, and Guy Moors. 2000. *Life course transitions and value orientations: Selection and adaption*. Presented at Contact forum: Values orientations and life cycle decisions, results from longitudinal studies, Brussels.
Lubbers, Marcel, Mérove Gijsberts, and Peer Scheepers. 2002. Extreme right-wing voting in Western Europe. *European Journal of Political Research* 41:345–378.
Meuleman, Bart, Eldad Davidov, and Jaak Billiet. 2009. Changing attitudes toward immigration in Europe, 2002–2007: A dynamic group conflict theory approach. *Social Science Research* 38:352–365.

Pichler, Florian. 2010. Foundations of anti-immigrant sentiment: The variable nature of perceived group threat across changing European societies, 2002–2006. *International Journal of Comparative Sociology* 51:1–25.

Quillian, Lincoln. 1995. Prejudice as a response to perceived group threat: Population composition and anti-immigrant and racial prejudice in Europe. *American Sociological Review* 60:586–611.

Quillian, Lincoln. 1996. Group threat and regional changes in attitudes toward African Americans. *American Journal of Sociology* 102:816–860.

Raijman, Rebeca, Moshe Semyonov, and Peter Schmidt. 2003. Do foreigners deserve rights? Determinants of public views towards foreigners in Germany and Israel. *European Sociological Review* 19:379–392.

Raijman, Rebeca, Eldad Davidov, Peter Schmidt, and Oshrat Hochman. 2008. What does a nation owe non-citizens? National attachments, perception of threat and attitudes to granting citizenship rights in a comparative perspective. *International Journal of Comparative Sociology* 49:195–220.

Rokeach, Milton. 1968. The role of values in public opinion research. *Public Opinion Quarterly* 32:547–559.

Rubin, Donald B. 1996. Multiple imputation after 18+ years (with discussion). *Journal of the American Statistical Association* 91:473–489.

Sagiv, Lilach, and Shalom S. Schwartz. 1995. Value priorities and readiness for out-group social contact. *Journal of Personality and Social Psychology* 69:437–448.

Schafer, Joseph L. 1997. Analysis of incomplete multivariate data. London: Chapman & Hall.

Scheepers, Peer, Mérove Gijsberts, and Marcel Coenders. 2002. Ethnic exclusionism in European countries. Public opposition to grant civil rights to legal migrants as a response to perceived ethnic threat. *European Sociological Review* 18:1–18.

Schlüter, Elmar, Peter Schmidt, and Ulrich Wagner. 2008. Disentangling the causal relations of perceived group threat and outgroup derogation: Cross-national evidence from German and Russian panel surveys. *European Sociological Review* 24:567–581.

Schlüter, Elmar, and Eldad Davidov. 2013. Contextual sources of perceived group threat: Negative immigration-related news reports, immigrant group size and their interaction, Spain 1996–2007. *European Sociological Review* 29:179–191.

Schlüter, Elmar, Bart Meuleman, and Eldad Davidov. 2013. Immigrant integration policies and perceived group threat: A multilevel study of 27 western and eastern European countries. *Social Science Research* 42:670–682.

Schwartz, Shalom H. 1992. Universals in the content and structure of values: Theory and empirical tests in 20 countries. In *Advances in experimental social psychology*, vol. 25, ed. Mark Zanna, 1–65. New York: Academic Press.

Schwartz, Shalom H. 1994. Are there universal aspects in the content and structure of values? *Journal of Social Issues* 50: 19–45.

Schwartz, Shalom H. 2006a. Les valeurs de base de la personne: Théorie, mesures et applications. *Revue Française de Sociologie* 47:249–288.

Schwartz, Shalom H. 2006b. A theory of cultural value orientations: Explication and applications. *Comparative Sociology* 5:137–182.

Schwartz, Shalom H. 2007. Value orientations: Measurement, antecedents and consequences across nations. In *Measuring attitudes cross-nationally. Lessons from the European Social Survey*, ed. Roger Jowell, Caroline Roberts, Rory Fitzgerald, and Gilian Eva, 169–203. London: Sage.

Semyonov, Moshe, and Anya Glikman. 2009. Ethnic residential segregation, social contacts and anti-minority attitudes in European societies. *European Sociological Review* 25:709–721.

Semyonov, Moshe, Rebeca Raijman, and Anastasia Gorodzeisky. 2006. The rise of anti-foreigner sentiment in European societies, 1988–2000. *American Sociological Review* 71:426–449.

Semyonov, Moshe, Rebeca Raijman, and Anastasia Gorodzeisky. 2008. Foreigners' impact on European societies: Public views and perceptions in a cross-national comparative perspective. *International Journal of Comparative Sociology* 49:5–29.

Semyonov, Moshe, Rebeca Raijman, Anat Yom-Tov, and Peter Schmidt. 2004. Population size, perceived threat, and exclusion: A multiple-indicators analysis of attitudes toward foreigners in Germany. *Social Science Research* 33:681–701.

Snijders, Tom A. B., and Roel J. Bosker. 1994. *Multilevel analysis: An introduction to basic and advanced multilevel modeling*. London: Sage.

Stephan, Walter G., C. Lausanne Renfro, Victoria M. Esses, Cookie White Stephan, and Tim Martin. 2005. The effects of feeling threatened on attitudes toward immigrants. *International Journal of Intercultural Relations* 29:1–19.

Strabac, Zan, and Ola Listhaug. 2008. Anti-Muslim prejudice in Europe: A multilevel analysis of survey data from 30 countries. *Social Science Research* 37:268–286.

Weldon, Steven A. 2006. The institutional context of tolerance for ethnic minorities: A comparative, multilevel analysis of Western Europe. *American Journal of Political Science* 50:331–349.

Eldad Davidov, 1971, Professor of Sociology at the University of Zurich, Switzerland. His research interests are applications of structural equation modeling to survey data, especially in cross-cultural and longitudinal research. Applications include human values, national identity, and attitudes toward immigrants and other minorities. Recent publications on these topics appeared in Social Science Research, Public Opinion Quarterly, Sociological Methods and Research, Survey Research Methods, International Journal of Comparative Sociology, International Journal of Public Opinion Research, European Sociological Review, and Political Analysis.

Bart Meulemann, 1965, Assistant Professor at the Centre for Sociological Research, University of Leuven (Belgium), where he teaches research methodology. His main research interests involve cross-cultural comparisons of attitude and value patterns, such as welfare attitudes, ethnocentrism, religiosity, and basic human values. In his work he mainly applies multilevel and structural equation models. Recent publications appeared in the Journal of Cross-Cultural Psychology, Journal of European Social Policy, Social Science Research, and International Journal of Social Welfare.

Shalom H. Schwartz, 1940, the Sznajderman Professor Emeritus of Psychology at the Hebrew University of Jerusalem, Israel and Co-chair of the Laboratory for Socio-Cultural Research at the State Research University Higher School of Economics (HSE) in Moscow (Russia). His recent work concerns two topics: the nature and sources of basic human values and their role as bases of attitudes and behavior, and the nature and sources of cultural value orientations as expressions of and influences on the institutional structures, policies, and prevailing norms and practices in different societies. He has published numerous papers on both topics.

Peter Schmidt, 1942, Professor Emeritus of Social Research Methods at the University of Giessen (Germany) and Co-chair of the Laboratory for Socio-Cultural Research at the State Research University Higher School of Economics (HSE) in Moscow (Russia). His research interests are the foundations and applications of structural equation models, analysis of panel data, and cross-cultural methodology. Applications include national identity, immigration, values, and environmental behavior. Recent publications appeared in Public Opinion Quarterly, International Journal of Public Opinion Research, International Journal of Comparative Sociology, Methodology, Psychological Methods, Journal of Social Issues, European Sociological Review, and Social Science Research.

Kontexteffekte von Wohngebieten

Jürgen Friedrichs

© Springer Fachmedien Wiesbaden 2014

Zusammenfassung Der Beitrag richtet sich darauf, Ergebnisse der Forschungen über die Effekte von Wohngebieten (neighbourhood effects) systematisch darzustellen. Im ersten Teil werden methodologische Probleme erörtert, z. B. die Wahl der räumlichen Einheit, die Zahl der Ebenen und sozialen Mechanismen. Weil die bisherigen Aufzählungen von Nachbarschaftseffekten unbefriedigend sind, schlage ich eine methodologische Differenzierung von Gebietsmerkmalen und Mechanismen vor. Anschließend werden Ergebnisse empirischer Studien sowohl für die Typen von Eigenschaften als auch die sozialen Mechanismen dargestellt. Am Beispiel von Studien zu den Gebietseffekten auf die Gesundheit der Bewohner werden nochmals die komplexen Zusammenhänge erörtert. In einem folgenden Kapitel werden Forschungsprobleme behandelt, darunter die Frage nach den Wirkungen unterschiedlicher Kontexte (Wohngebiete) auf Personen gleicher Merkmale. Das abschließende Kapitel enthält eine knappe Zusammenfassung und Folgerungen für weitere Forschungen.

Schlüsselwörter Wohngebiete · Nachbarschaftseffekte · Abweichendes Verhalten · Armut · Gesundheit

Neighbourhood effects

Abstract The article reviews findings on neighbourhood effects. First, methodological problems, such as the choice of spatial units, selection bias and social mechanisms are discussed. To overcome the problem of varying lists of neighbour-

---

J. Friedrichs (✉)
Institut für Soziologie und Sozialpsychologie, Universität zu Köln,
Greinstr. 2, 50939 Köln, Deutschland
E-Mail: friedrichs@wiso.uni-koeln.de

hood effects, I suggest a methodological distinction between characteristics of the neighbourhood and social mechanisms. In the following section, these typologies are applied to analyse findings from empirical studies on topics such as the impact of the physical environment, perceived social capital and income. The complex relationship between neighbourhood characteristics and individual outcomes is then examined using studies on the impact on physical and mental health.

Several research problems, such as the impact of different contexts on individuals of the same status are outlined in the following section. In the final chapter major findings are resumed and suggestions for further research are made.

Keywords Neighbourhood · Neighbourhood effect · Poverty · Deviant behavior · Disorder · Health

1 Einleitung

Die Analyse von Kontexten, hier: Effekten des Wohngebietes (neighbourhood effects), ist vermutlich das umfangreichste Gebiet der Kontextforschung. Diese erstaunliche Entwicklung geht darauf zurück, dass mit den Publikationen der Chicagoer Schule, vor allem dem Band von Shaw und McKay (1942), eine Tradition begründet wurde, in der nach den Wirkungen von Wohngebieten gefragt wurde. Hinzu kommt eine sehr breite und ebenfalls zunehmende Forschung über Nachbarschaftseffekte auf die Gesundheit.

Es ist schwierig zu entscheiden, wann zuerst die Frage nach den Kontexteffekten von Wohngebieten gestellt wurde. Sehr wahrscheinlich ist dies im Zusammenhang mit der Analyse von Armutsgebieten geschehen. Dann ist schon die neunbändige Arbeit „Life and Labour of People in London" von Charles Booth (1970), die 1902–1904 erschien, das erste umfangreiche Zeugnis von den entwürdigenden Lebensbedingungen in Armutsgebieten. Implizit unterstellt Booth einen Kontexteffekt neben den individuellen Effekten der Armut und der Eigenschaften der Bewohner (vgl. ausführlich Friedrichs 2013). Aber auch Studien der Chicagoer Schule wie „The Gold Coast and the Slum" (Zorbaugh 1929) oder „Juvenile Delinquency and Urban Areas" (Shaw und McKay 1942) haben die nachfolgende Forschung geprägt. Da die Kriminalitätsraten in den 75 Teilgebieten von Chicago sehr unterschiedlich waren, stellte sich für Shaw und McKay die Frage nach den Ursachen als auch nach den Wirkungen sozialer Desorganisation. Soziale Desorganisation war demnach ein Kontextmerkmal. Die neuere Diskussion hat wiederum mehrere Quellen. Zum einen ist es die bahnbrechende Studie von Wilson „The Truly Disadvantaged" (1987), der, wiederum am Beispiel von Chicago, zahlreiche negative Effekte von armen Nachbarschaften auf deren Bewohner darstellt. Erneut geht es auch hier nicht um Wohngebiete der Ober- oder Mittelschicht, sondern solche mit einem hohen Anteil von Armen, Alleinerziehenden, ethnischen Minderheiten. Der reale Hintergrund dieser Forschung war die zunehmende Armut – vor allem der Schwarzen – und deren räumliche Konzentration in wenigen Wohngebieten, dort aber mit Armutsquoten, die teilweise über 40 % lagen. Sein Buch löste eine wahre Welle von Folgestudien aus (vgl. den Überblick bei Small und Newman 2001), bis zum Jahr 2010 waren es rd. 1740 einschlägige Artikel (van Ham et al. 2012a, S. 3). Diese Frage nach den Auswirkungen von sozialer Desorganisation und Armut beschäftigt die

Stadtforschung bis heute; die neueste Publikation hierzu erneut am Beispiel Chicagos, ist die umfangreiche Studie von Sampson (2012) „Great American City".

Zu den einflussreicheren Arbeiten gehörten auch die Beiträge in dem Sammelband „Inner City Poverty" (Jencks und Mayer 1990). Insbesondere ihr eigener Beitrag gibt einen sehr guten Überblick über den (damaligen) Stand der Forschung. Es ist kaum verwunderlich, dass aufgrund dieser nordamerikanischen Tradition die meisten Beiträge zu Nachbarschaftseffekten aus den USA kamen. Seit etwa 2005 hat sich die Forschung internationalisiert, wie die Beiträge in Housing Studies in den Jahren 2005 und 2009 (Friedrichs et al. 2005; Blasius et al. 2009) und die drei Bände von van Ham et al. (2012b, 2013, 2014) dokumentieren.

Im Verlauf dieser Publikationen wurde erkennbar, dass die bislang in der Forschung getrennt verlaufenden Stränge von Nachbarschaftseffekten und sozialer Mischung methodologisch ein gleiches Problem behandeln (e. g. Ostendorf et al. 2001). In beiden wird ein Kontexteffekt des Aggregats, hier: des Wohngebiets, auf die Bewohner behauptet. Im Falle von Armutsgebieten ist dieser Effekt negativ, im Falle der erstrebten sozialen Mischung erhofft positiv.

Schließlich kam eine dritte Forschungsrichtung hinzu: diejenige zur Gentrification. Diese Entwicklung war folgerichtig, denn die politischen Programme zur Aufwertung von benachteiligten Wohngebieten, z. B. in Deutschland „Soziale Stadt", das französische „Gesetz zur Stadterneuerung und Solidarität" oder die „Right to Buy"- Programme in Großbritannien setzen durchgängig auf einen Zuzug der Mittelschicht, um die soziale Mischung zu erhöhen und für die bisherigen Bewohner positive Verhaltensvorbilder zu haben. Die wichtigste Maßnahme hierzu ist, Eigentumswohnungen und Eigenheime anzubieten. Diese Maßnahmen wiederum führten (je nach Sichtweise) zu der Frage oder Hypothese oder dem Vorwurf, Eigentum solle ein Gebiet aufwerten, hierdurch Haushalte der Mittelschicht anziehen– was zu einer „heimlichen Gentrification" (gentrification by stealth) führe, so der Untertitel des Bandes von Bridge et al. (2012). Wir haben es also seit den 2010er-Jahren mit einem wissenschaftlich erstaunlichen und zugleich produktivem Sachverhalt zu tun: die Theorie der Nachbarschaftseffekte erweitert ihren Objektbereich auf soziale Mischung und Gentrification von Wohngebieten.

Ich stelle Probleme und Ergebnisse der Nachbarschaftseffekte in mehreren Schritten dar. Zuerst behandle ich einige grundsätzliche, entwickle sodann in einer methodologischen Analyse eine neue Typologie von Nachbarschaftseffekten. Dieser doppelten Typologie folgend, berichte ich ausgewählte Ergebnisse für Gebietseffekte und soziale Mechanismen. In einem weiteren Schritt stelle ich Ergebnisse multipler Mechanismen am Beispiel der Forschungen zu dem Effekt des Wohngebiets auf die physische und mentale Gesundheit dar. In dem anschließenden Teil weise ich auf Forschungsdefizite hin. Der letzte Abschnitt enthält eine knappe Zusammenfassung der wichtigsten Ergebnisse der Analyse und einige Vorschläge für die weitere Forschung.

2 Methodologische Probleme

Bei der Analyse von Kontexteffekten von Wohngebieten stellen sich zahlreiche Probleme (vgl. Galster 2003, 2008):

1. Die Abgrenzung von Nachbarschaften
2. Die Art der Effekte
3. Individual- vs. Meso- vs. Makroeffekte
4. Gruppenspezifische Effekte und „exposure"
5. Schwellenwerte
6. Selektivität der Bewohnerschaft (selection bias).

2.1 Die Abgrenzung von Nachbarschaften

Wenn wir von „neigbourhood", „Wohngebiet", „Viertel" oder „Quartier" sprechen, dann sind stets räumliche Einheiten gemeint. Mithin muss ein Kontextmerkmal sich auf diese räumliche Einheit beziehen. Zwangsläufig ist es dann erforderlich, eine räumliche Einheit zu wählen, für die die entsprechenden Daten vorliegen, sofern man keine Primärerhebung durchführen will. (Aber auch bei einer Primärerhebung wird man meist zusätzliche statistische Daten einbeziehen wollen.) Die räumliche Einheit ist in den meisten nordamerikanischen Studien der census tract. In deutschen Studien wird man, je nach Verwaltungsbezeichnung in einer Stadt, „Viertel", „Ortsteile" oder als größere Einheiten „Stadtteile", wählen. Im Falle Kölns wären es 323 Viertel oder 86 (vormals 85) Stadtteile; im Falle Hamburgs 180 Ortsteile und 104 Stadtteile.

Es gibt aber noch andere Verfahren, um die räumliche Einheit „Nachbarschaft" zu bestimmen. Das eine ist, Baublöcke zu größeren räumlichen Einheiten zusammenzufassen. Dazu müssen die erforderlichen Daten auf der Ebene der Baublöcke vorliegen. Sodann bedarf es einer Regel, nach der Baublöcke zusammengefasst werden, z. B. jeweils angrenzende Blöcke ähnlicher Struktur. Auf diese Weise kann man zu räumlich gleich großen Einheiten gelangen. Ein Beispiel sind Studien mit schwedischen Daten: Hier sind SAMS die Einheiten (vgl. Galster 2008). Um Gebietsmerkmale zu erheben, eignet sich ein Verfahren bei dem in einzelnen census tracts Merkmale aller Gebäude, die zur Straße stehen („face blocks"), aufzunehmen (Raudenbush und Sampson 1999). Ein weiteres Verfahren besteht darin, die Bewohner anhand einer Karte ihres Wohngebiets „ihre" Nachbarschaft abgrenzen zu lassen. Wie eine entsprechende Studie von Reuber (1993) zeigt, führt das leider zu sehr unterschiedlichen Abgrenzungen, sodass sich hieraus keine klare Abgrenzung der Nachbarschaft aggregieren lässt.

2.2 Art der Effekte

In den Studien zu Nachbarschaftseffekten ist keinem Problem mehr Aufmerksamkeit gewidmet worden als dem der Effekte oder sozialen Mechanismen. Die erste Darstellung und Modellierung solcher Konntexteffekte stammt von Erbring und Young (1979), spätere u. a. von Dietz (2002), Durlauf (2004), Friedrichs (1998), Galster (2003, 2007, 2012), Jencks und Mayer (1990), Small und Feldman (2012). Es werden folgende Mechanismen angeführt:

1. Sozialisation
2. Ansteckung (contagion)
3. Kollektive Sozialisation

4. Rollenmodelle
5. Soziale Netzwerke
6. Soziales Kapital, soziale Kohäsion, soziale Kontrolle
7. Wettbewerb um knappe Ressourcen im Gebiet
8. Relative Deprivation der weniger erfolgreichen gegenüber den eher erfolgreichen Bewohner/innen
9. Gewalt ausgesetzt zu sein, Kriminalitätsfurcht
10. Physische Merkmale, z. B. Verwahrlosung („disorder"), Müll, Graffiti
11. Umweltqualität, z. B. Luftbelastung
12. Stigmatisierung des Gebiets
13. Ressourcen im Gebiet: (unzureichende) öffentliche Einrichtungen, z. B. Kindertagesstätten, Schulen, Krankenhäuser; (schlechte) Verkehrsverbindungen.

Betrachtet man diese Liste genauer, so fällt auf, dass sie in doppelter Hinsicht methodologisch unbefriedigend ist, weil Eigenschaften des Wohngebietes mit Mechanismen der Wirkung vermischt werden. So werden einerseits Mechanismen wie „Ansteckung" oder „Stigmatisierung" angeführt, aber es fehlt der Hinweis auf die Eigenschaften, z. B. Image oder Ruf des Wohngebiets. Andererseits werden Eigenschaften angeführt wie z. B. Kriminalitätsbelastung, aber es fehlt der Mechanismus.

Trennt man Eigenschaften von Mechanismen, so lassen sich die Kontexteffekte präziser darstellen (Tab. 1). Um die Merkmale näher zu bestimmen, ziehe ich die Klassifikation von Merkmalen nach Aggregatebenen heran, die Lazarsfeld und Menzel (1961) vorgeschlagen haben. Sie unterscheiden u. a. zwischen absoluten Merkmalen einer Einheit (Individuum, Gruppe) wie Geschlecht oder Zahl der Gruppenmitglieder und Merkmalen, die auf Verteilungen beruhen. Zu den letzteren gehören auf der Ebene der Individuen z. B. vergleichende (z. B. Stellung einer Person in einer Hierarchie) und auf der Ebene der Gruppe analytische (z. B. Häufigkeitsmaße, Mittelwerte). In der Tabelle sind nur Beispiele aufgeführt; im Folgenden stelle ich anhand von empirischen Studien die Beziehungen von Eigenschaften, Folgen und Mechanismen eingehender dar.

Typ1: Am häufigsten werden in Studien über Nachbarschaftseffekte Anteilswerte verwendet. Dabei handelt es sich um analytische Merkmale; sie sind durch mathematische Operationen der Individualmerkmale entstanden. In den meisten Studien wird dieser Typ von Merkmalen verwendet, so z. B. „Anteil Alleinerziehender", „Anteil Ausländer/ Migranten" oder als Indikator der Armut des Wohngebiets „Anteil Sozial-

Tab. 1 Eine Explikation von Kontexteffekten

Typ	Eigenschaften des Gebiets	Folgen (abh. Variablen)	Mechanismen
Typ 1	Anteil Armer, Anteil Wohlhabender	Fehlende Rollenvorbilder	Sozialisation, Ansteckung
Typ 2	Collective efficacy, soziales Kapital	Fortzüge, Kriminalität	Kollektive Sozialisation
Typ 3	4. Image, Ruf des Gebiets	Ablehnung bei Jobsuche	Diskriminierung
Typ 4	5. (Fehlende) Infrastruktur	z. B. weniger Freizeitaktivitäten	Reduktion, Kompensation oder Verzicht von/ auf Aktivitäten
Typ 5	Verwahrlosung	Depression, Übergewicht	Stress

hilfe-Empfänger". Sie beruhen meist auf amtlichen statistischen Daten. Als Beispiel wähle ich Studien zu den Effekten des Wohngebiets auf Einkommen und Arbeitslosigkeit der Bewohner.

In einer Reihe von Studien wurde der Einfluss des Einkommens im Wohngebiet auf die Einkommen der Bewohner untersucht (u. a. Galster et al. 2010; Ioannides und Loury 2004; Kleit 2001). McCulloch (2001) untersuchte mit den Daten der ersten acht Wellen der British Household Panel Study (4833 Männer und 5431 Frauen) den Effekt der Nachbarschaft (634 wards) auf verschiedene abhängige Variablen. In den benachteiligten Nachbarschaften war sowohl bei den Männern als auch bei den Frauen der Gesundheitszustand überdurchschnittlich schlecht; des Weiteren waren die Erwerbstätigkeit, die Einkommen als auch das Ausmaß der sozialen Unterstützung signifikant niedriger als in anderen Gebieten. Wurde zusätzlich der Wohnstatus berücksichtigt, so waren Mieter von Sozialwohnungen noch stärker benachteiligt als sie es ohnehin durch das schlechte Wohngebiet bereits waren; mithin stützen die Ergebnisse die These einer doppelten Benachteiligung. Bei Frauen, die in Sozialwohnungen lebten, trat die stärkere Benachteiligung jedoch in Nachbarschaften mit reicheren Bewohnern auf. McCulloch (2001, S. 681) erklärt dieses überraschende Ergebnis folgendermaßen: „The impact of a given level of deprivation is greater for an individual living in a generally more affluent district: perhaps because a sense of relative deprivation is more marked and has a more acute impact on the psychological state".

Galster et al. (2011) verwendeten Daten für rd. 124 000 Personen in 184 kleinräumigen Gebieten (SAMS) in Stockholm für die Jahre 1991 bis 2006. Sie fanden einen negativen Effekt des Anteils der Bewohner mit niedrigem Einkommen auf die Einkommen von erwerbstätigen männlichen Bewohnern; die Effekte traten bei Schwellenwerten der Anteile von 20 und 40 % Bewohner mit niedrigem Einkommen auf. Lebten die Personen jedoch länger als vier Jahre im Gebiet (= höhere exposure), betrugen die Schwellenwerte 10–20 % bzw. 30 %. In einer Studie mit dem gleichen Datensatz, $N = 90438$ Personen und die Periode 1995–2006, wurde ebenfalls ein negativer Effekt des Anteils niedriger, und ein noch höherer positiver des Anteils höherer Einkommen nachgewiesen (Hedman und Galster 2013). Ein weiterer wichtiger Befund der Studie bezieht sich auf das statistische Modell: Der Effekt der Einkommen im Wohngebiet wird unterschätzt, wenn man nur ein fixed-effects-Modell berechnet und steigt deutlich an, wenn die Autoren für unbeobachtete Variablen kontrollierten und ein Modell mit instrumenteller Variable und fixed-effects berechnen.

Es wurde ferner ein Zusammenhang von Arbeitslosigkeit im Wohngebiet und der Wahrscheinlichkeit, dass Bewohner arbeitslos bleiben, festgestellt.

Nonnenmacher (2009, 2013) geht von zwei Gebietsmerkmalen aus: Der Arbeitslosenquote und dem Anteil höherer Berufe, letzterer über die subjektive Wahrnehmung, wie viele Personen in leitender Tätigkeit die befragten Bewohner kennen, gemessen. Sie werden als Rollenvorbilder interpretiert. Ihre Stichprobe umfasst 1307 männliche Personen in 69 Stadtvierteln von Köln. Ihre Annahmen lauten: Die Arbeitslosenquote wirkt sich negativ auf den Anteil höherer Berufe aus, dieser Anteil beeinflusst deren Anteil im lokalen Netzwerk, diese die Normen zur Erwerbstätigkeit, und diese schließlich das Eintrittsrisiko zur Arbeitslosigkeit und deren Dauer. Empirisch zeigt sich der vermutete negative Effekt der Arbeitslosenquote auf die

Rollenvorbilder (mit einem Schwellenwert bei 25 %), je weniger zahlreich sie sind, desto geringer ist auch die individuelle Erwerbsnorm, ist sie hoch, vermindert sich das Risiko, arbeitslos zu werden.

Manley und van Ham (2012) verwendeten Daten der Scottish Longitudinal Study und berichten, dass die Wahrscheinlichkeit für Personen, die 1991 arbeitslos waren, im Jahre 2001 einen Job zu haben, sinkt, wenn der Anteil der Arbeitslosen zum früheren Zeitpunkt über 10 % lag. Der Effekt ist stärker für Männer als für Frauen: Frauen, die 1991 arbeitslos waren, hatten eine größere Chance als Männer 2001 erwerbstätig zu sein. Negative Effekte auf die Chance, einen Job zu haben, hat auch der Anteil der Sozialhilfeempfänger im Wohngebiet; diese treten verstärkt auf, wenn deren Anteil größer als 16 % ist (Musterd und Andersson 2005, 2006).

Die negativen Wirkungen der Arbeitslosenquote (auf der kleinräumigen Ebene von britischen wards) belegt die Untersuchung von Buck (2001): Bewohner in Gebieten hoher Arbeitslosigkeit haben signifikant weniger erwerbstätige Freunde, bleiben eher arbeitslos und schaffen es so nicht, sich aus der Armut zu befreien. Ein ähnliches Ergebnis berichten van der Klauw und van Ours (2003): Steigt die Arbeitslosenquote über 11 %, dann sinkt die Wahrscheinlichkeit, dass Bewohner nicht mehr von der Sozialhilfe leben müssen.

Diese negativen Effekte lassen sich auf die Einflüsse des Netzwerks der Bewohner zurückführen (Ioannides und Loury 2004) oder auf spezifische Normen, die eine geringere Bereitschaft, eine Arbeit (außerhalb des Gebiets) zu suchen, vermindern (Pinkster 2008, 2013; vgl. Kleit 2001). Schließlich kann auch die Diskriminierung eines Bewohners aufgrund des schlechten Images des Wohngebiets einen Einfluss haben. Welche der drei Erklärungen mit welchem Gewicht zutrifft, ist bislang nicht erforscht.

Zusammenfassend: Ohne Zweifel können fast alle Eigenschaften des Gebiets einen Einfluss auf alle oder einzelne Bewohnergruppen haben. Die Wirkung ist abhängig a) von der Stärke der Eigenschaft und b) dem Ausmaß, zu dem sie dem Merkmal ausgesetzt sind (exposure). Der Effekt selbst kann linear sein, dürfte aber nach vorliegenden Erkenntnissen eher Schwellenwerte aufweisen (vgl. Galster in diesem Band).

Typ 2: Prinzipiell zählen zum Typ 1 auch Merkmale wie das soziale Kapital, doch beruhen sie auf „subjektiven" Daten, meist Wahrnehmungen. Sie stellen eine Aggregation von Einstellungen einer Stichprobe von Bewohnern dar, die mit Skalen von Sampson et al. (vgl. Abschn. 3.5) wie „collective efficacy", „intergenerational closure" (beide Sampson et al.), „disorder" (Ross und Mirowsky 1999; Ross et al. 2001) gemessen wurden. Hierzu gehören auch die Eigenschaften wie „soziales Kapital", „bridging und bonding capital" (Gittel und Vidal 1998; Woolcock und Narayan 2000), die auf Angaben über die (ego-zentrierten) Netzwerke der befragten Bewohner beruhen. Es ist jedoch strittig, ob Merkmale des Typs 2 der Makroebene „Wohngebiet" zugeschrieben werden sollten oder nicht besser der Mesoebene. Letztere Interpretation legt das Modell von Sampson et al. nahe (siehe dazu Abschn. 4 weiter unten).

Dieser Sachverhalt kann auch am Beispiel der Beziehungen von Hausbesitzern und Mietern belegt werden. Hiscock (2001) untersuchte in einer schriftlichen Befragung in West-Schottland den Effekt der Mischung des Wohnstatus auf das soziale

Kapital von Wohngebieten. Das soziale Kapital wurde durch vier dichotome Indikatoren gemessen: ob man mit Nachbarn Gefälligkeiten tausche, ob man sich als Teil der Gemeinschaft fühle, ob man berufstätig sei, und ob das Ansehen des Wohngebiets ein Problem sei. Eine logistische Regression (unter Kontrolle von Alter, Geschlecht, Einkommen und Wohnstatus) erbrachte positive Effekte der Mischung auf Berufstätigkeit und Ansehen, wenn nur 29 % der Bewohner Sozialmieter waren, hingegen negative Effekte auf alle Indikatoren bis auf die Berufstätigkeit, wenn der Anteil bei 82 % lag (Hiscock 2001, S. 15). Somit ist ein nicht-linearer Effekt des Anteils der Sozialmieter auf das soziale Kapital zu vermuten. Des Weiteren hing das Ausmaß der Interaktionen von Merkmalen der Bewohner ab: „More interaction takes place when owners and renters have similar characteristics, especially when they have children" (2001, S. 6).

Ob soziales Kapital in einem Wohngebiet entsteht, hängt auch von den physischen Merkmalen im Wohngebiet ab, z. B. Balkone, Gehsteige, und Verkehrsberuhigung wirken positiv, Müll und Graffiti hingegen negativ, wie eine Studie in acht Wohngebieten in Portland gezeigt hat. Die Effekte bestanden auch dann, wenn Merkmale wie ethnische Zugehörigkeit, Wohndauer und Anteil der Hausbesitzer kontrolliert wurden (Wilkerson et al. 2011).

Umgekehrt kann man nach den Effekten des sozialen Kapitals fragen: Sind die Fortzüge aus einem Wohngebiet geringer, wenn das Gebiet über ein hohes soziales Kapital verfügt? Völker et al. (2013) untersuchten den Einfluss des sozialen Kapitals (einem Index aus Vertrauen in die Nachbarschaft, Kennen der Nachbarn und freundlicher Atmosphäre in der Nachbarschaft) in 3400 Wohngebieten mit Daten des Dutch Housing Survey für 2002 und 2006 auf die Fortzugsbereitschaft. Je niedriger das soziale Kapital in 2002 war und je stärker es von 2002 bis 2006 abgenommen hatte, desto höher war die Bereitschaft, fortzuziehen. Männer, Personen mit höherer Bildung, Migranten und Alleinerziehende, aber nicht Personen mit höherem Einkommen, waren eher bereit, fortzuziehen. Auch in dieser Studie zeigt sich, dass sich die Nachbarschaftsmerkmale ungleich auf einzelne soziale Gruppen auswirken.

Typ 3: Unter Diskriminierung lassen sich zwei verschiedene Sachverhalte verstehen: zum einen die Diskriminierung des Gebietes in der Form, dass sich dort bestimmte Geschäfte nicht ansiedeln, z. B. keine Banken oder nur wenige Ärzte. Die zweite Bedeutung besteht darin, dass Personen, die in dem Gebiet wohnen, bei Bewerbungen diskriminiert werden, man also das negative Bild des Gebietes auf alle Bewohner überträgt. Bei dieser Stigmatisierung wird die Eigenschaft: der schlechte (oder gute) Ruf oder Image des Wohngebietes, beispielsweise im Falle einer Bewerbung um einen Job, auf alle Bewohner übertragen und die Chance, den Job zu erhalten, auf den man sich beworben hat, vermindert (erhöht). Der Ruf wird dem Gebiet zugeschrieben und ist daher ein absolutes Merkmal. Allerdings beruht er auf den subjektiven Bewertungen entweder der Bewohner des Gebiets oder der restlichen Bewohner der Stadt. Häufig sind von solcher Diskriminierung Armutsgebiete oder Gebiete mit einem hohen Anteil von sozialem Wohnungsbau betroffen (Hastings 2009).

Typ 4: Hierbei geht es um die Auswirkungen einer fehlenden (oder vorhandenen) Infrastruktur, z. B. einem Kindergarten, einem Park, einem Krankenhaus, einer

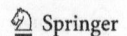

Bank(filiale), einer U-Bahn-Station. Es sind absolute Merkmale, die also nicht aus Individualdaten (d. h. Daten einer niedrigeren Ebene) konstruiert werden.

In „Problemgebieten" mit „problematischen Bewohnern" sind auch die Standards der Versorgung schlechter (Atkinson und Kintrea 2001), was zu einem schlechteren Service führt. Hastings (2009) vergleicht in einer qualitativen Studie 14 problematische und unproblematische Wohngebiete danach, welche infrastrukturellen Einrichtungen vorhanden sind, wie der Service ist und wie die Bewohner (196 Befragte) beides beurteilen. Er gelangt zu dem Ergebnis, dass in den stark benachteiligten Gebieten die angebotenen Dienstleistungen nur unzureichend den Bedürfnissen der Bewohner entsprechen, dies zu resignierten Reaktionen sowohl der Bewohner als auch des dienstleistenden Personals in den Einrichtungen führt. Das ist in den wohlhabenderen Gebieten nicht der Fall, dort verstärkt sich die „territoriale Ungleichheit" nicht. Ein weiteres Beispiel sind die negativen Effekte einer (schlechten) Ausstattung und Qualität von Schulen auf die Schüler in benachteiligten Wohngebieten, die für die USA nachgewiesen wurden (u. a. Condron und Roscigno 2003; Lankford et al. 2002).

Der Effekt des Wohngebietes besteht vor allem darin, „routine activities" (Sampson et al. 2002, S. 458) zu ermöglichen, zu erleichtern oder zu verhindern, weil einzelne Einrichtungen, z. B. Schule, Jugendtreffs, Freizeiteinrichtungen, Arztpraxen, vorhanden oder nicht vorhanden sind. Wie die aktionsräumliche Forschung (Heuwinkel 1981, S. 70 ff.) gezeigt hat, werden die Bewohner auf eine unzureichende Ausstattung in drei Weisen reagieren. Sie verzichten darauf, eine Aktivität auszuüben (Restriktion), oder sie versuchen, die Aktivität woanders auszuführen (Kompensation) oder sie üben andere Aktivitäten aus, für die auch im Wohngebiet die entsprechende Einrichtung vorhanden sind (Verlagerung).

Eine andere Einschränkung kann darin bestehen, dass das Wohngebiet eine schlechte Verkehrsanbindung hat, was es den Bewohnern erschwert, einen Job zu finden, weil sie auf eine rasche Verbindung mit einem öffentlichen Verkehrsmittel angewiesen sind. Wenn, wie in zahlreichen Großstädten der USA, Jobs im tertiären Sektor in die Suburbs verlagert wurden, haben die zu einem großen Anteil in der inneren Stadt wohnenden Schwarzen keine Chance, diese Arbeitsplätze zu erreichen, weil sie nicht über einen Pkw verfügen.

Typ 5: Werden negative Eigenschaften oder Ereignisse im Gebiet wahrgenommen, z. B. Verwahrlosung, Müll, Gewalttaten, Raub, Drogenhandel, dann wird dies von den Bewohnern als mangelnde Kontrolle, somit als ein Zustand der Normenlosigkeit interpretiert, was dann Unsicherheit und Kriminalitätsfurcht auslöst.

So untersuchen Ross et al. (2001; s. auch Ross und Mirowsky 1999) die wahrgenommene „disorder" in Wohngebieten und finden einen signifikanten Effekt auf das Gefühl der Machtlosigkeit bei den Bewohnern, das wiederum ihre schlechten Lebensbedingungen verstärkt. Auf dieser Studie aufbauend, zeigt eine Untersuchung in benachteiligten Wohngebieten, dass die wahrgenommene Verwahrlosung positiv mit den Fortzugsabsichten und negativ mit dem sozialen Kapital (collective efficacy und intergenerational closure) zusammenhängt (Blasius und Friedrichs 2007; Blasius et al. 2008). Aufgrund seiner umfangreichen empirischen Studien in Chicago gelangt Sampson (2012, S. 146) zu der These, die wahrgenommene Verwahrlosung habe einen stärkeren Effekt als die objektiv vorhandene: „Whether one is seeking to predict future poverty or outmigration, perceptions of disorder are equally, if not more significant than the usually cited structural variables".

Die geschilderten Probleme im Wohngebiet können sich auch als Stress auswirken, der seinerseits das Risiko körperlicher und mentaler Störungen erhöht. Diese in der soziologischen Forschung zu wenig beachteten Effekte wurden in Studien über Nachbarschaftseffekte auf die Gesundheit vielfach nachgewiesen; auf sie gehe ich im Abschn. 4 ein.

2.3 Mechanismen

Die bisherige Explikation zeigt, dass es im engeren Sinne nur sehr wenige Mechanismen gibt, die die Effekte der Makro-Eigenschaft auf ein individuelles Verhalten (oder das aggregierte individuelle Verhalten) beschreiben. Auffällig ist, dass es sich bei den Mechanismen weitgehend um Sozialisationsprozesse handelt. Entscheidend für die Analyse der Effekte ist, wie die Kette der Hypothesen lautet, die von einem gegebenen Kontextmerkmal zu Merkmalen der Bewohner und deren Handeln führt. Dazu steht uns die Theorie sozialen Lernens zur Verfügung (Bandura 1973; Bandura und Walters 1963; Akers 1985). *Die Theorie behauptet, Verhalten werde gelernt – und zwar sowohl durch Beobachtung als auch durch Interaktion in sozialen Situationen.* Diese Unterscheidung ist deshalb so bedeutsam, weil Verhalten demnach auch durch Beobachtung gelernt werden kann. „There is considerable evidence, however, that learning may occur through observation of the behavior of others even when the observer does not reproduce the model's responses during acquisition and therefore receives no reinforcement"... „Since eliciting and maintaining of imitative behavior are highly dependent on the response consequences to the model, an adequate social-learning theory must also take into account of the role of *vicarious reinforcement*, through which the behavior of an observer is modified on account of the reinforcement administered to the model" (Bandura und Walters 1963, S. 4; kursiv i. O.).

Ähnlich argumentiert Bandura (1973, S. 202, 203): „People repeatedly observe the actions of others and the occasions on which they are rewarded, ignored, or punished. Observed outcomes influence behavior in much the same way as directly experienced consequences (...). In general, observed rewards increase, and observed punishment decreases, the tendency to behave in similar or related ways". Und: „Observed rewards generally produce a greater increase in similar responding than if the exemplified actions have no evident effects". Bandura (1973, S. 205 f.) erklärt auch, wie diese Übertragung vor sich geht: „One explanation of vicarious reinforcement is in terms of the *informative function* of observed outcomes. Response consequences accruing to others convey information to observers about the types of actions that are likely to be approved or disapproved".

„Observed reinforcement is not only informative, but can also have *incentive motivational effects*. Seeing others positively reinforced can serve as a motivator by arousing in observers expectations that they will be similarly rewarded for analogous performances".

Es sind demnach die wahrgenommenen oder erfahrenen Konsequenzen des Handelns, die einen Akteur ein Verhalten übernehmen lassen. In der Sprache der Rational-Choice-Theorie formuliert: Der Nettonutzen der neuen Handlung ist größer als derjenige der alten, wobei die Wertschätzung der Umgebung, der Anderen, die individuelle Nutzenkalkulation (mit)bestimmt. Daher nehme ich an: Nur wenn der Akteur die Nutzenschätzung der Anderen übernimmt, wird die neue Handlung ausgeführt. Dies stimmt mit Akers (1985, S. 41) Reformulierung eines Postulats von Sutherlands (1968) „Theorie der differenziellen Assoziation" überein: „Deviant behavior is learned both in nonsocial situations that are reinforcing or discriminating and through that social interaction in which the behavior of other persons is reinforcing or discriminating for such behavior".

Nun haben wir in der Forschung über Kontexteffekte der Nachbarschaften keine Beispiele dafür, wo allein durch Beobachtung Verhalten übernommen wurde, obgleich sehr häufig „Rollenvorbilder" (role models) als Mechanismus angeführt werden. Wie die Übernahme durch Beobachtung und Imitation erfolgen kann, zeigt folgendes Zitat: „Observers tend to imitate modeled behavior if they like or respect the model, see the model receive reinforcement, see the model give off signs of pleasure, or are in an environment where imitation the model's performance is reinforced" (Baldwin und Baldwin 1981, S. 187; zit. nach Akers 1985, S. 46).

Beide „Kanäle", Beobachtung und Interaktion, durch die ein Verhalten V von Person A zu Person B übertragen wird, bestehen zweifellos. Es ist aber nicht ausgemacht, ob das Verhalten auch übernommen wird. Das erscheint insbesondere im Falle abweichenden Verhaltens nicht zwingend. Bandura formuliert nur die notwenige Bedingung, sie muss aber nicht hinreichend sein. Folgt man nämlich der Theorie der differenziellen Assoziation (Sutherland 1968), dann werden nicht nur Techniken abweichenden Verhaltens, z. B. *Wohnungsdiebstahl*, gelernt, sondern auch dessen (moralische) Rechtfertigung. Die Übernahme abweichenden Verhaltens erfolgt demnach auch, weil man Verhalten gut begründen kann. Wendet man diese Theorie auf die Kontexteffekte an, dann ist ein Effekt umso wahrscheinlicher, je stärker er sich aus einer Interaktion ergibt, denn nur in ihr können sowohl Techniken als auch Legitimation abweichenden Verhaltens gelernt werden. Wenn das zutreffend ist, stellt sich die weitere Frage, ob reine „Ausbreitung" von neuen Normen durch Beobachtung und Imitation erlernt werden kann oder ob es dazu persönlicher Kontakte mit Personen im Gebiet bedarf, um auch die Legitimation zu erlernen. Wie es also genau zur Übernahme oder Ablehnung abweichenden Verhaltens kommt, lässt sich nur aufklären, wenn die Wahrnehmung und Bewertung der Personen empirisch erfasst werden; solche Studien stehen aus.

3 Empirische Befunde zu einzelnen Mechanismen

Obgleich zu den Nachbarschaftseffekten eine umfangreiche und zunehmende Zahl von Studien vorliegt (vgl. Dietz 2002; Galster 2003, 2007; Friedrichs 1998; Friedrichs et al. 2003; Jencks und Mayer 1990; Leventhal und Brooks-Gunn 2000; Sampson et al. 2002; van Ham et al. 2012b, 2013, 2014), ist immer noch nicht hinreichend empirisch dargestellt, wie genau die Sozialisations- und Lernprozesse vor sich gehen. Ich stelle nun empirische Untersuchungen zu den einzelnen Mechanismen vor.

3.1 Kollektive Sozialisation und Rollenmodelle

Hier wird davon ausgegangen, der Effekt des Kontextes käme über die Sozialisation durch die Bewohner des Gebiets zustande, speziell durch Rollenmodelle. Eine häufig getestete Hypothese ist, ein hoher Anteil von Personen, die erwerbstätig sind und/ oder der Anteil der Personen, die in höheren Angestelltenberufen sind und den Freien Berufen angehören („managerial and professional"), habe einen positiven Einfluss auf das Erwerbsverhalten der Bewohner und einen negativen Effekt auf abweichendes Verhalten.

Crane (1991, S. 1233) berichtet, dieser Anteil von Personen mit relativ hohem sozialem Status habe auf die abhängigen Variablen „Schulabbrecher" und „Teenager-Schwangerschaften" einen stärkeren Effekt als andere Variablen, wie z. B. die Arbeitslosenquote, der Anteil alleinerziehender Frauen oder der Anteil der Erwerbstätigen. Unterstellt wird hier ein soziales Lernen.

In zwei deutschen Studien, Nonnenmacher (2009) sowie Rabold und Baier (2013) wurde dieser Anteil ebenfalls verwendet. Rabold und Baier untersuchten die Effekte der Stadtteile Hannovers auf Gewaltakzeptanz und ausgeübte Gewalt von $N=3232$ Jugendlichen im Alter von 15 Jahren. War der Anteil an solchen „Rollenvorbildern" im Stadtteil hoch, dann waren die Gewaltakzeptanz niedriger und die Selbstkontrolle höher. Ist hingegen das Konfliktniveau im Stadtteil hoch, erhöht sich die Wahrscheinlichkeit, dass ein Jugendlicher zu einer Gewalt akzeptierenden Gruppe gehört, fast um das 14-fache (Rabold und Baier 2013, S. 186).

Es ist unklar, ab welchem Anteil von Personen mit relativ hohem Status in einer Nachbarschaft die vermuteten positiven Effekte auftreten. Es ist ebenso möglich, dass bei einem Teil der Bewohner eine relative Deprivation auftritt, weil die Standards nicht erreicht werden können – was zu einem Rückzug („retreatism") im Sinne von Merton (1957, Kap. IV und V) führen kann.

Für Teenager, die mit 16 Jahren in einem Wohngebiet wohnten und dort vor dem 20. Lebensjahr ein Kind bekamen, wurde in einer britischen Studie der Effekt des Wohngebiets untersucht. Je höher der Anteil statushoher Bewohner, je höher die Quote der Verheirateten und je höher der Anteil junger Frauen, die eine weiterführende schulische Ausbildung machten, desto niedriger war die Quote von Teenager-Müttern (Lupton und Kneale 2012). Sowohl kollektive Sozialisation als auch Rollenmodelle können diese Effekte erklären.

Wie geht es vor sich, dass der Anteil von Personen mit höheren Positionen sich auf das Verhalten von Personen mit niedrigeren Positionen auswirkt? Wie können die unterstellten positiven Effekte solcher „Rollenmodelle" präziser formuliert werden? Es ist sinnvoll, hierzu auf die neueren Überlegungen zu „sozialen Mechanismen" zurückzugreifen (Hedström und Swedberg 1998; Mayntz 2005; Opp 2004, 2013; vgl. Kalter und Kroneberg in diesem Band); dieser Ausdruck wird zwar auch in einigen Arbeiten zu Nachbarschaftseffekten verwendet (z. B. Atkinson und Kintrea 2001; Sampson 2006; Sampson et al. 2002), aber ohne ihn mit konkreten Inhalten (Hypothesen) zu füllen.

Unter einem Mechanismus versteht Opp (2004, S. 362) einen „kausalen Prozess" oder eine „Wirkungskette". Es wird also nicht *eine* Hypothese formuliert, sondern eine Kette aufeinander bezogener Hypothesen, die spezifizieren, wie eine Bedingung

(Input) mit einem Ergebnis (Output) – auf plausible Weise – verbunden ist (Hedström und Swedberg 1998, S. 9). Den Kontexteffekt nach Opp solcherart zu modellieren hat den Vorteil, präziser zu bestimmen, welche Bedingungen gegeben sein müssen, damit ein Merkmal auf der Kontextebene sich auf die Handlungen der Individuen auswirkt.

Nehmen wir das Beispiel der Rollenmodelle. Die Kontexthypothese lautet: Je mehr Personen in höheren Angestelltenpositionen in einem Gebiet wohnen, desto niedriger ist die Rate abweichenden Verhaltens. Fasst man diese Hypothese genauer, so lautet der unterstellte Mechanismus: Personen der Gruppe A mit dem Verhalten V(Ai) sehen Personen der Gruppe B mit dem Verhalten V(Bj). Das Verhalten V(Bj) wird als abweichend vom eigenen Verhalten wahrgenommen, aber positiv von Angehörigen der Gruppe A bewertet. Diese positive Bewertung führt (zumindest einige) Personen der Gruppe A nun dazu, eher das Verhalten V(Bj) als das Verhalten V(Ai) auszuführen. So schreibt Crane (1991, S. 1227), arme männliche Jugendliche seien stärker als andere Bewohnergruppen für die Einflüsse von peer groups empfänglich, weshalb es zu stärkeren (delinquenten) jugendlichen Subkulturen käme.

3.2 Ansteckungseffekt

Diesem Effekt zufolge fördert ein höherer Anteil abweichenden Verhaltens in einem Wohngebiet auch die Bereitschaft, abweichendes Verhalten zu akzeptieren und zu übernehmen. Dies ist insbesondere für Jugendliche nachgewiesen worden (vgl. Browning et al. 2004, S. 508). Auch deutsche Studien in Hannover und Duisburg belegen diesen Zusammenhang (Kunadt 2013; Rabold 2011; Rabold und Baier 2013). Diese Annahme gehört aber auch zu den zentralen Hypothesen von Wilson (1987) über die Ausbreitung abweichender Verhaltensmuster, z. B. die Schule abzubrechen oder Schwangerschaften von Teenagern.

Anhand des im vorangegangenen Abschnitt dargestellten Beispiels kann man sich eine weitere Ausbreitung („Ansteckung") folgendermaßen vorstellen: Mehr Personen der Gruppe A mit dem Verhalten V(Bj) werden von anderen Mitgliedern der Gruppe A wahrgenommen und/ oder interagieren mit Personen der Gruppe A. Es kommt zur weiteren Übernahme des Verhaltens V(Bj) durch andere Personen der Gruppe A. Der Prozess lässt sich vermutlich als ein Diffusionsprozess beschreiben, der nur dann in Gang kommt, wenn eine kritische Masse im Sinne der Theorie von Oliver et al. (1985) besteht (siehe Abb. 1). Im Sinne dieser Theorie müssen wir bestimmen, wie groß die kritische Masse sein muss, deren Verhalten übernommen wird; es ist kein Anteil an den Bewohnern, sondern eine absolute Zahl: Wie viele Bewohner sind erforderlich, um einen solchen Diffusionsprozess zu bewirken? Man beachte, dass sich dieser Prozess sowohl auf die Übernahme abweichenden als auch normenkonformen Verhaltens beziehen kann.

Wie man an diesem Beispiel erkennen kann, machen wir die zusätzliche Annahme, Personen der Gruppe A würden das Verhalten V(Bj) der Gruppe B dem eigenen Verhalten V(Ai) vorziehen, weil sie es positiver bewerten. Einen solchen Maßstab müssen die Personen der Gruppe A sich jedoch ungeachtet der Neigung, V(Ai) auszuführen, bewahrt oder erarbeitet haben. Das ist nun keineswegs zwingend, denn z. B. Wilson (1987) lässt sich so interpretieren, dass mit dem Überwiegen von V(Bj)

Abb. 1 Verlauf des Ansteckungsprozesses mit kritischer Masse in t3

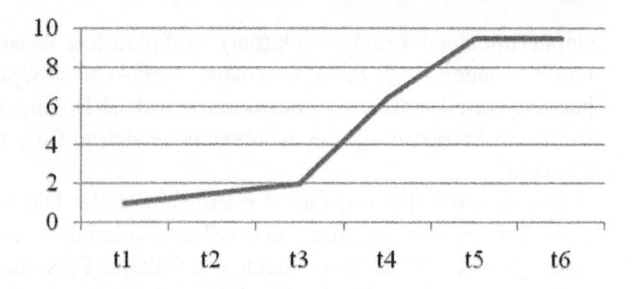

über V(Ai) in einem Wohngebiet auch die Maßstäbe der Bewertung sich zugunsten von V(Bj) verschoben haben – und sich nun die Bewohner daran als dem dominanten Verhaltensmuster orientieren. Das bedeutet: Wenn Wilson empirisch belegt, die Normen der Bewohner von Armutsgebieten wichen von den Normen der „mainstream society" ab, so dürfte dies auch einschließen, die Bewohner würden die Werte der Mehrheit nicht (mehr) akzeptieren.

3.3 Ausstattung des Gebiets

Die Ausstattung eines Wohngebiets beeinflusst das Verhalten der Bewohner insofern, als sie ihnen Aktivitäten ermöglicht oder nicht ermöglicht. Der „Mechanismus" ist sehr einfach: Opportunitäten und Restriktionen. So sind alleinerziehende Mütter vermutlich sehr stark auf einen Arbeitsplatz im Wohngebiet angewiesen, um bei einem engen Zeitbudget ihren vielfältigen Verpflichtungen nachkommen zu können. Auch soziale Programme, wie in Deutschland die „Soziale Stadt", richten sich darauf, Arbeitsplätze im benachteiligten Wohngebiet zu schaffen, weil sie den Bewohnern die Pendelkosten ersparen wollen.

Die Ausstattung des Wohngebiets wirkt sich ebenfalls (indirekt) auf die Gesundheit aus. Zu den Opportunitäten gehören auch die Qualität der Schulen, die Ausstattung mit Freizeiteinrichtungen, aber auch (unzureichende) Angebote an Nahrungsmitteln („food deserts"; vgl. Weinberg 2000). Fehlen Grünanlagen oder Parks, verringert sich die „walkability" des Wohngebiets und weniger Bewohner machen Spaziergänge, bewegen sich also körperlich (van Lenthe et al. 2005) oder sind eher übergewichtig (Sarkar et al. 2013). Fehlen Obst- und Gemüse-Geschäfte in der näheren Umgebung (zwei Kilometer Radius), so wird auch weniger Obst und Gemüse verzehrt – die Bewohner ernähren sich schlechter (Flint et al. 2013; Thornton et al. 2013). (Die Befunde belegen die oben formulierte Restriktions-Hypothese). Auch die Einflüsse von Kontexteffekten auf die Qualität und Inanspruchnahme medizinischer Versorgung wurden untersucht, es ergab sich aber entgegen den Hypothesen kein Effekt (Kubzansky et al. 2005; Law et al. 2005; Yip et al. 2002).

3.4 Andere Mechanismen

Ähnlich wie die Ausstattung können auch andere Merkmale des Gebiets den Effekt haben, Verhalten zu ermöglichen oder einzuschränken. Ein sehr gutes Beispiel ist der „male marriage pool", den Wilson (1987, S. 57 f.) beschreibt. In benachteiligten Wohngebieten mit vorwiegend schwarzen Bewohnern, ist der Anteil der Arbeitslosen hoch. Junge Frauen, mit dem Wunsch nach einem Partner finden mit großer Wahrscheinlichkeit nur einen arbeitslosen Schwarzen als (Ehe-)Partner. Aufgrund früher sexueller Kontakte kommt es eher zu einer Schwangerschaft. Nach einer Schwangerschaft der Frau verschwindet in vielen Fällen der Partner und lässt eine alleinerziehende Mutter zurück, die von der Sozialhilfe leben muss. Die Restriktion liegt hier vor allem in dem stark eingeschränkten pool von männlichen Partnern. Sie besteht aber zusätzlich darin, dass die jungen Frauen kaum Beziehungen zu Personen außerhalb des Wohngebiets haben: also über viel bonding aber sehr wenig bridging capital verfügen. Schließlich: Die junge Frau gelangt nicht aus dem Zirkel der Armut und dem Armutsgebiet heraus. Dieser Mechanismus erklärt auch, warum in diesen benachteiligten Gebieten ein sehr hoher Prozentsatz Alleinerziehender anzutreffen ist.

Beide Sachverhalte, die Schwangerschaft von jungen Mädchen im Alter von 13 bis unter 18 Jahren und der hohe Anteil von Alleinerziehenden, sind auch in anderen Studien nachgewiesen worden (u. a. Brooks-Gunn et al. 1993; Hogan und Kitagawa 1985; Jargowsky 1997; Jencks und Mayer 1990).

3.5 Individual- vs. Meso- vs. Makroeffekte

Die Analyse von Kontexteffekten beinhaltet, diese gegen Individualeffekte abzugrenzen. Gemeinhin sind die Kontexteffekte erheblich geringer als die Individualeffekte. Eine erste Schätzung der Anteile aufgrund eines Reviews der Literatur geben Leventhal und Brooks-Gunn (2000): Sie veranschlagen den Kontexteffekt auf maximal 8 %. Dabei sind diese Schätzungen noch relativ ungenau, weil sie von einem Modell mit nur zwei Ebenen ausgehen: Wohngebiet und Individuum. Tatsächlich ist aber sehr wahrscheinlich ein komplizierteres Modell erforderlich. Es enthält zusätzlich eine Mesoebene, auf ihr wiederum eine oder mehrere Institutionen, die als Kontexte ebenfalls Effekte haben.

Wenn die Einführung einer Mesoebene ein erforderliches Vorgehen ist, dann leiden fast alle Studien zu Nachbarschaftseffekten unter einer zu einfachen Spezifikation des Modells. Es wäre nun abzuwägen, ob der Effekt 1 verschwindet, wenn man die Effekte 4 und 5 berücksichtigt, ferner, dass nur die Effekte 2 und 3 als indirekte Effekte der Makroebene Bestand haben.

Ein gutes Beispiel sind die Skalen von Sampson et al. (Sampson 2006, 2012; Sampson und Groves 1989; Sampson et al. 1997), die auf eine Explikation der Desorganisations-Theorie von Shaw und McKay zurückgehen. Sampson et al. messen das Ausmaß des Vertrauens und der sozialen Kontrolle in einem Wohngebiet (collective efficacy), ferner das Ausmaß der Supervision von Kindern und Jugendlichen (intergenerational closure). Die Skalen sind eingebaut in ein Modell, das nach Ansicht der Autoren die zu einfache Beziehung zwischen Aggregat und Individuum spezifizieren soll (Sampson et al. 2002). Das Modell ist in Abb. 2 dargestellt.

Weil viele Studien sich auf benachteiligte Wohngebiete beziehen und die grundlegende Annahme lautet, abweichendes Verhalten sei eine Folge von Armut, unterstellen die Autoren, wahrgenommene Eigenschaften des Wohngebiets würden diese Beziehung moderieren. Wie ihre empirischen Studien (Sampson 2006, 2012, Kap. 7; Sampson et al. 1997; Sampson et al. 1999; Sampson et al. 2002; Sampson und

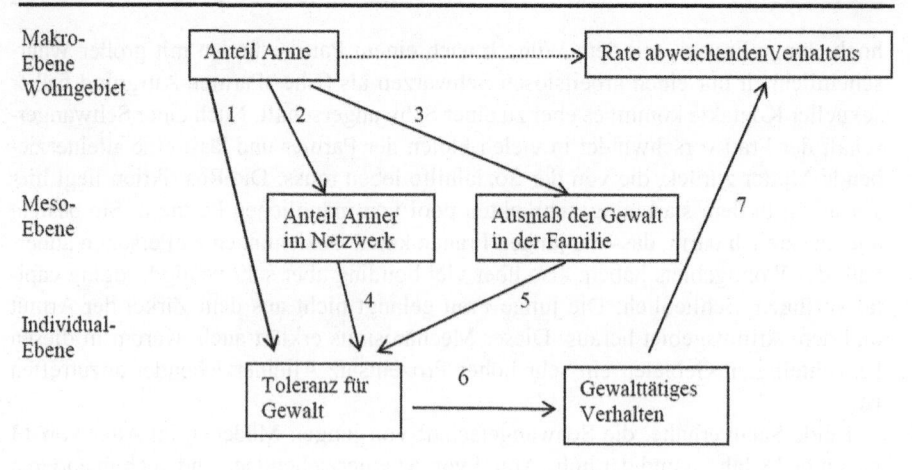

Abb. 2 Drei Ebenen Modell

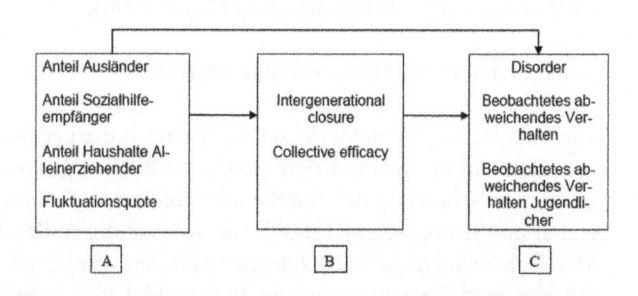

Abb. 3 Das Modell Sampson et al.

Raudenbush 1999) zeigen, führt die Wahrnehmung physischen Verfalls nicht direkt zu höherer Kriminalität, wie die „broken windows"-Hypothese von Wilson und Kelling (1982; vgl. dazu: Xu et al. 2005) postuliert, sondern wird durch das Ausmaß sozialer Kontrolle als intervenierender Variable bestimmt. Ist das soziale Vertrauen hoch, dann ist das Ausmaß abweichenden Verhaltens geringer. Dieser Effekt wurde auch in deutschen Studien nachgewiesen (Blasius et al. 2008; Friedrichs und Blasius 2003; Oberwittler 2007). Zugleich bewähren sich die beiden Skalen auch in den deutschen Studien (Abb. 3).

Die Skalenwerte in B sind aggregierte Werte der individuellen Antworten auf die Items der jeweiligen Skala. Weil dies auch für die Quoten in A gilt – ist B dann noch eine Moderator-Variable oder liegt sie auch auf der Makroebene A? Samson et al. wollen sie explizit als Moderator-Variable verstanden wissen, um den Effekt von A auf C besser zu erklären. Ich unterstelle, im Extremfall wird die Korrelation $r_{AC}=0$ aber sowohl die von r_{AB} und $r_{BC} > 0{,}30$ sein.

Nun müssen wir diese Effekte nicht nur darauf hin untersuchen, wie stark eine Person der Nachbarschaft ausgesetzt ist, sondern auch danach, wann die Effekte auftreten, das heißt mit welcher Zeitverzögerung. Das ist insofern bedeutsam, wenn wir Kontextmerkmale zu t_i auf mögliche Effekte zu t_{i+k} beziehen, z. B. die Arbeitslosenquote 1991 auf die Erwerbstätigkeit 2001 (Manley und van Ham 2012). Wir arbeiten hier u. a. mit folgenden Annahmen: a) die zeitliche Distanz ist korrekt gewählt, b) der

Kontexteffekt war konstant über diesen Zeitraum und c) der Kontexteffekt muss nur in den früheren Jahren der Sozialisation bestehen.

3.6 Gruppenspezifische Effekte und „exposure"

Die Effekte eines Wohngebietes müssen nicht alle Bewohnergruppen in gleichem Maße betreffen. Das zeigen z. B. Studien zu der Wirkung von sozialem Kapital auf Fortzüge (Völker et al. 2013), zu den Wirkungen von benachteiligten Nachbarschaften auf das Risiko, die Schule abzubrechen (Crowder und South 2010), Netzwerkstrukturen auf abweichendes Verhalten (Haynie 2001; Oberwittler 2007).

Oberwittler (2007) findet in einer postalischen Befragung von Schülern in Freiburg und Köln (5300 Befragte in 61 Nachbarschaften) nur für die deutschen Jugendlichen einen U-förmigen Zusammenhang zwischen dem Anteil der Sozialhilfequote in der Nachbarschaft und dem Ausmaß relativer Deprivation, das von den Jugendlichen berichtet wird. Hierbei ist die relative Deprivation in Nachbarschaften mit einem niedrigen Anteil und mit einem hohen Anteil von Sozialhilfeempfängern am höchsten; die entsprechenden Schwellenwerte liegen bei 3% und 18% Sozialhilfeempfänger.

Man kann aber grundsätzlich vermuten, dass der Nachbarschaftseffekt umso stärker ist, a) je mehr Zeit ein Bewohner im Gebiet verbringt und b) je größer der Anteil der lokalen Netzwerkpersonen an ihrem gesamten Netzwerk ist. Zusätzlich können wir einen (multiplikativen) Interaktionseffekt beider Merkmale annehmen. Demnach würden nichtberufstätige Personen wie Arbeitslose oder Hausfrauen, aber auch Schüler am stärksten den Gebietseffekt „ausgesetzt". Allgemein formuliert: Je höher die „exposure", desto stärker ist der Nachbarschaftseffekt (vgl. Galster et al. 2011; Galster in diesem Band).

3.7 Schwellenwerte und selektive Bewohnerschaft

Die Effekte eines Merkmals des Wohngebiets auf ein Verhalten der Bewohner müssen nicht linear sein, was zuerst Galster et al. (2000) herausgearbeitet haben. Seitdem hat die Forschung zahlreiche Beispiele für solche nicht-linearen Effekte erbracht, sodass wir von Schwellenwerten, die bei 20% und bei 40% des Wohngebiets-Merkmals liegen, ausgehen können. (Vgl. ausführlich den Beitrag von Galster in diesem Band.)

Nicht-lineare Effekte berichtet auch Gibbons (2002, S. 31 f.). Er untersuchte anhand der Daten der British National Child Development Study ($N=8175$ Befragte) den Einfluss des Anteil der Personen mit hoher Schulbildung (Level A und höher) in 5479 Wohngebieten auf die schulischen Erfolge von Jugendlichen. Er findet zunächst eine lineare Beziehung zwischen beiden Merkmalen. Kontrolliert man jedoch Merkmale der Familien, so zeigte sich, dass Jugendliche, die in Wohngebieten in den obersten 10% der höher Gebildeten wohnten, eine 5–6 Prozentpunkte höhere Wahrscheinlichkeit hatten, ebenso hohe Abschlüsse zu erzielen wie diejenigen mit gleichem familiären Hintergrund, die in den untersten 10% der Gebiete wohnten. Zudem beendeten Jugendliche aus den besten Nachbarschaften seltener die Schulausbildung ohne Abschluss. Der Nachbarschaftseffekt auf die Abschlüsse der Jugendlichen war im dritten Quartil der Verteilung (einem Anteil von 10–15% höher Gebildeter) vier Mal höher als der durchschnittliche Anstieg.

Das Problem der selektiven Bewohnerschaft ist insofern bedeutsam, weil wir nicht wissen, ob Personen oder Haushalte mit spezifischen Merkmalen in ein Wohngebiet gezogen sind, die wir nicht kennen (unobserved oder omitted variables). Wenn nun dem Gebiet ein Effekt der Armut auf ein Merkmal M der Bewohner, z. B. eine schlechte Wohnung, zugeschrieben wird, dann muss der Gebietseffekt Armut → Wohnung von dem Effekt, dass Haushalte mit sehr niedrigen Einkommen sich nur einfache Wohnungen leisten können, diese sich aber wiederum sehr viel häufiger in Armutsgebieten befinden, getrennt werden. Eine Lösung besteht darin, mit instrumentellen Variablen zu arbeiten, wofür die Studie von Hedman und Galster (2013) ein gutes Beispiel ist. (Vgl. dazu den Beitrag von Hedman in diesem Band.)

4 Multiple Effekte: Wohngebiet und Gesundheit

Die Studien zum Zusammenhang von Eigenschaften des Wohngebietes und Gesundheit haben in den letzten 15 Jahren enorm zugenommen. Sie sind nicht nur ihrer Ergebnisse wegen bedeutsam, sondern auch weil sich die theoretischen und methodologischen Probleme von Nachbarschaftseffekten hier besonders ausgeprägt darstellen. Zahlreiche sozio-demographische Merkmale sind mit gesundheitlichen Risiken verbunden, vor allem der soziale Status. Personen niedrigen sozialen Status ernähren sich schlechter, haben einen höheren Tabak- und Alkoholkonsum, sind häufiger übergewichtig und haben eine höhere Mortalitätsrate; sie schätzen ihre Gesundheit auch schlechter ein (Dalstra et al. 2005, Deutscher Bundestag 2005, Lampert und Mielck 2008). Deshalb stellen sich in diesen Untersuchungen in verstärktem Maße sowohl das Kompositionsproblem des Gebiets als auch das der Isolation von Gebiets- gegenüber Individual-Effekten.

Die Merkmale des Wohngebiets können nach Ellen et al. (2001, S. 392–394) auf vier Wegen die Gesundheit der Bewohner beeinflussen:

1. Institutionen und Ressourcen, z. B. medizinische Einrichtungen, Verkehrsanbindung;
2. Stress durch die physische Umwelt, z. B. Luftverschmutzung, Zustand der Wohngebäude;
3. Stress durch die soziale Umgebung, z. B. Kriminalität, Gewalt;
4. Netzwerke und Normen, z. B. Information, Isolation.

Folgende Wirkungen des Wohngebiets auf die Gesundheit von Bewohnern wurden vor allem untersucht: a) Krankheiten wie z. B. Asthma, Diabetes, b) Übergewicht, c) geistige Gesundheit (mental health), z. B. Depressionen, Stress, Angst, d) Ernährungsgewohnheiten und e) Konsum von Alkohol, Tabak und Drogen, f) körperliche Aktivitäten, sowie g) gesundheitliches Präventionsverhalten. Die Zahl der Studien hat in den letzten 15 Jahren stark zugenommen; sie belegen Effekte von physischen und von sozialen Merkmalen des Wohngebiets mit diesen Krankheiten (vgl. die Übersichten von Bryden et al. 2013; Curtis et al. 2013; Diez Roux 2001; Diez Roux und Mair 2010; Ellen et al. 2001; O'Campo et al. 2009; Pickett und Pearl 2001). Zum Beispiel finden Corburn et al. (2006) in benachteiligten Wohngebieten New Yorks einen Effekt auf die Häufigkeit der Inzidenz von Asthma.

Das Ausmaß der Deprivation eines Wohngebiets wies auch in einer schwedischen Studie mit 336 340 Erwachsenen einen Zusammenhang mit dem Auftreten von Diabetes auf: Die Risiken waren, unabhängig vom SES des Gebiets, in Gebieten mit hoher Deprivation doppelt so hoch als in solchen mit niedriger Deprivation (Mezuk et al. 2013).

Mehrere Studien belegen einen Zusammenhang von gebauter Umwelt auf mentale Störungen wie Depression (Galea et al. 2005; Weich et al. 2002) oder des Ausmaßes an Verwahrlosung (disorder) auf Depressionen und übermäßigen Alkoholkonsum (Hill und Angel 2005). Darüber hinaus ist ein Effekt des Gebiets auf das Übergewicht von Bewohnern nachgewiesen (e.g. Burdette und Hill 2008; Cummins und Macintyre 2006; Glass et al. 2006; Moffat et al. 2005; Ross et al. 2007). Wie Cohen et al. (2003) in einer Untersuchung von 107 nordamerikanischen Städten nachweisen, hat auch der Anteil verbarrikadierter unbewohnter Wohngebäude in einem Gebiet neben dem Anteil Schwarzer und dem Bildungsgrad der Bewohner einen Effekt: die Sterblichkeitsrate von Personen unter 65 Jahren ist erheblich höher.

In der Tradition der Studie von Faris und Dunham (1939) untersuchen Silver et al. (2002) anhand einer nordamerikanischen Befragung von 11 686 Personen, wie sich das Ausmaß der Benachteiligung eines Wohngebietes auf die mentalen Störungen auswirkt. In benachteiligten Gebieten sind die Depressionen und Drogenmissbrauch häufiger, ist die Mobilität höher, finden sich zusätzlich höhere Anteile von Personen, die an Schizophrenie erkrankt sind. Die Autoren erörtern auch eine andere Kausalkette: Personen, die an Schizophrenie erkrankt sind, haben einen niedrigeren SES und sie ziehen häufiger in benachteiligte Gebiete (ibid., S. 1466).

Für Jugendliche sind übereinstimmend negative Auswirkungen von Gewalt und Verwahrlosung im Wohngebiet sowohl auf deren Risiken, sich selbst gewalttätig zu verhalten (Externalisierung) oder aber depressiv (Internalisierung) zu reagieren, nachgewiesen worden (Curtis et al. 2013). Ein weiteres Beispiel sind die Auswirkungen auf Kinder. Martinez und Richter (1993) untersuchten 165 Kinder im Alter von 6–10 Jahren in einem statusniedrigen Wohngebiet von Washington. Die Hälfte der Kinder hatte Schießereien, Raub und Gewalttaten im Gebiet beobachtet; diese Kinder wiesen signifikant stärkere Symptome von Stress auf als jene Kinder, die derartige Ereignisse nicht beobachtet hatten.

Die Mehrzahl der Studien richtet sich auf die Unterschiede zwischen Wohngebieten unterschiedlichen sozialen Status (SES) und Indikatoren der Gesundheit. Methodologisch geht es um den Zusammenhang von Armut, Depression, Übergewicht, Tabak oder Alkohol- Konsum. Um aber den *Gebiets*effekt zu erklären, werden die von den Bewohnern wahrgenommenen (negativen) Eigenschaften des Gebiets in die Untersuchung einbezogen. Die Mechanismen, mit denen die Autoren diese Zusammenhänge aufklären, sind relativ ähnlich; es sind die in Abb. 4 dargestellten Zusammenhänge (für ähnliche Modellierungen vgl. Barrington et al. 2014; Burdette und Hill 2008; Kruger et al. 2007).

Bei den wahrgenommenen Gebietsmerkmalen geht es um ein breites Spektrum: Müll, Verwahrlosung (disorder), Raub, Gewalttaten, Drogenhandel, auf der Straße „herumhängende" Jugendliche, die als fehlende Kohäsion und mangelnde soziale Kontrolle wahrgenommen werden. Werden solche Mängel dauerhaft wahrgenommen, führt dies zu Stress (Brenner et al. 2013; Cohen et al. 2007; Schulz et al. 2013; Steptoe und

Abb. 4 Zusammenhang Gebietsmerkmal – Gesundheit

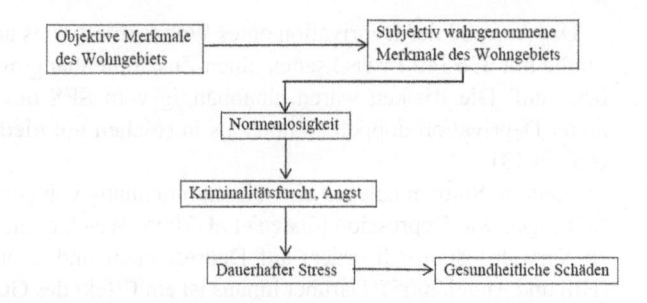

```
Objektive Merkmale   ──────▶   Subjektiv wahrgenommene
des Wohngebiets                Merkmale des Wohngebiets
         │                              │
         └──────────────┬───────────────┘
                        ▼
                 Normenlosigkeit
                        │
                        ▼
              Kriminalitätsfurcht, Angst
                        │
                        ▼
              Dauerhafter Stress ──────▶ Gesundheitliche Schäden
```

Feldman 2001), der sich z. B. in Angstzuständen äußert. Die Beziehung von Stress zu gesundheitlichen Schäden klären Burdette und Hill (2008, S. 39; vgl. Cohen et al. 2012) durch folgenden Mechanismus auf: Der Stress löst eine „fight or flight"-Reaktion aus, diese führt zu einem Ausstoß von Adrenalin, dieser zur Freigabe von Fettsäuren. Stress aktiviert die Hypophyse, sie leitet das Hormon Cortisol ins Blut ein. Es wandelt Nahrung in gespeicherte Fette um und bewirkt Hungergefühl und Nahrungssuche. Der psychologische Stress verstärkt diese Stoffwechsel-Prozesse; ein hoher Cortisol-Spiegel führt dann dazu, übermäßig Energie zu speichern; die Folge ist Übergewicht.

Damit ist ein komplexer sozio-medizinischer Mechanismus vollständig spezifiziert. Eigenschaften der Wohngebiete wirken nicht direkt, sondern vermutlich vor allem indirekt über Wahrnehmungen und somatische Prozesse auf die Gesundheit, allgemeiner: das Verhalten der Bewohner. Da der Mechanismus voraussetzt, dass die schlechten Zustände über längere Zeit wahrgenommen werden, müsste sich ein positiver linearer (?) Zusammenhang mit der Wohndauer als einen Indikator für exposure nachweisen lassen – oder stumpfen die Bewohner ab?

Wie bedeutsam die wahrgenommenen Eigenschaften des Wohngebietes sind, zeigen auch Baum et al. (2009) in einer Untersuchung in fünf unterschiedlich benachteiligten Wohngebieten in Adelaide, Australien. Sie finden einen signifikant positiven Zusammenhang zwischen wahrgenommener Sicherheit des Gebiets und selbst berichtetem Gesundheitszustand. Die ebenfalls erhobene Kohäsion im Gebiet (gemessen über eine Skala mit fünf Items zu Vertrauen und Kontrolle in der Nachbarschaft), wirkt sich stärker indirekt über die wahrgenommene Sicherheit aus.

5 Weitere Probleme

Die Mehrzahl der Studien richtet sich auf die Kontexteffekte „armer" Wohngebiete auf die Bewohner. So wird schon in der Einleitung des Reviews von Sampson et al. (2002) von Gebieten mit „concentrated poverty" gesprochen, auf die sich der Bericht über den kumulativen Forschungsstand dann auch bezieht. Wie aber sind die Kontexteffekte in „gemischten" oder „reichen" Wohngebieten, in denen es „arme", „mittlere" und „reiche" Haushalte gibt? Haben arme Haushalte bessere Chancen in weniger armen Gebieten? Welche Kontexteffekte treten in „reichen" Wohngebieten auf? Hierfür sind die oben berichteten Ergebnisse über die Wohngebietseffekte auf die Einkommen ein eindrucksvoller Beleg.

Tab. 2 Personen in armen und nicht-armen Wohngebieten, nach Status der Person, 85 Stadtteile von Köln, 2008, in Prozent

Status	Wohngebiet		
Person	Arm	Nicht-arm	Insg.
Arm	5,4	7,5	12,9
	A	B	
Nicht-arm	13,1	74,0	87,1
	C	D	
Insgesamt	18,4 % 183.472	81,6 % 811.344	100,0 % 994.816

Quelle: Berechnungen der Stadt Köln. Ungefähr 2400 Fälle bleiben unberücksichtigt, da diese den Stadtvierteln nicht zugewiesen werden konnten. Stand: Dezember 2008; Summe der Empfänger von Sozialleistungen nach SGB II, der Leistungen der Grundsicherung und der Hilfe zum Lebensunterhalt in Prozent der Bevölkerung mit Hauptwohnsitz in Köln.

Um diese Überlegungen zu verdeutlichen, gehe ich auf Weicher (1990, S. 69) zurück. Er verwendet Daten für 100 Großstädte der USA und führt deren Verteilung nach dem sozialen Status der Personen (arm, nicht-arm) auf arme und nicht-arme Wohngebiete auf. Der wichtigste Befund ist, dass mehr Nicht-Arme in armen Gebieten wohnen als Arme. Überträgt man diese Analyse auf Köln und bezeichnet Gebiete als „arm", wenn mindestens 20 % der Bewohner Sozialhilfe beziehen, so ergibt sich die Verteilung in Tab. 2. Im Jahr 2008 hatte Köln rd. 129 600 Empfänger von Sozialleistungen nach SGB II (Stadt Köln 2009), von diesen lebten 53 552 in jenen 20 % der Gebiete, die als arm (oder benachteiligt) bezeichnet wurden. Damit lebt der größte Teil der als „arm" klassifizierten Bevölkerung (74 790) in Gebieten, die als „nicht arm" bezeichnet werden, der Anteil der Nichtarmen in den „Armutsgebieten" ist damit noch deutlich größer ist als in den Großstädten der USA (Tab. 2).

An diesem Beispiel lassen sich eine Reihe von Forschungsfragen entwickeln, die in der Literatur zu Nachbarschaftseffekten bislang unzureichend beantwortet wurden, zum Beispiel: Worin unterschieden sich die Lebensbedingungen – die Kontexte – der Personen in den extremen Zellen A und D, wenn die individuellen Merkmale und Selektionseffekte kontrolliert werden? Ist der Effekt der Reichen auf alle Gruppen im Wohngebiet gleich? Sind die Lebensbedingungen für Arme in reichen (oder mittleren) Wohngebieten besser als in armen, wie es die Literatur zur sozialem Mischung behauptet?

Aufschlüsse über die möglichen Effekte gibt eine Studie von Atkinson und Kintrea (2001). Die Autoren verglichen je zwei Gebiete unterschiedlichen sozialen Status in Edinburgh und Glasgow. Die Eigentümerquoten betrugen in den status-niedrigen Gebieten 19 bzw. 23 %, in den statushöheren hingegen 67 und 68 %. Hält man den Wohnstatus (Eigentümer, Mieter Sozialwohnung, Mieter Genossenschaft, privater Mieter) konstant, dann hatten in den armen Gebieten weniger Bewohner am vorangegangenen Tag das Wohngebiet verlassen, waren weniger erwerbstätig und hatten mehr Bewohner lang andauernde Krankheiten. Zudem berichteten nur die Bewohner statusniedriger Gebiete, bei der Jobsuche diskriminiert worden zu sein. Obgleich die Autoren keine multivariaten Analysen vornehmen, sprechen die Ergebnisse dafür, dass es ärmeren Personen in gemischten Wohngebieten besser als in ärmeren geht, was auch Befunde zu den Gebietseffekten auf die Gesundheit der Bewohner zeigen (vgl. weiter unten).

Den meisten Studien liegt ferner die Annahme zugrunde, Familien mit höherem Einkommen hätten – als Rollenmodelle – einen positiven Effekt auf die Familien niedrigen Einkommens. Gibt es aber auch einen umgekehrten negativen Effekt des Unterschicht- auf das Mittelschicht-Verhalten? Ziehen Angehörige der Mittelschicht verstärkt aus solchen gemischten Wohngebieten aus, wie es die Ergebnisse von Friedrichs (1991) und Ostendorf et al. (2001, S. 379) nahe legen? Die Forschungsfrage lautet demnach: Bestehen Effekte der Armen auf Bewohner der Mittelschicht und Effekte der Mittelschicht auf reiche Bewohner – und wenn ja: welche?

Wir unterstellen also: Personen gleicher individueller Merkmale werden in Wohngebieten unterschiedlicher Sozialstruktur auch anders handeln, denn sonst wäre die Kontexthypothese falsifiziert. Diese Hypothese lässt sich streng genommen in einer Querschnitt-Studie nur begrenzt testen, geeigneter wären Panelstudien. Daher leisten drei nordamerikanische quasi-experimentelle Projekte zu Umzügen von armen Haushalten einen wichtigen Beitrag: Gautreaux (Popkin et al. 2000; Rosenbaum 1995), Moving to Opportunity (MTO) (Briggs et al. 2010; DeLuca et al. 2012; Goering und Feins 2003; Orr et al. 2003; Small und Feldman 2012) und HOPE VI (Cisneros und Engdahl 2009; Popkin et al. 2004).

Alle drei Programme gehen davon aus, Armutsgebiete hätten einen beträchtlichen negativen Effekt auf die Lebensbedingungen und Chancen der Bewohner. Der gleiche Nachbarschaftseffekt, nun aber positiver Art, wird unterstellt, wenn man Personen aus solchen Gebieten in Gebiete mit erheblich niedrigerer Quote von Sozialhilfeempfängern umsiedelt. In allen Projekten wurden Bewohner aus stark benachteiligten Wohngebieten in weniger benachteiligte vermittelt. Die Umzüge erfolgten bei den Projekten MTO und HOPEVI weitgehend durch eine randomisierte Zuweisung der Haushalte auf die neuen Wohngebiete und Wohnungen. Deshalb bestehen hier die Probleme des selection bias nicht.

Es ist hier nicht möglich, auf die differenzierten und z. T. umstrittenen Ergebnisse der drei Studien einzugehen; dazu sei auf die oben zitierten zusammenfassenden Darstellungen für das jeweilige Projekt verwiesen. Ich führe nur einige gesicherte Ergebnisse an: Der Umzug in ein weniger benachteiligtes Gebiet ist durchgängig mit geringerer Kriminalitätsfurcht, insbesondere der Frauen, verbunden. Damit sind weniger Stress (siehe oben) und mehr Aktivitäten im Gebiet verbunden. Mädchen bauen in stärkerem Maße neue soziale Netzwerke im Gebiet auf, Jungen hingegen besuchen zu einem höheren Anteil Freunde im alten Wohngebiet. Die schulischen Leistungen von Mädchen, aber kaum von Jungen, verbessern sich. Die erhofften positiven Auswirkungen auf höhere Erwerbstätigkeit und Einkommen lassen sich nicht nachweisen. Sehr zugespitzt kann man sagen: Die Projekte sind sozial, aber nicht ökonomisch erfolgreich. (Was allerdings nicht untersucht wurde, sind die längerfristigen Folgen für die Bewohner, die in den ursprünglichen MTO und HOPEVI-Gebieten zurück bleiben.) Der für die Frage dieses Kapitels entscheidende Befund ist, dass dieselben Personen in unterschiedlichen Kontexten auch unterschiedlich handeln können.

Ein weiteres Problem ist das der *Kombination von Effekten*. Auch hierzu fehlen Studien, in denen die relativen Effekte einzelner Merkmale des Wohngebiets *und* deren Interaktionseffekte auf die Einstellungen und das Verhalten von Bewohnern

	Hoher SES	Eigentümer	Migranten	Arbeitslose	Alleinerziehende
Gebiet A (%)	15	20	15	10	10
Gebiet B (%)	40	45	5	5	5

untersucht werden. Dieses Problem sei an einem Beispiel von zwei Gebieten, gemischt nach fünf Merkmalen und deren Ausprägungen, demonstriert:

Welche Effekte (auf welche abhängigen Variablen?) sind von der Mischung im Gebiet A und welche von der im Gebiet B zu erwarten? Zu eben diesem grundsätzlichen Problem der Effekte einer mehrdimensionalen sozialen Mischung und des Gewichts Gebietsmerkmale einzelner Merkmale liegen in der Literatur keine vergleichenden empirischen Ergebnisse vor.

6 Zusammenfassung und Folgerungen

Stark vereinfachend könnte man sagen, die Studien zu den abträglichen Effekten benachteiligter Wohngebiete seien durch zwei klassische Publikationen der Chicagoer Schule geprägt: Shaw und McKay (1942) für die soziale Desorganisation, Faris und Dunham (1936) für mentale Störungen. Im Gegensatz zur ersteren ist der Rückbezug auf die zweite weitgehend verloren gegangen; eine Ausnahme ist die Studie von Silver et al. (2002).

Die Analyse von Gebietseffekten ist ein prosperierendes Forschungsfeld, sowohl in der Soziologie als auch in der Medizinsoziologie. Die Grenzen zwischen den Disziplinen verwischen zudem, was fruchtbar für die Theorie, Methoden und statistischen Verfahren ist. Es hat nur den Nachteil, dass es kaum noch möglich ist, die Literatur zu rezipieren.

Die Erforschung der Kontexteffekte von Wohngebieten hat erhebliche Fortschritte gemacht. Fünf kumulative Befunde sind besonders wichtig:

1. Wohngebiete haben – unter Kontrolle individueller Variablen – einen Kontexteffekt.
2. Diese Kontexteffekte sind nicht gleichförmig, sondern für einzelne Bewohnergruppen verschieden.
3. Die Kontexteffekte sind häufig nicht-linear; es gibt Schwellenwerte. Vermutlich liegen diese Werte bei 10–20% und um die 40%, hängen aber von der Art der untersuchten Beziehung ab.
4. Die Schwellenwerte hängen auch von dem Ausmaß ab, zu dem eine Person einem gegebenen Gebietsmerkmal ausgesetzt ist (exposure). Daraus ergibt sich die Frage, wie lange eine Person, die einem negativen Kontexteffekt ausgesetzt war und nun in ein anderes Wohngebiet zieht, in diesem wohnen muss, damit der positive Effekt den ursprünglich negativen mildert oder gar aufhebt.
5. Objektive Merkmale des Gebiets sind vermutlich für Einstellungen und Verhalten der Bewohner weniger wichtig als die wahrgenommenen Eigenschaften.

Die künftige Forschung wird sich dennoch weiterhin darauf richten müssen, die sozialen Mechanismen genauer zu bestimmen. Wir müssen die Mechanismen „Rollenmodelle", „Sozialisation" und „Ansteckung" – also Prozesse sozialen Lernens, explizieren und in qualitativen oder „ethnografischen" Studien untersuchen, bevor wir eine standardisierte Befragung vornehmen können (vgl. Small und Feldman 2012). Das wird andere als die bislang verwendeten Methoden erfordern: eine teilnehmende Beobachtung von Situationen (Interaktionen), Gruppendiskussionen, als Erweiterung dessen concept mapping (Burke et al. 2005; Trochim 1989). Diese Methoden können dazu beitragen, die aufgeführten Mechanismen zu operationalisieren, um dann quantitative Studien durchzuführen, z. B. Surveys mit einem Vignetten-Design (Jasso und Opp 1997; Steiner und Atzmüller 2006). Schließlich bleibt, insbesondere in Studien einzelner Wohngebiete, das Problem des selection bias angemessen zu lösen.

Wenn der Archäologe Michael Smith (2010, S. 1) damit Recht hat, die „spatial division of cities in districts or neighborhoods is one of the few universals of urban life from the earliest cities to the present", dann kommt der Erforschung der Nachbarschaftseffekte künftig eine erheblich stärkere Bedeutung für die soziologische Forschung zu.

Literatur

Akers, Ronald L. 1985. *Deviant behavior. A social learning approach.* Belmont: Wadsworth.
Atkinson, Rowland, und Keith Kintrea. 2001. Disentangling area effects: Evidence from deprived and non-deprived neighbourhoods. *Urban Studies* 38:2277–2298.
Baldwin, John D., und Janice I. Baldwin. 1981. *Behavior principles in everyday life.* Englewood Cliffs: Prentice-Hall.
Bandura, Albert. 1973. *Aggression. A social learning analysis.* Englewood Cliffs: Prentice-Hall.
Bandura, Albert, und Richard H. Walters. 1963. *Social learning and personality development.* New York: Holt, Rinehart and Winston.
Barrington, Wendy E., Mai Stafford, Mark Hamer, Shirley A. A. Beresford, Thomas Koepsell und Andrew Steptoe. 2014. Neighborhood socioeconomic deprivation, perceived neighborhood factors, and cortisol responses to induced stress among healthy adults. *Health & Place* 27:120–126.
Baum, Fran E., Anna M. Ziersch, Guabyu Zhang und Katy Osborne. 2009. Do perceived neighborhood cohesion and safety contribute to neighborhood differences in health? *Health & Place* 15:925–934.
Blasius, Jörg, und Jürgen Friedrichs. 2007. Internal heterogeneity in a deprived urban area and its impact on resident's perceptions of deviance. *Housing Studies* 22:753–780.
Blasius, Jörg, Jürgen Friedrichs und Jennifer Klöckner. 2008. *Doppelt benachteiligt? Leben in einem deutsch-türkischen Stadtteil.* Wiesbaden: VS Verlag für Sozialwissenschaften.
Blasius, Jörg, Jürgen Friedrichs und George Galster. Hrsg. 2009. *Quantifying neighbourhood effects. Frontiers and perspectives.* London: Routledge.
Booth, Charles. 1970. *Life and labor of people in London.* [1902–1904]. New York: AMS Press.
Brenner, Allison B., Marc A. Zimmerman, Jose A. Bauermeister und Cleopatra H. Caldwell. 2013. Neighborhood context and perceptions of stress over time: An ecological model of neighborhood stressors and intrapersonal and interpersonal resources. *American Journal of Community Psychology* 51:544–556.
Brooks-Gunn, Jeanne, Greg J. Duncan, Pamela K. Klebanov und Naomi Sealand. 1993. Do neighborhoods influence child and adolescent development? *American Journal of Sociology* 29:167–207.
Browning, Christopher R., Seth L. Feinberg und Robert D. Dietz. 2004. The paradox of social organization: Networks, collective efficacy, and violent crime in urban neighborhoods. *Social Forces* 83:503–534.
Bridge, Gary, Tim Butler und Loretta Lees. Hrsg. 2012. *Mixed communities. Gentrification by stealth?* Bristol: Policy Press.
Briggs, Xavier de Souza, Susan J. Popkin und John Goering. Hrsg. 2010. *Moving to opportunity. The story of an American experiment to fight ghetto poverty.* Oxford: Oxford University Press.
Bryden, Anna, Bayard Roberts, Mark Petticrew und Martin McKee. 2013. A systematic review of the influence of community level factors on alcohol use. *Health & Place* 21:70–85.

Buck, Nick. 2001. Identifying neighbourhood effects on social exclusion. *Urban Studies* 38:2251–2275.
Burdette, Amy M., und Terrence D. Hill. 2008. An examination of processes linking perceived neighborhood disorder and obesity. *Social Science & Medicine* 67:38–46.
Burke, Jessica G., Patricia O'Campo, Geri L. Peak, Andrea C. Gielen, Karen A. McDonnell und William M. K. Trochim. 2005. An introduction to concept mapping as a participatory public health research method. *Qualitative Health Research* 15:1392–1410.
Cisneros, Henry G., und Lora Engdahl. Hrsg. 2009. *From despair to HOPE. HOPE VI and the new promise of public housing in America's cities*. Washington, DC: Brookings Institution Press.
Cohen, Deborah, Denise Janicki-Deverts, William J. Doyle, Gregory E. Miller, Ellen Frank, Bruce S. Rabin und Ronald B. Turner. 2012. Chronic stress, glucocorticoid receptor resistance, inflation, and disease risk. *Publications of the National Academy of Sciences* 109:5995–5999.
Cohen, Deborah, Karen Mason, Ariane Bedimo, Richard Scribner, Victoria Basolo und Thomas A. Farley. 2003. Neighborhood physical conditions and health. *American Journal of Public Health* 93:467–471.
Cohen, Sheldon, Denise Janicki-Deverts und Gregory E. Miller. 2007. Psychological stress and disease. *Journal of the American Medical Association* 298:1685–1687.
Condron, Dennis J., und Vincent J. Roscigno. 2003. Disparities within: Unequal spending and achievement in an urban school district. *Sociology of Education* 76:18–36.
Corburn, Jason, Jeffrey Osleeb und Michael Porter. 2006. Urban asthma and the neighbourhood environment in New York City. *Health & Place* 12:176–179.
Crane, Jonatha. 1991. The epidemic theory of ghettos and neighborhood effects on dropping out and teenage childbearing. *American Journal of Sociology* 96:1226–1259.
Crowder, Kyle, und Scoot J. South. 2010. Spatial and temporal dimensions of neighborhood effects on high school graduation. *Social Science Research* 40:87–106.
Cummins, Steven, und Sally Macintyre. 2006. Food environments and obesity – neighborhood or nation? *International Journal of Epidemiology* 35:100–104.
Curtis, Sarah, Rachel Pain, Sara Fuller, Yasmin Khatib, Catherine Rothon, Stephen A. Stanfeld und Shari Daya. 2013. Neighborhood risk factors for common mental disorders among young people aged 10–20 years: A structured review of quantitative research. *Health & Place* 20:81–90.
Dalstra Jetty A., Anton E. Kunst, Carme Borrell, Elizabeth Breeze, Emmanuelle Cambois, Giuseppe Costa, José J. M. Geurts, Eero Lahelma, Herman van Oyen, Niels K. Rasmussen, Enrique Regidor, Teresa Spadea und Johan P. Mackenbach. 2005. Socioeconomic differences in the prevalence of common chronic diseases: An Overview of eight European countries. *International Journal of Epidemiology* 34:316–326.
DeLuca, Stefanie, Greg J. Duncan, Micere Keels und Ruby Mendenhall. 2012. The notable and the null: Using mixed methods to understand the diverse impacts of residential mobility programs. In *Neighbourhood effects research: New perspectives*, Hrsg. Maarten van Ham, David Manley, Nick Bailey, Ludi Simpson und Duncan Maclennan, (2012b), 195–224. Dordrecht: Springer VS.
Deutscher Bundestag. 2005. *Lebenslagen in Deutschland. Zweiter Armuts- und Reichtumsbericht*. Drucksache 15/5015. Bonn: Deutscher Bundestag.
Dietz, Robert D. 2002. Estimation of neighborhood effects in the social sciences. *Social Science Research* 31:539–575.
Diez Roux, Ana V. 2001. Investigating neighborhood and area effects on health. *American Journal of Public Health* 91:1783–1789.
Diez Roux, Ana V., und Christina Mair. 2010. Neighborhoods and health. *Annals of the New York Academy of Sciences* 1186:125–145.
Durlauf, Steven N. 2004. Neighborhood effects. In *Handbook of regional and urban economics,* Vol. 4: *Cities and geography*, Hrsg. J. Vernon Henderson und Jacques-Francois Thisse, 7–42. Amsterdam: Elsevier.
Ellen, Ingrid G., Tod Mijanovich und Keri-Nicole Dillman. 2001. Neighborhood effects on health: Exploring the links and assessing the evidence. *Journal of Urban Affairs* 23:391–408.
Erbring, Lutz, und Alice A. Young. 1979. Contextual effects as endogenous feedback. *Sociological Methods & Research* 7:396–430.
Faris, Robvert E., und Warren H. Dunham. 1939. *Mental disorders in urban areas: An ecological study of schizophrenia and other psychoses*. Chicago: University of Chicago Press.
Flint, Ellen, Steven Cummins und Stephen Matthews. 2013. Do perceptions of the neighbourhood food environment predict fruit and vegetable intake in low-income neighbourhoods? *Health & Place* 24:11–15.

Friedrichs, Jürgen. 1991. Middle-class leakage in large new housing estates. Empirical findings and policy implications. *Journal of Architectural and Planning Research* 8:287–295.
Friedrichs, Jürgen. 1998. Do poor neighborhoods make their residents poorer? Context effects of poverty neighborhoods on residents. In *Empirical poverty research in comparative perspective*, Hrsg. Hans-Jürgen Andreß, 77–99. Aldershot: Ashgate.
Friedrichs, Jürgen. 2013. Sozialräumliche Kontexteffekte der Armut. In *Städtische Armutsquartiere – Kriminelle Lebenswelten?* Hrsg. Dietrich Oberwittler, Susann Rabold und Dirk Baier, 11–44. Wiesbaden: Springer VS.
Friedrichs, Jürgen, und Jörg Blasius. 2003. Social norms in distressed neighborhoods. Testing the Wilson hypothesis. *Housing Studies* 18:807–826.
Friedrichs, Jürgen, George Galster und Sako Musterd. 2003. Editorial. Neighbourhood effects in social opportunities: The European and American research and policy context. *Housing Studies* 18:797–806.
Friedrichs, Jürgen, George Galster und Sako Musterd. Hrsg. 2005. *Life in poverty neighbourhoods. European and American perspectives.* London: Routledge.
Galea, Sandro, Jennifer Ahern, Sasha Rudenstine, Zachary Wallace und David Vlahov. 2005. Urban built environment and depression: A multilevel analysis. *Journal of Epidemiology and Community Health* 59:822–827.
Galster, George C. 2003. Investigating behavioral impacts of poor neighborhoods: Towards new data and analytic strategies. *Housing Studies* 18:893–914.
Galster, George C. 2007. Neighborhoodsocial mix as a goal of housing policy: A theoretical analysis. *European Journal of Housing Policy* 7:19–43.
Galster, George C. 2008. Quantifying the effects of neighbourhood on individuals: Challenges, alternative approaches, and promising directions. *Schmollers Jahrbuch* 128:7–48.
Galster, George C. 2012. The mechanism(s) of neighbourhood effects: Theory, evidence, and policy implications. In *Neighbourhood effects research: New perspectives*, Hrsg. Maarten van Ham, David Manley, Nick Bailey, Ludi Simpson und Duncan Maclennan, (2012b), 23–56. Dordrecht: Springer VS.
Galster, George, Roberto G.. Quercia und Alvaro Cortes. 2000. Identifying neighborhood thresholds: An empirical exploration. *Housing Policy Debate* 11:701–732.
Galster, George, Roger Andersson und Sako Musterd. 2010. Who is affected by neighbourhood income mix? Gender, age, family, employment and income differences. *Urban Studies* 47:2915–2944.
Galster, George, Roger Andersson und Sako Musterd. 2011. Are males' incomes influenced by the incomes of their male neighbors? Explorations into nonlinear and threshold effects. Paper, presented at the European Network for Housing research Conference, Istanbul, July 2011.
Gibbons, Steve. 2002. *Neighbourhood effects on educational achievement: Evidence from the census and national child development study.* London: Centre for the Economics of Education, London School of Economics and Political Science.
Gittel, Ross, und Avis Vidal. 1998. *Community organizing: Building social capital as a development strategy.* Newbury Park: Sage.
Glass, Thomas A., Meghan D. Rasmussen und Brian S. Schwartz. 2006. Neighborhoods and obesity in older adults: The Baltimore memory study. *American Journal of Preventive Medicine* 3:455–463.
Goering, John, und Judith D. Feins. Hrsg. 2003. *Choosing a better life? Evaluating the moving to opportunity social experiment.* Washington, D.C: The Urban Institute.
Hastings, Annette. 2009. Neighbourhood environmental services and neighbourhood ‚effects': Exploring the role of urban services in intensifying neighbourhood problems. *Housing Studies* 24:503–524.
Haynie, Dana L. 2001. Delinquent peers revisited: Does network structure matter? *American Journal of Sociology* 106:1013–1057.
Hedman, Lina, und Maarten van Ham. 2012. Understanding neighbourhood effects: Selection bias and residential mobility. In *Neighbourhood effects research: New perspectives*, Hrsg. Maarten van Ham, David Manley, Nick Bailey, Ludi Simpson und Duncan Maclennan, (2012b), 79–99. Dordrecht: Springer
Hedman, Lina, und George Galster. 2013. Neighbourhood income sorting and the effects of neighbourhood income mix on income: A holistic empirical exploration. *Urban Studies* 50:107–127.
Hedström, Peter, und Richard Swedberg. 1998. Social mechanisms. An introductory essay. In *Social mechanisms: An analytical approach to social theory*, Hrsg. Peter Hedström und Richard Swedberg, 1–31. Cambridge: Cambridge University Press.
Heuwinkel, Dirk. 1981. *Aktionsräumliche Analysen und Bewertungen von Wohngebieten.* Hamburg: Christians.

Hill Terence D., und Ronald J. Angel. 2005. Neighborhood disorder, psychological distress, and heavy drinking. *Social Science & Medicine* 61:965–975.
Hiscock, Ruth. 2001. *Are mixed tenure estates likely to enhance the social capital of their residents?* Paper, presented at the Housing Studies Association Conference, Sept. 3–4, Cardiff, UK.
Hogan, Dennis P., und Evelyn M. Kitagawa. 1985. The impact of social status, family structure, and *Neighbourhood* on the fertility of black adolescents. *American Journal of Sociology* 90:825–855.
Ioannides, Yannis M., und Linda D. Loury. 2004. Job information networks, neighborhood effects, and inequality. *Journal of Economic Literature* 42:1056–1093.
Jargowsky, Paul A. 1997. *Poverty and place. Ghettos, barrios, and the American city*. New York: Russel Sage Foundation.
Jasso, G., und Karl-Dieter Opp. 1997. Probing the character of norms. A factorial survey analysis of the norms of political action. *American Sociological Review* 62:947–964.
Jencks, Christopher, und Susan E. Mayer. 1990. The social consequences of growing up in a poor neighborhood. In *Inner-city poverty in the United States*, Hrsg. Laurence E. Lynn und Michael G. H. McGeary, 111–186. Washington: National Academic Press.
Kleit, Rachel. 2001. The role of social networks in scattered-site public housing residents' search for jobs. *Housing Policy Debate* 12:541–573.
Kruger Daniel J., Thomas M. Reischl und Glibert C. Gee. 2007. Neighborhood social conditions mediate the association between physical deterioration and mental health. *American Journal of Community Psychology* 40:261–271.
Kubzansky, Laura D., S.V. Subramanian, Ichiro Kawachi, Martha E. Fay, Mah-J. Soobader und Lisa F. Berkman. 2005. Neighborhood contextual influences on depressive symptoms in the elderly. *American Journal of Epidemiology* 162:253–260.
Kunadt, Susann. 2013. Sozialräumliche Determinanten der Jugendkriminalität. Test eines Modells informeller Sozialkontrolle zur Erklärung des Gewalthandelns Jugendlicher aus verschiedenen Duisburger Stadtteilen. In *Städtische Armutsquartiere – Kriminelle Lebenswelten?* Hrsg. Dietrich Oberwittler et al., 141–168. Wiesbaden: Springer VS.
Lampert Thomas, und Andreas Mielck. 2008. Gesundheit und soziale Ungleichheit – Eine Herausforderung für Forschung und Politik. *Gesundheit + Gesellschaft Wissenschaft* 8:7–16.
Lankford, Hamilton, Susanna Loeb und James Wyckoff. 2002. Teacher sorting and the plight of urban schools: A descriptive analysis. *Educational Evaluation and Policy Analysis* 24:37–62.
Law, Michael, Kathi Wilson, John Eyles, Susan Elliott, Michael Jerrett, Tina Moffat und Isaac Luginaah. 2005. Meeting health need, accessing health care: The role of neighbourhood. *Health & Place* 11:367–377.
Lazarsfeld, Paul F., und Herbert Menzel. 1961. On the relation between individual and collective properties. In *A sociological reader on complex organizations*, Hrsg. Amitai Etzioni, 422–440. New York: Holt, Rinehart and Winston.
Leventhal, Tama, und Jeanne Brooks-Gunn. 2000. The neighborhood they live in: The effects of neighborhood residence on child and adolescent outcomes. *Psychological Bulletin* 126:209–337.
Livingston, Mark, Nick Bailey und Ade Kearns. 2008. *The influence of neighbourhood deprivation on people's attachment to places*. York: The Joseph Rowntree Foundation.
Lupton, Ruth, und Dylan Kneale. 2012. Theorising and measuring place in neighbourhood effects research: The example of teenage parenthood in England. In *Neighbourhood effects research: New perspectives*, Hrsg. Maarten van Ham, David Manley, Nick Bailey, Ludi Simpson und Duncan Maclennan, (2012b), 121–146. Dordrecht: Springer VS.
Manley, David, und Maarten van Ham. 2012. Neighbourhood effects, housing tenure and unindividual employment outcomes. In *Neighbourhood effects research: New perspectives*, Hrsg. Maarten van Ham, David Manley, Nick Bailey, Ludi Simpson und Duncan Maclennan, (2012b), 147–174. Dordrecht: Springer VS.
Martinez, Pedro, und John E. Richters. 1993. The NIMH Community Violence project: II. Children's distress symptoms associated with violence exposure. *Psychiatry* 56:22–35.
Mayntz, Renate. 2005. Soziale Mechanismen in der Analyse gesellschaftlicher Makro-Phänomene. In *Was erklärt die Soziologie?* Hrsg. Uwe Schimank und Rainer Greshoff, 204–227. Berlin: LIT Verlag.
McCulloch, Andrew. 2001. Ward-level deprivation and individual social and economic outcomes in the British household panel study. *Environment and Planning* A 33:667–684.
Merton, Robert K. 1957. *Social theory and social structure*. Glencoe: Free Press.
Messner, Steven, Baumer, Eric und Rosenfeld, Richard. 2004. Dimensions of social capital and rates of criminal homicide. *American Sociological Review* 69:882–903.

Mezuk, Briana, Asa Chikiat, Xinjun Li, Jan Sunquist, Kenneth S. Kendler und Kristina Sundquist. 2013. Depression, neighborhood deprivation and risk of type 2 diabetes. *Health & Place* 23:63–69.

Moffat, Tina, T. Galloway und J. Latham. 2005. Stature and adiposity among children in contrasting neighborhoods in the city of Hamilton, Ontario, Canada. *American Journal of Human Biology* 17:355–367.

Musterd, Sako, und Roger Andersson. 2005. Housing mix, social mix, and social opportunities. *Urban Affairs Review* 40:1–30.

Musterd, Sako, und Roger Andersson. 2006. Employment, social mobility and neighbourhood effects: The case of Sweden. *International Journal of Urban and Regional Research* 30:120–140.

Nonnenmacher, Alexandra. 2009. *Ist Arbeit eine Pflicht? Normative Einstellungen zur Erwerbsarbeit, Arbeitslosigkeit und der Einfluss des Wohngebiets*. Wiesbaden: VS Verlag für Sozialwissenschaften.

Nonnenmacher, Alexandra. 2013. Zur Nachweisbarkeit von Kontexteffekten der sozialräumlichen Umgebung. In *Städtische Armutsquartiere – Kriminelle Lebenswelten?* Hrsg. Dietrich Oberwittler, Susann Rabold und Dirk Baier, 293–319. Wiesbaden: Springer VS.

Oberwittler, Dietrich. 2007. Urban poverty and adolescent adjustment: A multilevel analysis of neighborhood effects on adolescent problem behavior differentiated by gender and ethnicity. *Housing Studies* 22:781–803.

O'Campo, Patricia, Christina Salmon und Jessica Burke. 2009. Neighbourhoods and mental well-being: What are the pathways? *Health & Place* 15:56–68.

Oliver, Pamela, Gerald Marwell und Ruy Texeira. 1985. A theory of critical mass. *American Journal of Sociology* 91:522–556.

Opp, Karl-Dieter. 2004. Erklärung durch Mechanismen: Probleme und Alternative. In *Angewandte Soziologie*, Hrsg. Robert Kecskes, Michael Wagner und Christof Wolf, 361–379. Wiesbaden: VS Verlag für Sozialwissenschaften.

Opp, Karl-Dieter. 2013. Rational choice theory, the logic of explanation, middle-range theories and analytical sociology: A reply to Gianluca Manzo and Petri Ylikoski. *Social Science Information* 52:394–408.

Orr, Larry, Judith E. Feins, Robin Jacob, Erik Beecroft, Lisa Sanbonmatsu, Lawrence F. Katz, Jeffrey B. Liebman und Jeffrey E. Kling. 2003. *Moving to opportunity interim impacts evaluation*. Washington, D.C: U.S. Department of Housing and Urban Development.

Ostendorf, Wim, Sako Musterd und Sjoerd de Vos. 2001. Social mix and the neighbourhood effect. Policy ambitions and empirical evidence. *Housing Studies* 16:371–380.

Pickett, Kate E., und M. Pearl. 2001. Multilevel analyses of neighbourhood socioeconomic context and health outcomes: A critical review. *Journal of Epidemiology and Community Health* 55:111–122.

Pinkster, Fenne. 2008. *Living in concentrated poverty*. Unveröff. Dissertation. Amsterdam: Universität Amsterdam, Department für Geographie.

Pinkster, Fenne M., und Beate Völker. 2009. Local social networks and social resources in two Dutch neighbourhoods. *Housing Studies* 24:225–242.

Pinkster, Fenne. 2013. Neighbourhood effects as indirect effects: Evidence from a Dutch case study on the significance of neighbourhood for employment trajectories. *International Journal of Urban and Regional Research*. DOI:10.1080/1369183X.2013.830503.

Popkin, Susan J., Larry Buron, Diane K. Levy und Mary C. Cunningham. 2000. The Gautreaux legacy: What might mixed-income dispersal strategies mean for the poorest public housing tenants. *Housing Policy Debate* 11:911–942.

Popkin, Susan J., Bruce Katz, Mary C. Cunningham, Karen D. Brown, Jeremy Gustafson und Margery Turner. 2004. *A Decade of HOPE VI: Research findings and policy challenges*. Washington, D.C.: The Urban Institute.

Rabold, Susann. 2011. *Zum Einfluss interethnischer Freundschaften auf Gewaltverhalten deutscher und nicht-deutscher Jugendlicher*. Baden-Baden: Nomos.

Rabold, Susann, und Dirk Baier. 2013. Sozialräumlicher Kontext und Jugenddelinquenz. Zum Einfluss von Stadtteileigenschaften auf gewalttätiges Verhalten von Jugendlichen am Beispiel Hannover. In *Städtische Armutsquartiere – Kriminelle Lebenswelten?* Hrsg. Dietrich Oberwittler et al., 169–191. Wiesbaden: Sringer VS.

Raudenbush, Stephen W., und Robert J. Sampson. 1999. Ecometrics: Toward a science of assessing ecological settings, with application to the systematic social observation of neighborhood. *Sociological Methodology* 29:1–41.

Reuber, Paul. 1993. *Heimat in der Großstadt*. Köln: Universität, Geographisches Institut.

Rosenbaum, James E. 1995. Changing the geography of opportunity by expanding residential choice: Lessons from the Gautreaux program. *Housing Policy Debate* 6:231–269.
Ross, Catherine S., und John Mirowsky. 1999. Disorder and decay: The concept and measurement of perceived neighbourhood disorder. *Urban Affairs Review* 34:412–432.
Ross, Catherine S., John Mirowsky und Shana Pribesh. 2001. Powerlessness and the amplification of threat: neighborhood disadvantage, disorder, and mistrust. *American Sociological Review* 66:568–591.
Ross, Nancy, Stephane Tremblay, Saeeda Khan, Daniel Crouse, Mark Tremblay und Jean-Marie Berthelot. 2007. Body mass index in Urban Canada: Neighborhood and metropolitan area effects. *American Journal of Public Health* 97:500–508.
Sampson, Robert. 2006. How does community context matter? Social mechanisms and the explanation of crime rates. In *Crime and its explanation: Contexts, mechanisms and development*, Hrsg. Per-Olof H. Wikström und Robert J. Sampson, 31–60. Cambridge: Cambridge University Press.
Sampson, Robert J. 2012. *Great American city*. Chicago: University of Chicago Press.
Sampson, Robert J., und W. Byron Groves. 1989. Community structure and crime: Testing social disorganization theory. *American Journal of Sociology* 94:774–802.
Sampson, Robert J., und Stephen W. Raudenbusch. 1999. Systematic social observation of public spaces: A new look at disorder in urban neighborhoods. *American Journal of Sociology* 105:603–651.
Sampson, Robert J., Stephen W. Raudenbush und Felton Earls. 1997. Neighborhoods and violent crime: A multilevel study of collective efficacy. *Science* 277:918–924.
Sampson, Robert J., Jeffrey D. Morenoff und Felton Earls. 1999. Beyond social capital: Spatial dynamics of collective efficacy for children. *American Sociological Review* 64:633–660.
Sampson, Robert J., Jeffrey D. Morenoff und Thomas Gannon-Rowley. 2002. Assessing „neighborhood effects": Social processes and new directions in research. *Annual Review of Sociology* 28:443–478.
Sarkar, Chinmoy, John Gallacher und Chris Webster. 2013. Built environment configuration and change in body mass index: The Caerphilly prospective study (CaPS). *Health & Place* 19:33–44.
Schulz, Amy J., Graciela Mentz, Laurie Lachance, Shannon N. Zenk, Jonetta Johnson, Carmen Stokes und Rebecca Mandell. 2013. Do observed or perceived characteristics of the neighborhood environment mediate associations between neighborhood poverty and cumulative biological risk? *Health & Place* 24:147–156.
Shaw, Clifford R., und Henry D. McKay. 1942. *Juvenile delinquency and urban areas*. Chicago: University of Chicago Press.
Silver, Eric, Edward P. Mulvey und Jeffrey W. Swanson. 2002. Neighborhood structural characteristics and mental disorder: Faris and Dunham revisited. *Social Science & Medicine* 55:1457–1470.
Skogan, Wesley G. 1990. *Disorder and decline: Crime and the spiral of decline in American neighborhoods*. New York: Free Press.
Small, Mario Luis, und Jessica Feldman. 2012. Ethnographic evidence, heterogeneity, and neighborhood effects after moving to opportunity. In *Neighbourhood effects research: New perspectives*, Hrsg. Maarten van Ham, David Manley, Nick Bailey, Ludi Simpson und Duncan Maclennan, (2012b), 57–78. Dordrecht: Springer VS.
Small, Mario L., und Katherine Newman. 2001. Urban poverty after the truly disadvantaged: The rediscovery of family, the neighborhood, and culture. *Annual Review of Sociology* 27:23–45.
Smith, Michel. 2010. The archeological study of neighborhoods and districts in ancient cities. *Journal of Anhtropological Archeology* 29:137–154.
Stadt Köln. 2009. Statistisches Jahrbuch 2009. Köln.
Steiner, Peter M., und Christiane Atzmüller. 2006. Experimentelle Vignettendesigns in faktoriellen Surveys. *Kölner Zeitschrift für Soziologie und Sozialpsychologie* 58:117–118.
Steptoe, Andrew, und Pamela J. Feldman. 2001. Neighborhood problems as sources of chronic stress: Development of a measure of neighborhood problems, and association with socioeconomic status and health. *Annals of Behavioral Medicine* 23:177–185.
Sutherland, Edwin H. 1968. Die Theorie der differentiellen Kontakte. In Kriminalsoziologie, Hrsg. Fritz Sack und René König, 394–399. Frankfurt a. M.: Akademische Verlagsgesellschaft.
Teitler, Julien O., und Christopher C. Weiss. 2000. Effects of neighborhood and school environments on transitions to first sexual intercourse. *Sociology of Education* 73:112–132.
Thornton, Lukar E., Karen E. Lamb und Kylie Ball. 2013. Employment status, residential and workplace food environments: Associations with women's eating behaviors. *Health & Place* 24:80–89.
Trochim, William. 1989. An introduction to concept mapping for planning and evaluation. *Evaluation and Program Planning* 12:1–16.

Van der Klaauw, Baas, und Jan C. van Ours. 2003. From welfare to work: Does the neighborhood matter? *Journal of Public Economics* 87:957–985.

Van Ham, Maarten, David Manley, Nick Bailey, Ludi Simpson und Duncan Maclennan. 2012a. Introduction. In *Neighborhood effects research: New perspectives*, Hrsg. Maarten van Ham, David Manley, Nick Bailey, Ludi Simpson und Duncan Maclennan, 1–22. Dordrecht: Springer.

Van Ham, Maarten, David Manley, Nick Bailey, Ludi Simpson und Duncan Maclennan. Hrsg. 2012b. *Neighborhood effects research: New perspectives*. Dordrecht: Springer VS.

Van Ham, Maarten, David Manley, Nick Bailey, Ludi Simpson und Duncan Maclennan. Hrsg. 2013. *Understanding neighborhood dynamics*. Dordrecht: Springer VS.

Van Ham, Maarten, David Manley, Nick Bailey, Ludi Simpson und Duncan Maclennan. Hrsg. 2014. *Neighborhood Effects or Neighborhood Based Problems?* Dordrecht: Springer VS.

Van Lenthe, Frank, Johannes Brug und Johan P. Mackenbach. 2005. Neighborhood inequalities in physical inactivity. The role of neighborhood attractiveness, proximity to local facilities and safety in the Netherlands. *Social Science & Medicine* 60:763–775.

Völker, Beate, Gerald Mollenhorst und Veronique Schutjens. 2013. Neighborhood social capital and residential mobility. In *Understanding neighborhood dynamics*, Hrsg. Maarten van Ham, David Manley, Nick Bailey, Ludi Simpson und Duncan Maclennan, 139–160. Dordrecht: Springer VS.

Weich, Scott, Martin Blanchard, Martin Prince, Elizabeth Burton, Bob Erens und Kerry Sproston. 2002. Mental health and the built environment: Cross-sectional survey of individual and contextual risk factors for depression. *British Journal of Psychiatry* 180:428–433.

Weicher, John C. 1990. How poverty neighborhoods are changing. In *Inner-city poverty in the United States*, Hrsg. Laurence E. Lynn und Michael G. H. McGeary, 68–110. Washington, DC: National Academy Press.

Weinberg, Zy. 2000. No place to shop: Food access lacking in the inner city. *Race, Poverty and the Environment* 7:22–24.

Wilkerson, Amy, Nichole E. Carlson, Irene H. Yen und Yvonne L. Michael. 2011. Neighborhood physical features and relationships with neighbors: Does positive physical environment increase neighborliness? *Environment and Behavior* 44:595–615.

Wilson, William J. 1987. *The truly disadvantaged*. Chicago: The University of Chicago Press.

Wilson, James Q., und George L. Kelling. 1982. Broken windows. *The Atlantic Monthly*, March 1982:29–38.

Woolcock, Michael, und Deepa Narayn. 2000. Social capital: Implications for development theory, research, and policy. *The World Bank Observer* 15:225–249.

Xu, Yili, Mora L. Fiedler und Karl H. Flaming. 2005. Discovering the impact of community policing: The broken windows thesis. Collective efficacy, and citizens' judgment. *Journal of Research in Crime and Delinquency* 42:147–186.

Yip, Alexandra M., George Kephart und Paul J. Veugelers. 2002. Individual and neighborhood determinants of health care utilization: Implications for health policy and resource allocation. *Canadian Journal of Public Health* 93:303–307.

Zorbaugh, Henry. 1929. *The gold coast and the slum: A sociological study of Chicago's near north side*. Chicago: University of Chicago Press.

Jürgen Friedrichs, 1938, Prof. Dr., Studium der Soziologie, Philosophie, Psychologie und Volkswirtschaftslehre. Nach der Promotion Assistentenstelle im Institut für Soziologie der Universität Hamburg, dort 1974 Berufung auf eine Professur für Soziologie; 1983 auf einen Lehrstuhl für Soziologie. Seit 1991 Lehrstuhl für Soziologie an der Universität zu Köln, Direktor des Forschungsinstitutes für Soziologie und Mitherausgeber der „Kölner Zeitschrift für Soziologie und Sozialpsychologie" (bis 2012). Seit 2007 emeritiert, aber weiterhin im Institut für Soziologie und Sozialpsychologie in der Lehre und Forschung tätig. Aktuelle Forschungsprojekte: Kontexteffekte, städtische Armutsgebiete, Gentrification. Aktuelle Veröffentlichungen: Städtische Armutsgebiete. In: *Städtische Armutsquartiere – Kriminelle Lebenswelten?* Wiesbaden 2013 (Hrsg. D. Oberwittler, S. Rabold und D. Baier); Armut und räumliche Polarisierung. In: Urbane Ungleichheiten. Wiesbaden 2014 (Hrsg. P.A. Berger et al.).

Schule und Schulklasse als soziale Kontexte der Entwicklung im Jugendalter

Katja Scharenberg

© Springer Fachmedien Wiesbaden 2014

Zusammenfassung Untersuchungen zur Bedeutung von sozialen Kontexten haben in der empirischen Sozial- und Bildungsforschung eine lange Tradition. Ein Anwendungsbereich der Kontextanalyse liegt im Mehrebenensystem Schule. Der Beitrag beschäftigt sich mit der Frage nach den relevanten Kontexten (Schulklasse und Schule) für die schulische Leistungsentwicklung als zentraler Aspekt der Entwicklung im Jugendalter. Dabei wird auch untersucht, ob die normative Kultur der Altersgruppe als Indikator für Vermittlungsprozesse zwischen Kontextmerkmalen und Schulleistung entwicklungsrelevant ist. Datengrundlage ist die Hamburger Schulleistungsstudie „Kompetenzen und Einstellungen von Schülerinnen und Schülern" (KESS), mit der die Leistungsentwicklung im Leseverständnis von 9681 Schülerinnen und Schülern in 467 Schulklassen und 142 Schulen in den Jahrgangsstufen 7 und 8 nachvollzogen werden kann. In schrittweisen Mehrebenenmodellen erweisen sich neben individuellen Schülermerkmalen die leistungsbezogene Klassenkomposition und die Schulformzugehörigkeit als bedeutsam. Die normative Kultur der Altersgruppe stellt hingegen nur im unmittelbaren Klassenkontext einen bedeutsamen Indikator für Vermittlungsprozesse von Kontexteffekten dar, wobei diese Prozesse geschlechtsspezifisch ausfallen.

Schlüsselwörter Schule · Schulklasse · Leistungsentwicklung · Jugendalter · Kontexteffekt · Vermittlungsprozesse

---

K. Scharenberg (✉)
Institut für Soziologie, Universität Basel,
Petersgraben 27,
4051 Basel, Schweiz
E-Mail: katja.scharenberg@unibas.ch

Schools and Classrooms as Social Contexts for the Development in Adolescence

Abstract Studies dealing with the importance of social contexts already have a long tradition in empirical sociological and educational research. One possibility of applying context analysis is to consider schools as multi-level systems. The contribution focuses on the question of the relevant context factors on classroom and school level for the development of school achievement as a key aspect of development in adolescence. It is also examined whether social responsibility goals and norms are indicators of mediating processes between context variables on the one hand and school achievement on the other hand. Data base is the study "Competences and attitudes of students" (KESS) that examines the development of Reading achievement from grade 7 to 8 of a whole student cohort (9,682 students in 467 classes and 142 schools in Hamburg, Germany). Stepwise multi-level regression analyses reveal individual student characteristics, the average ability composition on the class level and the attended track on the school level as relevant predictors of the development of achievement. Social responsibility goals and norms are relevant indicators of mediating processes within the proximal context of the classroom, but not within the context of the schools. These processes are, however, gender-specific.

Keywords School · Classroom · Achievement development · Adolescence · Contextual effect · Mediation processes

1 Einleitung

Kennzeichnend für das deutsche Schulsystem in der Sekundarstufe ist die institutionelle Differenzierung in verschiedene Schulformen und Bildungsgänge. Diese Differenzierung soll nach Leistungskriterien erfolgen und beruht auf der Annahme, dass der Unterricht in leistungshomogeneren Lerngruppen einfacher an individuelle Lernvoraussetzungen anzupassen sei, damit die Schülerinnen[1] und Schüler gezielt und ihrem Leistungsvermögen angemessen gefördert werden können (z. B. Barr und Dreeben 1983; Hallinan 1994; Harker und Tymms 2004; Hattie 2002; Slavin 1990b). Anhand verschiedener empirischer Studien wurde jedoch gezeigt, dass diese Differenzierung nicht ausschließlich leistungsbasiert erfolgt, sondern erheblich mit sozialen Herkunftsmerkmalen zusammenhängt (z. B. Baumert und Schümer 2001; Baumert et al. 2006). Die Schulformgliederung führt somit nicht nur zur gewünschten leistungsbezogenen Stratifizierung, sondern auch zu einer damit einhergehenden sozialen Segregation (Baumert et al. 2003, 2006). Gerade in Deutschland ist der Zusammenhang zwischen Sozialschichtzugehörigkeit und Lesekompetenz besonders eng – auf schulischer noch stärker als auf individueller Ebene (Baumert et al. 2009; Baumert und Schümer 2001). Dies führt zu einer Konzentration von Hauptschulen in den leistungsschwächeren, sozial benachteiligten sowie von Gymnasien in den

---

[1] Im Weiteren wird aus Vereinfachungsgründen von Schülern gesprochen, wenn Schülerinnen *und* Schüler gemeint sind.

leistungsstärkeren, sozial privilegierteren Bereichen der Verteilung bei gleichzeitig starker Überlappung der schulformspezifischen Leistungsverteilungen im mittleren Bereich (Baumert et al. 2006). Da eine Reihe weiterer leistungsrelevanter Merkmale mit der sozialen Herkunft eng zusammenhängt, können die spezifischen Kompositionsprofile der Schulformen zu einer kumulativen Benachteiligung oder Privilegierung von Schulen aufgrund einer für die jeweilige Schülerschaft unterschiedlichen Verfügbarkeit an ökonomischem, kulturellem oder sozialem Kapital führen. Nach Dreeben und Barr (1988) ist dabei nicht allein die soziale Zusammensetzung der Schülerschaft ausschlaggebend. Vielmehr scheinen sich Lehrkräfte v. a. an das damit variierende Leistungsniveau der Schülerschaft didaktisch, curricular und organisatorisch anzupassen. Auch schulformspezifische Traditionen der Didaktik und Lehrerbildung fördern die Herausbildung selektionsbedingter „differenzielle[r] Lern- und Entwicklungsmilieus" (Baumert und Schümer 2001, S. 462; Baumert et al. 2006, S. 98). Diese können dazu führen, dass die Entwicklung von Schülern unabhängig von und zusätzlich zu bereits existierenden individuellen Unterschieden je nach besuchter Schulform ungleich verläuft, erschwert oder sogar verhindert wird. Eine „faire", ausschließlich leistungsbezogene externe Differenzierung der Schülerschaft gelingt somit nicht (vgl. z. B. auch Artelt et al. 2001; Bos und Scharenberg 2010; Scharenberg 2012, 2013). Dies wirft Fragen auf

- nach der Gerechtigkeit und Chancengleichheit des deutschen Bildungssystems – und zwar auf individueller wie aggregierter Ebene (siehe hierzu Berkemeyer et al. 2012; Berkemeyer und Manitius 2013);
- danach, inwiefern die Entwicklung im Jugendalter – oder, in der Terminologie der Kontextanalyse ausgedrückt, das Explanandum auf der Mikroebene des Individuums – durch verschiedene institutionelle Kontexte auf Makro- und ggf. Mesoebene beeinflusst wird; und
- welcher der verschiedenen Kontexte im schulischen Bereich konkret welchen Anteil zum Bildungserfolg der Schüler beisteuert (Ditton 2013).

2 Schule und Schulklasse als soziale Kontexte der Entwicklung – ein Vermittlungsmodell

Gründe für Schereneffekte bei der Leistungsentwicklung zwischen verschiedenen Schulformen, die bereits mit Beginn der Sekundarstufe einsetzen und deren Auswirkungen sich über einen längeren Zeitraum kumulieren können (Bonsen et al. 2009a; Gröhlich et al. 2010a), liegen nach Baumert et al. (2006) darin, dass

1. Schüler in Abhängigkeit ihrer individuellen Lernausgangslagen unterschiedlich große Lernfortschritte machen (*individueller Matthäus-Effekt*);
2. *institutionelle Unterschiede* hinsichtlich der Unterrichtskulturen, Lehrpläne und Stundentafeln zwischen den Schulformen bestehen; und
3. sich die Schulformen auch hinsichtlich ihrer sozialen, kulturellen und leistungsbezogenen Zusammensetzung ihrer Schülerschaft, also in ihrer *Komposition*, unterscheiden (*institutioneller Matthäus-Effekt*).

Diese Auswirkungen der Schülerzusammensetzung auf die erzielten Lernstände und die Lern- und Persönlichkeitsentwicklung von Schülern werden auch unter dem Stichwort *Kompositionseffekte* behandelt. Beispiele für solche Effekte aggregierter Individualmerkmale (*Kompositionsmerkmale*) sind z. B. die durchschnittliche soziale Zusammensetzung und der prozentuale Anteil von Schülern mit Migrationshintergrund innerhalb von Schulen, ferner das durchschnittliche Leistungsniveau und die Leistungsheterogenität innerhalb von Schulklassen. Als Kompositionsmerkmale haben sie eine neue, eigenständige Bedeutung für die Vorhersage einer Kriteriumsvariablen, die sich nicht nur als Wirkung individueller Merkmale herausstellt:

> „In many school effects studies, achievement differences are found to be related to differences in the composition of the body of students. This is known as the ‚compositional' effect. Such an effect is often reported when a school-level aggregate of an individual-level variable makes an independent contribution to the explanation of outcome variance. In other words, the school-level aggregated variable makes a significant contribution to the explanatory model over and above the contribution of the same variable at the individual level" (Harker und Tymms 2004, S. 177).

Bezogen auf den Bereich Schule kann dies bedeuten, dass Schüler auch bei gleichen Lernausgangslagen und individuellen Voraussetzungen je nach Komposition des Lernkontextes (z. B. in leistungsstarken Schulklassen oder sozial eher günstiger zusammengesetzten Schulen) unterschiedliche Lernerfolge erzielen: „[T]wo pupils with similar prior scores but attending different schools can be predicted to have different scores depending on the average score of the other pupils in their schools" (ebd., S. 178). Erst wenn Institutions- oder Kompositionseffekte vorliegen, kann davon ausgegangen werden, dass verschiedene Schulkontexte differenzielle Lern- und Entwicklungsmilieus darstellen (Baumert et al. 2009, S. 37).

Von Effekten solcher Kompositionsmerkmale, die sich auf die Zusammensetzung der Schülerschaft beziehen, grenzen z. B. Harker und Tymms (2004) Effekte allgemeiner *Kontextmerkmale* ab, die nicht über die Aggregation individueller Merkmale operationalisiert werden.[2] Solche Kontextmerkmale sind Kennzeichen der weiteren Umgebung und z. B. von den Schulen selbst nicht direkt oder nur kaum zu beeinflussen, jedoch für die Entwicklung schulischer Leistungen relevant (Scheerens 1990). Zu den Kontextmerkmalen zählen demnach z. B. das schulische Einzugsgebiet und die Trägerschaft, regionale Unterschiede zwischen städtischen und ländlichen Gebieten, bundeslandspezifische Regelungen und Besonderheiten oder Unterschiede zwischen Schulsystemen verschiedener Staaten: „[T]he term ‚contextual effect' is now used in a way that includes other differences between schools [...]. [T]hese additional variables could be seen as other level-2 [...] variables to be examined for their mediating effects of a basic compositional effect" (Harker und Tymms 2004, S. 183).

Zur systematischen Analyse der Auswirkungen von Schule und Schulklasse als soziale Kontexte der Entwicklung im Jugendalter ist die Skizzierung eines theore-

---

[2] Andere Autoren verwenden den Begriff *Kontexteffekt* hingegen als Oberbegriff und bezeichnen damit den Effekt jeglicher Merkmale des Kontextes, z. B. auch die Auswirkungen von Kompositionsmerkmalen (z. B. Lüdtke et al. 2002).

Schule und Schulklasse als soziale Kontexte der Entwicklung im Jugendalter

Schulebene

Kontext — Komposition:
- Sozial- und Bildungsstatus
- Belastende Familienverhältnisse
- Migrationsstatus, kulturelle Vertrautheit
- Lernbiographische Belastung
- Leistungs- und Fähigkeitsniveau

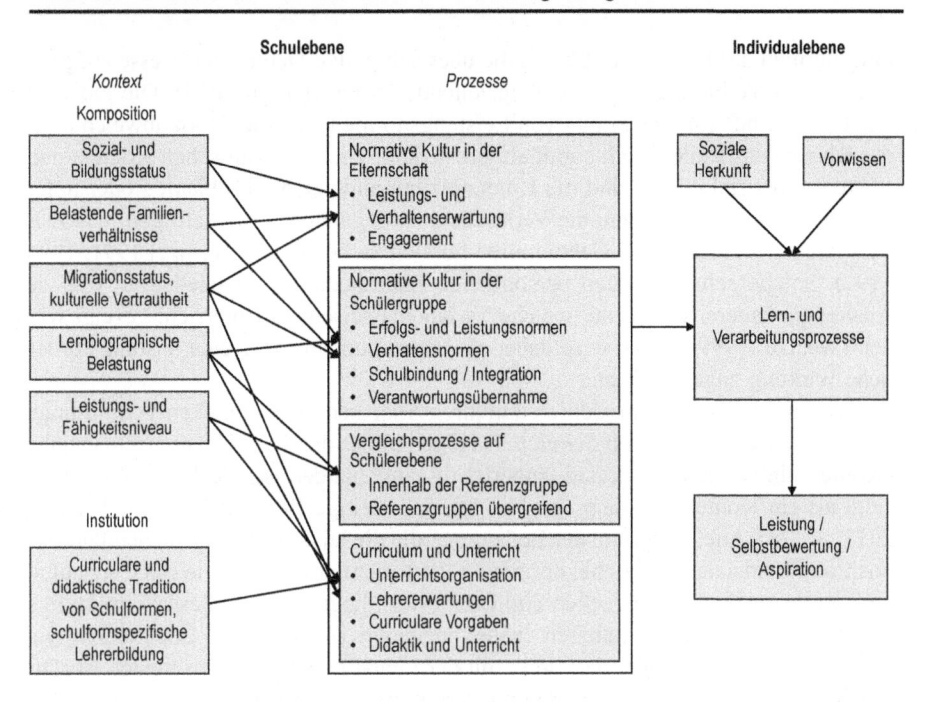

Institution:
- Curriculare und didaktische Tradition von Schulformen, schulformspezifische Lehrerbildung

Prozesse:
- Normative Kultur in der Elternschaft
  - Leistungs- und Verhaltenserwartung
  - Engagement
- Normative Kultur in der Schülergruppe
  - Erfolgs- und Leistungsnormen
  - Verhaltensnormen
  - Schulbindung / Integration
  - Verantwortungsübernahme
- Vergleichsprozesse auf Schülerebene
  - Innerhalb der Referenzgruppe
  - Referenzgruppen übergreifend
- Curriculum und Unterricht
  - Unterrichtsorganisation
  - Lehrererwartungen
  - Curriculare Vorgaben
  - Didaktik und Unterricht

Individualebene
- Soziale Herkunft
- Vorwissen
- Lern- und Verarbeitungsprozesse
- Leistung / Selbstbewertung / Aspiration

Abb. 1 Vermittlungsmodell für Kontexteffekte. (Quelle: Baumert et al. (2006, S. 126))

tisch fundierten Vermittlungsmodells (Abb. 1) erforderlich, das von Baumert et al. (2006) vorgeschlagen wurde: In ihrem Vermittlungsmodell zählen kompositionelle und institutionelle Merkmale von Schulen zu den Kontextbedingungen für schulische Lernprozesse. Kontextmerkmale wirken jedoch nicht unmittelbar auf Leistungs- und Entwicklungsprozesse ein. Vielmehr sind Makro- und Mikroebene durch verschiedene Vermittlungsmechanismen als Brückenhypothesen miteinander verbunden. Dreeben und Barr (1988) unterscheiden vier Transmissionswege, wonach Kontextmerkmale erstens durch die Unterstützungsbereitschaft der Elternschaft, zweitens durch die normative Kultur der Altersgruppe (z. B. über Leistungs- und Verhaltensnormen), drittens durch soziale Vergleichsprozesse (siehe hierzu Köller 2004; Köller und Baumert 2001) auf Schülerebene (referenzgruppenintern und -übergreifend) und viertens durch didaktische, curriculare und organisatorische Rahmenbedingungen vermittelt werden (z. B. wenn Lehrkräfte und Schulleitungen auf eine unterschiedliche Zusammensetzung der Schülerschaft mit verschiedenen Formen der Unterrichtsorganisation und Differenzierung, jeweils spezifischen Erwartungen und curricularen Vorgaben oder didaktisch adaptiv reagieren). Letztere werden von Dreeben und Barr (1988) in ihrer Bedeutung besonders hervorgehoben.

Soziologische Ansätze richten sich bei der Erklärung von Kontexteffekten hingegen eher auf die kollektiv geteilten und vorherrschenden Normen (vgl. bereits Blau 1960). Bezogen auf den schulischen Kontext wird dabei die normative Kultur der Altersgruppe als primärer Vermittlungsprozess und Bindeglied zwischen Kontextfaktoren einerseits und individuellem Verhalten andererseits angesehen. Demnach führen bestimmte Kompositionsmerkmale zu gemeinsam geteilten Erfolgs- und Leistungsnormen auf kollektiver Ebene, die über subjektive Deutungsprozesse aufgrund ihrer hohen Verbindlichkeit handlungsleitend werden (Ditton 2013). Die individuelle Bereitschaft zur Einhaltung von Leistungsnormen auch bei Normabweichungen der Klassenkameraden stellt somit ein prosoziales Ziel im schulischen Kontext dar.[3] Weitere prosoziale Ziele sind die Unterstützung anderer bei Problemen oder unterrichtsbezogenen Aktivitäten, die Verlässlichkeit gegenüber Gleichaltrigen, wie z. B. Versprechen zu halten und Geheimnisse für sich zu bewahren (Wentzel 1991, 1994, 1999). Solche selbstgesetzten persönlichen Ziele beeinflussen wiederum, wie viel Anstrengungsbereitschaft und welche Verhaltensweisen im Unterricht gezeigt werden (Wentzel 1999). Ihnen wird daher als Vermittlungsprozess eine leistungsförderliche Wirkung zugeschrieben.

Baumert et al. (2006) modellieren in ihren Analysen die komplexen Vermittlungsprozesse auf der Ebene von *Schulen*. Dagegen bildet die *Schulklasse* einen sozialen „Kontext, in den man stark und längerfristig eingebunden ist, [der] eher Wirkungen zeigt als ein Kontext, zu dem eine nur lose kurzzeitige Beziehung besteht" (Ditton 2013, S. 174). Auch aufgrund der Bedeutung, die die leistungsbezogene Schülerkomposition für soziale Vergleiche, normative Wertorientierungen sowie das Curriculum und den Unterricht hat (Dreeben und Barr 1988), liegt es nahe, diese Vermittlungsprozesse auch im unmittelbaren, nahe liegenden (*proximalen*) Lernkontext von Schulklassen zu vermuten, der direkt mit der Lehr-Lernsituation verbunden ist (Ditton 2000). Die Schulklassen stellen wiederum eine „normativ geregelte Verbindung bestimmter Formen des sozialen Handelns bestimmter Akteure" (Meulemann 2006, S. 224) dar mit einer sehr engen sozialräumlichen Umgebung (Friedrichs und Nonnenmacher 2010, S. 471) und Beziehung zwischen Individuum und Kollektiv (Ditton 2013, S. 174). In der Schul- und Unterrichtsforschung wird die Schulklasse deshalb als wirksame Entwicklungsumwelt angesehen und als eigenständige Analyseeinheit berücksichtigt (z. B. Schwetz 2003). Nach Fend (1991) stellen Schulklassen diejenigen sozialen Interaktionsfelder dar, in denen sich jeweils spezifische, gemeinsam geteilte Normen zur Bewertung von Schule, schulischer Leistungen und Anstrengungsbereitschaft herausbilden. So führen z. B. eine hohe Leistungsorientierung in der Schulklasse und die gemeinsame Verständigung auf leistungsbezogene Kriterien für Beliebtheit und gegenseitige Anerkennung unter den Gleichaltrigen dazu, dass sie ihre Selbstbewertung an der klassenspezifischen Leistungshierarchie festmachen, was sich langfristig über eine hohe subjektive Bedeutung von Motivation und Anstrengungsbereitschaft auf die Leistungsentwicklung niederschlagen sollte. Das soziale Lernumfeld hat demnach eine normative Funktion, wobei die Schulklasse die normgebende Bezugsgruppe bildet, in der sich eine jeweils spezifische Gruppen- und Lernkultur entwickelt und Verhaltensmodelle und -rollen bereitgestellt werden (z. B. Dar und Resh 1986).

Ausgehend von diesen Überlegungen soll nachfolgend mit Blick auf die Schule als einem Anwendungsbereich der Kontextanalyse das Ziel verfolgt werden, einen weiteren Beitrag, der sich hier nur auf einzelne Aspekte des theoretischen Vermitt-

---

[3] Die Akzeptanz von Leistungsnormen wird üblicherweise als Individualmerkmal erhoben, kann aber durch Aggregation auf höherer Ebene (z. B. Schulklasse oder Schule) als analytisches Kontextmerkmal behandelt werden, das unmittelbar mit dem Lernprozess verknüpft ist (Baumert et al. 2001).

lungsmodells von Baumert et al. (2006) beschränken kann, zur Klärung der Frage zu leisten, was der entwicklungsrelevante Kontext im Mehrebenensystem Schule ist und über welche Vermittlungsmechanismen sich Kontexteffekte auf die Schulleistung als zentraler Aspekt der Entwicklung im Jugendalter auswirken.

3 Empirische Forschungsbefunde

International ist der Forschungsstand zu den Auswirkungen unterschiedlicher Schulkontexte und der Zusammensetzung der Schülerschaft breit gefächert, insbesondere mit Fokus auf die soziale Komposition von Schulen (z. B. Harker und Tymms 2004; Hattie 2002; Oakes 1990; Opdenakker und van Damme 2001; Thrupp et al. 2002). Nachfolgend wird auf einige ausgewählte Forschungsbefunde näher eingegangen (für eine vertiefende Forschungsübersicht siehe z. B. Dumont et al. 2013; Maaz et al. 2008).

Für das deutsche Schulsystem wurden Kompositions- und v. a. Institutionseffekte nachgewiesen: Anhand der nationalen PISA-Ergänzungsstudie (PISA-E 2000) zeigte sich, dass 15-Jährige an Gymnasien unter Kontrolle von Merkmalen des individuellen und schulischen Lernkontextes signifikant höhere Lesekompetenzwerte gegen Ende der Pflichtschulzeit erzielen als Gleichaltrige an Hauptschulen (Baumert et al. 2006). Darüber hinaus wurde eine starke Konfundierung von Kompositions- und Institutionsmerkmalen deutlich: Das Intelligenzniveau der Schülerschaft scheint das bedeutendste Kompositionsmerkmal zu sein. Die soziale Zusammensetzung übt dagegen nur einen kleinen spezifischen, aber signifikanten Effekt auf die Lesekompetenz aus. Auch für den Kompetenzbereich Mathematik liegt empirische Evidenz zu differenziellen Entwicklungsverläufen an verschiedenen Schulformen vor: Im Rahmen einer Reanalyse der nationalen längsschnittlichen Erweiterung der dritten internationalen Mathematik- und Naturwissenschaftsstudie (TIMSS) zeigt sich anhand von Mehrgruppen-Strukturgleichungsmodellen, dass die um Messfehler bereinigten, latenten Lernzuwächse in den Jahrgangsstufen 7 und 8 an Gymnasien und Realschulen mehr als doppelt so hoch ausfallen wie an Hauptschulen (Becker et al. 2006). Die Befunde sind dabei mit Effektstärken in mittlerer Höhe von praktischer Relevanz.

Für den Stadtstaat Hamburg liegen hingegen andere Befunde vor: Im Gegensatz zu anderen Befunden für die Lesekompetenz (Baumert et al. 2006) stellen Gröhlich et al. (2010a) hinsichtlich der Entwicklung der Mathematikleistung in den Jahrgangsstufen 7 und 8 unter Kontrolle von Kompositions- und Institutionsmerkmalen keine höhere Lerneffektivität an Gymnasien fest. Allerdings fällt an Realschulen die Lernentwicklung im Vergleich zu Hauptschulen signifikant höher aus. Darüber hinaus scheinen sich institutionelle Effekte der Schulformgliederung nicht erst gegen Ende der Sekundarstufe, sondern bereits nach zwei Sekundarschuljahren zu manifestieren: Insbesondere an Gymnasien im Vergleich zu anderen Schulformen werden signifikant höhere Lernstände in Mathematik erzielt. Ihr Leistungsvorsprung kann nicht allein auf eine günstigere leistungsbezogene und soziale Komposition der Schülerschaft zurückgeführt werden (Bonsen et al. 2009a). Auch bei direkter Modellierung des Leistungs*zuwachses* in Mathematik als abhängiger Variable treten im Drei-Ebenen-Modell schulformspezifische Schereneffekte zugunsten der Hamburger Gymnasien und Realschulen gegenüber Hauptschulen auf, wobei auch das schulische Leistungsniveau für unterschiedliche Wissenszuwächse ausschlaggebend ist (Guill und Gröhlich 2013).

Die Annahme von Schereneffekten wird auch anhand einer nordrhein-westfälischen Stichprobe gestützt: Demnach führen schulformspezifische Zuwachsraten zu einer ungünstigeren Entwicklung der Mathematikleistung an Gesamt- und Hauptschulen bereits in den ersten beiden Sekundarschuljahren. Dies kann u. a. daran liegen, dass mit der Schulformzugehörigkeit soziodemografische Kompositions- und auch Unterrichtsmerkmale (z. B. Überforderung, Disziplin und Schülerorientierung) variieren (van Ophuysen und Wendt 2009). Es gibt allerdings auch Studien, die für die Kompetenzentwicklung in Lesen und Mathematik keine Schereneffekte zwischen Hauptschulen und Gymnasien nachweisen können (Schneider und Stefanek 2004).

Auch für die Schweiz gibt es Studien zu institutionellen Effekten der Leistungsdifferenzierung: So untersuchen z. B. Ramseier und Brühwiler (2003) in vertiefenden Analysen im Rahmen von PISA 2000 anhand von Pfadmodellen die Lese- und Mathematikleistungen von Schülern in den Kantonen Bern und St. Gallen. Unter Kontrolle der non-verbalen kognitiven Grundfähigkeit zeigt sich ein vergleichsweise hoher signifikanter Leistungsvorteil, wenn ein Schultyp mit erweiterten oder hohen Anforderungen besucht wird verglichen mit Schultypen mit Grundanforderungen. Der Schultyp erweist sich seinerseits als vermittelnde Variable zwischen personalen, kulturellen und sozialen Herkunftsmerkmalen einerseits sowie den Lese- und Mathematikleistungen andererseits, ist allerdings größtenteils mit diesen konfundiert. Neumann et al. (2007) zeigen anhand von Mehrebenenanalysen für Schüler der 8. Jahrgangsstufe, dass auch die Lernzuwächse im Fach Französisch als Fremdsprache unter Berücksichtigung zentraler Merkmale der Eingangsselektivität je nach Bildungsgang unterschiedlich ausfallen: Demnach werden an Schultypen mit erweiterten Anforderungen zwischen einem Drittel und einer halben Standardabweichung signifikant höhere Lernzuwächse erzielt als an Schultypen mit Grundanforderungen. Gleichzeitig erweisen sich Effekte von Bildungsgang und Leistungsniveau als konfundiert.

Zusammenfassend liegt also eine Reihe empirischer Forschungsbefunde zur Bedeutung unterschiedlicher Lernkontexte für die schulische Leistungsentwicklung in der Sekundarstufe vor, die jedoch über verschiedene Kompetenzbereiche hinweg nicht eindeutig sind (Baumert et al. 2009). In der Zusammenschau zeigen die Befunde jedoch, dass der mit der Schulformgliederung einhergehende Anspruch einer optimalen Förderung *aller* Schüler nicht erreicht werden kann. Die Frage, welche Rolle die normative Kultur der Altersgruppe als ein Aspekt von Vermittlungsmechanismen für Kontextmerkmale einnimmt und in welchem schulischen Kontext oder auf welcher Ebene diese wirksam werden, wurde zwar aufgeworfen, ist empirisch aber bislang weitgehend unbeantwortet geblieben. Es fehlt daher an Studien, die der Bedeutung von Vermittlungsmechanismen Rechnung tragen und die in der Lage sind, diese angemessen auf allen relevanten Kontextebenen zu berücksichtigen. In ihren Analysen zeigen Baumert et al. (2006) jedoch, dass normbezogene Vermittlungsprozesse auf schulischer Ebene nur in wenigen Schulformen leistungsförderlich sind. Die Autoren kommen zu dem Schluss, dass diese Prozesse offenbar nur auf individueller Ebene leistungsprädiktiv und schulformübergreifend auch weitgehend unabhängig von schulischen Kontextmerkmalen sind. Das postulierte Vermittlungsmodell sei demzufolge nicht haltbar, wenn Zusammenhänge nur auf aggregierter Ebene berücksichtigt werden. Somit ist „die Frage der Vermittlung der nachgewiesenen Kompositionseffekte weiterhin offen" (ebd., S. 149) und bislang „keineswegs eindeutig oder abschließend beantwortet" (Ditton 2013, S. 173).

4 Herleitung der Fragestellung und Hypothesen

Ausgehend von den theoretischen Überlegungen und den hierzu vorliegenden empirischen Forschungsbefunden lassen sich in dem für die Kontextanalyse typischen schrittweisen Vorgehen (ebd., S. 177) folgende Forschungsfragen mit Fokus auf die Kompetenzentwicklung als im Jugendalter zentraler Entwicklungsaspekt im schulischen Kontext konkretisieren:

1. In welcher Weise wirken sich Schule und Schulklasse als soziale Kontexte auf die Entwicklung im Jugendalter aus?

Zunächst wird gefragt, ob und inwieweit Schule und Schulklasse relevante Entwicklungskontexte darstellen, d. h., ob und in welcher Größenordnung signifikante Varianzanteile schulischer Kompetenzen auf Unterschiede zwischen Schulklassen und zwischen Schulen entfallen. In einem *ersten Schritt* wird also simultan die Varianzzerlegung der Kriteriumsvariable auf den Schul- und Klassenkontext bestimmt und gezeigt, welchem Kontext die größere Bedeutung zur Erklärung individueller Entwicklungsunterschiede zukommt. In einem *zweiten Schritt* wird regressionsanalytisch überprüft, welchen Beitrag bereits herkunfts- und personenbezogene Schülermerkmale zur Vorhersage unterschiedlicher Lernentwicklungen liefern. In einem *dritten Schritt* wird danach gefragt, ob und in welcher Richtung (positiv oder negativ) weitere schul- und klassenbezogene Merkmale über individuelle Schülermerkmale hinaus eine Rolle für die Leistungsentwicklung spielen: Lassen sich im Mehrebenenmodell Kompositionseffekte der leistungsbezogenen und sozialen Zusammensetzung von Schulen und Schulklassen sowie Institutionseffekte der Schulformgliederung in der Sekundarstufe nachweisen? Und ggf. auf welcher Ebene entfalten einzelne Kompositionsmerkmale ihre Wirkung?

Es wird erwartet, dass in der Varianzzerlegung signifikante Varianzanteile der abhängigen Variable auf den Schul- und Klassenkontext entfallen. Schule und Schulklasse sollten also entwicklungsrelevante Lernkontexte im schulischen Bereich darstellen, sodass es gerechtfertigt ist, beide Ebenen in die Analysen einzubeziehen. Regressionsanalytisch sollten analog zu Befunden anderer Studien (z. B. Baumert et al. 2006; Bonsen et al. 2009a; Gröhlich et al. 2010a, b; Guill und Gröhlich 2013; Neumann et al. 2007; Nikolova 2011) individuelle Schülermerkmale (Geschlecht, Migrationshintergrund, soziale Lage, allgemeine kognitive Grundfähigkeit und Ausgangsleistung zu einem früheren Erhebungszeitpunkt) die individuelle Lernentwicklung bereits gut vorhersagen können. Darüber hinaus wird auf Grundlage dieser Forschungsbefunde und als *Kontexthypothese* erwartet, dass eine günstige leistungsbezogene und soziale Zusammensetzung sowohl des Klassen- als auch Schulkontextes entwicklungsförderlich ist. Es wird vermutet, dass sich klassenbezogene Kompositionsmerkmale stärker durchsetzen, da der Klassenkontext die unmittelbare Lern- und Entwicklungsumwelt darstellt (z. B. Bellin 2009; Scharenberg 2012), in der das Lehren und Lernen stattfindet, und der Schulkontext weiter vom Unterrichtsgeschehen entfernt ist. Darüber hinaus wird vermutet, dass sich im schulischen Kontext Institutionseffekte der Schulformgliederung nachweisen lassen, die analog zu anderen Forschungsbefunden (z. B. Baumert et al. 2006; Bonsen et al. 2009a) v. a. in einer deutlichen, positiven Abgrenzung der Gymnasien zu anderen Schulformen bestehen sollten.

2. Durch welche Mechanismen werden Merkmale des Schul- und Klassenkontextes vermittelt?

In einem *vierten Schritt* wird das bereits auf der Schul- und Klassenebene wie oben beschrieben spezifizierte Mehrebenenmodell sozusagen in einer sukzessiven *Wirkungskette* um Vermittlungsmechanismen ergänzt. Nach Baumert et al. (2006) ist davon auszugehen, dass sich über solche Prozesse Kontextmerkmale höherer Ebenen auf individuelles Leistungsverhalten auf unterster Ebene auswirken. Dies entspricht dem von Friedrichs und Nonnenmacher (2010, S. 490) vorgeschlagenen Vorgehen, zunächst Effekte auf der Makroebene zu analysieren, bevor die Mechanismen, durch welche sich diese Effekte auf die Individuen auswirken, zu prüfen sind. Konkret wird anhand der verfügbaren Indikatoren überprüft, ob die mittlere Akzeptanz von Leistungsnormen innerhalb der Schulen und Schulklassen als ein möglicher Indikator für die normative Kultur der Altersgruppe auf der jeweiligen Kontextebene einen eigenständigen Erklärungsbeitrag leistet und von zusätzlichem Erklärungsmehrwert ist.

Es wird erwartet, dass bei einem hohen durchschnittlichen Ausgangsniveau der Leistungen im Schul- und Klassenkontext auch die gemeinsame Akzeptanz von Leistungsnormen überdurchschnittlich hoch ausfällt und diese ihrerseits zu höheren Testleistungen zu einem späteren Beobachtungszeitpunkt führen sollte (*Vermittlungshypothese*). Dementsprechend sollten sich diese Vermittlungsmechanismen in Verbindung mit den Kontextmerkmalen leistungsförderlich auf die individuelle Lernentwicklung auswirken. Die Spezifikation dieser Vermittlungsmechanismen auf den beiden Kontextebenen sollte einen eigenständigen Erklärungsbeitrag leisten und zu einem zusätzlichen Mehrwert des Gesamtmodells führen.

3. Sind Effekte des Klassen- oder Schulkontextes gruppenspezifisch?

In einem *fünften Schritt* wird untersucht, ob diese Vermittlungsmechanismen für alle Schüler gleichermaßen leistungsrelevant sind oder ob sie je nach individuellen Voraussetzungen unterschiedliche Auswirkungen haben. Durch die Modellierung von *Interaktionseffekten* lässt sich also prüfen, ob die Vermittlungsmechanismen des Klassen- oder Schulkontextes auf den Zusammenhang zwischen verschiedenen herkunfts- und personenbezogenen Schülermerkmalen und Kriteriumsvariable auf individueller Ebene wirken.

Es wird erwartet, dass sich die Vermittlungsmechanismen für Kontexteffekte in Abhängigkeit von individuellen Voraussetzungen unterschiedlich auswirken und dass sie bei ungünstigeren individuellen Lernausgangslagen kompensatorische Fördereffekte besitzen. So sollten z. B. Leistungsschwächere stärker von einer höheren Akzeptanz von Leistungsnormen hinsichtlich ihrer Leistungsentwicklung profitieren. Die

Annahme differenzieller Effekte von Merkmalen auf Aggregatebene beruht auf Befunden aus Meta-Analysen, die z. B. hinsichtlich der Leistungsheterogenität in Lerngruppen eine differenzielle Förderwirksamkeit für leistungsstarke und -schwächere Schüler belegt haben (z. B. Kulik und Kulik 1982; Lou et al. 1996; Slavin 1990a).

5 Datengrundlage und methodisches Vorgehen

5.1 Die Hamburger KESS-Studie

Datengrundlage ist die Hamburger Schulleistungsstudie „Kompetenzen und Einstellungen von Schülerinnen und Schülern" (KESS). Im Rahmen von KESS wurden die Lernstände in den Kompetenzbereichen Deutsch (Leseverständnis und Orthografie), Mathematik, Englisch und Naturwissenschaften am Ende der Jahrgangsstufe 4 (KESS 4, 2003; Bos et al. 2006), unmittelbar zu Beginn der Jahrgangsstufe 7 (KESS 7, 2005; Bonsen et al. 2009b) und am Ende der Jahrgangsstufe 8 (KESS 8, 2007; Bos et al. 2010a) erfasst.[4] Die Teilnahme an den Schulleistungstests war verpflichtend. Darüber hinaus wurden umfangreiche Hintergrundinformationen zu den individuellen und kontextspezifischen Rahmenbedingungen des schulischen Lehrens und Lernens mittels schriftlicher Befragungen der Schüler, ihrer Eltern, Lehrkräfte und Schulleitungen erhoben. Auftraggeberin der Studie war die Behörde für Schule und Berufsbildung der Freien und Hansestadt Hamburg. Die Organisation, Durchführung, Erfassung und Aufbereitung der Leistungsdaten erfolgten durch das Landesinstitut für Lehrerbildung und Schulentwicklung. Die Auswertung der Leistungsdaten in den Bereichen Leseverständnis und Mathematik fand am Institut für Schulentwicklungsforschung (IFS) der Technischen Universität Dortmund statt.

Das Hamburger Schulsystem zeichnete sich zum Zeitpunkt der KESS8-Studie im Jahr 2007 durch eine Reihe von Besonderheiten aus, die in Abb. 2 vereinfacht dargestellt sind (vgl. hierzu auch Bos et al. 2010a).[5]

In Hamburg erfolgt der Übergang in die weiterführende Schule nach dem Ende der vierjährigen Grundschulzeit. Mit dem Übergang in die Sekundarstufe findet dann eine zunehmende Differenzierung statt: An Haupt- und Realschulen, die in Hamburg eine organisatorische Einheit bilden, wird in den Jahrgangsstufen 5 und 6 im gemeinsamen Klassenverband ohne externe Leistungsdifferenzierung unterrichtet. Die Einrichtung dieser Beobachtungsstufe an Haupt- und Realschulen soll den Grundschulübergang entschärfen und eine Korrektur der Schulformentscheidung auch noch zu einem späteren Zeitpunkt ermöglichen. Ab der 7. Jahrgangsstufe wird innerhalb dieser Schulen in getrennten Hauptschul- oder Realschulklassen unterrichtet, in denen dann spä-

---

[4] Weitere Befragungen und Kompetenzmessungen des KESS-Jahrgangs erfolgten im Sommer 2009 am Ende der Sekundarstufe I (Jahrgangsstufe 10) bzw. zu Beginn der gymnasialen Oberstufe (Jahrgangsstufe 11), im Frühjahr 2011 am Ende der sogenannten Studienstufe an achtstufigen Gymnasien (Jahrgangsstufe 12) sowie ein Jahr später am Ende der Studienstufe der dreijährigen Oberstufe (Jahrgangsstufe 13) an Integrierten Gesamtschulen, Aufbaugymnasien und Beruflichen Gymnasien (Ivanov et al. 2011).

[5] Die Ausführungen beziehen sich auf die geltenden Regelungen zum Zeitpunkt der Durchführung der KESS-Studie. Auf die Besonderheiten, die sich durch die Hamburger Schulstrukturreform im Schuljahr 2010/11 ergeben haben, wird im Folgenden nicht näher eingegangen (vgl. hierzu z. B. Scharenberg 2012).

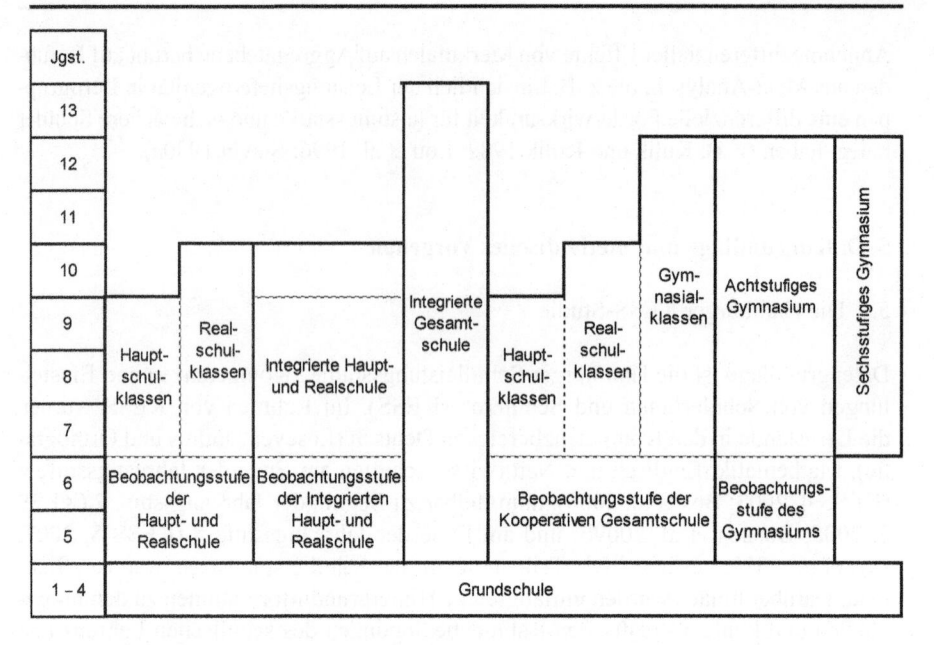

Abb. 2 Das Hamburger Schulsystem (Stand 2007).
(Quelle: BSB/IFS/LI, Kompetenzen und Einstellungen von Schülerinnen und Schülern© KESS 8)

ter auch schulformspezifische Abschlüsse erworben werden können. Die Berechtigung für den Übergang in die Hauptschule oder Realschule wird auf Grundlage der Zeugnisnoten am Ende der Jahrgangsstufe 6 ausgesprochen. An Integrierten Haupt- und Realschulen (IHR-Schulen) erfolgt hingegen eine innere Differenzierung nach Hauptschul- und Realschulstatus (H- und R-Status) bei gemeinsamer Unterrichtung im Klassenverband in den Fächern Deutsch, Mathematik und Englisch.

An den grundständigen achtstufigen Gymnasien erfolgt nach der zweijährigen Beobachtungsstufe der Übergang in die Mittelstufe. Das Abitur kann nach insgesamt 12 Schuljahren (mit zweijähriger Oberstufe) erworben werden. Ab der Jahrgangsstufe 7 steht das sechsstufige Gymnasium auch den leistungsstärkeren Haupt- und Realschülern offen. An Integrierten Gesamtschulen (IGS) findet eine jahrgangsweise Fachleistungsdifferenzierung in ein leistungsstärkeres Kursniveau I und ein leistungsschwächeres Kursniveau II nur in den Fächern Mathematik und Englisch statt. Der Erwerb des Abiturs ist hier nach insgesamt 13 Schuljahren (mit dreijähriger Oberstufe) möglich. An Kooperativen Gesamtschulen werden ab der Jahrgangsstufe 7 Hauptschul-, Realschul- und Gymnasialzweige getrennt.

5.2 Methodisches Vorgehen

Für die Analyse von Kontexteffekten empfiehlt sich ein mehrebenenanalytisches Vorgehen, bei dem Prädiktoren simultan auf mehreren Ebenen, d. h. als individuelle und als auf höherer Ebene aggregierte Merkmale, berücksichtigt werden können. Gerade im Zusammenhang mit der Analyse von Kompositionseffekten ist deshalb die Mehrebenenanalyse das methodische Vorgehen der Wahl (Dreeben und Barr 1988,

S. 129), um die hierarchisch geschachtelte Struktur der Daten, wie sie gerade für die Schule als ein Anwendungsbereich der Kontextanalyse kennzeichnend ist, angemessen zu berücksichtigen. Die einzelnen Beobachtungseinheiten sind ineinander verschachtelt (Schüler in Schulklassen in Schulen) und nicht unabhängig voneinander.[6] So sind sich z. B. Schüler derselben Schulklasse einander ähnlicher als diejenigen, die verschiedene Schulklassen oder Schulen besuchen. Gründe hierfür können z. B. darin liegen, dass sie gemeinsam von denselben Lehrkräften unterrichtet werden, d. h. gemeinsamen Rahmenbedingungen unterliegen, und in Altersgruppen sind, d. h. gemeinsame Sozialbeziehungen pflegen.

Verallgemeinert ausgedrückt ermöglicht die Mehrebenenanalyse, Effekte auf der Mikro- und Makroebene simultan zu schätzen. Zunächst müssen die zu untersuchenden Kontexte und deren Effekte (direkt vs. indirekt) auf das individuelle Verhalten bestimmt werden. Darüber hinaus kann es erforderlich sein, zusätzlich zur Mikro- und Makroebene auch eine Mesoebene einzubeziehen. Bezogen auf den Schulbereich und mit Blick auf die zuvor abgeleiteten Fragestellungen soll die schulische Leistungsentwicklung als ein zentraler Aspekt der Entwicklung im Jugendalter durch individuelle Schülermerkmale und Merkmale des schulischen Kontexts vorhergesagt werden. Diese Kontextmerkmale können in verschiedene Ebenen eingebettet sein, wobei die Schulklasse als die unmittelbare Lernumwelt und Bezugsgruppe der Schüler angesehen wird (Baumert et al. 2004; Dar und Resh 1986). Diese wird wiederum von schulischen Rahmenbedingungen beeinflusst (Opdenakker und van Damme 2006).

Zur Beantwortung der Frage nach der Kontextabhängigkeit schulischer Leistungen, den Vermittlungsmechanismen, deren Gruppenspezifität und differenzieller Effektivität für verschiedene Personengruppen wird folgende Modellspezifikation gewählt: Die individuelle Entwicklung schulischer Leistungen stellt bei den Analysen die abhängige Variable dar. Dabei beschränken sich die Analysen auf die Entwicklung des Leseverständnisses, das als „Werkzeug" für den selbstständigen Wissenserwerb auch in anderen Kompetenzbereichen eine grundlegende Voraussetzung ist (OECD 2001). Da schulische Kompetenzen durch eine Vielzahl von Determinanten bestimmt werden, welche die Rahmenbedingungen für individuelle Lernprozesse bilden (Helmke und Weinert 1997), werden zur Vorhersage der Kompetenzentwicklung in den Mehrebenenmodellen individuelle Schülermerkmale sowie weitere Merkmale des Klassen- und Schulkontextes hinzugezogen (zur Operationalisierung siehe Abschn. 5.3).

Die Modellgenese orientiert sich an dem von Hox (1995) vorgeschlagenen Vorgehen. Zunächst wird ein Modell ohne Prädiktoren (*Nullmodell*) spezifiziert, um die Varianzanteile der Kriteriumsvariablen zu bestimmen, die auf jeder der hier interessierenden Ebenen (Schüler, Schulklasse, Schule) maximal erklärt werden können sowie um entwicklungsrelevante Kontexte identifizieren und voneinander abgrenzen zu können. Dann werden zunächst auf unterster Ebene die Individualmerkmale Geschlecht, Migrationshintergrund, soziale Lage, kognitive Grundfähigkeit und

---

[6] Eine weitere Anwendungsmöglichkeit der Mehrebenenanalyse im schulischen Kontext ist z. B. die direkte Modellierung von Lernzuwächsen, wobei die Messwiederholungsdaten auf unterster Ebene verschachtelt sind und durch individuelle (zweite Ebene) und kontextuelle Merkmale von Schulen oder Schulklassen (dritte Ebene) vorhergesagt werden können (Anwendungsbeispiele finden sich u. a. in Bellin 2009; Guill und Gröhlich 2013).

Ausgangsleistung im Leseverständnis zu Beginn der Jahrgangsstufe 7 berücksichtigt (Variante I). Im nächsten Schritt werden als Kompositionsmerkmale des Klassenkontextes die soziale und leistungsbezogene Zusammensetzung der Schulklassen eingeführt, auf Schulebene wird zusätzlich die Schulformgliederung als Institutionsmerkmal berücksichtigt (Variante II). Anschließend wird die normative Kultur der Altersgruppe, welche nach Baumert et al. (2006) ein vermittelndes Prozessmerkmal zwischen Kontextfaktoren und individuellen Lernergebnissen darstellt, als zusätzlicher Prädiktor auf den beiden Aggregatebenen aufgenommen (Variante III).[7] Variante IV schätzt Effekte des Schul- und Klassenkontextes auf die Zusammenhänge auf individueller Ebene, um zu überprüfen, ob die angenommenen Vermittlungsmechanismen für alle Schüler gleichermaßen wirksam sind oder von individuellen Voraussetzungen moderiert werden.

Die Datenauswertung erfolgt mit der Software HLM 6.08 (Raudenbush et al. 2009). Kontinuierliche Prädiktoren werden auf individueller Ebene z-standardisiert und dann auf den höheren Ebenen aggregiert, sodass sich die Kompositionseffekte direkt ablesen lassen (Ditton 1998, S. 90 ff.). In den Varianten II und III werden ausschließlich direkte Effekte von Aggregatmerkmalen auf die abhängige Variable geschätzt. In Variante IV werden Interaktionseffekte (*Cross-level*-Interaktionen) zwischen einem Aggregatmerkmal und dem Zusammenhang zwischen verschiedenen individuellen Merkmalen und der abhängigen Variable zugelassen (für eine anschauliche Darstellung zur Schätzung dieser Effektarten siehe auch Snijders und Bosker 1999). Um abschließend beurteilen zu können, welche dieser Modellspezifikationen die empirischen Daten am besten repräsentiert, werden die verschiedenen Modelle anhand von Likelihood-Ratio-χ^2-Tests miteinander verglichen (Langer 2008, S. 119).

Fehlende Werte werden zunächst, sofern vorhanden, durch Angaben der Schüler zu früheren Messzeitpunkten ersetzt. Darüber hinausgehende fehlende Werte werden mittels eines einfachen Imputationsverfahrens auf Basis eines komplexen Modells an Hintergrundvariablen geschätzt (Software NORM 2.03; Schafer 1999). Hierfür werden Variablen verwendet, die inhaltliche Zusammenhänge und Korrelationen mit den analyserelevanten Variablen in mindestens mittlerer Höhe aufweisen ($|r| \geq 0{,}30$).[8]

Die Analysen beschränken sich auf die Entwicklung des Leseverständnisses in den Jahrgangsstufen 7 und 8, da Aspekte der normativen Kultur der Altersgruppe nur zum zweiten Messzeitpunkt der KESS-Studie (KESS 7) erfasst wurden und somit als Ausgangsbasis für die Lernentwicklung bis zum Ende der Jahrgangsstufe 8 verwendet werden können. Die Analysen erfolgen auf einem Signifikanzniveau von $p < 0{,}05$.

---

[7] In Anlehnung an Baumert et al. (2006, S. 145) wird die Akzeptanz von Leistungsnormen ausschließlich als Prädiktor auf aggregierter Ebene spezifiziert, um eine Überkontrolle des Modells auf Individualebene zu vermeiden, da davon ausgegangen werden kann, dass die individuelle Akzeptanz dieser Leistungsnormen wiederum von schulischen Qualitätsmerkmalen abhängt.

[8] Für die Imputation wurden Variablen aus den Schülerfragebögen verwendet, wie z. B. Anzahl der Bücher im Haushalt, soziales Kapital, allgemeines oder fachspezifisches Selbstkonzept, Zufriedenheit mit der Schule, Leistungsangst, Schüler-Lehrer-Verhältnis, Interesse der Eltern an den Freunden und Aktivitäten des Kindes, Verhältnis der Schüler zu ihren Eltern (zur Dokumentation der Erhebungsinstrumente vgl. Bos et al. 2009, 2010b).

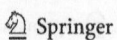

5.3 Operationalisierung der verwendeten Variablen

Prädiktoren auf Individualebene
Abhängige Variable ist die individuelle Testleistung im Kompetenzbereich „Leseverständnis" am Ende der Jahrgangsstufe 8. Das Leseverständnis wurde anhand verschiedener Testaufgaben erfasst, die sich bereits in anderen Schulleistungsstudien (z. B. PISA, IGLU, LAU) als valide und reliable Testinstrumente bewährt haben. Durch ein *Anker-Item-Design* wurden mehrere Messzeitpunkte miteinander verbunden (*fixed-parameters*-Methode; von Davier und von Davier 2007). Die Leistungsdaten wurden anhand des *einparametrigen Raschmodells* skaliert. Dadurch können die Testleistungen zu allen Messzeitpunkten auf einer gemeinsamen Metrik abgebildet werden (Bos et al. 2010a). Die Lernstände wurden für die KESS7-Population auf einen Mittelwert (M) von 500 und eine Standardabweichung (SD) von 100 Skalenpunkten standardisiert. Die Differenz der Testwerte zwischen zwei Messzeitpunkten bildet den Lernzuwachs ab.

Das *Geschlecht* (Referenz: Junge) wurde über die Schülerteilnahmeliste erfasst, die von den Testleitern ausgefüllt wurde. Der *Migrationshintergrund* wird über Angaben aus dem Elternfragebogen zu deren Geburtsland abgebildet. Bei diesem dichotomen Merkmal bilden die Schüler, deren Eltern beide in Deutschland geboren wurden, die Referenzkategorie gegenüber jenen mit mindestens einem im Ausland geborenen Elternteil. Die *soziale Lage* wird über den höchsten sozioökonomischen Status in der Familie (HISEI; Ganzeboom und Treiman 1996) erfasst, der auf den Elternangaben zu ihrer Berufstätigkeit basiert. Als ein Indikator für die *Intelligenz* wird die nonverbale kognitive Grundfähigkeit verwendet, die sprachfrei anhand von figuralen Analogien aus dem kognitiven Fähigkeitstest (KFT; Heller und Perleth 2000) erfasst wurde. Auf die Notwendigkeit korrekt spezifizierter Schätzmodelle, die ausleserelevante Leistungsmerkmale auf individueller und schulischer Ebene berücksichtigen, haben bereits Baumert und Schümer (2001) hingewiesen. Deshalb wird nachfolgend auch die *Ausgangsleistung* im Leseverständnis zu Beginn der Jahrgangsstufe 7 kontrolliert. Dadurch kann die vorhergesagte Variable indirekt als *Lernentwicklung* in den Jahrgangsstufen 7 und 8 interpretiert werden.[9]

Prädiktoren auf Ebene des Klassenkontextes
Die *soziale* und *leistungsbezogene Zusammensetzung* als Kompositionsmerkmale des Klassenkontextes werden anhand des arithmetischen Mittels der individuellen Merkmalsausprägungen über die Schulklassenzugehörigkeit in der Jahrgangsstufe 7 aggregiert. Im Unterschied zu globalen Merkmalen ohne weiteren Rückgriff auf individuelle Informationen (z. B. Schulträgerschaft) stellen solche Kompositions-

---

[9] Die *direkte* Modellierung des individuellen Lernzuwachses wäre auch anhand eines Drei-Ebenen-Modells mit der Schachtelung von Messwiederholungsdaten innerhalb von Individualeinheiten (Schüler) auf unterster Ebene möglich. Da in diesem Beitrag jedoch – neben individuellen Merkmalen – v.a. die gemeinsamen Auswirkungen des Schul- und Klassenkontextes auf zwei höheren Analyseebenen im Vordergrund stehen, die *direkte* Modellierung des Lernzuwachses aber nur die Berücksichtigung *einer* weiteren Aggregatebene erlaubt (Ditton 1998, S. 148), wird die am Ende der Jahrgangsstufe 8 erzielte Testleistung unter Kontrolle der Ausgangsleistung zu Beginn der Jahrgangsstufe 7 vorhergesagt und als Leistungs*entwicklung* in diesen beiden Schuljahren gedeutet.

merkmale nach Ditton (2013, S. 175) *analytische Merkmale* dar, die nur über die Aggregation individueller Merkmalsausprägungen innerhalb des Kontextes gewonnen werden.

Als ein Aspekt der normativen Kultur in der Altersgruppe, der im Rahmen der KESS-Studie als Indikator für Vermittlungsmechanismen von Kontexteffekten (Baumert et al. 2006) verfügbar ist, wird die *Akzeptanz von Leistungsnormen* auch bei Normabweichungen der anderen berücksichtigt, von der eine leistungsförderliche Wirkung vermutet wird. In KESS 7 wurde im allgemeinen Schülerfragebogen danach gefragt, wie sehr die Schüler darauf achten, im Unterricht nicht zu stören und Rücksicht auf andere zu nehmen. Die Akzeptanz von Leistungsnormen lässt sich über ihre Zustimmung zu den Fragen abbilden, wie oft sie versuchen,

- das zu tun, wozu die Lehrkraft sie auffordert;
- leise zu sein, wenn andere versuchen, im Unterricht zu lernen;
- weiterzuarbeiten, obwohl sie müde sind; und
- weiterzuarbeiten, obwohl die anderen nicht mehr ernsthaft bei der Sache sind.

Die Zustimmung zu diesen Aussagen konnte über ein vierstufiges Antwortformat (1 *immer*, 2 *oft*, 3 *selten*, 4 *nie*) ausgedrückt werden. Für die Analysen wurden die Antwortkategorien aller Items rekodiert, sodass höhere Skalenwerte für eine stärkere Akzeptanz von Leistungsnormen im Klassenkontext stehen. Die Skalenbildung erfolgte über den Mittelwert aller vier Items (Cronbachs $\alpha = 0{,}92$, Trennschärfe r_{it} bei allen Items $\geq 0{,}79$). Zur Dokumentation der Erhebungsinstrumente für die gesamte KESS7-Population sei auf Bos et al. (2009) verwiesen.

Prädiktoren auf Ebene des Schulkontextes
Analog zur Operationalisierung auf Klassenebene wird die *soziale* und *leistungsbezogene Zusammensetzung* der Schulen über die mittleren Ausprägungen der entsprechenden Merkmale über die Schulzugehörigkeit aggregiert. Als institutionelles Merkmal wird die *Schulformgliederung* in der Sekundarstufe berücksichtigt. Referenzkategorie bilden die Hauptschulklassen an Haupt- und Realschulen. Da die Leistungsdifferenzierung an Integrierten Gesamtschulen nur in den Fächern Mathematik und Englisch erfolgt, werden sie hier als organisatorische Einheit betrachtet (zu den für den KESS-Jahrgang geltenden Besonderheiten des Hamburger Schulsystems vgl. Abschnitt 5.1). Als Prozessmerkmal zwischen Kontextfaktoren der Schulen und den Lernergebnissen der Schüler fließt auch auf der Schulebene die *mittlere Akzeptanz von Leistungsnormen* mit in die Analysen ein, deren Operationalisierung analog zum Vorgehen auf der Klassenebene erfolgt.

Um inhaltliche Zusammenhänge zwischen den Analysevariablen identifizieren zu können, sind in Tab. 1 die Korrelationen zwischen Prädiktor- und Kriteriumsvariablen dargestellt. In der linken Spalte sind die Korrelationen (Pearsons *r*) der Merkmale Geschlecht, Migrationshintergrund, soziale Lage, kognitive Grundfähigkeit und Ausgangsleistung im Leseverständnis zu Beginn der Jahrgangsstufe 7 mit der Leseleistung am Ende der Jahrgangsstufe 8 auf individueller Ebene dargestellt. Da diese Einfachkorrelationen jedoch noch keine Rückschlüsse über Ursachen der Zusammenhänge erlauben und auch auf eine differenzielle Eingangsselektivität von Schulen und Schulformen zurückzuführen sein können, sind in der rechten Tabellen-

Tab. 1 Korrelationen der unabhängigen Variablen mit der Leseleistung am Ende der Jahrgangsstufe 8

	r	Partialkorrelation
Geschlecht[a]	**0,18**	**0,16**
Migrationshintergrund[b]	**−0,23**	**−0,09**
Soziale Lage	**0,37**	**0,18**
Kognitive Grundfähigkeit	**0,48**	**0,22**
Ausgangsleistung zu Beginn der Jgst. 7 (T1)	**0,69**	

[a]Referenz: Junge

[b]Referenz: beide Eltern in Deutschland geboren

Signifikante Korrelationen fettgedruckt ($p<0,05$). $n=9.681$.

Linke Spalte: Korrelationen auf individueller Ebene mit der Leseleistung am Ende der Jgst. 8 (T2)

Rechte Spalte: Korrelationen auf individueller Ebene mit der Leseleistung am Ende der Jgst. 8 (T2) unter Auspartialisierung der Ausgangsleistung zu Beginn der Jgst. 7 (T1)

spalte zusätzlich die Partialkorrelationen unter Kontrolle der Ausgangsleistung zu Beginn der Jahrgangsstufe 7 aufgeführt.

Bereits bivariat zeigen sich signifikante Zusammenhänge zwischen individuellen Schülermerkmalen und der Leseleistung: Mädchen erreichen am Ende der Jahrgangsstufe 8 eine höhere Leseleistung als Jungen. Schüler mit Migrationshintergrund erzielen dagegen niedrigere Lernstände als solche, deren Eltern beide in Deutschland geboren wurden. Mit einer höheren sozialen Lage oder einer höheren kognitiven Grundfähigkeit gehen ebenfalls höhere Lernstände einher. Der stärkste Zusammenhang besteht jedoch zwischen den Testleistungswerten zu den beiden Messzeitpunkten. Anders ausgedrückt: Fast die Hälfte der Varianz des Leseverständnisses am Ende der Jahrgangsstufe 8 wird bereits durch die Ausgangsleistung zu Beginn der Jahrgangsstufe 7 erklärt ($R^2 = 0,48$). Unter Berücksichtigung der Ausgangsleistung fallen die Zusammenhänge der Schülermerkmale mit der Leseleistung am Ende der Jahrgangsstufe 8 mit Ausnahme des Geschlechts geringer, aber immer noch signifikant aus. Ein Teil der Zusammenhänge lässt sich also bereits durch die differenzielle Eingangsselektivität der Schulen und Schulformen erklären.

5.4 Beschreibung der Analysestichprobe

Ausgangsbasis für die Analysen sind die Schüler, die an KESS 7 und KESS 8 teilgenommen haben ($n=11\,420$). In einem mehrschrittigen Ausschlussverfahren werden davon diejenigen Schüler ausgeschlossen,

- die eine Integrierte Haupt- und Realschule ($n=447$) oder Kooperative Gesamtschule ($n=356$) besuchen, da diese jeweils eine für Hamburg besondere, aber zahlenmäßig geringe Schülerschaft umfassen,
- die in Schulklassen oder Schulen gehen, für die weniger als zehn Schüler zugeordnet werden können ($n=187$), um für die über die Klassen- oder Schulzugehörigkeit aggregierten Kompositionsmerkmale realistische Schätzer der jeweiligen Lernumwelt zu erhalten,
- deren Schulen einzügig sind ($n=138$), um Klassen- und Schulkontext analytisch eindeutig voneinander trennen zu können,

Tab. 2 Mittlere Zusammensetzung der Schülerschaft in den verschiedenen Schulformen zu Beginn der Jahrgangsstufe 7

	Leseverständnis		Soziale Lage		Akzeptanz von Leistungsnormen		Anzahl Schüler
	M	SD	M	SD	M	SD	
Hauptschule	406,56[a]	77,73	38,94[a]	13,48	2,76[a]	1,02	805
Realschule	478,79[b]	73,40	44,50[b]	14,10	3,09[b]	0,86	1203
Gesamtschule	468,20[c]	89,94	46,69[c]	15,85	2,78[a]	1,00	3074
Gymnasium	564,93[d]	81,36	57,55[d]	16,25	2,91[c]	0,89	4599
Gesamt	510,34	99,41	50,93	17,00	2,88	0,94	9681

Schulformen mit ungleichen Suffixen (a, b, c, d) unterscheiden sich hinsichtlich der jeweiligen Zusammensetzung signifikant ($p<0,05$).

- die in Jahrgangsstufe 7 oder 8 die Schulklasse, Schule oder Schulform gewechselt haben ($n=611$), um die Klassen- und Schulkomposition über diese zwei Schuljahre hinweg konstant zu halten und um ein allzu „komplexes Ineinandergreifen unterschiedlicher Kontexte, an denen das Individuum teil hatte und aktuell (noch) teilhat" (Ditton 2013, S. 186), ausschließen zu können.

Somit verbleiben für die Analysen 9681 Schüler in 467 Schulklassen und 142 Schulen. Tabelle 2 beschreibt die Zusammensetzung dieser Schülerschaft hinsichtlich der mittleren Lernstände im Leseverständnis, der durchschnittlichen sozialen Zusammensetzung und der mittleren Akzeptanz von Leistungsnormen getrennt nach Schulform zu Beginn der Jahrgangsstufe 7.

An Hauptschulen liegt die durchschnittlich erzielte Testleistung rund eine Standardabweichung unter dem Gesamtdurchschnitt. An Integrierten Gesamtschulen und Realschulen fallen die mittleren Lernstände um mehr als eine halbe Standardabweichung höher aus. An Gymnasien bestehen die günstigsten Lernausgangslagen. Die Mittelwertsunterschiede fallen zwischen allen Schulformen signifikant aus. Integrierte Gesamtschulen umfassen eine insgesamt leistungsheterogenere Schülerschaft, die Leistungsstreuung fällt hier entsprechend etwas höher aus als an den anderen Schulformen. Insgesamt besteht jedoch auch innerhalb der verschiedenen Schulformen eine beträchtliche Leistungsheterogenität, die dem Anspruch des gegliederten Schulsystems nach Homogenisierung der Leistungen entgegensteht (Scharenberg 2012, 2013). Analog zu den leistungsbezogenen Lernvoraussetzungen zeigt sich auch hinsichtlich der sozialen Komposition, dass lediglich an Gymnasien überdurchschnittliche Werte erzielt werden. Während an Hauptschulen erneut die ungünstigsten Lernvoraussetzungen bestehen, ist die Schülerschaft an Gymnasien am privilegiertesten zusammengesetzt, wobei auch hier die Unterschiede zwischen allen Schulformen signifikant sind. Die Effektstärken für die Schulformunterschiede in der leistungsbezogenen ($0,12 \leq |d| \leq 1,96$) und sozialen Komposition ($0,40 \leq |d| \leq 1,17$) der Schülerschaft variieren jedoch je nach Wahl der Vergleichsgruppe beträchtlich, deuten aber auf bedeutsame und z. T. substanzielle Unterschiede zwischen den Schulformen hin.

Schulformspezifische Unterschiede zeigen sich auch für die normative Kultur der Altersgruppe: Die Akzeptanz von Leistungsnormen ist an Realschulen am stärksten ausgeprägt, gefolgt von Gymnasien. An Hauptschulen und Integrierten Gesamtschulen, die sich im Vergleich zu allen anderen Schulformen nicht signifikant voneinander unterscheiden, ist die mittlere Skalenausprägung hingegen am niedrigsten. Bei den signifikanten Schulformunterschieden handelt es sich um kleine Effekte ($0{,}14 \leq |d| \leq 0{,}36$). Die vergleichsweise großen Standardabweichungen an Hauptschulen und Integrierten Gesamtschulen indizieren eine erhebliche Variabilität selbst zwischen Schulen derselben Schulform.

6 Ergebnisse

Nachfolgend werden die Ergebnisse der multivariaten und mehrebenenanalytischen Auswertungen dargestellt. Dabei wird zunächst die Bedeutung individueller Herkunfts- und Personenmerkmale für die Entwicklung schulischer Kompetenzen am Beispiel des Leseverständnisses (Abschn. 6.1) beschrieben, bevor in einem Mehrebenendesign Merkmale des Klassen- und Schulkontextes (Abschn. 6.2) ergänzt werden. Abschließend wird auf gruppenspezifische Effekte (Abschn. 6.3) eingegangen.

6.1 Zur Bedeutung individueller Herkunfts- und Personenmerkmale

Zunächst wird in einem „leeren", d. h. vollständig unspezifizierten Modell die Varianz der abhängigen Variable in drei Komponenten zerlegt, und zwar in Varianzanteile, die auf

- Unterschiede zwischen Schülern (Ebene 1) innerhalb von Schulklassen,
- Unterschiede zwischen Schulklassen (Ebene 2) innerhalb von Schulen,
- Unterschiede zwischen Schulen (Ebene 3) entfallen.

57,2 % der Gesamtvarianz des Leseverständnisses am Ende der Jahrgangsstufe 8 entfallen auf individuelle Unterschiede. 34,1 % der Varianz können durch Schulmerkmale erklärt werden. Auf die Klassenebene entfallen im Drei-Ebenen-Modell hingegen nur 8,7 % der Varianz.[10] Diese Varianzzerlegung deutet bereits auf eine unterschiedliche Bedeutsamkeit der verschiedenen sozialen Kontexte für die Entwicklung schulischer Kompetenzen hin.

Tabelle 3 berücksichtigt zur Vorhersage des Leseverständnisses ausschließlich individuelle Schülermerkmale. Auf die Notwendigkeit eines korrekt spezifizierten Schätzmodells auf der Individualebene haben bereits Baumert et al. (2006) hingewiesen. Im Mehrebenenmodell gibt der Intercept den Wert im Leseverständnis am Ende

---

[10] Bei einer Spezifikation als Zwei-Ebenen-Modell (Scharenberg 2012) fällt der Varianzanteil des Leseverständnisses am Ende der Jahrgangsstufe 8, der durch die Klassenzugehörigkeit erklärt wird, mit 44,6 % deutlich höher aus und ergibt sich aus der Differenz der Gesamtvarianz (100 %) und dem Varianzanteil, der auf individuelle Schülermerkmale zurückgeht (55,4 %). Im Drei-Ebenen-Modell zeigt sich hingegen, dass diese Varianz zwischen den Schulklassen innerhalb einer Schule in erster Linie auf eine deutlich höhere Varianz zwischen den Schulen zurückzuführen ist. In beiden Fällen, d. h. im Zwei- wie im Drei-Ebenen-Modell, sind jedoch die Varianzanteile auf der Klassenebene signifikant. Die leicht unterschiedlichen Varianzanteile, die jeweils auf die Individualebene entfallen, sind durch die Wahl einer anderen Analysestichprobe begründet.

Tab. 3 Vorhersage des Leseverständnisses am Ende der Jahrgangsstufe 8 durch individuelle Schülermerkmale

	Koeffizient	SE
Intercept	−0,07	0,03
Individualebene		
Geschlecht[a]	**0,25**	0,02
Migrationshintergrund[b]	**−0,07**	0,02
Soziale Lage	**0,06**	0,01
Kognitive Grundfähigkeit	**0,13**	0,01
Ausgangsleistung zu Beginn der Jgst. 7 (T1)	**0,45**	0,01
Erklärte Varianz innerhalb der Schulklassen (in %)[c]	35,2	

[a]Referenz: Junge
[b]Referenz: beide Eltern in Deutschland geboren
[c]Varianzaufklärung im Verhältnis zum Nullmodell (vollständig unspezifiziert)
Varianzzerlegung im Nullmodell:
Ebene 1 (innerhalb der Schulklassen): 57,2 %
Ebene 2 (zwischen den Schulklassen): 8,7 %
Ebene 3 (zwischen den Schulen): 34,1 %
Kontinuierliche Prädiktoren auf der Individualebene z-standardisiert
Signifikante Koeffizienten fett ($p<0,05$).

der Jahrgangsstufe 8 an, den ein Junge ohne Migrationshintergrund mit durchschnittlicher sozialer Lage, kognitiver Grundfähigkeit und durchschnittlicher Ausgangsleistung zu Beginn der Jahrgangsstufe 7 erreichen würde. Handelt es sich hingegen um ein Mädchen oder einen Schüler mit einer überdurchschnittlichen Ausgangsleistung zum vorangegangenen Messzeitpunkt, so verändert sich die erreichte Testleistung am Ende der Jahrgangsstufe 8 um den jeweils angegebenen Parameter. Da neben dem Geschlecht, dem Migrationshintergrund, der sozialen Lage und der kognitiven Grundfähigkeit auch die Ausgangsleistung im Leseverständnis zum vorherigen Messzeitpunkt als ein Maß der differenziellen Eingangsselektivität kontrolliert wird, lassen sich die Koeffizienten auch als Prädiktoren der Lern*entwicklung* in den Jahrgangsstufen 7 und 8 interpretieren.

Die wichtigsten Prädiktoren auf individueller Ebene, allesamt signifikant, sind die Ausgangsleistung im Leseverständnis zu Beginn der Jahrgangsstufe 7 und das Geschlecht: Unter Kontrolle der jeweils anderen Merkmale erzielen leistungsstarke Schüler mit einer Ausgangsleistung, die zu Beginn der Jahrgangsstufe 7 eine Standardabweichung über dem Durchschnitt liegt, zwei Jahre später um rund eine halbe Standardabweichung höhere Testleistungen im Leseverständnis. Der Entwicklungsvorsprung der Mädchen fällt gegenüber Jungen um rund ein Viertel einer Standardabweichung höher aus. Die restlichen Prädiktoren folgen mit deutlichem Abstand und deuten auf individuelle Leistungsvorteile bei höherer kognitiver Grundfähigkeit und höherer sozialer Lage sowie auf Leistungseinbußen bei Schülern mit Migrationshintergrund hin, welche jedoch unter ansonsten gleichen Voraussetzungen nur sehr gering ausfallen.

Die Intraklassenkorrelation, die im Nullmodell bei $\rho=0,59$ lag, sinkt bei Spezifikation des Individualmodells auf $\rho_{res}=0,38$. 35,2 % der Varianz innerhalb der Schulklassen – das sind rund 20 % der Gesamtvarianz des Leseverständnisses am Ende der Jahrgangsstufe 8 – können bereits durch individuelle Herkunftsmerkmale der Schüler erklärt werden, die zu einer differenziellen Eingangsselektivität von Schulen und Schulformen führen.

6.2 Zur Bedeutung des Klassen- und Schulkontextes

Tabelle 4 ergänzt das zuvor bereits auf der Individualebene spezifizierte Modell um Merkmale des Klassen- und Schulkontextes. Auf der Klassenebene werden nun in

Tab. 4 Vorhersage des Leseverständnisses am Ende der Jahrgangsstufe 8 durch Individual-, Klassen- und Schulmerkmale

	Modell 1		Modell 2	
	Koeffizient	SE	Koeffizient	SE
Intercept	**−0,32**	0,13	**−0,33**	0,13
Individualebene				
Geschlecht[a]	**0,25**	0,02	**0,25**	0,02
Migrationshintergrund[b]	**−0,06**	0,02	**−0,06**	0,02
Soziale Lage	**0,06**	0,01	**0,06**	0,01
Kognitive Grundfähigkeit	**0,13**	0,01	**0,13**	0,01
Ausgangsleistung zu Beginn der Jgst. 7 (T1)	**0,42**	0,01	**0,43**	0,01
Klassenebene				
Mittlere Ausgangsleistung zu Beginn der Jgst. 7 (T1)	**0,21**	0,05	**0,19**	0,05
Mittlere soziale Lage	0,07	0,06	0,05	0,06
Mittlere Akzeptanz von Leistungsnormen			**0,10**	0,04
Schulebene				
Mittlere Ausgangsleistung zu Beginn der Jgst. 7 (T1)	0,05	0,09	0,05	0,09
Mittlere soziale Lage	−0,09	0,07	−0,07	0,07
Mittlere Akzeptanz von Leistungsnormen			−0,04	0,05
Schulform[c]				
Realschule	0,22	0,18	0,22	0,19
Integrierte Gesamtschule	0,12	0,12	0,13	0,12
Gymnasium	**0,32**	0,14	**0,33**	0,14
Erklärte Varianz (in %)[d]				
Innerhalb der Schulklassen (Individualebene)	35,4		35,4	
Zwischen den Schulklassen (Klassenebene)	48,0		51,7	
Zwischen den Schulen (Schulebene)	98,2		98,2	

[a]Referenz: Junge
[b]Referenz: beide Eltern in Deutschland geboren
[c]Referenz: Hauptschule
[d]Varianzaufklärung im Verhältnis zum Nullmodell (vollständig unspezifiziert)
Varianzzerlegung im Nullmodell:
Ebene 1 (innerhalb der Schulklassen): 57,2 %
Ebene 2 (zwischen den Schulklassen): 8,7 %
Ebene 3 (zwischen den Schulen): 34,1 %
Kontinuierliche Prädiktoren auf der Individualebene z-standardisiert
Signifikante Koeffizienten fett ($p < 0,05$).

Modellvariante 1 die durchschnittliche Testleistung innerhalb der Schulklassen zu Beginn der Jahrgangsstufe 7 und die mittlere soziale Lage (durchschnittlicher HISEI innerhalb der Schulklassen) aufgenommen. In Modellvariante 2 wird zusätzlich die mittlere Akzeptanz von Leistungsnormen als im Rahmen der gewählten Datenbasis verfügbarer Indikator für die normative Kultur der Altersgruppe berücksichtigt. Auf der Schulebene werden dieselben Kompositionsmerkmale (Modellvariante 1) sowie Vermittlungsmechanismen (Modellvariante 2) berücksichtigt, die dort jedoch über die Schulzugehörigkeit aggregiert werden. Außerdem fließt die Schulformzugehörigkeit in beiden Modellvarianten mit ein, um institutionelle Effekte der Leistungsdifferenzierung kontrollieren zu können. Der Intercept gibt nun den Wert an, den ein Junge ohne Migrationshintergrund mit durchschnittlicher sozialer Lage, kognitiver Grundfähigkeit und Ausgangsleistung im Leseverständnis am Ende der Jahrgangsstufe 8 erreicht, der eine im Hinblick auf die Merkmale auf den beiden höheren Ebenen durchschnittlich zusammengesetzte Schulklasse an einer durchschnittlich zusammengesetzten Hauptschule (Referenzkategorie) besucht. Ein solch durchschnittlicher Hauptschüler würde eine Leseleistung erreichen, die mit einem Drittel einer Standardabweichung signifikant unterhalb des Durchschnitts liegt.

Auf der Individualebene bleiben die Koeffizienten auch bei der Spezifikation von Aggregatmerkmalen im Vergleich zu Tab. 3 konstant: Signifikante und deutliche Leistungsvorteile am Ende der Jahrgangsstufe 8 ergeben sich bei günstigeren Lernausgangslagen und für die Mädchen. Auf der Klassenebene lassen sich Leistungsvorteile für leistungsstärkere Lernkontexte beobachten: Schüler aus Schulklassen, in denen die mittlere Ausgangsleistung eine Standardabweichung über dem Durchschnitt liegt, erzielen unter ansonsten gleichen Bedingungen knapp zwei Jahre später eine um rund ein Fünftel einer Standardabweichung signifikant höhere Testleistung im Leseverständnis im Vergleich zum Besuch von Schulklassen mit durchschnittlichem Ausgangsniveau. Unter Berücksichtigung der Leistungszusammensetzung lässt sich für die soziale Komposition der Schulklassen kein eigenständiger Effekt mehr nachweisen. Darüber hinaus erweist sich die normative Kultur innerhalb der Schulklassen (Modellvariante 2) als leistungsrelevanter Prädiktor: In Schulklassen, in denen die mittlere Akzeptanz von Leistungsnormen überdurchschnittlich hoch ist, werden um ein Zehntel einer Standardabweichung signifikant höhere Lernstände erzielt. Die Berücksichtigung dieses Prädiktors liefert einen zusätzlichen Erklärungswert von 3,7 Prozentpunkten gegenüber Modellvariante 1.

Auf der Schulebene ist in beiden Modellvarianten nur der institutionelle Lernkontext relevant für die Leistungsentwicklung: Schüler an Gymnasien erzielen unter ansonsten gleichen individuellen, klassenbezogenen und schulischen Voraussetzungen um ein Drittel einer Standardabweichung signifikant höhere Lernstände im Leseverständnis am Ende der Jahrgangsstufe 8 als jene an Hauptschulen. Auch an Realschulen und Integrierten Gesamtschulen zeichnet sich ein Leistungsvorsprung gegenüber Hauptschulen ab, der sich jedoch nicht zufallskritisch absichern lässt. Gleiches gilt für die Effekte der sozialen und leistungsbezogenen Zusammensetzung der Schulen. Hier deutet sich an, dass Kompositions- und Institutionseffekte auf der Schulebene stark miteinander konfundiert sind (vgl. z. B. auch Baumert et al. 2006; Scharenberg 2012). Insgesamt bestätigt sich hier der bereits bekannte Befund, wonach die verschiedenen Schulformen differenzielle Lern- und Entwicklungsmilieus darstellen, die den Schülern unabhängig von und zusätzlich zu individuellen Lernvoraussetzungen unterschiedliche Entwicklungschancen bieten – v. a. an Gymnasien (siehe z. B. auch Baumert et al. 2006; Gröhlich et al. 2010a, b; Guill und Gröhlich 2013). Die Akzeptanz von Leistungsnormen übt auf institutioneller Ebene der Schulen ebenfalls keinen signifikanten Effekt auf die erzielte Testleistung im Leseverständnis aus und ist ausschließlich im Klassenkontext entwicklungsrelevant.

Durch die in Tab. 4 dargestellte Modellspezifikation können auf individueller Ebene 35,4 % der Leistungsvarianz – das entspricht 20,3 % der Gesamtvarianz[11] –, 51,7 % der Varianz auf der Klassenebene – das entspricht 4,5 % der Gesamtvarianz[12] – und 98,2 % der Leistungsvarianz zwischen den Schulen – das entspricht 33,5 % der Gesamtvarianz[13] – erklärt werden. In der Summe liefert das Drei-Ebenen-Modell somit einen Erklärungsbeitrag von 58,2 % der Gesamtvarianz in den am Ende der Jahrgangsstufe 8 erzielten Leseleistungen. Somit bleibt noch ein Erklärungsspielraum von insgesamt 41,8 % der Gesamtvarianz. Herunter gerechnet verbleiben damit für Merkmale des Klassenkontextes noch 4,6 % und für Merkmale des Schulkontextes noch 0,6 % der Gesamtvarianz, die nicht bereits durch die hier berücksichtigten Merkmale erklärt werden. Der Löwenanteil der bislang noch unerklärten Varianz verbleibt jedoch mit 36,9 % für individuelle Schüler- und familiale Herkunftsmerkmale.

6.3 Gruppenspezifische Effekte

Die bisherigen Analysen haben gezeigt, dass nicht davon ausgegangen werden kann, dass die verschiedenen Dimensionen der Zusammensetzung der Schülerschaft gleichermaßen leistungsrelevant sind. Vielmehr scheint v. a. die Leistungszusammensetzung des Klassenkontextes für die Entwicklung des Leseverständnisses in den Jahrgangsstufen 7 und 8 bedeutsam zu sein. Darüber hinaus konnte gezeigt werden, dass auch eine hohe Akzeptanz von Leistungsnormen, welche hier als Indikator für Vermittlungsprozesse zwischen der Schülerzusammensetzung und individuellen Lernergebnissen herangezogen wird, leistungsförderlich ist. Bislang unbeantwortet geblieben ist jedoch die Frage, ob diese Vermittlungsprozesse für alle Schüler die gleichen Auswirkungen haben oder ob sie auch in Wechselwirkung mit individuellen Schülermerkmalen auftreten, ob also von differenziellen Effekten in Abhängigkeit individueller Voraussetzungen auszugehen ist. In einem nächsten Schritt werden deshalb im Mehrebenenmodell Interaktionseffekte zwischen der mittleren Akzeptanz von Leistungsnormen im Klassenkontext und den Individualmerkmalen zugelassen.

Tabelle 5 zeigt zunächst, dass bei der Modellierung von Interaktionseffekten im Vergleich zu einfacher spezifizierten Modellen die Auswirkungen von Individualmerkmalen, Kompositionsmerkmalen und der mittleren Akzeptanz von Leistungsnormen im Klassenkontext konstant bleiben. Darüber hinaus lässt sich ein zusätzlicher, negativer Interaktionseffekt zwischen dem Geschlecht und der mittleren Akzeptanz von Leistungsnormen auf die Lernentwicklung in den Jahrgangsstufen 7 und 8 beobachten: Je stärker die Akzeptanz von Leistungsnormen im Klassenkontext ist, desto

---

[11] $R^2 = 0{,}354 \cdot 0{,}572 = 0{,}203$.

[12] $R^2 = 0{,}517 \cdot 0{,}087 = 0{,}045$.

[13] $R^2 = 0{,}982 \cdot 0{,}341 = 0{,}335$.

Tab. 5 Interaktionseffekte zwischen individuellen Schülermerkmalen und mittlerer Akzeptanz von Leistungsnormen innerhalb der Schulklassen bei der Vorhersage des Leseverständnisses am Ende der Jahrgangsstufe 8

	Koeffizient	SE
Intercept	**−0,34**	0,13
Individualebene		
Geschlecht[a]	**0,25**	0,02
Migrationshintergrund[b]	**−0,06**	0,02
Soziale Lage	**0,06**	0,01
Kognitive Grundfähigkeit	**0,13**	0,01
Ausgangsleistung zu Beginn der Jgst. 7 (T1)	**0,43**	0,01
Klassenebene		
Mittlere Ausgangsleistung zu Beginn der Jgst. 7 (T1)	**0,19**	0,05
Mittlere soziale Lage	0,04	0,06
Mittlere Akzeptanz von Leistungsnormen	**0,12**	0,05
Interaktionseffekte auf der Klassenebene		
Mittlere Akzeptanz von Leistungsnormen * Geschlecht	**−0,08**	0,04
Mittlere Akzeptanz von Leistungsnormen * Migrationshintergrund	0,05	0,04
Mittlere Akzeptanz von Leistungsnormen * soziale Lage	0,00	0,02
Mittlere Akzeptanz von Leistungsnormen * kognitive Grundfähigkeit	0,02	0,02
Mittlere Akzeptanz von Leistungsnormen * Ausgangsleistung T1	−0,01	0,02
Schulebene		
Mittlere Ausgangsleistung zu Beginn der Jgst. 7 (T1)	0,05	0,09
Mittlere soziale Lage	−0,05	0,07
Mittlere Akzeptanz von Leistungsnormen	−0,04	0,05
Schulform[c]		
Realschule	0,23	0,18
Integrierte Gesamtschule	0,13	0,12
Gymnasium	**0,34**	0,14
Erklärte Varianz (in %)[d]		
Innerhalb der Schulklassen (Individualebene)	35,6	
Zwischen den Schulklassen (Klassenebene)	57,8	
Zwischen den Schulen (Schulebene)	97,7	

[a]Referenz: Junge
[b]Referenz: beide Eltern in Deutschland geboren
[c]Referenz: Hauptschule
[d]Varianzaufklärung im Verhältnis zum Nullmodell (vollständig unspezifiziert)
Varianzzerlegung im Nullmodell:
Ebene 1 (innerhalb der Schulklassen): 57,2 %
Ebene 2 (zwischen den Schulklassen): 8,7 %
Ebene 3 (zwischen den Schulen): 34,1 %
Kontinuierliche Prädiktoren auf der Individualebene z-standardisiert
Signifikante Koeffizienten fett ($p<0{,}05$).

geringer ist der Effekt, den das Geschlecht auf die Lernentwicklung ausübt. Da die Entwicklung des Leseverständnisses von Jungen unter ansonsten identischen individuellen, klassenbezogenen und schulischen Voraussetzungen an Hauptschulen (Referenzkategorie) ungünstiger verläuft als die der Mädchen, scheint eine hohe Akzeptanz

Tab. 6 Vergleich der verschiedenen Modellspezifikationen

Variante	I Tabelle 3	II Tabelle 4, Modell 1	III Tabelle 4, Modell 2	IV Tabelle 5
Spezifikation	Nur individuelle Schülermerkmale	+ Kompositions- und Institutionsmerkmale	+ Kompositions- und Institutionsmerkmale + Vermittlungsmechanismen	+ Interaktionseffekte
Kontextmodellierung		Klassen und Schulen	Klassen und Schulen	Effekte des Klassen- und Schulkontextes auf individuelle Leistungsentwicklung
Mittlere Devianz	19.103,54	18.941,65	18.933,39	18.906,28
df	141	136	135	130
Referenzvariante		(I)	(II)	(III)
Δ Devianz		161,89	8,26	27,11
Δ df		5	1	5
Prüfgröße		11,07	3,84	11,07
Veränderung des Modellfits[a]		+	+	+

[a]Nicht signifikante (0) bzw. signifikante Verbesserung (+) des Modellfits gegenüber dem Referenzmodell ($p<0{,}05$)

von Leistungsnormen einen leichten kompensatorischen Effekt zu besitzen, der diesen Nachteil der Jungen geringfügig, aber signifikant, verringern kann. Dieser geschlechtsspezifische Interaktionseffekt ist jedoch kein Effekt einer unterschiedlichen Geschlechterzusammensetzung innerhalb der Schulklassen, da er sich auch dann noch nachweisen lässt, wenn der Mädchenanteil innerhalb der Schulklassen zusätzlich kontrolliert wird (hier nicht dargestellt). Darüber hinaus lässt sich jedoch für die mittlere Akzeptanz von Leistungsnormen kein zusätzlicher Interaktionseffekt mit weiteren Schülermerkmalen beobachten. Es liegt also keine Mehrfachinteraktion oder eine Kombination mehrerer Benachteiligungsfaktoren auf individueller Ebene vor. Die Berücksichtigung von Interaktionseffekten mit allen Individualmerkmalen erhöht den Anteil der erklärten Varianz um rund 6 Prozentpunkte auf der Klassenebene auf nunmehr 57,8 % – das entspricht 5,0 % der Gesamtvarianz.[14]

6.4 Modellvergleichendes Resümee

Tabelle 6 gibt abschließend Auskunft über die Anpassungsgüte der verschiedenen Modellvarianten. In der ersten Modellvariante (Tab. 3) wurden nur individuelle Schülermerkmale spezifiziert. Die zweite Modellvariante (Tab. 4, Modell 1) berücksichtigte zusätzlich den Schul- und Klassenkontext und schätzte kompositionelle Effekte der leistungsbezogenen und sozialen Schülerzusammensetzung sowie institutionelle Effekte der Schulformzugehörigkeit. In einem dritten Schritt wurde ein Indikator für Vermittlungsmechanismen für Kontexteffekte ergänzt (Tab. 4, Modell 2). In der vierten Modellvariante (Tab. 5) wurden *Cross-Level*-Interaktionen zwischen Merkmalen

---
[14] $R^2 = 0{,}578 \cdot 0{,}087 = 0{,}050$.

des Schul- und Klassenkontextes und dem Zusammenhang von Herkunfts- und Personenmerkmalen und der abhängigen Variable auf individueller Ebene zugelassen.

Diese Modellvarianten können nun über ihre Anpassungsgüte an die empirische Datengrundlage anhand eines Likelihood-Ratio-χ^2-Tests miteinander verglichen werden. Dieser Test bestimmt die Devianzwerte und die Anzahl der Freiheitsgrade eines Alternativmodells im Vergleich zu einem Referenzmodell. Die daraus resultierenden Differenzwerte werden anhand eines χ^2-Tests daraufhin getestet, ob das jeweilige Alternativmodell zu einer signifikanten Verbesserung gegenüber dem Referenzmodell führt (siehe hierzu Langer 2008, S. 119).

Der Modellvergleich zeigt, dass die Berücksichtigung der Drei-Ebenen-Struktur (Variante II) zu einer signifikant besseren Modellanpassung gegenüber jenem Modell führt, das ausschließlich individuelle Schülermerkmale berücksichtigt (Variante I). Berücksichtigt man zusätzlich die Vermittlungsmechanismen (Variante III), von denen angenommen wird, dass Kontexteffekte über diese vermittelt werden, ergibt sich im Vergleich zu Variante II ebenfalls eine signifikante Modellverbesserung. Die Variante IV, bei der zusätzlich Interaktionseffekte zwischen Vermittlungsmechanismen auf aggregierter Ebene und Schülermerkmalen auf individueller Ebene zugelassen werden, weist schließlich die beste Modellanpassung auf.

7 Zusammenfassung und Diskussion

Ausgangspunkt des Beitrags war die Frage, welcher der verschiedenen Kontexte im Mehrebenensystem Schule entwicklungsrelevant ist und über welche Vermittlungsmechanismen sich Kontexteffekte auf die Schulleistung als zentraler Aspekt der Entwicklung im Jugendalter entfalten. Die Ergebnisse zeigen anhand von Daten der Hamburger KESS-Studie zunächst die unterschiedliche Bedeutung verschiedener sozialer Kontexte für die schulische Kompetenzentwicklung im Leseverständnis: Im vollständig unspezifizierten, also „leeren", Drei-Ebenen-Modell entfällt rund ein Drittel der Varianz der Kriteriumsvariable auf den Schulkontext, hingegen nur weniger als 10% auf den Klassenkontext. Die Variabilität zwischen den Schulklassen ist also schon von vornherein durch den Schulkontext eingeschränkt, der wiederum mit der Schulform und der sozio-kulturellen Zusammensetzung des Einzugsgebiets konfundiert ist. Zwar scheint dem Schulkontext eine höhere Bedeutung für die Leistungsentwicklung zuzukommen, dennoch ist der Varianzanteil, der auf den Klassenkontext entfällt, signifikant. Die Schulklasse ist somit als eigenständiger Entwicklungskontext im Jugendalter keineswegs zu vernachlässigen, stellt sie doch die unmittelbare Lernumwelt im schulischen Bereich dar, in der die Schüler über viele Jahre hinweg gemeinsam mit und von anderen lernen.

Mehr als die Hälfte der Leistungsvarianz entfällt im unspezifizierten Modell hingegen auf individuelle Unterschiede zwischen den Schülern. Diese werden zwar bereits v. a. durch unterschiedliche kognitive und leistungsbezogene Voraussetzungen, aber auch durch geschlechtsspezifische Disparitäten zugunsten der Mädchen erklärt. Allerdings lassen sich auf individueller Ebene auch migrationsbedingte und soziale Disparitäten nachweisen. Dies deutet darauf hin, dass auch der familiäre Kontext einen eigenständigen Beitrag zu ungleichen Entwicklungsverläufen leistet.

Insgesamt lässt sich in dieser *ersten Modellvariante* unter Berücksichtigung individueller Herkunftsmerkmale mehr als ein Drittel der Entwicklungsunterschiede auf individueller Ebene oder rund ein Fünftel der Gesamtvarianz erklären. Diese differenzielle Eingangsselektivität der Schulkontexte hatte sich zuvor bereits deskriptiv angedeutet.

Anschließend wurde anhand von Mehrebenenanalysen schrittweise überprüft, in welcher Weise sich Schule und Schulklasse als soziale Kontexte auf die Entwicklung im Jugendalter auswirken, durch welche Mechanismen verschiedene Kontextmerkmale vermittelt werden und ob solche Vermittlungsprozesse gruppenspezifisch auftreten. In einer *zweiten Modellvariante* zeigen sich dabei Vorteile eines leistungsstarken Klassenkontextes. Außerdem lässt sich eine höhere Lerneffektivität an Gymnasien, v. a. in Abgrenzung zu Hauptschulen, beobachten. Dies bestätigt die Befunde früherer Arbeiten (z. B. Baumert et al. 2006; Bonsen et al. 2009a; Gröhlich et al. 2010a, b; Neumann et al. 2007; Nikolova 2011). Es ist somit einerseits bedeutsam, *wo*, also in welchem Schulkontext die Schüler lernen. Andererseits macht es aber auch einen Unterschied, *mit wem* sie zusammen lernen. Schulklassen und Schulen stellen also gemeinsam differenzielle Lern- und Entwicklungsmilieus dar, die den Schülern, ungeachtet ihrer individuellen Unterschiede, je nach Kontextzugehörigkeit unterschiedliche Entwicklungsmöglichkeiten bieten. Es bestehen also neben *individuellen* auch erhebliche *institutionelle Matthäus-Effekte*. Überraschend erscheinen jedoch die ansonsten vielfach nachgewiesenen, hier in der Drei-Ebenen-Spezifikation aber ausbleibenden Kompositionseffekte des Schulkontextes. Bei gleichzeitiger Modellierung von Schul- und Klassenkontext schlagen sich Merkmale der sozialen und leistungsbezogenen Zusammensetzung von Schulen offenbar ausschließlich in Kompositionseffekten des Klassenkontextes *innerhalb* der jeweiligen Schul*formen* nieder. Dies legt vertiefende schulformspezifische Analysen nahe. Zudem wäre es interessant zu überprüfen, ob die hier ausbleibenden Kompositionseffekte der sozialen und leistungsbezogenen Schulzusammensetzung möglicherweise auf nicht-lineare Effekte zurückzuführen sind oder sich nur ab bestimmten Schwellenwerten nachweisen lassen (Friedrichs und Nonnenmacher 2010, S. 478).

In einer *dritten Modellvariante* wurden *Vermittlungsprozesse* auf den beiden Kontextebenen ergänzt, für die hier als Indikator die normative Kultur der Altersgruppe berücksichtigt wurde und von denen theoretisch anzunehmen ist, dass Effekte von Kontextmerkmalen über diese vermittelt werden (Baumert et al. 2006, S. 126). Als Ergebnis lässt sich festhalten, dass diese Vermittlungsprozesse auf schulischer Ebene unter Kontrolle kompositioneller und institutioneller Merkmale offenbar nur eine untergeordnete Rolle spielen. Im Klassenkontext zeigt sich hingegen ein direkter Effekt der geteilten Akzeptanz von Leistungsnormen als Vermittlungsprozess, der als Merkmal der unmittelbaren Lernumwelt der Schüler für die konkrete Lehr-Lernsituation im Unterricht kennzeichnend ist (Ditton 2000). Eine hohe Akzeptanz von Leistungsnormen scheint also durchaus leistungsförderlich zu sein und liefert einen zusätzlichen Erklärungswert bei der Vorhersage der Leistungsentwicklung. Der Nachweis von Vermittlungsprozessen innerhalb von Schulklassen als unmittelbare Entwicklungskontexte im Jugendalter ist auch theoretisch zu erwarten, da „*Vermittlungsprozesse über soziale Interaktionen* stattfinden und erst dadurch ein Kollektiv oder Kontext überhaupt für ein Individuum handlungsrelevant wird" (Ditton 2013, S. 178; Hervorhebung im Original). Die Überprüfung gruppenspezifischer Effekte dieser Vermittlungsprozesse ergab in einer *vierten Modellvariante*, dass eine hohe Akzeptanz von Leistungsnormen im Klassenkontext nur für männliche Hauptschüler (Referenzkategorie) einen leichten kompensatorischen Fördereffekt hat.

Zusammenfassend zeigte sich im Vergleich, dass mit jeder Modellvariante ein zusätzlicher Erklärungsbeitrag zur Vorhersage der Kompetenzentwicklung im Leseverständnis gewonnen werden konnte, sodass das vollständig spezifizierte Gesamtmodell die höchste Anpassung an die empirischen Daten lieferte. Zur Vorhersage der schulischen Leistungsentwicklung im Jugendalter muss also davon ausgegangen werden, dass diese nicht nur von individuellen Lernvoraussetzungen, sondern gleichzeitig auch von Bedingungen verschiedener Kontexte und von Vermittlungsprozessen abhängt, wobei letztere gruppenspezifisch auftreten. Bezogen auf den schulischen Bereich als ein Anwendungsgebiet der Kontextanalyse haben sich die Mehrebenenanalysen hier als geeignetes methodisches Verfahren erwiesen, das der hierarchischen Struktur der vorliegenden Daten gerecht wird und es ermöglicht, simultan Effekte der Makro- und Mesoebene auf die Mikroebene zu schätzen.

In methodischer Hinsicht eröffnen die hier präsentierten Befunde gleichzeitig vielfältige Anknüpfungspunkte für zukünftige Analysen: Einerseits legen sie die Überprüfung eines solchen Vermittlungsmodells für Kontexteffekte anhand einer weiteren Schülerpopulation, für einen anderen Kompetenzbereich sowie die Ausdehnung auf einen längeren Untersuchungszeitraum nahe. Andererseits wurde hier als im Rahmen der vorliegenden Datenbasis verfügbarer Indikator für Vermittlungsprozesse von Kontexteffekten lediglich die Akzeptanz von Leistungsnormen als ein Aspekt der normativen Kultur der Altersgruppe herausgegriffen. Neben diesen führen Baumert et al. (2006, S. 126) auch deviante Verhaltensnormen, Schulbindung und Verantwortungsübernahme sowie Vergleichsprozesse auf Schülerebene als bezugsgruppenbezogene Prozesse auf. Unberücksichtigt geblieben sind hier auch Engagement, Leistungs- und Verhaltensnormen der Elternschaft sowie curriculare und didaktische Aspekte. Eine Gesamtüberprüfung eines solch mehrfach gestuften Vermittlungsmodells steht also nach wie vor aus. Bereits eine Übertragung ihres komplexen Vermittlungsmodells auf den Klassenkontext ohne sonstige Modifikation wäre aufschlussreich, da sich ihr Vermittlungsmodell auf der Schulebene als nicht tragfähig erweist (ebd., S. 149).

Darüber hinaus wäre es wünschenswert, gemeinsame Effekte verschiedener Lern- und Entwicklungskontexte direkt auf individuelle Lern*zuwächse* zu modellieren. Die Mehrebenenanalyse wäre hierfür ein geeignetes Verfahren, da sie die Schachtelung von Messwiederholungsdaten innerhalb von Individualeinheiten ermöglicht. Vielversprechend wäre es auch – analog zu Baumert et al. (2006) – im Klassen- und Schulkontext Pfadmodelle zu konzipieren, bei denen die Kontextmerkmale die exogenen Variablen bilden und die Vermittlungsmechanismen als Mediatorvariablen fungieren. Der vorliegende Beitrag verdeutlicht also einmal mehr, „dass die Ermittlung von *Kontexteffekten* nicht trivial ist" (Ditton 2013, S. 175, Hervorhebung im Original).

Literatur

Artelt, Cordula, Petra Stanat, Wolfgang Schneider und Ulrich Schiefele. 2001. Lesekompetenz: Testkonzeption und Ergebnisse. In *PISA 2000. Basiskompetenzen von Schülerinnen und Schülern im internationalen Vergleich*, Hrsg. Jürgen Baumert, Eckhard Klieme, Michael Neubrand, Manfred Prenzel, Ulrich Schiefele, Wolfgang Schneider, Petra Stanat, Klaus-Jürgen Tillmann und Manfred Weiß, 69–137. Opladen: Leske + Budrich.
Barr, Rebecca, und Robert Dreeben. 1983. *How schools work*. Chicago: University of Chicago Press.
Baumert, Jürgen, und Gundel Schümer. 2001. Schulformen als selektionsbedingte Lernmilieus. In *PISA 2000. Basiskompetenzen von Schülerinnen und Schülern im internationalen Vergleich*, Hrsg. Jürgen Baumert, Eckhard Klieme, Michael Neubrand, Manfred Prenzel, Ulrich Schiefele, Wolfgang Schneider, Petra Stanat, Klaus-Jürgen Tillmann und Manfred Weiß, 454–467. Opladen: Leske + Budrich.
Baumert, Jürgen, Eckhard Klieme, Michael Neubrand, Manfred Prenzel, Ulrich Schiefele, Wolfgang Schneider, Klaus-Jürgen Tillmann und Manfred Weiß. 2001. *Soziale Bedingungen von Schulleistungen. Zur Erfassung von Kontextmerkmalen durch Schüler-, Schul- und Elternfragebögen*. http://www.mpib-berlin.mpg.de/pisa/Kontextmerkmale.pdf (Zugegriffen: 28. Okt. 2013).
Baumert, Jürgen, Ulrich Trautwein und Cordula Artelt. 2003. Schulumwelten und institutionelle Bedingungen des Lehrens und Lernens. In *PISA 2000. Ein differenzierter Blick auf die Länder der Bundesrepublik Deutschland*, Hrsg. Jürgen Baumert, Cordula Artelt, Eckhard Klieme, Michael Neubrand, Manfred Prenzel, Ulrich Schiefele, Wolfgang Schneider, Klaus-Jürgen Tillmann und Manfred Weiß, 261–331. Opladen: Leske + Budrich.
Baumert, Jürgen, Werner Blum und Michael Neubrand. 2004. Drawing the lessons from PISA 2000 – Long-term research implications: Gaining a better understanding of the relationship between system inputs and learning outcomes by assessing instructional and learning processes as mediating factors. *Zeitschrift für Erziehungswissenschaft, Beiheft* 3:143–157.
Baumert, Jürgen, Petra Stanat und Rainer Watermann. 2006. Schulstruktur und die Entstehung differenzieller Lern- und Entwicklungsmilieus. In *Herkunftsbedingte Disparitäten im Bildungswesen: Differenzielle Bildungsprozesse und Probleme der Verteilungsgerechtigkeit. Vertiefende Analysen im Rahmen von PISA 2000*, Hrsg. Jürgen Baumert, Petra Stanat und Rainer Watermann, 95–188. Wiesbaden: VS Verlag für Sozialwissenschaften.
Baumert, Jürgen, Kai Maaz, Petra Stanat und Rainer Watermann. 2009. Schulkomposition oder Institution – was zählt? Schulstrukturen und die Entstehung schulformspezifischer Entwicklungsverläufe. *Die Deutsche Schule* 101:33–46.
Becker, Michael, Oliver Lüdtke, Ulrich Trautwein und Jürgen Baumert. 2006. Leistungszuwachs in Mathematik. Evidenz für einen Schereneffekt im mehrgliedrigen Schulsystem? *Zeitschrift für Pädagogische Psychologie* 20:233–242.
Bellin, Nicole. 2009. *Klassenkomposition, Migrationshintergrund und Leistung. Mehrebenenanalysen zum Sprach- und Leseverständnis von Grundschülern*. Wiesbaden: VS Verlag für Sozialwissenschaften.
Berkemeyer, Nils, und Veronika Manitius. 2013. Gerechtigkeit als Kategorie der Analyse von Schulsystemen – das Beispiel Chancenspiegel. In *Schul- und Bildungsforschung: Diskussionen, Befunde und Perspektiven. Festschrift für Wilfried Bos*, Hrsg. Knut Schwippert, Martin Bonsen und Nils Berkemeyer, 223–240. Münster: Waxmann.
Berkemeyer, Nils, Wilfried Bos und Veronika Manitius. 2012. Chancenspiegel. Zur Leistungsfähigkeit und Chancengerechtigkeit der deutschen Schulsysteme. In *Chancenspiegel. Zur Leistungsfähigkeit und Chancengerechtigkeit der deutschen Schulsysteme*, Hrsg. Bertelsmann Stiftung und Institut für Schulentwicklungsforschung, 1–192. Gütersloh: Verlag Bertelsmann Stiftung.
Blau, Peter M. 1960. Structural effects. *American Sociological Review* 25:178–193.
Bonsen, Martin, Carola Gröhlich und Wilfried Bos. 2009a. Differentielle Lern- und Entwicklungsmilieus in der Hamburger Beobachtungsstufe? In *KESS 7 – Kompetenzen und Einstellungen von Schülerinnen und Schülern an Hamburger Schulen zu Beginn der Jahrgangsstufe 7*, Hrsg. Wilfried Bos, Martin Bonsen und Carola Gröhlich, 113–122. Münster: Waxmann.
Bonsen, Martin, Wilfried Bos, Carola Gröhlich und Anna Rau. 2009b. Ziele der Untersuchung KESS 7. In *KESS 7 – Kompetenzen und Einstellungen von Schülerinnen und Schülern an Hamburger Schulen zu Beginn der Jahrgangsstufe 7*, Hrsg. Wilfried Bos, Martin Bonsen und Carola Gröhlich, 13–21. Münster: Waxmann.

Bos, Wilfried, und Katja Scharenberg. 2010. Lernentwicklung in leistungshomogenen und -heterogenen Schulklassen. In *Schulische Lerngelegenheiten und Kompetenzentwicklung. Festschrift für Jürgen Baumert*, Hrsg. Wilfried Bos, Eckhard Klieme und Olaf Köller, 173–194. Münster: Waxmann.

Bos, Wilfried, Uta Brose, Svenja Bundt, Carola Gröhlich, Nina Hugk, Nike Janke, Peter May, Marcus Pietsch, Tobias C. Stubbe und Andreas Voss. 2006. Anlage und Durchführung der Studie „Kompetenzen und Einstellungen von Schülerinnen und Schülern – Jahrgangsstufe 4 (KESS 4)". In *KESS 4 – Kompetenzen und Einstellungen von Schülerinnen und Schülern am Ende der Jahrgangsstufe 4 in Hamburger Schulen*, Hrsg. Wilfried Bos und Marcus Pietsch, 9–32. Münster: Waxmann.

Bos, Wilfried, Martin Bonsen, Carola Gröhlich, Karin Guill und Katja Scharenberg. 2009. *KESS 7 – Skalenhandbuch zur Dokumentation der Erhebungsinstrumente*. Münster: Waxmann.

Bos, Wilfried, Carola Gröhlich, Karin Guill, Katja Scharenberg und Heike Wendt. 2010a. Ziele und Anlage der Studie KESS 8. In *KESS 8 – Kompetenzen und Einstellungen von Schülerinnen und Schülern am Ende der Jahrgangsstufe 8*, Hrsg. Wilfried Bos und Carola Gröhlich, 9–20. Münster: Waxmann.

Bos, Wilfried, Carola Gröhlich, Denisa-Felicia Dudas, Karin Guill und Katja Scharenberg. 2010b. *KESS 8 – Skalenhandbuch zur Dokumentation der Erhebungsinstrumente*. Münster: Waxmann.

Dar, Yehezkel, und Nura Resh. 1986. Classroom intellectual composition and academic achievement. A study of the effects of ability-based classes. *American Educational Research Journal* 23:357–374.

Ditton, Hartmut. 1998. *Mehrebenenanalyse. Grundlagen und Anwendungen des hierarchisch linearen Modells*. Weinheim: Juventa.

Ditton, Hartmut. 2000. Qualitätskontrolle und Qualitätssicherung in Schule und Unterricht. Ein Überblick zum Stand der Empirischen Forschung. *Zeitschrift für Pädagogik* 41:73–92

Ditton, Hartmut. 2013. Kontexteffekte und Bildungsungleichheit: Mechanismen und Erklärungsmuster. In *Bildungskontexte. Strukturelle Voraussetzungen und Ursachen ungleicher Bildungschancen*, Hrsg. Rolf Becker und Alexander Schulze, 173–206. Wiesbaden: Springer VS.

Dreeben, Robert, und Rebecca Barr. 1988. Classroom composition and the design of instruction. *Sociology of Education* 61:129–142.

Dumont, Hanna, Marko Neumann, Kai Maaz und Ulrich Trautwein. 2013. Die Zusammensetzung der Schülerschaft als Einflussfaktor für Schulleistungen. *Psychologie in Erziehung und Unterricht* 60:163–183.

Fend, Helmut. 1991. Schule und Persönlichkeit: Eine Bilanz der Konstanzer Forschungen zur „Sozialisation in Bildungsinstitutionen". In *Schule und Persönlichkeitsentwicklung. Ein Resümee der Längsschnittforschung*, Hrsg. Reinhard Pekrun und Helmut Fend, 9–32. Stuttgart: Enke.

Friedrichs, Jürgen, und Alexandra Nonnenmacher. 2010. Welche Mechanismen erklären Kontexteffekte? In *Komparative empirische Sozialforschung*, Hrsg. Tilo Beckers, Klaus Birkelbach, Jörg Hagenah und Ulrich Rosar, 469–497. Wiesbaden: VS Verlag für Sozialwissenschaften.

Ganzeboom, Harry B.G., und Donald J. Treiman. 1996. Internationally comparable measures of occupational status for the 1988 International Standard Classification of Occupations. *Social Science Research* 25:201–239.

Gröhlich, Carola, Karin Guill, Katja Scharenberg und Wilfried Bos. 2010a. Kumulative Effekte differentieller Lern- und Entwicklungsmilieus innerhalb der Sekundarstufe I am Beispiel der Mathematikleistung. In *Erziehungswissenschaftliche Forschung – nachhaltige Bildung. Beiträge zur 5. DGfE-Sektionstagung „Empirische Bildungsforschung"/AEPF-KBBB im Frühjahr 2009*, Hrsg. Bernd Schwarz, Peter Nenniger und Reinhold S. Jäger, 473–479. Landau: Verlag Empirische Pädagogik.

Gröhlich, Carola, Karin Guill, Katja Scharenberg und Wilfried Bos. 2010b. Differenzielle Lern- und Entwicklungsmilieus beim Erwerb der Lesekompetenz in den Jahrgangsstufen 7 und 8. In *KESS 8 – Kompetenzen und Einstellungen von Schülerinnen und Schülern am Ende der Jahrgangsstufe 8*, Hrsg. Wilfried Bos und Carola Gröhlich, 100–106. Münster: Waxmann.

Guill, Karin, und Carola Gröhlich. 2013. Individuelle Lernentwicklung im gegliederten Schulsystem der Bundesrepublik Deutschland. Fragen an die Sekundarstufe I. In *Schul- und Bildungsforschung: Diskussionen, Befunde und Perspektiven. Festschrift für Wilfried Bos*, Hrsg. Knut Schwippert, Martin Bonsen und Nils Berkemeyer, 51–69. Münster: Waxmann.

Hallinan, Maureen T. 1994. Further thoughts on tracking. *Sociology of Education* 67:89–91.

Harker, Richard, und Peter Tymms. 2004. The effects of student composition on school outcomes. *School Effectiveness and School Improvement* 15:177–199.

Hattie, John A.C. 2002. Classroom composition and peer effects. *International Journal of Educational Research* 37:449–481.

Heller, Kurt A., und Christoph Perleth. 2000. *KFT 4–12 + R. Kognitiver Fähigkeitstest für 4. bis 12. Klassen, Revision*. Göttingen: Beltz.

Helmke, Andreas, und Franz E. Weinert. 1997. Bedingungsfaktoren schulischer Leistungen. In *Psychologie des Unterrichts und der Schule*, Hrsg. Franz E. Weinert, 71–176. Göttingen: Hogrefe.
Hox, Joop J. 1995. *Applied multilevel analysis*. Amsterdam: TT-Publikaties.
Ivanov, Stanislav, Roumiana Nikolova und Ulrich Vieluf. 2011. Einführung. In *KESS 10/11. Kompetenzen und Einstellungen von Schülerinnen und Schülern an Hamburger Schulen am Ende der Sekundarstufe I und zu Beginn der gymnasialen Oberstufe*, Hrsg. Ulrich Vieluf, Stanislav Ivanov und Roumiana Nikolova, 9–13. Münster: Waxmann.
Köller, Olaf. 2004. *Konsequenzen von Leistungsgruppierungen*. Münster: Waxmann.
Köller, Olaf, und Jürgen Baumert. 2001. Leistungsgruppierungen in der Sekundarstufe I. Ihre Konsequenzen für die Mathematikleistung und das mathematische Selbstkonzept der Begabung. *Zeitschrift für Pädagogische Psychologie* 15:99–110.
Kulik, Chen-Lin C., und James A. Kulik. 1982. Effects of ability grouping on secondary school students: A meta-analysis of evaluation findings. *American Educational Research Journal* 19:415–428.
Langer, Wolfgang. 2008. *Mehrebenenanalyse. Eine Einführung für Forschung und Praxis*. 2. Aufl. Wiesbaden: VS Verlag für Sozialwissenschaften.
Lou, Yiping, Philip C. Abrami, John C. Spence, Catherine Poulsen, Bette Chambers und Sylvia d'Apollonia. 1996. Within-class grouping: A meta-analysis. *Review of Educational Research* 66:423–458.
Lüdtke, Oliver, Alexander Robitzsch und Olaf Köller. 2002. Statistische Artefakte bei Kontexteffekten in der pädagogisch-psychologischen Forschung. *Zeitschrift für Pädagogische Psychologie* 16:217–231.
Maaz, Kai, Ulrich Trautwein, Oliver Lüdtke und Jürgen Baumert. 2008. Educational transitions and differential learning environments: How explicit between-school tracking contributes to social inequality in educational outcomes. *Child Development Perspectives* 2:99–106.
Meulemann, Heiner. 2006. *Soziologie von Anfang an*. 2. überarb. Aufl. Wiesbaden: VS Verlag für Sozialwissenschaften.
Neumann, Marko, Inge Schnyder, Ulrich Trautwein, Alois Niggli, Oliver Lüdtke und Rico Cathomas. 2007. Schulformen als differenzielle Lernmilieus. Institutionelle und kompositionelle Effekte auf die Leistungsentwicklung im Fach Französisch. *Zeitschrift für Erziehungswissenschaft* 10:399–420.
Nikolova, Roumiana. 2011. *Grundschulen als differenzielle Entwicklungsmilieus. Objektive Kontextmerkmale der Schülerzusammensetzung und deren Auswirkung auf die Mathematik- und Leseleistungen*. Münster: Waxmann.
Oakes, Jeannie. 1990. *Multiplying inequalities. The effects of race, social class, and tracking on opportunities to learn mathematics and science*. Santa Monica: RAND Corporation.
Opdenakker, Marie-Christine, und Jan van Damme. 2001. Relationship between school composition and characteristics of school process and their effect on mathematics achievement. *British Educational Research Journal* 27:407–432.
Opdenakker, Marie-Christine, und Jan van Damme. 2006. Differences between secondary schools: A study about school context, group composition, school practice, and school effects with special attention to public and Catholic schools and types of schools. *School Effectiveness and School Improvement* 17:87–117.
Organisation for Economic Co-Operation and Development (OECD). 2001. *Lernen für das Leben. Erste Ergebnisse der internationalen Schulleistungsstudie PISA 2000. Ausbildung und Kompetenzen*. Paris: OECD.
Ramseier, Erich, und Christian Brühwiler. 2003. Herkunft, Leistung und Bildungschancen im gegliederten Bildungssystem: Vertiefte PISA-Analyse unter Einbezug der kognitiven Grundfähigkeiten. *Schweizerische Zeitschrift für Bildungswissenschaften* 25:23–58.
Raudenbush, Stephen W., Anthony S. Bryk und R. Congdon. 2009. *HLM 6.08 for Windows [Computer software]*. Lincolnwood: Scientific Software International, Inc.
Schafer, Joseph L. 1999. *NORM: Multiple imputation of incomplete multivariate data under a normal model, version 2*. Software for Windows 95/98/NT. http://www.stat.psu.edu/~jls/misoftwa.html (Zugegriffen: 01. Okt. 2013).
Scharenberg, Katja. 2012. *Leistungsheterogenität und Kompetenzentwicklung. Zur Relevanz klassenbezogener Kompositionsmerkmale im Rahmen der KESS-Studie*. Münster: Waxmann.
Scharenberg, Katja. 2013. Heterogenität in der Schule – Definitionen, Forschungsbefunde, Konzeptionen und Perspektiven für die empirische Bildungsforschung. In *Jahrbuch der Schulentwicklung, Bd. 17. Sprachliche, kulturelle und soziale Heterogenität in der Schule als Herausforderung und Chance der Schulentwicklung*, Hrsg. Nele McElvany, Miriam M. Gebauer, Wilfried Bos und Heinz Günter Holtappels, 10–49. Weinheim: Beltz Juventa.

Scheerens, Jaap. 1990. School effectiveness research and the development of process indicators of school functioning. *School Effectiveness and School Improvement* 1:61–80.
Schneider, Wolfgang, und Jan Stefanek. 2004. Entwicklungsveränderungen allgemeiner kognitiver Fähigkeiten und schulbezogener Fertigkeiten im Kindes- und Jugendalter. Evidenz für einen Schereneffekt? *Zeitschrift für Entwicklungspsychologie und Pädagogische Psychologie* 36:147–159.
Schwetz, Herbert. 2003. *Die Klasse macht den Unterschied. Mehrebenenanalytische Untersuchung der Effekte von Unterricht.* Landau: Verlag Empirische Pädagogik.
Slavin, Robert E. 1990a. Ability grouping in secondary schools: A response to Hallinan. *Review of Educational Research* 60:505–507.
Slavin, Robert E. 1990b. Achievement effects of ability grouping in secondary schools: A best-evidence synthesis. *Review of Educational Research* 60:471–499.
Snijders, Tom A. B., und Roel J. Bosker. 1999. *Multilevel analysis. An introduction to basic and advanced multilevel modeling.* Thousand Oaks: Sage Publications.
Thrupp, Martin, Hugh Lauder und Tony Robinson. 2002. School composition and peer effects. *International Journal of Educational Research* 37:483–504.
van Ophuysen, Stefanie, und Heike Wendt. 2009. Zur Veränderung der Mathematikleistung von Klasse 4 bis 6. Welchen Einfluss haben Kompositions- und Unterrichtsmerkmale? *Zeitschrift für Erziehungswissenschaft, Sonderheft* 12:302–327.
von Davier, Matthias, und Alina A. von Davier. 2007. A unified approach to IRT scale linking and scale transformations. *Methodology* 3:115–124.
Wentzel, Kathryn R. 1991. Relations between social competence and academic achievement in early adolescence. *Child Development* 62:1066–1078.
Wentzel, Kathryn R. 1994. Relations of social goal pursuit to social acceptance, classroom behavior, and perceived social support. *Journal of Educational Psychology* 86:173–182.
Wentzel, Kathryn R. 1999. Social-motivational processes and interpersonal relationships: Implications for understanding motivation at school. *Journal of Educational Psychology* 91:76–97.

Katja Scharenberg, 1980, Dr. phil., Senior Researcher an der Universität Basel am Lehrstuhl für Sozialforschung und Methodologie. Forschungsgebiete: Schulleistungs- und Schuleffektivitätsforschung, Bildungsverläufe und Übergänge im Schul- und Ausbildungssystem sowie ins Erwerbsleben, Leistungsgruppierung und -heterogenität, differenzielle Lern- und Entwicklungsmilieus, Belastung und Beanspruchung bei Lehrkräften. Veröffentlichungen: Schulische Belastung und Beanspruchung von Lehrkräften – eine Überprüfung des Erfurter Modells im Rahmen der Hamburger KESS-Studie. In: Schul- und Bildungsforschung: Diskussionen, Befunde und Perspektiven – Festschrift für Wilfried Bos (hrsg. von K. Schwippert, M. Bonsen und N. Berkemeyer), Münster 2013 (mit W. Rollett); Leistungsheterogenität und Kompetenzentwicklung – Zur Relevanz klassenbezogener Kompositionsmerkmale im Rahmen der KESS-Studie, Münster 2012; Lernentwicklung in leistungshomogenen und -heterogenen Schulklassen. In: Schulische Lerngelegenheiten und Kompetenzentwicklung – Festschrift für Jürgen Baumert (hrsg. von W. Bos, E. Klieme und O. Köller), Münster 2010 (mit W. Bos).

Evil Tidings: Are Reorganizations more Successful if Employees are Informed Early?

Rafael Wittek · Fernando N. Morales · Peter Mühlau

© Springer Fachmedien Wiesbaden 2014

Abstract Organizations represent deliberately designed social contexts that are characterized by multi-level hierarchies. Interests and opportunity structures at each level usually do not overlap. We suggest that one of the reasons why intentional change efforts often fail to reach their objectives is because they are likely to trigger *competing* social mechanisms at different levels of the hierarchy. In order to illustrate this argument, we analyze the consequences of timely communication of planned organizational changes on perceived success of reorganizations. Two competing mechanisms are derived and tested with data from a telephone survey (carried out in 2003), among a sample of $n=412$ Dutch business organizations that performed a reorganization. The *commitment perspective* predicts that early announcement of reorganization plans to middle management increases the likelihood of reorganization success, since it increases commitment and empowers middle management. The *influence mechanism* predicts that early information of non-managerial employees decreases the likelihood of reorganization success, because it enables employees to use the information to their own advantage, anticipate on the strategies of management, and organize opposition against the plans. We found that timely communication with middle management indeed increases chances for success, whereas timely communication

---

R. Wittek (✉) · F. N. Morales
Department of Sociology, University of Groningen,
Grote Rozenstraat 31, 9712 TG Groningen, The Netherlands
e-mail: r.p.m.wittek@rug.nl

F. N. Morales
e-mail: f.nieto.morales@rug.nl

P. Mühlau
Trinity College Dublin, The University of Dublin, College Green,
Dublin 2, Ireland
e-mail: muhlaup@tcd.ie

with employees correlates with reorganization failure. However, not communicating with employees has an even stronger negative effect on reorganization success. No evidence could be found for our argument that the severity of the reorganization's expected negative effects on the workforce moderates both mechanisms.

Keywords Communication · Commitment · Influence · Reorganization · Social mechanism · Single respondent organizational survey

Schlechte Nachrichten: Sind Reorganisationen erfolgreicher, wenn die Angestellten rechtzeitig informiert werden?

Zusammenfassung Organisationen sind absichtlich erzeugte soziale Kontexte mit mehreren hierarchischen Ebenen. Die Interessen und Gelegenheitsstrukturen jeder Ebene überschneiden sich meist nicht. Wir schlagen vor, dass einer der Gründe, warum absichtliche Anstrengungen sozialen Wandels häufig ihre Ziele nicht erreichen, darin zu sehen ist, dass sie in Wettbewerb stehende soziale Mechanismen auf unterschiedlichen Ebenen der Hierarchie hervorrufen. Um dieses Argument darzustellen, werden die Folgen einer rechtzeitigen Mitteilung eines geplanten Wandels der Organisation auf den wahrgenommenen Erfolg der Reorganisation untersucht. Zwei konkurrierende Mechanismen werden spezifiziert und mit Daten eines telefonischen Survey aus dem Jahr 2003 bei einer Stichprobe von $n=412$ niederländischen Geschäftsunternehmen untersucht, die eine Reorganisation vorgenommen haben. Der Commitment-Perspektive zufolge würde eine frühe Ankündigung der Reorganisation an das mittlere Management den Erfolg der Reorganisation erhöhen, weil es die Zustimmung erhöht und dem mittleren Management Mitwirkung erlaubt. Dem Einflussmechanismus zufolge würde eine frühe Information von Angestellten, die nicht auf der Managementebene beschäftigt sind, die Wahrscheinlichkeit einer erfolgreichen Reorganisation senken, weil es den Angestellten gestattet, die Information zu ihrem eigenen Vorteil zu verwenden, Strategien des Managements zu antizipieren und so einen Widerstand gegen die Pläne zu organisieren. Unsere Befunde zeigen, dass eine rechtzeitige Kommunikation mit dem mittleren Management in der Tat die Erfolgschancen erhöht, hingegen eine rechtzeitige Kommunikation mit den Angestellten mit einem Misserfolg der Reorganisation verbunden ist. Allerdings, wenn man die Angestellten gar nicht informiert, so hat dies noch einen stärkeren negativen Effekt auf den Erfolgt der Reorganisation. Schließlich fanden wir, dass die Stärke der negativen Effekte der Maßnahmen keinen Einfluss auf beide o. g. Mechanismen hat.

Schlüsselwörter Kommunikation · Verpflichtung · Einfluss · Reorganisation · Soziale Mechanismen · Organisationsstudie

1 Introduction

Formal organizations are particularly well suited for the study of social context and social mechanisms, because they have a *built-in macro-micro-macro structure*. For example, at the (macro) company level, human resource management policies are implemented with the intention to influence the (micro) motives and behaviors of individual organizational members in such a way that they contribute to the realization of some desired (macro) collective outcomes (e.g. productivity, profit).

But there are at least two characteristics through which organizations differ from other social contexts. First, since most organizations have some form of hierarchy, they define *multi-layered social contexts* in which the macro and the micro level are formally linked through chains of authority relations (e.g. employees of a department reporting to a department head, who in turn reports to top management). Second, those at the top of the hierarchy usually have the rights and the decision-making powers to deliberately change the organizational context. Such *planned top-down organizational interventions* at the macro level are supposed to trigger social mechanisms that in the end produce some desired macro level results.

Hence, many organizations represent deliberately designed social contexts that are characterized by multi-level hierarchies in which interests and opportunity structures at each level usually do not overlap. We suggest that one of the reasons why intentional change efforts, or 'reorganizations' for short, often fail to reach their objectives (IBM 2008; Kotter 2007) is because they are likely to trigger *competing* social mechanisms at different levels of the hierarchy.

In order to illustrate this argument, this article will elaborate and empirically test hypotheses on the consequences of the timing of information disclosure for the perceived success or failure of the change effort in a sample of Dutch business firms. In what follows, we first elaborate on the two competing mechanisms and develop hypotheses. Section three presents the research design, data, and results. Section four concludes.

2 Theoretical background

Among the many decisions that management has to take once it seriously considers to carry out a reorganization, is at which stage to inform employees and middle management. Should the plans to embark on change be communicated before major decisions and preparations have been taken, or after goals and plans have been determined and just shortly before the reorganization starts?

Though intra-organizational communication occupies a prominent position on the general agenda of both organization scholars (e.g. Eisenberg and Goodall 2004; Kreps 1990; Taylor 1993) and practitioners of organizational change (e.g. Harkness 2000; Kitchen and Daly 2002; Klein 1996; Quirke 1995), studies explicitly addressing the link between organizational change and the timing of messages are surprisingly scarce. Evidence for the importance of timing of announcements as a crucial determinant of the success of planned change comes from two case studies (Goodman and Truss 2004) and a formal model (Almeida Costa et al. 2003). Based on intra-organizational survey data in a public and a private U.S. company, Goodman and Truss (2004, p. 223) report that in both organizations, more than 70% of the employees complain that they had been informed after rather than before the implementation of the changes (Goodman and Truss 2004, p. 223). Almeida Costa et al.'s (2003) mathematical model explores the interrelationship between formal and informal network structure on the one hand, and the timing of information and attitude change on the other hand. Among other findings their study shows that socially isolated leaders with attitudes different from other members have a higher chance of changing other employees' attitudes in favor of a planned change if the information is first spread to the next lower level of the formal structure and only later to the rest of the organization.

While both studies underscore the important role of timing of information, they also show that theoretical foundations and empirical evidence on the effects of information timing on reorganization remain inconclusive. When deciding about the timing and openness of communicating anticipated changes to employees and middle management, top management has to consider a trade-off (Schweiger and Denisi 1991). In the case of early information, it increases the opportunity for participation and influence through middle management and employees. This can enhance commitment, and avoid the development of rumors. However, early announcement also creates the opportunity for influence attempts directed at the change of the goals of the reorganization into a direction not desired by top management (Eisenberg and Witten 1987). In case of late announcement, the opportunities for employees and middle management to participate during the goal formulation phase is reduced. This increases top management's grip on setting the agenda, the goals, and the desired road map for the implementation of the reorganization plans. However, it might also cause disappointment and de-motivation of employees and middle managers.

We suggest that depending on the level in the organizational hierarchy, early announcement triggers two competing mechanisms, with opposite effects on the success of a change effort. We refer to them as the commitment and the influence mechanism, respectively: whereas early disclosure is likely to enhance cooperation of middle management and therefore increase the likelihood of the change effort to be successful, it will decrease cooperation of lower level employees and therefore decrease the chances for the reorganization to be successful. Our theoretical argument is guided by a social rationality framework (Lindenberg 2001), according to which the degree to which individuals effectively pursue selfish vs. prosocial motives depends on the social context in which they take their decisions. Unlike canonical rational choice models which assume full rationality, selfishness and a preference for improving ones material condition as the default of human decision making, social rationality reasoning incorporates bounded rationality, social motives and non-material symbolic exchanges as they are prominent elements of the commitment mechanism.

2.1 Hierarchical Levels: Middle managers vs. non-managerial employees

Many studies have pointed to the crucial role of middle managers, in particular during periods of planned organizational change (Huy 2002; Rouleau 2005; Sharma and Good 2013). Middle manager support is fundamental for reorganizations to succeed. Maintaining a positive social environment, handling exceptions, and solving unexpected problems were found to be among the main expectations related to the middle manager role (Delmestri and Walgenbach 2005). The "buffer" function of middle management has been repeatedly demonstrated and analyzed: mediating between the

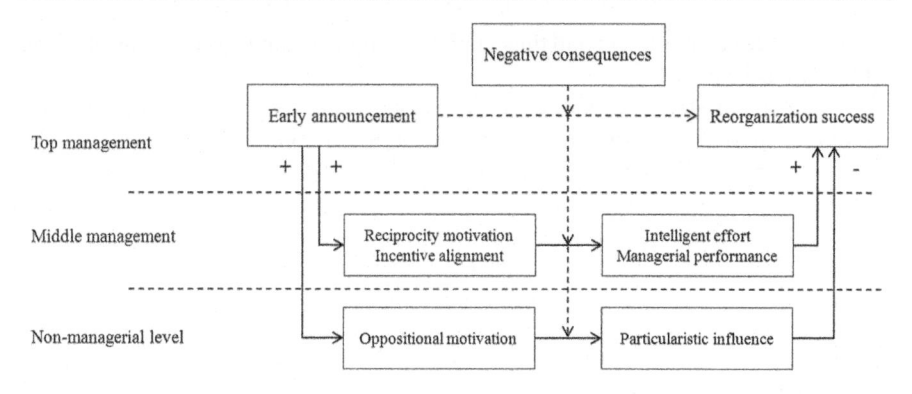

Fig. 1 Competing social mechanism explanations of the effect of early announcement on reorganization success

requirements defined by top managers and the claims of non-managerial employees is one of the key tasks defining the role of a middle manager. Also the successful implementation of new projects, including organizational change trajectories, often is part of middle managers' job description and performance evaluation. As a result, middle managers' career prospects are likely to improve to the degree that they demonstrate to be proactive change agents. Consequently, receiving timely information about top management's strategic intentions is likely to increase their commitment to organizational strategy because it increases their level of control and ability to implement the change (Barton and Ambrosini 2013, p. 278).

Middle management therefore will likely evaluate information on the change initiative from the angle of how to use it in decision-making about implementing the change. Formally, non-managerial employees have far less decision-making autonomy. For them, change related information will be evaluated in terms of the potential effects of the change on their own position and outcomes. We propose that this structural difference between the two levels in the organizational hierarchy triggers two opposite effects of timely information on reorganization success (see Fig. 1).

2.2 Mechanism I: Early announcement and commitment of middle management

Since the human relation movement, many practitioners and organization scholars favor the view that open communication and early involvement of the workforce during corporate restructuring are beneficial, not only for labor relations and organizational climate (Eby and Buch 1998), but also for organizational performance and the successful implementation of changes. "Effective change communication campaigns tend to reveal rather than conceal, reduce uncertainty through collective planning, and proactively establish and maintain trust." (DiFonzo and Bordia 1998). An open communication structure is seen as a major requirement for eliciting commitment (Pheng and May 1997, p. 162). If employees cannot acquire relevant information about the change initiative through official communication channels, uncertainty and mistrust will be likely (Tebbutt and Marchington 1997). Consequently, it is important to communicate, even if it is bad news. Continuous open communication before, during, and after reorganization increases the likelihood of success, because transparency enhances commitment and thus facilitates implementation (Goodman and Truss 2004; Klein 1996).

A number of studies found supporting evidence for a positive effect of (early) employee involvement and open communication on commitment to the organization and change (Fedor et al. 2006; Martin et al. 1995; Morgan and Zeffane 2003). An open communication climate, transparency of change processes, and employee involvement reflected in receiving timely, informative, and useful information about organizational change all were found to have positive effects on change related outcomes like employee commitment to the organization and commitment to change itself (Allen and Brady 1997; Giangreco and Peccei 2005; Guzley 1992; Schweiger and Denisi 1991; Wanberg and Banas 2000), identification with organization after change (Bartels et al. 2006; Chreim 2002), acceptance of the change (Kavanagh and Ashkanasy 2006), reduction of change related uncertainty (Kramer et al. 2004; Bordia et al. 2004), decreased resistance to change (Miller et al. 1994), and perceptions of procedural justice of change related layoffs (Gopinath and Becker 2000).

All these studies show that (timely) information and active involvement are likely to increase the commitment of the workforce (but see Barton and Ambrosini (2013), who could not corroborate the hypothesized effect in a stratified random sample of middle managers from 701 'high-tech' organizations in the UK). By communicating openly about its goals, top management signals its concern for the employees and the potentially negative effects that the change might have on them. Employees are given the opportunity to contribute ideas, and to actively influence the change initiative. This active involvement also facilitates the flow of information from lower to higher levels in the hierarchy, allowing change agents to calibrate interventions and thereby reduce transaction costs during implementation. The key assumption is that openness, transparency and involvement will trigger cooperative reactions of employees, which in turn will contribute to improving the implementation of the change initiative (Lines 2004; Morgan and Zeffane 2003).

An implicit assumption in most previous research is that this commitment effect holds across all levels of the organization. Based on the level assumption outlined in the previous section, we argue that the commitment effect holds for middle-management, but not for non-managerial employees, because early announcement differentially affects the preferences and constraints of both groups. Hence, the reasoning of the commitment perspective can be summarized by the following hypothesis:

H1: The earlier top management announces a reorganization to middle management, the more likely reorganization will be successful.

Organizational changes differ in terms of the severity of their consequences for the workforce. Whereas some changes may involve only slight adjustments in procedures and routines, others may consist of major restructurings, including massive layoffs. Such high impact change trajectories pose a major challenge for the involved change agents, since they are likely to trigger strong resistance and labor conflict. The earlier middle management is informed about change initiatives with such severe consequences, the better it can prepare itself, anticipate on potential negative reactions, and craft appropriate implementation and containment strategies. Hence, we expect the following interaction effect:

H2: The effect of early information of middle management on the success of reorganizations will be stronger positive for reorganizations with negative consequences for employees, than for reorganizations with no negative consequences.

Exhibit 1 summarizes the different steps underlying the commitment mechanism.

Exhibit 1: Stepwise explication of the commitment mechanism for middle management

1. Situational Mechanism (Macro-> Micro):
    a. Early announcement affects middle managers' opportunity structures by providing them with an information advantage, which allows them to anticipate on the change and its consequences, and improves their chances to take measures that lead to successful implementation.
    b. Early announcement affects middle managers' preferences in two ways. First, top management signals trust in middle managers, thereby triggering reciprocity motivations ("gift exchange mechanism"). Second, since middle managers are important change agents, the design and successful implementation of organizational change policies is usually part of their performance evaluation and therefore also affects their career prospects. As a result, early announcement will also provide an extra performance incentive for middle managers ("incentive alignment mechanism").
2. Action Generating Mechanism (Micro-> Micro): Information advantage, increased reciprocity motivation and performance incentives as they follow from early information will increase change related intelligent effort and performance of middle managers.
3. Transformation Mechanism (Micro-> Macro): The higher the number of middle managers whose change related efforts and performance increases, the higher the likelihood that the reorganization is successful.

2.3 Mechanism 2: Early announcement and influence attempts of non-managerial employees

The arguments of the commitment perspective have been challenged by scholars who emphasize that the costs of influencing and lobbying will rise to the degree that employees are informed about change. According to such an influence or Machiavellian perspective, the commitment view ignores the strategic nature of communication (Eisenberg and Witten 1987) and information asymmetries (Milgrom and Roberts 1988).

Influence perspectives predict that employees will likely use the information to their own advantage (Milgrom and Roberts 1988; Shaefer 1998) As a result, early announcement and information procurement may result in resistance, coalition forming, lobbying, and costly influence attempts (Matějka and De Waegenaere 2005). For example, Oreg (2006, p. 92), in a study of a merger of the two core units within an organization in the defense industry, reports a positive correlation between the amount of information and behavioral and cognitive resistance to change.

We suggest that the influence mechanism is more likely to become salient among non-managerial employees than among those with managerial responsibilities. The main reason is that non-managerial employees are usually not the purveyors of change, i.e. change agents with formal responsibility for implementation and success of the change, but targets who have to adjust to the change efforts (Bowen 2008). Unlike middle management, their career prospects and performance evaluations usually are not tied to their role in the design and implementation of reorganizations. Like middle management, being informed early allows them to anticipate on the impact of the reorganization on their own position, but unlike middle management, they do have far less incentives to use this information for the benefit of the reorganization. Joining forces with other employees will likely increase the chances to successfully influence change agents or to organize collective resistance. Being informed early extends the period through which effective counter-coalitions can be built, which in turn increases the chances of successful opposition or influence attempts.

In sum, the influence perspective predicts a negative effect of early announcement on reorganization success:

H3: The earlier top management announces a reorganization to non-managerial employees, the less successful the reorganization will be.

Influence and agency perspectives conceive employees as self-interested individuals, who try to minimize negative outcomes and improve their well-being. Organizational changes, which seriously threaten an employee's position or resource base, will therefore be taken much more seriously than changes, which do not have a direct impact on an employee's payoffs. Researchers have pointed to the strong motivating power of loss as a trigger for collective action in general (Van Assen 1998) and resistance to change in organizations (Gray 2002) in particular. It follows that the negative effects of early announcements on reorganization success will be much stronger in situations, in which the negative consequences for individual employees are severe, than in situations in which the consequences are less pronounced:

H4: The effect of early information of non-managerial employees on the success of reorganizations will be stronger negative for reorganizations with negative consequences for employees, than for reorganizations with no negative consequences for employees.

Exhibit 2 summarizes the different steps underlying the influence mechanism.

Exhibit 2: Stepwise explication of the influence mechanism for non-managerial employees

1. Situational Mechanism (Macro-> Micro):
   a. Early announcement affects employees' opportunity structures by providing them with an information advantage, which extends the time available to build coalitions and influence change agents.
   b. Early announcement affects employees' preferences in that it provides an incentive to improve their power position vis-à-vis management by forming oppositional coalitions. This incentive will increase the higher the potentially negative effects of the reorganization on the employees.
2. Action Generating Mechanism (Micro-> Micro): Information advantage and incentives to form oppositional coalitions will increase employees' efforts to influence change agents, and to exert pressure to adjust reorganization plans and objectives to their own advantage.
3. Transformation Mechanism (Micro-> Macro): The higher the number of employees who engage in particularistic influence attempts, the lower the likelihood that the reorganization is successful.

3 Research design and data

A strict empirical test of the two competing mechanisms would require a larger sample of organizations, for each of which one would collect information on a sizeable number of respondents at the level of (1) top-management (e.g. on the decision when and to whom to disclose reorganization plans, and on the outcome of the reorganization), (2) middle management (e.g. on performance evaluation, career prospects, commitment to change, perceived consequences of reorganizations etc.), and (3) non-managerial employees (e.g. on influence attempts, resistance to change, perceived consequences of change). Like most organizational research, also the present study faces the severe limitations with regard to the availability of high quality large scale in-depth organizational survey data (Liebig 2009). Though the recent attempts to create repositories of organizational datasets, and to develop more rigorous methodological standards with regard to research design and data quality are likely to improve the situation in the long run (Edler et al. 2012), encompassing multi-level organizational datasets of sufficient size, scope, and depth to subject our competing social mechanism explanations to a rigorous empirical test to date are non-existent.

For the present study, we used a Single Response Organizational Survey (SROS) design for our data collection. Though this design does not allow testing the causal chains of the two mechanisms, it nevertheless allows testing the macro (organization) level relationship between timing of information success and reorganization success. Data on reorganizations were collected by a telephone survey of key informants of establishments of private companies in the Netherlands. The target sample was randomly selected from a stratified sample of privately-owned establishments with 10 or more employees from the Chamber of Commerce central register. Registration is largely mandatory in the Netherlands, the few exceptions being irrelevant for this research (e.g., vendors). All industries with the exception of agricultural, health and education were involved. Only establishments that were created before 2000 and still existed in 2003 were sampled. These were first contacted by telephone in order to ask whether they would cooperate with the study, and if so, to identify the key informant who would be best informed about issues of organizational change and authorized to reveal this information. In more than 80% of cases, this key informant was the highest executive officer of the establishment or the owner/manager. The remaining respondents were senior managers of departments which were particularly involved in issues of organizational change. An introductory letter was sent to informants and an appointment for a telephone interview arranged. 32.1% of the contacted establishments cooperated in this research, resulting in 1131 telephone interviews on organizational processes and structures, including questions on ongoing or recently completed internal reorganization. No structural differences were observed between establishments that took part in our study and those that refused or declined to do so. The average length of interviews with 412 companies that experienced reorganization was 37 min. Our study is restricted to this subsample.

3.1 Measurements

Reorganization success was assessed with two questions. First, we asked informants "To what extent were the following goals important for the reorganization?" We offered ten goals: increase of efficiency, improvement of product or service quality, reduction of personnel costs, compliance to governmental regulations and product standards, improved internal communication, improved distribution of responsibilities, higher transparency, better controllability of the organization, change of corporate culture, and improvement of information management. Informants rated each one on a 5-point scale ranging from (0) not important at all to (4) extremely important. Second, we asked: "Judging the current situation, to what extent has each of the goals of the reorganization been achieved?" Response was coded in a 5-point scale ranging from (0) not achieved at all to (4) much better than expected. Figure 2 shows the distribution of (mean) achievement and (mean) importance per goal domain for the whole sample. The variable *reorganization success* represents the average of achievement across the 10 goal domains weighted by each goal's importance.

Early vs. late announcements. The timing of information was measured with the following two questions: "When did your top management inform middle management about the interventions that will follow from the reorganization?", and "When did your top management inform employees about the interventions that will follow from the reorganization?" Response categories were (1) [Middle management/employees] were informed before decisions about the reorganization were made; (2) they were informed after plans of the reorganization were defined; (3) just when the reorganization started; and (4) they were not informed at all. Two main dummy variables were created based on these two questions: *early information employees* was coded (1) if employees were informed before reorganization plans were defined, (0) otherwise. Similarly, *early information managers* was coded (1) if middle man-

Fig. 2 Reorganization success (per domain). Mean values per domain: (*1*) Efficiency, (*2*) Product or service quality, (*3*) Personnel costs, (*4*) Regulation and product standards, (*5*) Communication, (*6*) Responsibility, (*7*) Transparency, (*8*) Controllability, (*9*) Corporate culture, (*10*) Information

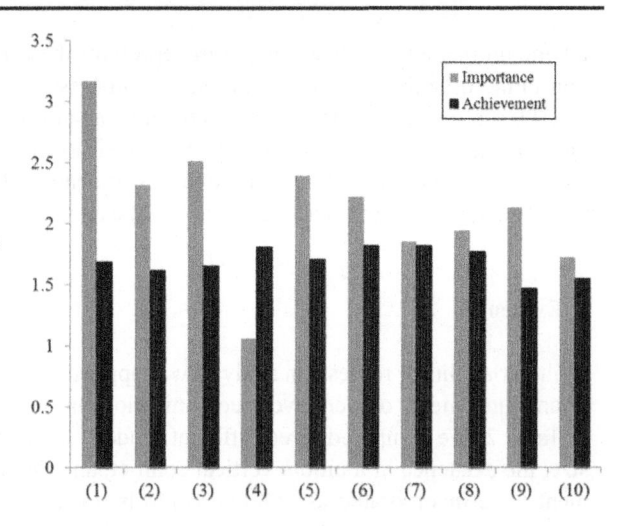

agement was informed in advance, or else (0). Further, given our interest in behavior triggered by information about change, we added a dummy for *employees not informed* [(1) if employees were not informed about the reorganization, (0) otherwise] to directly account for the effect of (early) information vis-à-vis no information among non-managerial employees. A similar treatment for the case of middle managers was not possible because the category "not informed at all" for this group did not occur in our sample.

Consequences of reorganization were elicited with the following question: "What are the most important consequences of the reorganization for employees? Response covered 11 dimensions (e.g. layoffs, reallocation of personnel to different functions, discretion over pace of work[1]). We used this set to generate the variable *negative consequences* indicating that the reorganization had no negative consequences for employees (0) or that at one or more of the following conditions held (1): layoffs, reallocations, lower skills required, increase in work pace, decrease in discretion, intensification of control, increase of work pressure, decrease in autonomy, and deterioration of career prospects. To test the moderation effects, two interaction variables were constructed by multiplying the negative consequences with, respectively, early information of middle management and early information of employees.

Controls. We included several control variables. *Size* of the organization was assessed with the question "How many individuals were on your payroll at the end of the year 2002?" We computed the natural logarithm of this value. *Employee council* indicates whether the organization has institutionalized employee representation or labor union (0 = no; 1 = yes). To account for the quality of labor relations in the organization, we measured *vertical conflict* based on whether or not there were problems with regard to conflicts between management and workers (3 = severe problems, 1 =

---

[1] The full list of consequences comprised the following items dimensions: (1) layoffs, (2) reallocation of personnel to different functions, (3) retraining, (4) changes to required skills and competences, (5) changes to task allocation, (6) discretion over work pace, (7) discretion over how to carry out work, (8) control over employees, (9) work pressure, (10) responsibilities, (11) changes to career prospects.

few/no problems). *Involvement culture* represents the extent of employees' participation in the organization's decision making processes, measured as the logarithm of a 0:100 score meaning 0 = no involvement whatsoever and 100 = thorough involvement. Finally, *share of affected employees* measures to the proportion of employees who directly experienced the consequences of change. Table 1 summarizes descriptive statistics for all measurements used in the analysis.

4 Evidence

Multivariate linear regression analysis was applied to analyze the effect of the timing of announcements on perceived reorganization success. The results are summarized in Table 2. We computed three different models. In all three models, organizational size, the existence of a union, vertical conflict, and the degree of employee involvement were incorporated as baseline controls. In the first model, we only included the 3 variables related to the announcement of change: whether or not workers were informed, early information of workers, and early information of middle management. In the second model, we added 2 characteristics of the reorganization (share of affected employees and negative consequences for employees). In the third model, we added interaction effects between information timing and negative consequences of the reorganization.

Model 1 shows a significant negative effect of not informing employees about the reorganization, as well as a negative effect of giving early information to employees. There is also a positive effect of early information of middle management on reorganization success. Model 2 —which accounts for two characteristics of the reorganization— shows that the effects of information timing remain significant and in the same direction. It also shows a positive and significant effect of the share of employees affected by reorganization —i.e. comprehensive reorganizations tend to be more successful also, given the conditions specified by model 2—. Finally, in model 3, the interaction effects between negative consequences and timing of announcement are not significant, and their inclusion into model 3 does not affect the main effects observed in the previous two models. None of the main effects of the control variables is significant in models 1, 2 and 3.

The findings support both the commitment and the influence perspective, differing for employees and middle managers in the predicted direction. First, as predicted, the effect of informing middle management early as compared to late information (i.e. information after reorganization plans were defined/just when the reorganization started) is significant and positive. This implies that timely communication to middle management *increases* reorganization success, supporting the commitment argument (*H1*). This result is independent of the potential negative consequences of change, since the hypothesized interaction effect is not significant, thereby disconfirming *H2*.

Second, informing workers early *decreases* the chances for reorganization success in comparison to late announcement. This finding is in line with the influence reasoning (*H3*). However, there is a negative effect of not sharing information with employees on reorganization success. This effect is stronger than the effect of early announcement, suggesting that not informing the workforce about change intentions

Table 1 Descriptive statistics

	N	Min : Max	M	SD	Correlations								
					10	9	8	7	6	5	4	3	2
1. Reorganization success	412	0 : 11.20	2.91	2.29	−0.04	−0.02	−0.02	0.00	0.01	0.11	0.07	0.01	−0.13
2. Employees not informed	401	0 : 1	0.04	–	−0.05	0.00	−0.14	−0.04	−0.05	−0.09	−0.09	−0.14	
3. Early information employees	401	0 : 1	0.28	–	0.08	0.00	0.04	0.03	−0.06	0.06	0.60		
4. Early information managers	390	0 : 1	0.52	–	0.03	−0.01	0.07	0.07	−0.08	−0.00			
5. Share affected employees	410	0 : 4.61	3.51	1.20	0.04	0.03	0.09	−0.02	−0.01				
6. Negative consequences	383	0 : 1	0.41	–	−0.02	0.09	0.05	0.03					
7. Size	411	0 : 11.16	4.71	1.45	0.03	0.00	0.47						
8. Employee council	412	0 : 1	0.60	–	0.16	0.01							
9. Vertical conflict	410	1 : 3	1.54	0.70	−0.00								
10. Involvement culture	410	0 : 4.62	3.97	1.13									

Highlighted correlations are significant $p<0.05$

Table 2 Multivariate regression: effect of information timing on reorganization success

	Model 1		Model 2		Model 3	
	Estimate	S.E.	Estimate	S.E.	Estimate	S.E.
Information						
Employees not informed	−1.79**	0.57	−1.59**	0.59	−1.61**	0.60
Early information employees	−0.70*	0.32	−0.75*	0.33	−0.85*	0.43
Early information managers	0.84**	0.29	0.90**	0.30	0.99*	0.40
Reorganization						
Share affected employees			0.27**	0.10	0.27**	0.10
Negative consequences			−0.03	0.24	−0.01	0.35
*Consequences * Information*						
Negative * Early info employees					0.23	0.69
Negative * Early info managers					−0.22	0.62
Controls						
Size	−0.01	0.09	−0.00	0.10	−0.00	0.10
Employee council	−0.29	0.28	−0.40	0.29	−0.40	0.30
Vertical conflict	−0.15	0.16	−0.18	0.17	−0.18	0.17
Involvement culture	−0.08	0.10	−0.08	0.11	−0.08	0.11
R^2	0.05		0.07		0.07	
N (listwise valid)	384		356		356	

**$p < 0.01$; *$p < 0.05$

in an early stage is far more detrimental than informing them. The effect of the interaction effect between negative consequences and early announcement to employees is positive (as predicted by *H4*) but not statistically significant, disconfirming *H4*.

In sum, our results corroborate the two hypothesized main effects, whereas no evidence could be found for the hypothesized moderating impact of the severity of the change.

5 Discussion and conclusion

This study explored the consequences of timely announcements of planned organizational change on the perceived success of changes. We explored two competing mechanisms explaining the impact of early information on reorganization success. According to the commitment mechanism, early information both empowers middle-management and increases its commitment to the change agenda, thereby contributing to a more successful change trajectory. According to the influence mechanism, early information provides strategic information that non-managerial employees will exploit to their own advantage, and will result in setbacks for the reorganization. We further argued that these effects could be moderated by the degree to which the reorganization has negative consequences for the workforce. In our empirical study, we found support for both mechanisms at the (macro) organizational level: timely communication with employees decreases the chances for successful change independently of the consequences of the change. In addition, lack of communication correlates with an even stronger negative effect on perceived success. Timely communication with middle management increases chances for success independently of the consequences of the change.

The findings on early information of middle management are in line with the commitment perspective, and confirm the pivotal role of this organizational segment for the functioning of organizations in general, and the planning and implementation of organizational changes in particular (Giangreco and Peccei 2005). A more complex picture emerges for communication with employees. The significant negative effect of early disclosure on perceived success of reorganizations suggests that early announcements of reorganization plans triggers politicking and strategic behavior in which the information is exploited to the detriment of the goals as they are defined by the dominant coalition. However, as the significant negative effect of not providing information at all shows, withholding information on change from employees can trigger negative consequences as well. Whereas early announcement may give employees a strategic advantage that is likely to be used against top management goals, not providing information can have an even worse effect in that lack of information might trigger stronger defection against change. There is a dilemma for top managers: revealing information too early may be a bad idea, but not disclosing information may be an even worse one. Perhaps the solution to this conundrum relates not only to the timing of the announcement but also to the quality and quantity of information, which may tame the negative influence of early information. Future research can benefit from addressing these subtle nuances in the decision of when, to whom and how to announce efforts of change.

Before concluding, it is appropriate to mention potential methodological limitations of our study. Single-response organizational surveys (SROS) like the one employed in this study are often criticized for relying fully on a single informant. Here, we address two of the more serious problems of SROS, and how we dealt with them: *insufficient knowledge* of the informant and increased risk of *common method bias*. The limitations of the expertise and detailed knowledge of key informants is an intensely discussed issue in strategic human resource research (see Gerhart et al. 2000a, b; Huselid and Becker 2000; Wright et al. 2001). In strategic human resource research, the bulk of the organizations surveyed are large corporations with multiple divisions and locations, which increases the problem of *insufficient knowledge* of informants. Earlier research concluded that the knowledge problem can be decreased if informants report on their establishments, and if establishments are small. In our study, the units of analysis are establishments with a very moderate median size. The single-informant problem of *insufficient knowledge* therefore appears to be not too severe.

The most likely reasons for a potential *common method bias* (see Podsakoff et al. 2003) are cognitive processes that result in overly coherent perceptions of the aspects of the reorganization episode ('consistency effect'), or the wish of the respondent to evoke a favorable impression of management's capability (a form of 'social desirability'). To evaluate the potential validity threat that may arise from common method variance, we applied Harman's single factor test on the set of indicators used in the analysis (cf. Podsakoff et al. 2003). We found that neither single factor solution nor a 'general' factor accounting for the lion's share of covariance emerges from our data. Principal component analysis on our variables yield 6 significant factors accounting for 62.4% of observed variance; loading all variables into a single factor only accounts for only 16.9% of variance. Therefore, we ruled out common method variance in our data.

Our findings contribute to extant research in two ways. First, our study illustrates the power of combining a multi-level approach with social mechanism reasoning when analyzing organizational processes. The same intervention may trigger completely different mechanisms at different levels of the organization. Our findings demonstrate the need to distinguish between middle management and employees as two different targets of top-down communication strategies. To our knowledge, our study is the first one disentangling the consequences of timely informing these 2 groups of organizational actors. Whereas not informing employees at all or giving away information to employees too early may fire back against reorganization efforts in our data, timely information of middle-management can contribute to the success of the change project.

Second, while confirming earlier claims concerning the necessity to incorporate the timing of announcements into models of organizational change (Almeida Costa et al. 2003; Goodman and Truss 2004), our study refines previous research, which mostly emphasized the positive effects of timely and open communication. By disentangling commitment and influence mechanisms, the findings remind us of the strategic nature that the disclosure of information and the timing of announcements has in principal-agent relations.

References

Allen, Myria, and Robert Brady. 1997. Total quality management, organizational commitment, perceived organizational support, and intra-organizational communication. *Management Communication Quarterly* 10:316–341.

Almeida Costa, Luis, Joao Amaro de Matos, and Miguel Pina e Cunha. 2003. The manager as change agent: Communication channels, timing of information, and attitude change. *International Studies of Management and Organization* 33:65–93.

Bartels Jos, Rynke Douwes, Menno.de Jong, and Ad. Pruyn. 2006. Organizational identification during a merger: Determinants of employees' expected identification with the new organization. *British Journal of Management* 17:S49–S67.

Barton, Lisa, and Veronique Ambrosini. 2013. The moderating effect of organizational change cynicism on middle manager strategy commitment. *The International Journal of Human Resource Management* 24:721–746.

Bordia, Prashant, Elizabeth Hobman, Elizabeth Jones, Cindy Gallois, and Victor J. Callan. 2004. Uncertainty during organizational change: Types, consequences, and management strategies. *Journal of Business and Psychology* 18:507–532.

Bowen, B. James. 2008. *After the downsizing: A case study of a commercial activities competition recognization*. ProQuest.

Chreim, Samia. 2002. Influencing organizational identification during major change: A communication-based perspective. *Human Relations* 55:1117–1113.

Delmestri, Giuseppe, and Peter Walgenbach. 2005. Mastering techniques or brokering knowledge? Middle managers in Germany, Great Britain and Italy. *Organization Studies* 26:197–220.

DiFonzo, Nicholas, and Prashant Bordia. 1998. A tale of two corporations: Managing uncertainty during organizational change. *Human Resource Management* 37:295–304.

Eby, Lillian T., and Kimperly Buch. 1998. The impact of adopting an ethical approach to employee dismissal during corporate restructuring. *Journal of Business Ethics* 17:1253–1264.

Edler, Susanne, Alexia Meyermann, Tobias Gebel, Stefan Liebig, and Martin Diewald. 2012. The German Data Service Center for Business and Organizational Data. *Schmollers Jahrbuch* 132:619–634.

Eisenberg, Eric M., and Harold Goodall. 2004. *Organizational communication: Balancing creativity and constraint*. Bedford: St. Martin's.

Eisenberg, Eric M., and Marsha G. Witten. 1987. Reconsidering openness in organizational communication. *Academy of Management Review* 12:418–426.

Fedor, Donald. B., Steven Caldwell, and David M. Herold. 2006. The effects of organizational changes on employee commitment: a multilevel investigation. *Personnel Psychology* 59:1–29.

Gerhart, Barry, Patrick M. Wright, and Gary C. McMahan. 2000a. Measurement error in research on the human resource and firm performance relationship: Further evidence and analysis. *Personnel Psychology* 53:855–872.

Gerhart, Barry, Patrick M. Wright, Gary C. McMahan, and Scott A. Snell. 2000b. Measurement error in research on the human resource and firm performance: How much error is there and how does it influence the effect size estimates? *Personnel Psychology* 53:803–834.

Giangreco, Antonio, and Riccardo Peccei. 2005. The nature and antecedents of middle manager resistance to change: Evidence from an Italian context. *International Journal of Human Resource Management* 16:1812–1829.

Goodman, Joanna, and Catherine Truss. 2004. The medium and the message: Communicating effectively during a major change initiative. *Journal of Change Management* 4:217–228.

Gopinath, Chirukandath, and Thomas E. Becker. 2000. Communication, procedural justice, and employee attitudes: Relationships under conditions of divestiture. *Journal of Management* 26:63–83.

Gray, Colin. 2002. Entrepreneurship, resistance to change and growth in small firms. *Journal of Small Business and Enterprise Development* 9:61–72.

Guzley, Ruth M. 1992. Organizational climate and communication climate: Predictors of commitment to the organization. *Management Communication Quarterly* 5:379–402.

Harkness, James. 2000. Measuring the effectiveness of change-the role of internal communication in change management. *Journal of Change Management* 1:66–73.

Huselid, Mark A., and Brian E. Becker. 2000. Comment on 'measurement error in research on human resources and firm performance: How much error is there and how does it influence effect size estimates?' *Personnel Psychology* 53:835–854.

Huy, Quy N. 2002. Emotional balancing of organizational continuity and radical change: The contribution of middle managers. *Administrative Science Quarterly* 47:31–69.

IBM Corporation. 2008. *Making change work*. http://public.dhe.ibm.com/common/ssi/ecm/en/gbe03100usen/GBE03100USEN.PDF. Accessed 28 June 2014.

Kavanagh Marie H., and Neal M. Ashkanasy. 2006. The impact of leadership and change management strategy on organizational culture and individual acceptance of change during a merger. *British Journal of Management* 17:S81–S103.

Kitchen, Philip, and Finbarr Daly. 2002. Internal communication during change management. *Corporate Communications* 7:46–53.

Klein, Stuart M. 1996. A management communication strategy for change. *Journal of Organizational Change Management* 9:32–46.

Kotter, John P. 2007. Leading change: Why transformation efforts fail. Harvard Business Review. http://hbr.org/2007/01/leading-change-why-transformation-efforts-fail/ar/1. Accessed 28 June 2014.

Kramer Michael W., Debbie S. Dougherty, and Tamyra A. Pierce. 2004. Managing uncertainty during a corporate acquisition—A longitudinal study of communication during an airline acquisition. *Human Communication Research* 30:71–101.

Kreps, Gary L. 1990. *Organizational communication: Theory and practice*. White Plains: Longman.

Liebig, Stefan. 2009. *Organizational Data. German Council for Social and Economic Data*. Working Paper No 67.

Lindenberg, Siegwart M. 2000. James Coleman. In *The Blackwell companion to major social theorists*, ed. Georg Ritzer, 513–544. Oxford: Blackwell Publishers.

Lindenberg, Siegwart M. 2001. Social rationality versus rational egoism. In *Handbook of Sociological Theory*, ed. Jonathan Turner, 635–668. New York: Kluwer Academic/Plenum.

Lines, Rune. 2004. Influence of participation in strategic change: Resistance, organizational commitment and change goal achievement. *Journal of Change Management* 4:193–215.

Martin, Christpher L., Charles K. Parsons, and Nathan Bennett. 1995. The influence of employee involvement program membership during downsizing: attitudes toward the employer and the union. *Journal of Management* 21:879–890.

Matějka, Michal, and Anja De Waegenaere. 2005. Influence costs and implementation of organizational changes. *Journal of Management Accounting Research* 17:43–52.

Milgrom, Paul, and John Roberts. 1988. An economic approach to influence activities in organizations. *American Journal of Sociology* 94:S154–S179.

Miller, Vernon D., John R Johnson, and Jennifer Grau. 1994. Antecedents to willingness to participate in a planned organizational change. *Journal of Applied Communication Research* 22:59–80.

Morgan, David, and Rachid Zeffane. 2003. Employee involvement, organizational change and trust in management. *International Journal of Human Resource Management* 14:55–75.

Oreg, Shaul. 2006. Personality, context, and resistance to organizational change. *European Journal of Work and Organizational Psychology* 15:73–101.

Podsakoff, Philip M., Scott B. MacKenzie, Jeong-Yeon Lee, and Nathan P. Podsakoff. 2003. Common method biases in behavioral research: A critical review of the literature and recommended remedies. *Journal of Applied Psychology* 88:879–903.

Pheng, Low Sui, and May Chan Foong. 1997. Quality management systems: A study of authority and empowerment. *Building Research and Information* 25:158–169.

Quirke, Bill. 1995. *Communicating change*. Maidenhead: McGraw Hill.

Rouleau, Linda. 2005. Micro-practices of strategic sensemaking and sensegiving: How middle managers interpret and sell change every day. *Journal of Management Studies* 42:1413–1441.

Schaefer, Scott. 1998. Influence costs, structural inertia, and organizational change. *Journal of Economics and Management Strategy* 7:237–263.

Schweiger, David M., and Angelo S. DeNisi. 1991. Communication with employees following a Merger. A longitudinal field experiment. *Academy of Management Journal* 34:110–135.

Sharma, Garima, and Darren Good. 2013. The work of middle managers sensemaking and sensegiving for creating positive social change. *The Journal of Applied Behavioral Science* 49:95–122.

Taylor, James R. 1993. *Rethinking the theory of organizational communication: How to read an organization*. Westport: Greenwood.

Tebbutt, Melanie, and Mick Marchington. 1997. Look before you speak. Gossip and the insecure workplace. *Work, Employment, and Society* 11:713–735.

Van Assen, Malm. 1998. Effects of individual decision theory assumptions on predictions of cooperation in social dilemmas. *Journal of Mathematical Sociology* 23:142–153.

Wanberg, Connie R., and Joseph T. Banas. 2000. Predictors and outcomes of openness to changes in a reorganizing workplace. *Journal of Applied Psychology* 85:132–142.

Wright, Patrick M., Timothy M. Gardner, Lisa M. Moynihan, Hyeon Jeong Park, Barry Gerhart, and John E. Delery. 2001. Measurement error in research on human resources and firm performance: Additional data and suggestions for future research. *Personnel Psychology* 54:875–902.

Rafael Wittek, professor of Theoretical Sociology and Research Director of the Department of Sociology, University of Groningen. He is also the Scientific Director of the Interuniversity Center for Social Science Theory and Methodology (ICS). His research interests are in the fields of the Sociology of Organziations, Social Network Research, and Sociological Theory. Recent publications: The Handbook of Rational Choice Social Research. Palo Alto 2013 (ed. by R. Wittek, T.A.B. Snijders, and V. Nee). Rational Choice. Oxford Bibliographies Online: Sociology 2013; Talking About the Boss: Effects of Generalized and Interpersonal Trust on Workplace Gossip. Group and Organization Management 37, 2012 (with L.R. Ellwardt and R. Wielers; won the best paper Award 2012 of the Journal Group and Organization Management).

Fernando Nieto Morales, 1984, doctoral candidate at the Department of Sociology, University of Groningen, and member of the Interuniversity Center for Social Science Theory and Methodology (ICS). His research interests include reorganizations, governance of organizational change, and public sector reform. Recent publication: After the reform: Change in Dutch public and private organizations. Journal of Public Administration Research and Theory 23, 2013 (with R. Wittek and L. Heyse; won the best paper award at the IV Latin American and European Meeting on Organizational Studies (LAEMOS)).

Peter Mühlau, assistant professor in European Employment Studies at the Department of Sociology at Trinity College Dublin. Main interests include comparative labor market and employment studies, the economic and social integration of immigrants and the changing organization of work and its implications for social inequality and employee well-being. Recent publications: Low expectations or different evaluations—What explains immigrants' high levels of trust in host country institutions? Journal of Ethnic and Migration Studies 39, 2012 (with A. Röder).Trust of immigrants in criminal justice institutions in Europe: The role of discrimination and expectations. European Journal of Criminology 9, 2012 (with A. Röder).

Der Einfluss der Gruppengröße auf die Aktivität von Parteimitgliedern

Alexandra Nonnenmacher · Tim Spier

© Springer Fachmedien Wiesbaden 2014

Zusammenfassung Ziel des Beitrags ist es zu prüfen, ob sich Olsons (The logic of collective action: Public goods and the theory of groups, Cambridge, Harvard University Press, 1965) Annahmen zum Einfluss der Gruppengröße auf die Neigung zum „Trittbrettfahren" in politischen Parteien bewähren. Die Mehrebenenanalyse von Daten der Deutschen Parteimitgliederstudie 2009 zeigt, dass ein solcher negativer Zusammenhang zwischen der Mitgliederzahl im Kreisverband und dem individuellen Aktivitätsniveau von Mitgliedern der CDU, CSU, SPD, FDP und Bündnis 90/Die Grünen nur für die neuen Bundesländer nachweisbar ist. Darüber hinaus stellen wir fest, dass selektive Anreize nicht geeignet sind, den negativen Einfluss steigender Mitgliederzahl zu mindern, während normative Anreize in den alten und neuen Bundesländern mit einer mit der Mitgliederzahl steigenden Neigung zum Trittbrettfahren einhergehen. Unsere Ergebnisse stützen nur teilweise die Annahmen zur Kollektivgutproblematik und verweisen auf weiteren theoretischen und empirischen Forschungsbedarf zu den Effekten der Gruppengröße und zur Rolle von Anreizen bei der Aktivität in politischen Parteien.

Schlüsselwörter Kollektivgutproblem · Parteien · Politische Partizipation · Innerparteiliche Aktivität · Mehrebenenanalyse

---

A. Nonnenmacher (✉)
Department Erziehungswissenschaft-Psychologie, Universität Siegen,
Adolf-Reichwein-Str. 2,
57068 Siegen, Deutschland
E-Mail: alexandra.nonnenmacher@uni-siegen.de

T. Spier
Seminar für Sozialwissenschaften, Universität Siegen,
Adolf-Reichwein-Str. 2,
57068 Siegen, Deutschland
E-Mail: tim.spier@uni-siegen.de

Group Size Effects on Party Members' Activity

Abstract In this paper, we aim to test Olson's (The logic of collective action: Public goods and the theory of groups, Cambridge, Harvard University Press, 1965) assumptions of group size effects on free-riding tendencies in political parties. Multilevel analyses of the *Deutsche Parteimitgliederstudie* (German Party Membership Study) 2009 reveal that for members of the CDU, CSU, SPD, FDP and Bündnis 90/Die Grünen, the assumed negative relationship between the number of party members in the district association and their individual level of activity can only be shown for the eastern states of Germany. Moreover, we show that selective incentives are not suitable for reducing the negative impact of a increasing membership figure, while normative incentives are associated with an increasing free-riding tendency with increasing number of members in the western and eastern *Bundesländer*. Our results only partly support the assumptions on collective action problems and point to a need for further theoretical and empirical research on group size effects and on the role incentives' play in explaining the activity in political parties.

Keywords Collective action problem · Political parties · Political participation · Inner-party activity · Multilevel analysis

1 Einleitung

Die Funktionen politischer Parteien in westlichen Demokratien lassen sich auf sieben zentrale Funktionen reduzieren (von Alemann et al. 2010, S. 216 f.): Partizipation, Transmission, Selektion, Integration, Sozialisation, Selbstregulation und Legitimation. Eine Voraussetzung für die Erfüllung jeder dieser Funktionen ist eine hinreichende Zahl von Parteimitgliedern, deren innerparteiliche Aktivität sich nicht nur auf die Zahlung des Mitgliedsbeitrags beschränkt, die also mehr Aktivität aufweisen als die von Klein (2006, S. 38) so bezeichneten „Karteileichen". Nur aktive Mitglieder formulieren und vertreten z. B. die sozialen Interessen unterschiedlicher Bevölkerungsgruppen (Transmission), übernehmen Ämter und Mandate (Selektion), erlernen demokratische Verfahrensweisen und Strukturen (Sozialisation) und tragen so letztendlich zur Legitimation und Stabilisierung eines politischen Systems bei, in dem Bürger die Möglichkeit haben, Einfluss auf die staatliche Willensbildung zu nehmen.

Eine vielfach bestätigte Erkenntnis der empirischen Parteienforschung ist jedoch, dass der Anteil aktiver Mitglieder in politischen Parteien länder- und parteiübergreifend relativ gering ist. In Deutschland betrachten sich nach den Ergebnissen der Deutschen Parteimitgliederstudie 2009 über alle zu dieser Zeit im Bundestag vertretenen Parteien nur rund 27 % als sehr oder ziemlich aktiv (vgl. Spier 2011, S. 99); in anderen Ländern ist der Wert ähnlich niedrig (vgl. Rüdig et al. 1991, S. 41; Seyd et al. 1996, S. 22 f.; Seyd und Whiteley 2002, S. 79 ff.; Pedersen et al. 2004; Hansen und Heidar 2005; Heidar und Saglie 2005)[1]. Da zudem die absolute Zahl der Parteimit-

---
[1] Fiers et al. (2007, S. 19) berichten für Belgien ein deutlich höheres Aktivitätsniveau von Parteimitgliedern, schreiben dies aber selbst einer durch die Erhebungsmethode bedingten selektiven Stichprobe zu.

glieder in den etablierten Demokratien innerhalb und außerhalb Europas stetig sinkt (Mair und van Biezen 2001; van Biezen et al. 2012; van Biezen und Poguntke 2014), stehen die Parteien vor der Aufgabe, ihre Mitglieder zu aktivieren oder zur Aktivität bereite Neumitglieder zu rekrutieren, um ihre Funktionen auch in Zukunft erfüllen zu können. Hierzu ist es notwendig zu wissen, was aktive von inaktiven Mitgliedern unterscheidet.

Da es sich bei der innerparteilichen Aktivität um eine typische, wenn auch besonders intensive Form der politischen Partizipation handelt, können die Erklärungsmuster der allgemeinen Partizipationsforschung prinzipiell zu ihrer Erklärung herangezogen werden (Whiteley und Seyd 2002, S. 1 ff.). In Anlehnung an die allgemeine Partizipationsforschung soll hier zwischen drei unterschiedlichen Faktorenbündel unterschieden werden, denen ein Einfluss auf das Aktivitätsniveau zugeschrieben wird: Ressourcen, Motivationen und Opportunitäten (vgl. so oder ähnlich Niedermayer 1989; Leighley 1995; Klein 2006; Morales 2009; Spier 2010). Bei den Ressourcen und Motivationen handelt es sich jeweils um individuelle Merkmale von Personen, wobei die Ressourcen das „Können", die Motivationen hingegen das „Wollen" erfassen (vgl. hierzu analog Klein 2006, S. 37). Bisher wurde innerparteiliche Aktivität fast ausschließlich mit Hilfe dieser beiden Faktorenbündel erklärt. Die Rolle politischer Gelegenheitsstrukturen (Opportunitäten) stellt dagegen eine Forschungslücke dar, die wir mit dem vorliegenden Beitrag zu füllen suchen. Konkret beschäftigen wir uns mit der sowohl in der Parteienforschung als auch in der allgemeinen Organisationssoziologie seit längerem diskutierten Frage, ob die Gruppengröße, d. h. die Zahl der Parteimitglieder auf der lokalen Organisationsebene der Kreisverbände, einen Einfluss auf das individuelle Aktivitätsniveau von Parteimitgliedern hat.

Der vorliegende Beitrag ist wie folgt strukturiert: Der folgende Abschnitt geht auf die theoretische Grundlagen und die aus ihnen abgeleiteten Hypothesen ein. Abschnitt 3 umreißt den aktuellen Stand der Forschung; Abschn. 4 die für die Hypothesenprüfung verwendeten Daten und die methodische Vorgehensweise. In Abschn. 5 werden die Ergebnisse unserer Analysen dargestellt und in Abschn. 6 zusammengefasst und diskutiert.

2 Theoretische Annahmen

Der Einfluss der Größe von Parteien auf das Aktivitätsniveau ihrer Mitglieder wird in der Literatur zu politischen Parteien und in der allgemeinen Organisationssoziologie schon lange diskutiert. Den verschiedenen Ansätzen ist trotz völlig unterschiedlicher theoretischer Hintergründe gemein, dass sie von einem negativen Zusammenhang zwischen Gruppengröße und individuellen Aktivitätsniveau ausgehen. Schon Michels (1925, S. 17 ff.) zufolge ist eine „Tendenz des Parteiwesens nach der größten Zahl" zu beobachten, die mit Ausdifferenzierung, Bürokratisierung und Immobilisierung der Organisation sowie einer daraus folgenden Inaktivität der Mitglieder verbunden ist. Scarrow (2000) geht von einer relativ konstanten Nachfrage nach Aktivität innerhalb von Parteien aus und damit auch von einer zunehmenden Inaktivität einzelner Mitglieder mit steigender Mitgliederzahl.

Der vorliegende Beitrag stützt sich konzeptionell aber vor allem auf Überlegungen von Olson (1965). Wir modellieren die Aktivität in Parteien als Kollektivgutproblem. Das Kollektivgut, für dessen „Produktion" innerparteiliche Aktivität notwendig ist, besteht in der Durchsetzung politischer Interessen, für die die eigene Partei steht. Um dies zu erreichen ist es notwendig, dass Ämter besetzt und Mandate übernommen werden, der Wahlkampf der eigenen Partei unterstützt wird, in Arbeitskreisen an der Formulierung politischer Aussagen mitgewirkt wird etc. Kollektivgüter haben allerdings erstens die Eigenschaft, dass niemand von ihrem Nutzen ausgeschlossen werden kann. Auch Parteimitglieder, die keine Kosten in Form von Zeit, Mühe etc. investieren, profitieren von der Durchsetzung politischer Interessen durch die Partei. Zweitens hat der individuelle Beitrag in der Regel keinen Einfluss darauf, ob das Kollektivgut produziert wird. Bezogen auf innerparteiliche Aktivität wird es z. B. für das Wahlergebnis der eigenen Partei praktisch unerheblich sein, ob ein bestimmtes Mitglied für einige Stunden Informationsmaterial verteilt hat. Der Nutzen aus dieser Investition ist also im Vergleich zu den Kosten gering.

Aus den beiden genannten Gründen ist es im Rahmen eines rational-choice-theoretischen Ansatzes für einen Akteur rational, sich nicht an der Produktion des Kollektivguts zu beteiligen. Solange er davon ausgehen kann, dass das Kollektivgut von anderen Gruppenmitgliedern produziert wird, d. h. solange der eigene Beitrag nicht entscheidend ist, werden seine Kosten den Nutzen übersteigen, er bleibt oder wird inaktiv, ein „Trittbrettfahrer". Diese Kollektivgutproblematik steigt mit der Gruppengröße, da der eigene Beitrag geringer wird und für die anderen Mitglieder die Chance sinkt, inaktive Mitglieder zu entdecken und zu sanktionieren, d. h. den Nettonutzen der Inaktivität zu senken. Nur in sehr kleinen Gruppen, in denen erstens die Wahrscheinlichkeit, dass Inaktivität entdeckt und sanktioniert wird, hoch ist und in denen zweitens der eigene Beitrag objektiv relevant ist für die Produktion des Kollektivguts, oder bei übersteigerten Überzeugungen von der Relevanz des eigenen Beitrags, wird ein individueller Akteur aktiv sein.

Mit Bezug auf das Aktivitätsniveau von Parteimitgliedern lässt sich aus Olsons (1965) Ausführungen ableiten, dass mit steigender Mitgliederzahl das individuelle Aktivitätsniveau der Mitglieder sinkt. Hierbei ist aber zu bedenken, dass es für den Einzelnen unerheblich sein dürfte, wie hoch die Mitgliederzahl im gesamten Land ist. Die Gruppe, innerhalb derer die zur Produktion des Kollektivguts notwendigen Aufgaben anfallen und organisiert werden, ist überwiegend die lokale Organisationseinheit. Hypothese 1 lautet entsprechend: Je größer die Mitgliederzahl in der lokalen Organisationseinheit einer Partei, desto geringer ist das Aktivitätsniveau des einzelnen ihr zugehörigen Parteimitglieds (*H1*).

Einen Ausweg aus der Kollektivgutproblematik können selektive Anreize darstellen. Selektive Anreize im engeren Sinne ergeben sich, wenn die Mitarbeit an der Produktion des Kollektivguts mit individuellem Nutzen verbunden ist, z. B. mit sozialer Anerkennung oder einem höheren Status innerhalb der Gruppe. Selektive Anreize im weiteren Sinne bestehen, wenn das Engagement in der Gruppe oder das – in unserem Fall politische – Handeln an sich einen Wert hat, weil es z. B. Freude bereitet. Wir vermuten, dass solche Mitglieder grundsätzlich aktiver sind als andere (*H2a*). Darüber hinaus können wir annehmen, dass der oben beschriebene negative Einfluss der Mitgliederzahl auf das individuelle Aktivitätsniveau schwächer ist für diejenigen

Abb. 1: Graphische Zusammenfassung der Hypothesen

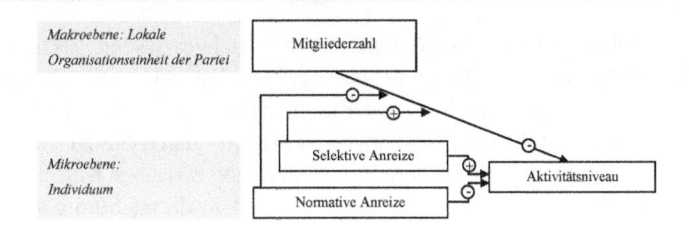

Mitglieder, für die die Aktivität mit einem Nutzen aus selektiven Anreizen verbunden ist (*H2b*).

Es ist möglich, dass der positiv wirkende Nutzen aus selektiven Anreizen den negativen Einfluss der lokalen Mitgliederzahl in einem Maß übersteigt, dass die Mitgliederzahl keinerlei Effekt auf das Aktivitätsniveau dieser Parteimitglieder hat.

Umgekehrt gibt es eine andere Gruppe unter den Parteimitgliedern, von der angenommen werden kann, dass sie eine stärkere Neigung zum Trittbrettfahren hat: diejenigen Mitglieder, für die nicht die Durchsetzung politischer Ziele der Grund für ihre Parteimitgliedschaft ist. Sie ziehen entsprechend geringen Nutzen aus dem Kollektivgut, ihre durch innerparteiliche Aktivität verursachten Kosten sind relativ hoch, und sie sollten somit eine geringe Bereitschaft zu innerparteilicher Aktivität aufweisen. Wir gehen davon aus, dass diejenigen Mitglieder, die sich vor allem aufgrund des Einflusses von Familienmitgliedern und Freunden einer Partei angeschlossen haben (im Folgenden als „normative Anreize" bezeichnet), einen geringen Nutzen aus dem Kollektivgut ziehen, und vermuten: Je wichtiger normative Anreize für die Mitgliedschaft in einer Partei sind, desto geringer ist das Aktivitätsniveau (*H3a*).

Zudem sollten diese Parteimitglieder, die einen geringen Nutzen aus der Produktion des Kollektivguts ziehen, ihre Entscheidung für oder gegen Aktivität vor allem von den Kosten abhängig machen, die (In-)Aktivität mit sich bringt. Mit steigender Gruppengröße sollten die Kosten für Inaktivität sinken, da erstens die Wahrscheinlichkeit sinkt, dass sie überhaupt entdeckt wird, und zweitens selbst bei „Entdeckung" weniger negative Sanktionen von Seiten anderer Mitglieder zu erwarten sind, da es zunehmend weniger auf den Beitrag jedes Einzelnen ankommt. Zusammenfassend sollte demnach der negative Einfluss der lokalen Mitgliederzahl auf die Intensität innerparteilicher Aktivität mit steigender Wichtigkeit normativer Anreize stärker werden (*H3b*).

In Abb. 1 werden die Hypothesen noch einmal zusammenfassend dargestellt.

3 Stand der Forschung

Der Stand der Forschung zum Einfluss von der Gruppengröße auf die innerparteiliche Aktivität ist lückenhaft und widersprüchlich. Tan (1998) weist für 23 Parteien aus acht vorwiegend europäischen Ländern eine negative Korrelation zwischen Parteigröße und dem durchschnittlichen Aktivitätsniveau ihrer Mitglieder auf der Aggregatebene nach. Ein Schluss auf den Zusammenhang zwischen Parteigröße und *individuellem* Aktivitätsniveau der Mitglieder aus diesem Befund ist nicht möglich, zudem wurden auf der Analyseebene der Parteien keine Kontrollvariablen berücksichtigt. Es ist also möglich, dass der nachgewiesene Zusammenhang, wenn er überhaupt für die Individualebene nachweisbar wäre, auf Kompositionseffekten beruht (z. B. könnten die Mitglieder kleiner Parteien politisch interessierter und aus diesem Grund durchschnittlich aktiver sein). Im Gegensatz zu Tan (1998) finden Fisher et al. (2006) einen positiven Zusammenhang zwischen Mitgliederzahl und Wahlkampfaktivitäten in britischen Parteien. Auch in dieser Studie wird der Einfluss relevanter Individual- oder Kontextmerkmale nicht kontrolliert. In beiden Untersuchungen wird zudem nicht berücksichtigt, dass nicht die Größe der gesamten Partei das für das Aktivitätsniveau der Mitglieder entscheidende Maß ist, sondern vielmehr der lokale Kontext, in dem die Mitglieder aktiv werden können (vgl. die Anmerkungen zu Hypothese *H1*).

Der positive Effekt der Bedeutung selektiver Anreize auf die individuelle Aktivität in Parteien ist relativ gut nachgewiesen (vgl. Whiteley und Seyd 1996; Gallagher et al. 2002; Seyd und Whiteley 2002; Spier 2011). Die Befunde zum Einfluss der Wichtigkeit normativer Anreize sind dagegen widersprüchlich. Seyd und Whiteley (2002, S. 110) finden den von uns erwarteten negativen Zusammenhang mit dem Aktivitätsniveau; Gallagher et al. (2002) dagegen keinen Zusammenhang. Eine Erklärung für diese Befunde mag in den unterschiedlichen Operationalisierungen von Aktivität (Gallagher et al. 2002, S. 102 f.; Seyd und Whiteley 2002, S. 62) sowie normativen Anreizen (Gallagher et al. 2002, S. 100; Seyd und Whiteley 2002, S. 77) oder an den unterschiedlichen nationalen Kontexten liegen.

4 Daten und Methode

4.1 Stichprobe und methodisches Vorgehen

Für die Hypothesenprüfung nutzen wir Daten, die im Rahmen der Deutschen Parteimitgliederstudie 2009 erhoben wurden.[2] Im Frühjahr 2009 wurden insgesamt 17000 Mitglieder der damals im Bundestag vertretenen politischen Parteien schriftlich befragt (jeweils 3000 Mitglieder von CDU, SPD, FDP, Bündnis 90/Die Grünen und der Linken sowie 2000 CSU-Mitglieder). Um eine ausreichende Beteiligung von Parteimitgliedern aus den neuen Bundesländern zu gewährleisten, war die Stichprobe disproportional geschichtet (jeweils 2000 Befragten aus den alten und 1000 Befragte aus den neuen Bundesländern für CDU, SPD, FDP und Bündnis 90/Die Grünen; 1000 Befragte aus den alten und 2000 Befragte aus den neuen Bundesländern für Die Linke). Der Versand der Fragebögen erfolgte aus den Parteizentralen; der Rücklauf war an die Universität Düsseldorf gerichtet, um den Befragten glaubhaft Anonymität zusichern zu können. Die Befragung wurde nach den Vorgaben der Total-Design-Method (Dillman 1978) durchgeführt (Details zur Stichprobenziehung und -zusammensetzung sind Klein 2011 zu entnehmen). Die Rücklaufquote betrug 49 % (CSU) bis 67 % (Die Linke), über alle Parteien 58 %.

---

[2] Das Projekt wurde gefördert durch die DFG, GZ AL 171/4-1 und KL 1385/1-1; Leitung: Ulrich von Alemann und Markus Klein.

Die zu prüfenden Hypothesen beziehen sich auf den Einfluss der Zahl der Mitglieder in der lokalen Organisationseinheit einer Partei (*H1*) sowie auf konditionale Effekte der Gruppengröße auf Mitglieder, für die die Parteiarbeit mit individuellem Nutzen verbunden ist (*H2b*) und solche, die einen geringen Nutzen aus dem zu produzierenden Kollektivgut „Durchsetzung politischer Interessen" ziehen (*H3b*). Um die Effekte solcher Individual- und Aggregatmerkmale gleichzeitig schätzen zu können, führen wir im Folgenden Mehrebenen-Regressionsanalysen durch. Hier wird als Kontextmerkmale auf die Mitgliederzahl der jeweiligen Parteien auf Kreisebene abgestellt. Für Die Linke liegen die Mitgliederzahlen auf Kreisebene zum Zeitpunkt der Auswertung leider nur unvollständig vor; die Analysen beziehen sich daher allein auf die Mitglieder von CDU, CSU, SPD, FDP und Bündnis 90/Die Grünen. Für die Regressionsanalysen wurden die Daten designgewichtet, um erstens die disproportionale Schichtung der Stichprobe und zweitens die unterschiedlich hohen Mitgliederzahlen der Parteien zu berücksichtigen. Die uni- und bivariaten Analysen wurden mit ungewichteten Daten durchgeführt.

In den Mehrebenen-Regressionsanalysen wird neben den für die Hypothesenprüfung zentralen Variablen eine relativ große Zahl an Kontrollvariablen berücksichtigt. Ziel dieser Vorgehensweise ist es, mögliche Selektions- oder Kompositionseffekte der lokalen Organisationseinheiten zu kontrollieren. Es ist beispielsweise möglich, dass ein negativer Zusammenhang zwischen Mitgliederzahl (Gruppengröße) und individuellem Aktivitätsniveau allein darauf beruht, dass a) mit dem politischen Interesse auch das Aktivitätsniveau steigt und b) in großen lokalen Organisationseinheiten mehr Mitglieder mit geringem politischen Interesse versammelt sind. Wir berücksichtigen Merkmale, deren Einfluss auf die Aktivität in bisherigen Untersuchungen wiederholt nachgewiesen wurde (vgl. z. B. Seyd und Whiteley 1992, 2002; Whiteley et al. 1993; Niedermayer 2002; Hansen und Heidar 2005; Klein 2006; S. 108 ff.; Spier 2011). Sie lassen sich zwei Faktorenbündeln zuordnen: Ressourcen (z. B. Bildungsniveau, Zeit, *efficacy* oder nach Verba und Nie 1972, S. 271: „time, money and civic skills") und Motivationen (z. B. Stärke der Parteiidentifikation, kollektive, ideologische, altruistische, expressive Anreize nach dem General-Incentives-Modell).

Sämtliche Analysen werden sowohl für alle befragten Parteimitglieder als auch getrennt für die alten und neuen Bundesländer durchgeführt. Mit dieser Vorgehensweise tragen wir der deutlich unterschiedlichen Situation in den beiden Regionen Rechnung. In Ostdeutschland sind die Parteiorganisationen erst 1989/90 aufgebaut worden, zudem weisen sie in der Regel absolut wie relativ deutlich weniger Parteimitglieder auf als im Westen der Republik. Schließlich kann auch nicht ausgeschlossen werden, dass die unterschiedlichen Sozialisationshintergründe in Ost- und Westdeutschland bewirken, dass innerparteiliche Aktivität jeweils anderen Determinanten unterliegt.

4.2 Operationalisierung

Aktivitätsniveau. Das individuelle Aktivitätsniveau als abhängige Variable wird mit Hilfe der Häufigkeit gemessen, mit der die befragten Parteimitglieder zwölf Formen der Parteiarbeit leisten. Auf die Frage „Es gibt verschiedene Formen der Mitarbeit in Parteien. Natürlich hat kaum jemand die Zeit und die Möglichkeit, dies alles zu tun.

Tab. 1 Hauptkomponentenanalyse der zwölf Items zur Messung des Aktivitätsniveaus

Item	Ladung	Anteil Befragter, die Aktivität … ausüben	
		Sehr häufig	Selten/nie
Bei der Organisation der Parteiarbeit mithelfen	0,869	10,9	40,0
Informationsstände der <Partei> besetzen und betreuen	0,837	12,3	44,7
Plakate kleben, Flugblätter und Informationsmaterial der <Partei> verteilen	0,815	14,1	39,1
Ein Amt in der Partei übernehmen	0,801	14,5	49,0
Die Parteiversammlungen besuchen	0,770	24,2	12,9
Bei Festen und anderen geselligen Veranstaltungen der Partei mitmachen	0,769	13,7	19,2
In Arbeitskreisen oder anderen Gremien der Partei an der Formulierung politischer Aussagen mitwirken	0,767	8,0	43,4
Im persönlichen Gespräch neue Mitglieder werben	0,698	4,1	37,2
In Beiträgen für Parteimedien (Parteizeitungen, Online-Angebote, etc.) die Ansichten der <Partei> deutlich machen	0,679	3,9	59,5
Für ein öffentliches Amt kandidieren	0,678	12,9	59,2
Bei sozialen Aktionen der Partei mitmachen (z. B. Senioren-betreuung, Kleidersammlung)	0,673	5,6	46,5
Bei Bedarf zusätzlich Geld spenden	0,512	5,6	35,1

Wie oft haben Sie in den letzten Jahren die nachfolgenden Aktivitäten ausgeübt?" wurden die befragten Parteimitglieder gebeten anzugeben, ob sie die jeweilige Aktivitätsform sehr häufig, weniger häufig, manchmal, eher selten oder selten/nie ausüben. Eine explorative Hauptkomponentenanalyse ergab, dass diese zwölf Items eine gemeinsame latente Dimension abbilden, auf der alle zwölf Items hoch laden (vgl. Tab. 1)[3]. Die gespeicherten Faktorwerte dienen uns im Folgenden zur Messung des Aktivitätsniveaus. Cronbachs Alpha für diesen Index beträgt 0,925.

In Tab. 1 sind außerdem die Anteile der Befragten aufgeführt, die die jeweilige Aktivität sehr häufig oder selten/nie ausüben. Die einzige Aktivität, die von einem größeren Anteil „sehr häufig" als „selten/nie" ausgeübt wird, ist der der Besuch von Parteiversammlungen. Fünf Aktivitäten werden von einem relativ großen Teil der Parteimitglieder selten oder nie ausgeübt und von einem relativ kleinen Teil sehr häufig, d. h. bleiben tendenziell einer kleinen Gruppe von Aktivisten und Funktionären innerhalb der Kreisverbände vorbehalten. Diese fünf Aktivitäten gliedern sich inhaltlich in zwei Gruppen, die unterschiedliche Arten von Hochkosten-Situationen („high-intensity participation", vgl. Seyd und Whitely 2002, S. 63 f.) darstellen: „an der Formulierung politischer Aussagen mitwirken" sowie „an Beiträgen für Parteimedien mitformulieren" sind mit hohen kognitiven Kosten verbunden, oder mit anderen Worten: Nur wenige Parteimitglieder verfügen über die notwendigen Kenntnisse, um diese Aktivitäten auszuüben. „Im persönlichen Gespräch neue Mitglieder werben", „bei sozialen

---

[3] Eine größtenteils mit dieser Operationalisierung übereinstimmende Liste an Aktivitäten bildet nach den Ergebnissen einer konfirmatorischen Hauptkomponentenanalyse (Seyd und Whiteley 2002, S. 63 f.) zwei Dimensionen ab: Hoch- und Niedrig-Intensitäts-Aktivitäten. Da die beiden Dimensionen aber mit $r=0,48$ (Labour Party) und $r=0,65$ (Conservative Party) korrelieren, ist es aus unserer Sicht angemessen, die Aktivitäten zur Messung eines allgemeinen Aktivitätsniveaus zusammenzufassen.

Aktionen mitmachen" sowie „zusätzlich Geld spenden" können dagegen prinzipiell alle Parteimitgliedern leisten, setzt aber die Bereitschaft voraus, zusätzliche Zeit und/ oder zusätzliches Geld zu investieren. Diese Unterschiede dürfen aber nicht überbewertet werden, da all diese Aktivitäten auf einer Komponente laden, sondern geben Nuancen innerhalb der Dimension „innerparteiliche Aktivität" wieder.

Motivationen. Für die Operationalisierung des „Wollens", der Motivationen, stützen wir uns auf das vor allem von Seyd und Whiteley (1992; vgl. auch Whiteley et al. 1993; Whiteley und Seyd 1996) geprägte General-Incentives-Modell politischer Partizipation, hier in der Umsetzung von Klein (2006). Wir unterscheiden sieben positive Anreize oder Nutzenfaktoren. Zwei dieser Anreize sind mit einem individuellen Nutzen verbunden und somit für die empirische Überprüfung der Hypothesen *H2a* und *H2b* geeignet: selektive, prozessbezogene Anreize (intrinsische Befriedigung durch Spaß an der politischen Arbeit, das Zusammenkommen mit netten Menschen oder aus der Entwicklung politischen Sachverstands) und selektive, ergebnisbezogene Anreize (Aktivität aus Interesse an einem Parteiamt oder öffentlichen Mandat sowie zur Erlangung beruflicher Vorteile).

Weitere vier Anreize beschreiben einen kollektiven politischen Nutzen: kollektive Anreize (Stärkung des Einflusses der Partei, Einsetzen für Ziele der Partei), ideologische Anreize (Mitgliedschaft, um den politischen Kurs der Partei zu beeinflussen oder einen bestimmten Flügel der Partei zu stärken), altruistische Anreize (um der eigenen Verantwortung als Bürger/in nachzukommen) sowie expressive Anreize (um Sympathie für die eigene Partei zu zeigen oder wegen beeindruckender Persönlichkeiten an der Spitze der Partei).

Normative Anreize stellen den siebten Nutzenfaktor da. Da er zwar ebenfalls einen kollektiven, aber keinen politischen Nutzen beschreibt, ist dieser Faktor geeignet, die Hypothesen *H3a* und *H3b* zu prüfen. Wir nehmen an, dass Personen, die vor allem wegen des Einflusses von Familie und Freunden Mitglied einer Partei werden, einen geringen Nutzen aus dem Kollektivgut „Durchsetzung politischer Interessen" ziehen, entsprechend wenig motiviert sind, Parteiarbeit zu leisten oder zentrale Funktionen zu übernehmen, und dass diese Zurückhaltung umso stärker wird, je mehr andere Parteimitglieder zur Verfügung stehen, die diese Arbeit übernehmen.

Ein weiterer motivationaler Faktor, dessen Einfluss auf das Aktivitätsniveau wir kontrollieren, ist die Parteiidentifikation („Wenn Sie es einmal insgesamt betrachten, wie stark neigen Sie der <Partei> zu?"), die sich in zahlreichen empirischen Untersuchungen als relevant für parteipolitische Partizipation erwiesen hat.

Ressourcen. Neben den Motivationen zur Aktivität in Parteien, dem „Wollen", ist es notwendig, den Einfluss von Ressourcen, dem „Können", zu kontrollieren. Wir berücksichtigen drei Formen kompetenzbezogener Ressourcen, die sich in der Partizipationsforschung als zentral erwiesen haben: politisches Interesse sowie interne und externe *efficacy*. Politisches Interesse wurde operationalisiert mit der Frage „Wie stark sind Sie selbst an Politik interessiert?" (5-stufig, „sehr interessiert" bis „überhaupt nicht interessiert"). Interne und externe *efficacy* wurden mit Hilfe von je zwei Items erhoben, die ebenfalls 5-stufig skaliert sind („stimme voll und ganz zu" bis

„stimme überhaupt nicht zu") und durch Mittelwertbildung zusammengefasst wurden. Die Items für die interne *efficacy* lauten: „Die ganze Politik ist so kompliziert, dass jemand wie ich nicht versteht, was vorgeht." (umgepolt) sowie „Ich traue mir zu, in einer Gruppe, die sich mit politischen Fragen befasst, eine aktive Rolle zu übernehmen." Die externe *efficacy* wird durch zwei weitere Items erfasst: „Die Politiker kümmern sich nicht viel darum, was die Leute denken." (umgepolt) sowie „Die Politiker bemühen sich im Allgemeinen darum, die Interessen der Bevölkerung zu vertreten."

Neben den kompetenzbezogenen Ressourcen kontrollieren wir außerdem den Einfluss derjenigen soziodemographischen Ressourcen, die sich in der Partizipationsforschung als bedeutsam für das Aktivitätsniveau von Parteimitgliedern erwiesen haben (vgl. z. B. Spier 2011): Geschlecht, Alter, schulisches Bildungsniveau sowie Erwerbs- und sozialer Status. Wir erwarten, dass mit sinkendem Alter und steigendem schulischem Bildungsniveau oder sozialem Status (gemessen am ISEI) das Aktivitätsniveau steigt und dass es bei Männern oder Erwerbstätigen höher ist als bei Frauen oder Nicht-Erwerbstätigen. Da einige der soziodemographischen Ressourcen als Voraussetzung für kompetenzbezogene Ressourcen betrachtet werden können (schulisches Bildungsniveau, sozialer Status), ist allerdings zu erwarten, dass wir in den folgenden multivariaten Analysen für die soziodemographischen Merkmale keinen direkten Einfluss auf das Aktivitätsniveau nachweisen können.

Opportunitäten. Unsere zentrale unabhängige Variable ist die Gruppengröße, d. h. die Zahl der Mitglieder auf der lokalen Organisationsebene einer Partei. Die deutschen Parteien unterscheiden sich allerdings darin, wo diese lokale Organisationsebene zu verorten ist: Die mitgliederstarken Parteien CDU, CSU und SPD verfügen zumeist über Ortsverbände, in denen die Basisarbeit organisiert ist, während sich FDP und Bündnis 90/Die Grünen auf grund ihrer deutlich geringen Mitgliederzahl in der Regel erst auf der Kreisebene organisieren. Um einen Vergleich dieser unterschiedlich großen Organisationseinheiten zu ermöglichen, betrachten wir im Folgenden die Zahl der Mitglieder der fünf untersuchten Parteien in 386 Kreisen und kreisfreien Städten[4] am 31.12.2008, also kurz vor der Befragung der Parteimitglieder, wobei die Verknüpfung mit den Individualdaten der Deutschen Parteimitgliederstudie 2009 durch ein Item erfolgt, dass nach dem Autokennzeichen des eigenen Hauptwohnsitzes fragt.

Da jede der fünf Parteien in jedem der 386 Kreise eine bestimmte Mitgliederzahl aufweist, besteht die für uns relevante Makroebene aus einer Kombination der beiden Merkmale Partei und Kreis. Die 7548 Befragten der Parteimitgliederbefragung sind 1235 Parteien-Kreisen zugeordnet (nicht alle der theoretisch möglichen 1544 Parteien-Kreise sind durch mindestens einen Befragten besetzt). Dies entspricht im Mittel 6,1 befragten Parteimitgliedern pro Parteien-Kreis, wobei rund 51 % der Parteien-Kreise mit drei Befragten oder weniger besetzt sind. Erstens ist aber die Zahl unserer Kontexteinheiten groß genug (vgl. Maas und Hox 2005) und zweitens werden mit einer solchen Datenstruktur vor allem die Standardfehler von Ebene 2-Regressionskoeffi-

---

[4] Die Stadtstaaten Berlin, Bremen und Hamburg werden mangels ausdifferenzierter Daten jeweils als ein Kreis behandelt.

zienten überschätzt (vgl. Theall et al. 2008). Sollte diese Datenstruktur also überhaupt Einfluss auf unsere Ergebnisse haben, dann in dem Sinne, dass wir unsere Hypothesen vorschnell ablehnen.

Zusätzlich zur Ebene der Parteien-Kreise beinhalten die Regressionsmodelle außerdem die Ebene der Kreise, da wir davon ausgehen müssen, dass erstens die Mitgliederzahl der Parteien im Kreis mit der Einwohnerzahl korreliert: In großen und einwohnerstarken Kreisen besteht ein größeres Rekrutierungspotenzial, entsprechend höher sollten auch die Mitgliederzahlen der Parteien-Kreise sein. Zweitens kann angenommen werden, dass auch das Aktivitätsniveau mit der Einwohnerzahl korreliert, und zwar negativ. In Großstädten sollte es durchschnittlich niedriger sein als in ländlichen Gebieten. Würden wir die Einwohnerzahl in den Regressionsmodellen nicht berücksichtigen, wäre es möglich, dass wir der Mitgliederzahl im Kreis einen Einfluss zuschreiben, der tatsächlich der Einwohnerzahl zukommt. Dasselbe gilt für die von uns vermuteten Interaktionseffekte, weshalb zusätzliche Cross-Level-Interaktionen mit der Einwohnerzahl im Kreis in die Regressionsmodelle aufgenommen werden.

Tabelle 2 gibt einen Überblick über alle in den folgenden Analysen verwendeten Variablen. Unter den Individualmerkmalen gibt es bis auf das höhere Bildungsniveau und den höheren Anteil an Erwerbstätigen in den neuen Bundesländern keine nennenswerten Unterschiede zwischen den beiden Regionen. Die Parteiidentifikation sowie das politische Interesse sind in beiden Landesteilen, nicht überraschend, sehr hoch. Selektive, ergebnisbezogene Anreize spielen mit einem Mittelwert von 1,92 bzw. 1,98 eine untergeordnete Rolle unter den Motivationen, während kollektive (Stärkung des Einflusses der Partei, Einsetzen für Ziele der Partei) und altruistische Anreize (um der eigenen Verantwortung als Bürger nachzukommen) wichtige Motive für die Parteimitglied sind.

Die scheinbar deutlich höheren durchschnittlichen Mitglieder- und Einwohnerzahlen in Ostdeutschland sind ausschließlich ein Effekt der Zuordnung Berlins. Wird Berlin ausgeschlossen, betragen die entsprechenden Mittelwerte 418 Mitglieder und 238 806 Einwohner.

5 Empirische Befunde

5.1 Deskriptive Analyse

Eine Analyse der bivariaten Zusammenhänge zeigt, dass alle motivationalen Faktoren positiv mit dem Aktivitätsniveau korrelieren (siehe Tab. 3). Für die selektiven Anreize sind die Zusammenhänge in den neuen Bundesländern etwas geringer als in den alten Bundesländern, gleichzeitig sind die Koeffizienten für normative, kollektive, ideologischen und expressive Anreize höher. Auch bei den kompetenzbezogenen Ressourcen sind Unterschiede feststellbar: Interne und externe *efficacy* weisen in den alten Bundesländern einen stärkeren Zusammenhang mit dem Aktivitätsniveau auf als in den neuen Bundesländern. Unsere Annahme, dass es in den beiden Regionen unterschiedliche Partizipationsstrukturen gibt, bestätigt sich hier, wenn auch die Unterschiede nicht groß sind.

Tab. 2 Analysierte Variablen; Mittelwerte bzw. prozentuale Anteile

Variable (Range)	Gesamt	N	Alte Bundesländer	N	Neue Bundesländer	N
Individualebene						
Aktivitätsniveau (−2,6–1,4)	0,000	7147	−0,014	5079	0,023	2068
Motivationen						
Selektive, ergebnisbezogene Anreize (0–10)	1,94	7143	1,92	5069	1,98	2074
Selektive, prozessbezogene Anreize (0–10)	4,45	7115	4,42	5045	4,51	2070
Normative Anreize (0–10)	2,19	7219	2,31	5131	1,91	2088
Kollektive Anreize (0–10)	6,97	7121	6,92	5057	7,11	2064
Ideologische Anreize (0–10)	4,56	7166	4,54	5090	4,60	2076
Altruistische Anreize (0–10)	6,39	7249	6,40	5151	6,35	2098
Expressive Anreize (0–10)	5,41	7195	5,44	5108	5,32	2087
Parteiidentifikation (1–5)	4,11	7385	4,11	5264	4,10	2121
Kompetenzbezogene Ressourcen						
Politisches Interesse (0–5)	4,49	7232	4,46	5216	4,55	2107
Interne Efficacy (0–5)	3,71	7336	3,66	5231	3,84	2105
Externe Efficacy (0–5)	3,03	7349	2,99	5239	3,11	2110
Soziodemographische Ressourcen						
Geschlecht: weiblich	27,9	7414	27,3	5302	29,6	2112
Alter (12–98)	54,8	7391	56,2	5285	51,3	2106
Schulabschluss						
Höchstens Hauptschule	15,8	1151	19,3	1001	7,2	150
Mittlere Reife/Realschulabschluss	18,9	1374	20,3	1051	15,4	323
(Fach-)Abitur	14,6	1060	14,2	736	15,5	324
(Fach-)Hochschulabschluss	50,7	3694	46,3	2399	61,9	1295
Erwerbstatus						
Vollzeit-erwerbstätig	49,2	3625	47,0	2470	54,8	1155
Teilzeit-erwerbstätig	13,3	978	13,7	722	12,1	256
Nicht erwerbstätig	37,5	2764	39,3	2067	33,1	697
Berufsstatus (ISEI) (16–90)	56,8	7360	55,8	5253	59,2	2107
Partei						
CDU	19,9	1503	18,4	989	23,8	514
CSU	12,8	966	12,8	966	–	–
SPD	22,1	1666	20,5	1105	26,0	561
FDP	20,9	1578	19,9	1074	23,3	504
Bündnis 90/Die Grünen	24,3	1835	23,3	1255	26,9	580
Kreisebene						
Mitgliederzahl	2346	386	1988	296	3225	90
Einwohnerzahl (in 1000)	666,9	386	394,9	296	1335,4	90

Für soziodemographische Ressourcen zeigen sich schon in der bivariaten Analyse kaum Zusammenhänge mit dem Aktivitätsniveau und entsprechend geringe Unterschiede zwischen Ost und West. Auch zwischen den Parteien gibt es nur geringe Unterschiede. FDP-Mitglieder sind leicht überdurchschnittlich aktiv, Grünen-Mitglieder leicht unterdurchschnittlich, und das Aktivitätsniveau der Mitglieder von

Tab. 3 Bivariate Zusammenhänge aller unabhängigen Variablen mit dem Aktivitätsniveau

Variable	Gesamt	Alte Bundesländer	Neue Bundesländer	Maß
Individualebene				
Motivationen				
Selektive, ergebnisbezogene Anreize	0,350	0,409	0,242	r
Selektive, prozessbezogene Anreize	0,467	0,489	0,426	r
Normative Anreize	0,114	0,103	0,139	r
Kollektive Anreize	0,334	0,324	0,355	r
Ideologische Anreize	0,326	0,319	0,339	r
Altruistische Anreize	0,233	0,253	0,202	r
Expressive Anreize	0,112	0,100	0,134	r
Parteiidentifikation	0,295	0,288	0,315	r
Kompetenzbezogene Ressourcen				
Politisches Interesse	0,269	0,269	0,267	r
Interne Efficacy	0,197	0,208	0,177	r
Externe Efficacy	0,088	0,119	0,043	r
Soziodemographische Ressourcen				
Geschlecht (Ref.: männlich)	−0,019	−0,008	−0,040	r
Alter	0,059	0,028	0,108	r
Schulabschluss				
Höchstens Hauptschule	−0,032	−0,033	−0,028	m
Mittlere Reife/Realschulabschluss	0,037	0,043	0,022	m
(Fach-)Abitur	−0,033	−0,039	−0,023	m
(Fach-)Hochschulabschluss	0,001	−0,025	0,033	m
Erwerbstatus				
Vollzeit-erwerbstätig	−0,031	−0,022	−0,047	m
Teilzeit-erwerbstätig	0,005	0,023	−0,038	m
Nicht erwerbstätig	0,027	−0,021	0,092	m
Berufsstatus (ISEI)	0,012	0,006	0,020	r
Partei				
CDU	−0,054	−0,071	−0,023	m
CSU	−0,092	−0,092	–	m
SPD	−0,002	−0,010	0,015	m
FDP	0,109	0,101	0,128	m
Bündnis 90/Die Grünen	−0,139	−0,033	−0,365	m
Kreisebene				
Mitgliederzahl	−0,116	−0,081	−0,175	r
Einwohnerzahl	−0,154	−0,109	−0,262	r

r Pearsons r, *m* Mittelwert

CDU, CSU und SPD entspricht dem Durchschnitt. Deutliche Unterschiede zwischen den Landesteilen gibt es nur bei Bündnis 90/Die Grünen. Hier sind die Mitglieder in den alten Bundesländern durchschnittlich aktiv (−0,033), während die Mitglieder in den neuen Bundesländern vergleichsweise inaktiv sind (−0,365).

Die Zusammenhänge zwischen Mitglieder- und Einwohnerzahl und individuellem Aktivitätsniveau sind wie erwartet negativ und in den neuen Bundesländern höher als in den alten Bundesländern. Hier deutet sich schon an, dass innerparteiliche Aktivität in den neuen Bundesländern stärker von Opportunitäten abhängig ist als in den alten Bundesländern. Die Korrelation zwischen Mitglieder- und Einwohnerzahl im Kreis beträgt $r=0{,}673$, bestätigt damit unsere Erwartung und verdeutlicht die oben beschriebene Notwendigkeit, den Einfluss der Einwohnerzahl in den Regressionsmodellen zu kontrollieren.

5.2 Mehrebenen-Regressionsmodelle

Der wie erwartet negative Zusammenhang zwischen Mitgliederzahl und individuellem Aktivitätsniveau in der deskriptiven Analyse weist schon darauf hin, dass sich die untersuchten Parteien-Kreise hinsichtlich ihres mittleren Aktivitätsniveaus unterscheiden, mit anderen Worten, dass es eine Zwischengruppenvarianz gibt, die durch Merkmale der Parteien-Kreise erklärt werden muss. Zur Bestimmung der potenziellen Erklärungskraft dieser Makroebene werden in Tab. 4 die Nullmodelle und Anteile der auf den drei Analyseebenen erklärbaren Varianz dargestellt. Für die gesamte Bundesrepublik Deutschland liegen 9,8 % der Gesamtvarianz auf der Ebene der Parteien-Kreise und 2,4 % auf der Ebene der Kreise. Bei getrennter Betrachtung der alten und neuen Bundesländer zeigt sich, dass das individuelle Aktivitätsniveau im Osten (15,6 %) deutlich stärker vom Parteien-Kreis abhängig ist als im Westen (6,1 %). Dasselbe gilt für die Ebene der Kreise.

In Tab. 5 sind schließlich die Ergebnisse der Regressionsanalysen abgetragen. Zwischen den Parteien gibt es keine statistisch signifikanten Unterschiede im Aktivitätsniveau ihrer Mitglieder, mit Ausnahme der SPD-Mitglieder in den neuen Bundesländern, die aktiver als CDU-Mitglieder sind. Unter den soziodemographischen Ressourcen haben lediglich das Alter und der Erwerbsstatus einen statistisch signifikanten Einfluss. Mit dem Alter steigt das Aktivitätsniveau (dieser Effekt schwächt sich aber mit steigendem Alter ab, wie der statistisch signifikante Effekt des quadratischen Terms zeigt), und nicht Erwerbstätige in den neuen Bundesländern sind aktiver als Vollzeit-Erwerbstätige. Das schulische Bildungsniveau und der Berufsstatus haben dagegen keinen Einfluss. Unter den kompetenzbezogenen Ressourcen wirkt sich nur die interne *efficacy*, also die Überzeugung, politisch selbst wirksam zu sein, in allen Modellen positiv auf die innerparteiliche Aktivität aus. Die externe *efficacy*, d. h. die Überzeugung, ob das politische System überhaupt beeinflussbar ist, hat hingegen keinen Einfluss. Das politische Interesse wirkt sich nur in Westdeutschland positiv auf das individuelle Aktivitätsniveau aus.

Tab. 4 Nullmodelle und ICCs

	Gesamte Stichprobe	Alte Bundesländer	Neue Bundesländer
Konstante	0,014 (0,018)	−0,018 (0,021)	0,133* (0,030)
Zufallseffekte	*Varianzkomp.*	*Varianzkomp.*	*Varianzkomp.*
Ebene 1: Individuum (e_{0j})	0,912 (0,015)	1,348 (0,028)	0,248 (0,007)
Ebene 2: Kreis*Partei (u_{0j})	0,102 (0,014)	0,089 (0,017)	0,052 (0,015)
Ebene 3: Kreis (v_{0j})	0,025 (0,010)	0,022 (0,012)	0,034 (0,013)
N (Ebene 1/2/3)	8363/1574/386	5196/1183/296	3167/458/90
Anteil erklärbarer Varianz auf			
Ebene 2	0,098	0,061	0,156
Ebene 3	0,024	0,015	0,102

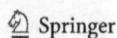

Tab. 5 Lineare Mehrebenen-Regressionsanalysen der innerparteilichen Aktivität

	Gesamte Stichprobe		Alte Bundesländer		Neue Bundesländer	
	B	S.E.	B	S.E.	B	S.E.
Konstante	−0,040	0,050	−0,004	0,053	−0,162	0,110
Fixe Effekte (Ebene 1: Individuum)						
Partei (Ref.: CDU)						
CSU	−0,024	0,055	−0,033	0,058	–	–
SPD	0,053	0,037	0,040	0,041	0,134*	0,065
FDP	0,090	0,064	0,130	0,079	0,031	0,084
Bündnis 90/Die Grünen	0,018	0,073	0,078	0,088	−0,167	0,114
Soziodemographische Ressourcen						
Geschlecht: weiblich	−0,002	0,026	−0,008	0,032	0,102*	0,043
Alter (/10)	0,338*	0,044	0,346*	0,054	0,304*	0,083
Alter (/10) quadriert	−0,022*	0,004	−0,022*	0,005	−0,022*	0,008
Schulabschluss (Ref.: höchstens Hauptschulabschluss)						
Mittlere Reife/Realschulabschluss	0,063	0,034	0,058	0,040	0,099	0,082
(Fach-)Abitur	−0,004	0,042	−0,010	0,050	0,035	0,085
(Fach-)Hochschulabschluss	−0,008	0,039	−0,022	0,047	0,070	0,083
Erwerbsstatus (Ref.: vollzeit-erwerbstätig)						
Teilzeit-erwerbstätig	0,018	0,038	0,011	0,046	0,087	0,065
Nicht erwerbstätig	−0,054	0,031	−0,068	0,037	0,115*	0,055
Berufsstatus (ISEI) (/100)	0,115	0,094	0,100	0,113	0,286	0,158
Kompetenzbezogene Ressourcen						
Politisches Interesse	0,140*	0,019	0,149*	0,023	0,058	0,034
Interne Efficacy	0,121*	0,016	0,119*	0,019	0,203*	0,029
Externe Efficacy	0,011	0,015	0,011	0,017	0,005	0,026
Motivationen						
Selektiv-ergebnisbezogene Anreize	0,089*	0,008	0,099*	0,009	0,044*	0,012
Selektiv-prozessbezogene Anreize	0,129*	0,008	0,132*	0,009	0,102*	0,011
Normative Anreize	−0,000	0,006	−0,003	0,006	0,007	0,009
Kollektive Anreize	0,043*	0,007	0,044*	0,009	0,042*	0,012
Ideologische Anreize	0,022*	0,005	0,020*	0,005	0,040*	0,008
Altruistische Anreize	0,014*	0,004	0,014*	0,005	0,013	0,007
Expressive Anreize	−0,065*	0,006	−0,067*	0,007	−0,044*	0,010
Parteiidentifikation	0,219*	0,019	0,208*	0,022	0,258*	0,033
*Fixer Effekt (Ebene 2: Kreis*Partei)*						
Mitgliederzahl (/100)	1,592	1,182	3,287*	1,406	−11,051*	4,872
*Cross-Level-Interaktionen: Mitgliederzahl**						
Selektiv-ergebnisbezogene Anreize	0,549	0,286	0,422	0,398	−0,199	0,363
Selektiv-prozessbezogene Anreize	−0,002	0,260	0,024	0,362	0,062	0,332
Normative Anreize	−0,546*	0,213	−0,680*	0,289	−0,520*	0,311
Fixer Effekt (Ebene 3: Kreis)						
Einwohner (/1.000.000)	−0,249*	0,067	−0,409*	0,092	−0,031	0,088

Tab. 5 (Fortsetzung)

	Gesamte Stichprobe		Alte Bundesländer		Neue Bundesländer	
	B	S.E.	B	S.E.	B	S.E.
Cross-Level-Interaktionen: Einwohnerzahl*						
Selektiv-ergebnisbezogene Anreize	−0,026	0,014	−0,013	0,026	0,004	0,015
Selektiv-prozessbezogene Anreize	−0,005	0,012	−0,010	0,024	−0,004	0,014
Normative Anreize	0,022*	0,010	0,045*	0,019	0,008	0,013
Zufallseffekte	*Varianzkomp.*		*Varianzkomp.*		*Varianzkomp.*	
Ebene 1: Individuum (e_{0j})	0,639	0,013	0,845	0,021	0,186	0,007
Ebene 2: Kreis*Partei (u_{0j})	0,072	0,012	0,062	0,013	0,031	0,015
Ebene 3: Kreis (v_{0j})	0,023	0,009	0,021	0,010	0,031	0,014
R^2 (Ebene 1/ 2/ 3)	0,299/0,294/0,081		0,373/0,303/0,045		0,250/0,404/0,088	
N (Ebene 1/ 2/ 3)	5.651/1.236/386		3.962/949/296		1.689/287/90	

*$p \leq 0,05$

Die motivationalen Faktoren zeigen mit wenigen Ausnahmen die zu erwarteten Effekte: Die Parteiidentifikation sowie sämtliche Anreize bis auf die normativen und expressiven korrelieren positiv mit dem Aktivitätsniveau, d. h. je wichtiger z. B. das Interesse an einem Parteiamt oder öffentlichen Mandat (selektive, ergebnisbezogene Anreize), der Spaß an der politischen Arbeit (selektive, prozessbezogene Anreize) oder die Stärkung des Einflusses der Partei (kollektive Anreize) für ein Mitglied sind, desto aktiver ist es. Altruistische Anreize (Parteimitgliedschaft aus Pflichtgefühl als Bürger eines Landes) haben allerdings nur in den alten Bundesländern einen statistisch signifikanten Effekt. Expressive Anreize haben einen negativen Einfluss, d. h. Personen, die vor allem aus Sympathie für die Partei oder wegen beeindruckender Persönlichkeiten an der Parteispitze Mitglieder einer Partei sind, gehören eher zu den Inaktiven. Die normativen Anreize haben in keiner (Teil-)Stichprobe Einfluss auf das Aktivitätsniveau. Da alle metrisch skalierten Variablen am Gesamt-Mittelwert der jeweiligen (Teil-)Stichprobe zentriert wurden und die Modelle einen Interaktionseffekt zwischen normativen Anreizen und Mitgliederzahl beinhalten, bildet dieser Haupteffekt den Einfluss normativer Anreize bei mittlerer Mitgliederzahl ab.

Unsere erste Hypothese zum negativen Einfluss der Mitgliederzahl im Kreis auf das individuelle Aktivitätsniveau bewährt sich nur für die neuen Bundesländer. Dies gilt nach weiteren, hier nicht abgebildeten Analysen auch dann, wenn Berlin als „Ausreißer" hinsichtlich der Einwohner- und Mitgliederzahl ausgeschlossen wird. In den alten Bundesländern ist der Einfluss der Mitgliederzahl unerwartet positiv, was bei gemeinsamer Analyse beider Regionen dazu führt, dass die Mitgliederzahl in Gesamt-Deutschland keinen statistisch signifikanten Einfluss hat.

Um eine Erklärung für das den theoretischen Annahmen widersprechende Ergebnis für die alten Bundesländer zu finden, haben wir in weiteren Analysen die fünf Parteien getrennt betrachtet. Die einzige Partei, bei der dieser positive Einfluss der Mitgliederzahl auf die Aktivität besteht, ist die SPD (vgl. Tab. 6 im Anhang). Weiterhin ist dieser Effekt nicht linear, sondern schwächt sich mit zunehmender Mitgliederzahl ab (der entsprechende Koeffizient für die quadrierte Mitgliederzahl verfehlt knapp das konventionelle Signifikanzniveau, zeigt aber an, dass eine lineare

Modellierung nicht angemessen wäre). Der positive Zusammenhang zwischen Mitgliederzahl im Kreis und Aktivitätsniveau beruht demnach nicht auf den Angaben der Mitglieder besonders aktiver SPD-„Hochburgen", sondern ausschließlich auf Kreisen mit relativ geringer Mitgliederzahl. Es ist möglich, dass es sich hierbei um Kreise handelt, in denen die CDU und CSU stark vertreten ist und dass diese „Konkurrenzsituation" zur Aktivierung der SPD-Mitglieder beiträgt. Da wir aber für die CDU und CSU keinen solchen Effekt in SPD-dominierten Kreisen gefunden haben, muss es noch mindestens einen weiteren Erklärungsfaktor geben. Es ist denkbar, dass die besondere Situation der SPD als „Juniorpartner" in einer großen Koalition und der Befragungszeitpunkt (ca. sechs Monate vor der Bundestagswahl) eine Erklärung bieten. Wir messen dieser Frage allerdings keine große Bedeutung zu, da der Erklärungsanteil des Kreises bei der West-SPD bei nur 1,5 % der Gesamtvarianz liegt (vgl. Tab. 7 im Anhang).

Hypothese *H2a* besagt, dass das Aktivitätsniveau mit der Wichtigkeit selektiver Anreize steigt. Diese Annahme bewährt sich für alle (Teil-)Stichproben. Mit Hypothese *H2b* haben wir angenommen, dass sich der negative Einfluss der Mitgliederzahl nicht bei denjenigen Parteimitglieder nachweisen lässt, die einen individuellen Nutzen aus der innerparteilichen Aktivität ziehen, d. h. für die selektive Anreize ein wichtiges Motiv für die Mitgliedschaft sind. Zu erwarten ist demnach, dass die Cross-Level-Interaktionen zwischen selektiven, ergebnisbezogenen oder prozessbezogenen Anreizen und der Mitgliederzahl positiv sind. Da in den alten Bundesländern der Haupteffekt der Mitgliederzahl positiv ist, kann sich Hypothese *H2b* hier ohnehin nicht bewähren. In den neuen Bundesländern ist ein solcher Effekt aber auch nicht nachweisbar; Hypothese *H2b* ist also falsifiziert.

Laut Hypothese *H3a* sollten Mitglieder, für die normative Anreize ein wichtiger Grund für die Parteimitgliedschaft sind, weniger aktiv sein als andere, und darüber hinaus sollte sich ihr Aktivitätsniveau laut Hypothese *H3b* mit steigender Mitgliederzahl noch weiter verringern. Diese Annahme lässt sich trotz positivem Haupteffekt für die alten Bundesländer (genauer: für die SPD) aufrechterhalten: Wir können vermuten, dass der positive Effekt der Mitgliederzahl bei den o. g. Mitgliedern schwächer ist. In beiden Fällen sollte sich dies an einer negativen Cross-Level-Interaktion zwischen der Wichtigkeit normativer Anreize (Wichtigkeit des Einflusses von Familie und Freunden für die Parteimitgliedschaft) und der Mitgliederzahl zeigen.

Hypothese *H3a* bewährt sich nicht, dagegen aber Hypothese *H3b*, unabhängig von der Richtung des Haupteffekts der Mitgliederzahl. Zusammengefasst neigen Mitglieder mit starken normativen Motiven stärker zum Trittbrettfahren, je größer ihr Kreisverband ist, sind aber in durchschnittlich großen Kreisverbänden nicht inaktiver als andere[5]. In kleinen Kreisverbänden sind sie sogar aktiver als andere Mitglieder, was dafür spricht, dass wie in Abschn. 2 angenommen, die Sanktionen anderer Mitglieder das Aktivitätsniveau bestimmen. Wer wegen des Einflusses von Familie und Freunden Parteimitglied wird, wird von diesen Personen vor allem in kleinen Kreisverbänden, in denen es stärker auf den Beitrag jedes Einzelnen ankommt, dazu angehalten,

---

[5] Der Unterschied zwischen den neuen und alten Bundesländern (genauer: der SPD) liegt darin, dass Mitglieder mit starken normativen Motiven in den neuen Bundesländern mit steigender Mitgliederzahl noch inaktiver werden als andere Mitglieder, während sie in der West-SPD nur weniger aktiv werden.

nicht nur passives Mitglied zu sein. Um diese Erklärung abschließend zu prüfen, würde es aber einer Netzwerkanalyse von Parteimitgliedern bedürfen.

6 Zusammenfassung und Diskussion

Ziel des vorliegenden Beitrags war es, den Einfluss der Mitgliederzahl in der lokalen Organisationseinheit politischer Parteien auf das Aktivitätsniveau individueller Mitglieder zu prüfen. Olsons (1965) Annahmen zur Kollektivgutproblematik bilden die theoretische Grundlage: Mit steigender Mitgliederzahl im Kreisverband, d. h. in der für den größten Teil aller Parteimitglieder wahrnehmbaren Organisationsebene, sollte die Aktivität des einzelnen Mitglieds geringer werden, da erstens der eigene Beitrag an der Produktion des Kollektivguts „Durchsetzung politischer Interessen" als unerheblich wahrgenommen wird und zweitens niemand von der Nutznießung dieses Kollektivguts ausgeschlossen werden kann. Insgesamt wird sich ein rational handelndes Parteimitlied mit steigender Mitgliederzahl eher für diejenige Handlungsalternative entscheiden, die mit einer günstigeren Kosten-Nutzen-Bilanz verbunden ist: Inaktivität (*H1*). Ausnahmen gelten für diejenigen Mitglieder, die aus der Aktivität einen zusätzlichen, individuellen (selektiven) Nutzen ziehen, z. B. weil sie mit ihrer Hilfe Ämter besetzen oder ausüben können oder weil die Parteiarbeit an sich mit positiven Konsequenzen (Spaß, Zusammentreffen mit anderen politisch Interessierten) verbunden ist (*H2b*). Diese Mitglieder sollten darüber hinaus unabhängig von der Mitgliederzahl in der lokalen Organisationseinheit der Partei mehr Aktivität zeigen (*H2a*). Gegenteilige Effekte können für Mitglieder angenommen werden, für die nicht die Durchsetzung politische Ziele der Grund für ihre Parteimitgliedschaft sind: Parteimitglieder, die sich vor allem wegen des Einflusses von Familie und Freunden einer Partei angeschlossen haben (normative Anreize). Sie ziehen einen geringen Nutzen aus dem Kollektivgut, ihre durch innerparteiliche Aktivität verursachten Kosten sind entsprechend relativ hoch, und sie sollten eine geringe Bereitschaft zu innerparteilicher Aktivität aufweisen (*H3a*). Zudem sollten diese Parteimitglieder ihre Entscheidung für oder gegen Aktivität ausschließlich von den Kosten abhängig machen, die (In-)Aktivität mit sich bringt. Da mit steigender Gruppengröße die Kosten durch negative Sanktionen von Seiten der anderen Mitglieder sinken, sollte der mit steigender Wichtigkeit normativer Anreize für die Mitgliedschaft der negative Einfluss der lokalen Mitgliederzahl auf die Intensität innerparteilicher Aktivität ebenfalls steigen (*H3b*).

Zur Prüfung der Hypothesen wurden Daten der schriftlichen Befragung der Deutschen Parteimitgliederstudie 2009 verwendet, die Aussagen über alle Mitglieder der CDU, CSU, SPD, FDP und Bündnis 90/Die Grünen zu diesem Zeitpunkt ermöglicht. Neben einer Betrachtung der gesamten Bundesrepublik Deutschland wurden alte und neue Bundesländer zusätzlich getrennt betrachtet, um den unterschiedlichen Organisationsstrukturen und politischen Traditionen der beiden Regionen Rechnung zu tragen.

Als Ergebnis der Mehrebenen-Regressionsanalysen kann festgehalten werden, dass sich Hypothese *H1* nur in den neuen Bundesländern bewährt hat: Mit steigender Mitgliederzahl sinkt das individuelle Aktivitätsniveau eines Parteimitglieds. In den alten Bundesländern ist der Einfluss der Mitgliederzahl dagegen wider Erwarten positiv. Weiteren Analysen zufolge ist dies allerdings ausschließlich auf die SPD zurückzuführen, und er ist in kleinen oder mitgliederschwachen Kreisen stärker als in den SPD-„Hochburgen". Es ist möglich, dass eine Kombination aus einer Konkurrenzsituation mit einer starken CDU/CSU in diesen Kreisen, der SPD als „Juniorpartner" in einer großen Koalition und die zeitliche Nähe zur nächsten Bundestagswahl zur Aktivierung der SPD-Mitglieder beitragen. Der geringe Erklärungsanteil des Kreises (1,5 % der Gesamtvarianz) weist aber darauf hin, dass die Frage, warum SPD-Mitglieder in den alten Bundesländern mit zunehmender Mitgliederzahl aktiver werden, für alle praktischen Zwecke von untergeordneter Bedeutung ist.

Das mit Hypothese *H2a* angenommene höhere Aktivitätsniveau von Parteimitgliedern, für die selektive Anreize wichtig sind, konnte übereinstimmend mit anderen Untersuchungen (vgl. Gallagher et al. 2002; Seyd und Whiteley 2002; Whiteley und Seyd 1996) nachgewiesen werden. Hypothese *H2b* hat sich nicht bewährt: Selektive Anreize stellen keinen „Schutz" vor dem negativen Einfluss einer steigenden Mitgliederzahl auf die individuelle Aktivität dar. Dafür hat sich übereinstimmend mit Hypothese *H3b* gezeigt, dass mit normativen Motiven eine verstärkte Neigung zum Trittbrettfahren einhergeht. Gleichzeitig beeinflussen normative Anreize nicht wie erwartet das Aktivitätsniveau unabhängig von der Mitgliederzahl (Hypothese *H3a*). Somit sind Mitglieder mit starken normativen Motiven nur in mitgliederstarken Kreisen relativ inaktiv, in kleinen Kreisen dagegen aktiver als andere, was für einen Einfluss unterschiedlich starker sozialer Sanktionen in großen und kleinen Kreisen spricht. Unsere Ergebnisse sprechen dafür, dass der Begriff des „individuellen Nutzens" weiter gefasst werden muss, als es gemeinhin der Fall ist. Soziale Sanktionen scheinen ähnlich wie ein Parteiamt oder der Spaß an der politischen Arbeit mit einem solchen Nutzen verbunden zu sein.

Die unterschiedliche Erklärungskraft, d. h. Bedeutung des Kontextes für das individuelle Aktivitätsniveau in Ost und West bedarf abschließend einer genaueren Betrachtung. Es ist grundsätzlich möglich, dass die höheren ICCs in den neuen Bundesländern lediglich auf Kompositionseffekte zurückzuführen sind, d. h. die Kreise nur deshalb unterschiedliche durchschnittliche Aktivitätsniveaus aufweisen, weil sich ihre Mitglieder in mindestens einem Individualmerkmal unterschieden, dass hoch mit dem Aktivitätsniveau korreliert. Gegen diese Erklärung spricht allerdings der hohe Anteil erklärter Varianz auf der Individualebene (25,0 %) sowie die Tatsache, dass wir diejenigen Variablen, die sich in anderen Studien als zentrale Erklärungsfaktoren für innerparteiliche Aktivität erwiesen haben, in den Regressionsmodellen berücksichtigt haben.

Es ist theoretisch auch möglich, dass unser Ergebnis ein Artefakt darstellt, dass durch die Verwendung von Kreis- statt Ortsverbänden auf der Makroebene verursacht wird. Die Betrachtung einer zu hohen Aggregatebene bedeutet in der Regel, dass durch die Homogenisierung von Kontextmerkmalen mögliche Kontexteffekte unentdeckt bleiben können (vgl. Nonnenmacher 2007, 2013), Kontexthypothesen also vorschnell abgelehnt werden. Zumindest theoretisch ist es aber auch möglich, dass durch die Zusammenfassung von Orts- zu Kreisverbänden der Anteil der Zwischengruppenvarianz an der Gesamtvarianz erhöht wird. Dies ist dann der Fall, wenn das mittlere Aktivitätsniveau in denjenigen Ortsverbänden, die zu einem Kreis gehören, stärker übereinstimmt als das mittlere Aktivitätsniveau in den Ortsvereinen verschiedener Kreise. Dies würde aber wiederum bedeuten, dass offensichtlich nicht der Ortsverein die für das Aktivitätsniveau entscheidende Ebene ist, sondern eben der Kreis. Sollte also diese unwahrscheinliche Konstellation auf unsere Daten zutreffen, hätten wir mit der Betrachtung der Kreise genau die inhaltlich relevante Analyseebene abgebildet.

Eine weitere methodische Erklärung läge darin, dass in unseren Regressionsmodellen mindestens eine zentrale Variable zur Erklärung des Aktivitätsniveaus fehlt, die für den Ost-/West-Unterschied entscheidend ist. Da wir aber alle Merkmale berücksichtigt haben, die nach derzeitigem Stand der Forschung das individuelle Aktivitätsniveau erklären, ist dies unwahrscheinlich.

Eine inhaltliche Erklärung könnte in einer stärkeren „Empfänglichkeit" der Parteimitglieder im Osten für Kontexteinflüsse liegen, genauer: für die Gruppengröße. Hier müssen wir auf die zukünftige Forschung verweisen.

Für politische Parteien in den neuen Bundesländern kann aus unseren Befunden die Schlussfolgerung abgeleitet werden, dass mögliche Bemühungen, neue Mitglieder zu werben, mit einem geringeren Aktivitätsniveau aller Mitglieder erkauft werden müssen. Dies wird in der Praxis nicht bedeuten, dass ab einer bestimmten Zahl ausschließlich inaktive Mitglieder in einem Kreisverband zu finden sind. Es wäre aber auch falsch davon auszugehen, dass mit einer Verdopplung der Mitgliederzahl auch doppelt so viel Parteiarbeit im Wahlkampf, an Informationsständen etc. geleistet werden kann. Um diesem Problem zu begegnen, müssten Parteien Maßnahmen zur Überwindung des Kollektivgutproblems treffen, z. B. zusätzliche selektive Anreize setzen. Besteht ein Kreisverband zu einem erheblichen Anteil aus Personen, die wegen des Einflusses von Familie und Freunden Parteimitglied sind, muss sogar damit gerechnet werden, dass das absolute Aktivitätsniveau sinkt und die Parteiarbeit von wenigen Engagierten geleistet werden muss.

Anhang

Tab. 6 Alte Bundesländer, parteispezifische Mehrebenen-Regressionsanalysen der innerparteilichen Aktivität

	CDU		CSU		SPD Modell 1		SPD Modell 2		FDP		Bündnis 90/ Die Gr90/I	
	B	S.E.	B	S.E.	B	S.E.	B	S.E.	B	S.E.	B	S.E.
Konstante	0,026	0,112	0,143	0,115	0,005	0,095	−0,082	0,109	0,401	0,213	−0,204	0,230
Fixe Effekte (Ebene 1: Individuum)												
Soziodemographische Ressourcen												
Geschlecht: weiblich	−0,013	0,080	−0,019	0,085	−0,005	0,068	−0,000	0,068	0,022	0,076	0,121*	0,054
Alter (/10)	0,518*	0,131	0,275*	0,121	0,122*	0,027	0,124*	0,027	0,167*	0,024	0,386*	0,117
Alter (/10) quadriert	−0,039*	0,012	−0,021*	0,011	–	–	–	–	–	–	−0,027*	0,012
Schulabschluss (Ref.: höchstens Hauptschulabschluss)												
Mittlere Reife/Realschulabschluss	0,054	0,097	−0,038	0,083	0,084	0,090	0,079	0,090	−0,163	0,114	0,098	0,130
(Fach-)Abitur	0,001	0,122	−0,239	0,124	0,014	0,108	0,010	0,108	−0,101	0,120	−0,097	0,127
(Fach-)Hochschulabschluss	−0,043	0,114	−0,126	0,103	0,011	0,107	0,005	0,107	−0,149	0,118	−0,005	0,124
Erwerbsstatus (Ref.: vollzeit-erwerbstätig)												
Teilzeit-erwerbstätig	−0,108	0,116	0,079	0,117	0,054	0,103	0,055	0,103	0,133	0,093	0,019	0,062
Nicht erwerbstätig	−0,036	0,093	−0,076	0,085	−0,104	0,076	−0,104	0,075	0,082	0,074	0,006	0,073
Berufsstatus (ISEI)	0,301	0,263	0,154	0,244	0,011	0,271	0,005	0,271	−0,146	0,257	−0,047	0,214
Kompetenzbezogene Ressourcen												
Politisches Interesse	0,157*	0,054	0,041	0,051	0,168*	0,053	0,164*	0,053	0,206*	0,053	0,126*	0,047
Interne Efficacy	0,152*	0,047	0,136*	0,043	0,110*	0,044	0,111*	0,044	0,097*	0,042	0,119*	0,037
Externe Efficacy	−0,035	0,042	−0,034	0,039	0,054	0,041	0,055	0,041	0,060	0,037	0,072*	0,031
Motivationen												
Selektiv-ergebnisbezogene Anreize	0,104*	0,026	0,108*	0,045	0,091*	0,022	0,091*	0,022	0,093	0,088	−0,018	0,097
Selektiv-prozessbezogene Anreize	0,123*	0,027	0,141*	0,041	0,150*	0,021	0,153*	0,021	0,129	0,081	0,026	0,085
Normative Anreize	−0,025	0,020	−0,051	0,030	0,009	0,015	0,009	0,015	−0,005	0,063	−0,127	0,067
Kollektive Anreize	0,042*	0,021	0,071*	0,019	0,042*	0,021	0,044*	0,021	0,047*	0,020	0,035*	0,016

Tab. 6 (Fortsetzung)

	CDU		CSU		SPD Modell 1		SPD Modell 2		FDP		Bündnis 90/ Die Gr90/l	
	B	S.E.	B	S.E.	B	S.E.	B	S.E.	B	S.E.	B	S.E.
Ideologische Anreize	0,026	0,014	0,012	0,012	0,016	0,012	0,015	0,012	0,039*	0,012	0,049*	0,009
Altruistische Anreize	0,032*	0,013	0,010	0,012	0,006	0,012	0,006	0,012	0,001	0,011	−0,001	0,008
Expressive Anreize	−0,055*	0,016	−0,069*	0,016	−0,072*	0,016	−0,074*	0,016	−0,063*	0,016	−0,087*	0,013
Parteiidentifikation	0,149*	0,056	0,218*	0,049	0,222*	0,051	0,221*	0,051	0,221*	0,051	0,212*	0,045
Fixer Effekt (Ebene 2: Kreis)												
Mitgliederzahl (/100)	0,660	2,842	−0,688	4,721	5,515*	2,186	12,269*	4,321	15,095	10,810	−8,403	11,431
Mitgliederzahl (/100)**2	–	–	–	–	–	–	−79,309**	42,201	–	–	–	–
Einwohner (/1 000 000)	−0,355*	0,176	−0,162	0,295	−0,527*	0,165	−0,419*	0,161	−0,295*	0,128	−0,285*	0,128
Cross-Level-Interaktionen: Mitgliederzahl *												
Selektiv-ergebnisbezogene Anreize	−0,633	1,314	−0,400	2,552	0,857	1,005	0,864	1,006	−0,149	5,041	−7,206	5,356
Selektiv-prozessbezogene Anreize	−0,750	1,353	−0,137	2,305	−0,008	0,869	−0,072	0,872	−0,496	4,673	−5,010	4,704
Normative Anreize	0,704	1,062	2,539	1,634	−1,678*	0,661	−1,658*	0,660	−0,191	3,632	−7,833*	3,731
Cross-Level-Interaktionen: Einwohnerzahl *												
Selektiv-ergebnisbezogene Anreize	0,004	0,078	0,050	0,156	−0,014	0,074	−0,020	0,075	−0,013	0,056	0,033	0,052
Selektiv-prozessbezogene Anreize	0,012	0,081	−0,038	0,140	0,007	0,067	0,011	0,067	−0,075	0,051	0,056	0,046
Normative Anreize	−0,003	0,066	−0,098	0,101	0,094	0,048	0,092	0,048	−0,034	0,042	0,040	0,039
Zufallseffekte	*Varianzkomp.*		*Varianzkomp.*		*Varianzkomp.*		*Varianzkomp.*		*Varianzkomp.*		*Varianzkomp.*	
Ebene 1: Individuum (e_{0j})	2,046	0,123	0,642	0,036	1,884	0,105	1,907	0,105	0,215	0,012	0,107	0,005
Ebene 2: Kreis (u_{0j})	0,008	0,000	0,004	0,010	0,029	0,019	0,016	0,017	0,022	0,018	0,033	0,014
N (Ebene 1/Ebene 2)	679/184		693/80		792/222		792/222		799/226		999/237	

*$p \leq 0{,}05$; **$p \leq 0{,}1$

Tab. 7 Alte Bundesländer, parteispezifische ICCs

	CDU		CSU		SPD		FDP		BDPle parte-Die Grünen	
	B	S.E.	B	S.E.	B	S.E.	B	S.E.	B	S.E.
Konstante	−0,078*	0,036	−0,086*	0,037	−0,005	0,038	0,109*	0,037	0,017	0,040
Zufallseffekte	Varianzkomp.		Varianzkomp.		Varianzkomp.		Varianzkomp.		Varianzkomp.	
Ebene 1: Individuum (e_{0j})	3,260	0,172	1,029	0,052	3,178	0,157	0,388	0,019	0,187	0,009
Ebene 2: Kreis (u_{0j})	0,016	0,023	0,019	0,016	0,048	0,027	0,031	0,026	0,135	0,033
N (Ebene 1/2)	854/193		854/92		974/238		969/239		1140/247	
ICC	0,005		0,018		0,015		0,074		0,419	

Literatur

Alemann, Ulrich von Philipp Erbentraut, und Jens Walther. 2010. *Das Parteiensystem der Bundesrepublik Deutschland* (4. Aufl.). Wiesbaden: VS Verlag für Sozialwissenschaften.

Dillman, Don A. 1978. *Mail and telephone surveys. The total design method.* New York: Wiley.

Fiers, Stefaan, Ine Vanlangenakker und Caroline Inglese. 2007. Who wants to/the party? The meaning of party membership in an eroding partitocracy. Working Paper for the ECPR Joint Sessions. Helsinki.

Fisher, Justin, David Denver und Gordon Hands. 2006. Party membership and campaign activity in Britain. The impact of electoral performance. *Party Politics* 12:505–519.

Gallagher, Michael, Vanessa Liston, Michael Marsh und Liam Weeks. 2002. Explaining activism levels among fine Gael members. A test of the general incentives model. *Irish Political Studies* 17:97–113.

Hansen, Bernhard, und Knut Heidar. 2005. *Party member activism in Denmark and Norway – A question of party?* Working Paper. Oslo.

Heidar, Knut, und Jo Saglie. 2003. A decline of linkage? Intra-party participation in Norway, 1991–2000. *European Journal of Political Research* 42:761–786.

Klein, Markus. 2006. Partizipation in politischen Parteien. Eine empirische Analyse des Mobilisierungspotenzials politischer Parteien sowie der Struktur innerparteilicher Partizipation in Deutschland. *Politische Vierteljahresschrift* 47:35–61.

Klein, Markus. 2011. Was wissen wir über die Mitglieder der Parteien? In *Parteimitglieder in Deutschland*, Hrsg. Tim Spier, Markus Klein, Ulrich von Alemann, Hanna Hoffmann, Annika Laux, Alexandra Nonnenmacher und Katharina Rohrbach, 31–38. Wiesbaden: VS Verlag für Sozialwissenschaften.

Leighley, Jan E. 1995. Attitudes, opportunities and incentives. A field essay on political participation. *Political Research Quarterly* 48:181–209.

Maas, Cora J., und Joop J. Hox. 2005. Sufficient sample size for multilevel modeling. *Methodology* 1:89–92.

Mair, Peter, und Ingrid van Biezen. 2001. Party membership in twenty European democracies, 1980–2000. *Party Politics* 7:5–21.

Michels, Robert. 1925. *Zur Soziologie des Parteiwesens in der modernen Demokratie* (2. Aufl.). Stuttgart: Kröner.

Morales, Laura. 2009. Joining political organisations. *Institutions, mobilisation and participation in western democracies.* Colchester: ECPR Press.

Niedermayer, Oskar. 1989. *Innerparteiliche Partizipation.* Opladen: Westdeutscher Verlag.

Niedermayer, Oskar. 2002. Beweggründe des Engagements in politischen Parteien. In *Parteiendemokratie in Deutschland* (2. Aufl.), Hrsg. Oscar W. Gabriel, Oskar Niedermayer und Richard Stöss, 297–311. Wiesbaden: Westdeutscher Verlag.

Nonnenmacher, Alexandra. 2007. Eignen sich Stadtteile für den Nachweis von Kontexteffekten? Eine empirische Analyse am Beispiel von Disorder und Kriminalitätsfurcht. *Kölner Zeitschrift für Soziologie und Sozialpsychologie* 59:493–511.

Nonnenmacher, Alexandra. 2013. Zur Nachweisbarkeit von Kontexteffekten der sozialräumlichen Umgebung. In *Städtische Armutsquartiere – Kriminelle Lebenswelten*, Hrsg. Dietrich Oberwittler, Susann Rabold und Dirk Baier, 293–319. Wiesbaden: Springer VS.

Olson, Mancur. 1965. *The logic of collective action: Public goods and the theory of groups.* Cambridge: Harvard University Press.

Pedersen, Karina, Lars Bille, Roger Buch, Jørgen Elklit, Bernhard Hansen und Hans Jørgen Nielsen. 2004. Sleeping or active partners? Danish party members at the turn of the millenium. *Party Politics* 10:367–383.

Rüdig, Wolfgang, Lynn G. Bennie und Mark N. Franklin. 1991. *Green party members. A profile.* Glasgow: Delta Publications.

Scarrow, Susan E. 2000. Parties without members? Party organization in a changing electoral environment. In *Parties without partisans. Political change in advanced industrial democracies*, Hrsg. Russell J. Dalton und Martin P. Wattenberg, 79–101. Oxford: Oxford University Press.

Seyd, Patrick, und Paul Whiteley. 1992. *Labour's grass roots. The politics of party membership.* Oxford: Clarendon Press.

Seyd, Patrick, und Paul Whiteley. 2002. *New Labour's grass roots. The transformation of the Labour party membership.* Basingstoke: Palgrave Macmillan.

Seyd, Patrick, Paul Whiteley und Jon Parry. 1996. *Labour and conservative party members 1990 – 92.* Aldershot et al.: Dartmouth.

Spier, Tim. 2010. Wer wird Funktionär? Determinanten der Erlangung lokaler politischer Ämter in den Bundestagsparteien. In *Parteien als fragmentierte Organisationen. Erfolgsbedingungen und Veränderungsprozesse*, Hrsg. Uwe Jun und Benjamin Höhne, 123–151. Opladen: Barbara Budrich.

Spier, Tim. 2011. Wie aktiv sind die Mitglieder in Parteien? In *Parteimitglieder in Deutschland*, Hrsg. Tim Spier, Markus Klein, Ulrich von Alemann, Hanna Hoffmann, Annika Laux, Alexandra Nonnenmacher und Katharina Rohrbach, 97–119. Wiesbaden: VS Verlag für Sozialwissenschaften.

Tan, Alexander C. 1998. The impacts of party membership size. A cross-national analysis. *The Journal of Politics* 60:188–198.

Theall, Katherine P., Richard Scribner, Sarah Lynch, Neal Simonsen, Matthias Schonlau, Bradley Carlin und Deborah Cohen. 2008. *Impact of small size on neighborhood influences in multilevel models.* Munich Personal RePEc Archive Nr. 11648.

van Biezen, Ingrid, und Thomas Poguntke. 2014. The decline of membership-based politics. *Party Politics* 20:205–216.

van Biezen, Ingrid, Peter Mair und Thomas Poguntke. 2012. Going, going, ... gone? The decline of party membership in contemporary Europe. *European Journal of Political Research* 51:24–56.

Verba, Sidney, und Norman H. Nie. 1972. *Participation in America. Political democracy and social equality.* New York: Harper Row.

Whiteley, Paul, und Patrick Seyd. 1996. Rationality and party activism. Encompassing tests of alternative models of political participation. *European Journal of Political Research* 29:215–234.

Whiteley, Paul, und Patrick Seyd. 2002. *High intensity participation. The dynamics of party activism in Britain.* Ann Arbor: University of Michigan.

Whiteley, Paul, Patrick Seyd, Jeremy Richardson und Paul Bissell.1993. Explaining party activism. The case of the British Conservative Party. *British Journal of Political Science* 24:79–94.

Alexandra Nonnenmacher, 1970, Prof. Dr., Studium der Soziologie, Psychologie und Philosophie. 2008 Promotion an der Universität zu Köln, 2008–2012 Akademische Rätin am Institut für Politische Wissenschaft der Leibniz Universität Hannover, 2009–2011 Vertretung der Professur für Empirische Sozialforschung im Fachbereich Gesellschaftswissenschaften der Universität Kassel. Seit 2012 Professorin für Methoden der empirischen Bildungs- und Sozialforschung an der Universität Siegen. Forschungsschwerpunkte: Kontexteffekte, insb. Methoden und Methodologie; städtische Armutsgebiete; politische Soziologie. Aktuelle Veröffentlichungen: Zur Nachweisbarkeit von Kontexteffekten der sozialräumlichen Umgebung, in: Städtische Armutsquartiere – Kriminelle Lebenswelten? Wiesbaden 2013 (Hrsg. D. Oberwittler, S. Rabold und D. Baier); The missing link: deficits of country-level studies. A review of 22 articles explaining well-being. Social Indicators Research 110, 2013 (mit J. Friedrichs); Parteimitglieder in Deutschland. Wiesbaden 2011 (hrsg. zusammen mit T. Spier, M. Klein, U. von Alemann, H. Hoffmann, A. Laux und K. Rohrbach).

Tim Spier, 1975, Prof. Dr., Studium der Politikwissenschaft und Rechtswissenschaft an der Georg-August-Universität Göttingen, Promotionsstudium am dortigen Graduiertenkolleg „Die Zukunft des Europäischen Sozialmodells" 2003–2006. 2007–2008 Wissenschaftlicher Mitarbeiter am Institut für Parteienrecht und Parteienforschung der Heinrich-Heine-Universität Düsseldorf, 2009–2012 Akademischer Rat am Institut für Sozialwissenschaften derselben Universität. Seit 2012 Juniorprofessor für Politikwissenschaft mit dem Schwerpunkt „Politisches System der Bundesrepublik Deutschland" an der Universität Siegen. Forschungsschwerpunkte: empirische Wahl-, Koalitions- und Parteienforschung. Aktuelle Veröffentlichungen: Parteien ohne Mitglieder? Baden-Baden 2013 (hrsg. mit U. von Alemann und M. Morlok); Parteimitglieder in Deutschland. Wiesbaden 2011 (hrsg. mit M. Klein, U. von Alemann, H. Hoffmann, A. Laux, A. Nonnenmacher und K. Rohrbach).

Social Networks and Social Settings: Developing a Coevolutionary View

Alessandro Lomi · Christoph Stadtfeld

© Springer Fachmedien Wiesbaden 2014

Abstract One way to think about social context is as a sample of alters. To understand individual action, therefore, it matters greatly where these alters may be coming from, and how they are connected. According to one vision, connections among alters induce local dependencies—emergent rules of social interaction that generate endogenously the observed network structure of social settings. Social selection is the decision of interest in this perspective. According to a second vision, social settings are collections of social foci—physical or symbolic locales where actors meet. Because alters are more likely to be drawn from focused sets, shared social foci are frequently considered as the main generators of network ties, and hence of setting structure. Affiliation to social foci is the decision of central interest in this second view. In this paper we show how stochastic actor–oriented models (SAOMs) originally derived for studying the dynamics of multiple networks may be adopted to represent and examine these interconnected systems of decisions (selection and affiliation) within a unified analytical framework. We illustrate the empirical value of the model in the context of a longitudinal sample of adolescent participating in the Glasgow Teenage Friends and Lifestyle Study. Social selection decisions are examined in the context of networks of friendship relations. The analysis treats musical genres as the main social foci of interest.

Keywords Networks · Affiliation · Social networks · Social selection · Social foci · Stochastic actor-oriented models

---

A. Lomi (✉) · C. Stadtfeld
Università della Svizzera italiana,
Via Guiseppe Buffi 13, 6904 Lugano, Switzerland
e-mail: alessandro.lomi@usi.ch

C. Stadtfeld
e-mail: christoph.stadtfeld@usi.ch

Soziale Netzwerke und Soziale Situationen: Ein co-evolutionäres Modell

Zusammenfassung Eine Möglichkeit, soziale Kontexte zu bestimmen, ist, sie als Stichprobe von Alteri zu definieren. Um individuelles Handeln zu verstehen, ist es wichtig zu wissen, woher diese Alteri kommen und wie sie miteinander verbunden sind. Einem Ansatz zufolge führen Beziehungen zwischen Alteri zu lokalen Abhängigkeiten. Es entstehen Regeln der sozialen Interaktion, die endogen die beobachtete Netzwerkstruktur von sozialen Situationen (settings) ausmachen. Hier geht es um die sozialen Wahlen. Einem anderen Ansatz nach sind soziale Situationen Sammlungen von sozialen Foci, also physischen oder symbolischen Räumen, in denen sich Personen treffen. Weil die Alteri eher aus den Foci stammen, werden soziale Foci häufig als die wichtigsten Ursachen für Netzwerk-Bindungen, und damit der Struktur der Situation, angesehen. Die Bindung an einen sozialen Focus ist das zentrale Interesse in diesem zweiten Ansatz. In unserem Beitrag zeigen wir, wie sich stochastische Akteurs-orientierte Modelle (SAOMs), die ursprünglich für die Analyse dynamischer multipler Netzwerke gedacht waren, auf miteinander verbundene Systeme von Entscheidungen (Wahl und Zugehörigkeit) in einem einheitlichen analytischen Bezugsrahmen anwenden lassen. Wir zeigen den empirischen Wert unseres Modells an einer Längsschnitt-Studie von Jugendlichen in der *Glasgow Teenage Friends and Lifestyle Study*. Die sozialen Wahlen werden im Kontext von Netzwerken von Freundschaften untersucht; dabei werden musikalische Genres als der wichtigste soziale Focus herausgearbeitet.

Schlüsselwörter Netzwerke · Soziale Wahlen · Zugehörigkeit · Soziale Foci · Stochastic actor-oriented models

1 Introduction

The notion of "alters"[1] as social context *(Die Anderen als sozialer Kontext)*—clearly articulated by Andreas Diekmann elsewhere in this special issue—brings to mind Jean Paul Sartre's vision of hell. It also prompts a fundamental question: Where do these alters come from? A major line of contemporary research in the analysis of social networks takes this question as the starting point for the specification of multiple dependence mechanisms between the network ties that link actors, and settings defined as subsets of possible alters (for recent comprehensive reviews see Rivera et al. 2010; Snijders 2011).

In a foundational contribution to the development of this line of research, Pattison and Robins (2002) propose the view of social networks as constructed locally through concatenation of local rules of social selection. These mechanisms operate in overlapping regions called social neighborhoods or—sites of interaction corresponding to subsets of possible network ties (Pattison and Robins 2002, p. 301). In

---

[1] Throughout the manuscript we use the less correct but more common plural form "alters" rather than "alteri".

this perspective, the composition of ego's social context (or setting)[2] is regulated by endogenous association-based mechanisms defined over local social neighborhoods. In recent years, substantial progress in statistical modeling of social networks has progressively refined and extended the menu of social mechanisms available for constructing and sustaining social settings (Snijders et al. 2006; Robins et al. 2007).

This view of social settings as local network neighborhoods that generate "Contingencies among possible network ties" (Pattison and Robins 2002, p. 305) is consistent with the notion of "setting as alters". This view also provides one possible analytical strategy to address associated questions about the mechanisms that regulate the selection of alters into social settings (Robins et al. 2001).

More recent research has revealed that local network neighborhoods are themselves embedded in larger structures that may span multiple levels of action—or layers of the social system (Wang et al. 2013). This is best illustrated by studies of formal organizations where individuals are members in units that are hierarchically nested in other—progressively more aggregate units connected by formal dependence relations (Borgatti and Foster 2003; Lazega et al. 2008; Lomi et al. 2014; Lusher et al. 2012; Rank et al. 2010).

The multilevel character of social settings that these more recent studies emphasize apparently exposes the view of "network neighborhoods as social settings" to the criticism that: "Unfortunately the study of social networks has often been carried out without concern for the origins in the larger social context. Most network analysis ends with the description and labeling of patterns; and when explanations of patterns are offered, they frequently rely upon inherent tendencies within networks to become consistent, balanced, or transitive" Feld 1981, p. 1015).

Clearly, this view is based on a sociological concept of context not simply as "alters," but rather as a collection of differentiated social foci or "Social, psychological, legal, or physical entit(ies) around which joint activities are organized (e.g., workplaces, voluntary organizations, families etc)" (Feld 1981, p. 1015). Like network neighborhoods, social foci tend to induce dependence relations among participants because: "[A]s a consequence of interaction associated with their joint activities, individuals whose activities are organized around the same focus will tend to become interpersonally tied and form a cluster" (Feld 1981, p. 1015). The consequence of this argument is that analysis of how individuals construct their social setting through interaction with a limited number of other individuals (their "alters") requires information about how individual interact in extra-network foci. According to Feld, (1981, p. 1016): "Without such contextual information, conclusions about networks and their consequences are likely to be incomplete and even misleading".

This argument reveals a clear tension in our theoretical understanding of social context and in our attempt to clarify the mechanisms through which contexts (settings) are constructed. Clearly, alters are not randomly sampled from populations of possible associates. Network ties create dependencies that affect this sampling process in predictable directions (Robins et al. 2005). Yet, alters are more likely to be

---

[2] Throughout the manuscript we do not provide explicitly different definitions for social "settings" and "contexts".

drawn from sets defined by joint participation in social foci—from "focused sets" in Feld's words (1982, p. 798).

In general, this discussion suggests that it would be desirable to have an analytical framework that allows both views to be integrated and their relative empirical value appraised. Such an analytical framework would be consistent with Pattison and Robins (2004) more comprehensive notion of social spaces—or contexts that are combined across multiple levels. To progress beyond programmatic statement, the notion of social space requires mutual articulation of the mechanisms through which actors construct their social setting, and the mechanisms through which actors choose the social foci in which they participate. The former set of mechanisms control social selection decisions ultimately giving rise to a social setting as defined by Pattison and Robins (2002). The latter set of mechanisms control participation in social foci ultimately giving rise to an affiliation network of individuals-by-foci, and hence to a social setting as defined by Feld (1981).

The objective of this paper is to illustrate how recent advances in Stochastic Actor Oriented Models (SAOMs) provide this analytical framework, and how such models may be adopted to reconcile the rival intellectual traditions we have briefly outlined. More specifically we adopt the recent SAOM for the co-evolution of one-mode and two-mode networks recently derived by Snijders et al. (2013) to specify multi-level mechanisms that connect individuals to social settings through social foci and social networks.

To establish the empirical value of the model we propose, we use data collected by Bush et al. (1997) in the context of the Glasgow Teenage Friends and Lifestyle Study. The analysis focuses on the coevolutionary relation linking change of friendship ties among adolescents and change in their preferences for music genres (See also Steglich et al. 2006 for a recent reanalysis of the same data). In the analysis we present, music genres play the role of social foci (Feld 1981)—occasions that facilitate the creation of direct network ties. The tendency of similarity in musical tastes (and patterns of cultural consumption in more general terms) to generate or stabilize social relation has been long recognized (Bryson 1996; van Eijck 2001; Lewis et al. 2008). We define affiliation-based closure as a multilevel network mechanism generating social relations through joint participation in focused activities (McPherson et al. 2001). We define association-based closure as a multilevel mechanism generating similarity in patterns of affiliation to social foci from the existence of network ties among adolescents (Wang et al. 2013). The objective of the analysis contained in the empirical part of the paper is to establish which one of these alternative mechanisms of multilevel closure better explains the coevolutionary dynamics of social setting and social networks among the adolescents in the sample.

2 Multilevel mechanisms linking networks and setting

Relations from nowhere do not exist. Like other social processes relations exist in settings. Settings are contingent times and places where actors meet and establish network ties—places in which individual action is situated (Abbott 1997).

For the purpose of the argument that we want to develop in this paper, the relevant feature of social settings is that they are internally differentiated in the sense that they: "Can be seen as consisting of a number of different foci and individuals, each individual is related to some foci and not to others" (Feld 1981, p. 1016). As we will see in the next section, it is precisely this internal articulation of social settings into differentiated foci that allows their representation as two-mode (or "affiliation") networks—i.e., networks containing two distinct sets of elements and for which relations are defined only between elements in different sets (Wasserman and Faust 1994).

This representation is commonly found, more or less explicitly, in a variety of studies. Examples of social foci include, among many others: (i) committees in which politicians participate (Padgett 1990); (ii) social events that actors attend (Borgatti and Everett 1997; Davis et al. 1941); (iii) investment syndicates formed by venture capital firms (Sorenson and Stuart 2008); (iv) physical locations where individuals meet like, for example, streets, bars or shops (Whyte 1943); (v) facts that team members know (Carley 1991); (vi) companies that students may be willing to consider as potential employers (Snijders et al. 2013); (vii) issue areas attracting the attention of Supreme Court justices (Breiger 2000); (viii) social identities that relief organizations associate to administrative practices (Breiger and Mohr 2004; Mohr and Duquenne 1997); (ix) companies connected by shared members in their board of directors (Robins and Alexander 2004), and (x) projects in which different kinds of organizations are involved within broader civic arenas (Mische and Pattison 2000).

In all these examples, social settings (e.g., civic arenas) are collections of differentiated social foci (e.g., projects) in which actors (e.g., organizations) are jointly involved (Mische and Pattison 2000). In all these examples, individuals participating in the same social foci have been found to be more likely to become connected by direct network ties than individuals participating in different foci. This is the case because joint affiliation to specific social foci increases mutual awareness and provides opportunities for commensuration (Stinchcombe 2002)—i.e., for the discovery and appraisal of similarities and differences that are frequently considered as the main antecedents of network ties (McPherson et al. 2001). Therefore, while obviously different, the various examples of social foci we have listed are also fundamentally similar in that: "[I]ndividuals whose activities are organized around the same focus will tend to become interpersonally tied and form a cluster" (Feld 1981, p. 1016). The examples discussed are also similar in that they all involve forms of bipartite association between the rows ("actor") and the columns ("foci") of an affiliation network.

In network terms, Feld's hypothesis implies that social settings affect the dynamics of social networks through a process of closure by affiliation or "affiliation-based closure": individuals becoming connected through social relations generated by joint participation (or interest) in specific dimensions of their settings. The process postulated by Feld (1981) is "affiliation-based" because individual decisions to establish direct network ties depend on joint affiliation to social foci. The process may be defined as "closure" because it induces bipartite clustering as illustrated in the lower panel of Fig. 1. Affiliation-based closure involves a multilevel process because it involves relations between entities defined at different levels of analysis and observation: individuals (white circles) and social foci (red squares).

Fig. 1 Closure by association (*above*), and closure by affiliation (*below*). *White circles* are individuals. *Red squares* are social foci. *Blue edges* represent social relations between individuals. *Black edges* represent affiliation ties linking individuals to social foci. *Dashed edges* are connections not yet existing at time *t*

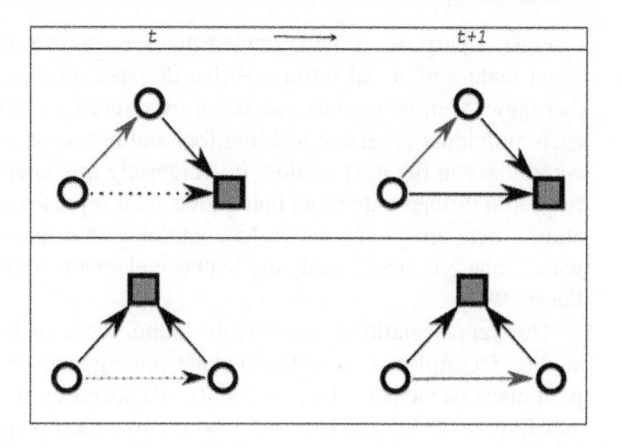

The argument that we have developed so far both hides, but at the same time reveals a fundamental duality linking individuals and social foci. Building on Breiger's notion of duality (2002, p. 303) we may say that a social focus "is" the set of actors jointly involved in it. In a fundamental sense, these actors "are" the multiple foci in which they participate. Relations between individuals, therefore, dually imply relations between social foci. This is probably what Feld had in mind when he recommended that (1981, p. 1019): "[I]t is important to remember that the formation of social networks and the relations to foci are interdependent. Once there is a tie between two individuals, these individuals will tend to find and develop new foci around which to organize their joint activity".

This view clearly resonates with the claim that social settings are contingent outcomes generated by social processes connecting individual actors (Pattison and Robins 2004). In this perspective, social networks may affect patterns of affiliation to social settings through a process of closure by association, or "association-based closure": individuals connected through social relations will be more likely to participate in (or build) shared social foci. This process is "association-based" because decisions to participate in specific foci are assumed to be driven by pre-existing social connections between actors. As before, we describe the process as "closure" because it induces a specific form of 2-mode network clustering as illustrated in the upper panel of Fig. 1.

Similarly to affiliation-based closure, association-based closure involves a multi-level process because it involves relations between individuals and social foci that are defined at different levels of analysis (Conaldi et al. 2012).

As it is readily apparent from Fig. 1 (see figures at time t+1 in the column to the right), affiliation-based and association-based closure mechanisms produce outcomes that are observationally indistinguishable in cross-sectional samples, i.e., connected individuals who are affiliated to the same foci. This is an outcome that that students of social networks typically associate with homophily (McPherson et al. 2001) or other forms of attribute-dependent assortative mixing (Rivera et al. 2010). The underlying trajectories responsible for this outcome, however, are very different and may reveal important details on how affiliation to social foci come to link social settings and social networks.

More specifically, mechanisms of affiliation-based closure are consistent with social selection arguments according to which individuals expressing preferences toward the same social foci are more likely to become connected by network ties (Snijders et al. 2013). Mechanisms of association-based closure are more consistent with social influence arguments according to which individuals connected by network ties tend to assimilate the preferences and behavioral orientations of their network partners. While the problem of separating the effects of social selection from those of social influence is well recognized in contemporary social network research (Steglich et al. 2010), available studies have restricted this problem to the analysis of social networks and individual behavioral outcomes. We are aware of no research that has recognized the multilevel character of social selection and social influence process. In the next section we outline a stochastic actor-oriented model recently derived by Snijders et al. (2013) for the coevolution of 1-mode and 2-mode networks that speaks directly to this concern.

3 Social networks coevolving with social settings

One way of linking social networks to social settings to facilitate empirical investigation is to see both as outcomes of coupled processes of change unfolding across different levels.

The first is the level of social ties between actors—the level at which change in network connections between individuals is observable. The second is the level of affiliation ties linking actors to constitutive dimensions of their social setting. Hypotheses about the specific coupling mechanisms connecting these two levels represent the core of the recent extension of stochastic actor-oriented models (SAOMs) proposed by Snijders et al. (2013). Wasserman and Iacobucci (1991) and Skvoretz and Faust (1999) provide earlier example of models inspired by a similar objective.

The model was originally derived for examining the coevolutionary dynamics of change in one-mode and two-mode networks. The model involves two interdependent processes. The first is a social selection process controlling change in network ties defined over the set of all possible ties that may connect social actors. The second is a bipartite affiliation process linking social actors to constitutive dimensions of their social setting ("social foci") defined over the set of all possible associations. The model provides an analytical framework to examine how network ties affect participation in social foci and—at the same time—how joint participation in those foci affects the dynamics of network ties. The former process, operating from ties to settings, is what we called association-based closure. The second process—operating from setting to ties—is what we have called affiliation-based closure. Both processes entail multilevel network closure mechanisms controlling tendencies toward clustering across levels of action (Wang et al. 2013).

To fix ideas, suppose that observations are available at T time points (with $T>2$) on a one-mode ("social") network X with node set N and directed tie variables X_{ij} for $i, j \in N$ ($i \neq j$), indicating the presence of absence of a tie from actor i to actor j (Snijders et al. 2013). In network X, ties connect pairs of actors (i, j) through the existence of a specific social relation. In the empirical case that we present later in the paper, for example, social connectivity in X is determined by change in friendship ties between the adolescents analyzed by Steglich et al. (2006).

Suppose, further, that observations are also available at T time points (with T>2) on a two-mode network Y with tie variables Yia (for i ∈ N, a ∈ A), and with Yia=1 if actor i participates in activity a, and Yia=0 otherwise (Snijders et al. 2013). In the network Y, ties (i, a) affiliate actors to activities, events, sites or any other object that may serve as social foci (Feld 1981). In the empirical example that we present later in the paper Y affiliates actors to musical genres interpreted as social foci (Bush et al. 1997; Pearson and West 2003).

The process of social selection operating on X may be defined in terms of change in network ties (Xij) controlled by the following network evaluation function:

$$f_i^x(x, y) = \sum_k \beta_k^x s_{ki}^x(x, y), \quad (1)$$

The network evaluation function (1) represents the relative propensity of actor i to make a change toward state x of the social network, given that the affiliation network is in state y. In the network evaluation function, $s_{ki}^x(x, y)$ are called effects, and β_k^x are parameters which tell how strongly and in what direction the associated effect affects the change in the network of observed social relations.

The process of bipartite affiliation operating on Y may be defined similarly in terms of change in ties of association (Yia) controlled by the following setting evaluation function:

$$f_i^y(x, y) = \sum_k \beta_k^y s_{ki}^y(x, y), \quad (2)$$

The setting evaluation function (2) represents the relative propensity of actor i to make a change toward state y of the two-mode network, given that the one-mode network has state x. As before, $s_{ki}^y(x, y)$ are called effects, and β_k^y are parameters which tell how strongly and in what direction the associated effect affects the change in the observed affiliation network.

A basic assumption of the model is that actors change at most one tie variable at a time, that is actors decide to create only one new link or dissolve only one existing link at a specific time point. Because in the model the ties are defined as dichotomous, changes in social and affiliation ties can be seen as a toggle of the tie variables, i.e., as changes of Yia or Xij into (1−Yia) or (1−Xij), respectively. Of course, the model also admits the possibility of no change (Snijders et al. 2013).

Both $s_{ki}^x(x, y)$ and $s_{ki}^y(x, y)$ are statistics computed on the observed social and affiliation networks, respectively. They may defined in terms of linear combinations of: (i) endogenous network dependencies created by mechanisms such as, for example, "reciprocity" and "transitivity"; (ii) endogenous 2-mode dependencies such as, for example, the tendency of specific elements of the social setting to attract affiliation ties ("popularity"), and (iii) cross-level dependencies such as, for example, the different types of closure that we have discussed in the prior section (Snijders et al. 2013). Finally, network effects may interact with actor-specific or relation-specific covariates such as, for example, gender, age and spatial distance to control for sources of exogenous variation in the dynamics of social and affiliation networks.

As discussed in Snijders et al. (2010) separate endowment functions may be defined to specify the factors that affect the termination, rather than the creation, of a tie. Such endowment functions may be defined for endogenous as well as exogenous effects. Endowment effects are both conceptually relevant as well as empirical important because a large proportion of observed relationships are replicated—i.e., they exist today because they existed in a prior time period. It is substantially important, therefore, to estimate models that specify mechanisms underlying the creation of new network ties, while controlling for the stabilizing force (or inertia) of preexisting ties. As we will see in the empirical part of the paper, different kinds of multilevel closure display asymmetric tendencies with respect to creation and dissolution processes.

In the section that follows, we situate the model in the analysis of an empirical case that we have selected to illustrate specific aspects of the coevolution of social networks and social settings. More specifically we will narrow the analytical focus on the specification and identification of different paths to multilevel closure as discussed in the prior section. The case is based on data originally collected by Bush et al. (1997) in the context of their Glasgow Teenage Friends and Lifestyle Study. Studies based on these data include Michell (1997); Michell and West (1996); Michell and Amos (1997), Pearson and Michell (2000), and Pearson and West (2003). More recent analyses may be found in Steglich et al. (2006), and in Steglich et al. (2010).

4 Illustration

4.1 Data

The data we use in the empirical part of the paper come from the "Teenage Friends and Lifestyle Study" (Michell and West 1996; Pearson and Michell 2000) that was conducted from 1995–1997 among teenage secondary school pupils in Glasgow, Scotland[3]. We focus on a cohort of 160 adolescent pupils aged 12–14 years at the beginning of the study. Data were collected in three waves with approximately one year between two subsequent measurements. All of the 129 pupils in the sample we analyze were present at the three measurement points.

The longitudinal data set include both individual and relational information. The individual part of the questionnaire is designed to elicit personal information on address, family background, and the consumption of tobacco, alcohol and drugs (Michell and West 1996). The questionnaire also elicited information on individual preferences for music genres (Steglich et al. 2006). The relational part of the questionnaire focused on friendship relations. Each participant could name up to six friends per wave that could potentially be outside the study cohort. On average, pupils named more than three friends within the cohort. In earlier studies, the change of friendship relations was investigated as a dynamic process that partly co-evolves with behavioral variables (not modeled as two-mode structures) such as alcohol consumption or music taste (Steglich et al. 2006; Steglich et al. 2010). We use music

---

[3] We use the data set that is publicly available and may be accessed by visiting: http://www.stats.ox.ac.uk/~snijders/siena/Glasgow_data.htm.

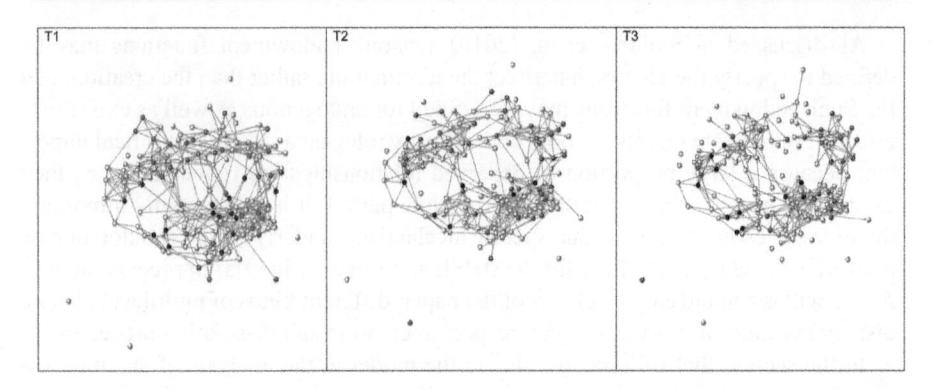

Fig. 2 Friendship networks in the three time periods. Different colors indicate different music tastes. *Back nodes* are "rockers" (adolescents declaring preference for rock music genres) *red nodes* are "ravers" (adolescents declaring preference for rave music genres). The three networks all have the same layout to make structural changes more readily comparable

genres as instances of social foci because received research has long recognized similarity in music tastes to affect the formation, stabilization and erosion of social relations (Lewis et al. 2008).

Figure 2 shows friendship relations among the 160 participants over three data collection waves (1995–1997). Students are marked as circles (nodes). An arrow from a person A to a person B indicates that A nominated B as a friend in the questionnaire of the corresponding wave. Many of the relations are reciprocal. Denser areas in the network indicate that social forces are at play that cause clustering. The colors of the people indicate music preferences: Black nodes are "rockers"—people who indicated their music preference to contain at least three types of rock music in one of the waves. Red nodes are "ravers" and listen to at least four types of electronic ("rave") music. This rough classification already indicates that music taste and friendship seem to be related: Colored nodes seem not to be randomly distributed in the networks but slightly cluster together.

Figure 3 shows the local relational structure of affiliation to seven exemplary music genres interpreted as social foci. As it should be clear from the figure, student one manifests less focused preferences than, say, student 2 who seems to like only rave—a genre (red square) that appears to be particularly popular in the sample. Less popular foci ("techno") are not direct generators of relations between the three adolescents (white circles) depicted in Fig. 3.

Figure 4 aggregates the personal affiliation networks to show the affiliation of all the 139 pupils to 15 different music genres in wave 3. As before, circles represent people, squares represent music genres. A link between a person and a music genre shows that this person indicated that he/she listen to this genre in wave 3. The very popular music genre "chart" is not represented to simplify the visualization. Proximity of two or more music genres in the plot indicates that the same people tend to listen to all these music genres. The visualization reveals several of such clusters of similar music types: electronic or rave music ("rave", "techno", "dance") in the upper part of the figure, rock music and sixties in the right part and classical ("folk", "jazz",

Fig. 3 Affiliation of students 1, 2 and 3 to 8 of 16 musical genres

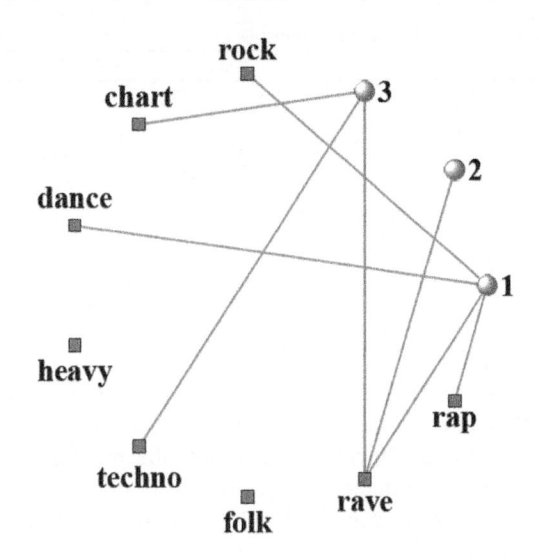

Fig. 4 Two-mode network describing the affiliation of students to 15 music genres (except for "chart"; wave 3 only). The presence of a tie denotes an expressed preference relation

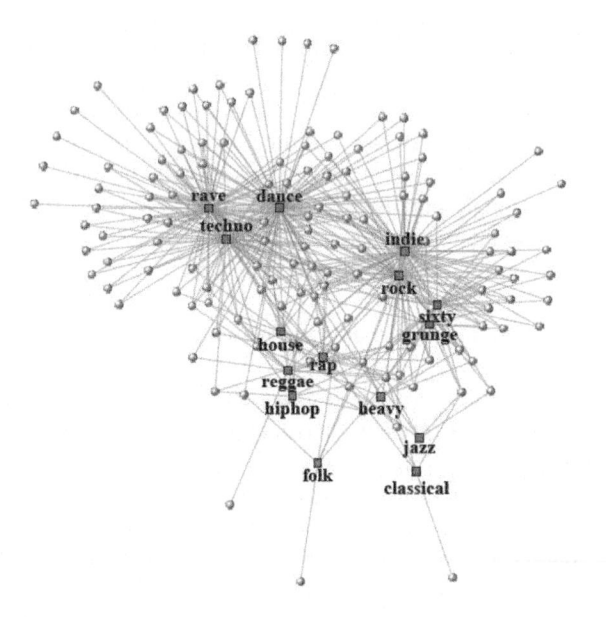

"classical") in the lower part. This observation corresponds to the music genre classification derived by Steglich et al. (2006, p. 52).

Descriptive statistics of the friendship networks in the three data collection waves (1995–1997) are given in Table 1. The number of participants is 160 in total and ranges from 153 in wave 1 to 139 in wave 3. The network density varies between 2.2 and 2.6% which corresponds to average degrees (number of nominated friends within the cohort) between 3.4 (wave 2) and 3.8 (wave 1). The percentage of reciprocal relations ranges between 53.9% (wave 2) and 63.9% (wave 3). Gender homoph-

Table 1 Network descriptive statistics

	Wave 1	Wave 2	Wave 3
Number of participants	153	152	139
Density (%)	2.5	2.2	2.6
Avg. degree	3.8	3.4	3.6
Reciprocity (%)	56.3	53.9	63.6
Same-gender ties (%)	88.6	90.1	90.1
Clustering coefficient (%)	35.8	30.9	41.8
Avg. music genre nominations	3.8	3.3	3.3

ily is an important social force in the formation of the observed friendship networks. This is indicated by the fact that 88.6–90.1 % of all friendship ties are between people of the same gender. Transitivity or local clustering seems to be relevant as well: The clustering coefficient that measures the proportion of closed triangular friendship structures over unclosed triads ranges from 35.8 % (wave 1) to 41.8 % (wave 3). The final descriptive explains the average number of music genre nominations of people which ranges from 3.3 to 3.8.

A further overview of the music genres is given in Table 2. It shows the sixteen music genres from the questionnaire in a ranked list per wave.

"Chart" (which was not shown in Fig. 4) is consistently the most popular music genre and is chosen by between 91 (wave 3) and 104 (wave 1) people. "Classical", on the other hand, is ranked last in two of three waves and only nominated by 4–5 people. The popularity of other music genres is less stable over time. The genres "Indie" and "Sixty" (rank 10 and 11 with 20 and 15 nominations in wave 1) become increasingly popular over time. In wave 3 they are ranked 4 and 7 with then 67 and 31 nominations. "Heavy" rock music (rank 9 with 20 nominations in wave 1) loses popularity. It is only ranked 13 in wave 3 with merely seven nominations.

4.2 Individual attributes and network mechanisms

In our analyses we use three demographic variables as controls: gender, age and spatial distances between parental homes of pupils. Descriptive statistics are reported in Table 3.

Female students represent 47.5 % of the sample. The average age in wave 1 is 13.3 years and ranges from 12.4 to 14.6 years. On average, the parental homes of the pupils are 1.6 km apart with a maximum distance of 9.2 km.

The network mechanisms included in the empirical model specification are summarized in Table 4. Note that the table includes both mechanisms operating at the network level (like, for example, reciprocity) as well as mechanisms operating across levels (like, for example, the various types of bipartite closure we have discussed).

The precise definition of the effects can be found in the R-Siena manual (Ripley et al. 2013). The one-mode effects in the table are defined and discussed in Snijders et al. (2010). Koskinen and Edling (2012), Conaldi et al. (2012) and Snijders et al. (2013) discuss and interpret some of the two-mode and mixed one-mode-two-mode effects included in the model and listed in Table 4. We refer interested readers to consult directly the original sources.

Table 2 Expressed preferences for music genres

Rank	Wave 1		Wave 2		Wave 3	
1	Chart	104	Chart	103	Chart	91
2	Rave	95	Dance	81	Dance	78
3	Dance	90	Rave	80	Rave	68
4	Techno	87	Techno	66	Indie	67
5	Rock	48	Rock	42	Techno	59
6	Rap	43	Indie	39	Rock	48
7	Reggae	33	Rap	30	Sixty	31
8	Grunge	23	Sixty	19	Rap	15
9	Heavy	20	Reggae	17	Reggae	14
10	Indie	20	Heavy	10	House	12
11	Sixty	15	House	10	Grunge	11
12	House	11	Grunge	10	Hiphop	8
13	Hiphop	9	Hiphop	8	Heavy	7
14	Jazz	5	Jazz	7	Folk	6
15	Classical	5	Folk	6	Jazz	5
16	Folk	3	Classical	4	Classical	5

Table 3 Sample descriptive statistics

	Mean	Std. dev.	Min	Max
Gender (% female)	47.5	50.1	0.0	100.0
Age in wave 1	13.3	0.3	12.4	14.6
Spatial distance (km)	1.6	1.2	0.0	9.2

4.3 Empirical model specification and estimation

The model for the coevolution of one-mode (1M or "social") networks and two-mode (or 2M or "affiliation") networks derived by Snijders et al. (2013) is a recent addition to the class of Stochastic Actor Oriented or SAOMs (Snijders 1996). A non-technical introduction of SAOMs can be found in Snijders et al. (2010). More detailed treatments are provided in Snijders (2001), Snijders (2005), and Steglich et al. (2010).

Estimation of the 1M-2M SAOM requires repeated observations on a social network (X) and a related affiliation network (Y) of interest. Both networks are observed in discrete time but (unobserved) change between successive panels takes place in continuous time.

In SAOMs change is decomposed into a two component sub-processes. The first is the timing component which controls the number of opportunities for change that actors face per unit time—the amount of change, as it were. This is captured by a rate function that incorporates assumptions about the distribution of waiting times (Snijders 2005). In the model we estimate in the next section the time component is represented by period-specific rate parameters.

The second is the choice component which summarizes the preferences of the actors. In our case, preference driving change in social network ties are specified in the network evaluation function defined in (1). Preferences driving change in affiliation ties to settings are summarized by the setting evaluation function defined in (2). Further details on model specification are discussed in Snijders et al. (2013).

Table 4 Association and affiliation-based effects included in the model[a]

Effect	Qualitative pattern	Description
Outdegree (friendship)		Tendency to maintain a limited number of friends
Reciprocity		Tendency to reciprocate friendship ties
Transitive triplets		Tendency to become friend with friends of friends
Three-cycles		Tendency towards generalized exchange
Indegree popularity (friendship)		Tendency to nominate popular people as friends
Out-in degree assortativity		Assortative mixing of high outdegree with high indegree individuals: Tendency of students who mention many friends to mention students who are mentioned by many as friends
Affiliation-based closure		Choosing friends with a similar music taste (operationalized as the number of shared preferences)
Outdegree (music genre)		Tendency to maintain a limited set of music preferences
Four-cycles (similar music genre)		Tendency to adopt a music preference that is similar to the music preferences expressed by others with similar preferences
Indegree popularity (music genre)		Tendency to choose music genres that are liked by many others
Association-based closure		Choosing music genres that friends like as well (operationalized as the number of friends who like a particular music genre)

[a]*Red square* Social foci (music genres), *White circles* Individuals (adolescents), *Blue arrows* link between individuals (1-Mode connections), *Black arrows* affiliate individuals to foci (2-mode connections), *Squiggly arrows* potential ties at time t that may become observable at time t+1

The models that we estimate in the next section contain both endogenous effects as well as covariate-related effects. In the friendship network endogenous effects are, for example, the tendency of people to maintain a limited outdegree, to reciprocate friendship nominations and to form and maintain transitive structures in the friendship network. We further control for degree-related effects like indegree popularity. In the music taste network we control for three endogenous effects: the outdegree, the tendency of people to like music tastes that are liked by others with similar preferences (four-cycle effect) and the tendency of individuals to choose music genres that are popular (have a high indegree).

Covariate-related effects in the friendship network are related to the three demographic variables in Table 3. We control for age homophily (the tendency to select friends who have a similar age) and gender homophily. Additionally, we allow differences in the number of sent and received friendship nominations between genders by including an "ego" (sender) and an "alter" (receiver) gender covariate. Further we test whether spatial distance between parental homes influences the tendency to become friends. In the music genre sub model we control whether people who choose a type of music from a certain category (e.g., the rock music genre "grunge") are more likely to choose other music genres from the same category (e.g., the rock music genre "heavy"). Further parameters that are specified are two rate parameters per sub process that indicate the average number of changes per actor per period (e.g., from wave 1 to wave 2) in the two coupled dynamic networks (friendship and music genre affiliation).

Significantly positive (negative) parameters in the network evaluation function suggest that subjects act as if they preferred network configurations in which the correspondent effects have a higher (lower) value. For example, a positive reciprocity parameter may be taken as indication that subjects act *as if* they preferred reciprocated to non-reciprocated relations with partners. As discussed in Snijders et al. (2010) separate endowment functions may be defined to specify the factors that affect the termination, rather than the creation, of a tie. Significantly positive parameters corresponding to the endowment effect associated with reciprocity could be taken as evidence that reciprocated relations are costly to break. As a consequence organizations would prefer to maintain such relations.

In the section that follows, the parameters in the models are estimated by the method of moments using the stochastic approximation algorithms described in Snijders et al. (2007), and implemented in RSiena—an R-based software package designed for the analysis of SAOMs (Ripley et al. 2013).

5 Results

We estimate two models in which we focus on the distinction between "affiliation-based closure" and "association-based closure" while controlling for a number of additional variables.

Each model consists of two sub-models that describe changes in the friendship network and in the music genre affiliation network. By including "affiliation-based closure" in the friendship process and "association-based closure" in the music genre process, both processes become interdependent (coupled) sub processes.

In the first model, we test the general tendency to create *and* to maintain affiliation- and association-based closure structures. In the second model, we model the creation and maintenance of ties within selection and association-based closure structures as separate social processes. Beside these focal "cross-network effects" we control for a number of endogenous effects (changes in a network depending on the state of the same network) and covariate-related effects (changes in the network depending on covariates).

The results of the first model are presented in the left side of Table 5 (Model 1). The focal effects are shown in line 14 (affiliation-based closure) and line 21 (association-based closure). We find no evidence of affiliation-based closure in model 1. The estimate is positive but not significant. However, there is strong evidence for association-based closure. The estimate of 0.43 is highly significant and the effect

Table 5 Estimates of SAOMs for the coevolution of social networks and social settings

	Model 1					Model 2			
	Effect	Estimate	S.E			Effect	Estimate	S.E	
1	Rate 1 (friendship)	14.68	1.41		1	Rate 1 (friendship)	14.80	1.63	
2	Rate 2 (friendship)	11.96	1.09		2	Rate 2 (friendship)	11.62	1.21	
3	Outdegree (friendship)	−2.77	0.19	***	3	Outdegree (friendship)	−2.68	0.19	***
4	Reciprocity	2.07	0.11	***	4	Reciprocity	2.11	0.11	***
5	Transitive triplets	0.73	0.04	***	5	Transitive triplets	0.74	0.05	***
6	Three-cycles	−0.41	0.09	***	6	Three-cycles	−0.42	0.09	***
7	Indegree popularity (friendship)	−0.01	0.03		7	Indegree popularity (friendship)	−0.01	0.03	
8	Out-in degree assortativity	−0.06	0.05		8	Out-in degree assortativity	−0.08	0.05	
9	Age difference	−0.03	0.11		9	Age difference	−0.03	0.11	
10	Spatial distance	−0.13	0.03	***	10	Spatial distance	−0.13	0.04	***
11	Alter female	−0.14	0.09		11	Alter female	−0.17	0.09	
12	Ego female	0.01	0.10		12	Ego female	0.03	0.10	
13	Same gender	0.77	0.09	***	13	Same gender	0.75	0.08	***
14	*Affiliation-based closure*	*0.04*	*0.04*		14	*Maintain: affiliation-based closure*	*−0.38*	*0.17*	*
15	Rate 1 (music genre)	5.29	0.41		15	*Create: affiliation-based closure*	*0.43*	*0.18*	*
16	Rate 2 (music genre)	5.34	0.43		16	Rate 1 (music genre)	5.14	0.39	
17	Outdegree (music genre)	−1.72	0.06	***	17	Rate 2 (music genre)	5.14	0.38	
18	Four-cycles (sim. music tastes)x10	0.01	0.01		18	Outdegree (music genre)	−1.68	0.07	***
19	Indegree popularity (musicgenre)x10	0.02	0.02		19	Four-cycles (sim. music tastes)x10	0.02	0.01	
20	Choosing music in the same category	0.14	0.03	***	20	Indegree popularity (music genre)x10	0.02	0.02	
21	*Association-based closure*	*0.43*	*0.05*	***	21	Choosing music in the same category	0.15	0.03	***
					22	*Maintain: association-based closure*	*0.17*	*0.10*	
					23	*Create: association-based closure*	*0.58*	*0.11*	***

*$p<0.10$; **$p<0.05$; ***$p<0.01$

size is large. Having a friend with a specific music taste increases the probability of adopting or maintaining the same genre preference by 53 % ($e^{0.43}$) compared to a genre no friend is affiliated to. If several friends are affiliated to a specific music genre, the influence effect gets even stronger. Three friends who share a music taste will increase the probability for creating or maintaining an affiliation with this music genre by 260 % ($e^{3*0.63}$) compared to a music genre that is not liked by a friend.

In model 2 (right side of Table 5), we distinguish between the creation and maintenance (using "creation" and "endowment" effects) of the focal closure mechanism. The effects for maintaining vs. creating a friendship tie with people who have the same music taste (affiliation-based closure) are in lines 14 and 15. The effects for maintaining vs. creating the preference for a music genre that is liked by friends are in lines 22 and 23.

Interestingly, now that we distinguish between these fine-grained social processes we indeed find two significant effects for affiliation-based closure that, however, point in different directions. The creation of ties with others who are similar regarding music taste is facilitated (positive "creation" effect 15) but these ties also tend to be easier dropped compared to friendship ties with people who have different music tastes (negative "maintenance" effect 14). The effects sizes are rather large. For example, the probability of becoming friends (create) with someone who shares a preference for a music genre is increased by 53 % ($e^{0.43}$) as compared to a person who does not share any music genre interests.

Both association-based closure effects are positive, however, only the creation effect is significant and the estimate is significantly higher. The general tendency towards association-based closure that we observed in model 1 is, therefore, mostly explained by a very strong creation effect. Students in the sample are very likely to establish ties of affiliation with new music genres based on what they learn from their friends. We find no significant evidence for the process that they will also be more likely to maintain these music tastes over time.

6 Discussion and conclusions

Considering alters as social contexts requires understanding of how the *actual* alters that compose personal networks are selected from populations of *potential* alters. One contemporary analytical tradition rooted in the work of Pattison and Robins (2002) on neighborhood-based models for social interaction addresses this question by emphasizing processes of network self-organization. The structure of social settings emerges from concatenation of local network dependencies involving subsets of relational entities providing possible sites of social interaction (see also Pattison and Robing 2004). A second tradition rooted in the work of Feld (1981, p. 1982) emphasizes the internal segmentation of social setting into social foci to which actors are differentially affiliated. In this perspective, the structure of social settings emerges from contingent patterns of overlapping affiliations to social foci.

Building on recent advances in stochastic actor-oriented models (Snijders et al. 2013), in this paper we have offered a model which attempts to integrate these two analytical traditions by portraying individual association and affiliation decisions as interdependent components of a broader co-evolutionary system. We have defined two multilevel closure mechanisms of theoretical interest: association and affiliation-based closure. We illustrated the empirical value of the model in the context of data on a sample of adolescents collected during the Glasgow Teenage Friends and Lifestyle Study (Bush et al. 1997; Pearson and Michell 2000; Pearson and West 2003). The data were recently re-analyzed by Steglich et al. (2010).

The model we presented was explicitly inspired by models for social space outlined by Pattison and Robins according to whom (2004, p. 11): "Social space cannot be specified simply in geographical, network or sociocultural terms but, rather, requires an understanding of the interdependence of relationships among different types of social entities, such as persons, groups, sociocultural resources and places. We also suggest that social space cannot be regarded as fixed: unlike the Euclidean space of Newtonian mechanics, social space is constructed, at least in part, by the social processes that it supports." The "social space" that Pattison and Robins (2004) define, encompasses both processes of association (generating network ties) and affiliation (generating connections to social foci).

The distinction that our model supports between mechanisms of closure by association (association-based closure), and closure by affiliation (affiliation-based closure) helped us to illuminate important dynamic aspects of the social context we have examined. For example, we found that adolescents affiliated to the same music genres (i.e., sharing membership in the same social foci) are more likely to establish friendship ties and hence become members of the same social neighborhood. Yet, the ties contributing to affiliation-based closure are more fragile than the less frequent ties established between adolescents affiliated to different music genres—ties that are part of open multilevel triads. This result is important because it demonstrate that social foci are not completely impermeable to cross-cutting ties (Lomi et al. 2014). We also found that adolescents associated through direct friendship ties are more likely to participate in similar social foci (association-based closure)—and hence construct overlapping social circles in a Simmelian sense (1955). We found no evidence, however, that friendship ties stabilize patterns of affiliation to social foci (music genres, in the case we have examined).

In conclusion, it seems appropriate to return to the need that Pattison and Robins (2004) identified in their prescient essay on social spaces to: "Introduce an explicit dynamic framework so that we can model the evolution of relational structures, and ultimately the joint evolution of interdependent social processes *at multiple levels of analysis*" (2004, p. 26. Emphasis in the original). One way to frame the contribution of the present paper is as an attempt to heed this call. Our intention has been to make a preliminary step towards establishing an analytical framework for combining social networks and social settings into a broader social space whose constructive mechanisms provide appropriate material for direct empirical investigation.

Acknowledgements Financial support provided by the Swiss National Science Foundation and the European Science Foundation is gratefully acknowledged (Project: Social Influence in Dynamic Networks, Grant number: 133273).

We are grateful to Professor Patrick West and Lynn Michell of the MRC Social and Public Health Sciences Unit, Glasgow University, for making publicly available the data that we use in this article. The original data collection was funded by the Chief Scientist's Office of the Scottish Home and Health Department.

References

Abbott, Andrew. 1997. Of time and space: The contemporary relevance of the Chicago school. *Social Forces* 75:1149–1182.
Borgatti, Steve, and Martin Everett. 1997. Network analysis of 2-mode data. *Social Networks* 19:243–269.
Borgatti, Steve, and Pacey Foster. 2003. The network paradigm in organizational research: A review and typology. *Journal of Management* 29:991–1013.

Breiger, Ronald L. 1974. The duality of persons and groups. *Social Forces* 53:181–190.
Breiger, Ronald L. 2000. A toolkit for practice theory. *Poetics* 27:91–115.
Breiger, Ronald L. 2002. Poststructuralism in organizational studies. In *Social structure and organizations revisited. Research in the sociology of organizations*, eds. Michael Lounsbury and Marc J. Ventresca, 295–305. Bingley: Emerald Group Publishing Limited.
Breiger, Ronald L, and John W. Mohr. 2004. Institutional logics from the aggregation of organizational networks: Operational procedures for the analysis of counted data. *Computational & Mathematical Organization Theory* 10:17–43.
Bryson, Bethany. 1996. "Anything but heavy metal": Symbolic exclusion and musical dislikes. *American Sociological Review* 61:884–899.
Bush, H., Patrick West, and Lynn Michell. 1997. *The role of friendship groups in the uptake and maintenance of smoking amongst pre-adolescent and adolescent children: Distribution of Frequencies.* Working Paper No. 62. MRC Medical Sociology Unit Glasgow.
Carley, Kathleen. 1991. A theory of group stability. *American Sociological Review* 56:331–354.
Conaldi, Guido, Alessandro Lomi, and Marco Tonellato. 2012. Dynamic models of affiliation and the network structure of problem solving in an open source software project. *Organizational Research Methods* 15:385–412.
Davis, Allison, Burleigh B. Gardner, Mary R. Gardner. 1941. *Deep south*. Chicago: The University of Chicago Press.
Diekmann, Andreas. 2014. Die Anderen als sozialer Kontext. Zur Bedeutung strategischer Interaktion. In *Soziale Kontexte und soziale Mechanismen*. Sonderheft 54 der *Kölner Zeitschrift für Soziologie und Sozialpsychologie*, eds. Jürgen Friedrichs und Alexandra Nonnenmacher, 47–68. Wiesbaden: Springer VS.
Feld, Scott L. 1981. The focused organization of social ties. *The American Journal of Sociology* 86:1015–1035.
Feld, Scott L. 1982. Social structural determinants of similarity among associates. *American Sociological Review* 47:797–801.
Koskinen, Johan, and Christopher Edling. 2012. Modelling the evolution of a bipartite network—peer referral in interlocking directorates. *Social Networks* 34:309–322.
Lazega, Emmanuel, Marie Thérèse Jourda, Lise Mounier, and Rafael Stofer. 2008. Catching up with big fish in the big pond? Multilevel network analysis through linked design. *Social Networks* 30:157–176.
Lewis, Kevin, Jason Kaufman, Marco Gonzalez, Andreas Wimmer, and Nicholas Christakis. 2008. Tastes, ties, and time: A new social network dataset using Facebook.com. *Social Networks* 30:330–342.
Lomi, Alessandro, Dean Lusher, Philippa Pattison, and Garry Robins. 2014. The focused organization of advice relations: A case study of boundary-crossing ties in a multi-unit business group. *Organization Science* (Forthcoming).
Lusher, Dean, Garry Robins, Philippa Pattison, and Alessandro Lomi. 2012. Trust Me: Differences in expressed and perceived trust relations in an organization. *Social Networks* 34:410–424.
McPherson, Miller, Lynn Smith-Lovin, and James Cook. 2001. Birds of a feather: Homophily in social networks. *Annual Review of Sociology* 27:415–444.
Michell, Lynn. 1997. Pressure groups: Young people's accounts of peer pressure to smoke. *Social Sciences in Health* 3:3–17.
Michell, Lynn, and Amanda Amos. 1997. Girls, pecking order and smoking. *Social Science and Medicine* 44:1861–1869.
Michell, Lynn, and Patrick West. 1996. Peer pressure to smoke: The meaning depends on the method. *Health Education Research* 11:39–49.
Mische, Ann, and Philippa Pattison. 2000. Composing a civic arena: Publics, projects and social settings. *Poetics* 27:163–194.
Mohr, John, and Vincent Duquenne. 1997. The duality of culture and practice: Poverty relief in new York city, 1888–1917. *Theory & Society* 26:305–356.
Padgett, John. 1990. Mobility as control: Congressmen through committees. In *Social mobility and social structure*, ed. Ronald L. Breiger, 27–58. New York: Cambridge University Press.
Pattison, Philippa, and Garry Robins. 2002. Neighborhood-based models for social networks. *Sociological Methodology* 32:301–337.
Pattison, Philippa, and Garry Robins. 2004. Building models for social spaces: Neighborhood-based models for social networks and affiliation structures. *Mathematics and Social Sciences* 42:1–29.
Pearson, Michael, and Patrick West. 2003. Drifting smoke rings: Social network analysis and Markov processes in a longitudinal study of friendship groups and risk-taking. *Connections* 25:59–76.

Pearson, Michael, and Lynn Michell. 2000. Smoke rings: Social network analysis of friendship groups, smoking and drug-taking. *Drugs: Education, Prevention & Policy* 7:21–37.

Rank, Olaf, Garry Robins, and Philippa Pattison. 2010. Structural logic of intraorganizational networks. *Organization Science* 21:745–764.

Ripley, Ruth, Tom A. B. Snijders, and Paulina Preciado. 2013. *Manual for RSiena. June 18*. Oxford: University of Oxford, Department of Statistics.

Rivera, Mark T., Sara B. Soderstrom, and Brian Uzzi. 2010. Dynamics of dyads in social networks: Assortative, relational, and proximity mechanisms. *Annual Review of Sociology* 36:91–115.

Robins, Garry, and Malcolm Alexander. 2004. Small worlds among interlocking directors: Network structure and distance in bipartite graphs. *Journal of Computational and Mathematical Organization Theory* 10:69–94.

Robins, Garry, Peter Elliott, and Philippa Pattison. 2001. Network models for social selection processes. *Social Networks* 23:1–30.

Robins, Garry, Philippa Pattison, and Josie Woolcock. 2005. Small and other worlds: Global network structures from local processes. *American Journal of Sociology* 110:894–936.

Robins, Garry, Tom A. B. Snijders, Peng Wang, Mark Handcock, and Philippa Pattison. 2007. Recent developments in exponential random graph (p*) models. *Social Networks* 29:192–215.

Simmel, Georg. 1955. *Conflict and the web of group affiliations* (translated by Kurt H. Wolff, R. Bendix). Glencoe: The Free Press.

Skvoretz John, and Katherine Faust. 1999. Logit models for affiliation networks. In *Sociological Methodology*, eds. Mark Becker and Michael Sobel, 253–280. New York, Basil Blackwell.

Snijders, Tom A. B. 2001. The statistical evaluation of social network dynamics. *Sociological Methodology* 31:361–395.

Snijders, Tom A. B. 2005. Models for Longitudinal Network Data. In *Models and methods in social network analysis*, eds. Peter Carrington, John Scott, and Stanley Wasserman, 215–247. New York. Cambridge University Press.

Snijders, Tom. 2011. Statistical models for social networks. *Annual Review of Sociology* 37:131–153.

Snijders, Tom A. B., Alessandro Lomi, and Vanina J. Torlo. 2013. A model for the multiplex dynamics of two-mode and one-mode networks, with an application to employment preference, friendship, and advice. *Social Networks* 35:265–276.

Snijders, Tom A. B., G. van de Bunt, and C. Steglich. 2010. Introduction to stochastic actor-based models for network dynamics. *Social Networks* 32:44–60.

Snijders, Tom A. B., P. E. Pattison, G. L. Robins, M. S. Handcock. 2006. New specifications for exponential random graph models. *Sociological Methodology* 36:99–153.

Snijders, Tom A. B., Christian Steglich, and Michael Schweinberger. 2007. Modeling the co-evolution of networks and behavior. In *Longitudinal models in the behavioral and related sciences*, eds. Kees van Montfort, Han Oud, and Albert Satorra, 41–71. Mahwah: Lawrence Erlbaum.

Sorenson, Olav, and Toby E. Stuart. 2008. Bringing the context back in: Settings and the search for syndicate partners in venture capital investment networks. *Administrative Science Quarterly* 53:266–294.

Steglich, Christian, Tom A. B. Snijders, and Michael Pearson. 2010. Dynamic networks and behavior: Separating selection from influence. *Sociological Methodology* 40:329–393.

Steglich, Christian, Tom A. B. Snijders, and Patrick West. 2006. Applying SIENA: An illustrative analysis of the co-evolution of adolescents' friendship networks, taste in music, and alcohol consumption. *Methodology* 2:48–56.

Stinchcombe, Arthur L. 2002. New sociological microfoundations for organizational theory: A postscript. In *Social structure and organizations revisited. Research in the sociology of organizations*, eds. Michael Lounsbury and Marc J. Ventresca, 415–433. Bingley: Emerald Group Publishing Limited.

van Eijck, Koen. 2001. Social differentiation in musical taste patterns. *Social Forces* 79:1163–1185.

Wang, Peng, Garry Robins, Philippa Pattison, and Emmanuel Lazega. 2013. Exponential random graph models for multilevel networks. *Social Networks* 35:96–115.

Wasserman, Stanley, and Dawn Iacobucci. 1991. Statistical modeling of one-mode and two-mode networks: Simultaneous analysis of graphs and bipartite graphs. *British Journal of Mathematical and Statistical Psychology* 44:13–44.

Wasserman Stanley, and Katherine Faust. 1994. *Social network analysis: Methods and applications*. New York. Cambridge University Press.

Whyte, William F. 1943. *Street corner society: The social structure of an Italian slum*. Chicago: University of Chicago Press.

Alessandro Lomi, professor in organization theory and behavior at the Faculty of Economics at the University of Italian Switzerland, Lugano. He is a life member of Clare Hall College, University of Cambridge (UK), a honorary senior research fellow at the Melbourne School of Psychological Sciences, University of Melbourne (Australia), and a fellow of the European Academy of Sociology (EAS). His research interests include the analysis of social networks within and between organizations. He received his PhD from Cornell University (Ithaca, New York).

Christoph Stadtfeld, postdoctoral research fellow in the Faculty of Economics at the University of Italian Switzerland, Lugano, and a member of the ICS at the University of Groningen (The Netherlands). His research focuses on dynamic processes in social networks. He received his PhD in Economics from Karlsruhe Institute of Technology (Germany).

… Kölner Zeitschrift für Soziologie und Sozialpsychologie

Kontexteffekte in Familien – Angleichung von Paaren und intergenerationale Transmission am Beispiel Religiosität

Oliver Arránz Becker · Daniel Lois · Anja Steinbach

© Springer Fachmedien Wiesbaden 2014

Zusammenfassung Der vorliegende Beitrag zeigt konzeptuelle und methodische Ansätze zur Untersuchung von sozialen Kontexteinflüssen innerhalb von Familien auf. Familienmitglieder repräsentieren füreinander jeweils gegenseitig den sozialen Kontext, innerhalb dessen sich familiales Handeln und individuelle Persönlichkeitsentwicklung abspielen. Soziale Einflüsse in Familien äußern sich empirisch in einer überzufälligen Ähnlichkeit der Familienmitglieder hinsichtlich einer großen Bandbreite von Merkmalen. Der vorliegende Beitrag fokussiert auf die intrafamiliale Homogenisierung hinsichtlich Religiosität, wobei in einem empirischen Datenbeispiel a) horizontale Paar-Angleichungsprozesse sowie b) vertikale intergenerationale Transmissionsprozesse untersucht werden. Neben dem Befund, dass Sozialisationserfahrungen im Elternhaus bedeutsamer sind als spätere Partnereinflüsse, zeigen die Analysen, dass soziale Kontexteffekte umso stärker ausfallen, je größer die Kohäsion in der jeweiligen Interaktionsdyade ist (hier operationalisiert über die Beziehungsqualität).

O. Arránz Becker (✉)
Fakultät für Sozialwissenschaften, Universität Mannheim,
A5,6, 68131 Mannheim, Deutschland
E-Mail: arranz-becker@sowi.uni-mannheim.de

D. Lois
Wirtschafts- und Sozialwissenschaftliche Fakultät, Eberhard Karls Universität Tübingen,
Haußerstr. 11, 72076 Tübingen, Deutschland
E-Mail: daniel.lois@uni-tuebingen.de

A. Steinbach
Institut für Soziologie, Universität Duisburg-Essen,
Lotharstr. 65, 47057 Duisburg, Deutschland
E-Mail: anja.steinbach@uni-due.de

Schlüsselwörter Intergenerationale Transmission · Homogamie · Religion ·
Dyadische Datenanalyse · Sozialisation · Sozialer Kontext

Context effects in families: Couple alignment and intergenerational transmission using the example of religiosity

Abstract The present contribution shows conceptual and methodological approaches for the study of social context effects within families. Family members mutually constitute the social context in which family behavior and personality development take place. Social influence in families becomes evident empirically in family members' significant similarity concerning a wide variety of characteristics. The present study focuses on intrafamily convergence with regard to religiousness. In an empirical illustration, both (a) horizontal intracouple alignment and (b) vertical intergenerational transmission processes are examined. Besides the finding that experiences during religious socialization in the parental home have a stronger impact than partner influences in adulthood, our analyses show that social context effects are more pronounced the stronger the cohesion of the respective interaction dyad is (e.g., according to measures of relationship quality).

Keywords Intergenerational transmission · Homogamy · Religion ·
Dyadic analysis · Socialization · Social context

1 Problemstellung und theoretischer Hintergrund

Eine zentrale Aufgabe der Soziologie besteht in der Analyse sozialen Handelns (Esser 1996). Soziales Handeln wiederum ist nach Weber (1972, S. 1) insbesondere durch den Bezug auf das Verhalten anderer Personen, d. h. auf soziale Kontexte, charakterisierbar. Derartige soziale Bezüge können auf zweierlei Arten zustande kommen: zum einen durch Koorientierung, d. h. indem Akteure sich durch gegenseitigen Vergleich in ihrem Handeln aneinander orientieren, zum anderen durch soziale Interdependenz, d. h. aufgrund des gegenseitigen aufeinander Angewiesenseins mit dem Ziel des Tauschs wechselseitig benötigter Ressourcen (Esser 2000a; Meulemann 2012).

Nicht nur innerhalb von Gesellschaften, sondern auch für das familiale Handeln sind diese beiden grundlegenden Sozialformen relevant. Sie lassen sich recht gut verschiedenen basalen Funktionen der Familie (vgl. Nave-Herz 2013) zuordnen: Einerseits kann in Familien im Rahmen der Haushaltsfunktion die instrumentell-arbeitsteilige Produktion wichtiger Basisgüter (sogenannter commodities, vgl. Becker 1981) gesichert werden, andererseits dient die Familie als Netz expressiver Sozialbeziehungen in der Regel auch der Weitergabe von Werten sowie der psychischen Reproduktion und Rekreation. Diese beiden Aspekte, die auch mit den soziologischen Grundkonzepten der funktionalen (Rollen-)Differenzierung und der kulturellen Verbundenheit oder Differenzierung (Esser 2000b) korrespondieren, tragen in Bezug auf die Ausstattung der Familienmitglieder mit Ressourcen oder kulturellen Merkmalen zu gegensätzlichen Konstellationen bei: Während Arbeitsteilung und funktionale Differenzierung unterschiedliche Merkmalsausprägungen der Personen (z. B. hinsichtlich des marktfähigen Humankapitals) implizieren, führen Sozialisationsprozesse, die sowohl innerhalb als auch zwischen Generationen stattfinden können, zu ähnlichen Ausprägungen (z. B. zu Werteähnlichkeit). Die Gemeinsamkeit beider Prozesse besteht darin, dass jeweils eine (stochastische) Abhängigkeit resultiert, die sich bei funktionaler Differenzierung in einer negativen, bei Sozialisationsprozessen hingegen in einer positiven Korrelation der interessierenden Merkmale zwischen den Familienmitgliedern niederschlägt (vgl. hierzu die Unterscheidung von komplementären und substituierbaren Merkmalen bei Gary Becker (1993, S. 241 f.)). Wir fokussieren im Folgenden auf die Sozialisationsfunktion der Familie, methodisch-analytisch lassen sich die beschriebenen Überlegungen jedoch ohne weiteres auf Spezialisierungsprozesse übertragen.

Allgemein können zwei Prozesse für die Entstehung von Ähnlichkeit in Familien verantwortlich gemacht werden (vgl. Arránz Becker und Lois 2010): a) Selektionsprozesse, d. h. die aktive Wahl von Kontexten, u. a. nach dem Kriterium der Ähnlichkeit (z. B. Partnerwahlprozesse oder auch spätere Trennung im Fall eines „mismatch"),[1] und b) Sozialisationsprozesse, d. h. die Angleichung der Mitglieder über die Zeit. Konkret impliziert Sozialisation, dass, vermittelt über persönliche Interaktion, im Laufe der Zeit eine (wechselseitige) Anpassung an die Werthaltungen und Einstellungen der übrigen Familienmitglieder erfolgt. Jedes Familienmitglied kann dabei als Teil des sozialen Kontexts für die übrigen Familienmitglieder konzeptualisiert werden und einen mehr oder weniger starken sozialen Einfluss auf diese ausüben. Das Ausmaß dieser Einflüsse ist im Rahmen einer angemessenen statistischen Modellierung zu quantifizieren. Sozialisation wird hier in Anlehnung an die angelsächsische familiensoziologische Literatur (z. B. Oppenheimer 1988) in einem weiten Sinn gebraucht, der über Primärsozialisation und Enkulturation im Sinne der Werte- und Norminternalisierung bei Kindern hinausgeht und explizit wertebezogene Angleichung innerhalb einer Generation (z. B. bei Paaren) einschließt.

In einer historischen Betrachtung der Familienforschung fällt auf, dass bis in die 1990er Jahre hinein Kontexteffekte auf familiales Handeln, z. B. über die Berücksichtigung der Merkmale von Partnern oder anderen Familienmitgliedern, kaum untersucht wurden, obwohl dies aus theoretischer Sicht bereits seit längerem explizit gefordert worden war (Thompson und Walker 1982). Der späte Zeitpunkt der „dyadischen Wende", welche sich inhaltlich in der zunehmenden Berücksichtigung von Partnermerkmalen (Corijn et al. 1996) sowie in einer parallel dazu einsetzenden Methodenentwicklung (Kenny 1988; Gonzalez und Griffin 1997) niederschlug, überrascht insofern, als sich zu diesem Zeitpunkt bereits längst einflussreiche theoretische Paradigmen wie Austauschtheorie (Nye 1982) und Familienökonomie (Becker 1981) etabliert hatten, in denen Dyaden oder familiale Haushalte als theoretische Analyseeinheit gesehen wurden.

---

[1] Die Wahl von Kontexten im Rahmen von Selektionsprozessen wird ausführlich in einem eigenen Beitrag von Hedman in diesem Heft behandelt. Sie wird im vorliegenden Beitrag auch deswegen ausgeblendet, da sie zwar für horizontale (Paar-)Beziehungen eine bedeutsame Rolle spielt, jedoch weniger für vertikale Generationenbeziehungen, die in aller Regel lebenslang bestehen.

Der vorliegende Beitrag verfolgt zwei Ziele: Inhaltlich geht es um die Frage nach dem Prozess der intrafamilialen Diffusion von Werthaltungen, wobei mit der Religiosität eine grundlegende Wertedimension untersucht wird, die auch in modernen Gesellschaften eng mit familialen Übergängen wie Heirat und Familiengründung verknüpft ist (Lois 2009). Aus methodischer Perspektive sollen außerdem neuere Modellierungstechniken für soziale Einflüsse innerhalb von Dyaden und Familien vorgestellt werden. Im Folgenden wird zunächst in (Abschn. 2) der Forschungsstand zu religiösen Transmissionsprozessen und zu religiösen Angleichungsprozessen innerhalb von Familien referiert. Im Anschluss daran werden (Abschn. 3) aktuelle Entwicklungen im Bereich statistischer Analysemethoden aufgearbeitet, mittels derer sich Kontexteffekte bei Paaren und in Familien modellieren lassen, bevor (Abschn. 4) an einem eigenen empirischen Beispiel Partnereinflüsse und intergenerationale Transmission von Religiosität illustriert werden. Im Fazit (Abschn. 5) werden schließlich zentrale Befunde resümiert, der mögliche Erkenntnisgewinn aus derartigen Analysen eingeschätzt sowie potenzielle zukünftige Forschungslinien identifiziert.

2 Forschungsüberblick

Im Folgenden wird der aktuelle Forschungsstand hinsichtlich familialer Kontexteinflüsse auf die Entstehung von Werthaltungen und Lebensstilen aufgearbeitet, unter besonderer Berücksichtigung der im vorliegenden Beitrag untersuchten Religiosität. Dabei wird zunächst intergenerationale Transmission behandelt, anschließend Anpassung innerhalb von Partnerschaften.

2.1 Intergenerationale Transmission

Unter intergenerationaler Transmission wird die soziale Vererbung von Merkmalen der Eltern auf ihre Kinder verstanden (Martin-Matthews und Kobayashi 2002, S. 923).[2] Aufgrund des demographischen Wandels und des damit verbundenen Anstiegs der durchschnittlichen Lebenserwartung geraten inzwischen aber auch Großeltern und ihre Enkelkinder zunehmend in den Blick der Wissenschaft, wenn es um die vertikale Weitergabe von Einstellungen, Werten oder Verhaltensweisen in der Familie geht (siehe z. B. Copen und Silverstein 2007). Die empirische Messung des Effekts intergenerationaler Transmissionsprozesse erfolgt üblicherweise über die Betrachtung von Ähnlichkeiten der Angehörigen verschiedener Generationen in der jeweils interessierenden Merkmalsausprägung. In der inzwischen relativ umfangreichen Literatur zu intergenerationalen Transmissionsprozessen werden verschiedene Dimensionen sozialer Vererbung behandelt, die sich grob in drei Bereiche aufteilen lassen (Fend 2009, S. 83 ff.): In der Soziologie und den Bildungs- und Erziehungswissenschaften genießt die Vererbung des sozioökonomischen Status der Eltern auf

---

[2] Es wird zwar inzwischen auch die umgekehrte Richtung des Einflusses von Kindern auf ihre Eltern diskutiert sowie die Möglichkeit von Selbstsozialisation (Stecher und Zinnecker 2007); diese Perspektiven sollen hier jedoch vernachlässigt werden, da sie keine große Rolle für die Ausprägung der in diesem Beitrag interessierenden Kulturelemente wie religiöse Orientierungen und Praxen spielen.

ihre Kinder besonderes Interesse. Hier wird vor allem die intergenerationale Transmission des Bildungs- und Berufsstatus in den Blick genommen (Brake und Büchner 2003; Rössel und Beckert-Zieglschmid 2002; Fend 2009). Der familialen Reproduktion kulturellen Kapitals in Migrantenfamilien kommt hierbei besondere Aufmerksamkeit zu (Steinbach und Nauck 2004). Ein weiterer Bereich sozialer Vererbung bezieht sich auf die intergenerationale Transmission von verschiedenen Verhaltensweisen, wie zum Beispiel ehrenamtliches Engagement (Bekkers 2007; Mustillo et al. 2004) oder Gewaltausübung (Uslucan und Fuhrer 2009). Besonders umfänglich ist die empirische Forschung, die auf Ähnlichkeiten zwischen Eltern und erwachsenen Kindern in Bezug auf partnerschaftliche und familiale Verhaltensweisen wie z. B. Ehe- oder Beziehungsqualität (Perren et al. 2005; Yu und Adler-Baeder 2007; Erzinger 2009), Erziehungsstile (Chen et al. 2008), Scheidung (Dronkers und Harkonen 2008; Teachman 2002; Berger 2009) oder auch das Timing familialer Übergänge wie Alter bei Heirat oder erster Geburt (Steenhof und Liefbroer 2008; Van Poppel et al. 2008) fokussiert. Ein dritter großer Bereich betrifft die intergenerationale Transmission von Einstellungen und Wertorientierungen. Hierzu zählen Geschlechtsrolleneinstellungen (Moen et al. 1997) ebenso wie die Übertragung der Leistungsorientierung von Eltern auf ihre Kinder (Baier und Hadjar 2004). Aber auch politische und religiöse Orientierungen haben Eingang in eine Reihe von empirischen Untersuchungen gefunden (Fend 2009; Bengtson et al. 2009; Grob 2009).

Die folgenden Ausführungen konzentrieren sich ausschließlich auf die intergenerationale Transmission von kulturellen Werten, wobei mit Blick auf die empirischen Analysen im vierten Abschnitt insbesondere die Transmission von Religiosität im Vordergrund der Betrachtungen steht. Die soziale Vererbung von kulturellen Werten in Familien ist nicht nur deshalb von besonderem Interesse, weil sie wichtige Einflussfaktoren für individuelle Entscheidungen im Lebensverlauf darstellen und damit letztendlich Bedeutung für die Strukturierung desselben haben, sondern auch weil dadurch das Ausmaß der kulturellen Tradierung einer Gesellschaft bestimmt wird (Schönpflug 2001, S. 175; Trommsdorff 2009, S. 126). Bevor jedoch genauer auf die empirischen Ergebnisse eingegangen wird, soll zunächst kurz dargestellt werden, welche theoretischen Überlegungen bezüglich des Vorgangs der sozialen Vererbung von kulturellen Werten existieren. Es ist hier auf die Bedeutung hinzuweisen, die der Familie (neben Peers und Schule) als Entwicklungskontext im kindlichen Sozialisationsprozess zugeschrieben wird. Dabei stehen insbesondere die familialen Lebensumstände und das Engagement der Eltern im Mittelpunkt der Betrachtungen (Vollebergh et al. 2001; Roest et al. 2009; Kraul und Radicke 2012). Die Relevanz der Familie, in diesem Zusammenhang natürlich insbesondere der Eltern, zur Schaffung sogenannter „transmission belts" (Schönpflug 2001) ergibt sich daraus, dass die kulturelle Transmission (im Gegensatz zur genetischen Transmission) soziales Lernen erfordert (Bandura 1976). Da Eltern und Kinder, bis die Kinder im Erwachsenenalter eine eigenständige Lebensführung beginnen, (zumindest in der überwiegenden Zahl) in einem gemeinsamen Haushalt leben und dort alltäglich miteinander kommunizieren und interagieren, fungieren die Eltern in der Regel als wichtigste Vorbilder für soziale Lern- und Imitationsprozesse der Kinder (Schönpflug 2001). Die Verbundenheit der Generationen endet aber natürlich nicht mit dem Auszug der Kinder, sondern Eltern und Kinder bleiben in der Regel ein Leben lang miteinander verbunden. Für die Eltern-Kind-Beziehung gilt deshalb, wie für keine andere soziale Beziehung in diesem Maße, das Prinzip der „linked lives" (Elder 1994), nach dem Individuen während ihres gesamten Lebens in soziale Beziehungen mit anderen Menschen eingebettet sind. Das Verhältnis von Eltern und Kindern ist entsprechend über den gesamten Lebenslauf zu sehen, wobei Lebenslaufstadien und sozialhistorische Entwicklungen jeweils miteinander interagieren (Bengtson et al. 2002). In einem „ecocultural model of intergenerational relations" werden die verschiedenen, bereits erwähnten Komponenten miteinander verbunden, indem der Prozess, die Richtung und das Ergebnis kultureller Transmission als von „the *persons* (*agents*) who are involved in the transmission process, their respective *relationships*, the *issue* (*contents*) that are transmitted, and the *cultural context* in which transmission takes place" beeinflusst beschrieben werden (Trommsdorff 2009, S. 127 f. Hervorhebung im Original). An die Daten für eine empirische Untersuchung von intergenerationalen Transmissionsprozessen werden entsprechend hohe Anforderungen gestellt (Baier und Hadjar 2004). Im Idealfall enthalten die erforderlichen Datensätze unabhängig voneinander gewonnene Informationen mehrerer Generationen, die über verschiedene Messzeitpunkte hinweg erhoben wurden. Die empirischen Arbeiten zur intergenerationalen Transmission von religiösen Werten, deren Ergebnisse im Folgenden berichtet werden, erfüllen diese Kriterien zum überwiegenden Teil.

Verschiedene Studien zeigen, dass die intergenerationale Transmission in Bezug auf die kirchlich-religiösen Orientierungen der nachfolgenden Generationen, auch im Vergleich zu anderen kulturellen Orientierungen wie politischen Werthaltungen oder Interessen und Kompetenzen im musikalischen Bereich, besonders erfolgreich ist (Bengtson et al. 2009; Zinnecker und Hasenberg 1999). Empirisch lässt sich generell ein sehr hoher intergenerationaler Vererbungsgrad in Bezug auf religiöse Praktiken und Überzeugungen feststellen (Zinnecker 1998; Fend 2009; Bao et al. 1999; Pearce und Thornton 2007; Domsgen 2008). Hier konnte sowohl eine Kurzzeitübertragung (Eltern-Adoleszente) als auch eine Langzeitübertragung (Eltern-erwachsene Kinder) nachgewiesen werden (Fend 2009; Myers 1996; Domsgen 2008). Übereinstimmend kommen die verschiedenen empirischen Untersuchungen zu dem Ergebnis, dass sowohl das Geschlecht der Eltern als auch das Geschlecht der Kinder eine Rolle für den Erfolg des Transmissionsprozesses spielt. Für die kulturelle Übermittlung von Religion und religiösen Überzeugungen kommt den Müttern offensichtlich größere Bedeutung zu als den Vätern (Bao et al. 1999; Zinnecker und Hasenberg 1999). Der Grund dafür wird in der immer noch sehr dominanten Rolle von Müttern für die Entwicklung von Werten bei Kindern aufgrund ihrer expressiven Rolle im familialen Sozialisationsprozess, der größeren Wahrscheinlichkeit psychologischer Kontrolle und der größeren Interaktionsdichte mit dem Nachwuchs gesehen (Bao et al. 1999, S. 371). Als weiteres Ergebnis bezüglich der Relevanz des Merkmals Geschlecht ist zu konstatieren, dass die Übernahme von religiösen Überzeugungen bei Töchtern stärker ausgeprägt ist als bei Söhnen (Fend 2009; Zinnecker 1998; Zinnecker und Hasenberg 1999).

In einem Strukturgleichungsmodell kann Zinnecker (1998) weiterhin zeigen, dass die Eltern bei der religiösen Erziehung ihrer Kinder Synergieeffekte erzielen, da die religiöse Interessen und Absichten von Müttern und Vätern empirisch eng zusammenhängen, obwohl die Aussagen der Eltern getrennt erhoben wurden. Zinnecker

(1998, S. 349) schließt daraus, dass die Werthaltungen von Mutter und Vater ein übergeordnetes Konstrukt elterlicher Familienreligiosität bilden, wobei die kulturelle Homogenität in Bezug auf Religiosität als Ergebnis von Entwicklungs- und Verständigungsprozessen interpretiert wird.[3] Es wird aber auch noch auf eine weitere Komponente des empirischen Modells Bezug genommen: die Erfahrungen der kirchlich-religiösen Erziehung der Eltern in ihrer eigenen Kindheit. Die Einschätzungen der Mütter und Väter bezüglich ihrer eigenen religiösen Erziehung zeigen, dass die Eltern sehr homogene religiöse Sozialisationserfahrungen aufweisen, die bei ihrer Partnerwahl offensichtlich eine Rolle gespielt haben. Zinnecker (1998, S. 350) bezeichnet dies als „Beharrlichkeit kirchlich-religiöser Familienmilieus". Weitere Synergieeffekte sind auch dadurch zu erwarten, dass religiös aktive Eltern nicht nur kulturell adäquate Institutionen für ihre Kinder auswählen (z. B. religiöser Kindergarten), die ihre innerfamiliale religiöse Erziehung unterstützen, sondern sich auch in einem religiös geprägten sozialen Netzwerk bewegen und ihre Kinder diesen Netzwerkeinflüssen aussetzen (Pearce und Thornton 2007, S. 1229; siehe auch Wolf 1995). Zu diesem sozialen Netzwerk gehören natürlich auch die Eltern der Eltern, also die Großeltern dieser Kinder. Auf Basis einer Längsschnittstudie, die drei familiale Generationen umfasst, wird gezeigt, dass „parents and grandparents simultaneously serving as independent and joint agents of religious socialization" (Bengtson et al. 2009, S. 340). Als wichtige positive Einflussgröße auf den Transmissionserfolg wird auch hier wieder das weibliche Geschlecht ausgemacht, aber auch der sozialhistorische Kontext spielt eine wichtige Rolle.

In Bezug auf die Eltern-Kind-Transmission von religiösen Praktiken und Orientierungen zeigen die empirischen Ergebnisse verschiedener Studien aus den späten 1980er Jahren und den frühen 1990er Jahren außerdem, dass eine hohe Qualität sowohl der Paar- als auch der Eltern-Kind-Beziehung (in der Kindheit spielt insbesondere ein gutes Familienklima eine wichtige Rolle) die soziale Vererbung von Religiosität fördern (Myers 1996; Luft und Sorell 1987; Dickie et al. 1997). Auch eine neuere US-amerikanische Studie (Bao et al. 1999), die sich mit der Frage beschäftigt, inwieweit die Wahrnehmung elterlicher Akzeptanz die intergenerationale Transmission religiöser Praktiken und Überzeugungen moderiert, kommt zu dem Ergebnis, dass ein unterstützender und zugewandter Erziehungsstil eine große Bedeutung für den Erfolg religiöser Sozialisation in der Familie hat.

Zusammenfassend ist zu sagen, dass dem Bereich der intergenerationalen Transmission von kulturellen Werten eine besondere Rolle im Prozess der Sozialisation zukommt. Auf der Mikroebene kann hier ein starker Einfluss von Eltern (oder Großeltern) auf die Kinder (bzw. Enkelkinder) zur Vorbereitung auf das Erwachsenenleben durch die Entwicklung einer bestimmten Sicht auf die Welt konstatiert werden. Auf der Makroebene vollzieht sich in diesem Prozess gleichzeitig die Tradierung von Kultur in einer Gesellschaft. Die soziale Vererbung von religiösen Praktiken und Orientierungen ist von besonderem Interesse, da einerseits zwar inzwischen seit Jahrzehnten empirisch eine sehr starke Übertragung zwischen den Generationen belegt wurde, andererseits aber auch eine Abnahme der Bedeutung von Religion und Religi-

---

[3] Zur Frage der Herkunft von Ähnlichkeiten in Partnerschaften siehe ausführlich die Ausführungen im nächsten Abschnitt dieses Beitrags.

osität in modernen Gesellschaften zu beobachten ist (siehe zu weiteren Ausführungen bezüglich der Säkularisierungsdebatte Pickel 2010, 2013). Vielleicht hat das damit zu tun, dass, wie Fend (2009) zeigen konnte, bereits eine geringfügig distanziertere Haltung der Eltern zur Religion dazu führt, dass die Kinder im Erwachsenenalter eine völlige Institutionenferne zeigen, was vermutlich auch mit der mangelnden Einübung religiöser Praktiken zusammenhängt. An dieser Stelle muss allerdings hinzugefügt werden, dass hier lediglich die Kirchenbindung (gemessen über die Kirchgangshäufigkeit) betrachtet wurde und deshalb auch keine Aussage über das Ausmaß der Religiosität getroffen werden kann. Wenn aber immer weniger Kinder religiös sozialisiert werden und damit auch immer weniger religiöse Personen dem Partnermarkt zur Verfügung stehen, scheint es eine besonders interessante Frage zu sein, inwieweit Anpassungsprozesse bezüglich der Religiosität in Partnerschaften stattfinden und welche Richtung diese nehmen.

2.2 Gegenseitige Anpassung bei Paaren

Ähnlichkeit in Partnerschaften ist auf Selektions- und Sozialisationseffekte zurückführbar (Kalmijn 1998). Selektionseffekte bestehen in sozial vorstrukturierte Gelegenheiten des Kennenlernens („assortative meeting") und der erhöhten Instabilität unähnlicher Paare („assortative mating"). Unter Sozialisationseffekten wird dagegen die gegenseitige Anpassung von Partnern verstanden, d. h. die Entstehung von Ähnlichkeit im Verlauf der partnerschaftlichen Beziehung. Vor der Zusammenfassung des Forschungsstandes wird zunächst die theoretische Basis für Anpassungseffekte dargestellt, die vor allem auf der Balancetheorie (Heider 1958; Newcomb 1953) aufbaut. Die Grundannahme dieser Theorie lautet, dass Kognitionen in harmonischer Art und Weise organisiert sind, sodass kognitive Dissonanzen vermieden werden. Wenn sich zum Beispiel ein Akteur (A) und sein Partner (P) sympathisch finden, fühlen sich A und P wohl, wenn sie beide ähnliche d. h. positive oder aber negative Einstellungen gegenüber dem Objekt X haben. Ist die A-P-X-Triade dagegen unausgeglichen, da sich A und P in der Valenz ihrer Einstellung gegenüber X unterscheiden, kommt es zu negativen psychischen Reaktionen. Diese sind aus der Perspektive von A umso stärker, je attraktiver sich A und P finden, je wichtiger das Einstellungsobjekt X für A ist oder je stärker sich A seiner eigenen Haltung gegenüber X verpflichtet fühlt und je relevanter das Einstellungsobjekt für die Beziehung von A und P ist (vgl. Davis und Rusbult 2001).

Im Falle einer unausgeglichenen A-P-X-Triade gibt es mehrere Möglichkeiten zur Wiederherstellung der Balance: A kann seine Beziehung zu P verändern (z. B. durch Verringerung der Sympathie oder, im Extremfall, auch durch Abbruch der Beziehung), oder A und P können versuchen, das Einstellungsobjekt X aus ihrer Beziehung auszublenden. Die dritte und im vorliegenden Fall interessante Möglichkeit besteht in einer Anpassung, d. h. entweder A oder P (oder beide) ändern ihre Einstellung gegenüber X in Richtung des jeweils anderen. Davis und Rusbult (2001) postulieren nun, dass es sich bei der Anpassung an den Partner um eine Reaktionsweise handelt, die mit einem relativ geringen (psychologischen) Aufwand verbunden ist. Dies gilt vor allem dann, wenn die Sympathie zwischen A und P stark ausgeprägt ist.

Im folgenden Forschungsüberblick wird darauf eingegangen, bei welchen Merkmalsklassen Anpassung bisher festgestellt wurde, von welchen Bedingungen das Ausmaß der gegenseitigen Anpassung über die Zeit abhängt und welche Konsequenzen Anpassungsprozesse für den Fortbestand von Partnerschaften haben. Bisher liegen allerdings nur vergleichsweise wenige Studien vor, die derartige Anpassungsprozesse in Partnerschaften untersucht haben. Ein Grund dafür mag in den hohen Anforderungen an die Daten liegen, die nicht nur im Längsschnitt vorliegen müssen, sondern darüber hinaus auch unabhängige Messungen für beide Partner enthalten sollten. Neben einer experimentellen Studie (Davis und Rusbult 2001) handelt es sich vorwiegend um Untersuchungen auf der Basis von Surveydaten, in denen das Actor-Partner-Interdependence-Model (APIM) eingesetzt wird. Anpassung wird hier über einen sogenannten Partnereffekt gemessen. Dieser gibt an, inwiefern der „idiosynkratische" Anteil einer bestimmten Merkmalsausprägung des *Partners* in einer vorangehenden Befragungswelle, also der Anteil, der sich nicht auf Basis der entsprechenden zeitgleichen Ausprägung des Akteurs vorhersagen lässt, die Ausprägung des *Akteurs* zum aktuellen Messzeitpunkt beeinflusst. Eine ausführlichere methodische Erläuterung dieses Modells findet sich in Abschn. 3 dieses Beitrags.

Zunächst lässt sich festhalten, dass sich für eine ganze Reihe von Merkmalsdimensionen Hinweise auf die Existenz von Anpassungsprozessen über die Zeit feststellen lassen. Hierbei handelt es sich, thematisch geordnet, um traditionale Geschlechtsrollenorientierungen (Kalmijn 2005) und Einstellungen zum vorehelichen Geschlechtsverkehr (Caspi et al. 1992), politisch-machtbezogene Werte (Caspi et al. 1992) und sozialkritische Haltungen (etwa Durchsetzung gegenüber herrschenden Machtverhältnissen; Roest et al. 2006), religiöse Werte (Caspi et al. 1992), Kirchgangshäufigkeit und konfessionelle Zugehörigkeit (Lois 2013), hedonistische Werte (Caspi et al. 1992) sowie gemeinsame Freizeitaktivitäten des Paares (Arránz Becker und Lois 2010). Gegen eine universelle Anpassungstendenz spricht allerdings, dass sich für einige weitere Merkmale keine signifikanten Partnereffekte feststellen lassen. Dazu zählen rational-ökonomische Werte, Werte der ehelichen Treue, Einstellungen zur ehelichen Alltagsinteraktion, traditionale familiale Werte sowie Selbstwirksamkeitswerte (Caspi et al. 1992; Roest et al. 2006).[4]

Von der reinen Existenz von Angleichungstendenzen ist zudem die relative Stärke der Anpassungseffekte zu unterscheiden. Arránz Becker und Lois (2010) kommen in diesem Zusammenhang zu dem Ergebnis, dass Partnereffekte beim Hochkulturschema (Schulze 1992), das Freizeitaktivitäten wie Malen, Musizieren oder einen Theater- und Opernbesuch umfasst, signifikant schwächer sind als beim Spannungsschema, unter dem anregende Aktivitäten wie Sport oder Kino- und Discobesuche subsumiert werden. Eine Erklärungsmöglichkeit für diesen Befund besteht darin, dass das Hochkulturschema durch seine Bildungsabhängigkeit in höherem Maße voraussetzungsvoll und distinktiv ist. Lois (2013, S. 184–209) findet zudem Hinweise darauf, dass Partnereffekte bei der Häufigkeit von Gottesdienstbesuchen deutlich

---

[4] Caspi et al. (1992) stellen in ihrer sehr differenzierten Analyse zudem fest, dass Ehepartner in ihren Einstellungen und Werten über die Zeit zwar in bestimmten Bereichen nicht ähnlicher werden (Anpassung), die Initialähnlichkeit durch gleichsinnige Veränderungen jedoch häufig über die Zeit erhalten bleibt. Hierfür können geteilte soziale Randbedingungen („common fate"), aber auch genetische Faktoren, verantwortlich sein.

schwächer sind als bei nicht religiösen Freizeitaktivitäten wie der Vergnügungsfreizeit im Sinne des Spannungsschemas. Dieses Ergebnis spricht für die biografische Trägheit religiöser Prägungen, für die frühe elterliche Sozialisationseinflüsse möglicherweise von vergleichsweise größerer Bedeutung sind als die spätere Anpassung an neue Sozialisationsagenten wie den Lebenspartner. Das Ziel der empirischen Analysen dieses Beitrags (Abschn. 4) besteht darin, diese Frage vertiefend zu untersuchen.

Die bisher vorliegenden Forschungsergebnisse verdeutlichen ferner, dass das Ausmaß der Anpassung, neben der zugrundeliegenden Merkmalsdimension, von weiteren moderierenden Faktoren abhängt. So können Davis und Rusbult (2001) in einem laborexperimentellen Setting verschiedene Annahmen der Balancetheorie bestätigen. Es zeigt sich, dass Akteure vor allem dann bereit sind, sich im Hinblick auf verschiedenste Einstellungsdimensionen aneinander anzupassen, wenn sie eine Partnerschaft miteinander eingegangen sind (verglichen mit der Anpassung zwischen „Fremden"), wenn es sich um Paare mit hoher Partnerschaftsqualität handelt, wenn das Einstellungsobjekt für den Partner zentral ist und wenn Diskrepanzen gegenüber einem Einstellungsobjekt als salient empfunden werden.

Einige dieser Befunde werden auch durch Studien auf der Basis von Surveydaten unterstützt. Roest et al. (2006) können das Ergebnis replizieren, dass die Partnereffekte allgemein stärker sind, wenn die Partner eine hohe eheliche Zufriedenheit aufweisen. Zudem ist das Institutionalisierungsniveau der Partnerschaft insofern bedeutsam, da Anpassungsprozesse bei Freizeitaktivitäten nach Arránz Becker und Lois (2010) stärker sind, wenn es sich um Ehen (verglichen mit nichtehelichen Lebensgemeinschaften) und zusätzlich um Paare mit langer Ehedauer handelt. Auch eine sozialstrukturelle Homogamie der Partner scheint Anpassung zu begünstigen. So berichten Roest et al. (2006), dass Partnereffekte bei konfessioneller Homogamie und Bildungshomogamie der Partner stärker sind. Arránz Becker und Lois (2010) zeigen, dass sich Partner umso mehr im Hinblick auf das Hochkulturschema anpassen, je weniger sich ihr Bildungsniveau unterscheidet.

Weiterhin findet sich in bisherigen Studien empirische Evidenz für die Annahme, dass sich Partner vor allem dann angleichen, wenn das zugrundeliegende Merkmal für die Partnerschaft allgemein oder in spezifischen Lebensphasen sehr relevant (salient) ist. Nach Lois (2013, S. 184–209) werden konfessionell heterogame Paare, etwa ein katholischer Mann und eine evangelische Frau, vor allem dann durch Konvertierung konfessionell homogam, wenn es sich um ein religiös aktives Paar handelt, wenn der Übergang in die (erste) Ehe vollzogen wird und wenn Kinder in einem Alter ab fünf Jahren im Haushalt leben. Ähnliche Ergebnisse zeigen sich auch für die Anpassung der Kirchgangshäufigkeit in Partnerschaften. Hierzu ist anzumerken, dass konfessionell heterogame Paare, die kirchlich heiraten wollen, durch die strengen Endogamienormen in einigen Religionsgemeinschaften quasi zur Herstellung von Homogamie gezwungen sind. Nach den Ergebnissen von Musick und Wilson (1995) konvertieren Personen im Zuge der Eheschließung selbst dann in die Religionsgemeinschaft des zukünftigen Ehepartners, wenn dessen Glaubensgemeinschaft ihrer vormaligen Konfession kulturell sehr unähnlich ist. Kinder im Schulalter rufen darüber hinaus wahrscheinlich deshalb einen Anpassungsbedarf hervor, da sich die Frage nach einer konsistenten religiösen Sozialisation in diesem Altersbereich mit erhöhter Dringlichkeit stellt. Im Hinblick auf Freizeitaktivitäten zeigen die Befunde von Arránz Becker und Lois (2010), dass sich der Erwerbseinstieg und die Familiengründung hemmend auf eine Harmonisierung der Freizeitaktivitäten auswirken, während Anpassungsprozesse durch den Übergang ins „empty nest", der weniger eine Spezialisierung als eine Harmonisierung der Zeitressourcen und Lebensstile fördert, begünstigt werden. Kalmijn (2005) kann dagegen für die Geschlechtsrollenorientierung zeigen, dass Männer sich stärker an Frauen anpassen, wenn der Übergang zur Familiengründung vollzogen wird. Dieser (vordergründig) widersprüchliche Befund erklärt sich wahrscheinlich dadurch, dass die Geschlechtsrollenorientierung einen starken Bezug zu der Erwerbsbeteiligung der Partner hat, die, insbesondere im Zuge der Familiengründung, im Rahmen einer traditionellen Arbeitsteilung substituierbar ist.[5]

Eine weiterführende Frage besteht ferner darin, welche Konsequenzen Anpassungsprozesse für den Fortbestand von Partnerschaften haben. Kann die Angleichung an den Ehe- oder Lebenspartner als eine Investition in die Partnerschaft interpretiert werden, die gegen eine Trennung „immunisiert"? Die bisherige empirische Evidenz unterstützt diese Hypothese. Nach Arránz Becker und Lois (2010) senkt nicht nur eine zeitkonstante, also schon beim Kennenlernen der Partner vorhandene Ähnlichkeit von Vorlieben im Freizeitbereich das Trennungsrisiko, sondern zusätzlich auch die Entstehung von Ähnlichkeit durch Anpassung über die Zeit. Zu ähnlichen Ergebnissen kommen Lehrer und Chiswick (1993) sowie Lois (2013, S. 189–209) für die Merkmale konfessionelle Zugehörigkeit und Kirchgangshäufigkeit. Lehrer und Chiswick (1993) unterscheiden z. B. bei ihrer Analyse der Partnerschaftsstabilität zwischen Ehepaaren, die bereits zu Beginn der Ehe der gleichen Glaubensgemeinschaft angehört haben und Paaren, die erst während der Ehe durch Konvertierung homogam geworden sind. Im Falle von homogam protestantischen Ehen zeigt sich, dass Ehen mit Konvertierung während der Ehe stabiler sind als bereits im Ausgangszustand homogame Paare. Dieser Effekt ist jedoch auf andere Religionsgemeinschaften, zum Beispiel katholische Ehen, nicht übertragbar.

3 Neuere methodische Ansätze zur Untersuchung familialer Kontexteinflüsse

Empirische Analysen von Paar- oder Familienmerkmalen (sogenannte „*between variables*", vgl. Kenny et al. 2006), zu denen per definitionem auch Ereignisse wie Übergänge im Familienzyklus gehören, erfordern lediglich a) die Verfügbarkeit von Informationen zu denselben Merkmalen aller potenziell relevanten Familienmitglieder sowie b) deren Berücksichtigung als zusätzliche Kovariaten, nicht hingegen besondere Auswertungsverfahren. Methodisch interessanter (und aufwendiger) wird es immer dann, wenn als Explanandum individuell variierende Merkmale („*mixed variables*"), z. B. Wahrnehmungen oder Einstellungen, untersucht werden. In diesem Fall ist die Annahme unabhängiger Beobachtungen in den gängigen statisti-

---

[5] Für das spezielle Beispiel der Anpassung religiöser Konfessionen finden sich zudem Hinweise auf einen Periodeneffekt im Sinne des allgemeinen Säkularisierungstrends. Nach Lois (2013, S. 189–209) geht die Neigung zu religiöser Anpassung durch Konvertierung im Zuge der historischen Zeit zurück. Dieser Befund korrespondiert mit Studien, die im Langfristtrend einen zunehmenden Anteil konfessioneller Mischehen feststellen (Hendrickx et al. 1994; Klein und Wunder 1996).

Abb. 1 Actor-Partner Interdependence Model (APIM) für nicht unterscheidbare Dyaden

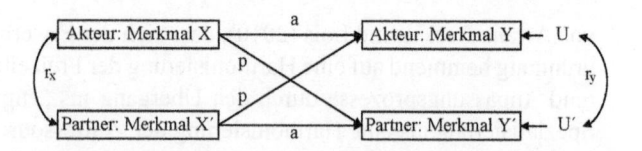

schen Verfahren aufgrund der „Clusterung" der Individuen in Paare oder Familien verletzt. Eine einfache Lösung dieses Problems besteht in der Adjustierung der Standardfehler, die zumindest bei überzufälliger Ähnlichkeit der Personen innerhalb der „Klumpen", systematisch unterschätzt werden (Kenny 1995). Allerdings nutzt diese Auswertungsstrategie, welche die Abhängigkeit der Daten lediglich als „statistisches Ärgernis" betrachtet, die inhaltlichen Möglichkeiten der Modellierung sozialer Interdependenz nicht und ist daher in der Regel suboptimal.

Inhaltlich angemessener erscheinen Modellierungstechniken, mittels derer Konttexteinflüsse in Dyaden oder Familien mit Hilfe sogenannter Partnereffekte spezifiziert werden können. Nachdem in der Literatur zunächst relativ aufwendige, da manuelle Berechnungen auf Basis bivariater Korrelationen erfordernde Verfahren beschrieben wurden (Gonzalez und Griffin 1999; Neyer 1998), hat in den vergangenen zehn Jahren eine prosperierende Weiterentwicklung multivariater dyadischer Analyseverfahren stattgefunden; entgegen ihrer Bezeichnung ist die Anwendung dieser Verfahren nicht auf Dyaden beschränkt, sondern diese können auch auf kleinere Gruppen angewendet werden (vgl. im Überblick Kenny et al. 2006). In der internationalen Forschung hat sich insbesondere das Actor-Partner-Interdependence-Model (APIM) durchgesetzt (Cook und Kenny 2005). Das Hauptcharakteristikum des APIM besteht darin, dass jeder Positionsinhaber innerhalb eines sozialen Gebildes oder Netzwerks gleichzeitig als Sender und als Ziel sozialen Einflusses betrachtet wird (vgl. Abb. 1). Im APIM können zwei Arten von Effekten differenziert werden: sogenannte Akteureffekte a), d. h. Zusammenhänge zwischen einem Merkmal X und einem Merkmal Y innerhalb derselben Person, und Partnereffekte b), d. h. dem Zusammenhang eines Merkmals X einer Person und dem Merkmal Y eines anderen Dyaden- oder Gruppenmitglieds. Beide Effekte werden jeweils unter Kontrolle des Ausmaßes an (Un-)Ähnlichkeit zwischen den Dyadenmitgliedern (r_x) berechnet. Die residuale Ähnlichkeit hinsichtlich Merkmal Y unter Kontrolle des Merkmals X beider Individuen wird mittels r_y als Korrelation der Residuen U und U' geschätzt.

APIM lassen sich mit weitgehend identischen Ergebnissen prinzipiell entweder als Mehrebenen- oder als Strukturgleichungsmodelle schätzen (Kenny et al. 2006, Kap. 7). Wir verwenden im Folgenden eine Zwei-Ebenen-random intercept-Spezifikation. Aufgrund der Tatsache, dass im einfachen Regressionsansatz jeweils nur eine abhängige Variable analysiert werden kann, müssen die Ausprägungen beider Partner[6] „untereinander" in dieselbe (Akteur-)Variable codiert werden. Außerdem werden zur Berechnung der Partnereffekte (d. h. der sozialen Einflüsse) die Ausprägungen des jeweils anderen Partners in eine (Partner-)Variable codiert; eine zusätzliche Dummy-Statusvariable (S) zeigt den Personentyp des Akteurs (z. B. Geschlecht

---

[6] In der Erhebung müssen nicht notwendigerweise beide Partner auch selbst befragt worden sein; insofern lassen sich APIM auch über Proxyangaben spezifizieren, wobei allerdings mit einer Überschätzung der Effekte aufgrund gemeinsamer Methodenvarianz zu rechnen ist (Perren et al. 2005).

Tab. 1 Fiktive pairwise-Datenmatrix für dyadische Längsschnittdaten (long-long-Format)

Welle	Paar-ID	Partner-ID (S)	Y_a	Y_p	X_a	X_p
1	1	1	5	2	3	1
1	1	2	2	5	1	3
2	1	1	4	2	5	2
2	1	2	2	4	2	5
3	1	1	4	3	4	2
3	1	2	3	4	2	4
1	2	1	2	4	2	5
1	2	2	4	2	5	2

des Ehepartners oder Generationenstatus) an. Im Fall von Dyaden ergibt sich durch dieses Vorgehen, bei dem jede Person pro Welle einmal als Akteur und einmal als Partner im Datensatz vorkommt, das sogenannte „pairwise-Format" mit paarweise gekreuzten Akteur- und Partner-Ausprägungen; im Längsschnitt wiederholt sich dieses Codierschema für jede Welle (Datensatz im long-long-Format, vgl. Tab. 1).

In der einfachen dyadischen Formulierung des APIM ergibt sich die folgende Zweiebenen-Regressionsgleichung (mit Paarindex i, zur Vereinfachung ohne weitere Kovariaten, vgl. Kenny und Kashy 2011, S. 344):

Ebene 1 (Personen):

$$Y_a = \beta_{0i} + \beta_{1i}X_a + \beta_{2i}X_p [+\beta_{3i}S + \beta_{4i}X_a \cdot S + \beta_{5i}X_p \cdot S] + U \quad (1)$$

Ebene 2 (Paar/Familie):

$$\begin{aligned}
\beta_{0i} &= \gamma_0 + U_i \\
\beta_{1i} &= \gamma_1 \\
\beta_{2i} &= \gamma_2 \\
[\beta_{3i} &= \gamma_3 \\
\beta_{4i} &= \gamma_4 \\
\beta_{5i} &= \gamma_5]
\end{aligned} \quad (2)$$

β_{0i} ist ein random intercept, der zwischen Paaren variiert. β_{1i} ist der *Akteureffekt* von Merkmal X auf Merkmal Y, innerhalb der Personen; β_{2i} ist der *Partnereffekt* von Merkmal X des einen auf Merkmal Y des anderen Partners, unter Kontrolle der Ausprägung von X des anderen Partners. In dem Fall, dass es sich bei X um eine zeitlich vorhergehende Messung[7] der abhängigen Variable Y handelt, liegt damit ein sogenanntes cross-lagged- oder auch dynamisches Panelmodell vor (Engel und Reinecke

---

[7] In unserem empirischen Beispiel verwenden wir Daten aus zwei Wellen, sodass aufgrund der Modellierung mittels zeitverzögerter Kovariaten nur eine Beobachtung pro Person, ohne Clusterung nach Zeitpunkten, vorliegt. Bei Längsschnittanalysen über mehr als zwei Wellen (vgl. Tab. 1) wird die Modellierung deutlich komplizierter. Eine Modellierungsoption bildet dann z. B. das sogenannte two-intercept model (Kenny et al. 2006, S. 344 ff.)

1996); der Partnereffekt zeigt dann das Ausmaß der Anpassung des einen Partners an die (residuale) Veränderung des anderen Partners an. Bei inhaltlich sinnvoller Unterscheidbarkeit der Personen innerhalb der Dyade (z. B. anhand des Geschlechts bei heterosexuellen Paaren) lassen sich je zwei Akteur- und Partnereffekte (von Männern auf Frauen und umgekehrt) getrennt schätzen, indem Akteur- und Partnereffekt mit der Statusvariablen multipliziert werden (vgl. die eckige Klammer in Gl. 1). In diesem Fall quantifiziert der jeweilige Haupteffekt β_{1i} (β_{2i}) den Akteureffekt (Partnereffekt) in der Referenzkategorie der Statusvariablen S (z. B. bei Männern), während das unstandardisierte Regressionsgewicht des Interaktionseffekts dann die numerische Effektdifferenz zwischen den beiden durch S indizierten Gruppen (also z. B. bei Männern vs. Frauen) anzeigt. Obwohl der Ansatz prinzipiell auf mehr als zwei Personen pro Gruppe generalisierbar ist (für ein empirisches Beispiel vgl. Roest et al. 2009), verliert die Spezifikation mit zunehmender Anzahl von Personen pro Gruppe schnell an Übersichtlichkeit, sodass die hier beschriebenen dyadischen Analyseverfahren insgesamt für größere soziale Gebilde (z. B. Netzwerke) oder für Gruppen mit stark variierender Größe wie Schulklassen oder Firmen weniger gut geeignet sind. Innerhalb von Paaren oder Familien, die meist durch unterscheidbare Rollen oder Positionen und eine überschaubare Größe charakterisiert sind, lassen sich damit jedoch sehr differenziert soziale Interdependenzstrukturen herausarbeiten.

Für die vorliegende Fragestellung sind insbesondere die Partnereffekte relevant, durch die sich bei einer longitudinalen Modellierung die gegenseitige Anpassung innerhalb von Dyaden über die Zeit schätzen lässt. Sollen darüber hinaus soziale Bedingungen identifiziert werden, unter denen Anpassung (oder Stabilität) begünstigt oder abgeschwächt wird, können zusätzliche Interaktionseffekte zwischen den Bedingungsfaktoren und den Partnereffekten (oder den Akteureffekten) spezifiziert werden (vgl. hierzu unser empirisches Beispiel im folgenden Abschnitt).

4 Empirisches Beispiel: Familiale Kontexteinflüsse auf Religiosität

4.1 Datensatz, Methode und Operationalisierungen

Um die Bedeutung des familialen Kontextes für die individuelle Religiosität empirisch zu verdeutlichen, greifen wir auf Daten des Bamberger Ehepaarpanels (BEP, ZA Nr. 4266) und des Nichteheliche Lebensgemeinschaften-(NEL-)Panels (ZA Nr. 4665) zurück. Beim BEP (Vaskovics und Staatsinstitut für Familienforschung an der Universität Bamberg (ifb) 2007; zur Studienbeschreibung vgl. Rost et al. 2003) handelt es sich um eine in Bayern, Hessen und Niedersachsen erhobene Längsschnittstudie zur Familien- und Beziehungsentwicklung mit insgesamt fünf Panelwellen (1988, 1990, 1992, 1994 und 2002). Das in Bayern erhobene NEL-Panel (Vaskovics und Rupp 2009; vgl. auch Vaskovics et al. 1997, S. 48–54) fand im Zeitraum 1988–1994 parallel zum BEP statt. Die erste Welle des BEP umfasst 1528 kinderlose Paare, in denen die Frau das Alter 35 noch nicht überschritten hat. Im NEL-Panel wurden in der ersten Welle 900 ledige Paare befragt, die mindestens seit einem Vierteljahr in einer gemeinsamen Wohnung zusammenleben und in einem für Fertilitätsprozesse relevanten Alter sind.

Abb. 2 APIM für unterscheidbare Dyaden zu religiösen Transmissionsprozessen in Partnerschaften. (Quelle: Bamberger Ehepaar- und NEL-Panel (Welle 1988); Koeffizienten basierend auf Tab. 3, Modell 1)

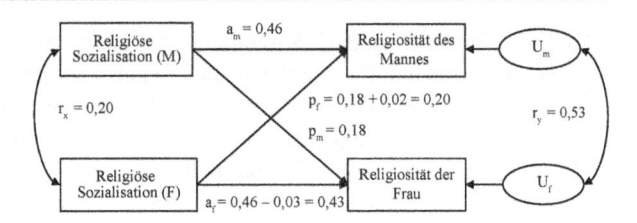

Trotz ihrer primären Ausrichtung auf die Analyse der Übergänge zum ersten Kind oder in die erste Ehe sind beide Datengrundlagen sehr gut für die vorliegende Fragestellung geeignet. Sie erlauben nicht nur die Konstruktion einer reliablen Multi-Item-Skala zur individuellen Religiosität (s. u.), sondern beinhalten zusätzlich alle Informationen, die für eine Analyse von Transmissions- und Anpassungsprozessen notwendig sind. Da beide Partner überwiegend (zu 95 %) unabhängig voneinander und zudem wiederholt befragt wurden, stehen zur Analyse der partnerschaftlichen Anpassung dyadische Längsschnittdaten zur Verfügung, wobei jeweils zwei Messzeitpunkte mit identischen Operationalisierungen verwendet werden (die Wellen 1988 und 1992 für Ehen und die Wellen 1988 und 1990 für nichteheliche Lebensgemeinschaften). Die Untersuchung von Transmissionsprozessen wird darüber hinaus dadurch ermöglicht, dass für beide Partner sowohl Informationen zur religiösen Sozialisation im Elternhaus zur Verfügung stehen als auch Variablen zu aktuellen Eigenschaften der intergenerationalen Beziehung.

Im ersten Schritt wird empirisch untersucht, wie sich die Religiosität der Eltern auf ihre Kinder transmittiert und unter welchen Bedingungen Transmissionseffekte stabil bleiben. Zugrunde liegen die gepoolten Querschnittdaten der ersten Welle (1988) des BEP und des NEL-Panels ($n=2307$ Paare mit gültigen Werten auf der abhängigen Variable und mindestens einem lebenden Elternteil).[8] Die Daten sind im sogenannten Pairwise-Format angeordnet (vgl. Tab. 1), d. h. beide Partner fließen jeweils einmal als Akteur in den Datensatz ein. Die Modellierung erfolgt im Rahmen eines APIM, welches als Multilevel-Modell geschätzt wird (siehe Abschn. 3 sowie Kenny et al. 2006, S. 173 ff.). Die jeweils zwei partnerspezifischen Zeilen auf Level 1 (siehe die Partner-ID in Tab. 1) sind in Dyaden auf Level 2 (siehe die Paar-ID in Tab. 1) geschachtelt, wodurch die statistische Abhängigkeit der Partner modelliert wird. Im Regressionsmodell wird die Religiosität des Akteurs durch die religiöse Sozialisation, die von seinen eigenen Eltern ausgeht (Akteureffekt), und durch die religiöse Sozialisation seitens der Eltern des Partners (Partnereffekt), vorhergesagt (siehe Abb. 2). Da es sich um unterscheidbare Dyaden (heterosexuelle Paare) handelt, werden geschlechtsspezifische Unterschiede in den Akteur- und Partnereffekten durch Interaktionsterme getestet.

Folgende Operationalisierungen wurden zugrundegelegt:
Die Religiosität des Akteurs wird durch eine einfaktorielle Skala gemessen, die aus vier Items besteht. Dazu zählen die Wichtigkeit des Lebensbereichs Religion und Kirche (von 1 = „unwichtig" bis 4 = „besonders wichtig"), der Einfluss religiöser Überzeugungen auf das Leben des Befragten (von 1 = „spielen gar keine Rolle" bis 4 = „spielen eine große Rolle"), die Verbundenheit mit der Kirche (von 1 = „gar nicht"

---

[8] Fehlende Werte bei den unabhängigen Variablen wurden einfach mittels EM-Algorithmus imputiert.

bis 4 = „sehr stark") und die Kirchgangshäufigkeit (von 1 = „nie" bis 4 = „mindestens einmal pro Woche"). Die Kirchgangshäufigkeit wurde zunächst auf die Anzahl jährlicher Gottesdienstbesuche hochgerechnet. Anschließend wurden alle Items z-standardisiert und durch Mittelwertbildung kombiniert. Cronbach's Alpha rangiert, je nach Messzeitpunkt, zwischen 0,78 und 0,89.

Die religiöse Erziehung durch die Eltern wird durch folgende beiden Items gemessen, die im Mittel mit $r=0{,}71$ korrelieren und daher durch Mittelwertbildung zusammengefasst werden: „Meine Eltern waren in meiner Kindheit sehr religiös" und „Die Religiosität meiner Eltern spielte damals eine große Rolle für das Familienleben" (Antwortformat jeweils von 1 = „stimmt gar nicht" bis 5 = „stimmt voll und ganz").

Um Variationen des intergenerationalen Transmissionseffekts im Lebensverlauf zu untersuchen, werden jeweils aus Akteurperspektive neben dem Lebensalter die Kontakthäufigkeit sowie eine Gesamteinschätzung des Verhältnisses zu den Eltern (im Folgenden: intergenerationale Beziehungsqualität) als Moderatoren berücksichtigt. Die Kontakthäufigkeit wurde über eine 6-fach abgestufte Frage erhoben (von 0 = „gar nicht" bis 5 = „täglich oder fast täglich") und die Beziehungsqualität über die Frage „Wie würden Sie Ihr derzeitiges Verhältnis zu Ihren Eltern einschätzen? (von 1 = „eher schlecht" bis 5 = „sehr gut"). Das Verhältnis zur Mutter und zum Vater wurde getrennt abgefragt. Da beide Angaben im Mittel mit $r=0{,}52$ korrelieren, wurden beide Informationen zu einer Skala zusammengefasst.

Im zweiten Schritt steht die gegenseitige Anpassung der Partner über die Zeit im Mittelpunkt. Gegenstand der Analysen sind 1391 Paare (60,3 % der Ausgangsstichproben in Welle 1), die für zwei Messzeitpunkte (1988 und 1992 sowie 1988 und 1990) gültige Werte auf der abhängigen Variablen aufweisen. Die Daten liegen wiederum im Pairwise-Format vor, und die Schätzung erfolgt im Rahmen des oben beschriebenen Mehrebenenmodells (Level 1: Partner, Level 2: Dyaden). Um Veränderungen über die Zeit modellieren zu können, wird die Religiosität des Akteurs zum Zeitpunkt t (Welle 1992 für Ehen und 1990 für NEL) durch seine Religiosität zum Zeitpunkt t-1 (1988, Akteureffekt) und durch die Religiosität des Partners zum Zeitpunkt t-1 (Partnereffekt) vorhergesagt (siehe Abb. 3). Mit der zeitverzögert („cross-lagged") aufgenommenen abhängigen Variablen wird gemessen, wie stabil die Religiosität des Akteurs zeitlich ist; der Partnereffekt bildet den „Einfluss" des Partners ab, d. h. inwieweit sich der Akteur über die Zeit in die Richtung des Partners bewegt, sich also an seinen Partner anpasst.

Neben der schon beschriebenen Religiositäts-Skala und dem Geschlecht des Akteurs fließen die folgenden Moderatorvariablen ein:

In der ersten Welle des BEP oder NEL-Panels wird für jede Person die Konfession in fünf Ausprägungen (katholisch, evangelisch, sonstige christliche Religionsgemeinschaft, sonstige nicht-christliche Religionsgemeinschaft, konfessionslos) abgefragt. 52 % der Frauen und 50 % der Männer sind katholisch und 38 % der Frauen bzw. 35 % der Männer evangelisch. Der Anteil der Konfessionslosen liegt bei 9 % (Frauen) und 13 % (Männer). Bezogen auf das Paar ist die Dummy-Variable „konfessionelle Homogamie" dadurch definiert, dass beide Partner derselben Konfession angehören, soweit sich dies auf der Basis der fünf berücksichtigten Kategorien messen lässt. Zusätzlich wird eine Dummy-Variable „beide Partner konfessionslos" aufgenommen, womit die Referenzkategorie konfessionell gemischte Paare darstellen (unter

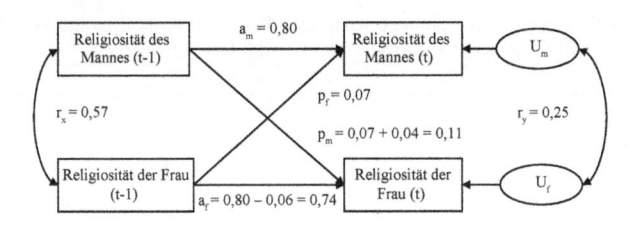

```
                                    a_m = 0,80
    ┌─────────────────┐                          ┌─────────────────┐
    │ Religiosität des│─────────────────────────▶│ Religiosität des│      ⎛   ⎞
    │  Mannes (t-1)   │                          │   Mannes (t)    │◀─────⎝ U_m⎠
    └─────────────────┘╲                       ╱ └─────────────────┘
                        ╲      p_f = 0,07    ╱
  r_x = 0,57              ╲                ╱                        r_y = 0,25
                            ╲            ╱
                              ╲        ╱
                      p_m = 0,07 + 0,04 = 0,11
                            ╱            ╲
                          ╱                ╲
    ┌─────────────────┐ ╱                    ╲ ┌─────────────────┐
    │Religiosität der │╱                      ╲│Religiosität der │      ⎛   ⎞
    │   Frau (t-1)    │─────────────────────────▶│    Frau (t)   │◀─────⎝ U_f⎠
    └─────────────────┘  a_f = 0,80 − 0,06 = 0,74└─────────────────┘
```

Abb. 3 Cross-lagged APIM für unterscheidbare Dyaden zu religiösen Anpassungsprozessen in Partnerschaften. (Quelle: Bamberger Ehepaar- und NEL-Panel (Wellen 1988, 1990 bzw. 1992); Koeffizienten basierend auf Tab. 4, Modell 1)

Einschluss des Falls, dass nur ein Partner konfessionslos ist). 54 % der Paare sind nach dieser Definition in Welle 1 homogam, 41 % sind heterogam und in 5 % der Fälle sind beide Partner konfessionslos.

Für jedes Paar wird für den jeweiligen Zeitpunkt t mit Dummy-Variablen gemessen, ob es sich um eine NEL (0) oder Ehe (1) handelt und ob die Familiengründung bereits vollzogen wurde.

Die Partnerschaftszufriedenheit (gemessen aus Akteurperspektive zum Zeitpunkt t-1) basiert auf der Frage, wie glücklich die jeweilige Person insgesamt derzeit mit ihrer Ehe bzw. Partnerschaft ist (von 1 = „sehr unglücklich" bis 5 = „sehr glücklich").

4.2 Empirische Ergebnisse zu religiösen Transmissions- und Anpassungsprozessen

Die in Tab. 2 dargestellte Korrelationsmatrix gibt zunächst einen Überblick über die Zusammenhänge zwischen Akteurs-, Partner- und Elternmerkmalen im familialen Kontext. Die substanziellen Korrelationen zwischen der religiösen Elternsozialisation und der Religiosität des Akteurs ($r=0{,}50$ für Ehen und $r=0{,}40$ für NEL) deuten in Übereinstimmung mit den in Abschn. 2.1 dargestellten Studien auf relativ starke vertikale Transmissionsprozesse hin. Wovon es abhängt, dass derartige Prägungen durch die elterliche Sozialisation im Lebensverlauf stabil bleiben, wird nachfolgend mit multivariaten Modellen untersucht.

Die noch höhere Korrelation zwischen Akteur und Partner ($r=0{,}67$ in Ehen und $r=0{,}43$ in NEL) zeigt zudem, dass es sich bei der Religiosität, vor allem bei verheirateten Paaren, offensichtlich um ein komplementäres, d. h. im Vergleich der Partner sehr ähnlich ausgeprägtes Merkmal handelt. Die Erklärungsmöglichkeiten für diesen gut abgesicherten Befund reichen von sozial vorstrukturierten Gelegenheiten des Kennenlernens, über die erhöhte Instabilität unähnlicher Paare bis hin zu Anpassungsprozessen als eine Art von horizontaler Sozialisation. Letztere werden im Folgenden mit Längsschnitt-APIM vertiefend analysiert.

Schließlich bestehen, wiederum vor allen in Ehen, auch zwischen der Religiosität des Akteurs und den Eltern des Partners oder zwischen den Eltern des Akteurs und den Eltern des Partners signifikante, wenngleich deutlich schwächere Korrelationen. Diese Zusammenhänge können möglicherweise auf eigenständige Kontexteffekte, etwa Sozialisationseinflüsse der Schwiegereltern, zurückgeführt werden. Eine Alternativerklärung besteht jedoch darin, dass es sich um ein reines „Nebenprodukt" der Partnerwahl handelt: Religiös ähnlich geprägte Personen gehen eher Partnerschaften

Tab. 2 Horizontale und vertikale familiale Kontexteinflüsse auf die Religiosität (Korrelationsmatrix). (Quelle: Bamberger Ehepaar- und NEL-Panel (Wellen 1988, 1990 bzw. 1992))

	A	P	EA	EP
Ehen				
Religiosität Akteur (A)	1			
Religiosität Partner (P)	0,67	1		
Religiöse Sozialisation durch Eltern des Akteurs (EA)	0,50	0,34	1	
Religiöse Sozialisation durch Eltern des Partners (EP)	0,34	0,50	0,27	1
NEL				
Religiosität Akteur (A)	1			
Religiosität Partner (P)	0,43	1		
Religiöse Sozialisation durch Eltern des Akteurs (EA)	0,40	0,12	1	
Religiöse Sozialisation durch Eltern des Partners (EP)	0,12	0,40	0,04	1
n (Personen)			4674	
n (Paare)			2337	

Mit Ausnahme der Korrelation EP-EA bei NEL sind alle Korrelationen signifikant mit $p<0,05$

miteinander ein und weisen gleichzeitig eine ähnliche religiöse Erziehung in ihren jeweiligen Elternhäusern auf (Zinnecker 1998).

Das in Tab. 3 dargestellte APIM trennt die Einflüsse der eigenen Eltern und der Eltern des Partners, die in bivariaten Korrelationen grundsätzlich vermischt sind. Die vertikale religiöse Transmission lässt sich eindeutig bestätigen. Der entsprechende Koeffizient für den Akteureffekt ($b=0,46$) entspricht, da es sich um z-standardisierte Variablen handelt, einem standardisierten Effekt. Eltern übertragen folglich, in Übereinstimmung mit dem in Abschn. 4.1 zitierten Studien (Zinnecker 1998; Fend 2009; Bao et al. 1999; Pearce und Thornton 2007), ihre eigene Religiosität in relativ starkem Maße auf ihre Kinder.

Zusätzlich ist ein positiver, wenn auch schwächerer Zusammenhang zwischen der Religiosität des Akteurs und der religiösen Elternsozialisation des Partners feststellbar ($b=0,18$). Die Existenz dieses direkten, unvermittelten Partnereffektes spricht dafür, dass die Eltern des Partners, im Sinne eines kirchlich-religiösen Familienmilieus (Zinnecker 1998), eigenständige Sozialisationseinflüsse auf den Akteur, über die u. a. aus dem „assortative mating" resultierende Ähnlichkeit der religiösen Sozialisation beider Partner hinaus, ausüben.

In Abb. 2 findet sich eine grafische Darstellung des vollständigen APIM für unterscheidbare Dyaden, also unter Differenzierung nach dem Geschlecht (Modell 1 in Tab. 3). Hier werden die bisher besprochenen, auf *männliche Akteure* bezogenen Zusammenhänge ($b=0,46$ für den Akteureffekt und $b=0,18$ für den Partnereffekt), um die entsprechenden Effekte für weibliche Akteure ergänzt. Dies geschieht durch die Verrechnung von Haupt- und Interaktionseffekten. Beispielsweise entspricht der Akteureffekt für weibliche Akteure einem Wert von $b=0,43$ (Akteureffekt für Männer plus negativer Interaktionseffekt). Die beiden insignifikanten Interaktionseffekte ($b=-0,03$ und $b=0,02$) in Modell 1 dokumentieren jedoch, dass das Geschlecht des Akteurs für die Stärke der Akteur- und Partnereffekte keine Rolle spielt.[9] Mit den vor-

---
[9] Aus diesem Grund werden in den Modellen 2–4 kombinierte, d. h. geschlechtsunspezifische Akteur- und Partnereffekt geschätzt.

Tab. 3 Bedingte Einflüsse der Elternsozialisation auf die Religiosität in Ehen und Nichtehelichen Lebensgemeinschaften (APIM-Modell, b-Koeffizienten mit z-Werten in Klammern). (Quelle: Bamberger Ehepaar- und NEL-Panel (Welle 1988))

	Modell			
	1	2	3	4
Akteur- und Partnereffekte				
Religiöse Sozialisation des Akteurs (Akteureffekt)	0,46** (26,4)	0,45** (38,6)	0,45** (38,3)	0,45** (38,0)
Religiöse Sozialisation des Partners (Partnereffekt)	0,18** (10,2)	0,19** (15,8)	0,19** (15,9)	0,19** (15,8)
Moderatoren				
Akteureffekt × Frau	−0,03 (−1,0)			
Partnereffekt × Frau	0,02 (0,7)			
Akteureffekt × Alter Akteur[a]		−0,01** (−3,1)		
Akteureffekt × Kontakthäufigkeit Akteur[a]			0,03** (3,9)	
Akteureffekt × IGB-Beziehungsqualität Akteur[a]				0,05** (3,9)
Kontrollvariablen				
Frau	0,02 (1,5)	0,02 (1,2)	0,02 (1,4)	0,02 (1,5)
Alter des Akteurs[a]		−0,03** (−10,5)		
Kontakthäufigkeit des Akteurs[a]			0,05** (4,8)	
IGB-Beziehungsqualität des Akteurs[a]				0,06** (4,6)
Intercept	0,01 (0,7)	0,01 (0,6)	0,01 (0,7)	0,01 (0,7)
Varianz innerhalb der Dyade	0,34** (33,9)	0,33** (33,9)	0,34** (33,8)	0,34** (33,8)
Varianz zwischen Dyaden	0,38** (22,3)	0,36** (22,0)	0,37** (22,1)	0,37** (22,2)
n (Paare)		2307		
n (Beobachtungen)		4614		

⁺$p<0,1$; *$p<0,05$; **$p<0,01$
[a]Zentriert

liegenden Daten kann der Forschungsbefund, wonach die Übernahme von religiösen Überzeugungen bei Töchtern stärker ausgeprägt ist als bei Söhnen (Bao et al. 1999), somit nicht bestätigt werden. Die Residualkorrelation zwischen der Religiosität von Mann und Frau ($r_y = 0,53$) entspricht dem Teil der religiositätsbezogenen Partnerähnlichkeit, der weder über die eigenen religiösen Sozialisationserfahrungen im Elternhaus noch durch den Einfluss der religiösen Sozialisation des Partners erklärbar ist.[10]

Die weiteren Modelle (2–4) in Tab. 3 dienen dem Zweck, Bedingungen zu identifizieren, unter denen die vertikale Transmission von Religiosität stärker oder schwächer ausfällt. Der signifikante Interaktionseffekt „Akteureffekt × Alter" in Modell 1 ($b=-0{,}01$) dokumentiert einerseits, dass die Vererbung religiöser Prägungen mit dem Alter des Akteurs an Bedeutung zu verlieren scheint. Dieses Resultat korrespondiert mit dem gut abgesicherten Befund aus der Religionssoziologie, dass sich religiöse Orientierungen beim Übergang vom Jugend- ins Erwachsenenalter, der auch durch eine Ablösung vom Elternhaus gekennzeichnet ist, abschwächen (siehe für einen Überblick: Lois 2013, S. 120–135).

Andererseits ergeben sich Hinweise darauf, dass eine enge, durch emotionale Nähe und häufige Kontakte geprägte, intergenerationale Beziehung die nachhaltige Transmission religiöser Orientierungen wahrscheinlicher macht. Sehen sich Eltern und erwachsene Kinder häufig (Modell 3) und schätzen die erwachsenen Kinder die Beziehung zu ihren Eltern insgesamt als sehr gut ein (Modell 4), fallen die Akteureffekte jeweils signifikant stärker aus.[11] Auch dies steht im Einklang zu den in Abschn. 2.1 zitierten, US-amerikanischen Studien (Bao et al. 1999; Myers 1996; Luft und Sorell 1987; Dickie et al. 1997).

Die in Tab. 4 dargestellten Längsschnittmodelle behandeln horizontale Sozialisation durch den Partner, d. h. die gegenseitige Anpassung der Partner über die Zeit. Der Akteureffekt in Modell 1 ($b=0{,}80$) bezieht sich wiederum auf Männer und dokumentiert eine ausgeprägte zeitliche Stabilität der Religiosität über die beiden untersuchten Messzeitpunkte. Bei Frauen ist der Akteureffekt, wie der Interaktionsterm ($b=-0{,}06$) verdeutlicht, geringfügig, aber signifikant, schwächer.

Der signifikante Partnereffekt in Höhe von $b=0{,}07$ ist im vorliegenden Zusammenhang von besonderem Interesse. Er dokumentiert, dass sich Männer im Hinblick auf ihre Religiosität über die Zeit an ihre Frauen anpassen, d. h. sich zum zweiten Messzeitpunkt (t) in Richtung der Initialausprägung der Frau zum Zeitpunkt t-1 bewegen, statistisch bereinigt um die eigene Ausprägung zu diesem Zeitpunkt. Männer mit ursprünglich überdurchschnittlich religiösen Frauen werden also tendenziell selbst religiöser, bei Männern mit anfänglich wenig religiösen Frauen ist häufig eine Abnahme der Religiosität zu beobachten. Der, als standardisiert interpretierbare Partnereffekt ist allerdings relativ schwach. Dies stimmt mit den Analysen von Lois (2013, S. 184–210) zur Kirchgangshäufigkeit überein und deutet darauf hin, dass die Religiosität ein in der Identität fest verankertes und daher nur schwer veränderbares Merkmal ist. Auch die Anpassung von Frauen an ihre Männer ist, wie die insignifi-

---

[10] Diese Korrelation entspricht der Intraklassenkorrelation und wird berechnet als Anteil der Varianz zwischen Dyaden an der Gesamtvarianz ($0{,}38/(0{,}34+0{,}38)=0{,}53$). Im Fall negativer Abhängigkeit (d. h. dyadischer Unähnlichkeit) lassen sich mittels einer modifizierten Schätzung auch negative ICCs berechnen (zu Details vgl. Kenny et al. 2006, Kap. 4).

[11] Zur Interpretation der konditionalen Haupteffekte sei Folgendes angemerkt: Da eine Mittelwertzentrierung vorgenommen wurde, beziehen sich die Akteureffekte in den Modellen 2–4 jeweils auf eine mittlere Ausprägung der Moderatoren (Alter, Kontakthäufigkeit, Beziehungsqualität). Die Haupteffekte der Moderatorvariablen beziehen sich auf den Fall, dass die Religiosität des Akteurs null (d. h. durchschnittlich) ist.

Tab. 4 Bedingte Partnereinflüsse auf die Religiosität des Akteurs in nichtehelichen Lebensgemeinschaften und Ehen (Cross-lagged Actor-Partner Interdependence-Modelle, b-Koeffizienten mit t-Werten in Klammern). (Quelle: Bamberger Ehepaar- und NEL-Panel (Wellen 1988, 1990 bzw. 1992))

	Modell			
	1	2	3	4
Akteur- und Partnereffekte				
Religiosität des Akteurs, Zeitpunkt t-1 (Akteureffekt)	0,80** (42,9)	0,77** (49,4)	0,78** (50,2)	0,78** (50,0)
Religiosität des Partners, Zeitpunkt t-1 (Partnereffekt)	0,07** (3,7)	0,05** (2,7)	0,06** (2,9)	0,09** (7,4)
Moderatoren				
Akteureffekt × Frau	−0,06* (−2,2)	−0,03 (−1,5)	−0,03 (−1,4)	−0,03 (−1,6)
Partnereffekt × Frau	0,04 (1,6)			
Partnereffekt × Konfessionelle Homogamie		0,06* (2,4)		
Partnereffekt × Beide konfessionslos		0,04 (0,3)		
Partnereffekt × Ehe (Ref.: NEL)			0,06* (2,2)	
Partnereffekt × Familie gegründet			−0,04 (−1,4)	
Partnereffekt × Partnerschaftszufriedenheit[a]				0,03+ (1,9)
Kontrollvariablen				
Frau	0,05** (3,3)	0,05** (3,4)	0,05** (3,4)	0,05** (3,4)
Konfessionelle Homogamie		−0,03 (1,3)		
Beide konfessionslos		0,02 (0,9)		
Ehe (Ref.: NEL)			0,01 (0,9)	
Familie gegründet			−0,03 (−1,5)	
Partnerschaftszufriedenheit				−0,02 (−1,3)
Intercept	−0,05** (−4,0)	−0,07** (−4,2)	0,01 (0,5)	−0,05** (−4,3)
Varianz innerhalb der Dyade	0,15** (25,4)	0,15** (25,3)	0,15** (23,4)	0,15** (25,4)
Varianz zwischen Dyaden	0,05** (8,7)	0,05** (8,7)	0,05** (8,6)	0,05** (8,8)
n (Paare)	1291			
n (Beobachtungen)	2582			

+$p<0,1$; *$p<0,05$; **$p<0,01$

[a]zentriert

kante Wechselwirkung ($b=0{,}04$) zeigt, nicht stärker. Aus diesem Grund wird in den Modellen 2–4 erneut ein kombinierter Partnereffekt geschätzt.

In Abb. 3 findet sich die Darstellung des vollständigen APIM (ohne Moderatorvariablen). Die Residualkorrelation zum Zeitpunkt t ($r_y=0{,}25$) entspricht in diesem Fall dem „idiosynkratischen" Teil der Partnerähnlichkeit zum zweiten Messzeitpunkt, der nicht auf die vorhergehenden Ausprägungen der Partner zurückführbar ist. Hierbei kann es sich z. B. um außergewöhnliche gemeinsame Erlebnisse („common fate"), welche die Religiosität tangieren (z. B. kritische Lebensereignisse), handeln.

In den Modellen 2–4 wird erneut nach Bedingungen für die Stärke von Anpassungsprozessen gesucht. Ein naheliegendes Argument ist zunächst, dass eine Anpassung an den Partner vor allem dann erleichtert wird, wenn beide Partner der gleichen Konfession angehören, die religiösen Überzeugungen und Praktiken also in einen gemeinsamen kulturellen Rahmen eingebettet sind. Die empirischen Ergebnisse unterstützen diese Annahme: Der Partnereffekt ist, wie die Wechselwirkung „Konfessionelle Homogamie × Partnereffekt" ($b=0{,}06$) verdeutlicht, signifikant stärker, wenn die Partner der gleichen Konfession angehören. Ein ähnlicher Verstärkungseffekt ist dagegen für den Fall eines homogam konfessionslosen Paares nicht zu beobachten.

In den Modellen 3 und 4 wird die aus der Balancetheorie ableitbare Hypothese getestet, dass Anpassungsprozesse vor allem dann wahrscheinlich sind, wenn die Beziehung zwischen Akteur und Partner stark ist (vgl. Abschn. 2.2). Als Indikatoren für die Stärke werden beziehungsspezifische „Investitionen" (Ehe, Familiengründung) sowie die Gesamteinschätzung zur Beziehungsqualität verwendet. Während sich für die Familiengründung kein Effekt zeigt, sind religiöse Anpassungsprozesse in Ehen signifikant stärker ausgeprägt als in Nichtehelichen Lebensgemeinschaften (Model 3).[12] Außerdem bestätigen die Ergebnisse in Modell 4 zumindest tendenziell, dass sich der Partnereffekt in Abhängigkeit von der Beziehungsqualität verstärkt. Einen ähnlichen Moderatoreffekt berichten Davis und Rusbult (2001) sowie Roest et al. (2006) für verschiedene andere Einstellungsdimensionen (Abschn. 2.2). Trotz der relativ ausgeprägten zeitlichen Trägheit der Religiosität und der entsprechend geringen Tendenz zur Anpassung ist das Ausmaß der Partnereinflüsse somit insgesamt nicht invariant gegenüber der konfessionellen Homogamie sowie Merkmalen der Partnerschaft.

5 Fazit und Ausblick

Der vorliegende Beitrag hatte das Ziel, theoretische und empirische Ansätze aufzuzeigen, mittels derer soziale Kontexteinflüsse innerhalb von Familien konzeptualisiert und analysiert werden können. Innerhalb der Familie finden Interaktionsprozesse statt, die offenbar in der Summe zu einer zunehmenden kulturellen Homogenisierung von Familien im Laufe der Zeit beitragen können. Im speziellen Fall der Religiosität ist der Einfluss der Sozialisation im Elternhaus augenscheinlich deutlich stär-

---

[12] Vertiefende Analysen zeigen, dass die Dauer der Partnerschaft als Moderator darüber hinaus keine Rolle spielt.

ker als spätere Partnereinflüsse. Gleichwohl ist dieser Prozess keine Einbahnstraße: Das Ausmaß des sozialen Einflusses der jeweiligen Interaktionspartner hängt nach unseren Befunden aus den vorgestellten Moderatoranalysen, ganz im Einklang zu den Vorhersagen der Balancetheorie (Heider 1958), offenbar entscheidend von der Kohäsion der jeweiligen (Paar- oder Generationen-)Beziehung ab. Hier deutet sich an, dass es bei einer Verringerung der Kontaktintensität oder bei einer kritischeren Beziehungsbewertung durchaus auch zu einer Abnahme des sozialen Einflusses des betreffenden Interaktionspartners und möglicherweise zu divergenten Entwicklungen (d. h. zu einer zunehmenden Einstellungsheterogenität) kommen könnte, welche wiederum (im Extremfall unüberwindbarer Differenzen) zum „Verlassen" der Dyade oder Familie führen kann. Umgekehrt, so zeigen beispielsweise die Befunde von Lois (2013), stärkt wertebezogene Homogenität wiederum die Kohäsion zwischen den Mitgliedern und damit die Resilienz gegenüber Trennungen oder Kontaktabbruch; insofern handelt es sich hier um einen sich selbst verstärkenden Prozess, zumindest solange keine exogenen „Störungen" (z. B. kritische Lebensereignisse) oder sonstige interpersonale Dynamiken hinzutreten.

Weiterer Forschungsbedarf besteht hinsichtlich der relativen Bedeutung von Selektions- und Sozialisationsprozessen (vgl. Arránz Becker und Lois 2010). Es ist zu bedenken, dass sich Längsschnittanalysen zu familialen Kontexteffekten stets auf das selektive Sample der über die Zeit fortbestehenden Interaktionsbeziehungen beschränken, sodass Selektionseffekte darin *per definitionem* ausgeblendet werden. Aber auch die „anfängliche" Werteähnlichkeit ist freilich ein Konglomerat aus zeitlich zurückliegender Selektion (insbesondere in horizontalen Paarbeziehungen) und Anpassung; für eine akkurate Dekomposition beider Prozesse müssten alle Familienmitglieder vor oder ab dem Beginn der Paar- oder Familienbildung über die Zeit beobachtet werden. Diese Anforderung an das Datenmaterial ist jedoch im Hinblick auf Familien, anders als beispielsweise in Studien zur Einstellungsähnlichkeit vor und nach der Entstehung von Freundschaftsbeziehungen in Gruppen mit relativ konstanter Zusammensetzung wie Schulklassen (Laursen et al. 2008), nahezu unerfüllbar.

Der vorliegende Beitrag illustriert, dass moderne multivariate Analyseverfahren wie das Actor-Partner Interdependence Model (APIM) das Potenzial besitzen, intrafamiliale Interaktions- und Interdependenzstrukturen detailliert herauszuarbeiten. In Anknüpfung an die vorgestellten Analysen wäre es beispielsweise möglich, horizontale und vertikale Transmission prinzipiell nicht nur abwärts-, sondern auch aufwärtsgerichtet in einem Längsschnittmodell simultan zu untersuchen. Bislang existieren allerdings kaum derartige Studien (Roest et al. 2009), vermutlich wegen der damit verbundenen hohen Anforderungen an das Datenmaterial. Der besondere Erkenntnisgewinn solcher systemischer Analysen bestünde darin, die „Nettoeinflüsse" der verschiedenen Sozialisationsagenten besser isolieren und vergleichen zu können. Trotz der reichhaltigen Analysemöglichkeiten ist aus methodischer Sicht allerdings kritisch darauf hinzuweisen, dass in der bisherigen Forschung Anpassung (zumindest bezüglich metrischer Merkmale) überwiegend darüber definiert wird, dass sich der Akteur über die Zeit in Richtung der Initialausprägung des Partners bewegt. Dies ist jedoch nur eine von mehreren Definitionsmöglichkeiten. So ist z. B. denkbar, dass sich Partner A über die Zeit in Richtung von Partner B bewegt, die *Differenz* der Partner in Bezug auf das betrachtete Merkmal gleichzeitig aber unverändert bleibt oder sogar ansteigt. In diesem Zusammenhang ist auch die (alleinige) Verwendung des Längsschnitt-APIM kritisch zu sehen. Dieser Analyseansatz vermischt, wie für dynamische Panelmodelle mit zeitverzögerter abhängiger Variable typisch, die beiden Varianzquellen zwischen Paaren und innerhalb von Paaren über die Zeit (vgl. Brüderl 2010). Dadurch werden die Schätzmodelle potenziell anfällig für Selektionseffekte, da vermeintliche Anpassung teilweise auf eine Ähnlichkeit der Partner hinsichtlich zeitkonstanter Drittvariablen zurückzuführen sein könnte. Daher erscheint es für die zukünftige Forschung lohnenswert, Fixed-Effects- oder Hybrid-Modelle (Allison 2009) auch für die dyadische Datenanalyse stärker nutzbar zu machen; eine explizite Formalisierung steht unseres Wissens jedoch bislang noch aus.

Insgesamt zeigt der vorliegende Beitrag, dass Familien als Interaktionssysteme mit multiplen reziproken sozialen Einflüssen zwischen den Familienmitgliedern theoretisch konzeptualisiert und mittels des vorgestellten Analyseansatzes auch modelliert werden können. Solche sozialen Kontexteinflüsse sind theoretisch von sozialräumlichen Kontexteffekten (beispielsweise regionale konfessionelle oder religiöse Prägung) abzugrenzen; empirisch lassen sich beide Prozesse jedoch ohne weiteres simultan modellieren, indem etwa eine weitere regionale Ebene (z. B. Gemeinden oder Kreise) inklusive entsprechender Merkmale in die Gleichung aufgenommen wird. Daher sind dyadische Analysen direkt anschlussfähig an die in diesem Band beschriebenen Modellierungstechniken für andere Arten von Kontexteffekten; sie sollten daher zukünftig immer dann zur Anwendung kommen, wenn haushalts- oder familienbezogene Daten analysiert werden. Inhaltlich beschränkt sich die Anwendbarkeit keineswegs auf Werte und Einstellungen, sondern es eröffnen sich bei Anwendung auf Sozialstatus- oder Prestigeindikatoren auch im Bereich der Ungleichheits- und Mobilitätsforschung interessante neue Fragestellungen.

Literatur

Allison, Paul D. 2009. *Fixed effects regression models.* Thousand Oaks: Sage.
Arránz Becker, Oliver, und Daniel Lois. 2010. Selection, alignment, and their interplay: Origins of lifestyle homogamy in couple relationships. *Journal of Marriage and Family* 72:1234–1248.
Baier, Dirk, und Andreas Hadjar. 2004. Wie wird Leistungsorientierung von den Eltern auf die Kinder übertragen? Ergebnisse einer Längsschnittstudie. *Zeitschrift für Familienforschung* 15:156–177.
Bandura, Albert. 1976. *Lernen am Modell: Ansätze zu einer sozial-kognitiven Lerntheorie.* Stuttgart: Klett.
Bao, Wan-Ning, Les B. Whitebeck, Danny R. Hoyt und Rand D. Conger. 1999. Perceived parental acceptance as a moderator of religious transmission aomg adolescent boys and girls. *Journal of Marriage and family* 61:362–374.
Becker, Gary S. 1981. *A treatise on the family.* Cambridge: Harvard University Press.
Becker, Gary S. 1993. *Der ökonomische Ansatz zur Erklärung menschlichen Verhaltens.* Tübingen: Mohr.
Bekkers, Rene. 2007. Intergenerational transmission of volunteering. *Acta Sociologica* 50:99–104.
Bengtson, Vern L., Timothy J. Biblarz und Robert E. L. Roberts. 2002. *How families still matter. A longitudinal study of youth in two gerenations.* Cambridge University Press.
Bengtson, Vern L., Casey E. Copen, Norella M. Putney und Merril Silverstein. 2009. A longitudinal study of the intergenerational transmission of religion. *International Sociology* 24:325–345.
Berger, Fred. 2009. Intergenerationale Transmission von Scheidung. In *Lebensverläufe, Lebensbewältigung, Lebensglück. Ergebnisse der LifE-Studie,* Hrsg. Helmut Fend, Fred Berger und Urs Grob, 267–303. Wiesbaden: VS Verlag für Sozialwissenschaften.
Brake, Anna, und Peter Büchner. 2003. Bildungsort Familie. *Zeitschrift für Erziehungswissenschaft* 6:618–638.

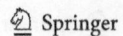

Brüderl, Josef. 2010. Kausalanalyse mit Paneldaten. In *Handbuch der sozialwissenschaftlichen Datenanalyse*, Hrsg. Christof Wolf und Henning Best, 963–994. Wiesbaden: VS Verlag für Sozialwissenschaften.
Caspi, Avshalom, Ellen S. Herbener und Daniel J. Ozer. 1992. Shared experiences and the similarity of personalities: A longitudinal study of married couples. *Journal of Personality and Social Psychology* 62:281–291.
Chen, Zeung-Yin, Ruth X. Lui und Howard B. Kaplan. 2008. Mediating mechanism for the intergenerational transmission of constructive parenting: A prospective longitudinal study. *Journal of Family Issues* 29:1574–1599.
Cook, William, und David Kenny. 2005. The actor-partner interdependence model: A model of bidirectional effects in developmental studies. *International Journal of Behavioral Development* 29:101–109.
Copen, Casey E., und Merril Silverstein. 2007. Transmission of religious beliefs across generations: Do grandparents matter? *Journal of Comparative Family Studies* 38:497–510.
Corijn, Martine, Aart C. Liefbroer und Jenny De Jong Gierveld. 1996. It takes two to tango, doesn't it? The influence of couple characteristics on the timing of the birth of the first child. *Journal of Marriage and the Family* 58:117–126.
Davis, Jody L., und Caryl E. Rusbult. 2001. Attitude alignment in close relationships. *Journal of Personality and Social Psychology* 81:65–84.
Dickie, Jane R., Amy K. Eshleman, Dawn M. Merasco, Amy Shepard, Michael Vanderwilt und Melissa Johnson. 1997. Parent-child relationships and children's images of god. *Journal for the Scientific Study of Religion* 36:25–43.
Domsgen, Michael. 2008. Kirchliche Sozialisation: Familie, Kindergarten, Gemeinde. In *Kirche empirisch. Ein Werkbuch*, Hrsg. Jan Hermelink und Thorsten Latzel, 73–94. Gütersloh: Gütersloher Verlagshaus.
Dronkers, Jaap, und Juho Harkonen. 2008. The intergenerational transmission of divorce in cross-national perspective: Results from the fertility and family surveys. *Population Studies* 62:273–288.
Elder, Glen H. Jr. 1994. Time, human agency, and social change. Perspectives on the life course. *Social Psychological Quarterly* 57:4–15.
Engel, Uwe, und Jost Reinecke. Hrsg. 1996. *Analysis of change. Advanced techniques in panel data analysis*. Berlin: Walter de Gruyter.
Erzinger, Andrea B. 2009. Langzeitfolgen familiärer Beziehungserfahrungen im Jugendalter für partnerschaftliche Beziehungen im Erwachsenenalter – Wird die Qualität der Partnerbeziehung über die Generationen „vererbt"? In *Lebensverläufe, Lebensbewältigung, Lebensglück. Ergebnisse der LifE-Studie*, Hrsg. Helmut Fend, Fred Berger und Urs Grob, 245–265. Wiesbaden: VS Verlag für Sozialwissenschaften.
Esser, Hartmut. 1996. *Soziologie. Allgemeine Grundlagen*. Frankfurt a. M.: Campus.
Esser, Hartmut. 2000a. *Soziologie. Spezielle Grundlagen, Band 3: Soziales Handeln*. Frankfurt a. M.: Campus.
Esser, Hartmut. 2000b. *Soziologie. Spezielle Grundlagen, Band 2: Die Konstruktion der Gesellschaft*. Frankfurt a. M.: Campus.
Fend, Helmut. 2009. Was die Eltern ihren Kindern mitgeben – Generationenbeziehungen aus Sicht der Erziehungswissenschaft. In *Generationen. Multidisziplinäre Perspektiven*, Hrsg. Harald Künem und Marc Szydlik, 81–103. Wiesbaden: VS Verlag für Sozialwissenschaften.
Gonzalez, Richard, und Dale Griffin. 1997. On the statistics of interdependence: Treating dyadic data with respect. In *Handbook of personal relationships 2*, Hrsg. Steve Duck, 271–301. New York: Wiley.
Gonzalez, Richard, und Dale Griffin. 1999. The correlational analysis of dyad-level data in the distinguishable case. *Personal Relationships* 6:449–469.
Grob, Urs. 2009. Die Entwicklung politischer Orientierungen vom Jugend- ins Erwachsenenalter - Ist die Jugend eine spezifisch sensible Phase in der politischen Sozialisation? In *Lebensverläufe, Lebensbewältigung, Lebensglück. Ergebnisse der LifE-Studie*, Hrsg. Helmut Fend, Fred Berger und Urs Grob, 329–372. Wiesbaden: VS Verlag für Sozialwissenschaften.
Heider, Fritz. 1958. *The psychology of interpersonal relations*. New York: Wiley.
Hendrickx, John, Osmund Schreuder und Ultee Wouter. 1994. Die konfessionelle Mischehe in Deutschland (1901–1986) und den Niederlanden (1914–1986). *Kölner Zeitschrift für Soziologie und Sozialpsychologie* 46:619–645.
Kalmijn, Matthijs. 1998. Intermarriage and homogamy: Causes, patterns, trends. *Annual Review of Sociology* 24:395–421.
Kalmijn, Matthijs. 2005. Attitude alignment in marriage and cohabitation: The case of sex-role attitudes. *Personal Relationships* 12:521–535.

Kenny, David A. 1988. The analysis of data from two-person relationships. In *Handbook of personal relationships*, Hrsg. Steve Duck, 57–77. New York: Wiley.
Kenny, David A. 1995. The effect of nonindependence on significance testing in dyadic research. *Personal Relationships* 2:67–75.
Kenny, David A., und Deborah A. Kashy. 2011. Dyadic data analysis using multilevel modeling. In *Handbook of advanced multilevel analysis*, Hrsg. Joop Hox und J. Kyle Roberts, 344–360. New York: Routledge.
Kenny, David A., Deborah A. Kashy und William Cook. 2006. *Dyadic data analysis*. New York: The Guilford Press.
Klein, Thomas, und Edgar Wunder. 1996. Regionale Disparitäten und Konfessionswechsel als Ursache konfessioneller Homogamie. *Kölner Zeitschrift für Soziologie und Sozialpsychologie* 48:96–125.
Kraul, Margret, und Christina Radicke. 2012. Familiale Erziehung zwischen Tradierung, intergeneratioeller Dynamik und Aneignung. In *Tradierungsprozesse im Wandel der Moderne: Religion und Familie im Spannungsfeld von Konfessionalität und Pluralisierung*, Hrsg. Dimitrij Owetschkin, 137–161. Essen: Klartext.
Laursen, Brett, Danielle Popp, Wiliam J. Burk, Margaret Kerr und Håkan Stattin. 2008. Incorporating interdependence into developmental research: Examples from the study of homophily and homogeneity. In *Modeling dyadic and interdependent data in the developmental and behavioral sciences*, Hrsg. Noel A. Card, James P. Selig und Todd D. Little, 11–38. Milton Park: Routledge.
Lehrer, Evelyn L., und Carmel U. Chiswick. 1993. Religion as a determinant of marital instability. *Demography* 30:385–399.
Lois, Daniel. 2009. *Lebensstile und Entwicklungspfade nichtehelicher Lebensgemeinschaften. Eine empirische Analyse mit dem Sozioökonomischen Panel*. Wiesbaden: VS Verlag für Sozialwissenschaften.
Lois, Daniel. 2013. *Wenn das Leben religiös macht. Altersabhängige Veränderungen der kirchlichen Religiosität im Lebensverlauf*. Wiesbaden: Springer VS.
Luft, Gary A., und Gwendolyn T. Sorell. 1987. Parenting style and parent-adolescent religious value consensus. *Journal of Adolescent Research* 2:53–68.
Martin-Matthews, Anne, und Karen M. Kobayashi. 2002. Intergenerational transmission. In *International encyclopedia of marriage and family relationships 2*, Hrsg. J. J. Ponzetti, 922–927. New York: MacMillan.
Meulemann, Heiner. 2012. *Soziologie von Anfang an: eine Einführung in Themen, Ergebnisse und Literatur*. Wiesbaden: Springer VS.
Moen, Phyllis, Mary Ann Erickson und Donna Dempster-Mcclain. 1997. Their mother's daughters? The intergenerational transmission of gender attitudes in a world of changing roles. *Journal of Marriage and family* 59:281–293.
Musick, Marc, und John Wilson. 1995. Religious switching for marriage reasons. *Sociology of Religion* 56:257–270.
Mustillo, Sarah, John Wilson und Scott M. Lynch. 2004. Legacy volunteering: A test of two theories of intergenerational transmission. *Journal of Marriage and family* 66:530–541.
Myers, Scott M. 1996. An interactive model of religiosity inheritance: The importance of family context. *American Sociological Review* 61:858–866.
Nave-Herz, Rosemarie. 2013. *Ehe- und Familiensoziologie. Eine Einführung in Geschichte, theoretische Ansätze und empirische Befunde*. Weinheim: Beltz Juventa.
Newcomb, Theodore M. 1953. An approach to the study of commicative acts. *Psychological Review* 60:393–404.
Neyer, Franz J. 1998. Zum Umgang mit dyadischen Daten: Neue Methoden für die Sozialpsychologie. *Zeitschrift für Sozialpsychologie* 29:291–306.
Nye, Frank I. Hrsg. 1982. *Family relationships. Rewards and costs*. Beverly Hills: Sage.
Oppenheimer, Valerie Kincade. 1988. A theory of marriage timing. *American Journal of Sociology* 94:563–591.
Pearce, Lisa D., und Arland Thornton. 2007. Religious identity and family ideologies in the transition to adulthood. *Journal of Marriage and Family* 69:1227–1243.
Perren, Sonja, Agnes Von Wyl, Dieter Bürgin, Heidi Simoni und Kai Von Klitzing. 2005. Intergenerational transmission of marital quality across the transition to parenthood. *Family Process* 44:441–459.
Pickel, Gert. 2010. Religiosität versus Konfessionslosigkeit. In *Deutsche Kontraste 1990-2010. Politik – Wirtschaft – Gesellschaft – Kultur*, Hrsg. Manuela Glaab, Werner Weidenfeld und Michael Weigl, 447–484. Frankfurt a. M.: Campus.

Pickel, Gert. 2013. Die Situation der Religion in Deutschland – Rückkehr des Religiösen oder voranschreitende Säkularisierung? In *Religion und Politik im vereinigten Deutschland. Was bleibt von der Rückkehr des Religiösen?*, Hrsg. Gert Pickel und Oliver Hidalgo, 59–94. Wiesbaden: Springer VS.
Roest, Annette M.C., Judith Semon Dubas, Jan R. M. Gerris und Rutger C. M. E. Engels. 2006. Disentangling value similarities and transmissions in established marriages: A cross-lagged longitudinal study. *Journal of Marriage and Family* 68:1132–1146.
Roest, Annette M. C., Judith Semon Dubas und Jan R. M. Gerris. 2009. Value transmission between fathers, mothers, and adolescent and emerging adult children: The role of family climate. *Journal of Family Psychology* 23:146–155.
Rössel, Jörg, und Claudia Beckert-Zieglschmid. 2002. Die Reproduktion kulturellen Kapitals. *Zeitschrift für Soziologie* 31:457–513.
Rost, Harald, Marina Rupp, Florian Schulz und Laszlo A. Vaskovics. 2003. *Bamberger-Ehepaar-Panel*. ifb-Materialien 6/2003. Bamberg: Staatsinstitut für Familienforschung.
Schönpflug, Ute. 2001. Intergenerational transmission of values: The role of transmission belts. *Journal of Cross-Cultural Psychology* 32:174–185.
Schulze, Gerhard. 1992. *Erlebnisgesellschaft: Kultursoziologie der Gegenwart*. Frankfurt a. M.: Campus.
Stecher, Ludwig, und Jürgen Zinnecker. 2007. Kulturelle Transferbeziehungen. In *Handbuch Familie*, Hrsg. Jutta Ecarius, 389–405. Wiesbaden: VS Verlag für Sozialwissenschaften.
Steenhof, Liesbeth, und Aart C. Liefbroer. 2008. Intergenerational transmission of age at first birth in the Netherlands for birth cohorts born between 1935 and 1984: Evidence from multiple registers. *Population Studies* 62:69–84.
Steinbach, Anja, und Bernhard Nauck. 2004. Intergenerationale Transmission von kulturellem Kapital in Migrantenfamilien. Zur Erklärung von ethnischen Unterschieden im deutschen Bildungssystem. *Zeitschrift für Erziehungswissenschaft* 7:20–32.
Teachman, Jay D. 2002. Childhood living arrangements and the intergenerational transmission of divorce. *Journal of Marriage and Family* 64:717–729.
Thompson, Linda, und Alexis J. Walker. 1982. The dyad as the unit of analysis: Conceptual and methodological issues. *Journal of Marriage and Family* 44:889–900.
Trommsdorff, Gisela. 2009. Intergenerational relations and cultural transmission. In *Cultural transmission. Psychological, developmental, social, and methodological aspects*, Hrsg. Ute Schönpflug, 126–160. Cambridge: Cambridge University Press.
Uslucan, Haci-Halil, und Urs Fuhrer. 2009. Intergenerational transmission of violence. In *Cultural transmission. Psychological, developmental, social, and methodological aspects*, Hrsg. Ute Schönpflug, 391–418. Cambridge: Cambridge University Press.
Van Poppel, Frans, Christiaan Monden und Kees Mandemakers. 2008. Marriage timing over the generations. *Human Nature* 19:7–22.
Vaskovics, Laszlo A., und Marina Rupp. 2009. *Bamberger NEL-Panel. ZA4665 Datenfile Version 1.0.0*, doi:10.4232/1.4665. Köln: GESIS Datenarchiv.
Vaskovics, Laszlo A., und Staatsinstitut für Familienforschung an der Universität Bamberg (Ifb). 2007. *Bamberger Ehepaar-Panel. ZA4266 Datenfile Version 1.0.0*, doi: 10.4232/1.4266. Köln: GESIS Datenarchiv.
Vaskovics, Laszlo A., Marina Rupp und Barbara Hofmann. 1997. *Nichteheliche Lebensgemeinschaften. Eine soziologische Längsschnittstudie*. Opladen: Leske und Budrich.
Vollebergh, Wilma A. M., Jurjen Iedema und Quinten A. W. Raaijmakers. 2001. Intergenerational transmission and the formation of cultural orientations in adolescence and young adultshood. *Journal of Marriage and Family* 63:1185–1198.
Weber, Max. 1972. *Wirtschaft und Gesellschaft*. Tübingen: Mohr.
Wolf, Christof. 1995. Religiöse Sozialisation, konfessionelle Milieus und Generation. *Zeitschrift für Soziologie* 24:345–357.
Yu, Tianyi, und Francesca Adler-Baeder. 2007. The intergenerational transmission of relationship quality: The effects of parental remarriage quality on young adults' relationships. *Journal of Divorce and Remarriage* 47:87–102.
Zinnecker, Jürgen. 1998. Die Tradierung kultureller Systeme zwischen den Generationen. Die Rolle der Familie bei der Vermittlung von Religion in der Moderne. *Zeitschrift für Soziologie der Erziehung und Sozialisation* 18:343–356.
Zinnecker, Jürgen, und Ralph Hasenberg. 1999. Religiöse Eltern und religiöse Kinder: Die Übertragung von Religion auf die nachfolgende Generation in der Familie. In *Entwicklung im sozialen Wandel*, Hrsg. Rainer K. Silbereisen und Jürgen Zinnecker, 445–457. Weinheim: Beltz.

Oliver Arránz Becker, 1973, Prof. Dr., Juniorprofessor für Bildungs- und Familiensoziologie, Universität Mannheim. Forschungsgebiete: Familiensoziologie, Gesundheitsforschung, sozialwissenschaftliche Methoden. Veröffentlichungen: What narrows the stepgap? Closeness between parents and adult (step) children in Germany. Journal of Marriage and Family 75, 2013 (mit V. Salzburger, N. Lois und B. Nauck); Institutional regulations, opportunity, and the kinship solidarity of women. Results from thirteen regions in Asia, Africa, Europe and North America. European Sociological Review 29, 2013 (mit B. Nauck); Competing pleasures? The impact of leisure time use on the transition to parenthood. Journal of Family 34, 2013 (mit D. Lois).

Daniel Lois, 1978, PD Dr., Juniordozent für Methoden, Universität Tübingen. Forschungsgebiete: Familiensoziologie, Religionssoziologie, Sozialstrukturanalyse, sozialwissenschaftliche Methoden. Veröffentlichungen: Zur Erklärung sozialer Ansteckung beim Übergang zur Elternschaft. Ein Test vermittelnder Mechanismen. Kölner Zeitschrift für Soziologie und Sozialpsychologie 65, 2013; Competing pleasures? Quantity and quality of leisure and the transition to parenthood. Journal of Family Issues 34, 2013 (mit O. Arránz Becker); Religious affiliation and church attendance across time. A trend study considering differences between East and West Germany. Comparative Population Studies. Zeitschrift für Bevölkerungswissenschaft 36, 2011.

Anja Steinbach, 1974, Prof. Dr., Professorin für Soziologie an der Universität Duisburg-Essen. Forschungsgebiete: Familiensoziologie, Bevölkerungssoziologie und Migrationssoziologie. Veröffentlichungen: Generationenbeziehungen in Stieffamilien. Der Einfluss leiblicher und sozialer Elternschaft auf die Ausgestaltung von Eltern-Kind-Beziehungen im Erwachsenenalter, Wiesbaden 2010; Intergenerational relations across the life course. Special Issue of Advances in Life Course Research 17, 2012; Family structure and parent-child contact: A comparison of native and migrant families. Journal of Marriage and Family 75, 2013.

Springer VS

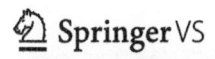

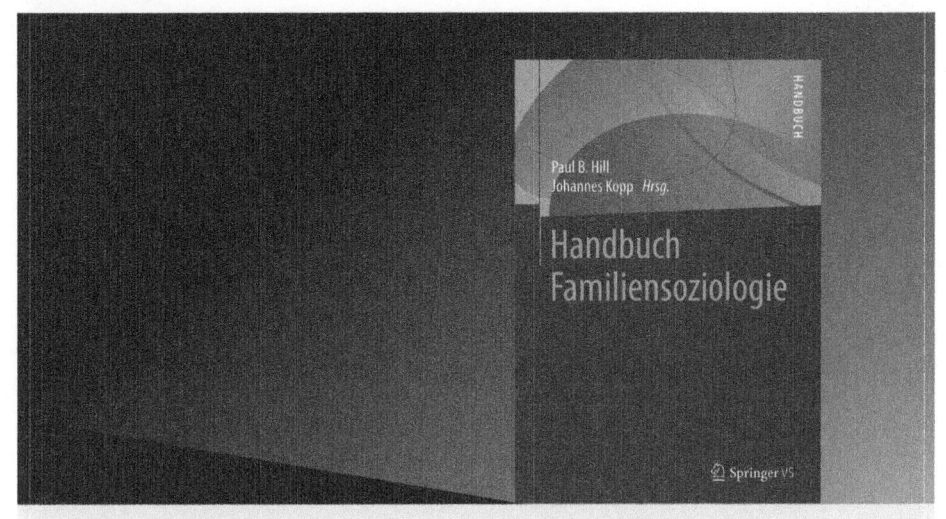

springer-vs.de

Familie aus soziologischer Perspektive

Paul B. Hill, Johannes Kopp (Hrsg.)
Handbuch Familiensoziologie
2014. 815 S. 55 Abb. Geb.
ca. € (D) 89,99 | € (A) 92,51 | *sFr 112,00
ISBN 978-3-658-02275-4

Dieser Band bietet einen umfassenden Einblick in die große thematische Breite und Tiefe der familiensoziologischen Forschung. Dabei geht es um die Konstanten und Differenzierungen des familialen Lebens in den verschiedensten Regionen der Welt sowie die unterschiedlichen methodischen und theoretischen Ansatzpunkte in der Familienforschung. Schließlich wird eine Vielzahl familialer und sozialstruktureller Fragestellungen einschließlich ihrer empirischen Fundierung aufgegriffen, referiert und kritisch kommentiert. Heiratsmarkt, Fertilität, Arbeitsteilung, Generationenbeziehungen, Interaktionsstile, Trennung, Bildung, Mobilität sind nur einige Beispiele für den breiten thematischen Zugriff des vorliegenden Bandes, welcher in vier thematischen Abschnitten und fünfundzwanzig Beiträgen systematisch das Feld der Familiensoziologie beschreibt.

€ (D) sind gebundene Ladenpreise in Deutschland und enthalten 7% MwSt. € (A) sind gebundene Ladenpreise in Österreich und enthalten 10% MwSt. Die mit * gekennzeichneten Preise sind unverbindliche Preisempfehlungen und enthalten die landesübliche MwSt. Preisänderungen und Irrtümer vorbehalten.

Jetzt bestellen: springer-vs.de

Springer VS

springer-vs.de

Highlights aus dem Methoden-Programm

Nina Baur, Jörg Blasius (Hrsg.)
Handbuch Methoden der empirischen Sozialforschung
2014. XL, 1086 S. Geb.
ca. € (D) 69,99 | € (A) 71,95 |
*sFr 87,50
ISBN 978-3-531-17809-7

- Das Buch bietet einen umfassenden Überblick über die Methoden der empirischen Sozialforschung

Rainer Diaz-Bone, Christoph Weischer (Hrsg.)
Methoden-Lexikon für die Sozialwissenschaften
2014. 600 S. Brosch.
ca. € (D) 39,90 | € (A) 41,02 |
*sFr 50,00
ISBN 978-3-531-16629-2

- Lexikalischer Zugang zu allen Aspekten sozialwissenschaftlicher Methoden

€ (D) sind gebundene Ladenpreise in Deutschland und enthalten 7% MwSt. € (A) sind gebundene Ladenpreise in Österreich und enthalten 10% MwSt.
Die mit * gekennzeichneten Preise sind unverbindliche Preisempfehlungen und enthalten die landesübliche MwSt. Preisänderungen und Irrtümer vorbehalten.

Jetzt bestellen: springer-vs.de

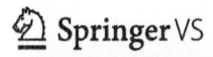

Neu in der Reihe: Neue Bibliothek der Sozialwissenschaften

Günter Dux, Jörn Rüsen (Hrsg.)
Strukturen des Denkens
Studien zur Geschichte des Geistes
Reihe: Neue Bibliothek
der Sozialwissenschaften
2014. VI, 244 S. 7 Abb.,
6 Abb. in Farbe. Geb.
€ (D) 29,99 | € (A) 30,83 | *sFr 30,00
ISBN 978-3-658-06254-5

Wir haben in der Neuzeit die ganze Geschichte im Blick. Das gilt auch für die Geistesgeschichte. Von den mythischen Weltbildern der Frühzeit über die monotheistischen Religionen und Epen der Hochkulturen bis zum Umbruch des Weltbildes am Beginn der Neuzeit zieht sich die Spur unseres Wissens. Es gibt in dieser Geschichte des Geistes eine Sequenz, die von der Entwicklung des Denkens bewirkt wird. Zum einen haben sich dessen formal-logische Strukturen entwickelt. Ihre Entwicklung lässt sich durch die Entwicklung der algebraischen Logik dokumentieren. Zum andern haben sich ihre material-logischen Strukturen entwickelt. Die der Welt immanente Prozessualität wird in der Neuzeit anders verstanden als in der Vergangenheit. Der Entwicklung beider Strukturen geht der vorliegende Band nach. Geschichte lässt sich unter den erkenntniskritischen Vorgaben einer säkular gewordenen Welt verstehen. Das ist die Botschaft, die der Band vermitteln möchte.

€ (D) sind gebundene Ladenpreise in Deutschland und enthalten 7% MwSt. € (A) sind gebundene Ladenpreise in Österreich und enthalten 10% MwSt. Die mit * gekennzeichneten Preise sind unverbindliche Preisempfehlungen und enthalten die landesübliche MwSt. Preisänderungen und Irrtümer vorbehalten.

Jetzt bestellen: springer-vs.de